I0120637

Henry Francis Walling, Alexander Winchell

Tackabury's Atlas of the State of Michigan

Henry Francis Walling, Alexander Winchell

Tackabury's Atlas of the State of Michigan

ISBN/EAN: 9783743448070

Printed in Europe, USA, Canada, Australia, Japan

Cover: Foto ©Suzi / pixelio.de

More available books at **www.hansebooks.com**

TACKABURY'S

ATLAS

OF THE STATE OF

MICHIGAN,

INCLUDING STATISTICS AND DESCRIPTIONS

OF ITS

TOPOGRAPHY, HYDROGRAPHY, CLIMATE, NATURAL AND CIVIL HISTORY, RAILWAY AND STEAM BOAT HISTORY, EDUCATIONAL INSTITUTIONS, MATERIAL RESOURCES, ETC.

BY

ALEXANDER WINCHELL, LL.D., PROFESSOR OF GEOLOGY AND PALEONTOLOGY IN THE UNIVERSITY OF MICHIGAN, ORAMEL HOSFORD, ESQ., AND RAY HADDOCK, ESQ.

DRAWN AND COMPILED BY

H. F. WALLING, C. E.,

TOPOGRAPHER TO UNITED STATES GEOLOGICAL SURVEY, LATE PROFESSOR OF CIVIL ENGINEERING IN LAFAYETTE COLLEGE, AND AUTHOR OF MAPS AND ATLASES OF MAINE, NEW HAMPSHIRE, VERMONT, MASSACHUSETTS, RHODE ISLAND, NEW YORK, PENNSYLVANIA, OHIO, INDIANA, ILLINOIS, IOWA, CANADA, ETC., ETC.

PUBLISHED BY

GEORGE N. TACKABURY,

DETROIT, MICH., AND CANASTOTA, N. Y.

1884.

STEREOTYPED AND PRINTED BY THE FREE PRESS PRINTING HOUSE,
DETROIT, MICH.

NOTE.—ERRORS AND OMISSIONS.—It is quite impossible to avoid errors and omissions in a work of this extent. Some of them, indeed, arise from changes which occur while the work is in progress. Persons who notice them will confer a favor by indicating them so that they may be rectified in future editions.

Address GEO. N. TACKABURY, DETROIT, MICH., or CANASTOTA, N. Y.

CONTENTS.

INDEX TO MAPS.

NOTE.—The Counties of the *Lower Peninsula* are drawn to the scale of three miles to an inch. They are arranged in geographical order, commencing at the northern extremity of the Peninsula, with Emmet county, and following across the State from west to east and from east to west to its southern boundary. The Counties of the *Upper Peninsula* are drawn to a scale of four miles to an inch.

PREFACE.

SALUTATORY.

The Editor and Publishers to the Patrons of the Atlas of Michigan.

WE greet you with congratulations, which we feel should be mutual, on the completion of our arduous labors, editing, compiling, drawing, engraving and publishing the work now placed before you. The difficulties which attend the preparation of such a work by individual enterprise can be understood only by those who have been engaged in similar undertakings. We believe, however, that the great labor and expense bestowed upon this atlas have been productive of highly remunerative results, to you at least, as well as to all interested in the welfare of the State, if not to ourselves.

VALUE OF MAPS.

Maps of States, complete in comprehensive entirety as well as in plenitude of minute detail, such as we here present to you of Michigan, possess an intrinsic and a *practical* value far beyond that due to the mere pleasure they afford in regarding them as pictorial representations of the territory represented as it might appear, could it be looked down upon from a great elevation. Only the more thoughtful, however, fully recognize how closely and extensively the prosperity of a country depends upon the existence of accurate maps of its domain with general facility of access to them. We take the liberty to suggest, to those who have not given much attention to the subject, a few of the many considerations which indicate this dependence.

EXPLORATIONS AND SURVEYS.

It will easily be seen that before a new country can become settled, it must be *explored*, to ascertain what portions of it, if any, are available for the residence of a future population. Exploration, to be serviceable, should be carefully and intelligibly recorded, and to accomplish this, accurate instrumental *surveys* are required. The original records of these surveys are taken in the surveyor's note-books in the field. The notes, however, are far from being in a convenient form for reference, and a stranger wishing to gain information from the note books or from a verbal abstract of them, would find himself involved in much difficulty and perplexity.

TOPOGRAPHICAL MAPS.

The most convenient and intelligible mode of presenting the results of the surveys is that of topographical maps drawn to a suitable scale. In this way the relative positions of all parts of the country are preserved, and every representation of an object upon the paper bears an invariable proportion to the corresponding object upon the ground. Thus the scale of the county maps in this atlas is $\frac{1}{190080}$; or one inch upon the paper represents a distance of 190,080 inches or three miles upon the ground. The same proportion holds good if any other standard of measure than that of inches is used. A length of one centimetre, for instance, on the paper would represent 190,080 centimetres or 1900.8 metres upon the ground.

IMAGINARY POINT OF VIEW.

The apparent size of an object depends upon the magnitude of the visual angle it subtends, or in less technical language, upon the size of the angle or opening between two straight lines extending from the opposite sides of the object to the eye. This angle diminishes as the distance increases and by the familiar law of proportion in similar triangles, we can calculate the elevation above the earth which would give the same apparent magnitude or visual angle to objects, which their representations have in the atlas. Supposing the atlas page to be viewed at a distance of fifteen inches from the eye, then, since the scale of the map is three miles to an inch, fifteen inches above the maps correspond to forty-five miles above the ground. Of course the more comprehensive maps upon smaller scales represent the country as if seen from a correspondingly greater elevation of the point of view.

VALUE OF MAPS IN PROMOTING IMMIGRATION.

If the surveyor is accurate in his field work, and the topographer skillful in reproducing the results of the surveys in graphical form, we obtain reliable and valuable maps. In no other way could one who contemplated emigrating to a new country obtain so correct an idea of its topographical features, its rivers, lakes, marshes, forests, prairies etc., and their relations to each other as by a correct map of the country, particularly if the map also presents to view the means of access to the region, whether by sailing vessels or navigable rivers and lakes, or by artificially constructed roads and rail roads. The immigrant is thereby enabled to compare advantages held out to induce him to settle in different localities, in the way of convenience of access, proximity to earlier settlers and to markets for his produce, prospects of future increase in value, etc., and thus to come to a satisfactory decision in locating his new home. In the absence of such information most men would naturally shrink from a leap in the dark. Other things being equal, a country which has been explored and its attractive features intelligibly represented on a good map would far more rapidly become settled than a "terra incognita."

VALUE IN PROMOTING PUBLIC IMPROVEMENTS.

But the usefulness of maps does not cease with the first occupation of a country. On the contrary the more a state becomes settled and improved the greater the need of an exact and minute knowledge of its topography. New facilities for conveyance and travel are continually required. Wagon roads, canals and railroads must be built to accommodate the ever increasing travel and traffic attendant upon the increasing population and the consequent development of agricultural and mechanic arts. Centres of trade, of manufactures, of the administration of government and of great educational institutions grow up to meet the wants of the people. Easy access to these cities and villages, and from them to more distant places, becomes indispensable, whence occurs a continued multiplication of the public highways. The location and construction of these public works must be preceded by a careful determination of the most favorable routes. The necessity for first constructing an accurate map of the different routes proposed is obvious. Upon it the peculiar advantages and disadvantages of each route will more distinctly appear than in any other way, and unnecessarily expensive if not irreparable errors of construction are thereby avoided. Officers and promoters of railroads and other public works, while constantly availing themselves of these important aids in their operations, frequently fail to appreciate their great indebtedness to them. If there is any one interest which, more than another, among the various branches of industry in the social economy, is indebted to topographical engineering, it is the enormously great and constantly increasing *Railroad* interest.

GENERAL USES.

It would be impossible to designate or enumerate all the various practical uses which are continually being made of maps by persons in nearly every class of life, from the traveller who, for business or pleasure, desires to ascertain the shortest and most convenient route from place to place, to the railroad engineer, county officer or state legislator who considers the relations of any particular engineering project or concomitant course of legislative action to the welfare of the parties for whom he is empowered to act. So clearly has the value, to a State, of accurate topographical maps been perceived by the Governments of Europe that, with scarcely an exception, they have each expended many millions of dollars to obtain them, instead of leaving the matter, as in this country, almost entirely to individual enterprise.

EDUCATIONAL USES.

Besides the direct practical uses of local maps they have an educational value, of which it is well not to lose sight. Instruction in the geography of the whole world is very properly taught, in an elementary way, even in the primary schools, as a branch of the most common education. There can be no doubt that this would be most advantageously supplemented if not preceded, by a *careful* study of the minute geography of the student's own state, county and immediate vicinity. Even a child forms a better idea of the nature and uses of a map when he is able to observe and compare the relative position of familiar haunts and to trace out the routes of his rambles about his home. Clearly his conceptions of the relations, as to position and magnitude, between his town, county, state, country, and the entire world will be far more correct than would be possible without the aid of accurate local maps. No intelligent, public spirited citizen therefore, who feels interested in the prosperity of the community in which he resides, in his own personal prosperity and in the education and intellectual welfare of his children, can afford to be without the best maps attainable, of his township, county and state. This is especially true in a state like Michigan which is increasing with such wonderful rapidity, in population wealth and importance.

UNITED STATES SYSTEM OF LAND SURVEYS.

The sources of information made available in preparing the maps for this atlas were various. The basis of the whole work was obtained by carefully copying all the township plats in the State Land Office at Lansing, some eighteen hundred and fifty in number. These were originally made under the direction of the United States Land Commissioner, in accordance with the system of Surveying and Laying out the Public Lands established by Congress in 1785. This system was planned with a wise foresight of the needs of a new and growing country and its execution has, in general, been conducted in as faithful and skillful a manner as the circumstances would permit.

A brief description of the United States system as applied to the public lands of Michigan, will also describe, in its general features the uniform method for all the public lands of the United States except in a few special cases.

PRINCIPAL MERIDIAN AND BASE LINE.

A meridian line, running through the State from north to south, and a base line running across from east to west, were first surveyed out, very carefully, by competent engineers, great care being taken that the former should be truly on a meridian or due north and south line, and the latter on a parallel of latitude or due east and west line. These two lines serve as bases or datum lines for all the surveys in the State, including the upper and lower peninsulas and those islands belonging to the State. They correspond in some measure to the co-ordinate axes of analytical mathematics, affording a simple method of locating surveys.

The Michigan meridian was the first one located for the United States Public Lands, before the State was organized, and is known as the "First Principal Meridian." It forms the boundary between Lenawee and Hillsdale counties, passes through the middle of Jackson and Ingham, divides Clinton from Shiawassee and Gratiot from Saginaw, Crawford from Oscoda and Otsego from Montmorency, and, passing through the eastern part of Cheboygan county, strikes Lake Huron nearly south of the eastern extremity of Bois Blanc island. The Base Line for this meridian runs from Lake Michigan to Lake Huron, along the northern boundaries of Van Buren, Kalamazoo, Calhoun, Jackson, Washtenaw and Wayne counties.

RANGES AND TOWNSHIPS.

After the establishment of the Meridian and Base Line, the surveyor proceeds to lay off the country into Townships, six miles square. Each Township accordingly contains thirty-six square miles or 23,040 acres "as nearly as may be." Having measured a distance of six miles along the base line to the east or west of the Principal Meridian a monument is erected at the six mile point and another meridian is surveyed out north and south from this monument. The strip of land six miles wide lying between and extending in a north and south direction entirely across the State is called a *Range*. The Range adjacent to the Principal Meridian is called Range Number One East, if on the east side, or Range Number One West, if on the west side of the Principal Meridian. A second strip six miles wide adjoining the first, is called Range Number Two, east or west as the case may be, and so in the same manner on both sides of the Principal Meridian until the entire State is divided into Ranges.

These Ranges are subdivided into Townships, by east and west lines six miles apart. The Township adjoining the Base Line is called Township Number One North, if on the north side, and Township Number One South, if on the south side of the Base Line. The next Township is Township Number Two, north or south as the case may be, and so on to the northern and southern boundaries of the State. Portions of Townships which are not complete where the Ranges are bounded by irregular lines or bodies of water are called Fractional Townships.

By this comprehensive and simple method of designation the description of the smallest tract of land becomes admirably succinct and definite. An adequate description for purposes even of legal conveyance of a forty acre lot might read as follows.—"The south-east quarter of the north west quarter of section Seventeen in Township Eight North, Range Three East of the First Principal Meridian." No farther description could make its exact location plainer or more certain. Of course reference to other Principal Meridians would fix the position of the lands in other States or Territories.

Upon the county maps in this atlas the numbers of the Ranges are indicated by Roman Numerals in the border at the *top and bottom* of the maps; the letters R. W. and R. E. near the corners signifying Ranges west and Ranges east of the Principal Meridian. Township numbers are in figures at the *sides*, $\frac{T.}{N.}$ and $\frac{T.}{S.}$ denoting Townships North and Townships South of the Base Line.

SECTIONS.

Each Township is cut up into thirty-six Sections by lines running parallel to the side of the Township. Each section is one mile square and contains 640 acres "as nearly as may be."

The accompanying diagram exhibits the manner of numbering the sections of a single township, commencing with Number One in the northeast corner.

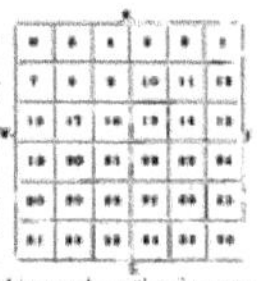

In fractional Townships each section is numbered the same as the corresponding section in whole Townships.

It will be noticed that in this Atlas only those section numbers are engraved which mark the eastern and western sections of each lateral row, thus:—Crowding the map with figures is thereby avoided, while the number of any section is easily ascertained.

Each Section is usually subdivided into half mile squares called quarter Sections each containing one hundred and sixty acres, and sometimes the subdivision is carried still farther into half quarter or quarter quarter sections.

CONVERGENCE OF MERIDIANS.

It will be perceived, on a little reflection, that if north and south lines are true meridians, they will not be parallel, but will approach each other or *converge* towards the north. In fact if continued sufficiently far they would all meet in one point at the north pole. The convergence in a single township is small, though quite perceptible, the actual excess in length of its south over its north line being, in Michigan, about three rods. The townships north of the Base Line, therefore become narrower and narrower than the six miles width with which they commence, by that amount; and those south of it become as much wider than six miles.

CORRECTION LINES.

If continued for too great a distance this narrowing or widening would cause serious inconvenience, and to obviate this effect of the curvature of the earth's surface it is found necessary to establish, at stated intervals, *standard parallels* commonly called "*Correction Lines.*" These are usually sixty miles apart, though in some localities it has been found convenient to establish them nearer together. It will be seen that Michigan has five Correction Lines, all north of the Base Line. The "First Correction Line" is sixty miles north of the Base Line and accordingly runs between Townships 10 and 11. The second is between Townships 20 and 21 and so on. On these parallels, which form new base lines, fresh measurements are made from the Principal Meridian, and the corners of new Townships are fixed six miles apart, as on the original Base Line. This method of procedure not only takes up the error due to convergency of meridians, but checks and arrests errors which arise from want of precision or carelessness in the surveys already made. Its effects will be noticed on the maps at all the correction lines whose position is indicated above, by the offsets which occur there, in the north and south lines. These offsets, of course, increase in amount by a *cumulative* process, as their distance from the Principal Meridian increases. Another precaution against errors in surveying is taken by running, at convenient intervals, usually about forty-eight miles, "*Guide Meridians*". These are surveyed with more exact instruments and with greater care than the ordinary Range lines.

FRACTIONAL SECTIONS.

The reason is now apparent for using the words "as nearly as may be" in the law which defined the area of Townships and Sections. Upon the subdivision of a Township into sections, the surplusage or deficiency is by law "added to or deducted from the western or northern ranges of sections according as the error may be in running the lines from east to west or from north to south." The northern or western sections of a township, (and any others), which contain more or less than 640 acres are accordingly called *Fractional Sections.*

LAKE SURVEYS.

In accordance with Congressional Laws the War Department of the United States Government is carrying on elaborate surveys of the Northern and North western Lakes under the charge of the U. S. Engineer officers. These surveys are based upon very careful and accurate triangulations and astronomical observations and exhibit the topography and hydrography of the Lakes and navigable rivers with great minuteness, giving full sailing directions etc., for navigators. By the courtesy of the accomplished Engineers connected with that most important work the U. S. Lake Survey we have been supplied with all the published charts relating to Michigan as follows:—"West End of Lake Erie," Lieut. Col. James Kearney, 1849, "Maumee Bay," Capt. Geo. G. Meade, 1857, "River Ste. Marie (No. 1)," Capt. Geo. G. Meade, 1857, "River Ste. Marie (No. 2)," Capt. Geo. G. Meade, 1858, "Lake Huron," Capt. Geo. G. Meade, 1860, "North End of Lake Michigan," Brev. Brig. Gen'l W. F. Raynolds, 1867, "Lake Superior (No. 1)," Brev. Brig. Gen'l W. F. Raynolds, 1868, "Lake Superior (No. 2)," Brev. Brig. Gen'l W. F. Raynolds, 1868, "Lake Superior (No. 3)," Brev. Brig. Gen'l C. B. Comstock, 1870, "St. Clair River," Brev. Brig. Gen'l C. B. Comstock, 1872. Gen. Godfrey Weitzel has since held the appointment. The present incumbent is Gen. O. M. Poe.

These charts have not only afforded a means of verifying the general outlines obtained by plotting the United States Land Surveys, and of correcting the coast and river details, so far as they extend, but they have furnished the only available data for projecting the map of Michigan upon correctly drawn meridians and parallels of latitude.

PROJECTION OF THE MAPS.

We have already shown that in drawing a map of a portion of the earth's surface we have to represent it on a reduced scale with all its parts maintaining a uniform proportion to the objects represented. In doing this of a territory of considerable extent we encounter the difficulty or rather the *impossibility* of representing in this way a spherically curved surface upon a flat or plain surface, like that of a map. In a single county the discrepancy arising from this source would be inappreciable, but it becomes quite apparent in a large map of the whole State of Michigan.

If we represent parallels of latitude by straight parallel lines, meridians cannot be accurately drawn for they must either converge, in which case only one of them can make right angles with the parallels of latitude, or if all are drawn at right angles they cannot converge, while on the ground both the convergence and the rectangularity occur.

As it was intended eventually to publish the map of Michigan entire, as a wall map as well as in atlas form, it became necessary to draw the map continuously and to adopt such a mode of "*projection*" as would best adapt it for both purposes by preserving the rectangularity of parallels and meridians without too great a disturbance of the scale or distortion of the true proportions of the map. Various projections have been devised by geographers with these objects in view and different plans are adopted by them for representing the whole earth, for a single hemisphere, or for a portion of a hemisphere, near the equator, near the poles etc. The best now known for our present purpose is that devised by the officers of the United States Coast Survey and called by them the

"RECTANGULAR POLYCONIC PROJECTION."

Imagine huge hollow tin cones, like candle extinguishers, to be placed over the north part of the earth so as to just touch it all around on any particular parallel of latitude which we wish to draw. Of course as we take parallels farther north the cones will become flatter or more blunt at the angle or apex. Suppose these cones removed by some mighty hand, slit from base to apex and then unrolled or "developed," as the mathematicians have it, so as to become flat. The line where the parallel of latitude touched the cone would roll out forming a part of a circle, the point which had formed the apex of the cone being its centre. Now this arc of a circle reduced to its proper scale is what we draw upon the map for the corresponding parallel of latitude. The term "Polyconic" is used because it is necessary to develope a different cone for each different parallel of Latitude represented. For areas not too large all the meridians and parallels will cross at sensibly right angles. There will be more or less distortion on the sides of the map according to the extent of territory represented, but for a state no larger than Michigan the distortion will be practically inappreciable. The Coast Survey tables, published in the Report for 1853, are very convenient for drawing this projection and have been used in the construction of the large map from which all the county maps in this atlas are taken.

TOPOGRAPHICAL DETAILS.

The parallels and meridians being projected, we drew the Principal Meridian and its Base line, the latter on a parallel of latitude. Both were fixed as nearly as possible in their proper places by comparison with the Lake Charts already mentioned. The termini of these lines were approximately marked upon the charts by careful comparison of the adjacent topography with that of the Land Surveys and thus the true positions of the lines as to Latitude and Longitude were approximately determined.

We next proceeded to "build up" the surveys upon the projection about in the same order in which they were made, carefully measuring the distances recorded in the second or revised surveys made for subdividing townships into sections. This was a somewhat difficult and perplexing task but it was most faithfully performed. The Lakes and Water courses were next laid down from the Land Surveys and corrected from such more modern sources of information as could be obtained, and finally the villages, post-offices, highways, railroads etc., were carefully located.

CO-OPERATION.

The compilation of the details of the map has been attended with a vast amount of research and labor, including correspondence etc. We are happy to acknowledge the kind interest which has almost universally been manifested in the work throughout the State and the cordiality and effectiveness of the co-operation by numerous and well informed correspondents. It is hardly possible to enumerate all the persons to whom we are under deep obligations. The supervisors of nearly every organized township in the State have responded cheerfully to our inquiries.

It is now ten years since the First Edition of our work made its appearance, and similar reasons to those which then conspired to make it a necessity exist now, only in an intensified degree, in their application to the Second Edition. While the general topography of the country has undergone no material change, and the boundaries of our noble State are still the same, her unparalleled advancement in all the great interests identified permanently with her material fortunes could not be satisfactorily illustrated save by the revision of all the county maps. Some new counties and a still greater number of new townships have been formed; new railways, including some of which are of the vastest importance to the agricultural, commercial, and a number of other great interests of the State, have been constructed, while others, previously in operation, have been extended, developments tending directly to vindicate the wisdom of those whose liberality, enterprise and public spirit called them into existence: new wagon roads have been opened; new towns and villages have sprung up as if under the wand of enchantment, and new cities have been chartered. In many counties so great have been the changes that the maps prepared for this edition would hardly be recognized by those familiar with their physical features only as they existed ten years ago. The work of revising and correcting these maps has proved a far more elaborate and arduous task than was anticipated, hence a longer time has been required for its final completion than was expected, but the work has been conscientiously performed, and we are confident that in the important details referred to this edition will be found very generally correct. For the results attained we are largely indebted to county and other local surveyors, as well as to other intelligent and capable gentlemen in almost every county, who have lent their kind offices in behalf of our enterprise. We would also express a sense of our obligation to railroad officers for the stations upon their several lines, and to the honorable the Secretary of State and the Commissioner of Roads and Swamp Lands for valuable information. It is of course next to impossible to produce a work of such interminable detail which shall prove absolutely perfect. Changes are liable to transpire even while the work is in progress. But it is hoped and believed that the result will, as a general rule, prove acceptable to even the most exacting. Should any errors or omissions be discovered by the patrons of the work we would be greatly obliged if those noting them would make memoranda of the same and forward by post to G. N. Tackabury, Detroit, in order that the proper corrections may be made in future editions.

We are confident that our new map of the Upper Peninsula will be found entirely satisfactory. It is upon a plan worthy of the mighty interests developed and in process of development in that interesting region, the scale being four miles to the inch, instead of six miles as in the first edition.

It is hardly necessary to invite attention to the various papers treating of all the great questions of interest to the State respectively, which are comprised in our letter press. The historical, educational and scientific papers are the work of gentlemen who have long been recognized as among the very ablest and most scholarly writers upon the themes referred to. As to the historical sketches of steamboats and railroads, we are confident that none will dispute our claim that they are to-day the only full and comprehensive histories extant upon those important subjects. Our compilation upon the Forest and Mineral Wealth of the State—thanks in no small degree to the very reliable authorities to whom proper credit is given—is graphic and exhaustive. The letter press of the second edition exceeds in length that of the first, by eighteen pages. With these brief remarks, it is not without a fair degree of confidence in the result that we submit the fruits of our labors on the question of their value to the verdict of the people.

TOPOGRAPHY AND HYDROGRAPHY.

BY ALEXANDER WINCHELL, LL. D.,

PROFESSOR OF GEOLOGY AND PALEONTOLOGY IN THE UNIVERSITY OF MICHIGAN. LATE DIRECTOR OF THE STATE GEOLOGICAL SURVEY.

THE STATE OF MICHIGAN occupies a position approximating the centre of the continent of North America. The geographical centre of the continent is not far from the Lake of the Woods, which is 560 miles in a straight line from the centre of the State, and 280 miles from its western extremity. The centre of the State is marked by the position of Carp Lake, in Lelanau county, which is 670 miles in a straight line from New York, the nearest point on the Atlantic Seaboard. The State is limited by natural boundaries on all sides except the south. Politically,* it has 708.5 miles coterminous with the Dominion of Canada; 55.5 miles coterminous with Minnesota; 571 miles coterminous with Wisconsin; 58 miles bordering on Illinois; 129.2 miles on Indiana, and 92.8 miles on Ohio; making a total length of boundary line, amounting to 1615 miles.

The land area of the State consists of two natural divisions, known as the Upper and Lower Peninsulas, to which are attached the contiguous islands. The Upper Peninsula is bounded by portions of the lakes Superior, Michigan and Huron, the river St. Mary and the State of Wisconsin. The Lower Peninsula is embraced by lakes Michigan, Huron, St. Clair and Erie, and the St Clair † and Detroit rivers; and is bounded on the south by the States of Ohio and Indiana.

The main land of the State is embraced between the parallels of 41° 692 and 47° 478 north latitude, and the meridians of 82° 407 and 90° 536 of longitude west from Greenwich. The most northerly point is the north side of Keweenaw Point, five miles west of the Light House at Copper Harbor; and the most southerly is the north-west corner of Ohio. The most easterly point is at Port Huron, near the outlet of Lake Huron; and the most westerly is at the mouth of Montreal river. The most northern territory belonging to the State, is Gull Islet, off the extremity of Ile Royale, which attains the latitude of 48° 211.

The following table exhibits the latitudes and longitudes of the principal points of the State:

TABLE OF GEOGRAPHICAL POSITIONS.

STATIONS.	LATITUDE. ° ′ ″	LONGITUDE. ° ′ ″
Detroit, St. Paul's Church,	42 19 46.82	83 02 22.73
" Congregat'l Church,	42 19 45.64	83 02 20.27
" Intersection Fort and Griswold Sts.,	42 19 49.85	83 02 20.83
Fort Gratiot, Light House,	43 00 21.86	82 24 43.98
Pt. aux Barques, Light House,	44 01 23.35	82 47 09.87
Saginaw, Light House,	43 38 27.84	83 50 54.46
Tawas, Light House,	44 15 35.44	83 28 14.57
Mouth of Thunder Bay River,	45 03 38.90	83 25 32.63
Detour Light House,	45 57 20.11	83 54 23.71
Fort Holmes, Mackinac I.,	45 51 27.81	84 36 24.48
Waugoshance Light House,	45 47 18.38	85 04 56.53
N. E. cor. Big Beaver Island,	45 45 12.67	85 29 38.00
Sand Point, Escanaba,	45 44 35.04	87 02 25.80
Menominee,	45 06 19.32	87 35 25.20
Grand Haven, Court House,	43 03 47.25	
" Lake Survey Sta.	43 03 50.14	86 14 21.30
Marquette, Light House,	46 32 55	87 22 12.40
Vulcan, near Copper Harbor,	47 28 44.28	
Ann Arbor, Observatory,	42 16 48.20	83 43 43.05
New Buffalo, Intersection of middle of Whittaker Ave. and Mechanics St.,	41 47 47.00	86 44 53.35
Niles, Steeple of Trinity Church,	41 49 48.10	86 15 36.60
Monroe, Light House,	41 53 28.77	83 19 22.29
Adrian,	41 54 36	83 59 27
Hillsdale,	41 55 19	84 33 46
Coldwater,	41 52 30	85 01 32
White Pigeon,	41 44 59	85 39 42
Ypsilanti,	42 14 12	83 37 06
Jackson,	42 14 46	84 23 01
Marshall,	42 13 38	84 56 09
Kalamazoo,	42 17 39	85 35 53
Allegan,	42 31 49	85 52 37
Lansing,	42 43 53	84 30 42
Pontiac,	42 37 44	83 17 21
Owosso,	43 00 17	84 18 21
Grand Rapids,	42 57 59	85 39 59
Muskegon,	43 13 54	86 15 51
Flint,	43 01 01	83 40 58
Tuscola,	43 19 31	83 39 20
East Saginaw,	43 26 25	83 55 43
Manistee,	44 13 41	86 18 42
Traverse City, E. and Hannah, Lay & Co's Pier,	44 45 59.74	85 36 53.11
Ontonagon, Light House,	46 52 16.35	89 18 29.46
Houghton,	47 07 15.06	88 33 27.12

The foregoing positions, as far as Vulcan, inclusive, are selected from the numerous determinations of the United States Lake Survey; Ann Arbor has been determined by the Director of the Observatory; New Buffalo and Niles are from Col. Graham's determinations; Monroe, Traverse City, Ontonagon and Houghton are from the Lake Survey Charts, and the co-ordinates of the remaining localities have been calculated from Farmer's large sectional map of the State.

The following table exhibits the difference of time between Detroit and some important points in the State:

TABLE OF LOCAL TIME.

LOCALITIES.	Time difference from Detroit Time. m. s.	LOCALITIES.	Time difference from Detroit Time. m. s.
Port Huron,	3 30.57*	Battle Creek,	8 34.89
Pontiac,	0 58.85	Kalamazoo,	10 13.13
Monroe,	1 07.87	Traverse City,	10 18.08
Ypsilanti,	2 18.89	Grand Rapids,	10 20.39
Flint	2 34.35	Allegan,	11 20.84
Ann Arbor (Obs.,)	3 45.85	Grand Haven,	12 47.90
East Saginaw,	3 33.84	Niles (Trinity Ch.,)	12 52.93
Adrian,	3 48.83	Muskegon,	12 55.91
Owosso,	5 03.91	Manistee,	13 65.25
Hillsdale,	5 05.55	Escanaba,	16 00.19
Jackson,	5 22.54	Marquette (L. H.,)	17 16.85
Lansing,	5 53.30	Menominee,	18 12.16
Mackinac,	6 16.01	Houghton,	21 04.25
Marshall,	7 35.85	Ontonagon,	25 04.42
Coldwater,	7 56.84	Mouth Montreal River,	29 59.15

* Faster than Detroit Time.

FOREIGN LOCALITIES COMPARED WITH DETROIT.

Greenwich, England,	5 h. 32 m.	2.51 sec.	faster.
N. Y. City, (Custom House,)	36 "	9.31 "	"
Washington, D. C. (Observ.)	24 "	8.51 "	"
Chicago, Ill. (Old Court House,)	18 "	22.34 "	slower.
San Francisco, Cal.,	2 h. 37 "	23.60 "	"

The geographical centre of the main land of the Upper Peninsula is on Sec. 36, T. 46, N. R. 25, W., about three miles east of the Peninsula Railroad, in Marquette County. The geographical centre of the main land of the Lower Peninsula is on Sec. 24, T. 13, N. R. 3, W., township, of Coe, Isabella County. The geographical centre of the main land of the entire State is on Sec. 3, T. 21, N. R. 8, W., in Missaukee County. The geographical centre of the entire state, within its political boundaries (including the lake-areas belonging to the State) is on the S. W. ¼ Sec. 30, T. 30, N. R. 11. W., very near Provemont in Lelanau County.*

The extreme length of the main land of the Upper Peninsula is 318.104 miles, and its extreme breadth 164.286 miles. The extreme length of the main land of the Lower Peninsula, from north to south, is 277.009 miles; and its extreme breadth is 259.056 miles. The greatest actual width of the Peninsula, however, measured along a parallel of latitude, is between Forestville, on Lake Huron, and Little Point Sable, on Lake Michigan. The width here is 197.057 miles.†

The Base Line of the land surveys of the State runs "seven miles north of Detroit" (probably the Old Capitol), and the Michigan Meridian (which rules south to the old territorial boundary) is 84° 37′ west of Greenwich. The land area of the State is 56,457 square miles, or 36,128,640 acres.

There are 179 islands included within the political boundaries of the State, which have an area from one acre upwards. The total area of these islands is 404,730 acres.

The total length of the lake-shore line within the State is 1620 miles. Besides the larger lakes lying upon the frontiers, the State includes within its bounds 5173 smaller lakes, having an area of 712,864 acres. The following Table sets forth the leading data respecting the "Great Lakes."

	Length miles.	Width miles.	Depth feet.	Shore Line in Michigan miles.	Elevation above sea feet.	Area sq. miles.
Superior,	460	180	988	524	600.2	32,000
Michigan,	380	108	900	637	580.6	20,000
Huron,	270	160	300	424	580.6	20,000
Erie,	250	80	200	39	565	6,000
Ontario,	180	65	500		232	6,000
	1,620			1,624		84,000

*The political boundaries of the State are defined by the following documents: Sixth Article of the Treaty of Ghent; Report of Commissioners provided by that Article, and dated June 18, 1822; Act admitting Michigan into the Union, June 15, 1836; Act of April 18, 1818, Sec. 2; Act admitting Wisconsin, Aug. 6, 1846; Act of April 20, 1836, Sec. 2. For the original boundary of Ohio on the north, see Act of April 30, 1802.

† The river St. Clair was originally named Sinclair from Patrick Sinclair, a British military officer, who purchased of the Indians, in 1765, 4000 acres of land on the river. Lake St. Clair was so named from a French officer. (American State Papers, Public Lands, Vol. 1, p. 216.)

* These determinations have been made by ascertaining the centres of gravity of sheets of paper of uniform thickness, cut to the exact limits of the mapped boundaries of the areas whose centres were sought.

† These dimensions are based on the latitudes and longitudes of the points referred to, and the calculated lengths of the degrees of latitude and longitude in the different positions.

The two natural divisions of the State are distinguished by marked physical characteristics. They are completely cut off from each other by the Straits of Mackinac. The northern is rugged, with numerous rocky exposures; the southern consists of plains, plateaux, gentle undulations and moderate hills, with very few outcrops of rocky strata. The northern peninsula is a mineral region; the southern, agricultural. The climates of the two peninsulas are as distinct as their locations and their topography; and, in all statements respecting the climatic features of the State, the two peninsulas ought to be separately treated. The meteorological means for the whole State convey very inadequate impressions respecting either of its natural divisions.

The topographical configuration of the State has been the subject of very careful study. The attempt has been made to collect all the important information obtained in running the various levels for railroad and canal surveys, from 1836 to the present time. The recent progress of these enterprises is so rapid, that it has been impossible to make the tables of elevation absolutely complete, but over 6900 elevations have, nevertheless, been tabulated, which give the height of the surface at every point along the surveyed lines, at which the superficial slope exhibits any considerable change. The planes of reference of the various surveys have been elaborately compared with each other, and all the elevations reduced to the Chicago City Datum—which is low water in Lake Michigan in 1847. These elevations, transcribed upon the map of the State, have served, in the Lower Peninsula, for the construction of a system of contour lines, or lines drawn through points having the same elevation above a given plane. We have undertaken to draw a contour line for every fifty feet of elevation above Lake Michigan, and these are exhibited upon the accompanying map.

Throughout all that portion of the State south of Houghton Lake, this map presents a good general picture of the surface configuration. North of that latitude, the data are insufficient; and the contour lines must be regarded as only rudely approximative. Combining, however, the exact data at hand, with our personal familiarity with the northern portion of the Peninsula, and with the inferences to be drawn from a good map of the water courses, we have produced results which, with many persons, may be regarded as quite preferable to the absence of all information.

These tortuous lines, to the casual observer, may seem to be very easily laid down, and to possess little interest or value; but every intelligent person will be able to appreciate their importance, and to understand that they represent months of careful labor.

A general glance at the superficial configuration of the Lower Peninsula, reveals a surface swelling gently from the lake shores toward the interior regions. The lake waters are hemmed in by no mountainous barriers or rocky ranges of hills. Generally the lake shores are depressed. This is especially the case around the upper half of Saginaw Bay, and along the region from Lake Huron to Maumee Bay. Yet, in almost all cases, the land rises, within a few miles—sometimes quite rapidly, or even abruptly—to the height of one or two hundred feet above the contiguous lake. Steep, or even precipitous shores, are presented in the northern and eastern part of Huron county; through a large part of Presq' Ile county, around Little Traverse Bay in Emmet county; and throughout Charlevoix, Antrim, Leelanau and Benzie counties; and the statement may be extended to Manistee, Mason and Oceana counties. Sleeping Bear Point in Leelanau county is a bluff of incoherent materials facing the lake, and attaining an elevation of 600 feet. The limestone ridge forming the northern angle of the county, rises somewhat precipitously to altitudes of 200 to 300 feet.* Similar elevations approach the shore of Little Traverse Bay. The Sliding Banks on Hammond's Bay of Lake Huron are 77 feet high, and the rocky cliffs about Point aux Barques, rise to the height of 12 to 20 feet.

Along the border of Lake Michigan, stretches a series of sand-dunes or piles of fine, mostly silicious sand, blown up by the prevailing westerly winds. These attain elevations up to 100 and 200 feet. At Grand Haven, the highest reaches an altitude of 215 feet. This is on the north side of Grand river. The highest on the south side attains an elevation of 205 feet. In the neighborhood of New Buffalo, they reach heights of 30, 40, 50 and 93 feet. Back of these dunes the surface is generally depressed, and not unfrequently, occupied by a marsh, a lakelet, a lagoon or an estuary. As a rule, these sands are continually shifting before the wind. They are, accordingly, making constant encroachments upon areas occupied and improved by man. Sometimes, as at Grand Haven and Sleeping Bear, the forest becomes submerged beneath these accumulations, and presents the singular spectacle of withered tree tops projecting a few feet above a waste of sands.

The origin of these sands is in the disintegration or solution of rocks more or less arenaceous, and located along the shores to the windward, or in the bottom of the lake within reach of the agitations of the waters. The liberated silicious grains are either thrown directly upon the beach, or, through a process of bar formation, a new beach rises to the surface, with the characteristic lagoon between it and the original beach. Thus, in many situations, the land is extended lakeward, and, while the sands are encroaching on the landward side, compensation is made by the westward retreat of the sand-laden beach which supplies the encroaching sands.

Proceeding from the littoral belt of the Peninsula toward the interior, we find a region considerably more elevated and better drained than ancient official misrepresentations had led the general public to believe. Though presenting no mountainous districts, and no indications of the agency of forces of upheaval, we have a land-area attaining throughout a large portion of the peninsula, an elevation averaging from 400 to 1000 feet. Erosions, dating back into geological time, have pared down the original surface, and established the existing slopes to the lake shores, and even to the lake bottoms. Later fluviatile erosions have scored deep and broad valleys, which mark off the prominent portions into several distinct regions.

Viewing the Peninsula as a whole, we discover, first of all, a remarkable depression stretching obliquely across from the head of Saginaw Bay, up the valley of the Saginaw and Bad rivers, and down the Maple and Grand rivers, to Lake Michigan. This depression attains, nowhere, an elevation greater than 72 feet above Lake Michigan. This elevation is in the interval of three miles separating the waters flowing in the opposite directions. This spot was chosen, in 1837, as the location for a canal, connecting Saginaw Bay with Lake Michigan. It is obvious, that when the lakes stood at their ancient elevations, their waters communicated freely across this depression, and divided the Peninsula into two portions, of which the northern was an island. This depression, for convenience of reference, may be designated the "Grand-Saginaw Valley."

That lobe of the peninsular swell which lies to the south-east of the dividing belt, has its salient longitudinal axis stretching somewhat arcuately from north-east to south-west through Huron, Sanilac, Lapeer, Oakland, Washtenaw and Hillsdale counties. This, which may be called the South-eastern Water-shed, is not broken through by any of the streams, though it is deeply excavated by the Huron river, in Washtenaw county. Various passes exist across it, and the crest rises in four isolated summits. The Oakland Summit, located in the north part of Oakland county, attains an elevation, on the surveyed lines,* of 529 feet, and gives rise to tributaries of the Flint, Clinton and Belle rivers. The Washtenaw Summit, in the north-eastern portion of Washtenaw county, rises to the height of 394 feet, and over, and gives origin, on opposite sides, to tributaries of the Huron river. The Franciscan Summit on the borders of Jackson and Washtenaw counties, is 411 feet high, on the measured lines, and divides the waters flowing into the Huron and Grand rivers. The Hillsdale Summit is located in the centre of Hillsdale county, and attains two culminations, one in the south-western part, between Cambria and Reading, where it reaches an elevation of 613 feet, and another in the north-eastern part, in the township of Somerset. This is, therefore, the highest summit south of the

* For a more particular account of the topography and hydrography of this portion of the State see the writer's *Report on the Grand Traverse Region*. 8 vo. pp. 92 with map. 1866.

* It must be remembered that the following discussion is based on elevations along lines of survey for railroads and canals. Generally, therefore, the numerical values given do not represent the highest elevations nor the lowest depressions.

MICHIGAN
SHOWING
CONTOUR LINES
BY
ALEXANDER WINCHELL, LL.D.
Professor of Geology and Paleontology in the University of Michigan.
Late State Geologist of Michigan Etc.
LAKE HURON
SAGINAW BAY
MICHIGAN
LAKE ST. CLAIR
DETROIT
LAKE ERIE
ALPENA
OSCODA
OGEMAW
MANISTEE
WEXFORD
MASON
OCEANA
NEWAYGO
MONTCALM
GRATIOT
OTTAWA
CLINTON
LIVINGSTON
INGHAM

Grand-Saginaw valley. It stretches south-westward into Indiana, and, on the borders of that State, presents a culmination of 546 feet, while, through the southern portion of Branch county, it maintains an elevation of 400 to 500 feet. The Hillsdale Summit stretches also into the south-western part of Jackson county, with an elevation of 450 feet, while a spur 400 feet high, extends to Springport in the north-western corner of the county. From Hillsdale Summit rise the headwaters of the St. Joseph, Kalamazoo and Grand rivers, flowing into Lake Michigan, and the Maumee and Raisin, flowing into Lake Erie. Tributaries of the Maumee and St. Joseph rise within a mile of each other, in the townships of Reading and Allen. Tributaries of the Kalamazoo and St. Joseph rise within half a mile of each other, in the township of Adams; and these two streams approach again within two miles, at Homer, Calhoun county. The head waters of the Raisin are within a mile of those of the Kalamazoo, in the township of Somerset, and those of the Maumee approach equally near in the adjoining township of Wheatland. In the northern part of Somerset are two peaks which, perhaps, constitute the real culminations of the Hillsdale Summit. Here, within an area of two miles by three, we may view the head waters of the St Joseph, Kalamazoo, Grand and Raisin rivers; and an area of four miles square would include, with these, the highest tributaries of the Maumee.

The broad north-westerly slope of the south-eastern Water-shed is intersected by six great rivers—the Shiawassee, the Cedar and Grand, which unite at Lansing, the Thornapple, which unites with the Grand at Ada, the Kalamazoo and the St. Joseph rivers, all pursuing a general north-westerly course, except the latter, which flows south-westerly to South Bend in Indiana, and thence north-west. The surface between these river valleys rises into a corresponding number of swells. Of these, the one between the Shiawassee and Cedar rivers, lying chiefly in Livingston county, and reaching an elevation of 350 feet, may be regarded as a spur of the Oakland Summit. The Ingham Summit, which is the next, lies between the Cedar and Grand rivers, in the south-eastern portion of Ingham county and the contiguous parts of Jackson, and attains an elevation of 391 feet, on the measured lines. The Grand Ledge Summit, between the Grand and Thornapple rivers, stretching across the northern part of Eaton county and into Ionia, attains an elevation of only 250 feet. The Barry Summit, between the Thornapple and Kalamazoo rivers, is a mass exscinded by Battle Creek from the northwestern prolongation of the Hillsdale Summit. It occupies the south-eastern part of Barry county, reaching, with an altitude of 250 feet, into Eaton, Calhoun and Kalamazoo. The north-western prolongation of this, cut off by Gun river, which unites with the Kalamazoo at Otsego, forms the Kent Summit, occupying the eastern part of Allegan county and the southern part of Kent, and having a culmination of 213 feet in the latter county. Between the Kalamazoo and St. Joseph rivers, is placed the north-easterly-elongated mass of the Cass Summit, which is cut off from the western extension of the Hillsdale Summit by the south-western reach of the St. Joseph river. It covers the north-eastern half of Cass county, extending into the south-western part of Kalamazoo, where it finds a culmination at an elevation of 349 feet, while another culmination in the vicinity of Cassopolis reaches an altitude of 384 feet.

Gathering together the foregoing results, we may here present the following compendious summary:

RELIEF FEATURES IN THE LOWER PENINSULA.

[illegible]

South-eastern Watershed.		Oakland Summit,	529 ft.
		Washtenaw Summit,	394 "
		Francisco Summit,	411 "
	Hillsdale Summit	Somerset culmination,	600?"
		Cambria "	613 "
		California "	548 "
North-western Slope.		Livingston Summit,	350 "
		Ingham Summit,	391 "
		Grand Ledge Summit,	250 "
		Barry Summit,	250 "
		Kent Summit,	213 "
	Cass Sum't	Oshtemo culmination,	349 "
		Cassopolis "	384 "

That Lobe of the Peninsular swell which lies to the north of the Grand-Saginaw Valley is placed, as a mass, midway between lakes Huron and Michigan, with its northwestern borders crowding somewhat upon the region of Grand and Little Traverse Bays of Lake Michigan. It exemplifies, like the Southern Lobe, a strong tendency to a north-east south-west disposition. The primary division of the Northern Lobe is effected by the valleys of the Manistee and Sable rivers, which take their rise upon the highest summit, and flow thence toward the south-west and south-east into their respective Lakes. The Sable has excavated a valley which, in Wexford county and the western part of Oscoda, sinks from 10 to 100 feet below the highest levels, and in the eastern part of Oscoda, and in Alcona County, 200 to 300 feet below the highest levels—the general plains being 90 to 125 feet above the river. The valley of the Manistee (as well as its tributary, the Pine) is similarly sunken in an undulating plateau.

The southern division is bounded south-easterly by a continuous slope toward Saginaw Bay. In its central part it is indented by the hydrographical basin of Houghton and Higgins Lakes. In this rests Houghton Lake at an elevation of 589 feet above Lake Michigan. From this lake, the Muskegon river, the largest of the Peninsula, takes its rise, and, flowing south-westerly, marks the position of a broad deep valley, leaving, on the south-east, an elongated watershed stretching from Mecosta County through Clare and Roscommon, into Ogemaw County. This may be distinguished as the Central Watershed. It presents a general elevation of 700 feet and over, throughout its entire length. The Roscommon Summit of the Watershed, upon the eastern borders of the county by that name, attains an altitude of at least 820 feet, and the Clare Summit, in the central part of Clare County, is believed to attain an elevation of 750 feet.

The prolongation of the Central Watershed toward the north-east is nearly cut off by the South Branch of the Sable river, forming thus what may be designated as the Ogemaw Summit, occupying the region around the junction of the four counties, Ogemaw, Roscommon, Crawford and Oscoda. The culminating point is believed to be about 800 feet above Lake Michigan, while the pass separating it from the Roscommon Summit is not depressed below 625 feet.

To the north-west of the central lakes and the valley of the Muskegon, rise three summits detached from each other by shallow passes. The Crawford Summit, with an elevation of over 700 feet, besides occupying the south-western portion of the county by this name, stretches into Kalkaska, Missaukee and Roscommon Counties. Being bounded on the north-west by the valley of the Manistee, on the north-east by the bifurcated valley of the North and South Forks of the Sable, it is limited on the south-west by interlocking tributaries of the Manistee and Muskegon rivers.

The Wexford Summit, in the south-eastern portion of Wexford county and contiguous portions of Missaukee and Osceola counties, includes Clam Lake, and is believed to attain an elevation exceeding 700 feet. By the Pine river, a tributary of the Manistee, whose higher waters issue from the neighborhood of the head-waters of an affluent of the Muskegon, this Summit is isolated, on the south, from the Osceola Summit, located near the centre of Osceola County, and reaching an elevation of over 700 feet.

The northern division of the Northern Lobe of the Peninsula embraces the most elevated land south of the Straits of Mackinac. It appears to consist of two principal summits separated from each other by the pass which gives place to the head waters of the Thunder Bay river, and one of the affluents of the Sable. The eastern, which we may designate the Oscoda Summit, because located chiefly in the northern part of that county, has an elevation of 800 feet or more. Otsego Summit, to the west, occupies a large part of Otsego county, and is said to attain an elevation of 1200 feet. Within its limits, take their rise the streams which water the Grand and Little Traverse regions, as well as those which find outlet in the vicinity of the Straits.*

RELIEF FEATURES IN THE LOWER PENINSULA

[illegible]

Southern Division.	[illegible]	Roscommon Summit,	820? ft.
		Clare Summit,	750? "
		Ogemaw Summit,	800? "
		Crawford Summit,	700? "
		Wexford Summit,	700? "
		Osceola Summit,	700? "
Northern Division.		Oscoda Summit,	800? "
		Otsego Summit,	1200? "

The enumeration of the foregoing 18 Summits, in the whole Peninsula, must not be

* Otsego Lake is represented on the maps as having an outlet into the North Branch of the Sable river. This is an error. There are evidences, however, of an ancient outlet, at a time when the water of the lake stood at a higher level. Recently, moreover, a canal has been dug for "lumbering" purposes, which opens connection with the Sable. The lowering of this lake, like that of Houghton and Higgins Lakes, is one of the numberless evidences of a gradual process of desiccation taking place all over the continent—to the east as well as the west of the Rocky Mountains.

allowed to produce the impression of any very marked irregularities of surface. The summit-districts are not generally mere hill-tops, but level or gently undulating plateaux, through which atmospheric and fluviatile erosions have excavated drainage valleys of moderate depths or with gently bounding slopes. This conformation of the surface exists to a marked extent in the Northern Lobe of the Peninsula. There are, consequently, few precipitous hill-sides, and but very limited regions which cannot be subjected readily to the operations of agriculture.

It may convey, in a more exact form, some idea of the nature of the surface, to present the following statistics of the construction of the Jackson, Lansing and Saginaw railroad. On the 120 miles of the road between Wenona and Otsego Lake, the average amount of earth-work per mile was 10,000 cubic yards; the maximum mile, 40,000, and the minimum, 1,000 cubic yards. The deepest cut is 23 feet; the deepest filling, 28 feet, and the longest cut, 5,000 feet. The total amount of culverting is 500,000 feet, board measure; total amount of bridging, 1,320 feet; number of bridges, 15; longest bridge, 200 feet; highest, 28 feet.

As to the Upper Peninsula, the data accumulated do not enable us to speak with so much detail; and no attempt has been made to lay off contour lines. It seems, nevertheless, appropriate to complete our account of Michigan topography by offering some descriptive statements in reference to that Peninsula.

The region between Lake Superior and the northern bend of Lake Michigan, limited on the east by St. Mary's river, and on the west by the Whitefish river, may be referred to as the Monistique Peninsula, from the large Lake Monistique, occupying nearly a central position in it. The principal portion of the drainage, to the west of this lake, is into Lake Michigan, the water-shed running east and west, by a zig-zag line, within six to ten miles of Lake Superior. East of Lake Monistique, the drainage is chiefly into Lake Superior and other waters east of the meridian of the Straits. The streams, however, throughout the whole interior of the Peninsula, are sluggish, and the regions to the east of Point Iroquois, and about the upper waters of the Tequamenon, are largely occupied by marshes abounding in peat and bog iron ore.

The southern border of the Monistique Peninsula is lined by ranges of limestone hills, which, in the vicinity of Point Detour, are but slightly elevated, with intervening marshes, but, farther west, in the vicinity of Mackinac, attain elevations of 150 to 300 feet. Drummond's Island and the Manitoulin Islands are but the eastward prolongation of the same range of hills, and exhibit elevations quite as considerable as those in the vicinity of the Straits. The cliffs at the eastern extremity of Drummond's Island are over 100 feet high, while the surface toward the interior, rises to the height of 200 and 300 feet. The escarpments of Mackinac Island are 140 feet high, and the central plateau is 300 feet high. Westwardly, the same range of hills extends to Little Bay de Noquet, where, as at Mackinac Island, it presents some strongly marked scenery. In approaching the coast, this elevated limestone region is cut by erosions into innumerable islands ranging in extent from a mere point of rock to several hundreds, or even thousands of acres. These, in the vicinity of Drummond's Island, and Point Detour, become a literal labyrinth with almost inextricable passages.

Toward the north shore, a prominent range of hills begins in the region back of Point Iroquois, and extends in a nearly westerly direction, to the coast of Lake Superior, where it abuts in the famous escarpment known as the "Pictured Rocks," and re-appears in Grand Island with its towering promontories. These smoothly rounded and densely wooded hills attain elevations of 300 to 600 feet above Lake Superior. The streams which break through the range are interrupted by falls. The principal of these is the Tequamenon, which has falls of 40, 45 and 15 feet. The Au Train, eight miles above its mouth, has a fall of 95 feet, and nearer the lake, another of 40 feet.

The immediate shore, between Point Iroquois and the Pictured Rocks, is an alternation of low, sometimes marshy, plains, and rounded sand-hills and promontories. The latter, in the vicinity of Carp river, reach an elevation of 100 feet, while the Grand Sable stands 345 feet above the lake.

The Whitefish river marks the location of a well characterized Valley of Erosion, from one to three miles wide, and bounded by unconsolidated banks 100 to 120 feet above the limestone bottom. The river rises in a series of lakelets within nine miles of the shore of Lake Superior; and the Au Train river, flowing into the latter lake, takes its rise in the same vicinity. Along this valley, the most elevated point is not more than 150 feet above Lake Superior. The writer has elsewhere* suggested that this valley is probably the site of an ancient outlet of Lake Superior, whose waters then passed through Little Bay de Noquet, Green Bay, and the Wisconsin depression occupied by Lakes Winnebago, Horicon and Koshkonong, into the valley of Rock river, and thence to the Mississippi.

Of the region west of Whitefish river, the southeastern portion, between the Menominee river and Green Bay, is mostly a gently undulating surface, presenting a general slope in the direction of the water-courses. This slope, in the south-western part of Delta county, is 430 feet, and near the head waters of the Chocolate river, in Marquette county, 550 feet above Lake Michigan. North and north-west of this, is the mountainous district, comprising the Iron and Copper regions, each of which is characterized by its own topography.

The water-shed of the mountainous region strikes in a serpentine course, north-west from the head-waters of the Chocolate river, to within ten miles of the head of Keweenaw Bay, whence it bends, by a course still more serpentine, south-westward to Lac Vieux Desert, on the boundary of Wisconsin. In the first reach of its course, it passes through the midst of the Marquette Iron District. The elevation at Negaunee is 775 feet above Lake Michigan; at Ishpeming, to the west of the water-shed, 865 feet, and at the Champion mine, near Lake Michigami, 1011 feet. The summit, on the Marquette, Houghton and Ontonagon railroad, is 1186 feet. Lake Michigami lies 906 feet above Lake Michigan. The hills north of the lake, reach an elevation of 1215 feet. The greatest elevation on the water-shed is in the vicinity of the sources of the Michigami river, which are 1250 feet above Lake Michigan. The Huron Mountains, east of Keweenaw Point, abut upon the shore of Lake Superior, and rise in rugged eminences which give a marked expression of the mountainous character of the Upper Peninsula. Mount Huron attains an elevation of 932 feet, and other Summits rise from 760 to 887 feet above Lake Superior. The region of the water-shed, south-west from Lake Michigami, becomes first less broken, and then a gently undulating plain, to the Wisconsin boundary.

Keweenaw Point is a rocky ridge, which, beginning with the promontory at the head of the Point, forms a water-shed nearly along the central line. From the base of the Point, the range trends south-west into Ontonagon county. Mount Houghton, near the head of the Point, is 884 feet above Lake Superior, and the range attains nowhere a greater elevation than 900 feet above the lake.

Beyond the Ontonagon river, the Porcupine Mountains may be regarded as a fresh development of the range. Rising somewhat abruptly from the immediate vicinity of the lake shore, they trend at first south-south-west for about 30 miles, whence their course is more westerly. The greatest altitude attained near Lake Superior, is 950 feet; but several knolls further inland, attain elevations from 1100 to 1380 feet above the lake.

In concluding this synoptical sketch of the topographical features of Michigan, it remains to direct attention to one interesting generalization which has not heretofore been pointed out. This is what may be styled the *diagonal system* in the physical features of the State. By this expression it is meant to say that the longitudinal axes of the topographical and hydrographical features of the State, especially of the Lower Peninsula, lie in directions which are diagonals between the cardinal points of the compass. It would extend this paper too far, to point out the leading *facts* which illustrate and establish this proposition; but it is believed that a brief study of the topographical Chart will render the truth of the proposition apparent.

* *American Naturalist*, Vol. IV., p. 368. Through inadvertence, it is stated in the *Naturalist* that the valley is hemmed in by "limestone" cliffs. The cliffs are of unconsolidated materials, though limestone frequently appears in the bottom of the valley. The existence of this valley is not the only evidence that it has been a water-course, since the limestone bed is, in some places, seen to be worn into pot-holes.

The subject will be elsewhere adequately amplified.

The diagonal system in American physiography is not by any means confined to Michigan. The Maumee river of Ohio, with its tributaries, is a striking reproduction of the Saginaw and its affluents. The Maumee, flowing east-north-east, is fed by the Au-Glaize and St. Mary's, from the south-east, the (little) St. Joseph from the north-east, and the Tiffin from the north-west—the last named, in its higher reaches, flowing from Hillsdale county, Michigan, first south-east and then south-west. In Wisconsin, the north-east south-west basin of Green Bay is prolonged through the Fox river into Lake Winnebago. The same trend is seen in the shore-lines about Chegowawegon Bay, the Apostle Islands and the western extremity of Lake Superior. Even the upper Mississippi, whose general course is meridional, divides itself into a succession of reaches, conforming strangely to the law of diagonism, while, on the other hand, the river and Gulf of St. Lawrence are a further indication that something in the course of events which have fashioned the actual surface, has exerted a greater energy in the direction of the diagonals than in the direction of the cardinal points of the compass.

This is not the place to discuss the causes of this well-marked method in the surface-configuration of the north-west. It would be easy to show that these features sustain relations to the underlying rocky structure. It would be equally easy to demonstrate that they are closely connected with the movements of the continental glacier, which geologists believe to have moved, in the lake region, from north-east to south-west, during the epoch immediately preceding the advent of man upon the earth. But, at the same time, it would appear that these features do not conform exclusively to either set of agencies; and that their actual relation to each may be expressed in the following proposition: *The actual topographical and hydrographical axes of Michigan and the whole lake-region, are the resultant of two forces—a* GLACIAL, *acting from the north-east, and a* STRATIGRAPHICAL, *acting along the lines of strike of the rocky formations.*

As a corollary, we should find that where the rocky formations are most consolidated, the resultant lies nearest the line of the stratigraphical force; and where the rocky formations are little consolidated, the resultant approximates the line of the glacial force.

As a second corollary, physical features determined by causes which have *obliterated* the glacial and stratigraphical trends, do not, necessarily, express relations to either force. Of this kind are the small streams whose courses over the diluvial beds have been determined by post-glacial erosions; and river courses, like the St. Clair and Detroit, marked out across lacustrine or other post-glacial deposits which have concealed the surface-features due to geological structure or glacial erosion.

BRIEF OUTLINE OF THE HISTORY OF MICHIGAN.

BY THE HON. C. I. WALKER.

MICHIGAN, although a comparatively new State, has a history not only of deep and romantic interest, but a history that reaches back beyond the clearly defined regions of fact into the dim and shadowy regions of romance. But a sketch of the limits to which this is confined can only deal with a dry and meager outline of fact. This, however, may not be without its use in awakening an interest in a wider and deeper research.

UNDER FRENCH DOMINION.

Precisely when the territory now included in the State of Michigan was first visited by civilized man cannot now be determined. The first authentic record of such visit is that of the Jesuit Fathers, Charles Raymbault and Isaac Jogues, to the Sault St. Mary in July, 1641. They planted the cross and preached its doctrines to the docile Chippeways. They left with the expectation of soon returning and establishing a mission, but Raymbault died of consumption the following year, and Jogues soon met a martyr's death among the Iroquois. Doubtless long previous to this time French traders had traversed both the woods and the waters of this distant wild.

In October, 1660, Father Mesnard, after a voyage of two months in which he suffered terribly from toil, and from the insults and cruelty of his savage attendants, reached one of the bays of Lake Superior, probably Keweenaw; where with no white man nearer to him than the region of Montreal he spent a long, cold winter, preaching the cross and bearing it. In the following summer he started to visit some Christianized Hurons, and was never seen more. In 1665, the well known Jesuit Father, Claude Allouez, founded the Mission at Lapoint, Lake Superior, just over the Michigan boundary. In 1668, the revered Father Marquette founded the first Christian Mission within the limits of Michigan at Sault St. Mary, and in 1671, he founded the Mission of St. Ignace near Mackinaw, and these became permanent posts as well as great centres of Indian trade. In 1671, an envoy of the French King gathered a grand Indian Council, at Sault St. Mary, of all the Western tribes and formally took possession of all the country between Montreal and the South Sea. From this time, the North-West was under the dominion of France until it was ceded to Great Britain by the treaty of peace of 1763. For the most part, the territory of Michigan, at this time, was occupied by the Chippeways and Ottawas. Some Pottawatomies and Miamis were on the southern borders, and the Sacs and Foxes skirted the southern shore of Lake Superior.

In 1679, La Salle passed through the Detroit River in the Griffin, on his way from Black Rock to Green Bay and the Illinois, and Father Hennepin, the historian of the voyage, who accompanied him, graphically describes the beautiful country bordering upon its banks.

In 1686, Fort St. Joseph was erected where Fort Gratiot afterwards stood near Port Huron by the De Luht or De Luth, and soon after another fort was erected upon the eastern border called Fort Detroit, but its precise locality is not known. One purpose of the erection of these Forts was to command the passage, through which the Iroquois and the English of New York sought to gain access to the upper Lakes and share its rich fur trade. In 1688, a strong force of about sixty Englishmen and several Indians attempted to reach Mackinaw by this route with a large supply of goods, but were captured by the French.

About this time a Fort was built on the St. Joseph River, near its mouth, which continued to be occupied up to the time of the Revolutionary war.

Fort St. Joseph and Fort Detroit were temporary structures and were soon abandoned, so that when Detroit was founded in 1701 the only points in Michigan then occupied were Sault St. Mary, Mackinaw and the post on the St. Joseph River.

In 1694, De La Motte Cadillac, a man of noble birth, great ability and energy, was placed in command at Mackinaw, then the most important point in the Northwest. It had a garrison of one hundred soldiers, and was the center of a large and lucrative trade in furs, in which the English of New York were determined to share. It was while in command here, that he conceived the plan of founding a permanent post and settlement on the Detroit, with especial reference to holding the English and Iroquois in check. In 1699, he visited France, where his worth and services were well known, and in 1700, had interviews with Count Pontchartrain, the Prime Minister of Louis XIV, to whom he fully explained his plan.

It was cordially approved, and he was commanded to return without delay and proceed with its execution. The result was that, on the 24th day of July, 1701, he landed at Detroit with fifty soldiers and fifty traders and citizens, and at once proceeded to erect Fort Pontchartrain, a stockade of pickets with four wooden bastions. With characteristic energy, De La Motte took effective measures to draw around the new post Indians from Mackinaw and elsewhere, until in 1705, there were 2,000 Indians near the fort; 400 of whom were warriors. He also sought to encourage permanent agricultural settlements by the French, but with very limited success. In 1706, the Ottawas becoming dissatisfied, attacked the Miamis near the Fort, killed a priest and a soldier, and kept the fort in something like a state of siege for forty or fifty days. A still greater danger threatened the new post in the bitter hostility of the Jesuits, who disliked the commandant, and that of the Governor General of Canada, who was opposed to this whole project of a post at Detroit and made great efforts to bring about its abandonment

The commandant however succeeded in retaining the confidence of the court and Detroit remained. In 1711, he was appointed Governor of Louisiana and left Detroit. The following year, 1712, while the Indians belonging to Detroit were absent on their hunting grounds, the post was surrounded by a large force of the Foxes, who threatened its destruction. The commandant, Du Buisson, "did not know on what Saint to call" as his force was very small. But the return of the friendly Indians not only raised the siege but the Foxes were in their turn besieged, and, for the most part, utterly destroyed under circumstances of peculiar and ferocious cruelty. About one thousand of them perished.

From this time, during the remainder of the French dominion, no great event occurred in Michigan history, although Indian hostility sometimes threatened its overthrow. About 1749, there was quite an emigration from France to the banks of the Detroit, and settlers were encouraged with grants of land and with advances of stock.

Major Rogers, in 1761, estimates the whole number of inhabitants of this settlement at 2500, of whom 500 were capable of bearing arms.

UNDER BRITISH RULE

The victory of Wolfe upon the plains of Abraham in 1759, led to the surrender of Detroit and the other North-western posts to the English in the following year, and by the treaty of peace of 1763, France ceded her dominion over the Canadas, including Michigan and the North-West, to Great Britain; and the British power was firmly established. The French inhabitants submitted to this change with a much better grace than did their Indian allies. Pontiac, an Ottawa chief of remarkable ability, organized "The Conspiracy of Pontiac," being a combination among the Indian tribes for reducing, by a simultaneous attack, all the British posts from Niagara to Green Bay. Pittsburgh, Niagara and Detroit alone escaped the threatened destruction. In this State St. Joseph and Mackinaw fell into their hands. Detroit was besieged by Pontiac in person for nearly four months. The history of this conspiracy and, especially of the siege of Detroit forms one of the most remarkable chapters in the history of Indian warfare, and it has found in Parkman a fitting historian.

From this time, until the passage of the famous Quebec Act by Parliament in 1774, Michigan was without the pale of civil government. The commandant was not only the Military Commander but combined within himself the Legislative, judicial and executive powers. By the Quebec Act the North-West became a part of the Province of Quebec, and was brought nominally under civil government; and under it Col. Henry Hamilton was appointed "Lieut. Governor and Superintendent of Detroit." He had doubtless been selected because of his capacity, energy and zeal and with reference to the impending difficulties between the Colonies and the Mother Country. Henceforth, and during the entire revolution, Detroit became the center of British power in the North-West. The relentless and cruel Indian warfare, that was carried on against the border settlements of Pennsylvania, Virginia and Kentucky, received its inspiration and direction from this point. The Indian power of the North-West was at this period fearfully great. It was mainly under the control of British influence and British gold, and it was used without scruple to harass, cripple and destroy the struggling Colonies; and, in its cruel ferocity, it spared neither sex, infancy nor age. When George Rogers Clarke made the conquest of the British posts in Illinois in 1778, Governor Hamilton with a force of British and Indians left Detroit to reconquer them. He wintered at Vincennes; and on the 25th of February 1779 was captured by Clarke, and all his force taken prisoners.

Major Lernoult, who was in command during the absence of Hamilton, was succeeded by Major De Peyster in October 1779, and it was under his command that the famous Indian expedition against Kentucky was sent forth under Capt. Byrd in 1780.

MICHIGAN AS A TERRITORY.

By the treaty of peace of 1783, Michigan, heretofore a part of Canada, became a part of the United States, but possession was not actually surrendered until July, 1796, and under the provisions of Jay's treaty.

It then became a part of the North-Western Territory, of which General St. Clair was the Governor; and on the 11th of August, 1796, Wayne County was organized, including all of Michigan, Northern Ohio and Indiana, and a part of Illinois and Wisconsin. It elected delegates to the first Territorial Legislature which met at Cincinnati, Sept. 16, 1799. By an Act of Congress of April 30, 1802, the North-Western Territory ceased to exist, the State of Ohio was organized and the Territory of Indiana was formed, of which Michigan formed a part. Gen. Wm. H. Harrison was the Governor of this new Territory.

On the 11th of January, 1805, Congress passed an Act for the organization of the Territory of Michigan, the Governor and Judges exercising the legislative power. On the 26th of February, the President nominated the Territorial Officers. Gen. Wm. Hull was made Governor. On the 11th of June following, and before the organization of the new government, Detroit was utterly destroyed by fire. Not a dwelling was saved.

On the 1st of July, Governor Hull arrived, and on the following day the Territorial Legislature, consisting of the Governor and Judges was organized, and the Government of Michigan commenced its existence.

It included within its boundaries the present State of Michigan except the upper Peninsula. When Illinois was admitted as a State, in 1818, all of what is now Wisconsin was added to the Territory, and in 1834, Iowa and Minnesota were added for the purposes of temporary government. Gen. Hull continued Governor until the shameful surrender of Detroit to Gen. Brock on the 17th of August, 1812. On the breaking out of the war he was put in command of the army provided for the defence of this frontier. For this position he was utterly incompetent from his age and his habits; but of his patriotism there is no reasonable doubt. On the surrender of Detroit to the British, martial law was declared and they remained in possession until after the victory of Perry on Lake Erie, on the 10th of September in the following year, when on the approach of the army under Harrison, Detroit was evacuated and the subsequent victory of Harrison at the Thames secured it from further danger. On the 13th of October, 1813, Col. Lewis Cass was appointed Governor, an office which he held until he was called to the Cabinet of General Jackson in 1831. Under his wise administration Michigan commenced that career of prosperity which has made it what it now is.

In 1818, some of the public lands, which had recently been surveyed, were brought into market. This, with the introduction of steam navigation upon the lakes, the improvements of the roads leading from the east and the opening of the Erie Canal somewhat later, induced a large emigration to the Territory, so that her population increased from 8,876 in 1820 to 31,639 in 1830, and to 212,267, in 1840. In 1819, Michigan was authorized to elect a delegate to Congress, and in 1823 a Legislative Council was authorized; to consist of nine members to be appointed by the President, by and with the advice and consent of the senate, from eighteen persons elected by the people. From this time the Judges ceased to exercise Legislative power. In 1825, the council was increased to thirteen.

By the ordinance of 1787, it was provided that the Territory North-West of the Ohio, should be divided into not less than three States or more than five, as Congress should decide. Congress had the power to form one or two States of the territory lying "north of an East and West line drawn through the southerly bend or extreme of Lake Michigan." By the creation of the three States of Ohio, Indiana, and Illinois, and leaving a large territory north of the line, Congress had clearly determined to create at least four if not five States out of this territory. The ordinance further provided that whenever any of the States had Sixty Thousand free inhabitants they might form a State Constitution and be admitted into the Union. In 1802 Congress authorized the inhabitants of Ohio to form a State Constitution, fixing for the northern boundary of the new State the line indicated by the ordinance viz.: "an East and West line drawn through the Southerly extreme of Lake Michigan." But the Constitution of Ohio described a different line, viz. "one running from the Southern bend of Lake Michigan to the Northerly cape of Maumee Bay." By the line of the Ordinance and the act of Congress the mouth of the Maumee and the site of Toledo would be in Michigan; by the line of the Constitution of Ohio they would be in Ohio. Congress admitted Ohio into the Union under her Constitution without any allusion to the boundary question. As early as 1812 Congress passed an act authorizing the Surveyor General to run and mark the line described in the act of Congress 1802, but the war with Great Britain came and nothing was done at the time. In 1831 Congress authorized a survey to enable them to determine the line.

ADMISSION INTO THE UNION.

In 1834, a census of the inhabitants of the Territory of Michigan was taken, under the authority of the Legislative Council, when it was ascertained that the population was 87,273, more than enough to enable it to be admitted as a State under the ordinance of 1787. In January, 1835, an act was passed by the Legislative Council, authorizing a convention to form a State Constitution. The convention met in May following, and formed a Constitution, which was submitted to and adopted by the people in October following. At the same time, State Officers and a Legislature were elected to act under the Constitution.

The Legislature met in November, 1835. The Governor, Stevens P. Mason, entered upon the duties of his Office and the whole machinery of State Legislation and action went into operation, except the judiciary, which was not organized until July 4th, 1836. At the same time John S. Horner claimed to be Governor of the *Territory* of Michigan under an appointment of President Jackson, and he continued to act as such until some time in 1836. The history of this contest, and of the admission of Michigan into the Union forms a very curious and interesting chapter in our annals, including as it does a history of that serio-comic performance "The Toledo War." But it can only be glanced at here.

Michigan claimed that the ordinance of 1787 was a compact of binding force, and that the line there described must govern. Ohio claimed that the ordinance had been superseded by the Constitution of the United States and that Congress had full power to regulate the boundary question.

When Michigan sought admission into the Union the question of boundary became a vital one, especially as the territory included the port and site of Toledo, and a decision became inevitable.

The Legislature of Ohio and the Council of Michigan in February and March 1835 passed acts asserting jurisdiction over the disputed territory and providing for its exercise.

In March, an army of Michigan braves, from 800 to 1200 strong, under the leadership of the young and gallant acting Governor Mason, marched to Toledo and took possession. Governor Lucas of Ohio was preparing for an attack on the invaders, but actual hostilities were prevented by the timely arrival of commissioners from Washington. A state of semi-war was kept up for many months, sometimes seriously threatening real hostilities, but the ludicrous incidents far outnumbered the tragic ones. In the meantime Michigan applied for admission under her new Constitution, and, on the 15th of June, 1836, Congress passed an act admitting Michigan into the Union, upon condition that she, by a convention of delegates elected by the people for that purpose, assented to the boundary line, as claimed by Ohio, and giving her, in the place of the territory claimed, the Upper Peninsula. A convention, elected under a call from the Governor, met at Ann-Arbor in September following, and rejected the proposed terms of admission, but the result was not acquiesced in. The machinery of a State government was already in operation, and there were many public and some private reasons for desiring full admission into the Sisterhood of States. The Democratic Central Committee called upon the people to elect another set of delegates, which they did. This second convention met at Ann Arbor on the 14th of December, 1836, and, on the following day, assented to the conditions of admission. A sharp debate ensued in Congress as to whether this assent of a second convention, called without authority, was such a one as the act of Congress contemplated; but on the 27th of January, 1837, Congress, by an act, declared such assent sufficient, and Michigan was admitted into the Union. The Constitution of 1835 remained the fundamental law of the State until superseded by the Constitution of 1850. A convention to revise the constitution was elected in 1867 and submitted to the people a new constitution which was rejected.

MICHIGAN AS A STATE.

The history of Michigan as a State of the Union has for the most part transpired within the memory of the present generation, and needs no especial record here. Then too, for the most part, it has been a history of peace, of growth, of material prosperity and of steady advancement in all the elements of real progress, including those higher interests upon which, in a great degree, the ultimate prosperity and greatness of a people depends. It is therefore a history marked by few incidents of stirring interest.

In no State have the interests of Education been more carefully and wisely promoted. One of the earliest acts of the State Government was the establishment of the University of Michigan upon a broad, firm basis and the making of ample provision for a system of Common Schools, and to-day her University and her common Schools are a just ground of State pride and of hope for the future.

Her Institutions for the care of the Insane, the Deaf and Dumb and the Blind, are worthy of the State; while a hopeful advance is being made in providing for the care of other helpless persons. Her Penal and Reformatory Institutions are being brought more and more into harmony with the true purposes for which they should exist, viz. the prevention of crime and the reformation of the offenders.

Michigan was among the earliest in abolishing imprisonment for debt, and in giving to married women the control of their own property.

Her mines, her forests, her soil and her waters are all contributing to her wealth and increase. Her past is secure and she may well be proud of it. Her future, under God, is in her own hands.

TERRITORIAL GOVERNORS.

William Hull,	1805 to 1813
Lewis Cass,	1813 to 1831
George B. Porter,	1831 to 1834
Stevens T. Mason, (Acting Gov.)	1834 to 1835
John S. Horner,	1835 to 1836

STATE GOVERNORS.

Stevens T. Mason,	Nov., 1835 to Dec. 31, 1839
William Woodbridge,	1840 and part of 1841
James Wright Gordon, (Acting Gov.)	part of 1841
John S. Barry,	1842, 1843, 1844, 1845
Alpheus Felch,	1846
William L. Greenly, (Acting Gov.)	1847
Epaphroditus Ransom,	1848, 1849
John S. Barry,	1850, 1851
Robert McClelland,	1852 and part of 1853
Andrew Parsons, (Acting Gov.)	Part of 1853, 1854
Kinsley S. Bingham,	1855, 1856, 1857, 1858
Moses Wisner,	1859, 1860
Austin Blair,	1861, 1862, 1863, 1864
Henry H. Crapo,	1865, 1866, 1867, 1868
Henry P. Baldwin,	1869, 1870, 1871, 1872
John J. Bagley,	1873, 1874, 1875, 1876
Charles M. Croswell,	1877, 1878, 1879, 1880
David H. Jerome,	1881, 1882
Josiah W. Begole,	1883, 1884

LIEUTENANT GOVERNORS.

Edward Mundy,	1835, 1837, 1838, 1839
James Wright Gordon,	1840, 1841
Origen D. Richardson,	1842, 1843, 1844, 1845
William L. Greenly,	1846, 1847
William M. Fenton,	1848, 1849, 1850, 1851
Calvin Britain	1852
Andrew Parsons,	1853, 1854
George A. Coe,	1855, 1856, 1857, 1858
Edmund B. Fairfield,	1859, 1860
James Birney,	1861, 1862
Charles S. May,	1863, 1864
Ebenezer O. Grosvenor	1865, 1866
Dwight May,	1867, 1868
Morgan Bates,	1869, 1870, 1871, 1872
Henry H. Holt,	1873, 1874, 1875, 1876
Alonzo Sessions,	1877, 1878, 1879, 1880
Moreau S. Crosby,	1881, 1882, 1883, 1884

SENATORS IN CONGRESS.

John Norvell,	1835 to 1841
Lucius Lyon,	1836 to 1840
Augustus S. Porter,	1840 to 1845
William Woodbridge,	1841 to 1847
Lewis Cass,	1845 to 1848
Thomas H. Fitzgerald, Session of	1848-9
Alpheus Felch,	1847 to 1853
Lewis Cass,	1849 to 1857

Charles E. Stuart,	1853 to 1859
Zachariah Chandler,	1857 to 1875
Kinsley S. Bingham,	1859 to 1861
Jacob M. Howard,	1861 to 1871
Thomas W. Ferry,	1871 to 1883
Isaac P. Christiancy, (Resigned Feb. 10, 1879)	1875 to 1881
Zachariah Chandler, (to fill vacancy; died Nov. 1, 1879)	
Henry P. Baldwin, (to fill vacancy)	1879 to 1881
Omar D. Conger,	1881 to 1887
Thomas W. Palmer,	1883 to 1889

JUDGES OF TERRITORIAL SUPREME COURT.

Augustus B. Woodward,	1805 to 1824
Frederick Bates,	1805 to 1808
John Griffin,	1806 to 1824
James Witherell,	1808 to 1828
Solomon Sibley,	1824 to 1836
John Hunt,	1824 to 1827
Henry Chipman,	1827 to 1832
William Woodbridge,	1828 to 1832
George Morell,	1832 to 1836
Ross Wilkins,	1832 to 1836

CHANCELLORS OF THE STATE.

Elon Farnsworth,	1837 to 1842 and 1846
Randolph Manning,	1842 to 1846

JUDGES OF THE SUPREME COURT UNDER CONSTITUTION OF 1835.

William A. Fletcher,	1836 to 1842
Epaphroditus Ransom,	1836 to 1847
George Morell,	1836 to 1842
Charles W. Whipple,	1837 to 1848 and 1852 to 1855
Alpheus Felch,	1842 to 1845
Daniel Goodwin,	1843 to 1846
Edward Mundy,	1848 to 1851
Warner Wing,	1845 to 1852 and 1854 to 1857
George Miles,	1846 to 1850
Sanford M. Green,	1844 to 1854 and 1856 to 1858
George Martin,	1851 to Jan., 1858
Joseph T. Copeland,	1852 to 1857
Samuel T. Douglass,	1852 to 1857
David Johnson,	1852 to 1857
Abner Pratt,	1851 to 1857
Nathaniel Bacon,	1855 to 1858
E. H. C. Wilson,	1856 to 1858
Benjamin F. H. Witherell, vacancy in latter part	1857
Benjamin F. Graves, vacancy in latter part	1857
Josiah Turner, " " "	1857
Edwin Lawrence, " " "	1858

JUDGES OF SUPREME COURT UNDER PRESENT ORGANIZATION.

George Martin,	1858 to 1868
Randolph Manning,	1858 to 1864
Isaac P. Christiancy,	1858 to 1875
Benj. F. Graves,	1868 to 1883
Isaac Marston, (Resigned 1883)	1875 to ——
James V. Campbell, 1858—Term expires	1887
Thomas M. Cooley, 1864— " "	1885
Thos. R. Sherwood, 1883— " "	1889
John W. Champlin, 1883— " "	1891

Population of Michigan at each Decade, according to Census of the United States:

CENSUS OF 1820,	8,896
" " 1830, (Territory)	31,639
" " 1840, (State)	212,267
" " 1850,	397,654
" " 1860,	749,113
" " 1870,	1,184,059
" " 1880,	1,636,937

A SUMMARY

OF THE

HISTORY OF EDUCATION IN MICHIGAN.

BY ORAMEL HOSFORD, Esq.

THE first School Law of the Territory of Michigan, was enacted in 1827. That Law ordained that the citizens of any township, having fifty house-holders, should provide themselves with a schoolmaster, of good morals, to teach the children to read and write. Any township with two hundred house-holders, was required to have a schoolmaster who could teach Latin, French and English. For neglect to comply with the requirements of the law, the town became liable to a fine of $ 50 to $ 150.

In 1833, this law gave place to another creating the office of Superintendent of Common Schools, and providing for three Commissioners, and ten Inspectors, who were to have charge of the School lands, which had, by act of Congress, in 1828, been under the supervision of the Territorial Governor and Council.

As early as 1787, an ordinance was passed by Congress for the government of the North Western Territory, in which it was declared that "Schools and the means of education, shall forever be encouraged."

SCHOOL LANDS.

An act passed in 1804, providing for the sale of lands in the Indian Territory, afterwards formed into the States of Indiana, Illinois, Michigan and Wisconsin—expressly reserved from sale Section 16 in every township "for the support of schools."

All the rights and privileges which these acts conferred, were confirmed to the Territory of Michigan organized in 1805. The ordinance admitting the State of Michigan into the Union in 1836 declares, that "Section number 16 in every township of the public lands, and where such section has been sold, or otherwise disposed of, other lands equivalent thereto, and as contiguous as may be, shall be granted to the *State* for the use of schools."

The original Constitution, as well as the present, required that the proceeds of these lands, should "remain a perpetual fund for that object." The original design of Congress was to grant to each township the avails of the section found within its limits, or to give to the township, the section to be managed by them, as they might think best. In many of the townships, these lands were nearly worthless, being near swamps or covered with water. These grants led to most serious difficulties in other states, as they attempted to manage the lands, as proposed by Congress. Townships having worthless lands would apply to Congress for additional aid, and failing there, would apply to their Legislature. In addition to all this, different parts of the same township, and different townships, presented their conflicting claims, which could not possibly be adjusted, satisfactorily.

To escape these troubles the people of Michigan, when they came, in 1835, to form a State government, included in the ordinance submitted to Congress, that "Section 16, &c., shall be granted to the *State*, for the use of schools." The wisdom of this arrangement is seen in the ease with which the land grant has been managed, and the slight expense attending the sale of the lands and the appropriation of the School Fund.

Another great advantage has been, that all the schools of the State have shared in the School Fund as soon as such fund has accrued. Townships having poor or worthless sections, suffered no *special* loss on that account; it was a loss shared by the whole State, and those townships lying at a distance from the more settled portions of the State, were not compelled to go without schools, or conduct them at their own expense, until the school section of their township could be disposed of—but they at once shared, with all the schools of the State, in the Common School Fund.

The success of our school system is largely owing to this wise foresight of those who had the responsibility of its organization.

The first State Superintendent, Hon. J. D. Pierce, estimated the amount of land thus donated by Congress for the use of public schools, to be 1,148,160 acres, and that there would be realized from them a sum not less than $6,000,000. This estimate, as it now appears, was too large, the actual amount being not far from 1,000,000 acres. A little more than one half has been sold, and the fund arising therefrom is $3,393,115, which added to $844,194 derived from swamp lands, gives a total of $ 4,237,309 as the present School Fund. The State pays 7 per cent. on the School land fund, and 5 per cent. on the swamp land fund. The school lands are sold at four dollars per acre. The purchaser can pay the full amount and secure his patent at once, or he can pay one fourth at the time of purchase, and the balance at his own convenience—the land reverting to the State, on a failure to pay the interest. About 380,866 acres are yet unsold. This should eventually increase the fund to nearly four and one half millions of dollars, and, adding the amount to be received from swamp lands, we may reasonably expect that ultimately the fund will reach $4,700,000.

UNIVERSITY LANDS.

The act of 1804, for the disposal of the public lands in the Indian Territory, reserved three townships "for the use of seminaries of learning,"—one of these was for that part of the Territory now constituting the State of Michigan.

In 1824, the township reserved for the University, not having been located, it was found difficult to secure a township of good land, of which none had been sold. Through the exertions of Gov. Woodbridge, and Hon. Austin E. Wing, then delegate to Congress, an act was passed, giving permission to select the land in detached sections, and adding another township, or its equivalent, to the original grant. The moneys arising from the sale of these lands, together with that obtained from the three sections granted by Congress in 1817 to the "College of Detroit," constitute the "University Fund."

The Constitution provides that all lands granted for educational purposes "shall be inviolably appropriated and annually applied to the specific objects of the original gift, grant or appropriation."

Thus the University Fund, arising from these grants of lands, is inalienable, and can not be diverted from the University, without a gross breach of faith and a violation of the Constitution.

In addition to the permanent Fund, the University has received, from successive Legislatures, large appropriations. These will doubtless not only be continued, but largely increased.

THE UNIVERSITY AND ITS BRANCHES.

The University was established by the Legislature in 1837, but did not complete its buildings and make other necessary arrangements, so as to enter upon its appropriate work, until 1841.

The act establishing the University also provided for the creation of "Branches," as preparatory schools, to be located in various parts of the State. With no capital, and without any hope of any, except the anticipated income from the future sales of land, those having the responsibility erected the University buildings with borrowed capital. The State borrowed $100,000 and re-loaned it to the University with the understanding that it should be refunded, principal and interest, from the income from University Lands. The University was opened in 1842, having a preparatory school connected with it. There were but two Professors appointed to active duty, with a salary of $500 each, but they were also entitled to whatever tuition might be paid in the preparatory school. The University however soon rose to a commanding position among the Colleges of the country, notwithstanding the multitude of hindrances in the way of its advancement. It required the most vigilant and constant watchfulness, on the part of its friends, to prevent a diversion of its funds to other purposes during the great monetary pressure suffered by the State, during the early history of the University.

To these friends, is the Institution largely indebted for its present efficiency and standing. To these men the State will ever owe a debt of gratitude, for their untiring zeal and patience in caring for an Institution which is now the crowning work of our educational system.

Soon after the opening of the University, several Branches were established in different parts of the State. These were to be supported, in part, by appropriations from the University Fund. It was estimated that the income from this fund would be, at least, $50,000, and $25,000 was deemed an ample sum to meet the current expenses of the University, leaving $25,000 to be expended in these Branches, and the several Counties, in which they were located, were to raise an amount equal to the sum appropriated, which would, together with a moderate tuition fee, meet the wants of these Branches. A few years' experience, however, satisfied the most ardent supporters, that the plan was impracticable, as all the money arising from the University Fund was not sufficient for the University alone, and the Branches could not be continued without endangering the University itself; indeed for a time, the danger of its suspension was imminent; consequently, the Branches were very soon closed or assigned to private corporations.

NORMAL SCHOOL.

The suspension of these schools was felt to be a great loss, as they gave much attention to the training of Teachers. Urgent petitions were sent to the Legislature, by parents and teachers, for the establishment of a Training School.

In 1849, an act was passed, creating a Normal School which was located at Ypsilanti. This school was opened in Oct. 1852.

The history of this Institution is familiar to all, and its influence has reached every primary school in the State.

OTHER COLLEGES.

During the years occupied in organizing and developing these State Institutions, there sprang up Academies and Seminaries in various places, either private or local in their character. None of them, however received aid from any public fund. All that was granted them, was permission to live. In 1856, there were about 40 of these chartered schools. Six of them have since received charters, giving them full College powers.

AGRICULTURAL COLLEGE.

The Agricultural College was established in 1855. From the first, it has met violent opposition, but has overcome, thus far, every obstacle, and now stands first among the Agricultural Colleges of this country, and is honorably doing its peculiar work, as an efficient co-worker with the other educational institutions of the State.

PRIMARY SCHOOLS.

The Primary School Law was enacted in 1837, by the first State Legislature. This Law was a transcript of the Law of the State of New York. It provided for the division of the State into districts, containing a sufficient number of inhabitants to support a school having a single teacher. The schools were composed of pupils of all grades, pursuing the usual branches of study. As the population increased, and the school house became crowded, the district was divided. This process was continued in the villages, until there were five or six of these schools in the same village; many of the school houses, being hardly a stone's throw apart. Some of the schools were very good, others nearly worthless. Some were continued nine months, some six, and others not more than three. The purpose of the founders of our school system, was to adopt that of Prussia, so far as it was found adapted to the genius of our government, and the character and condition of our people.

The Primary Schools constitute the foundation of the system, and the University its crowning glory. The design was, to have the primary schools connected with the University, by those of different grades, which should have courses of study, such as would prepare the pupils to enter the University.

GRADED SCHOOLS.

The several Branches that were established having expired, a new system was devised. In the cities and villages, where a number of districts were contiguous, they were united, forming a single school district. These were, at first, called Union Schools. They were divided into several departments, called primary, intermediate, grammar and high school, and each department was divided into different grades or classes, for pupils of different degrees of advancement. These schools are now called by the more appropriate name of Graded Schools. The Curriculum for the High School department, is the same as that usually adopted by the best Academies, and pupils are here prepared for the Colleges and University.

SCHOOL HOUSES.

For ten or twelve years after the organization of our school system, but little attention was given to the building of School houses. They were of the cheapest character, small and insignificant and as inconvenient as they could well be made, and entirely inadequate to meet the wants of a rapidly growing population.

The successful management of a graded school, demanded a better class of school houses, and a new era in school architecture appeared. The various cities and villages vied with each other in erecting the best school edifice, and now it is no rare thing to find, in a village of two or three thousand inhabitants, a school house which cost $20,000 or $30,000, while in the cities and larger towns the cost of those edifices has been from $60,000 to more than $100,000.

There are now six thousand eight hundred and ninety school houses in the state, the value of which is estimated at $10,435,860.

EDUCATIONAL INSTITUTIONS.

The following is a list of the Educational Institutions of the State.

THE UNIVERSITY OF MICHIGAN.

This is under the control of a Board of Regents, consisting of eight members, elected by the people, and their term of office continues six years. The President of the University is ex-officio President of the Board. The University is organized in three departments, as follows: the Department of Literature, Science and the Arts; the Department of Medicine and Surgery; and the Department of Law. Each department has its Faculty of Instruction, who are charged with its special management. These several Faculties constitute the University Senate, which decides all questions of common interest in all the Departments.

THE STATE NORMAL SCHOOL.

This is under the control of the State Board of Education, consisting of three members, chosen by the people, and their term of office is six years.

The Superintendent of Public Instruction is, ex officio, Secretary of the Board.

THE AGRICULTURAL COLLEGE.

This is under the control of the State Board of Agriculture, consisting of six members, appointed by the Governor, with the approval of the Senate whose term of office is six years. The Governor and the President of the College are, ex officio, members of the Board.

OTHER CHARTERED COLLEGES.

The following are the chartered Colleges of the State:

Hillsdale College,	at Hillsdale.
Albion College,	at Albion.
Adrian College,	at Adrian.
Olivet College,	at Olivet.
Kalamazoo College,	at Kalamazoo.
Hope College,	at Holland.
Battle Creek College,	at Battle Creek.
Grand Traverse College,	at Grand Traverse.

These are under the control of Boards chosen either by some religious body, or are made, by their charters, self-perpetuating.

All the above named Institutions are subject to visitation, by committees, appointed by the Superintendent of Public Instruction.

The "Detroit College" has been instituted within a few years, under the management of the Jesuits, with nine professors.

The Michigan Female Seminary, at Kalamazoo, is another modern institution.

The character of the College at Grand Traverse is outlined as classical, scientific, normal and commercial.

There are about 300 graded schools, taking the place and doing the work of Academies.

The State Superintendent of Public Instruction has the general supervision of the work of education, and it is his duty to make an annual report of the condition of all the Institutions and public schools of the State. His term of office is two years.

The most radical changes within the past ten years affecting local interests are the amendment of the law creating a County Superintendent, abolishing that office, and the creation of County Boards of Examiners, consisting of three members, who are charged with the duty of examining teachers and visiting the schools.

THE NUMBER OF TEACHERS AND CHILDREN REPORTED IN 1881.

Number of male teachers, ...	4,024
Number of female teachers, . . .	10,448
Total, ...	14,472
Number of children between the ages of five and twenty years, . . .	518,201
Number reported in 1872, . . .	404,285
Number in attendance 1881, . . .	371,748

STEAMBOATS AND LAKE TRANSPORTATION.

BY RAY HADDOCK, Esq.

THE far-reaching importance of the influence exerted upon the settlement of the country, especially of the West, by the solution of the steamboat problem, is beyond the power of man to compute. The geographical configuration of the country seemed to hold out unwonted incentives to the Genius of Progress, while the bold and enterprising character of the population was found to be equal to the occasion. When we remember that some of the single river channels of the West adapted to steam navigation exceed in length the distance across the Atlantic, while there are many other navigable streams almost equal in majestic grandeur to those referred to, we may be able to realize at a glance the extent and character of the field opened to enterprise by this great innovation in the mode of transit. That this event should be coeval with the settlement of that important part of the Northwest which borders upon the great chain of lakes seems somewhat in the nature of a coincidence, while it has had no insignificant influence in molding the character of the people.

From the immense water-line of Michigan, her vast interests are very intimately connected with the lake marine. Her commercial metropolis is one of the greatest centers of first class steamboat lines on the globe, while almost every port on her lakes and rivers owns more or less tonnage. This wide diffusion of proprietorship is quite a prominent feature, our Custom House books exhibiting the fact that, excluding steam yachts and canal boats, there are in Michigan more different points at which this important class of property is owned than in the States of New York, Massachusetts and Ohio combined, those States being the next highest in this particular classification.

In the infancy of our carrying trade our iron, lumber and other coarse commodities found a market by means of sail craft, but when its volume had attained enormous proportions, steam began to supersede that mode of conveyance, and is now largely depended upon, especially so far as concerns steam barges.

BRIEF HISTORICAL SKETCH OF STEAM POWER.

It is known that steam boilers were in use to some little extent for philosophical demonstrations, if for no other purpose, some three generations before the Christian era, and the fact is well authenticated that paddles as a means of propulsion were among the evidences of progress belonging to a still earlier antiquity. According to all this, the ancients lacked only the proper application of machinery to inaugurate a steamboat era which would naturally have led to the discovery of America hundreds, perhaps thousands, of years before that event actually happened.

In a valuable work recently brought out by Rear-Admiral Preble, of the United States navy, an account is given of the efforts of Blasco de Garray, a native of Biscay, who, in June, 1543, propelled a vessel "without visible machinery, except an immense cauldron of boiling water, a complicated number of wheels within and gyrating paddles without." But it is hardly necessary to add that the invention was only a partial success. The names of a score of inventors and experimenters are mixed up with the great problem in its various stages. The fame of Watt is, of course, world-wide as the inventor who did incomparably more toward bringing about the successful application of steam than any who had preceded him. Watt obtained his first patent for a steam engine in 1769, but prior to that time there were those who deserve a passing notice. In 1630 Charles I. of England granted a patent to David Ramseye "to make boats, shippes and barges to go against strong wind and tide." While Denis Papin, a French engineer, is claimed to have been the inventor of the steam engine in 1690, Jonathan Hulls, who in 1736 obtained a patent for propelling a boat by steam, which by the way, never amounted to anything practically, was, no doubt, the first Englishman who proposed to apply that power to marine purposes. Oliver Evans constructed a steam engine prior to 1786, at which date he had it in operation, and the first tubular boiler was invented by Nathan Reed, of Salem, Mass. The first locomotive boiler was planned by M. Seguin, in France, and Booth, in England, and was used by George Stephenson in 1828 or 1829. The earliest water tubular boilers were those of Voight, Rumsey and Fitch, and were invented and known as "pipe boilers" as early as 1785. William Henry, of Chester Co., Pa., had the model of a steamboat on the Conestoga River in 1763. On July 27, 1786, an invention of John Fitch was brought to a successful experiment on the Delaware, and it may be called the first adaptation of steam to marine purposes. It consisted of a skiff propelled by oars or paddles at the sides which were set in motion by means of cranks worked by the engine. Fitch was assisted in perfecting his plan by Voight, an ingenious Philadelphia watchmaker. The year previous to the culmination of this most important invention, James Rumsey, of Richmond, had exhibited a rude model of a steamboat to a party at Berkeley Springs, Va., George Washington being among those present. In the meantime some three or four patents were issued in connection with steam and its machinery, one to Fitch among the rest. In 1788 the last-named inventor loomed up above all competitors, having brought out a boat sixty feet long and eight beam. The oars were in the stern and pushed against the water, and the engine was a 12-inch cylinder. In July of the above named year she was propelled from Philadelphia to Burlington, twenty miles, the longest trip made by any boat up to that time. In October she took thirty passengers from Philadelphia to Burlington in three hours and ten minutes. Previous to these demonstrations, on the 6th of March, Rumsey's boat "with more than half her capacity, about three tons, made a progress of four miles an hour against the current of the Potomac River."

It will thus be seen that Fitch and Rumsey seem to have pretty nearly divided the honors attaching to the first invention of steamboats. Fitch's actual successful experiment antedated that of Rumsey by about two years, although the latter may have brought out the first model. Fulton had been an ingenious and persevering inventor in other fields, and he doubtless deserved all the honors that have been awarded him. He built a steamboat on the Seine in 1803, and about the same time the invention was offered to Napoleon Bonaparte, then First Consul, but no encouragement was offered, that great conqueror having placed his affections wholly upon land enterprises. Fulton's first successful voyage was made from New York to Albany August 7, 1807. His boat, the Claremont, was 130 feet long, eighteen feet beam and six feet hold. Her engine a low pressure, was built by Boulton & Watt, in England.

The first steamer to cross the Atlantic was the Savannah in 1819, which ran from New York to Liverpool in twenty-six days. She was built at Corlaers Hook. The first steamers to ascend the Mississippi were three little government boats in 1819.

Within four years from the invention of the locomotive boiler, the "Detroit & St. Joseph Railroad" (now the Michigan Central) was chartered by the Legislative Council, Michigan being then a Territory. A more striking illustration of Western enterprise could hardly be presented.

EARLY LAKE NAVIGATION.

The aboriginal inhabitants availed themselves of the facilities for transit afforded by our magnificent lakes and rivers long before the tread of the European had awakened the forest echoes of the new world. Their deftly fashioned canoes were wont to glide along the bright waters, pointed toward favorite hunting grounds and anon toward the strongholds of hostile tribes. Some of the traditions of grim war among these tribes that have come down to us from the shadowy past are full of romantic but tragical interest. As civilization extended westward, the bark canoe was supplanted by improved means of conveyance, the batteau being introduced by the French and other styles of boat by the English and Americans. The voyages were of the most tedious description; nevertheless a work of wonderful importance was gradually accomplished in the establishment of missions and trading posts, thus paving the way to the settlement of the country. It is not far from 200 years since the first sail craft vexed the waters of the upper lakes, yet up to the lapsing of another century only a few lake craft had ever spread their white pinions to the breeze. The first vessel was the Griffon, built by La Salle near the foot of Lake Erie in 1679. She was lost before the completion of a round trip. It has been a received tradition that she was wrecked on Lake Huron on her return from Green Bay, but she probably never reached Mackinac. At the latter point it had been arranged that she should take on a quantity of furs, but she never made her appearance. She left Green Bay, September 18, 1679, and is believed to have been lost on the following day in a gale. The only vestige of her ever brought to light was a small lot of furs picked up by Indians on the shore of Lake Michigan. Not a soul was saved to recount the story of her fate.

THE EARLIEST LAKE STEAMBOATS.

The first Lake steamers were the Ontario, built at Sackett's Harbor in 1816, and the Canadian steamer Frontenac, built at Bath near Kingston, the same year. The Ontario was of 231 tons burden, and was 110 feet long. She had a beam engine, thirty-four-inch cylinder and four feet stroke. Capt. James Van Cleve, who is still living in Ontario, directly opposite Detroit, was for a time master of the Ontario. The Frontenac was a fine steamer of about 700 tons, and her coming out occasioned no little enthusiasm in Canada, which had its effect in enlivening trade. The keel was laid in October, 1816, and she was completed the following year, as already stated. The contract price was seven thousand pounds, and the engine cost a like amount. The contract for building her was awarded to an American, the representative of a Sackett's Harbor firm, but the enterprise reflects great credit upon the Canadians, of whom it may be justly said that relatively considered as to their means they have at least not been behind their neighbors in steamboat enterprise. The Walk-in-the-Water, the first steamer on Lake Erie, was built at Black Rock in 1817. She was of 342 tons burden and was propelled by a low-pressure engine. She made several trips to Mackinac and Green Bay, and was lost on the night of November 1, 1821, near Buffalo in a gale.

When the first steamers were launched, the Erie Canal had not been commenced, and slavery had not yet become entirely extinct in the Empire State. The canal was commenced in 1817, and was finally completed in 1825.

THE "OUTLOOK" AT THE OUTSET.

It seemed to require extraordinary prescience to enable the builders of the first Lake steamers to see their way clear. The country was new and it became a question whether they were to build up the country or the country build up them, with the chances in favor of the former hypothesis. Many of the appliances requisite in building, everything in fact except timber, were difficult to procure, and the skilled labor wherewith to run the boats was at a high premium. There was no grain or other farm produce to move from the "Great West;" in fact, what little movement might be expected was in the opposite direction. There were, of course, no improved harbors at that early day, and Erie was the only good natural harbor on Lake Erie, and even that was good only in a comparative sense. At that port, during the war a few years previous, the American fleet had to be floated out by means of scows. In 1820 Detroit was a comparatively little, insignificant French town, with only one dock. The only towns on the lake were Cleveland, Sandusky and Erie, with a few houses at Huron, ten miles from Sandusky.

Ship-building, which even now is not one of the exact sciences, was at the period referred to prosecuted in a much cruder manner. An owner to find himself in possession of a good, trim craft, propelled at a good rate of speed by a well-constructed engine, and managed by a competent and trustworthy master, would be lucky in a three-fold way, for not a few of the boats put afloat were found either "crank" or supplied with engines that were below the mark, while in addition to these difficulties, there must have been fortunes swamped through mismanagement unless the jade Rumor has egregiously lied. Despite all these drawbacks a golden era was inaugurated for steamers as well as for the country, and the lake region was rapidly settled. Nearly all the business of the country for forty years was transacted through the agency of the boats. The freighting was not remunerative, a good, modern steamer's load of merchandise being adequate to the then wants of a community like that of Detroit for an entire month, but the passenger trade assumed magnificent proportions. With good boats well-managed, money-making was assured. Superadded to the travel in the way of current trade, especially from pioneers and those prospecting for homes in the West, the route became all the rage for excursions by capitalists and others from New York, Philadelphia, Boston, Albany, Washington, Baltimore and other points. The steamboat passenger trade was at its maximum at about the period running from 1834 to 1837. Old citizens say that they have seen the decks of the Chicago-bound steamers as black with human beings as are those of the Windsor ferries or boats for Sandwich during any portion of the "heated term." Two steamboat trips can now be made between given points in the time required for one upon the first introduction of Lake steamers.

Nearly all of the better class of sail craft had from two to six berths fitted up for passengers, and numerous emigrant families reached the West in that way.

HULL AND ENGINE BUILDING.

The steamboat era inaugurated a new departure in shipbuilding, and improved skill was demanded, a want which was supplied fully as soon as it could be reasonably expected, taking into consideration the fact that a pressing demand for the same class had sprung up all over the country. There were good builders at Black Rock, Cleveland, Huron, Detroit and other points. A Capt. Goodsell was the earliest at Detroit, and he built all or nearly all of Commodore Newberry's steamers. Huron, O., also soon became a favorite port, there being two good builders there, Messrs Church and Bates, one of whom had come from New York expressly to establish himself there. Jones of Cleveland, was also celebrated. He was the father of the family of that name so widely known in marine circles. At a later period Bidwell & Banta, of Buffalo, modeled and built a great many fine boats, while the reputation of Cleveland was well maintained. Marine City, Trenton and Gibraltar have all become noted for shipbuilding. The best of the old-time steamers would not stand comparison with those of a modern date, either for show or service. The improvements that have been made in one way and another, suggested by ingenuity and experience, it would be almost tedious to recount. The changes as to shape are so elaborate and extensive that between two boats of exactly the same size, one according to the old and the other the modern style, the carrying capacity of the latter is more than double that of the former.

A number of engines were at first brought from the seaboard, but Pittsburg early became a favorite point for procuring them. Detroit had not at that period embarked in the business. Subsequently first-class engines were built in Cleveland and Buffalo, and Black Rock also engaged in the business to some extent. The well known engine of the Ocean, of the Detroit and Cleveland line, was built expressly for an ocean steamer, but was purchased in New York by Capt. E. B. Ward, who built the Ocean.

SCREW PROPULSION.

In 1841 a conference was held at the East between some of our lake steamboat men and representatives of Ericsson, which resulted in the right to use the screw, of which he was the alleged inventor. The first boat of this class was the Vandalia, built at Oswego in 1841. She was sloop-rigged, and was of 138 tons burden. She would not compare very favorably in point of speed with some of the fast sail craft of the present day, yet she was equal in that regard to some of her successors. Ericsson, the *soi-disant* inventor of the screw, deserves high praise for some of his subsequent achievements in the way of naval armaments, but the principle of screw propulsion is one to whose development the ingenuity of mechanical inventors was addressed with partial success at a very early period.

A PARTIALLY EXTINCT TYPE OF MEN.

The introduction of steamboats caused an immediate want for a peculiar type of men to command them, and the result was the coming to the fore of a class who are always referred to, by those yet living who knew their traits, with interest, and often with enthusiasm. Ethical philosophers will no doubt draw a pleasing deduction from the fact that they were exactly the kind wanted—skillful and intrepid to a degree, and brimful of energy and enterprise.

"A race of nobles may die out,
A royal line may leave no heir;
* * * * * *
But they fail not, the kinglier breed."

Our owners being obliged to have them at all hazards, inducements were offered that brought them from various quarters—some from the ocean service, and others from the coast, the Sound, the North River and other quarters. In the meantime many good captains were at an early day educated here, some of them having had an experience with sail craft that qualified them, with a little practice, to take the command of steamers. One who achieved a most respectable rank commenced his marine experience in the capacity of cook, and other cases very nearly parallel might be cited. These men were not without their faults; but to say that, taken as a whole, their noble qualities greatly overbalanced their foibles, would be drawing it exceedingly mild. They were a frank, bluff, warm-hearted set, a part of whose creed it was to take care of each other and of their friends. They were ever alive to appeals to their sympathy and were equally at home among the roughest of one sex and the most refined of the other. They seemed pretty nearly a cross between the weather-beaten sons of Neptune of the ocean steamers and the more courtly semi-cavaliers of the western rivers. So far as relates to the respective duties of the last-named class and those of our lake captains, there is a marked difference, the management of the river steamers, when running, being entirely under the control of the pilots, whose office is a very important one from the intricate nature of their calling, the more especially upon streams where the channel is constantly changing, like the Mississippi. The duties of masters are confined to the business management. The almost complete monopoly of the carrying trade, saving the coarser commodities, by the railroads has resulted in confining the operations of our lake side-wheel steamers, so far as concerns lucrative business, to pleasure travel or to a few particular routes. Two or three routes may be designated where the business yet retains some few vestiges of its olden glory, but the Jasons and their Argos have passed away. In old times it was difficult to procure skilled labor, but common help was easily accessible. Although engineers were scarce, their wages would seem low from the standpoint of the present, running from $30 to $40 per month.

PERSONAL MENTION.

At the risk of appearing invidious, the names of a few of the more eminent captains of the past generation may be perhaps appropriately given, such as the following: Capts. Whitaker, Blake, Howe, Van Cleve, the Allens, Averill, Atwood, Burke, Cotton, Chase, Davis, Goldsmith, Edmonds, Van Allen, Appleby, Miller, Hart, Hazard, Wilkins, Shalcross, Caverly, Pheatt, Nickerson, Wagstaff, Kelsey, Lundy, S. G. Langley, Pease, Stannard, Stone, Travers, Wilkeson, Willoughby, Roby, T. F. Richards, etc. Captains Whitaker, Van Cleve, Gager and Atwood are the only ones left of the more ancient class, all of whom are between 80 and 83 years of age. Capts. Evans (of the Detroit & Cleveland Line), Ralph, Dustin, Caverly *et al* belong to a somewhat later era. Capts. Whitaker, Blake, Van Cleve, Howe, Willoughby, Wilkeson and Appleby were among the more conspicuous. Capt. Blake died at the residence of his son, back of Milwaukee, in 1851. During the last year or two of his life he was wont to pass considerable of his time in summer in traveling with his old friends. Capt. B. was a gallant soldier of the war of 1812. Capt. Howe died in Cleveland in 1853, Willoughby in Quebec in 1862, and Wilkeson in Perrysburg in 1873. Capt. S. G. Langley, so well remembered as the commander of the steamer Mississippi, died in St. Joseph in 1868 at the age of 63. Capt. Wilkeson was seemingly of a rather morose disposition, especially noticeable in his intercourse with strangers; but, like his numerous compeers, his heart overflowed with kindly sympathies, and he was the impersonation of integrity and manliness.

Tried by the law of cause and effect, it would seem to be undeniable that the old line of captains as well as the engineers, well understood their calling. Capt. Whitaker states that for two decades succeeding the introduction of lake steamers, only eight lives were lost, six on the Peacock and two on the Commodore Perry. The frequent occurrence of disasters on the Mississippi River, particularly explosions, cannot have been forgotten. Doubtless many of these unfortunate occurrences, were owing to causes that seem totally inexplicable; at the same time many must have been due to the bad character of the water and defective boilers as well as to the incompetency or carelessness of those in charge.

HEROIC DEEDS.

Modern marine annals bear the names of at least two or three men who have performed deeds of heroism that richly entitle them to enrollment alongside the very noblest known to our steamboat history. One of these is that of Capt. John Wilson, of the Lady Elgin, sunk by collision with the schooner Augusta in 1860 upon an excursion between Chicago and Milwaukee, by which memorable catastrophe about 300 lives were lost. Captain Wilson was in a position to have easily saved himself, but he deemed life not worth having if saved at the cost of or the neglect of those who had been intrusted to his care, and he was lost in endeavoring to save the lives of ladies belonging to the party. Another incident, in which an equal degree of heroism was displayed with happier results, was that wherein Capt. William McKay, of the Detroit and Cleveland line, accompanied by his mate, George McKay, put out from Cleveland in a terrible gale, at the imminent hazard of their lives, to the rescue of the crew of the wrecked United States steamer Winslow. On the occasion of the burning of the G. P. Griffith, nineteen miles below Cleveland, in 1850, Capt. Roby displayed all the heroism possible under the trying circumstances. He was one of the very last to leave the seething ruins and thereby surrender the chance to aid the unfortunates who were exposed to the dreadful ordeal. The statement of these incidents, so honorable to our nature, might be largely extended.

The more terrible of the disasters not already directly referred to were the burning of the Erie in 1841, when nearly 200 lives were lost; the sinking of the Keystone State in 1862 or 1863, the memorable sinking of the Atlantic in 1852, by which about 400 lives were lost; the burning of the Niagara 2d, in 1856, by which about 300 were lost; the burning of the E. K. Collins, in 1854, by which over 300 lives were lost; the sinking of the Lady Elgin, in 1860, by which 400 were lost; the burning of the Northern Indiana, in 1856, with the loss of nearly 400; and the sinking of the Chesapeake in 1846, by which about 100 were lost. The Keystone State went down in Saginaw Bay with about 100 on board, of whom not a soul was saved. The burning of the Griffith was a fearful calamity. Although the trip was partly one for pleasure, the boat swarmed with emigrants. There have been many other terrible disasters, while the name of the minor ones is legion.

CAPT. WHITAKER'S RECOLLECTIONS.

Capt. Harry Whitaker, the Nestor of steamboat men, is still living in Detroit, in the enjoyment of a green old age, having reached 82 years, with his eye yet beaming with all its olden fire. In one sense he has doubtless been the most successful man that ever trod a deck. He has commanded consecutively no fewer than eighteen steamers, though, of course, some of them only briefly, yet he has never lost a human life or a pound of freight. Such a record it is impossible to surpass, and in the nature of things it would be next to impossible to equal. His memories comprise well-nigh a full history of steamboating on the lakes.

Capt. Whitaker states that his first marine service was on the sloop Huntington at $6 a month. In 1821, he was wheelsman on the Walk-in-the-Water, and in 1824 he commanded the schooner Macedonia, and in 1828 the steamers Peacock and Pioneer, both temporarily by way of relieving others. The first steamer to ascend Grand River, as well as the first to reach Sault Ste. Marie, were those commanded by Capt. Whitaker. At that period an entire week was required to make the round trip between Buffalo and Detroit. The steamers all carried two masts, and sails were unfurled whenever they could be made available. Wood was used exclusively for fuel, coal not having even been thought of for that purpose.

The A. D. Patchin, a much finer steamer than any of her predecessors, was built by Capt. Whitaker in 1847. Some notable improvements were introduced in her construction, but Capt. W. neglected to take out a patent, and others, especially builders at the East, reaped the benefit of his inventions. The Patchin was wrecked in 1850, by which disaster the fortunes of the worthy captain were almost literally swamped.

A FEW OF THE FAVORITES

Among the favorite boats of the "old timers" as regards excellence of construction or some other peculiarly good quality may be named the following: Walk-in-the-Water, A. D. Patchin, Daniel Webster (fair), North America, Superior 1, Com. Perry, Monroe, Robert Fulton, Troy, Enterprise, Columbus, United States, De Witt Clinton, St. Clair, Rochester, Madison, Boston, Baltic, Baltimore, Ohio 2, Globe, Bunker Hill, Constitution, Anthony Wayne, Great Western, Fairport, Washington 2, Gen. Scott, Harrison 2, Empire, New Orleans, Buffalo, Chesapeake, Henry Clay, Pioneer, (crank), Michigan 2, Detroit 1, Jefferson, Sandusky, Illinois 1, Cleveland 1, Erie, Lexington, John Owen, Champion 1, Superior 2, Niagara 2, Sultana, Pacific, Sam Ward, Empire State, Queen City, New England 2.

A LIST FROM THE EARLIEST PERIOD.

The following is a list of side-wheel steamers built on Lake Erie and intercommunicating waters from 1817 to 1847 inclusive, omitting to avoid repetition those named above, the Canadian boats being designated by an asterisk, viz.: Chippewa, Niagara 1, Newburyport, Ohio 1, Adelaide*, Gen. Gratiot, Gen. Brady, Champlain, Perseverance, Lady of the Lake, Gov. Marcy, Oliver Newberry, Delaware, Victory, Jefferson, Mazeppa, Minnesetunk*, Jackson, Little Western*, Sheldon Thompson, Columbus, Chicago, Cincinnati, W. F. Taylor, Thames*, Julia Palmer, Don Quixote, Little Erie, Barcelona*, United, St. Clair, Rochester, Macomb, Rhode Island, Star, Goderich*, Commerce, Mason, Buffalo, Red Jacket, Geo Vance, James Allen, Detroit 2, Waterloo, Ben Franklin, Union, Emerald*, Tecumseh, J. Wolcott, Indian Queen, Boston, London*, Helen Strong, Romeo, Albany, Louisiana, Canada 1*, Baltic, Baltimore, Diamond, Southerner, Cataract, Michigan 1, Ontario, Saratoga, Vermillion, Missouri, Pennsylvania, Oregon, Hendrick Hudson, New York, Superior 2, Charles Townsend, Wisconsin, St. Louis, Indiana, Nile, Constellation, Lexington, Milwaukee, Washington 1, Gen. Porter, Sophia, Charlotte*, Dalhousie*, Chippewa, Toronto*, Queenston*, Caroline*, Martha Ogden, Canada 2*, Wm. Penn, Enterprise*, Alciope*, Sir James Kempt*, Wm. Peacock, Brownville*, Great Britain*, Charles Carroll, Iroquois*, Uncle Sam, William Fourth*, John By*, Transit*, Brockville*, Coburg*, Kingston 1*, Oswego, Black Hawk, New York, Delaware, Britannia*, Union*, Rapid*, Constitution*, Com. Barry*, Traveler*, Highlander 1*, Telegraph, Oneida, Oakville*, St. George*, Gore*, Sir Robert Peel*, New England, Queen Victoria*, Experiment, Express, St. Lawrence, H. Gildersleeve*, Ontario*, Chautauqua, Brothers*, Kent*, Huron 1, Harrison 1, Waterloo, America 1*, Sovereign*, Frontenac 2*, City of Toronto*, Princess Royal*, Despatch*, Prince of Wales*, Harrison 1, George Clinton, Admiral*, Chief Justice Robinson*, Welland*, Mohawk* (iron), Cherokee* (naval), Sir C. Napier*, Eclipse*, Nile, Union, Michigan (U. S.), Albert (U. S.), Troy, Louisiana, British Queen*, Passport*, Sultana, Chieftain, England*, Jenny Lind, Prescott*.

The following is a list of those built in the same localities from 1848 to 1859 inclusive, viz: Arrow, Alabama, F. Moore, J. D. Morton, Empire State, Queen City, Columbus, Charter, Albion, J. Hollister, Mayflower, Telegraph Dart, Dover, Ocean, Fox, Gore*, May Queen, Arctic, Ruby, Bay City, Buckeye State, Northerner, Swan, Magnet, Pearl, Ploughboy*, Queen*, Mazeppa*, Minnesota, Forest City, Caspian, Golden Gate, Traveler, Crescent City, Queen of the West, Mississippi, St. Lawrence, E. K. Collins, Ariel, Garden City, Canadian*, Kaloolah, T. Whitney, Northern Indiana, Southern Michigan, R. N. Rice, Forester, Plymouth Rock, Western World, North Star, R. R. Elliott, Clifton*, Forest Queen, Planet, Island Queen, Amity*, Magnet, Western Metropolis, City of Buffalo, City of Cleveland, Princess, Olive Branch, Gazelle, Sea Bird, Detroit, (s. s.) Milwaukee, (s. s.) Bonny Boat, Ottawa, Geo. Moffat*, Alida, Comet, Cygnet, Dart, Fox, Leviathan, (wrecking steamer), L. L. Lyon, Illinois 2, Globe, Albion, St. Helen*, New Era*, Ottawa*, St. Lawrence*, Bay State, Atlantic, America, Keystone State, Wave 1, Hector, Lady Elgin*, Ocean Wave*, British Empire*, Northerner, Cora Linn, Belle, Champion 2, Maple Leaf*, Highlander 2*, Brownsville*, New York, Swan, Cleveland 2, Huron 2, Arabian*, Bay of Quinte*, Banshee*, Huron*, International, Maid of the Mist, Clifton*, Canada 3*, America*, Abyssinian, Zimmerman*, Europa*, Welland 2*, Monarch*, Provincial*, Ironton*, Amity*, John P. Ward, Hercules*, Pierpont*, Valley City*.

The following is a list of the side-wheel steamers put afloat as above from 1860 to 1888, inclusive, viz., Comet, Heather Bell, Canada, Morning Star, Emerald, Corinthian (iron), S. Clement, Ajax, Philo Parsons, Reindeer, Susan Ward, River Queen, J. B. Smith, New York, Marine City, Mackinaw, Manitoba*, Metropolis, Chief Justice Waite, Milton D. Ward, Admiral, Alaska, Alpena, W. R. Burt, John A. Dix, Emerald, Evening Star, Great Western*, Grace Grummond, Marine City, Maud*, Minnie, Peerless*, Ruby 2, Westover, City of Sandusky, City of Toledo, W. R. Clinton, Jay Cooke, Dove, Eureka, B. F. Ferris, Geo. S. Frost, Ivanhoe (iron), Keweenaw, Cora Locke, R. N. Rice, John Sherman, Canadian*, City of Cleveland, City of Detroit, City of Milwaukee (iron) City of Toronto 2*, Mary Ethel, Flour City, Ella G., R. G. Stewart, City of Mackinac, New William*, Emily May*, Prince of Wales*, Bruce*, City of the Bay*, Young America, Rochester*, Silver Spray, W. J. Spicer*, Wave 2, Corinthian*, Garibaldi*, Watertown*, Waubuno*, Gen. Sheridan, McDonald*, Spartan*, Saginaw, Union*, J. A. McDonald*, Frances Smith*, Dominion*, Ivanhoe, Pearl, R. B. Hayes, Cumberland*.

LAKE MICHIGAN STEAMERS.

The following, in addition to the steamer Northwest, were built during the above periods at various points on or near Lake Michigan, viz., Sunbeam (lost on Lake Superior), L. G. Mason, Muskegon, Sheboygan, Chicago, Corona, Geo. L. Dunlap (condemned) Union, Sarah Van Epps (dismantled), Flora M. C. Hawley, James Allen, Morning, Orion, Manitowoc, North Star, Astor. In addition to these a number of lower lake built steamers have been diverted to that trade.

[Our statement is confined exclusively to sidewheels and the list is placed on record for future reference, as belonging to a class that has now in a great measure passed away. Boats of tonnage under 100 are not included.]

About 400 propellers were built during the same period.

Sail vessels were engaged in the Lake Superior trade as long ago as the beginning of the present century, but the commerce of that region did not assume important proportions until the opening of the Ste. Mary's ship canal, an event which at once gave a great impetus to mining as well as commerce both by steam and sail. With characteristic enterprise our steamboat owners undertook and successfully carried forward the work of transporting steamers across the portage before the completion of the canal. In 1845 the propeller Independence, the first steamer that ever woke the echoes of Lake Superior, was taken across, being followed the ensuing year by the Julia Palmer, the first sidewheel steamer. In the winter of 1848–9 the schooner Napoleon was converted into a propeller. In 1850 the Manhattan was hauled over by the Messrs. Turner, of Cleveland, and the Monticello in 1850 by Col. Sheldon McKnight. The latter was lost during the autumn of the same year, and Col. McKnight supplied her place the ensuing winter with the Baltimore. In 1853 or 1854 Capt. E. B. Ward took over the Sam Ward and Col. McKnight took over the propeller Peninsula about the same time. In the spring of 1855 the canal was opened.

PALATIAL RAILROAD STEAMERS.

Soon after the completion of the various railroads having lake ports as their termini large and elegant steamers were built and placed on the lake, running in connection with the lines respectively to Buffalo. They were exceedingly popular, but were finally all withdrawn. The boats running to and from Detroit were the Plymouth Rock and Western World; from Toledo the Southern Michigan and Northern Indiana, subsequently the Western Metropolis, City of Buffalo and Empire State; from Sandusky the St. Lawrence and Mississippi, and from Cleveland the Crescent City and Queen of the West. Some of these steamers made excellent time. Upon one occasion, without special effort, the Western Metropolis made the run from Cleveland to Buffalo in ten hours and ten minutes. The Sandusky trade did not "pan out" very beautifully, owing in part to inadequate depth of water, and the Mississippi was brought to Detroit and made the third boat in the Michigan Central Line. When these boats were finally broken up, the hulls of one or two of them were devoted to dry-dock purposes.

DETROIT & CLEVELAND STEAM NAVIGATION COMPANY

For over a quarter of a century this has been the line of "palatial steamers" par excellence, "giving no sign" of the "decadence of the side-wheel steamboat interest."

Routes: Cleveland to Detroit and return and Detroit and Cleveland to Mackinac and intermediate ports.

Steamers: City of Detroit, Northwest, City of Cleveland, City of Mackinac. The Detroit and Northwest ply between Cleveland and Detroit, and the Cleveland and Mackinac make the Mackinac trip.

THE STAR LINE

Operates boats from Detroit to Port Huron, Port Austin and intermediate ports, as follows: Steamers Idlewild and Evening Star.

THE WHITE STAR LINE.

Both Star lines operate under a pool arrangement under the auspices of the Detroit & Cleveland Steam Navigation Company. The White Star boats are the steamers Milton D. Ward and Saginaw. These boats run between Detroit, Port Huron, Port Austin and intermediate ports.

ASHLEY & MITCHELL'S LINE.

These gentlemen have their wharf and office at the foot of First street, their boats being as follows: Steamer Pearl, Detroit and Mackinac; steamer Alaska, Detroit to Lake Erie Islands and Sandusky, and steamer Riverside, Detroit to Amherstburg and intermediate points.

DETROIT, BELLE ISLE AND WINDSOR FERRY COMPANY.

The corporation owns five boats, two of which are on the Belle Isle Park route and two on the Windsor ferry route, with one for varied service as business on either of the above named routes may demand. The boats are the Victoria, Fortune, Excelsior, Hope and Garland.

THE WALKERVILLE, WINDSOR & DETROIT COMPANY.

This company is a new organization, having, as yet, but two boats. The route is between Detroit and Walkerville, touching at Belle Isle Park and Windsor. The boats are the Sappho and Ariel.

GRUMMOND'S MACKINAC LINE.

This line of boats is owned by S. B. Grummond. Semi-weekly trips are made to Alpena, Cheboygan, Mackinac and intermediate ports, and the boats are the steamers Flora and Atlantic.

DETROIT AND SAGINAW LINE.

The Oconto and Sanilac form a semi-weekly line on this route.

OTHER OUT-BOUND BOATS.

The steamer City of New Baltimore runs to St. Clair by the way of New Baltimore and the North Channel Club House. The steamer R. J. Gordon runs to Grosse Ile, Wyandotte, Sugar Island and intermediate ports. The steamer Hattie runs to Fairhaven and the steamer Byron Trerice to Wallaceburg and Dresden.

WARD'S DETROIT & LAKE SUPERIOR LINE.

Capt. Eber Ward, one of the pioneers in the shipping interests of the great lakes, conducts a line of fine steamers, which make regular trips between Detroit and all Lake Superior ports, touching at intermediate river ports. The boats of the line are as follows: Steamers St. Paul, Samuel Hodge, Toledo, Keweenaw and Osceola.

LAKE SUPERIOR TRANSIT COMPANY.

The following boats run in this line: China, Nyack, Japan, Badger State, India, Arctic, Empire State, Winslow, St. Louis; J. T. Whiting agent. Mr. W. is as well posted in everything pertaining to Lake Superior as if he were the actual inventor of that great inland sea.

STEAMERS TOUCHING AT DETROIT.

While the boats named above make regular trips out of and with Detroit as the chief terminal point, passage may be obtained to most of the ports on the rivers and lakes, on any one of the following boats:

At the wharf of Wm. Livingstone, Jr., the steamers Fountain City and Oneida make weekly calls on their passages between Chicago and Buffalo. At the wharf of A. Chesebrough & Co., fourteen boats of the Union Line, fourteen boats of the Anchor Line and five boats of the Commercial Line call on their way between Buffalo and Chicago.

Besides the Detroit companies having headquarters at Hutchings & Co.'s wharf, the Ogdensburg & Chicago Transportation Company, the Western Express Line and the Tonawanda Transportation Company land their boats at the wharf named. The Ogdensburg & Chicago Company operate the following boats: Propellers Roanoke, Northerner, Davidson, Saginaw Valley, Pacific, Nashua. The boats of the Western Express Line are the propellers Myles, St. Magnus, Alcadia, Glenfinlas, Shickaluna, Scotia, Canada, Prussia, Europe, Lake Michigan, Lake Ontario. The Tonawanda Transportation Company operate two propellers, the Alleghany and Weston.

BLANCHARD'S LINE.

This is a transportation line, composed of the steamer Don M. Dickinson, propeller Mayflower, tugs Wm. Parke and A. T. Bartlett, and several sail barges. It is engaged in transporting lumber, coal, stone, and coarse freights generally, between the various lake and river ports. The line is owned in Detroit.

MICHIGAN NAVIGATION CO.

This company own the propeller T. W. Palmer and tug Charles Kellogg, running between Buffalo, Erie, Cleveland, Detroit and Lake Michigan ports, and any other points where business may be presented. Headquarters in Detroit.

FARWELL TRANSPORTATION CO.

This line consists of the steamer Jesse H. Farwell and propeller Northerner, and is engaged in carrying grain, lumber, coal, etc. Headquarters in Detroit.

COLE & HOLT'S ALPENA AND BAY CITY LINE.

This line consists of the steamers Arundel and Metropolis, making daily trips between the above ports and Harrisville, Greenbush, Oscoda, East Tawas, Tawas City and Alabaster.

GRAHAM & MORTON TRANSPORTATION CO.

The steamers Dora and Messenger run in this line, making daily trips between Benton Harbor and Chicago.

CHICAGO AND LAKE SUPERIOR LINE.

This line is owned in Chicago, but is included in our list with other lines plying between Michigan ports. Those enterprising and well known gentlemen, Leopold & Austrian, for many years proprietors of this line, have consolidated their navigation interests with those of the Spencer, Lake Michigan and Lake Superior Transportation Co., their boats running between Chicago and Duluth, touching at all intermediate ports in Illinois, Michigan and Wisconsin. The steamers are the Peerless, J. L. Hurd, City of Duluth, City of Fremont and barge Whiting.

LAKE SUPERIOR LOCAL LINES.

Holt's Lake Superior Line consists of propeller R. G. Stewart, making daily trips between Duluth and Agate Bay, a point 23 miles down the shore. The steamer Dove is engaged in plying between Duluth and Port Arthur, running in connection with the Canada Pacific Railway. The steamer Agnes runs between Duluth and Isle Royale.

The iron steamer Ivanhoe makes daily trips between Houghton and L'Anse.

The passenger steamer Manistee runs between Portage Lake and Duluth, touching at Ontonagon, Ashland and Bayfield, and giving occasional excursions to the "North Shore."

FLINT AND PERE MARQUETTE R. R. LINE.

The steamers Flint and Pere Marquette No. 1, and Flint and Pere Marquette No. 2, make daily trips between Ludington and Milwaukee. Both are steel-plated.

DETROIT, GRAND HAVEN AND MILWAUKEE R. R. LINE.

The steamers Michigan and Wisconsin run daily between Grand Haven and Milwaukee. Both are doubly bottomed with iron.

HANNAH, LAY & CO.'S LINE.

The steamer City of Grand Traverse, owned as above, in Traverse City, makes semi-weekly trips between that port and Chicago.

DETROIT, MACKINAC AND MARQUETTE LINE.

The steel clad steamer Algomah performs ferry service for this line between Old Mackinac and St. Ignace.

GOODRICH TRANSPORTATION CO.'S LINE.

The company representing this line has long been recognized as one of the most enterprising in the Northwest. Its headquarters are in Chicago, but its steamers run to almost every port of the Lower Peninsula on the west side, and to Escanaba and Menominee in the Upper Peninsula. There are seven large and elegant steamers, four of them side-wheelers, forming six separate lines.

The side-wheel steamers Chicago, Sheboygan and Muskegon—the only boats of this company's line not running to Michigan ports—form a daily line between Chicago, Racine and Milwaukee.

The side-wheel steamer Corona makes daily trips between Manitowoc and Menominee, connecting at the former port with the Chicago and Sheboygan.

The propeller City of Ludington makes daily trips, Sundays excepted, between Milwaukee and Ludington. She also makes trips every Wednesday and Sunday morning between Manistee and Frankfort, leaving from the former port and arriving at the latter the same afternoon.

The propeller De Pere leaves Chicago every Saturday morning for Escanaba and all intermediate ports.

The steamer Menominee makes tri-weekly trips between Chicago, Grand Haven and Muskegon, leaving Muskegon for Chicago every Tuesday, Thursday and Sunday afternoon, and Grand Haven the same evenings.

The arrangements given for the various lines are those for 1883.

SOUTH HAVEN AND CHICAGO LINE.

The steamer Grace Grummond runs in this line, making daily trips during the fruit season and tri-weekly the rest of the season.

CHICAGO AND ST. JOSEPH LINE.

The new propeller City of St. Joseph runs in this line, making the round trip daily.

ALGONAC AND PORT HURON LINE.

The steamer Pickup makes daily trips on this route.

ACKNOWLEDGMENT.—In the compilation of our chapter upon Steamboats and Lake Transportation we have drawn freely from the columns of THE DETROIT DAILY FREE PRESS.

For Historical Sketch of Michigan Railroads, see page 145.

STEAM CRAFT OF ALL CLASSES.

NAME.	TONNAGE.	WHERE OWNED.
A. McMillan	14.48	Saugatuck.
A. B. Ward	20.62	Grand Haven.
A. B. Watson	15.33	Muskegon.
A. C. Van Raalte	178.68	Cheboygan.
A. D. Perkins	9.90	Detroit.
A. F. Bartlett	10.74	Monroe.
A. H. Hunter	28.10	East Saginaw.
A. H. Morrison	108.40	St. Joseph.
A. M. Calhoun	110.30	Saugatuck.
A. W. Wright	17.91	East Saginaw.
Aberdeen	345.79	Marine City.
Agate	7.86	Marquette.
Agnes	41.86	St. Clair.
Agnes	8.07	Muskegon.
Alaska	810.59	Detroit.
Albert Miller	228.91	Manistee.
Alcona	784.00	Detroit.
Alfred P. White	56.18	Ludington.
Algomah	456.28	Detroit.
Alice Purdy	24.16	Saugatuck.
Alice E. Gray	29.09	Muskegon.
Alice Wanner	9.77	Houghton.
Alpena	653.00	Detroit.
Alvin A. Turner	309.87	Detroit.
Angler	19.73	Detroit.
Annie Smith	420.99	Detroit.
Anne Moiles	73.98	Bay City.
Antelope	11.08	Sault Ste. Marie
Ariel	201.47	Detroit.
B. W. Aldrich	49.34	Ludington.
B. W. Jenness	339.04	Detroit.
Badger	390.19	Detroit.
Bay City	271.48	Marine City.
Ben Drake	47.37	Escanaba.
Benton	332.78	Bay City.
Bob Anderson	112.77	Detroit.
Bob Anderson	33.16	Marquette.
Bob Stevenson	19.42	Marquette.
Bob Mills	89.61	Marquette.
Boss	11.59	St. Joseph.
Brunswick	1,030.11	Detroit.
Buffalo	19.66	Bay City.
Burlington	278.50	Port Huron.
C. Hickox	309.02	Muskegon.
C. Williams	62.07	Manistee.
C. H. Green	750.46	East Saginaw.
C. M. Farrar	17.46	Bay City.
C. W. Moore	307.54	Douglas.
Carrie Maher	21.77	Muskegon.
Carrie E. Bird	58.93	Marine City.
Centennial	38.47	Muskegon.
Challenge	17.47	East Saginaw.
Champion	364.88	Detroit.
Charles Kellogg	276.61	Detroit.
Charles Lee	17.50	East Saginaw.
Charles D. Holt	14.60	Bay City.
Charles C. McDonald	14.15	Bay City.
Charles E. Bird	14.15	St. Joseph.
Charles E. Pendell	18.87	East Saginaw.
Charles W. Liken	38.98	Sebewaing.
Charlie W. Greenough	19.60	Manistee.
Charlotte Gray	7.19	Montague.
Chauncy Hurlbut	1,908.70	Detroit.
Christian A. Forbes	21.43	Bay City.
City of Cheboygan	47.37	Cheboygan.
City of Cleveland	1,772.88	Detroit.
City of Concord	446.58	Port Huron.
City of Detroit	1094.08	Detroit.
City of Grand Rapids	332.66	Grand Haven.
City of Marquette	19.98	Marquette.
City of Mt. Clemens	53.90	Mt. Clemens.
City of New Baltimore	50.30	Marine City.
City of St. Joseph	771.48	St. Joseph.
City of Traverse	1,453.33	Grand Haven.
Clara	84.61	Detroit.
Clara Belle	46.79	Grand Haven.
Clara Ivy	13.50	Bay City.
Claude	61.09	Grand Haven.
Cleveland	380.31	East Saginaw.
Col. Ferry	17.08	Grand Haven.
Col. Ferry	15.24	Grand Haven.
Col. I. Camp	7.87	Bay City.
Colonial	1,501.37	Marquette.
Continental	1,500.67	Marquette.
Cora B.	36.99	East Saginaw.
Cora Fuller	24.98	Muskegon.
Crawford	26.50	Grand Haven.
Crusader	190.02	Detroit.
Cupid	21.62	South Haven.
Cuyahoga	422.31	Bay City.
Cyclone	29.39	Ludington.
Cygnet	8.39	Cheboygan.
D. F. Rose	228.82	Marine City.
D. P. Dell	34.30	Frankfort.
Daisy	18.58	Detroit.
Daisy Lee	30.27	East Saginaw.
Diamond	11.89	Muskegon.
Doctor Hanley	49.96	Port Sherman.
Don M. Dickinson	424.97	Detroit.
Douglas	779.09	Saugatuck.
Dove	148.12	Bay City.
D. Cutler, Jr.	34.48	Montague.
E. C. [illegible]	23.87	Grand Haven.
E. M. Miller	30.14	Alpena.
E. D. Martin	43.45	L'Anse.
E. M. Peck	36.60	Sault Ste. Marie
E. M. Peck	30.27	Bay City.
E. T. Carrington	37.77	Bay City.
East Saginaw	336.97	Alpena.
Edgar Haight	13.07	Bay City.
Edith	18.46	Benton Harbor.
Edwin Eddy	38.45	East Saginaw.
Eighth Ohio	144.64	Detroit.
Eliza Williams	87.31	Marquette.
Ella Williams	9.30	Alpena.
Elizabeth White	11.08	East Saginaw.
Ella M. Smith	171.97	Algonac.
Elmer	31.17	Manistique.
Emerald	215.42	Bay City.
Empire	785.85	Detroit.
Escanaba	1,480.88	Marine City.
Essex	9.05	Mt. Clemens.
Eva English	11.34	Cheboygan.
Eva Wadsworth	23.67	Marquette.
Evening Star	381.85	Detroit.
Excelsior	702.59	Detroit.
Ezra Stevens	48.85	Muskegon.
F. A. Jennings	12.15	Detroit.
F. L. Danforth	28.60	Marquette.
Fairy	30.02	Marquette.
Fanny Shriver	79.77	Holland.
Favorite	499.30	Menominee.
Fawn	9.56	Escanaba.
Fisherman	19.70	Detroit.
Flora	501.69	Detroit.
Florence	9.18	East Saginaw.
Florence	36.99	Detroit.
Forest City	1,330.79	Detroit.
Fortune	199.77	Detroit.
Frank Canfield	40.16	Manistee.
Frank Goole	14.79	Muskegon.
Frank Moffat	122.38	Port Huron.
Frank Terry	6.50	Sault Ste. Marie
Frank C. Fero	22.40	Marquette.
Fred Nellson	44.97	Grand Haven.
Frank H. Peavy?	58.38	Muskegon.
G. P. Heath	132.48	Saugatuck.
G. P. Kingsbury	79.98	Port Sherman.
G. J. Truesdell	400.87	Ludington.
Ganges	29.48	Saugatuck.
Garden City	371.52	Alpena.
Garland	246.38	Detroit.
Gazelle	30.00	Charlevoix.
Gazelle	182.53	Detroit.
Gem	9.54	Pentwater.
G. D. Stanford, Jr.	81.77	Grand Haven.
George P. Savidge	30.09	Grand Haven.
George W. Cuyler	48.39	Cheboygan.
George Hand	21.79	East Saginaw.
George King	582.88	Bay City.
George Rickett?	21.49	Grand Haven.
George R. Dickson	82.71	Bay City.
Geo. B. McClellan	108.18	Detroit.
George L. Colwell	490.09	Bay City.
Geo. E. Brockway	164.00	Ludington.
George W. Sagnaw?	99.10	Alpena.
George W. Wood	77.12	Cheboygan.
Gordon Benson?	6.08	Muskegon.
Gracie	12.80	Detroit.
Glasgow	808.81	Detroit.
Grace Dormer	85.90	Port Huron.
Grace Greenwood	188.11	Detroit.
Grace Patterson	119.99	Manistee.
Grace Truesdell?	13.54	Detroit.
Gracie Barker	78.22	Grand Haven.
Granite State	428.61	Grand Haven.
Grayling	17.92	Detroit.
H. A. Ballentine	86.05	Detroit.
H. C. Akeley	1,187.87	Grand Haven.
Hancock	46.65	Grand Haven.
Handy Boy	196.27	Mt. Clemens.
Handy Boy	58.50	Bay City.
Hannah Sullivan	88.32	St. Joseph.
Hattie	68.90	New Baltimore.
Hattie T. Brown	7.20	Bay City.
Henry Howard	280.38	Detroit.
Henry F. Brower	90.17	Holland.
Hercules	61.59	Detroit.
Hiram Warner	78.40	Grand Haven.
Houghton	48.08	Sault Ste. Marie
Hunter Savidge	14.57	Manistee.
I. C. Mason?	125.10	Detroit.
Ida	27.15	Detroit.
Ida	10.27	Saugatuck.
Ida Burton	43.83	Mt. Clemens.
Ida M. Stevens	22.35	Ludington.
Idlewild	222.33	Detroit.
Inter Ocean	1,068.36	Marine City.
Ira Chaffee	103.63	Detroit.
Ira O. Smith	59.85	Muskegon.
Iona L. Wheeler?	51.07	Manistee.
Iron Age	850.45	Detroit.
Iron Duke	1,152.32	Detroit.
Ivanhoe	277.64	Houghton.
J. A. Rhomberg	22.11	Grand Haven.
J. B. Smith	85.16	Detroit.
J. C. Liken	79.16	Sebewaing.
J. C. Clapsaddle?	51.80	Manistee.
J. E. Martel?	20.06	Saugatuck.
J. G. Hatswell?	8.90	Bay City.
J. J. Mosley?	60.80	Detroit.
J. L. Hurd	82.10	Detroit.
J. S. White	36.34	Marquette.
J. N. Westcott?	18.59	Detroit.
J. P. Clark	98.73	Detroit.
J. S. Ruby?	138.69	New Baltimore.
J. S. Seaverns	175.08	Saugatuck.
J. W. Hale	19.77	Escanaba.
J. W. Johnston	28.88	Grand Haven.
J. W. Peabody	21.41	St. Clair.
James Beard	86.74	Port Huron.
James Davidson	1,456.11	Marine City.
James Fay	55.50	East Saginaw.
James McGordon	32.96	Muskegon.
James Reid	129.52	Detroit.
James H. Martin?	28.79	Port Huron.
James H. Shrigley	499.82	Manistee.
James L. Beckwith	100.91	Port Huron.
James N. Brooks	10.15	Escanaba.
James P. Donaldson	212.82	Marine City.
James T. Thompson?	15.51	Detroit.
James W. Bennett?	61.37	Mackinac.
Jay C. Morse	99.51	Marquette.
Jennie Hall?	68.74	Frankfort.
Jennie A. Sutton?	10.29	Grand Haven.
Jesse H. Farwell	1,306.96	Detroit.
Jim Hayes?	16.86	Marquette.
Joe Gordon	6.78	Bay City.
Joe D. Dudley	52.07	Marquette.
John Chesnut?	17.84	Marquette.
John Ely	20.19	Marquette.
Jessie?	19.68	Grand Haven.
John Martin	182.73	Detroit.
John Owen	229.50	Detroit.
John Pridgeon, Jr.	1,211.60	Detroit.
John Smith	11.73	Manistee.
John Torrent?	18.35	Muskegon.
John A. Dix	320.61	Manistee.
John G. Campbell	34.75	Grand Haven.
John M. Osborn	846.04	Marine City.
Joseph Heald	43.41	Montague.
Joseph E. Bramble, Jr.	10.90	Grand Haven.
Julia	162.20	St. Clair.
Julia E. Drake?	26.61	Grand Haven.
Kaiser Wilhelm	38.01	Grand Haven.
Kasota	88.24	Marquette.
Kate Buttironi	965.81	Marine City.
Kate Moffat	314.11	Detroit.
Kate Williams	184.89	Detroit.
Kelly Brothers	27.20	Muskegon.
Keweenaw	869.24	Detroit.
Kittie Garfield?	13.55	Ludington.
Kitty O'Neill	5.38	Marquette.
L. G. Mason	120.70	East Saginaw.
L. L. Lyon	98.61	Detroit.
L. Q. Rawson	78.59	Detroit.
Lady May	14.87	Charlevoix.
Lady Washington	72.80	Grand Haven.
Lakeside	79.71	Bay City.
Lark	22.59	Marquette.
Laura Gibbs?	15.96	Au Sable.
Lawrence	647.37	Grand Haven.
Lewis Gilbert	92.90	Manistee.
Lewis Wallace	41.80	Grand Haven.
Lillie?	18.80	Detroit.
Lillie?	41.55	Detroit.
Little Eastern	36.35	East Saginaw.
Lizzie Frank	28.59	Grand Haven.
Lizzie Sutton	32.50	Houghton.
Lord	516.09	Benton Harbor.
Lowell	400.17	St. Clair.
Luther Westover	133.85	Bay City.
M. F. Merick	505.03	Detroit.
M. S. Youngs	79.96	Sault Ste. Marie
M. W. Wright	34.60	Charlevoix.
Mackinaw	262.00	Harrisville.
Maggie Marshall	308.59	Grand Haven.
Maggie L. Wilson?	30.59	Marine City.
Magnet	43.91	Ludington.
Mamie	381.59	Detroit.
Mamie	15.60	Detroit.
Manistique	478.50	Detroit.
Maple Leaf	9.47	Charlevoix.
Margaret	41.09	Ludington.
Maria B. M.	12.06	Grand Haven.
Marion Teller	22.12	Bay City.
Marine City	663.62	Marine City.
Marion	223.49	Marine City.
Marshall F. Butters	270.39	Grand Haven.
Martin Swain	206.39	Detroit.
Mary	32.71	Cheboygan.
Mary Bell	24.15	Saginaw.
Mary Groh	138.45	South Haven.
Mary Lily	41.74	Detroit.
Mary Martini	61.40	Sebewaing.
Mary Mills	249.53	Marine City.
Mary Pringle	204.68	Marine City.
Mary E. Wells?	16.06	Houghton.
Maud Fish?	4.37	East Saginaw.
Maud Lilley?	12.79	Grand Haven.
Maud Sampson?	18.92	Mackinac.
Maud S.	47.44	Bay City.
May Flower	42.20	Detroit.
May Flower	413.38	Detroit.
May Graham	81.67	Grand Haven.
Maythorn?	86.74	Marquette.
Menominee Ring?	78.61	Menominee.
Mentor	29.47	Marquette.
Messenger	444.87	Benton Harbor.
Messenger	46.15	Detroit.
Metropolis	422.49	Bay City.
Michigan	394.35	Detroit.
Middlesex	387.50	Detroit.
Mildred	10.19	East Saginaw.
Milton D. Ward	544.10	Detroit.
Milwaukee	419.11	Manistee.
Mineral Rock	498.09	Detroit.
Minnie?	77.46	Detroit.
Minneapolis	1,072.22	Detroit.
Minnie T.	8.87	Marquette.
Minnie Brown	8.28	Houghton.
Minnie Warren	23.52	Charlevoix.
Mocking Bird	143.54	Port Huron.
Music?	220.40	Bay City.
Myra	22.24	Detroit.
Myrtle L. McClure	14.14	Grand Haven.
Mystic	87.94	Marquette.
N. McGraft?	17.74	Muskegon.
N. Mills	381.02	Port Huron.
Nashua?	440.52	Grand Haven.
Nat. Hickney?	77.55	East Saginaw.
Newell Avery	58.62	Muskegon.
New Era	522.98	Grand Haven.
Niagara	278.87	Detroit.
Norman	880.66	Manistee.
North Muskegon	33.58	Muskegon.
North Star	62.20	Charlevoix.
North West	1,939.19	Detroit.
Northerner?	1,214.43	Detroit.
O. Wilcox	140.14	Detroit.
Odd Fellow	22.40	Marquette.
Ogemaw	626.18	St. Clair.
Old Jack	27.73	Detroit.
Olean?	377.65	Au Sable.
Oliver C. Williams	37.78	Saugatuck.
Omar D. Conger	199.56	Port Huron.
Ontario	34.38	Marquette.
Ontonagon	877.71	East Saginaw.
Osceola	878.00	St. Clair.
Oswegatchie	580.55	Detroit.
Oswego	546.59	Detroit.
Pacific	42.00	Detroit.
Passaic?	844.61	Detroit.
Pearl	28.58	Grand Haven.
Pearl	321.96	Detroit.
Peter Dalton	49.31	Montague.
Peter Smith	181.55	Bay City.
Phebe	17.59	Grand Haven.
Pioneer	19.22	Marquette.
Pony	12.20	Muskegon.
Porter Chamberlain	207.00	East Saginaw.
R. McDonald	348.78	Muskegon.
R. C. Brittain	530.17	Saugatuck.
R. C. Wilson	18.02	Cheboygan.
R. G. Peters	295.04	Manistee.
R. J. Gordon	198.61	Marine City.
R. J. Hackett	1,129.27	Detroit.
R. P. Easton?	12.39	Muskegon.
Red Wing	19.56	Detroit.
Reindeer	24.66	Grand Haven.
Republic	1,343.29	Marquette.
Rescue?	22.80	Detroit.
Rhoda Stewart	447.13	Detroit.
River Queen	52.16	Detroit.
Riverside	152.08	Detroit.
Robert Boyd	30.85	East Saginaw.
Robert Ingersoll	79.78	South Haven.
Rosalie?	28.80	St. Clair.
Rose	8.50	Marquette.
Rover	41.59	Detroit.
Roys J. Cram	19.57	East Saginaw.
Ruby	16.10	Grand Haven.
S. C. Baldwin	412.34	Detroit.
S. D. Caldwell	780.42	East Saginaw.
S. S. Hoag?	66.68	Bay City.
Saginaw	727.47	Detroit.
Saginaw Valley	739.17	Bay City.
St. Albans	432.73	Grand Haven.
St. Marie?	102.44	Sault Ste. Marie.
St. Mary	36.44	Manistee.
Salina	915.32	Marine City.
Salmo?	17.33	Marquette.
Samuel F. Hodge	582.82	Detroit.
Sanilac	810.21	Oscoda.
Sarah E. Sheldon?	17.82	Escanaba.
Saugatuck	85.79	Mackinac.
Sea Gull	74.74	Bay City.
Sea Wing	21.43	Detroit.
Sergeant?	9.12	Manistee.
Silvanus J. Macy	646.42	Detroit.
Sky Lark	126.00	Benton Harbor.
Southern Belle	23.78	Mackinac.
Sport	81.09	Ludington.
Standard Rock	92.01	Grand Haven.
Stephen C. Hall	467.00	Port Sherman.
Stewart Edward	13.77	Grand Haven.
Stillman Witt	76.79	Marquette.
Stranger	72.69	Detroit.
Swallow	336.47	Muskegon.
Sweepstakes	227.60	Detroit.
Sylph	8.86	Detroit.
Syphax?	9.00	Houghton.
T. M. Moore?	30.64	Marine City.
T. R. Merrill	31.13	Detroit.
T. S. Faxton	153.66	Grand Haven.
T. W. Ferry	97.51	Grand Haven.
T. W. Snook	168.54	Montague.
Tempest	377.92	Grand Haven.
Third Michigan	40.15	Muskegon.
Thomas Coleman	42.08	Detroit.
Thomas Quayle	545.20	Detroit.
Thomas W. Palmer	1,090.00	Detroit.
Tiger	13.22	Muskegon.
Trinity?	742.33	Detroit.
Tom Dowling	25.90	East Saginaw.
Torrent	700.72	Detroit.
Trader	180.95	Pentwater.
Transport?	1,324.90	Detroit.
Triton?	82.14	Detroit.
Twilight	38.54	Muskegon.
Twilight	28.90	Grand Haven.
Uarda	88.30	Grosse Isle.
Uncle Sam	24.21	East Saginaw.
Victoria	190.11	Detroit.
Vulcan	349.42	Detroit.
W. B. Castle	178.77	Port Huron.
W. D. Cushing	89.74	Sault Ste. Marie
W. E. Quimby	86.79	East Saginaw.
W. H. Gratwick	474.86	Detroit.
W. A. Avery	70.28	Bay City.
Walter Crysler	27.50	Charlevoix.
W. Batchelor	48.93	Grand Haven.
W. R. Hart	252.94	East Saginaw.
Westford	392.20	Alpena.
White Swan	9.89	Grand Haven.
White and Friant	429.97	Grand Haven.
Wm. Rudolph	297.82	Mt. Clemens.
Wm. LaChapelle	5.28	Detroit.
Wm. Cowie	208.81	Marine City.
Wm. Richards	19.79	Montague.
Wm. A. Moore	812.80	Detroit.
Wm. B. Nixter?	15.61	Mackinac.
Wm. H. Barrett?	119.36	Grand Haven.
Winslow	237.97	Detroit.
Witch of the West	59.39	Bay City.
York State	38.90	Muskegon.
Young America	87.86	Algonac.
Zouave	117.34	East Saginaw.
Antelope	756.02	Bay City.
Argonaut	1,119.39	Marine City.
Comet	81.88	Muskegon.
G. R. Green?	18.18	Escanaba.
Gladiator	256.08	Detroit.
Nellie Booth?	73.08	Charlevoix.
Sweet Brothers?	23.48	St. Joseph.
City of Mackinac	594.72	Detroit.
E. K. Roberts	168.15	Detroit.
Romeo	99.84	Detroit.
Mayflower	13.12	Detroit.
George E. Fisher?	54.12	Detroit.
Neptune?	540.22	Detroit.
Walter L. Frost	1322.24	Detroit.
Alice B. Wilde?	183.74	Detroit.
Edward Smith	535.88	Marine City.
Pauline	14.10	Mt. Clemens.
Sigma	100.35	Detroit.

RAILROADS OF MICHIGAN

NOW COMPLETED, WITH

STATIONS AND DISTANCES.

CHICAGO & GRAND TRUNK.

[illegible]

CINCINNATI, WABASH & MICHIGAN.

[illegible]

DETROIT, GRAND HAVEN & MILWAUKEE.

[illegible]

DETROIT, LANSING & NORTHERN.

[illegible]

DETROIT, MACKINAC & MARQUETTE.

[illegible]

FLINT AND PERE MARQUETTE.

[illegible]

GRAND RAPIDS & INDIANA.

[illegible]

GRAND TRUNK RAILWAY.

[illegible]

CHICAGO & WEST MICHIGAN.

[illegible]

(Continued on page [illegible].)

(Concluded from page 27.)

Brodie's 66
Kinmount 76
Mylne Railway Junction 78
Minden 87
Ingoldsby 91
Dysart 93
Gould's 98
Haliburton 99

GRAND JUNCTION DIVISION.

Peterborough to
Hilliard's J'n 1
Heath's J'n
Auburn Mills 3
Nassau Mills 4
Lakefield 11
Ashburnham 2
Drummond's 9
Keene 11
Blezard's 13
Birdsall's 18
Hastings 24
Campbellford 34
Hoard's 43
Stirling 46
N'th Hastings Junction 52

Eldorado
Madoc 6
Moira Lake 9
[illegible] 12
Ivanhoe 16
West Huntingdon 19
N'th Hastings Junction 21

N'th Hastings Junction 58
Holloway 56
Foxboro 59
Corbyville 64
Belleville G. T. R. 65
Belleville City 67
Belleville Har. 68

GEORGIAN BAY AND LAKE ERIE DIV.

Wiarton to
Clavering 8
Hepworth 6
Park Head 11
Allenford 14
Tara and Invermay 20
Dobbington 28
Chesley 32
Elmwood 37
Hanover 44
Neustadt 50
Ayton 54
Alsfeldt 56
Drew 58
Harriston 64
Palmerston 70
Gowanstown 74
Listowel 79
Britton 83
Peffers 88
Milbank 90
Milverton 93
Brunner 94
Gadshill 99
Stratford J'n
Stratford 105
Tavistock J'n 112
Tavistock 113
Strathallan 119
C. V. R. Junc. 126
Woodstock 127
Curries 132
Burgessville 138
Norwich 142
Brantford J'n 144
Otterville 146
Hawtrey 148
C. S. R. Junc. 149
Brandy Creek 151
Gilbert 154
Simcoe 160
Lynn Valley 163
Port Dover 167

DURHAM BRANCH.

Durham to
Varney 6
Holstein 9
Mount Forest 6
Palmerston 11

GREAT WESTERN DIVISION.

SUSP. BRIDGE TO LONDON.

Susp. Bridge to **Niagara Falls**
St. Davids 5
Merritton 8
St. Catharines 11
Jordan 17
Beamsville 23
Grimsby 27
Winona 32
Stoney Creek 37
Hamilton 43
Junction Cut 45
Dundas 49
Copetown 55
Lynden 59
Harrisburg 62
St. George 64
Dumfries 67
Paris 71
Princeton 79
Gobles 81
Governor's R'd 84
Eastwood 88
Woodstock 91
Beachville 95
Ingersoll 100
Putnam's Sid. 104
Dorchester 109
Westminster 113
London East 118
London 119

LONDON TO WINDSOR.

London to
Hyde Park J'n 4
Komoka 10
Mt. Brydges 15
Longwood 21
Canada South. Crossing 24
Appin 26
Glencoe 31
Pratt's 34
Newbury 37
Bothwell 42
Thamesville 50
Lewisville 56
[illegible] 59
Chatham 65
Jeannette's C'k 76
[illegible] 84
St. Clair 88
Belle River 92
Tecumseh 100
Windsor Ship Dock 104
Windsor 110

LOOP LINE.—FORT ERIE TO GLENCOE.

Fort Erie to
Stevensville 7
Humberstone 13
Welland J'n 16
Welland Canal 17
Feeder Siding 20
Marshville 24
Moulton 28
Dunn 30
Darling Road 40
Canfield J'n 41
Cayuga 45
Nelles Corn's 52
Jarvis 61
Renton 67
Simcoe 72
Nixon 76
Delhi 81
Courtland 88
Tilsonburg 93
Tilsonburg J'n 93
Corinth 99
Aylmer 107
New Sarum 117
Canada South. Crossing 119
St. Thomas 121
Payne's 123
Canada South. Crossing 130
[illegible] 126
Lawrence 129
Thames River 131
Middlemiss 134
Ekfrid 139
Glencoe 145

TORONTO TO HAMILTON.

Toronto to Northern R'y Junction
Queen's Wharf 1
Parkdale 3
High Park 4
The Humber 5
Mimico 7
Port Credit 13
Clarkson's 16
Oakville 21
Bronte 25
Burlington 30
Waterdown 35
Junction Cut 37
Hamilton 39

SARNIA BRANCH.

Komoka to
Strathroy 10
Kerwood 16
Watford 24
Wanstead 32
Wyoming 36
Petrolia Junc. 38
Mandaumin 41
Sarnia 51
Pt. Edward 54

PETROLIA BRANCH.

Wyoming to
Petrolia Junc. 1
Petrolia 5

LONDON, HURON AND BRUCE R'WAY.

London to
Hyde Park J'n 4
Birr 7
Ilderton 11
Brecon 15
Clandeboye 20
Centralia 26
Exeter 32
Hensall 37
Kippen 39
Brucefield 43
Clinton 50
Londesborough 56
Blyth 60
Belgrave 67
Wingham J'n 73
Wingham 74

WELLAND RAILWAY AND ALLANBURG BRANCH.

Niagara Falls to
Clifton Junc. 1
Stamford 3
Allanburg J'n 9
Merritton J'n
Thorold
Allanburg
Port Robinson 10
Welland 14
Welland J'n 17

LONDON AND PORT STANLEY BRANCH.

London to
Westminster 5
Glanworth 9
Yarmouth 12
St. Thomas 15
White's 19
Port Stanley 24

W. G. & B.—MAIN LINE.

Southampton to
Port Elgin 4
Turner's 9
Paisley 17
Pinkerton 23
Cargill 26
Dunkeld 29
Walkerton 32
Mildmay 38
Clifford 46
Harriston 52
Palmerston 56
Moorefield 63
Drayton 68
Goldstone 73
Alma 79
Fergus 85
Elora 89
Soper's 94
Guelph 100
Guelph Cross
Hespeler 109
Preston 112
Galt 115
Branchton 123
Harrisburg 126

W. G. & B.—SOUTH EXTENSION.

Kincardine to
Ripley 9
Lucknow 15
Whitechurch 22
Wingham 28
Wingham J'n 29
Bluevale 33
Brussels 40
Ethel 44
Henfryn 47
Atwood 51
Listowel 57
Gowanstown 61
Palmerston 66

BRANTFORD AND TILSONBURG LINE.

Tilsonburg J'n to
Tilsonburg 2
Old Station
Springford 9
C. S. & L. E. Crossing 13
Norwich 16
Hatchley 20
Harley 21
Burford 25
Mt. Vernon 28
Mt. Pleasant 30
Brantford B. & T. 34
Brantford B. & G.
"T" Switch 35
Harrisburg 43

LAKE SHORE & MICHIGAN SOUTHERN.

Detroit to
Toledo 64
Cleveland 176
Buffalo 361
Monroe 40
Adrian 70
Chicago 285

MARQUETTE HOUGHTON & ONTONAGON.

EASTERN DIVISION.

Marquette to
[illegible] 2
Bruce 5
Morgan
Eagle Mills 8
Carp 11
Negaunee 12
Ishpeming 14

MIDDLE DIVISION.

Ishpeming to
Ontonagon J'n 16
Saginaw 18
Greenwood 21
Boston Junc. 23
Clarksburgh 25
Humboldt 30
Champion J'n 30
Champion 33
Northampton Junction 36
Michigamme 38

WESTERN DIVISION.

Michigamme to
Spurr Mine 38
Beaufort Junc. 41
Three Lakes 44
C.'s Siding 45
Sturgeon 47
Summit 52
Taylor Junc. 55
L'Anse 59
Baraga 58
Minnesota 70
Powerville 71
Newton's 76
Robinson's 87
Houghton 94

REPUBLIC BRANCH.

Humboldt to
Midway 3
Republic 6

MICHIGAN CENTRAL.

Detroit to
Springwells 3
Junction Yard 4
Dearborn 10
Inksters 15
Wayne 17
Wayne Junc. 19
Denton's 24
Ypsilanti 29
Geddes 33
Ann Arbor 37
Delhi 42
Scio 46
Dexter 47
Chelsea 54
Francisco 61
Grass Lake 65
Leoni 68
Michigan Cen. 71
Jackson Junc. 74
Jackson 75
Trumbull's 80
Parma 86
North Concord 89
Bath Mills 92
Albion 96
Marengo 101
Marshall 107
Ceresco 113
Wheatfield 114
Nichols 119
Battle Creek 120
Bedford 126
Augusta 130
Galesburg 134
Comstock 138
Kalamazoo 143
Oshtemo 149
Mattawan 152
Lawton 160
White Oaks 162
Decatur 167
Glenwood 173
Dowagiac 176
Pokagon 185
Niles 191
Buchanan 196
Dayton 200
Galien 205
Avery's 209
Three Oaks 211
New Buffalo 218
Corymbo 222
M. C. Yard 227
Mich. City 228
Furnessville 234
Porter 238
Christman's 243
Lake 246
Tolleston 255
Gibson's 260
Hammond 264
Kensington 270
22d Street 280
Chicago 285

AIR LINE DIV.

Jackson to
Jackson Junc.
[illegible]
Snyder's 8
Spring Arbor 10
Concord 14
Pulaski 18
Homer 23
Clarendon 28
Tekonsha 32
Burlington 37
Union City 41
Sherwood 46
Colon 53
Wasepi 56
Centreville 58
Three Rivers 66
Conley's 70
Jones 73
Vandalia 84
Diamond Lake 87
Forrest Hall 92
Cassopolis 95
Dailey 94
Barron Lake 99
Niles 106

BAY CITY DIV.

Detroit to
M. C. Junc. 2
L. S. & M. S. Joint Track 3
G'd River Ave. 4
Woodward Av. 5
L. S. & M. S. & G. T. R. Cross'g 6
D. G. H. & M. Jc. 7
Norris 10
[illegible] 14
Warren 17
Spaldings 19
Utica 24
Depew's Siding 29
Rochester Jc. 30
Rochester 31
Goodison's 33
[illegible] 39
Orion 40
Bailey's Siding 42
Oxford 45
P. O. & P. A. Crossing 45
Thomas 47
Metamora 52
Hunter's Creek 55
Walker's Mill 56
Lapeer Junc. 59
Lapeer 60
L. & N. Junc. 60
Carpenter's 61
Columbiaville 66
Otter Lake 71
Smith's Siding 77
Millington 80
Crampton's 83
F. P. & N. W. Crossing 86
Vassar 89
Caro Junction 91
Grand Pt. Siding 93
Denmark Junc. 94
S. T. & H. R. R. Crossing 95
Reese 98
Mulgrew's 101
Bay City 108

BRIDGE DIVISION.

Slocum Junc. to
Stock Yards
Grosse Isle Shops
Grosse Isle Station
Stony Island 8

CARO BRANCH.

Vassar to
Caro Junction
Watrousville 5
Wahjamega 8
Caro 13

GRAND RAPIDS DIVISION.

Jackson to
Prison Track 1
Vanhorn's 6
Rives Junction 10
[illegible] 14
Onondaga 17
Eaton Rapids 24
Charlotte 34
Chester 39
Vermontville 45
Nashville 49
Morgan 54
Thorn Apple 56
Quimby 57
Hastings 61
Irving 69
Middleville 73
Parmelee 77
Caledonia 79
Dutton 83
Bowen 87
C. & W. M. Junc.
Grand Rapids 93

JOLIET DIVISION.

Lake to
Liverpool 3
Ross 5
P. C. & St. L. Crossing 12
Dyer 14
[illegible] 20
Matteson 25
Frankfort 32
Spencer 37
Joliet 41

LAPEER AND NORTHERN BRANCH.

Lapeer to
L. & N. Junc.
[illegible] 5
Five Lakes 9

MACKINAW DIV.

West Bay City to
West Bay City Yards
Kawkawlin 4
Terry's 10
State Road 13
Pinconning 18
Pinconning Jc. 19
White Feather 21
Saganing 23
Estey's 26
Standish 30
Deep River 30
Sterling 33
[illegible] 35
Wells 39
Culver 41
Summit 43
Greenwood 44
Welch 47
West Branch 52
Ogemaw 52
Beaver Lake 60
St. Helens 64
Roscommon 73
Cheney 84
Grayling 92
Frederic 106
Wright's Lake 109
Otsego Lake 114
Bagley 118
Gaylord 119
Vanderbilt 127
Wolverine 132
Indian River 143
Topinabee 152
Riverside 158
Mullet Lake 166
Cheboygan 165
Freedom 172
Mackinaw City 182

SAGINAW DIV.

Jackson to
Prison Side Track 1
Van Horns 6
Rives Junction 10
Leslie 15
Eden 20
Mason 24
Holt 30
Lansing 36
North Lansing 37
Chandler's 41
Bath 44
Laingsburg 51
Bennington 56
Owosso Junc. 62
Owosso 64
Henderson's 69
Oakley's 73
Chesaning 77
Paines 82
St. Charles 85
Garfield 89
Swan Creek 91
Paines 95
Saginaw City 99
S. R. Junction 100
North Saginaw 101
F. & P. M. Junc. 102
Carrollton 103
Zilwaukee 106
Crooks 109
Salzburg 111
West Bay City 115
West Bay City Yards
Bay City 116

SAGINAW BRANCH.

Vassar to
Caro Junc.
Denmark Junc. 4
Tuscola 9
Buena Vista 14
F. & P. M. Crossing 19
East Saginaw 20
S. B. Junc. 21
Saginaw City 22

SOUTH BEND DIV.

Niles to
Main Street
Bertrand 5
Notre Dame 9
South Bend 11

SOUTH HAVEN DIV.

Kalamazoo to
[illegible] 4
Alamo 9
Williams 11
Kendall 14
Pine Grove 17
Gobles 19
Bloomingdale 22
Berlamont 24
Columbia 27
Grand Junc. 28
Brown's Mills 30
Lacota 31
Kibbie 34
South Haven 39

TOLEDO DIVISION.

Detroit to
Bay City Junc. 2
Springwells 3
South Yard 4
Woodmere 5
River Rouge Siding 6
Ecorse 9
Wyandotte 10
Sibley's 13
Trenton 15
Slocum Junc. 17
Gibraltar 19
S. Rockwood 23
Newport 27
Stony Creek 30
Frenchtown 33
Warner 34
Monroe 35
LaSalle 40
Vienna 44
Alexis 49
Tremainsville 52
Wagon Works Junction 53
Wagon Works Station 56
Toledo 59
C. S. Junction 57

CANADA SOUTHERN DIVISION.

Buffalo to
Susp. Bridge Clifton
Niagara Falls 1
Falls View
Montrose Junc. 3
Montrose 4
Welland 14
Moulton 18
Perry 20
Wellandport 26
Attercliffe 31
Moorhead 33
Canfield 38
Evans 43
Dufferin 50
Hagersville 55
Townsend 61
Villa Nova 64
Waterford 69
Windham 74
Pt. Dover Jc. 76
Hawtrey 80
Cornell 83
Tilsonburg 86
Brownsville 93
Springfield 100
Kingsmill 102
Yarmouth 108
St. Thomas 115
St. Clair Junc. 116
[illegible] 120
Shedden 124
Iona 127
Dutton 132
Bismarck 140
Rodney 144
Taylor 148
Muirkirk 150
Highgate 153
Ridgetown 156
Harwich 164
E. & H. Junc. 169
Charing Cross 171
Buxton 176
Fletcher 182
Tilbury Centre 189
Comber 195
Ruscomb 200
Woodslee 204
Essex Centre 210
Maidstone Cross 214
Pelton 220
[illegible] 224
Windsor 225
Detroit 227

AMHERSTBURG DIV.

Essex Centre to
Elford 4
Colchester 7
Engine House 14
Amherstburg 15

FORT ERIE DIV.

Buffalo to
Black Rock 4
Fort Erie 3
Victoria 5
Niagara Junc. 7
Stevensville 12
Brookfield 15
Welland 20

MICHIGAN MIDLAND DIVISION.

St. Clair to
Adair 8
Ridgeway 18

NIAGARA DIVISION.

Niagara to
Queenston 8
Clifton 13
Niagara Falls 14
Falls View
Montrose Junc. 15
Chippawa 17
Black Creek 22
Niagara Junct. 23
Victoria 26
Fort Erie 30
Black Rock
Buffalo

PETROLIA DIVISION.

Petrolia to
Petrolia Junc. 2

ST. CLAIR DIVISION.

St. Thomas to
St. Clair Junc. 5
Air Line Crossing 5
Southwold 9
Delaware 15
Melbourne 19
G. W. R. Crossing 29
Ekfrid 32
Walkers 31
Alvinston 42
Inwood 49
Oil City 49
Petrolia Junc. 51
Brigden 56
Courtright 66

MICHIGAN & OHIO.

Toledo to
Manhattan Jc. 2
Alexis Junc. 5
Hawthorn 9
Samaria 12
Lulu 17
Monroe Junc. 16
Dundee 22
[illegible] 34
Tecumseh 38
Tipton 45
Cambridge 46
Addison 60
Jerome 67
Moscow 70
Hanover 74
Pulaski 79
Homer 88
Marshall 100
Ceresco 105
Battle Creek 112
Augusta 123
Yorkville 138
Richland 139
Montieth 144
Pine 148
Kellogg 151
Allegan 156

PAW PAW AND TOLEDO AND S. HAVEN.

Lawton to
Paw Paw 4
Lawrence 13
Hartford 19

PONTIAC, OXFORD AND PT. AUSTIN.

Pontiac to
Barnes 6
Cole 9
Oxford 14
Shoup 16
Dryden 27
Imlay City 33
King's Mills 43
North Branch 48
Clifford 55
Kingston 62
Wilmot 65
Deford 68
Cass City 74
Gagetown 80
[illegible] 84
Wisner 87
Berne 92
Caseville 100

PORT HURON AND NORTH-WESTERN.

EAST SAGINAW DIV.

Port Huron to
Thomas Street 1
12th Street 2
Gratiot Center 4
North Street 6
50 Feet Grade 10
Kingsley 11
Saginaw J'n 13
Gravel Siding 15
Fair's 16
Brown's Corners 19
Brockway Centre 24
Melvin 25
Yorks 28
Brown's City 36
[illegible] 40
Marlette 45
Clifford 50
Silver Creek 53
Mayville 58
Juniata 65
D. & B. C. J'n 71
Vassar 72
Tuscola 75
Frankenmuth 82
East Saginaw 91

ALMONT DIVISION.

Port Huron to
10th Street 3
Grand Trunk Junction 2
Kimball 9
Burns 13
Wales 16
Lamb 23
Memphis 29
Berville 33
Smith's 38
Almont 34

SAND BEACH AND PORT AUSTIN DIV.

Port Huron to
Thomas Street 1
12th Street 1
Gratiot 4
North Street 6
50 Foot Grade 10
Kingsley 11
Saginaw J'n 13
Grant Centre 14
Jeddo 17
Amadore 20
Croswell 25
Tidball 28
Applegate 32
Park's Siding 34
Carsonville 37
Deckerville Rd 40
Wilbur Road 41
Downing 44
Deckerville 45
Cooley Road 48
Palms 51
Tyre 56
Ubly 61
Wadsworth 66
Bad Axe 22
Filion 28
Dwight 75
Port Austin 67
Minden 60
Adams' Corn's 59
Sand Beach 70

SAGINAW, TUSCOLA & HURON.

East Saginaw to
Cheese Creek 5
Reeseville 9
Reese 12
Gilford 17
Kinner 19
Fair Grove 22
Akron 25
Wardman 27
Caseville 31
State Road 34
Sebewaing 37
Bay Port 48

SAGINAW VALLEY & ST. LOUIS.

East Saginaw to
Saginaw City 2
Paines 8
Swan Creek 11
Graham [illegible]
Sand Ridge 19
Hemlock 16
Porters 18
Merrill 21
Doyle 23
Wheeler 27
Breckenridge 28
St. Louis 35
Alma 38
Ithaca 45

TOLEDO, ANN ARBOR & G'D TRUNK.

Toledo to
Manhattan Jc. 1
Alexis Junc. 4
Hawthorn [illegible]
Samaria 11
Lulu 13
Monroe Junc. 15
Dundee 18
Azalia 22
Milan Junc. 26
Milan 31
Nora 33
Urania 35
Pittsfield 40
Ann Arbor 45
Leland 52
Worden 55
South Lyon 61

WABASH ST. LOUIS & PACIFIC.

DETROIT AND INDIANAPOLIS DIV.

Detroit to
Delray 4
Hood 7
Romulus 15
Belleville 18
Willis 24
Whittaker 28
Milan 32
Ocean 37
Britton 42
Holloway 48
Adrian 55
Sand Creek 61
N. Morenci 70
North Fayette [illegible]
Alvordton [illegible]
Kunkle 86
Montpelier 94
Blakesley 104
Butler 114
Auburn 121
Laotto 130
Churubusco 136
Columbia City 156
South Whitley 167
N. Manchester 177
Lagro 191
Roann 197
Chili 203
Denver 205
Peru 214
Miami 219
Kokomo 233
Fairfield [illegible]
Tipton 251
Arcadia 263
Noblesville 273
Indianapolis 296

FOREST AND MINERAL WEALTH,

COMPILED FROM OFFICIAL AND OTHER AUTHENTIC SOURCES.

IT may no doubt be justly claimed that the extent and diversified character of the natural wealth and resources of Michigan surpass those of any region of similar geographical extent on the globe. The leading interests are those of lumber, iron, copper, salt and gypsum, and to these our statement will be mainly confined, although there are others that are not undeserving of mention, and in whose development the attention of capitalists must to a greater or less extent become enlisted. With a water line of 2,000 miles, the shipping advantages of our noble State are in keeping with her vast resources, and when in addition to these unrivaled elements of wealth we take into consideration her immense agricultural resources, the important character of her manufactures and the extent of her fisheries, it would really seem that her elements of material prosperity were filled to overflowing.

COPPER.

The subject of minerals very naturally calls to mind the Upper Peninsula, in which region are located the valuable mines which have wielded so large an influence in conducing to the general prosperity, and which have exerted and will continue to exert so important an influence in financial, commercial, marine and manufacturing circles. The location of the above named region will be understood by those not conversant with it by consulting our maps. Its greatest length is about three hundred miles, and its average width about one hundred and twenty.

When the French Jesuits visited this country as early as 1640, they discovered its rich mineral resources, and reported the fact to the head of their order at Paris. Consequently, we see Dr. Franklin in 1783, when he was negotiating our treaty of peace with the British Government, carefully insisting that the line which was to divide the British from the American possessions on the North, should run to the North of Isle Royale on Lake Superior; for the purpose, as far as stated, of securing the rich deposits of copper that were known to exist on that island.

When Gen. Cass visited the country in 1822 he discovered that celebrated mass of native copper which is now in the Patent Office at Washington. This mass of copper had been detached from its native hill and been transported several miles from it to the bank of the Ontonagon River, with the evident intention of taking it down that stream to the lake. By what race of men this mass was removed from its native bed, and carried to where Gen. Cass discovered it, will probably never be known. There are traces of these "ancient miners" throughout the whole mineral range of Lake Superior. Mining "pits" or excavations in the copper-bearing rock are so extensive and distinct, that after removing the soil and debris that fill them, the modern miner, without any geological knowledge whatever, has no difficulty in tracing the copper veins from one end of the country to the other. That it is three or four centuries since these people made the excavations, does not seem to admit of a doubt, for trees, whose ages can be calculated for that length of time, have been found growing within the excavations referred to. Copper chisels and spears, in great variety and abundance have been taken from underneath the roots of these huge trees. Who the people were and who worked these mines at that early day, whence they came, or whither they went, will probably never be known by us moderns. It is imagined by some that if they were not actually the "mound-builders" they were, at least, contemporary with them, but all is conjecture. That they were infinitely farther advanced in civilization than the "North American Indians" of our day, does not admit of a doubt. If the Jesuit missionaries of 1640 failed to learn anything respecting them, we, of this day, must content ourselves to remain in ignorance. In 1835 when the people of the then Territory of Michigan, applied to the Congress of the United States to be admitted as a State into the Union—the Congressional delegation of Ohio resisted the application most strenuously, for reasons best known to themselves. A "Compromise" was finally effected, whereby the Ohioans agreed to relinquish their opposition, on condition that Michigan should allow the northern line of Ohio to be carried six miles further north than it had been originally located. To this Michigan's delegate objected, but the whole controversy was finally settled by giving Michigan what is now known as her "Upper Peninsula," in lieu of the rich belt of land, six miles in width, traversing her whole Southern border; which Congress awarded to Ohio. Long and loud was the wail sent up by every Michigander when this settlement of the admission of their Territory as a State, was made known to them. They denounced the Upper Peninsula as an "American Siberia," a land of eternal snows and ice, entirely uninhabitable! This was the cry of the masses. A few of her citizens were willing to admit that some "specimens" of copper had been seen there, but no one dreamed that it would ever amount to anything as a mineral region. Little did our people at that time think that they were getting a second "California" by the trade!

As soon as the Indian title to this country was extinguished, in 1843, the United States Government established a military post on Keweenaw Point, known as Fort Wilkins. The usual number of citizen attachees and hangers on accompanied our troops to the Fort. These adventurers were not long in discovering the extensive existence of native copper in the rocky hills in its vicinity.

In 1844 the State Government of Michigan commenced a systematic geological survey of the country. This was prosecuted with vigor, until the death of the lamented Doctor Houghton, its chief, in 1846.

This partial geological examination showed that a portion of the country from Keweenaw Point to the Porcupine Mountains, was well filled with "native copper"—that a belt of copper-bearing rock, about three miles in width, and from three to twelve miles inland, which is nearly one hundred miles in length, contained more or less copper. A wild rush of speculation filled the country with adventurers in 1845 and '46. Most of these persons knew no more about mining for copper than children, and the consequence was, that Lake Superior copperdom was denounced a humbug—for the simple reason that they had neither experience or the necessary cash capital to open the mines. In two instances, however, men of experience took hold with a will and some cash means. A number of gentlemen from New York and Pittsburgh embarked in the real business of mining. They organized two companies as early as 1848, known as the Cliff and Minnesota companies, the one near Keweenaw Point, and the other on the Ontonagon River, near the western terminus of what is thus far known as the "Mineral Range."

The history of mining in Michigan presents a somewhat checkered phase. The Cliff mine was worked three years without much sign of success. It changed hands at the very moment when the vein was opened which proved afterward to be exceedingly rich in copper and silver. The Minnesota for the first three years gave no very encouraging results. The discovery of the ancient pit with the large mass of native copper above alluded to, led to the operations at this mine, but it was long before any adequate return was received for the money expended. The Pewabic mine was commenced in 1855, with an expenditure of $26,357, which produced $1,080 worth of copper; the second year it expended $40,820 and produced $31,492 worth of copper; in 1857, $54,484 of expenses produced $44,058 worth of copper; in 1858, the amount expended was $109,159 and the receipts for copper $76,588. Other mines met with similar, or even more disastrous experiences. Mining operations were then carried on at a great disadvantage. Owing to the rapids in the St. Mary's River, the country could not be approached by water with large craft from below. Being more than a thousand miles distant from any centre of supplies or market for mine products, destitute of all the requirements for the development of mines; every tool, every part of machinery, every mouthful of provisions had to be hauled around the rapids, boated along the shores for hundreds of miles to the copper region, and thence often carried on the back of man or beast to the place where copper was supposed to exist. Every stroke of the pick cost tenfold more than in populated districts; every disaster delayed the operations for weeks and months. But the opening of the Sault Ste. Marie Ship Canal gave a new impetus to mining operations and tended largely to develop the mineral resources of the Upper Peninsula.

The discovery of the rich deposits of the world-renowned Calumet and Hecla mine, which are worked in the interest of a consolidation, amazed copper miners and baffled some of their theories. These mines have yielded colossal fortunes to stockholders.

The want of adequate scientific and practical knowledge, on the part of many who early embarked in the business, led to much loss of capital and often to the embarrassment of those interested, and the abandonment of enterprises which, if they had been conducted with the same care and judgment that is ordinarily bestowed upon other branches of business, would have proved profitable and permanent investments. The fact of an inexhaustible quantity of this valuable mineral, and of a quality which in richness is not surpassed in the world, led to numerous scientific explorations of the territory and to the employment of a large amount of capital, which has, for many years past, by judicious management, been yielding a rich percentage. It, in fact, ranks among the most important products of the Northwest, and a careful study and exposition of the different geological peculiarities of the copper districts, and an attentive observation of the local and general mineralogical and vein phenomena are being bestowed upon these vast metallic deposits, which will lead to still more important developments, affecting very materially the wealth and the commerce of the country.

The ore now mined is of a very superior quality, yielding fully 80 per cent. of ingot copper. In many instances masses weighing hundreds of tons, of pure native copper, have been taken out. The copper is smelted at Portage Lake, Detroit, Cleveland and Pittsburgh. There are now 28 mines in operation, employing about 7,000 men. The district embraces the counties of Houghton, Keweenaw, Ontonagon and Isle Royale. In quality the product is now universally conceded to be the best in the world. Prices are at present having a low range with, however, some promising symptoms of a rally.

The Hon. A. P. Swineford, at the close of his exhaustive and admirable "Annual Review" for 1882, presents the following carefully prepared statistics:

	Net Tons.	Pounds.	Market Value.
Adventure	......	439	78 91
Allouez	561	1,327	205,943 84
Atlantic	1,815	1,709	484,797 44
Aztec	1	1,175	525 81
Calumet & Hecla	15,097	1,349	3,801,098 59
Central	676	1,387	248,197 94
Cliff	39	53	12,160 35
Conglomerate	567	349	189,446 47
Copper Falls	293	1,506	108,153 78
Franklin	1,622	196	598,224 49
Grand Portage	379	1,080	139,679 43
Hancock	270	933	99,512 56
Huron	180	379	67,119 05
Isle Royale	14	1,739	5,472 39
Mass	336	56	122,294 49
Minnesota	5	673	1,904 71
Mitong	10	1,380	3,835 65
Norwich	23	494	8,323 18
Osceola	2,066	737	758,942 36
Pewabic	761	686	279,260 81
Phoenix	280	665	102,777 53
Quincy	2,858	1,795	1,042,398 64
Ridge	51	698	18,908 53
Sheldon Columbian	1	1,600	607 59
St. Clair	42	1,136	15,689 06
National	8	1,560	2,828 78
Salt Mines	2	1,776	1,033 68
Wolverine	59	1,457	12,096 58
Total	25,421	780	$13,456,028 33

The following table shows the product (refined copper) of the Lake Superior copper mines for each year since 1854, together with the approximate value:

Year.	Tons.	Pounds.	Value.
1854 and previous	6,029	1,797	$2,148,400
1855	2,964	1,004	1,596,100
1856	4,109	1,808	2,219,860
1857	4,763	836	2,095,300
1858	4,579	1,916	2,190,435
1859	4,462	1,692	2,222,391
1860	6,094	275	2,604,960
1861	7,519	697	3,457,000
1862	6,789	328	3,604,382
1863	6,420	1,344	4,413,580
1864	6,243	1,945	3,879,300
1865	7,179	338	5,832,553
1866	6,575	42	4,639,625
1867	6,722	1,807	4,442,841
1868	10,467	124	4,849,434
1869	12,819	1,300	6,335,615
1870	12,815	960	5,996,783
1871	12,972	849	5,798,455
1872	12,278	1,359	7,979,406
1873	15,047	1,325	8,758,100
1874	17,156	1,309	8,008,334
1875	18,019	1,487	8,180,426
1876	19,152	987	7,986,432
1877	19,513	471	7,427,308
1878	20,843	1,366	6,990,540
1879	21,439	1,399	7,327,360
1880	24,885	867	9,947,979
1881	23,574	1,766	9,025,891
1882	25,421	763	10,456,828
Total	356,920	180	$180,307,798

From the foregoing tables it will be seen that there was an increase of 1,917 tons of copper, as compared with the preceding year. The values given are approximate, that of the copper being figured at the average price for the year, which was 18.41 cents per pound.

On the amount of copper produced in 1882 the several companies paid dividends amounting to *two million, nine hundred thousand dollars*, the same mines having previously paid to their shareholders an aggregate of $25,315,000, by much the larger half of which has been paid during the last ten years. The net earnings of the iron mines cannot be given, for the reason that the companies are close corporations, and not being required by law to do so, make no public announcement of dividends. While we know that the net earnings of some of them have been very large, it is at the same time true that others, only partially developed, have so far not more than paid expenses, while still others, through mismanagement, have become involved in debt, and are likely to remain so until a change of ownership is brought about. Nevertheless, as a whole, the net earnings of iron mines have been very large, even during the depression which followed in the wake of the great panic of 1873—how large, we cannot definitely state, and would not if we could, for the reason that we would be charged in many quarters with meddling with private business affairs with which the public have no concern. We venture the opinion, however, that the percentage of profit made by the copper companies, would not be an exorbitant guess at a basis upon which to figure the net earnings of the iron mines. It would be rather below than above the actual figure.

In closing this review of the iron and copper mining industry of the Upper Peninsula, we cannot do better than quote the following table, showing the dividends paid by the mines of the several states and territories in 1882:

	1882.	Total to date.
Arizona	$1,065,300	$4,097,500
California	5,715,408	14,517,407
Colorado	2,040,900	4,165,650
Dakota	907,500	6,179,500
Georgia	48,000	80,000
Idaho	47,000	47,000
Michigan	2,900,000	28,215,000
Missouri	60,000	390,000
Montana	302,113	748,613
Nevada	792,382	51,626,590
New Mexico	904,875	904,875
North Carolina	6,000	6,000
Utah	2,350,000	6,433,000
	$18,140,900	$79,658,648

The Mining Stock Register, a publication devoted exclusively to gold and silver mining, gives a list, with the ratings, of nearly *eight thousand gold and silver* mining companies now in existence, of which only 61 were reported as paying dividends in 1882, whereas the entire list of iron and copper mines on Lake Superior last year numbered just 103, the *copper companies alone* contributing the dividends credited to Michigan in the foregoing table.

To quote from Mr. Swineford: "With the foregoing record before him, how can the capitalist hesitate where and how to invest his surplus funds? Iron mining is a legitimate business, not a doubtful speculation; there have been no losses not directly traceable to bad management, or a wretched lack of judgment in the selection of property in which to invest. No where, and in no other business, is the man of means so certain of a handsome return on the amount invested; the stocks of our principal mines are as nearly an absolute security as a government bond, while yet returning to the holder tenfold as much annually in the way of interest. Men who have squandered hundreds of thousands, nay millions, of dollars only to pauperize themselves in speculative gold and silver mining, could easily have made immense fortunes by investing half the amount thus thrown away in the much more legitimate business of mining iron or copper on Lake Superior—a region the mines of which return to their owners annually *a larger amount of profit than is yielded by all the gold and sil-*

ver mines *of the United States.* Indeed, no other region of the same extent and population—no matter what its industries may be—can present a showing of profits which will at all compare with the exhibit which can truthfully be made in behalf of the iron and copper mining industries of the Upper Peninsula of Michigan, and to prove the truth of the assertion the author respectfully invites a comparison of figures, past and present."

THE COPPER PRODUCT FOR 1883.

Official returns show the total product of the Portage Lake, Keweenaw Point and Ontonagon districts for the past year to be 37,434 tons, against 35,671 for 1882. The statement for 1883 is as follows:

	Yield in 1883 Tons
Portage Lake District.	
Calumet and Hecla	20,404
Quincy	2,322
Osceola	2,459
Franklin	2,130
Atlantic	1,909
Pewabic	907
Peninsula	581
Hancock	452
Grand Portage	440
Huron	435
Wolverine	430
Centennial	31
Other sources	30
Keweenaw Point District.	
Allouez	1,264
Central	911
Copper Falls	328
Phoenix	405
*Conglomerate	185
St. Clair	62
Cliff	9
Ontonagon District.	
Mass	452
Ridge	34
National	17
Belt	8
Knowlton	9
Minnesota	8
Evergreen Bluff	1
Adventure	....

The following companies have declared dividends this year.

Calumet and Hecla (quarterly)	$500,000
Quincy	180,000
Franklin	80,000
Atlantic	40,000
Osceola (quarterly)	25,000

IRON.

The existence of iron ore in the Upper Peninsula was known to the Indians and white traders who visited that locality at an early day. In June, 1845, the Jackson Iron Co. was organized with a view to operations in the copper district. Mr. P. M. Everett, one of the original corporators, visited Lake Superior as the agent of the company to locate lands. He was provided with a number of permits from the Secretary of War for the location of such lands as he might select for the company. While on his way to that country Mr. Everett was informed by the Indians of the existence of iron, and through their instrumentality he was able to find it, and then located what are now the Jackson and Cleveland mines. On his return to the lower country, Mr. Everett brought with him some of the ore. A portion of this was sent to Pittsburgh to be tested and was there pronounced worthless. Another small quantity was sent to an old forge at Coldwater, and there was made the first iron from Lake Superior ore. This was a small bar, a portion of which Mr. Everett had made into a knife, the better to test its qualities. It was a year later before the Jackson company made the first opening and commenced the erection of a forge. This forge was put in operation in the spring of 1847, and the first ore taken out at the Jackson mine was there manufactured into blooms. The first blooms were sold to E. B. Ward, and the iron was used in the walking-beam of the steamboat "Ocean." Other forges were begun from time to time, but the business was slow at starting, owing to the difficulty of shipping. In 1853 three or four tons of Lake Superior iron were shipped to the World's Fair at New York, but regular shipments did not commence until the spring of 1856.

*No stamping done till near the end of the year.

The ores thus far developed are mainly in the county of Marquette. They are generally found in hills, which are from 400 to 600 feet high, and which are nothing more nor less than solid masses of iron partially covered by layers of earth and rock. These hills are in a range of about six miles wide by one hundred miles in length, extending from Lake Fairbanks to Keweenaw Bay. There is another extensive range of equally rich hills in Menominee county, but which have not yet been much developed. This range also crops out near Bayfield, and at other points large deposits of magnetic ores have been found, which have been proved to be almost pure native iron.

Five varieties of ore have been developed. The most valuable is the specular hematite, which is a very pure anhydrous sesqui-oxyde, giving a red powder and yielding in the blast-furnace from 60 to 65 per cent. of metallic iron, which is slightly red short. The ore occurs both slaty and granular or massive. The next in order of importance is probably the soft hematite, which much resembles the brown hematite of Pennsylvania and Connecticut. This ore is generally found associated with the harder ores, from which many suppose it is formed by partial decomposition or disintegration. It contains some water chemically combined, is porous in structure, yields about 50 per cent. in the furnace, and is more easily reduced than any other ore of the district. It forms an excellent mixture with the speculars. The magnetic ore of the district has thus far only been found to the west of the other ores—at the Michigan, Washington, Edwards and Champion mines—at which none of the other varieties have been found except the specular, into which the magnetic sometimes passes. The flag ore is a slaty or shistose silicious hematite, containing rather less metallic iron, and of a more difficult reduction than either of the varieties above named. It is often magnetic and sometimes banded with a dull red or white quartz. The iron is cold short, which is one of the best qualities of this ore, the other ores of the district being red short. It is believed to be the most abundant ore in the district. A silicious iron ore containing a variable amount of oxyde of manganese is found at several points accompanying the flag ore, and is of great value as a mixture.

As previously stated the first shipments of Lake Superior ore were from the Jackson mine in 1856, up to which year the aggregate product amounted to 25,000 tons. The Cleveland mine was opened about the same time, and in 1856 shipped about 6,000 tons. The Marquette mine was the next one opened and made its first shipment in 1858. Other mines followed in due time, the attention of capitalists having been attracted in that direction. Railroads and immense docks have been built to facilitate the shipping of ores and furnaces have been erected to reduce the ores on the spot.

Twenty-six blast furnaces have been built and put in operation in the Lake Superior mining region. The first was the "Pioneer," built in 1857, and the last the "Vulcan," blown in May, 1882.

We again refer to the Annual Review of Mr. Swineford, from which publication are extracted all of the statistics appended.

Amount of iron ore shipped in 1882, and the approximate market value of the same:

Name of Mine.	Gross tons.	Value.
Argyle	15,431	$117,[illegible]
Barnum	41,779	208,[illegible]
Bay State	1,309	7,418
Beaufort	5,142	46,430
Bessemer	27,494	104,964
Boston	18,345	179,[illegible]
Brier Hill	19,309	90,045
Cambria	61,545	[illegible]
Champion	150,008	1,590,[illegible]
Chapin	247,908	2,156,[illegible]
Cleveland	206,159	1,820,145
Commonwealth	115,982	757,[illegible]
Calumet	5,947	49,[illegible]
Crystal Falls	1,281	8,718
Cory	13,874	114,778
Cyclops	18,507	535,442
Columbia	15,068	105,[illegible]
Dalliba	64,966	346,369
Detroit	3,405	22,412
East Champion	4,082	30,012
Erie	2,721	21,946
Fairbank	8,045	64,347
Florence	130,185	950,[illegible]
Foster	11,642	90,[illegible]
Great Western	537	5,228
Goodrich	9,999	84,[illegible]
Hewitt	9,365	80,136
Humboldt	42,408	415,[illegible]
Indiana	4,226	38,[illegible]
Iron River	20,113	149,047
Jackson	90,[illegible]	809,[illegible]
[illegible]	15,029	119,946
Keel Ridge	30,436	190,113
Lake Angeline	54,258	337,445
Lake Superior	296,208	2,504,[illegible]
Ludington	97,183	648,[illegible]
Mastodon	8,477	22,[illegible]
McComber	40,408	282,415
Metropolitan	22,824	134,[illegible]
Michigamme	43,712	415,104
Milwaukee	40,981	345,346
Mitchell	102,398	800,479
Nanaimo	2,466	16,126
National	29,468	202,377
Negaunee Concentrating Works	1,177	11,[illegible]
New York	56,966	509,[illegible]
New York Hematite	3,105	22,[illegible]
New Dun	5,612	47,061
Norway	165,347	1,076,[illegible]
Quinnesec	44,[illegible]	341,[illegible]
Paint River	6,514	50,842
Pendill	9,097	54,099
Perkins	72,940	526,[illegible]
Pittsburgh & Lake Superior	41,456	379,[illegible]
Republic	335,[illegible]	2,821,[illegible]
Rolling Mill	108	900
Saginaw	41,208	396,860
Salisbury	43,243	347,450
Section 13	2,287	17,979
Spurr	9,673	72,[illegible]
St. Lawrence	5,466	42,440
Swanzy	21,446	135,[illegible]
Sterling	8,006	76,307
Taylor	15,146	82,[illegible]
Titan	1,779	2,779
Union	12,505	109,[illegible]
Vulcan	94,862	799,677
Webster	4,443	34,438
West Republic	27,885	264,737
Wheat	9,354	76,400
Wetmore	1,771	8,778
Wick	196	1,606
Winthrop	33,006	189,035
Youngstown	8,198	77,189
[illegible]	110	1,054
Total	2,948,307	$24,363,745

Name of Mine.	Gross tons.	Value.
QUARTZ.		
Carp River Iron Co.	5,386	$27,675
Powell Bros. & Co.	1,840	5,313
McVickle & Co	5,395	26,953
Total quartz	12,623	$60,115
Total ore and quartz	2,961,696	$24,326,637

The following table shows the aggregate product of each Lake Superior iron mine since the beginning of mining operations in 1853:

	Gross tons.		Gross tons.
Argyle	243,513	McComber	392,781
Barnum	320,624	Metropolitan	58,524
Bay State	38,095	Michigamme	493,859
Beaufort	3,571	Milwaukee	56,936
Bessemer	114,317	Mitchell	109,127
Boston	44,543	Nanaimo	2,496
Brier Hill	20,593	National	213,061
Cambria	108,398	Negaunee Con. W'ks	1,177
Champion	1,138,913	New York	1,091,395
Chapin	418,564	New York Hematite	97,307
Chicago	12,516	New Buri	3,957
Cleveland	2,355,164	Norway	503,319
Columbia	24,119	Paint River	6,515
Commonwealth	220,015	Pendill	38,379
Calumet	3,017	Perkins	198,713
Crystal Falls	1,348	Pittsb'gh & L. Sup.	279,849
Curry	45,462	Quinnesec	308,302
Cyclops	97,495	Republic	1,482,508
Dalliba	58,093	Rolling Mill	221,977
Detroit	3,448	Saginaw	472,583
East Champion	62,740	Salisbury	372,092
Erie	8,763	Section 12	32,696
Fairbank	8,933	Spurr	153,465
Foxdale	274,799	St. Lawrence	9,096
Foster	120,503	Sterling	18,305
Goodrich	31,564	Swanzey (and Ch'rs)	156,538
Great Western	252	Taylor	22,795
Hewitt	13,859	Titan	3,778
Humboldt	456,058	Union	15,648
Indiana	4,380	Vulcan	365,649
Iron River	22,115	Webster	4,448
Jackson	4,771,998	West Republic	95,329
Jim Pascoe	19,696	Wetmore	1,777
Keel Ridge	35,962	Wheat	93,569
Lake Angeline	343,728	Wick	196
Lake Superior	2,991,963	Winthrop	379,303
Ludington	54,212	Youngstown	6,199
Mastodon	8,477	Mines now idle	848,938
Total			30,568,867

The following table shows the product of the Lake Superior charcoal furnaces in 1882, together with its approximate value in market:

	Gross tons.	Value.
Carp River Iron Co's furnace	11,526	$653,490
Deer Lake	8,532	313,926
Jackson	8,461	324,977
Pioneer	8,430	146,590
Menominee	12,400	386,600
Martel	11,217	385,467
Pioneer	12,819	417,992
Total	72,962	$2,698,450

The following table shows the aggregate product of all the furnaces that have been built and put in operation on the Upper Peninsula:

Pioneer (two stacks)	198,219
Northern	15,098
Collins	41,967
Michigan	41,501
Greenwood	40,392
Bancroft	34,618
Morgan	37,578
Champion	32,048
Deer Lake (two stacks)	48,844
Jackson (two stacks)	127,008
Bay (two stacks)	50,708
Manistique	28,312
Grace	11,048
Escanaba	6,636
Carp River Iron Co. (three stacks)	87,871
Menominee	66,138
Cliff	6,302
Florence	8,114
Martel	13,338
Total	916,919

Total aggregate production of the Upper Peninsula iron mines and furnaces from 1856 to 1882, inclusive, with approximate value of product:

YEAR.	Ore.	Pig Iron.	Ore and Pig.	VALUE.
1856*	36,319	......	36,319	$ 358,677
1857	25,646	......	25,646	76,938
1858	32,278	1,629	34,505	122,795
1859	68,832	7,258	76,090	873,859
1860	114,401	5,660	120,061	738,446
1861	114,209	7,970	122,399	719,432
1862	124,169	8,590	132,759	984,977
1863	203,055	9,513	212,568	1,416,890
1864	247,059	13,932	260,991	1,867,310
1865	193,758	13,982	207,740	1,390,453
1866	296,713	18,437	315,150	2,405,903
1867	465,504	20,311	485,815	3,415,826
1868	510,522	38,246	548,768	3,993,413
1869	639,097	39,003	678,100	4,969,633
1870	859,507	49,298	908,805	6,303,773
1871	813,984	51,225	865,209	6,115,898
1872	954,512	65,355	1,019,867	9,156,893
1873	1,195,234	70,507	1,265,741	11,380,981
1874	935,488	86,484	1,021,972	7,399,819
1875	910,549	81,725	992,274	7,709,765
1876	992,811	61,511	1,054,322	6,397,796
1877	1,025,129	29,362	1,054,491	5,380,583
1878	1,125,392	17,404	1,142,796	6,004,484
1879	1,414,182	39,395	1,453,577	12,419,117
1880	1,997,309	48,394	2,045,703	19,457,430
1881	2,321,315	52,462	2,373,777	20,427,613
1882	2,948,307	72,363	3,020,670	26,370,908
Total	20,390,963	916,919	21,307,882	$154,963,780

*And previous years.

THE PRODUCT FOR 1883.

Below are given tables showing the entire output of the Lake Superior district in iron ore and pig iron for the year ending December 31, 1883—the statement of ore output, including all ore shipped by lake or rail and hauled by train to furnaces—also the estimated value of the same in the market. The output of ore shows a falling off of about 600,000 tons compared with 1882:

Pig Iron.

Furnace.	Gross tons.	Value.
Carp River Iron Company	430	$ 9,473
Deer Lake	10,163	238,991
Jackson	5,688	159,743
Florence	5,830	137,158
Menominee	6,738	151,560
Pioneer	15,048	361,096
Vulcan	4,130	93,355
Martel	8,243	199,807
Total	57,004	$1,351,140

Iron Ore.

Name of Mine.	Gross tons.	Value.
Argyle	13,730	$ 81,300 00
Barnum	63,759	378,518 00
Beaufort	18,978	66,823 00
Bay State	694	3,989 50
Bessemer	3,172	8,774 00
Boston	22,090	121,140 00
Brier Hill	4,090	26,838 00
Cambria	47,308	287,387 00
Champion	104,660	784,730 00
Calumet	29,346	175,634 00
Chapin	365,630	2,394,098 00
Chicago	117	526 50
Cleveland	109,219	1,080,614 00
Columbia	714	4,284 00
Commonwealth	91,949	639,715 00
Curry	3,479	22,658 00
Cyclops	32,571	186,630 00
Dalliba	1,483	7,387 50
Detroit	13,814	41,375 00
Dexter	4,873	29,385 00
Delphic	6,419	15,345 00
East Champion	6,036	30,364 00
Erie	6,403	37,993 00
Emma	1,255	3,453 00
Fairbank	435	2,047 50
Florence	60,302	391,641 00
Foster	10,059	65,130 50
Great Western	32,633	209,712 50
Hewitt	7,519	45,036 00
Humboldt	31,895	191,106 00
Indiana	4,362	22,172 00
Iron River	100,595	505,643 00
Jackson	71,279	437,868 00
Keel Ridge	3,958	22,196 00
Lake Angeline	27,338	163,834 00
Lake Superior	300,790	1,804,724 00
Lillie	2,442	14,652 00
Ludington	102,525	615,325 00
Mangusue	327	1,975 00
Mastodon	16,877	95,602 00
McComber	14,675	75,030 00
Metropolitan	86,946	516,682 00

Name of Mine.	Gross tons.	Value.
Michigamme	43,330	$260,198 00
Milwaukee	966	4,080 00
Nanaimo	28,361	148,136 00
National	31,178	197,962 00
Negaunee Concentrating Works	13,894	69,264 00
Norway	114,959	574,315 00
Northwestern	7,200	43,212 00
Paint River	5,971	36,969 56
Pendill	819	1,590 00
Perkins	79,514	459,364 00
Pittsburgh & L. S.	19,414	116,484 00
Quinnesec	34,578	180,056 00
Republic	128,565	1,067,915 00
Rolling Mill	1,330	7,810 00
Saginaw	8,103	34,840 00
Salisbury	17,028	82,140 00
Spurr	9,067	34,402 00
St. Lawrence	10,961	49,324 50
Sterling	3,600	21,798 00
Swanzy	10,730	69,600 00
Taylor	6,155	36,773 00
Titan	18,138	82,075 00
Union	4,894	31,376 00
Vulcan	79,674	479,364 00
West Republic	60,344	294,401 00
Wetmore	2,777	12,995 50
Wheat	6,653	32,125 00
Winthrop	50,143	350,733 00
Youngstown	15,293	76,480 00
Miscellaneous	468	2,340 00
Quartz Rock	2,271	15,984 00
Total	2,353,979	$15,077,909 06

LUMBER.

Our State embraces a large number of important interests, including some few that are not shared by any other part of the country. With due deference to other interests, it cannot be denied that up to this time decidedly the greatest of all of them—save only that of agriculture—and the most magnificent in its general aspects, is that of lumber. In this regard she has probably been without a peer in any similar extent of territory on the globe, taking into the account both quantity and quality. In both these respects Michigan has for the past thirty-five years been a continuous marvel, while as to the question of material wealth the trade has been the very life blood of the prosperity of much of the greater part of the State. The product of our forests has been at different periods shipped to each of the four quarters of the globe, a fact which probably cannot be said of that of any other one region. Of the Lower Peninsula, embracing about 25,000,000 acres, considerably more than one-half might very properly have been classed as a pine region, for the product was found growing upon all the streams, and was interspersed in almost every township with hardwood. It is a well known peculiarity that the choicest pine is always thus interspersed with other timber, and that the lands having such varieties are always admirably adapted to agricultural purposes. It was through the operations of our lumbermen that the true character of the soil of the northern portion of the Lower Peninsula first became generally known. Up to the period of these demonstrations the quality of the soil of that region had been greatly underrated, through causes not necessary to dwell upon at length at this time, but which are understood by all the more intelligent of our old citizens. Hence the pioneer operators in lumber consisted mainly of adventurers, very few of whom had any intention of becoming permanent residents. Gardens were cultivated in the vicinity of the mills, partly by way of experiment, and it was the unexpectedly prolific yield of vegetable products so planted that led to the settlement of the country by agriculturists. Although nearly all kinds of pine are found in various parts of the State, ours consists mainly of the white pine, so highly prized in commerce, and it is the great preponderance of this choice variety that has contributed so largely toward making the State famous.

Of the probable future date of the exhaustion of the supply of pine lumber in this State there have been speculations and estimates without end. Some of these estimates have been regarded as very careful ones, yet they have proved illusory, as all calculations up to a comparatively recent period have been imminently liable to prove. Those making these predictions in former years were not able to see "through the woods," but now it is quite different. Then the armies of lumbermen belonging respectively to the eastern and western coasts had not met. They have now not only crossed and recrossed each other's track, but every quarter section of valuable pine lands has been crossed and recrossed, and claims either staked out at the land offices of Uncle Sam or the precious right secured from first, second, third or fourth hands, generally by large operators who are able to hold. The development of the railway system, which has so immensely facilitated shipping operations, has also contributed its aid toward denuding the State of this inestimable source of wealth. The time has therefore actually arrived when predictions such as those above referred to are in order. Our prominent operators now concur in the opinion that if our forests should be made to disappear at the same ratio for the ensuing six or eight years as they have for the past three, the end will virtually have been reached. This is, however, put forth not without some qualification, for the ratio of slaughter referred to will not be witnessed, for the very good reason that the great body of the timber yet spared is in the hands of intelligent operators who intend to hold it for contingencies not yet fully foreshadowed. Monopolists are odious as a rule, but this class, who are bent on preserving intact some few segments of our forests, deserve the gratitude of the public. That the supply from our world-renowned pineries is actually approaching its end will come over the minds of thousands and tens of thousands like waking from a long dream, but the fact is too patent to leave room for doubt. Of all our domains of pine, which once seemed practically inexhaustible, those of the rich Saginaw Valley and half a dozen other prominent points were all that had been invaded no longer than three decades since. Throughout all the rest of our almost interminable pine forests no clash and clangor of machinery rendered back music to the merry whistle of the passing steamer or the tread of the lonely hunter or trapper; but this solemn stillness is succeeded by a change such as could never have been dreamed of. Instead of lumbering operations being confined to the margins of streams, as was so long the case, the ax has found the very marrow of this great source of wealth, and the problem as to what use a large share of the costly machinery of our lumbermen will be diverted will soon be presented for solution. A considerable proportion of this property will doubtless be required for many years in working up inferior qualities of lumber. As regards the absolute extinction of our soft woods, especially the lower grades—irrespective of the question whether the business will be a paying one—a prediction probably cannot even now be made, judging from analogous cases in Pennsylvania and other localities.

A new field for the operations of our enterprising lumbermen has been opened within a few years in the Upper Peninsula, and the trade there has assumed large proportions.

At the close of the year there is not a very buoyant feeling, although the Eastern markets are not in large stock so far as concerns the upper qualities. Prices of the raw material at the leading points of production are about $2 per M below those of one year ago, and possibly may not rally to any great extent at an early day, for it is notorious that Presidential election years are rather unfavorable to trade generally, although why this should be so it is sometimes difficult to divine. Possibly it serves as a pretext for the ultra-conservatives and "unbelieving Thomases" among the business fraternity to retire within their shells and thereby contribute to make business slow instead of throwing their influence in behalf of a more hopeful state of things.

The relative production of choice lumber has steadily tended to diminution. While formerly the manufacturer turned out from ten to fifteen per cent. of this quality, it cannot now be estimated at over about three per cent. To intensify the dullness in the lower grades our manufacturers are practically deprived of an Eastern demand to any extent worth speaking of for these particular grades, the consumption in that quality being largely confined to hemlock, spruce, etc., produced in New York, Pennsylvania, and, perhaps to some extent, in Maine. A method of imparting a healthier tone to the market for coarse lumber by neglecting the production has been projected, and will perhaps be followed to some extent.

The following is a statement of the population of all the important cities and villages of the pine lumber regions according to the census of 1880. The production of salt contributes its potent influence in conducing to the prosperity of the cities of the Saginaw Valley. With regard to the others, the lumber trade is the very life blood of the prosperity of all of them excepting Grand Rapids, Port Huron, and a very few others:

Alpena	6,153	Midland City	[illegible]
Au Sable	1,259	Muskegon	11,262
Bay City	20,693	Newaygo	1,097
Big Rapids	3,552	Port Huron	8,883
East Saginaw	19,016	Saginaw	10,525
Flint	8,409	Standish (vil.)	[illegible]
Grand Haven	4,862	Stanton	1,700
Grand Rapids	32,016	St. Clair	1,928
Lexington	[illegible]	St. Louis	1,875
Ludington	4,190	Tawas City	772
Manistee	6,930	West Bay City	6,397
Menominee	[illegible]		

Some of these places are growing so rapidly, and are the centers of such important interests, that the above figures do not serve to convey an adequate idea of their relative status.

The following is a statement of the aggregate production of pine lumber in this State from 1876 to 1882 inclusive:

Years.	Feet.
1876	[illegible]
1877	2,457,[illegible]
1878	[illegible]
1879	[illegible]
1880	[illegible]
1881	[illegible]
1882	[illegible]

The grand total of the product of the Northwest for 1882 is stated at 7,513,866,191 feet of lumber and 5,000,000,000 shingles.

The stocks on hand in Chicago compared with last year are as follows:

	Lumber and Timber.	Shingles.
December 1, 1882	[illegible]	[illegible]
December 1, 1881	[illegible]	[illegible]
Increase		[illegible]
Decrease	[illegible]	

It is only one or two decades since active operations were commenced toward utilizing the unparalleled stores of choice hard woods in which the State abounds, and the value of these products, unrivalled in excellence in many varieties, must continue to increase with every year. The time may not, indeed, be far distant when the hardwood product of this section will equal in yearly value the present pine lumber traffic. The oak stave trade and the business in ship timber have assumed positions of importance. The special industries which may grow up and be supplied by the hardwood forests are almost innumerable, and include all manufactures into which our native woods enter.

Forestry Bulletin No. 6, issued by the United States Census Bureau on December 1, 1881, contained this estimate of the amount of merchantable timber standing in Michigan on May 31, 1880:

Standing White Pine in Michigan in 1880.

LOCATION.	Feet, Board Measure.
On banks of streams flowing into Saginaw Bay	7,000,000,000
On banks of streams flowing into Lake Huron	6,000,000,000
On banks of streams flowing into Lake Michigan (Lower Peninsula)	14,000,000,000
In Menominee River Valley	1,800,000,000
In Schoolcraft, Chippewa, Mackinac and Delta Counties	3,400,000,000
In remainder of the Upper Peninsula	[illegible]
Total	35,000,000,000

Standing Hard Wood in Michigan in 1880.

LOCATION.	Cords.
Lower Peninsula	575,600,000
Upper Peninsula	184,500,000

SALT.

The existence of saline deposits in Michigan was known at an early day, and at one time Dr. Douglass Houghton, the eminent geologist, made extensive researches under the auspices of the State. Very little was accomplished, however, practically prior to 1859, when important investigations in East

Saginaw led at once to the development of this interest.

Of late years the Michigan product has exceeded that of any other State, and as bearing on this point the following statistics are presented:

PRINCIPAL SALT PRODUCTS OF THE CENSUS YEAR 1880.

STATES.	Value of Product.	Average Strength of Brine.	Average No. of Employes.	Capital Invested.
Michigan	$2,771,843	81½	1,268	$2,147,206
New York	1,298,742	69¼	1,016	2,366,085
West Virginia	390,365	35½	758	909,500
Ohio	386,795	36½	451	829,600
Pennsylvania	177,413	29	137	224,500
Virginia	127,878	68	98	1,000,000
California	121,360	....	684	361,030

The pre-eminence of Michigan as a salt-producing State (says the report of the Commissioner of Immigration) is due to a combination of causes. The abundance and superior strength of its brine do not alone explain it; neither does the fact that the careful inspection by State authority through a series of years, has, as a rule, kept its salt unsurpassed in chemical purity and in preserving qualities. The fortunate location of the wells upon the shores of navigable waters has given this industry the advantages of cheap transportation and easy access to markets in all the central and northwestern States. Still more important is the economy with which the salt blocks are worked. In connection with saw-mills their operation involves a large saving of expense. Power is furnished by the same engines; the evaporation of the brine is forced, during the day, by the exhausted steam from the mills, and during the night by live steam generated in the boilers by burning the refuse slabs and sawdust; and the barrels are made of staves cut from the rejected lumber and slabs. By this system a superior salt is obtained at a minimum cost of manufacture. The same advantages cannot fail to accrue to the salt trade of the State in its competition with other States hereafter.

The chief center of the salt manufacture is the Saginaw river, and the blocks on its banks produce about three-fourths of the entire yield of the State. There are salt blocks at Caseville, Port Crescent, Port Austin, New River, Port Hope, Sand Beach, and White Rock, in Huron county; at Oscoda, East Tawas, and Tawas City, in Iosco county; at St. Louis in Gratiot county; at Midland, and at Manistee. The latter is the pioneer district of the Lake Michigan shore, and was developed in 1881. Recently there have been very important developments in Marine City and arrangements are being made for manufacturing upon an extensive scale at that point.

No rock salt has been found in the State, and the brine is procured by boring deep wells and pumping. The salt is obtained by evaporation, and steam is mainly used for this work, although the solar process is employed by a few companies. All the product is carefully inspected and branded by officers appointed by the State, and the purity of the brine and the perfection of the methods of manufacture are such that the yield of 1882 did not contain two per cent of second quality salt. The bulk of the Michigan salt is shipped to Chicago, but it also finds distributing points at Milwaukee, Racine, Duluth, Detroit, Toledo, Sandusky, Cleveland, Dunkirk, Erie, St. Louis, Cincinnati, and Hannibal, Mo. Of late it has been shipped by rail as well as by water.

The chief reservoir of Michigan brine is a series of sandstones and shales, from 1,000 to 1,200 feet in thickness, called by geologists the Waverly group. It is a sea-coast rock, in which the prints of sea-weeds and the fossil remains of enormous marine growths are found, and is saturated, sponge-like, with the brine. Presumably centuries ago the waves of a pre-Adamite ocean broke upon that shore, and impregnated it with its saline riches. In his inaugural address Gov. Jerome said: "The salt producing territory of Michigan as now developed covers over 8,000 square miles; * * it is fair to presume that the supply is inexhaustible, and the increase in manufacture will continue as the demand increases with the growth of the great West."

The average depth of the Saginaw wells is about 900 feet. Productive wells elsewhere have been sunk to distances ranging from 1,000 to 2,000 feet, and they indicate other brine-carrying basins belonging to another group which will reward deeper borings. The brine is easily pumped, and the yield of the wells varies from 12 to 20 gallons per minute. A single well has yielded 25,000 barrels of salt in a manufacturing season of eight months, and the annual product of some companies has reached 120,000 barrels.

State Salt Inspection was established in 1869. The salt inspection year closes November 30. The product for the year just closed falls considerably short of that of 1882, owing to various causes, such as idle mills, late starting up, etc. The following is a comparative statement of the number of barrels inspected since the State Inspection law went into effect:

1869	561,288	1877	1,660,997
1870	621,352	1878	1,855,884
1871	728,175	1879	2,058,040
1872	724,481	1880	2,676,589
1873	823,346	1881	2,750,299
1874	1,026,979	1882	3,037,317
1875	1,081,865	1883	2,985,140
1876	1,462,729		

The average price obtained for the salt product during the past year was about eighty-two cents a barrel.

The following table will show the amount of the various grades of salt inspected in Michigan for the years named:

KIND OF SALT.	1879. Bbls.	1880. Bbls.	1881. Bbls.	1882. Bbls.
Fine	1,967,530	2,588,087	2,672,310	2,908,343
Packers	18,041	16,651	13,880	17,398
Solar	16,886	23,327	8,483	31,833
Second quality	59,087	48,532	56,621	80,782
Total	2,058,043	2,676,598	2,750,299	3,037,307

At Marine City a new well has been put down by the Marine City Stave Company. At the depth of 1633 feet, solid salt rock was found. They drilled 115 feet into the salt rock, their well then producing a good flow of brine, and stopped at this point. There have been quite recently some further important developments, and manufacturing on an extensive scale will soon be in progress.

At Manistee there are three wells completed, producing large quantities of very pure brine. And three salt blocks will be completed and ready for operation upon the opening of navigation. There are four more wells being put down, and blocks will be built the coming season. This point is destined to produce a large amount of salt in the near future.

At Cheboygan, Ludington and Jackson, test wells are being sunk with fair prospect of success.

The State is divided into seven inspection districts.

The revenues collected by the State Salt Inspector for the fiscal year ending November 30, 1882, are as follows:

RECEIPTS.

Duties on 3,037,311 barrels at 3 mills per barrel....		$9,111 93

EXPENDITURES.

Salary of State Salt Inspector	$1,500 00	
Printing and office expenses	200 00	
Salaries of Deputy Inspectors	7,330 36	
		9,030 36
Balance		$ 81 57

GYPSUM.

Immense deposits of a very superior quality of gypsum have been found at Grand Rapids and Alabaster, in Iosco county, near Lake Huron. The beds at Grand Rapids were discovered about thirty-seven years ago, at which period a mill for grinding was promptly erected, but up to 1856 the quantity of the product disposed of was not very considerable, the then means of shipment not being adapted to the carriage of freight of that description. This difficulty was in due time obviated, and the beds have proved a source of immense wealth to the locality in which they are situated. The stratum is about thirteen feet in thickness, and extends over an area of ten or twelve square miles. When taken from the mine, the product is usually piled up in large blocks and suffered to remain several months exposed to the atmosphere in order that the moisture may be in a measure evaporated. When taken to the mill, the large lumps are broken with heavy hammers and the commodity is then passed through two heavy run of stone, the first of which crushes it into small pieces and the last reduces it to powder. Some of the finer grained masses are frequently carved and polished into ornaments. The business at the beds at Alabaster is also a very prosperous one. In 1878 the Commissioner of Mineral Statistics estimated the total product of the State up to that time at 500,000 tons of land plaster and 700,000 barrels of calcined plaster. His report showed that at that date there were seven companies engaged in this business, and that the total product of the two preceding years was 95,000 tons of land plaster and 100,000 barrels of calcined plaster.

COAL.

We again quote from the report of the State Commissioner of Immigration: It is estimated by geologists that one-fifth of the lower peninsula of Michigan is underlaid by coal-bearing deposits. These "coal measures," as they are termed, are supposed to cover an area of 8,000 square miles, and their limits, as far as ascertained, would be roughly defined by a line drawn from Sebewaing, on Saginaw bay, successively through Holly, Jackson, Albion, Hastings, and Big Rapids, and thence through Osceola, Clare, and Gladwin counties to the mouth of the Rifle river in Bay county. The coal is bituminous and easily broken, possesses excellent heat-producing qualities, and burns with a bright flame leaving but a small residuum of ashes. It has not been found as yet in large quantities at any one point, and is not sufficiently exposed in the formation to make exploring easy or cheap, while it is, in its natural state too highly bituminous or not pure enough to make its use possible for smelting, blacksmithing, or the manufacture of gas. The result is that it has been mined, thus far to a limited extent only. Still, profitably workable beds of coal have been opened at Jackson and Corunna, and their yield has proved equal to any imported coal for the purposes of steam production. Bulletin 273 of the United States Census Bureau gave these statistics of coal production in Michigan: Number of mines, 6; tons mined in year ending June 1, 1880, 100,800; value of mines, $224,500; employees, 412. The total product of the State up to the close of 1881 may be estimated at over 700,000 tons.

STONE, SLATE AND EARTHS.

Michigan is rich in sandstones and limestones of commercial importance. Building stone of excellent quality has been found at many points in the State, and quarries have been opened in the counties of Calhoun, Eaton, Ingham, Ionia, Jackson, Marquette and Monroe. The Marquette brown stone is of particularly fine texture and capable of receiving a high finish; it does not suffer by comparison with any of the free stones known to American builders. Its supply is practically inexhaustible, and its quarrying is an infant industry which must inevitably develop into great importance. The grindstones of the Huron county quarries have no superior in the Northwest, and gritstones of good quality are found elsewhere in the State. The slates of the Huron Bay district in Baraga county, in the Upper Peninsula, are of excellent quality and cannot be surpassed in the American market in durability and color; these quarries can be developed to a practically unlimited extent and must certainly become the centre of a large and thriving industry. The iron district produces a quartz rock which is supplanting the foreign quartz long imported for the lining of Bessemer steel converters, and similar purposes. Clays and sands of commercial value are found everywhere in abundance. Brick and tile yards are numerous and successful potteries are in operation at different points. At Raisinville, Monroe county, is found a superior quality of glass sand, suitable for use in the manufacture of the finer grades of cylinder and plate glass. This has been shipped in large quantities to Pittsburg and Ontario, and is also used in the manufactory of window glass located at Delray, below the city of Detroit.

GOLD AND SILVER.

Gold-bearing quartz has been found near Ishpeming at what is known as the Ropes Gold Mine. Developments have been made with very encouraging results, and arrangements are being completed for the continuation of the work. Native silver has been found in small quantities in the Upper Peninsula. It was taken from time to time from the opening of the Minnesota and the Cliff, and in the stamp mills of some of the mines upon the Pewabic lode the washed mineral is looked over for this metal. Seams of rock carrying granular silver have also been found in the Iron river district of Ontonagon county and occasioned some excitement at the time of their original discovery. The systematic mining of this metal has never been attended in this State with profitable results.

GEOLOGY.

BY ALEXANDER WINCHELL, LL.D.,

PROFESSOR IN MICHIGAN UNIVERSITY, MEMBER OF THE PHILADELPHIA ACADEMY OF NATURAL SCIENCES, THE BOSTON SOCIETY OF NATURAL HISTORY, ETC., ETC. ALSO MEMBER OF THE GEOLOGICAL SOCIETY OF FRANCE; CORRESPONDING MEMBER OF THE GEOLOGICAL SOCIETIES OF LIVERPOOL, GLASGOW, DRESDEN, ETC.

A synoptical sketch of Michigan geology will naturally be embraced under three general heads: 1. STRUCTURAL GEOLOGY. 2. HISTORICAL GEOLOGY. 3. ECONOMICAL GEOLOGY.

I. STRUCTURAL GEOLOGY.

The Lower Peninsula occupies the central part of a great synclinal basin, toward which the strata dip from all directions. The basin structure is bounded on all sides by anticlinal swells and ridges. Thus, north of Lake Ontario, Georgian Bay and Lake Huron, is a portion of the great Laurentian ridge whose branches extend from this region toward the north-east and north-west. On the north-west is the elevated granitic and dioritic region stretching from Marquette south-west through northern Wisconsin. On the south-west, south and south-east is a bifurcating gentle swell of the outcropping Devonian and Silurian strata, which stretches southward to Cincinnati and central Kentucky.

The limits of this great geological basin exceed, somewhat, the bounds of the Lower Peninsula, as the centripetal dip can be traced, on the east, as far as London, Ont.; on the west, to Madison, Wis.; on the north-west, to the vicinity of Marquette, and on the north, to the Sault Ste. Marie. Within these limits, the outcropping edges of strata older and older in the series, are passed over in traveling from the centre of the Peninsula outward. The whole series of strata may be likened to a nest of wooden dishes. The great hydrographic features of the region present a striking conformity to the trends of these outcropping strata, as will readily be seen by comparing the longitudinal axes of Lakes Erie, Huron and Michigan, as of Georgian, Little Traverse and Green Bays, with the strikes of the neighboring formations, as delineated on the Geological Map.

The Upper Peninsula is divided by the Marquette-Wisconsin anticlinal into two geological areas. The eastern, as just stated, belongs to the great Michigan basin, while the western belongs to what may be styled the Lacustrine Basin, since Lake Superior covers a large part of its surface. The southern rim of the latter is seen uplifted along Keweenaw Pt., and the south shore of the Lake, while, from this rim, the strata dip north-westerly under the Lake, re-appearing in Ile Royale, and, to a limited extent, along the north shore of the Lake. Between the Michigan and Lacustrine basins the metalliferous Marquette-Wisconsin axis interposes a separating belt of about 50 miles.

We here present, in tabular form, a list of the geological formations of the State.

TABLE OF FORMATIONS.

EOZOIC GREAT SYSTEM.			
I. LAURENTIAN SYSTEM.			
II. HURONIAN SYSTEM.			
PALÆOZOIC GREAT SYSTEM, 2040 ft.			
III. SILURIAN SYSTEM,	920 ft.		
Lake Superior Sandstone,		800 ft.	
Calciferous Sandrock,		100	
Trenton Group,		60	
Cincinnati Group,		60	
Niagara Group,		250	
Niagara Limestone,			218
Clinton Sub-group,			32
Salina Group,		50	
Lower Helderberg Group,		100	
IV. DEVONIAN SYSTEM,	1040 ft.		
Corniferous Group,		130	
Little Traverse Group,		200	
Huron Group,		720	

Black Shale,			20
Portage Sub-Group,			500
Chemung Sub-Group,			200
V. CARBONIFEROUS SYSTEM,	720 ft.		
Marshall Group,		190	
Michigan Salt Group,		185	
Carboniferous Limestone,		70	
Coal-bearing Group,		305	
Parma Conglomerate,			100
Coal Measures,			125
Woodville Sandstone,			80
CÆNOZOIC GREAT SYSTEM.			
VI. QUATERNARY SYSTEM.			
Boulder Deposits,			
Modified Drift,			
Lacustrine Clays,			
Bogs, Marls, Dunes, Soils, etc.			

I. The LAURENTIAN SYSTEM.—This System embraces the oldest known stratified deposits. It therefore underlies all the other strata, and its outcropping border constitutes the barrier which limits the great geological basins. Only a small portion of the Laurentian falls within the State of Michigan, and its geographical limits have not been completely determined. It rises in four distinct bosses within the bounds of the Upper Peninsula, three of which lie between the meridians of Keweenaw Bay and Marquette, while the fourth lies south of Ontonagon, on the State boundary, and stretches far into Wisconsin. This System is composed largely of granitic, syenitic and gneissoid rocks. The latter, in Michigan, are known to embrace gneiss, hornblendic and syenitic gneiss, and micaceous and hornblendic schists. Granite proper rarely occurs; syenite is common. It is probable that some of the deposits of white crystalline marble north-west of Menominee will be found to belong to this System.

II. The HURONIAN SYSTEM.—This System comprises the mass of imperfectly stratified rocks with which the great deposits of iron ore, in Michigan, are associated. The area occupied by them stretches in a widening belt from Marquette south and south-westward into Wisconsin,—the Laurentian bosses protruding through the belt. Lithologically, the rocks consist chiefly of diorites, quartzites, chloritic and talcose schists, marbles and iron ores. The results of the most recent studies in these rocks have not as yet been published; but Major T. B. Brooks, under the direction of the State Survey of 1869, '70, determined the usual order of superposition of the rocks, in the Marquette iron region, to be as follows: 1. Laurentian rocks; 2. Quartzite; 3. Talcose schist; 4. Diorite; 5. Ferruginous Quartzite; 6. Diorite; 7. Ferruginous Quartzite; 8. Diorite; 9. Ferruginous Quartzite; 10. Diorite; 11. Ferruginous Quartzite; 12. Hæmatitic and magnetic ores; 13. Quartzites. The quartzites are whitish or rusty, and vitreous. The diorites are composed of feldspar and hornblende—the feldspar being generally albite, but sometimes orthoclase or oligoclase. These minerals vary greatly in degree of coarseness, but the rock is generally distinctly granular. The talcose schist ranges from an almost pure talc rock to chloritic, argillaceous, and sometimes, micaceous, talcite. The ferruginous quartzites are, in other words, silicious or lean hæmatites, which have been many times mistaken for productive deposits, and so reported, to the great disappointment of investors. The productive iron ores are chiefly hæmatite, undergoing alteration, in contact with water, to red chalk and limonite ("soft hæmatite"), though magnetite occurs abundantly. The mode of occurrence of these ores is not in eruptive outbursts (as formerly supposed), but in vast lenticular masses crowded into the stratification of the schists. Their origin is yet a matter of discussion, but they seem to be masses segregated from the contiguous rocks by some geologic action—perhaps through heat. One of these masses, consequently, is not inexhaustible. Indeed, several of them have already been worked out.

The Laurentian and Huronian Systems are, in this State, wholly destitute of organic remains, as far as known. For this reason, they were styled, collectively, "Azoic" by Foster and Whitney. It is yet uncertain whether the supposed animal structures found in rocks of Laurentian age in Canada and Massachusetts, are truly of organic origin.

III. The SILURIAN SYSTEM.—1. *Lake Superior Sandstone.*—This is the whitish, reddish, mottled or drab sandstone—sometimes shaly—occurring along the south shore of Lake Superior, from the St. Mary's river to Superior City, and beyond. There has been much discussion in reference to its geological age. The prevailing opinion, at present, makes that portion of it east of Keweenaw Point the equivalent of the Calciferous and Chazy formations of New York. The portion west of the Point is thought by some to be of the same age, while others regard it as the equivalent of the sandstones in Wisconsin and Minnesota, which are generally ranged in the horizon of the Potsdam of New York. As the uplift of Keweenaw Point has tilted the sandstones on the west, while those on the east have retained their horizontality, there is reason for supposing that the eastern strata are of more recent origin. It may nevertheless be true that the sandstones on both sides of the Point are of the same age, though those on the eastern side were not permanently tilted by the convulsion which upheaved the others. As we find apparently superincumbent strata which answer to the Calciferous, we shall continue to parallelize the Lake Superior Sandstone, presumptively, with the Potsdam.

The geographical extent and surface features of this formation are set forth in the article on Topography. In its geological structure, it consists, as first pointed out by Dr. Houghton, of an upper division composed chiefly of gray sandrock, and a lower division composed of thinner beds of reddish sandrock. These two divisions are further subdivided, as follows:

(f) Sandstone, light colored, thick bedded, rather incoherent, with bands of conglomerate, one of which caps the mass,	20 to 45 ft.
(e) Sandstone, whitish, friable, thin-bedded, with shaly seams,	75 to 100 ft.
(d) Sandstone, white, friable, massive,	50 ft.
(c) Sandstone, laminated, micaceous, banded with white and red layers, alternating with red arenaceous shales,	35 ft.
(b) Sandstone, uniformly red, somewhat argillaceous, thick-bedded,	12 ft.
(a) Sandstone, red or speckled, thick-bedded, hard and coarse-grained,	20 ft.

In the Ontonagon district, the upper division of the sandrock seems to be wanting, and its character is generally laminated or shaly, sometimes becoming decidedly argillaceous.

Keweenaw Point is a ridge of more recent origin than the Huron mountains and the associated upheavals. It consists of an immense dyke or wall of volcanic rock, constituting the axis of the Point, against which rest, on the westerly side, alternating strata of sandstone, conglomerate and bedded dolerite, aggregating many thousand feet in thickness. These features, due to igneous action, continue westward to the Porcupine mountains. Ile Royale marks the site of another igneous outburst, which has also brought into view, along the south-easterly side of the island, a reddish sandstone undoubtedly the equivalent of that upon the southern shore.

No animal remains have been discovered in the Lake Superior Sandstone; but the writer has described some forms of fucoids found near the Montreal river and in the Porcupine mountains, under the names of *Palæophycus arthrophycus* and *Palæophycus informis*.

2. The *Calciferous and Chazy Formation.*—This formation enters the Upper Peninsula at the Grand Rapids of the Menominee river, and, trending nearly north in a broad belt, as far as township 45, bends eastward to follow the strike of the Lake Superior Sandstone, and crosses the St. Mary's river at Sugar island. Its contact with the underlying sandstone is seen near Munising Furnace, on Sailor Encampment island and elsewhere; and the limestones of the following group are seen in contact with it at the rapids of the Menominee, on the Escanaba river, on Sailor Encampment island, and at other localities.

The formation is a more or less calcareous, often coarse-grained, sandstone, with alternations of dolomitic limestone, recalling the prevailing character of the Calciferous formation west of the Mississippi river. The following is a section on the Menominee river.

(f) Limestone, fine, crystalline, evenly and thinly bedded, with argillaceous partings,	4 ft.
(e) Limestone, nodular, concretionary,	3 ft.
(d) Dolomitic limestone, compact, arenaceous,	2 ft.
(c) Limestone, finely argillo-arenaceous, red-banded or variegated with red blotches, in thin and even-bedded layers,	3 ft.
(b) Limestone, hard, dolomitic, with oölitic belts,	4 ft.
(a) Sandstone, white, coarse, with seams of arenaceous shales,	5 ft.

The formation is almost destitute of fossils.

3. The *Trenton Group.*—These rocks are predominantly calcareous. They form an outcropping belt, about four miles wide, across St. Joseph and Great Sailor Encampment islands, stretching thence westerly in a gradually widening band which bends around to the south-west, lying with its southern border on the west shore of Little Bay de Noquet and Green Bay, and continuing thence across Wisconsin into northern Illinois.

The limestones of this Group form the Little and part of the Grand Rapids, in the Menominee river, and the so-called falls of the Escanaba and other affluents of Little Bay de Noquet, from the west.

The following section from the Escanaba river will serve as a representation of the stratigraphical constitution of the western portion of the Group:

(g) Limestone, impure and dolomitic, in beds 4 to 10 inches thick,	8 ft.
(f) Limestone, thin-bedded, nodular, with irregular seams of argillaceous and cherty matter,	12 ft.
(e) Shales, alternating with arenaceous limestones, highly fossiliferous,	30 ft.
(d) Limestone, light, sub-crystalline, underlaid by dark-blue, crystalline limestone,	7 ft.
(c) Limestone, thin-bedded, uneven, nodular, with silicious veins and concretions,	15 ft.
(b) Dolomitic limestone, thick-bedded and crystalline,	8 ft.
(a) Limestone, greenish-ashen, with concretions,	6 ft.

In the region of the eastern outcrops, we may dispose the strata of the Group into three divisions, as follows:

III. Limestone, light, brittle, breaking with conchoidal fracture, weathering into uneven, wedge-shaped slabs. Highly fossiliferous.
II. Limestone, dark, thin-bedded, nodular, with shaly intercalations. Highly fossiliferous.
I. Arenocalcareous shales, dusky green or bluish. Abounding in fossils.

Besides the main outcropping belt, an isolated area of horizontally stratified Trenton limestones, 75 feet thick, covering about four square miles, is found about 14 miles northwest of the head of L'Anse Bay. Sulphur island, also, four miles north of Drummond's island, seems to be an uplifted dome of Huronian quartzite, flanked by steeply inclined strata of silico-argillaceous limestone belonging to this group.

4. The *Cincinnati Group* (Formerly "Hudson River Group.")—The outcropping belt of these prevalently argillaceous limestones is nearly concentric with the preceding formations, but lies nearer the centre of the geological basin. The strata are well seen on the north side of Drummond's island, in a belt about four miles wide, which extends with equal width across St. Joseph island, and intercepts the southern extremity of Sailor Encampment island. On the northwest, the Group occupies the space between Great and Little Bays de Noquet, forming cliffs 15 to 30 feet high along the shore of the latter. Excavated along its outcropping border to form the basin of Green Bay, it reappears at the southern extremity, and continues in the direction of Winnebago and Horicon lakes in Wisconsin. Dipping from the regions exterior to the Lower Peninsula of Michigan concentrically toward the centre of the Peninsula, the formation underlies the whole of it, making its appearance, on the south, in southern Ohio, and thence to Cincinnati and central Kentucky.

The following section of strata belonging to this Group, is furnished on the east side of Little Bay de Noquet, SE ¼ Sec. 26 T 39 N 22 W:

(f) Limestone, massive, argillaceous, bluish or ashen, and highly fossiliferous,	20 ft.
(e) Blue indurated shale,	2½ ft.
(d) Limestone, very argillaceous and fossiliferous, with irregular patches of shale intermixed,	2½ ft.
(c) Blue shale, greenish on fresh exposures,	54 ft.
(b) *Limestone*, very argillaceous, bluish and fossiliferous,	11 ft.
(a) Blue shale, greenish on fresh exposures,	64 ft.

The fine exposure upon the north shore of Drummond's island presents strata of a similar character, and abounding in beautiful fossil corals.

5. The *Niagara Group.*—This eminently calcareous group of strata forms a belt arching around the northern borders of lakes Michigan and Huron. Constituting the principal mass of Drummond's island, it trends westward, underlying the region west of the southern half of St. Mary's river, and dipping beneath the water of the lakes, where it remains visible, sometimes, to the depth of thirty or forty feet. It is deeply and irregularly eroded along the lake shores, presenting innumerable passes through a labyrinth of small rocky islands. Continuing westward, it underlies the peninsula between Lake Michigan and Big Bay de Noquet, and forming the islands south of Pt. Detour, reappears in the Wisconsin peninsula east of Green Bay, and follows the coast of Lake Michigan thence to Chicago. Along the shore of Big Bay de Noquet, it rises in picturesque cliffs to the height of 100 and 175 feet.

Eastward from Drummond's island, the solid masses of this group constitute the Little and Great Manitoulin islands, and reappear at Cape Hurd, to form the peninsula between Lake Huron and Georgian Bay. Thence it strikes south-east to the Niagara river, which gives its name to the group.

In Michigan, the group divides itself into two divisions, consisting of the Niagara limestone above, and the Clinton limestone below. In New York, further divisions are noted. The Niagara limestone, as a whole, may be described as a gray, crystalline, rather fine-grained, compact, moderately fossiliferous, dolomitic mass, attaining a maximum measured thickness (on Green Bay, Wisconsin) of 217 ft. 10 in. A portion of the mass is generally very thick-bedded, more coarsely crystalline, vesicular, and abounding in *Pentamerus oblongus*, whence it was styled by Dr. Houghton the "Pentamerus limestone." These beds seem generally to occupy a middle position, but observations in the vicinity of Bay de Noquet tend to indicate that the Pentamerus beds are not always in the same horizon. The Clinton limestone is more homogeneous, aluminous and fine-grained, and contains a paucity of fossils.

This group is finely exhibited on the eastern portion of Drummond's island, where the following section of limestones was carefully measured by the writer:

(p) Hard, crystalline, light gray, weathering rough, abounding in *Pentamerus* and corals, constituting the highest ledge,	6.00 ft.
(o) Very thin layers, much broken,	8.00
(n) Rough, crystalline, geodiferous, abounding in *Pentamerus* and corals,	23.93
(m) Concealed slope, which, allowing for dip, makes,	18.87
(l) Gray, crystalline, hard, highly calcareous, burned for lime. Forms upper ledge south of the quarry,	7.00
(k) Areno-calcareous, weathering harsh, abounding in fossils. Uppermost rock seen in the quarry,	5.00
(j) Argillo-calcareous below, resembling (h); areno-calcareous above, resembling (k); weathers unequally; some *Cystiphyllum* at top,	2.75
(i) Dark, coarsely crystalline, exceedingly tough,	.25
(h) White layer, very fine-grained, weathering white, cherty-mottled in the lower part,	3.50
(g) Areno-calcareous with some cherty mottlings; the lower half very hard, the upper, softer and striped with brown,	4.25
(f) Arenaceous, with hard, interlaminated layers; becomes vesicular,	2.00
(e) Dark gray, very hard, with small geodes. Beautifully ripple-marked at top,	2.00
(d) Arenaceous, thinly laminated, dark colored; traces of fucoids or branching corals on the upper surface. Coated with lamellar crystal cavities,	1.35
(c) Brown limestone, exceedingly tough,	.75
(b) Dark, areno-calcareous, with alumina disseminated and in wavy streaks,	1.75
(a) Argillo-calcareous, ashen colored, very fine-grained, thick-bedded—a single stratum being 4½ feet. Contains *Cytherina*, sp. *Avicula* and *Murchisonia*,	6.00
Distance to the water surface,	1.50
Total Elevation,	98.30 ft.

North of this locality, lower strata are seen which, added to the above, give us a thickness here of 75 feet for the Niagara limestones, and 32 feet for the Clinton.

On the opposite side of the State, in the vicinity of the Jackson Iron Furnace, on Big Bay de Noquet, the following detail of limestones appears:

(j) Thin-bedded and argillaceous,	8 ft.
(i) Talus, sloping back 20 rods,	20
(h) Coarse, vesicular, massive, fossiliferous,	14
(g) Very hard, sub-crystalline, fine-grained, compact, flint-like, argillaceous, unfossiliferous, weathering buffish,	8 ft. 2 in.
(f) Rough, massive, vesicular, fossiliferous,	5 ft. 10 in.
(e) Fine-grained, crystalline, very compact and hard,	2 ft.
(d) Rather thin-bedded, banded with argillaceous matter, fine-grained, unfossiliferous,	1 ft. 8 in.
(c) Hard and sub-crystalline, with conchoidal fracture, unfossiliferous,	11 ft.
(b) Rough, vesicular, coarse, weathering into irregular flags or chips, fossiliferous,	5 ft.
(a) Fine, hard, sub-crystalline, in beds of 11 to 14 inches, resembling (c),	7 ft. 8 in.
Total thickness of exposure,	83 ft. 4 in.

The total thickness of the Clinton strata in this part of the State is 38 ft. 10 in., with a persistent, mixed conglomeritic bed of 8 to 12 inches or more, separating them from the Niagara.

The Niagara limestones pass southward beneath the Lower Peninsula, but do not reach the surface within the southern limits of the State, though they have been penetrated in Artesian borings at London in Monroe County.

6. The *Salina Group.* (Formerly "Onondaga Salt Group.")—This is a thin series of argillaceous magnesian limestones and marls, embracing beds and masses of gypsum, and, in some regions, strata of rock salt. It is the lowest stratified rock in the Lower Peninsula. In the Upper Peninsula, its belt of outcrop stretches across the point of land north of the Straits of Mackinac, from Little Point au Chene to near the mouth of Carp river, and following the vicinity of the shore, from that Point to West Moran Bay. The formation, with the characteristic gypsum, is seen, beneath the water-surface, at the Little St. Martin island, and at Goose island near Mackinac. Dipping beneath the Southern Peninsula, it re-appears in Monroe county, where it has been exposed in some of the

MAP
MICHIGAN
PALÆOZOIC
SUPERIOR
MICHIGAN
CANADA

deepest quarries. Near Sandusky, Ohio, it affords valuable deposits of gypsum. The formation has also been reached in numerous Artesian borings, as at Mt. Clemens, Caseville and Alpena. At the two latter places, a thick bed of rock-salt was penetrated, which is undoubtedly the equivalent of the bed worked at Goderich, on the opposite side of Lake Huron. The total thickness of the formation is not accurately established, but probably, aside from the salt-bed, it does not exceed 50 or 60 feet. The stratification, by combining observations at remote outcrops, may be set down as follows:

III. Calcareous clay, seen at Bois Blanc.
II. Fine ash-colored limestone, with acicular crystals, as at Ida, Otter Creek and Plum Creek quarries, Monroe County, and at Mackinac, Round and Bois Blanc islands.
I. Variegated gypseous marls, with imbedded masses of gypsum, as at Little Point au Chêne and the St. Martin islands.

7. The *Lower Helderberg Group*.—This group of argillaceous and magnesian limestones was not known to the public to exist within the State until announced by the writer in 1870. They form some of the lower portions of Mackinac island and the contiguous shores, and, passing under the Peninsula, outcrop along the western end of Lake Erie, and constitute a large part of some of the islands in that region of the lake. At their northern outcrop, they consist of a series of chocolate-colored, magnesian limestones, more or less argillaceous, occurring in regular layers 4 to 8 inches in thickness, and passing upward by irregular gradations into the brecciated mass of the next group, showing a thickness of perhaps 50 feet. At the southern outcrops, the strata are evenly bedded, rather dark-ashen in color, argillaceous, and lined, sometimes, with darker argillaceous seams. They are often exposed in the quarries of the eastern part of Monroe county, and may be stated to attain the thickness of about 60 feet. They seem to correspond to the Waterlime group of the New York series. The fossils seen in Michigan are *Leperditia alta* and *Spirifer modesta*. *Eurypterus remipes* is also found on Put-in Bay and other contiguous islands of Lake Erie.

III. The DEVONIAN SYSTEM. 8. The *Corniferous Group*.—This comprises the conspicuous and durable limestone which forms the mass of Mackinac, Round and Bois Blanc islands, and the elevated promontories of that vicinity on both sides of the Straits. It underlies a large part of Emmet and Presqu' Ile counties, and forms the Fox and Beaver islands of Lake Michigan. On the south, it underlies a large part of Monroe county, and stretches southward into Ohio and Indiana. It is the prominent limestone seen at Columbus and Sandusky, Ohio; at Monroe and London, Michigan; and at London and Woodstock, Ontario. This and the Niagara are the great limestone masses which enter into the relief of the physiognomy of the northern states, from New York to the Mississippi river, and furnish sites for the most valuable limestone quarries. The formation everywhere abounds in fossils, and furnishes us, in the form of fish-remains, the relics of the oldest vertebrates which inhabited our planet. Within the limits of Michigan, it is everywhere divisible into two well marked divisions: a lower, brecciated mass, about 150 feet thick, and an upper, somewhat evenly stratified mass, about 100 feet thick. At Mackinac and vicinity the stratification may be generalized, as follows:

IV. Limestone, more or less oölitic, regularly bedded,	25 ft.
III. Limestone, unevenly and thinly bedded, with silicious veins, and cherty nodules,	75 ft.
II. Brecciated limestone, the individual fragments being angular, various in composition, and sometimes little displaced from original juxtaposition, all re-cemented by an indurated calcareous mud,	150 ft.
I. Conglomeritic bed, consisting of a mass of cherty and agatoid pebbles. This occupies the place of the "Oriskany Sandstone" of New York, though not yet identified with it.	3 ft.

In the southern part of the State, the brecciated division presents conspicuous and remarkable features along the shore of Lake Erie, in the vicinity of Pt. aux Peaux and Stony Pt., where it abounds, also, in the mineral strontianite. A generalized section of the group in this part of the State is here presented:

IV. Brown bituminous limestone, seen in most of the quarries of Monroe county; also in Presqu' Ile and Emmet counties,	75 ft.
III. Arenaceous limestone, sometimes resolving itself into beds of friable sandstone and incoherent sand. Monroe county, also Crawford's quarry.	4 ft.
II. Oölitic limestone, as in Bedford and Raisinville, Monroe county.	25 ft.
I. Brecciated limestone, sometimes concretionary,	50 ft.

The Corniferous limestone, as its name implies, abounds everywhere in masses of hornstone. These however, do not occur in all parts of the formation. The very general presence of bituminous matter imparts a prevailing dark color to the rock. This is also frequently seen disposed in very thin partings between the strata. Petroleum often saturates the formation, and, in many places, imparts its characteristic odor. In some localities, it may be seen to ooze from the crevices and float upon the surface of water. Naturally, these manifestations have led to an unlimited amount of confident, but ignorant and wasteful well-boring. In consequence of the more or less shattered condition of the whole formation, streams of water have coursed through it, and worn out extensive subterranean passages and caverns. In these, considerable creeks sometimes wholly disappear; while they serve also, as means of communication between Lake Erie and some of the inland lakes.

9. The *Little Traverse Group*.—This is composed chiefly of the "Hamilton Group" proper, of the New York geologists; but, as the lower limits of the Hamilton have not yet been clearly fixed upon in this State, we apply the above term to a series of limestones outcropping in the vicinity of Little Traverse and Thunder Bays, and constituting physically a single mass. They have been made the subject of considerable study. In 1860 we made an official survey of the Little Traverse strata; in 1866, a special survey and report; and in 1869 the ground was again officially examined. As the result of all our studies, we submit the following generalized arrangement:

IV. Chert Beds.
III. Buff, vesicular magnesian limestone, overlaid by characteristic crinoidal beds.
II. Bituminous shales and limestone, composed of
(b) Acervularia Beds above and
(a) Bryozoa Beds below.
I. Pale-buff, massive limestone, comprising
(b) Cœnostroma Beds above, and
(a) Fish Beds below.

The total thickness was set down provisionally at 141 feet, which is probably too low.

This grouping will apparently hold good over extensive regions. The Cœnostroma and Acervularia Beds are extremely conspicuous on the opposite side of the State, while the Acervularia Beds outcrop at Iowa City, and the Bryozoa Beds at New Buffalo, Iowa. The following is a section of the Cœnostroma Beds near the head of the Bay.

(d) Dolomitic limestone, pale-buff, very massive, breaking into regular blocks, somewhat arenaceous,	12 ft.
(c) Dolomitic limestone, similar to above, vesicular, brecciated in places, having a rude concretionary structure,	20 ft.
(b) Limestone, thin-bedded below, thicker above, broken, with a 10 inch band of dark bituminous mud at top, and thinner ones below,	10 ft.
(a) Talus, or sloping beach of fragments,	4 ft.

Section of Bryozoa Beds (SE ¼ Sec 1 T 34 N 6 W)

(e) Limestone, argillaceous, sub-crystalline, the thinner layers shaly, terminated by a few inches of black shale,	14 ft.
(d) Limestone, very dark chocolate-colored, argillaceous, compact, much broken,	3 ft.
(c) Limestone, very dark, bituminous, in beds from 6 inches to one foot thick, shaly or subcrystalline,	12 ft.
(b) Limestone, dark brown, argillaceous, unevenbedded, breaking with a ragged uneven fracture,	5 ft.
(a) Limestone, dark, compact, argillo-calcareous, breaking with smooth, conchoidal fracture, much shattered,	1 ft.

Section of Acervularia Beds (SW ¼ Sec 2 T 34 N 6 W)

(d) Shale, bluish, argillaceous, imperfectly seen at top of bank,	2 ft.
(c) Limestone, varying from dark to light gray, in beds from one to four feet thick, with a rough, somewhat granular fracture. Few fossils.	23 ft.
(b) Limestone, light or yellowish-buff, varying to dark chocolate, argillo-calcareous, breaking with smooth fracture into irregular, sharply angular fragments, rather even-bedded in layers 6 inches to 2 feet thick. In the upper part, alternating with bands of black bituminous calcareous shale and blue clay. The clay beds abounding in beautifully preserved corals.	17 ft.
(a) Limestone, grayish-brown, compact, argillaceous, uneven-bedded, with smooth conchoidal fracture, embracing in its upper part a 4 inch stratum of black, bituminous argillaceous limestone replete with characteristic fossils.	14 ft.

The strata embraced in the above section seem to be the equivalents of the eminently fossiliferous and often argillaceous beds well known at Partridge Point in Thunder Bay, at Widder and Saul's Mills, Ontario, and Eighteen-mile Creek, N. Y., and the less known localities near the head of Cheboygan lake and in Alpena county.*

The belt of strata of the group under consideration, arches across the northern portion of the Lower Peninsula, occasionally outcropping, and everywhere manifesting their proximity by characteristic fossils in the soil

* For further particulars, see "*Report on the Grand Traverse Region*," pp. 40 to 48 and 53 to 71.

(especially *Acervularia*, *Cœnostroma* and *Atrypa reticularis*) and appearing again in extensive exposures in Alpena county, especially along Thunder Bay river, and in the bluffs and islands about Thunder Bay. Without entering here into details of stratification, we may offer the following summarized statements:

The Cœnostroma Beds are extensively developed at the water-surface on Thunder Bay island and contiguous localities.

The Bryozoa Beds are seen immediately overlying, on the island, and at Nine-mile Point, and are extensively exposed along the lower valley of the Thunder Bay river.

The Acervularia Beds are seen in the cliffs along the lake shores north of the mouth of the Bay, and in the interior, in Sunken Lake and at the head of Cheboygan Lake.

The Crinoidal Beds are observed at the top of the bluff on Cheboygan Lake; and the gray, coarse, magnesian limestones are found in Sunken Lake.

The strata of this age, passing from Thunder Bay under Lake Huron, reappear in Ontario, and passing under the eastern part of Lake Erie, traverse centrally the western half of the State of New York. On Kelley's island, in Lake Erie, generally reputed to be formed of the Corniferous limestone, we find many of the fossils of this group, and it hence appears that the limits of the Hamilton and Corniferous are as obscure here as in northern Michigan.

The Little Traverse group abounds in most interesting fossil remains. Besides a large number of new species, we have signalized the occurrence of three new genera of corals occurring in the northern part of the Peninsula.

10. The *Huron Group*.—(The "Genesee Shale," the "Portage" and the "Chemung" groups of New York.) This series of preeminently argillaceous strata constituting a single mass, physically, not only in Michigan, but also in Ohio, Indiana, Kentucky and other regions, we perpetuate the general designation first employed by us in 1859. These strata underlie extensive areas in the northern and the southern portions of the Peninsula. Northward their outcropping belt strikes arcuately across the Peninsula between the regions south of Grand Traverse and Thunder Bays; while, southward, a considerable part of Allegan, Van Buren, Kalamazoo, Branch and Lenawee counties is underlaid by it. The physiognomy of these regions is generally plain without rocky outcrops.

The general features of the group may be stated as follows:

The *Black Shale*, at the bottom, attains a thickness of perhaps 20 feet. It is sometimes laminated and fissile, but frequently somewhat massive and indurated. It is a very persistent formation, known, with increasing thickness, in Ontario and all the western States east of the Mississippi river. In Michigan, we see it outcropping in Grand Traverse Bay, on Pine Lake, on Sulphur island of Thunder Bay, on the coast east of Pt. aux Barques, at several localities in Sanilac and St. Clair counties, and in Kalamazoo and Branch counties; and it is pierced in numerous Artesian borings. It is often mistaken for a coal shale, or even for coal itself; but, though it blazes in a fire, its geological position is far below any valuable coal deposits.

The *Portage Shales* come next in order above, and consist of a series of whitish and greenish, more or less calcareous shales and clays almost wholly destitute of fossils, and attaining a thickness of probably 500 feet. They outcrop at several points around the shores of Grand Traverse Bay, and again, extensively, at Port Hope and other localities on Lake Huron, southward. They are frequently encountered in river bluffs and artificial excavations in the southern part of the State. Nodules of Kidney Iron ore are everywhere characteristic of the formation, as may be seen at Coldwater and Union City. At the latter place they have been worked for iron. These nodules are found abundantly in the surface deposits of the whole southern portion of the Peninsula. At Pt. aux Barques, the shales are seen to be interstratified with thin beds of crystalline and fossiliferous limestone; and such strata are also encountered to a limited extent in the Artesian borings farther south.

The *Chemung Shales*, following next in ascending order, cannot be sharply distinguished from the preceding. They may be assigned a thickness of 200 feet. If these are more, the Portage shales are correspondingly less, since the thickness of the two has generally been found in Artesian borings, to attain about 700 feet. Toward their upper portion, they become more arenaceous, and terminate in a series of laminated, argillaceous, micaceous, friable sandstones, and pass into the lower beds of the next group.

IV. The Carboniferous System. 11. The *Marshall Group*. This arenaceous and generally ferruginous series of strata corresponds to the upper or fossiliferous portion of the "Waverly Sandstone Group" of Ohio, and is probably represented by the Catskill Group of New York, as now restricted. It answers, probably, to the upper portion of the Old Red Sandstone series of Scotland, which, with the Catskill, seems to occupy the base of the Carboniferous System. The Marshall Group was, for a long time, confounded with the Portage and Chemung, but was assigned a distinct place and designation by the writer, in 1859 and 1860. It is seen outcropping in the sandstone bluffs of Pt. aux Barques; and, trending thence southward through Huron, Sanilac, Oakland and Washtenaw counties, it forms the southeastern watershed of the Peninsula. In the southern part of Jackson and most parts of Hillsdale county, it rises in frequent outcrops, and is not unfrequently worked as a quarry stone. It is mostly a somewhat friable rock, with a reddish, buffish or olive color, though in some regions becoming gray or bluish gray. The coloring ferruginous matter is very often arranged in imperfect concentric layers, presenting, on a large scale, a rude concretionary structure. At Battle Creek, it becomes decidedly calcareous, and thence toward the northwest, this consolidating constituent causes the formation to present a marked contrast with the friable condition of the rock on the eastern side of the Peninsula.

This formation is generally rich in fossils, though they exist, chiefly, in the form of casts and impressions. Marshall, Battle Creek, Holland, Pt. aux Barques and numerous localities in Hillsdale county, are quite productive. Fish and crustacean remains are not abundant. The molluscous fauna embraces many species of *Nautilus*, *Goniatites*, *Orthoceras*, *Bellerophon*, besides *Nuculana*, *Solen*, *Cardiomorpha*, and many other genera. Brachiopoda, except *Rhynchonella*, are of infrequent occurrence.

12. The *Michigan Salt Group*.—This is eminently argillaceous, but the included stores of Gypsum and brine confer upon it a great degree of commercial importance. Stratigraphically, it consists of beds of clay and shale, with thin intercalated strata of limestone, and an apparently persistent bed of gypsum, having a thickness of ten to twenty feet. As the group embraces no porous stratum capable of serving as a reservoir of the brine, no considerable supplies of brine are obtained in the formation, but they occur in the underlying sandstones of the Marshall group.

This Group outcrops characteristically, near Grand Rapids, and, on the eastern side of the State, on the shore of Saginaw Bay, at Alabaster. At both these localities the gypsum is extensively worked. Evidences of the persistence of the gypseous deposits are known to exist many miles toward the interior. The formation becomes excessively thinned in the southern bend of its circuit.

The only fossils discovered in the Group are obtained from Alabaster. They present marked affinities with the fauna of the Carboniferous limestone; and the writer entertains little doubt that this Group is a mere local condition of the lower portion of the Carboniferous limestone. This phenomenon is understood to be reproduced in Nova Scotia. Thickness about 185 feet.

13 The *Carboniferous Limestone*.—This formation answers to some portion of the great calcareous deposits of the Mississippi Valley, which, for that reason, might be styled the Mississippi River Group. In Michigan, it outcrops quite frequently in Spring Arbor and neighboring portions of Jackson county, and very extensively at Bellevue and Grand Rapids, and, on the opposite side of the Peninsula, at Pt. au Gres, the Charity islands and Wild Fowl Bay. In the eastern outcrops, it presents a mass of calciferous sandstone at bottom, while elsewhere the formation is almost exclusively calcareous. At Grand Rapids it encloses a stratum of red ferruginous, argillaceous limestone, five feet thick, which, like some of the other argillaceous strata, possesses hydraulic properties. Total thickness does not exceed 70 feet.

The limestones are generally quite fossiliferous. *Lithostrotion Canadense* may be regarded as indicating some representation of the St. Louis member of the Mississippi Valley limestones, while *Spirifera Keokuk*, and perhaps other forms, establish the existence of the Keokuk member. It is probable that the highest member—the Chester limestone, is unrepresented, as in other northern regions, while the lowest member may yet be shown to be present in the Michigan Salt Group.

14. *The Coal-bearing Group.*—This occupies the central portion of the Peninsula, extending from Jackson on the south, to Town 20 on the north, and from Range X. west, to Range VIII. east, of the meridian. We may distinguish three members, as follows:

(a) The *Parma Conglomerate* is the well-known "Conglomerate" of the coal regions of Ohio and other western States. This is the oldest geographical designation bestowed upon the formation, and is derived from Parma, Jackson county, where it outcrops in a quarry of whitish, glistening, somewhat friable, massive sandstone, with scattered pebbles. It attains a somewhat uniform thickness of 100 feet.

(b) The *Coal Measures*, consisting essentially of a series of carbonaceous shales, sandstones, clays, and one persistent bed of bituminous coal, from three to four feet thick. To these are added local beds of black-band iron ore and considerable Kidney ore, though neither ore possesses economical importance in Michigan. The total thickness of these measures does not exceed 125 feet. The following is an average section:

V. Bituminous shales and clays, 40 ft.
IV. Black-band, passing into black limestone, 2 ft.
III. Bituminous and cannel coal, in one or more seams, with aggregate thickness of 3 to 11 feet.
II. Fire-clay and sandstone, 20 ft.
I. Shale, clay, sandstones and thin seams of coal, 50 ft.

(c) The *Woodville Sandstone*, a persistent deposit, presenting variable characters, but generally more or less friable, ferruginous and gritty. At Woodville it is buffish in color, in Shiawassee county, buffish-gray, in Ionia county, red and gray-mottled. Thickness 80 feet.

The Coal-bearing Group of strata presents no general dip. Their normal position is nearly horizontal; but local dips are of frequent occurrence. Slight geological disturbances have caused numerous anticlinal ridges on which the denudation which leveled the country has worn to a greater or less depth—sometimes leaving the Woodville sandstone at the surface, sometimes exposing the coal measures, and at other times even bringing to view the Parma Sandstone. Hence the local details of the geology within the geographical bounds of the Group, are exceedingly complex and difficult to settle.

V. The Quaternary System.—The surfaces of the Laurentian, Huronian and Palæozoic rocks above described are overlaid generally by a sheet of unconsolidated materials consisting of clay, boulders and sand, with frequent superincumbent beds of marl and peat. Along the shores of the great lakes, these are seen to consist chiefly of strictly and horizontally stratified clays, mostly of bluish and coppery colors. In the interior, we find partially and obliquely stratified, alternating beds of sands and clays, with occasional courses of boulders. In the Northern Peninsula, and, to a great extent, in the Southern, a bed of wholly unstratified clay and rounded boulders rests immediately upon the rocky surface. The superficial beds of marl and peat, with not infrequent bogs of iron and manganese, connect the history of the past with the present. The sand dunes along the lake shores are merely piles of sand blown up by the winds, as explained in the article on topography.

2. HISTORICAL GEOLOGY.

The first land within the limits of the State, was that which we have mapped as Laurentian and Huronian. No part of the existing continent is older; while nearly all other portions were still sea-bottom, except an angulated belt north of the Great Lakes and the river St. Lawrence. This original area has been subjected to a vast amount of subsequent erosion, and correspondingly diminished in its elevation and contracted in its dimensions. Its upheaval marked the close of Eozoic, and the dawn of Palæozoic, Time.

At the end of the first period of Palæozoic Time, an igneous outburst called into existence Keweenaw Point, the Porcupine Mountains, and the intervening copper ranges, together with Ile Royale and limited areas, upon the immediate shore of Lake Superior.

After this time, there were no local disturbances of special importance. The whole continental mass, east of the Rocky Mountain region was, by degrees, bodily uplifted. The Michigan region slowly emerged. The valley which was to become the basin of Lake Superior, was, at first, a bay of salt water. With the progress of continental upheaval, it became isolated from the sea, and was, for ages, a salt lake. The sea still set up the valley of the St. Lawrence to the head of the present hydrographical basin of Lake Ontario.

At the end of the Silurian Age, the whole Upper Peninsula had emerged, but the Lower Peninsula was still sea-bottom. On the west, the continent reached down to Chicago, and, on the opposite side, its shore trended southeast to London and the Niagara river. At the close of Devonian Time, the Lower Peninsula marked the position of a vast bay opening southward. It is not certain whether the anticlinals on the south of the Peninsula had an existence at this early period, or not. It is more probable that the coal-making marshes of Michigan were continuous with those of Ohio, Indiana and Illinois, but this is far from certain.

At the end of the Carboniferous Age, all Michigan was dry land. But none of the great lakes existed, except Superior. The region which is now the centre of the Lower Peninsula was probably less elevated than the regions which now lie upon the borders and in the beds of Lakes Huron and Michigan. The surface denudations going forward through Mesozoic and Cænozoic Time, isolated the coal regions of Michigan and Ohio, if they were ever connected, depressed the regions which were to become the basins of Lakes Michigan, Huron and Erie, and excavated the first Niagara gorge. The drainage of the great northern sea changed it to a lake of fresh water, in which rose the St. Lawrence, flowing into the Atlantic, and probably another great stream flowing through the hydrographical basin now occupied by Lake Michigan and the Illinois river, to the Mississippi and the Gulf of Mexico. No traces of the Flora and Fauna of Michigan, during this long period, have been preserved; but without doubt, forms of animal and vegetable life adapted to the physical situation, were abundant.

At length the region which was to become Michigan, was buried, in common with the entire northern part of the continent, beneath a burden of accumulated snow and ice. This, like modern glaciers, underwent a slow motion which imparted a grinding action to the sheet of ice, and materially modified the surface features of the underlying country. The direction of this movement, on the eastern side of the State seems to have been from the north-east; on the western side, it may have been more from the north. The erosion of the continental glacier gave origin to the boulders and finer materials which occupy the present surface, and its movement transported them southward. By such action were deepened, if not originated, the valleys of Lake Erie, Lake Huron, Saginaw Bay and Lake Michigan with its appended bays. This action, combined with the strike of the underlying strata, has determined those trends in the physiographic features of the State, which we have designated as the "Diagonal System."

In due time, a change of climate, dissolving the glacier, originated torrents of water which imparted an imperfect stratification to the superficial portion of the drift materials. There was, perhaps, a subsidence which buried the whole State again beneath the waters of the ocean. Whether this were so or not, the great valleys excavated by Mesozoic and glacier agencies, were left filled with the water which either was, originally, or in time became, fresh water. The breadth of the great lakes exceeded vastly their present dimensions. Lakes Erie, St. Clair and Huron were one. Through Saginaw Bay and the valley of the Grand River, Lake Huron connected with Lake Michigan. The latter spread over the prairie region of Illinois. By the removal of the eastern barriers, the lakes were slowly drained to their present dimensions.

The surface of the Lower Peninsula was, at first, dotted with almost numberless small lakes. Many of these, by filling with sediments, marl and peat, have become converted into marshes or even meadows and arable lands; and the remainder of them are undergoing the same process.

It is likely that in America, as in Europe, man made his appearance while the dissolution of the continental glacier was in progress. We have, at least, some evidence of his presence in Illinois, while the prairies were a lake-bottom.

3. ECONOMICAL GEOLOGY.

As the commercial statistics of Michigan are presented in a separate article, we shall content ourselves, in this connection, with little more than a catalogue of the economical products of the geology of the State.

I. METALS AND THEIR ORES. 1. IRON.—(a) *Hæmatite* and *Magnetite*, in immense lenticular masses of unsurpassed purity, in the Huronian rocks of the Upper Peninsula. The Hæmatite presents itself as granular, slaty, micaceous, specular, crystalline, and earthy. Under the action of water, it becomes soft hæmatite and red chalk, and by a chemical union with water, assumes the character of Limonite, which is also styled by the miners, soft hæmatite. It also occurs to a limited extent in crystalline forms. The magnetite is generally massive and granular, with distinct crystallizations, which are sometimes also disseminated through the contiguous chloritic schists. (b) *Limonite*, altered from the Huronian hæmatites, as an earthy ore or ochre, or, not unfrequently, re-deposited in stalactitic, mammillary, botryoidal and velvety forms of great beauty. Limonite occurs, also, in immense quantities, and widely distributed over the State, in the forms of bog ore, shot ore, yellow ochre, or even in some cases, massive rock-like beds. (c) *Kidney Ore* abounds in the Huron clays, presenting, like the bog ores, various degrees of purity, and, like them, employed to a limited extent. for iron-making. (d) *Black-band* in the Coal Measures, but not known to possess economical importance.

2. COPPER.—(a) *Native* in the "trap" of Lake Superior, in *sheets*, and *strings*, and masses; also in certain conglomerates and grits associated with the beds of trap, where it occurs in grains and in powder, like the other detrital materials. This is its condition in the famous so-called "Calumet Vein," also in parts of the Porcupine mountains. (b) *Chalcopyrite* or Copper Pyrites and other ores, in the Eozoic and other metamorphic rocks. While these ores sustain an important industry in the dominion of Canada (Bruce and Wellington mines) native copper is the chief resource in Michigan.

3. SILVER.—(a) *Native*, existing, to some extent, in most of the native copper, and not unfrequently associated with it in a state of purity. (b) Existing as a *vein ore*, in limited abundance, in the trappean rocks; and, at Silver islet (Canada) and vicinity, developing an important special industry. Also, as a sulphide in union with galena, in the dolerites of Lake Superior, but not existing to any important extent.

4. LEAD.—*Galena* in unimportant and unpromising veins in the dolerites.

5. GOLD.—*Native*, existing, to a limited extent, in the Lake Superior region.

6. MANGANESE.—(a) In connection with certain hæmatites of Lake Superior. (b) In numerous bogs in the Lower Peninsula, where it is sometimes used as a black pigment.

II. SALT.—Occurring in the form of brine which has its origin in three different formations: 1. The *Salina Group*, which underlies the Lower Peninsula, and has been pierced and found to afford brine at Port Austin, Caseville, Mt. Clemens, Jackson, Lansing, Grand Haven, Alpena and other localities. Only in the first three does the supply sustain the manufacture of salt. At Alpena and Caseville rock salt occurs as at Goderich. 2. The *Michigan Salt Group*, which supplies most of the wells along the Saginaw river and vicinity, and affords a brine of remarkable strength, but containing considerable chloride of calcium which, nevertheless, as manipulated, does not interfere seriously with the manufacture of salt. These wells average about 800 feet in depth, and pass through the whole thickness of the coal-bearing group to the Marshall sandstone, into which the brine descends and accumulates. The brine is obtained from these Artesian borings by pumping. 3. The *Coal Measures*. Some of the shallow wells in the lower portion of the Saginaw Valley are supplied from this source with weaker but purer brine than that obtained from the group below. The Parma conglomerate serves as the reservoir for this group of salt-bearing strata. It may be added that the dish-like conformation of the strata of the Lower Peninsula, preventing the passage of water from side to side, retains the soluble constituents of the rocks, and hence they are all somewhat saliferous.

III. MINERALS USED IN CERTAIN CHEMICAL MANUFACTURES.—1. The BITTERNS rejected in the salt manufacture, are now extensively employed in the production of soda. 2. IRON PYRITES occurs in the Huron Group in such abundance as to promise availability, at some future time, in the process of alum-making. 3. LIMESTONE suitable for fluxing, occurs in unlimited quantities in the Trenton and Huronian rocks of the Upper Peninsula, as also in the form of calc-spar veins in the cupriferous region. In the Lower Peninsula the limestones of the Little Traverse and Corniferous Groups are equally available.

IV. MINERALS USED IN AGRICULTURE.—1. GYPSUM in remarkable abundance, purity and beauty, in the *Michigan Salt Group*, at Grand Rapids and Alabaster. Occurs also in the *Salina Group* at Little Pt. au Chene, and may be found, perhaps, in Monroe county. 2. MARL, generally distributed, and occuring at the bottom of lakelets and marshes. 3. PEAT, as the uppermost layer on the sites of filled lakelets, and around the low borders of existing lakelets.

V. MINERALS USED AS PIGMENTS.—1. IRON and MANGANESE OCHRES, in bogs and marshes through the Lower Peninsula and the Monistique Peninsula. 2. FERRUGINOUS SHALES.

VI. COMBUSTIBLE AND CARBONACEOUS MATERIALS. 1. COAL underlying about 8000 square miles of the central portion of the Lower Peninsula. Generally bituminous and of the character of the average Illinois coals. Cannel coal exists to some extent, but has not yet been developed. The principal coal mines are at Corunna and Jackson. At Grand Ledge and other points, the facilities for mining are equally good. The undisturbed condition of the strata has left the coal deposit generally so low that drainage of the mines is impracticable except by pumps. 2. BITUMINOUS SHALE, in the Huron Group, capable of furnishing oil, gas, stearine &c. 3. PETROLEUM in the Huron Shales; but which, from the absence of anticlinal axes and overlying porous strata, has not accumulated in reservoirs. 4. PEAT, in bogs, throughout the State.

VII. REFRACTORY MATERIALS. 1. SANDSTONE. 2. FIRE-CLAY of superior quality, in the Coal Measures. 3. MOULDING SAND: (a) *White*, in the Corniferous Limestone of Monroe County; (b) *Colored*, in the drift.

VIII. MATERIALS FOR BRICKS etc. 1. CLAY, in the Huron Group (as at Coldwater) and in the lacustrine deposits and the ordinary drift, suitable for (a) *Common Bricks* and pottery, (b) *Buffish* (or "Milwaukie") *bricks*, and even *white* bricks and pottery, as at Spring Lake. 2. WHITE SAND of superior quality for glass, in Monroe county, and in the Woodville Sandstone of Jackson county.

IX. MATERIALS FOR CEMENTS AND MORTARS.—1. HYDRAULIC LIMESTONES, in the Salina and Lower Helderberg Groups of Monroe County, and probably, also, in the Hamilton of Alpena County and elsewhere; also, in the Michigan Salt Group of Grand Rapids and Alabaster. 2. STONE FOR QUICK-LIME, in great abundance. Used extensively from the Corniferous, in Monroe County, and from the Carboniferous, in Eaton and Kent counties. 3. PLASTER, in the Michigan Salt Group and the Salina Group.

X. GRINDING AND POLISHING MATERIALS.—1. GRITSTONES, of superior quality, from the Marshall Group at Pt. aux Barques, and coarser ones at Napoleon. The Huron grindstones have a national celebrity. 2. HONESTONES, in the Huronian strata near Marquette, from the silicious schists. 3. POLISHING POWDERS, in the drift in many places.

XI. BUILDING MATERIALS.—1. GRANITE, SYENITE, DIORITE, GNEISS, etc., equal to any in the world, in the Upper Peninsula. 2. ROOFING SLATES, in the vicinity of L'Anse and at other points. 3. SANDSTONES: (a) *Brown freestone*, somewhat reddish or mottled; otherwise very similar to the Portland (Ct.) brown sandstone. Occurs near Marquette, and somewhat inferior qualities at many other points in the Upper Peninsula. (b) *Reddish* and *mottled freestone*, from the Woodville formation at Ionia and vicinity. (c) *Bluish* and *gray freestone*, at Pt. aux Barques—same as Cleveland stone. (d) *Buffish freestone*, at Napoleon and Hanover, Jackson County. (e) *Whitish freestone*, in

Parma formation at Parma. 4. LIMESTONES, in the Corniferous, at London, Monroe County, and in Presqu' Ile County; also in the Hamilton in Little Traverse Bay; also in the Niagara of Drummond's island and Little Bay de Noquet—the same as at Lockport, N. Y., and Joliet, Ill. 5. SAND and GRAVEL, from the drift. 6. BOULDERS, from the drift, extensively used for foundations, and even sometimes for superstructures.

XII. MATERIALS FOR ORNAMENTAL PURPOSES.—1. MARBLES: (a) *Statuary* in the Menominee region. (b) *Mottled* and silicious in the Huronian of Marquette County. (c) *Coralline* from the Little Traverse Group of Presqu' Ile and Alpena counties. 2. ALABASTER, variously colored, from the Michigan Salt Group of Grand Rapids; also, *white* and *clouded*, from the same group at Alabaster. 3. PRECIOUS STONES. *Agates*: banded, fortification and moss agates; *jasper*, *chalcedony*, *chrysocolla*, *chlorastrolites*, *etc.*,—all in the doleritic rocks of the Upper Peninsula.

XIII. MINERAL WATERS. 1. SALINE WATERS.—(a) *Brines*, used for salt-making, as before stated. (b) *Medicinal*, of insufficient strength for salt-making, but containing carbonate and sulphate of potash, soda and iron, with sometimes traces of lithia and other ingredients, occurring in the form of springs, as at Ann Arbor, St. Joseph and other localities, or obtained by boring, as at St. Louis, Lansing, Spring Lake and many other points. 2. CARBONATED waters, with more or less of soluble salts, as at Eaton Rapids. 3. SULPHUR WATERS, issuing in springs, as occurs most copiously at Raisinville and on the shore of Lake Erie in the town of Erie, Monroe County; also at Ann Arbor and many other points. Also, issuing from Artesian borings, especially in the Corniferous limestone and the Huron Group. As before remarked, the conformation of the strata has retained all their original soluble constituents; hence, all Artesian waters in the State, save some outlying, leached-out patches of the Parma sandstone, will be found mineralized. The so-called "Magnetic" waters of the State are not themselves magnetic; but marked magnetic phenomena manifest themselves about the wells. These certainly arise, in part, through induction from the earth, without regard to the waters; but some experiments seem to indicate a power of *excitation* of magnetism possessed by the waters themselves.

XIV. MISCELLANEOUS. 1. LITHOGRAPHIC STONES, of coarse quality, in the Clinton and Salina Groups. 2. STATIONERS' SAND. Magnetic iron-sand assorted by the waves upon the lake-beaches. 3. PAVING STONES from the drift.

CLIMATE

BY ALEXANDER WINCHELL, LL.D.,

CHANCELLOR OF THE SYRACUSE UNIVERSITY, VICE-PRESIDENT OF THE AMERICAN ASSOCIATION FOR THE ADVANCEMENT OF SCIENCE; MEMBER OF THE AMERICAN PHILOSOPHICAL SOCIETY, ETC., ETC.

THE meteorology of the region of the "Great Lakes" is singularly interesting, and is, also, closely connected with the industrial resources and the civilization of that portion of our country. We have, accordingly, bestowed upon this subject, a large amount of study, some of the general results of which will be embodied in the present paper. Our investigations have extended to all the elements of climate—temperature, pressure, moisture, precipitation, cloudiness, winds and occasional phenomena; and we have compiled voluminous tables giving mean monthly results for series of years at a large number of localities, both within and without the State of Michigan. Our tables and results represent all the meteorological observations ever published from within the limits of the State, as well as many observations yet unpublished. For purposes of comparison, we have collected similar data, respecting more than fifty selected localities lying outside of the State of Michigan. The Michigan observations aggregate 284 years, and those of other localities, 493 years.

In the present paper we direct especial attention to the subject of temperature; and, instead of offering a body of statistical tables, we present the reader a series of *isothermal charts*, which, with the explanatory remarks with which we accompany them, will exhibit intelligibly to the eye, the general thermometric features of the different parts of the State. For the purpose of exhibiting a comparison between the climate of Michigan and that of the states contiguous, on the west, we have extended the territory covered by these charts, as far west as the Missouri river, and as far south as Springfield, Illinois. The sinuosities of the several lines will demonstrate, at a glance, the peculiar character of the climate of Michigan, and the fact that, both in summer and winter, it is better adapted to the interests of agriculture and horticulture, and probably, also, to the comfort and health of its citizens, than the climate of any other northwestern state.

The marked peculiarity of the climate of Michigan, in these respects, is attributable to the influence of the Great Lakes, by which the State is nearly surrounded. It has long been known that considerable bodies of water exert a local influence in modifying climate, and especially, in averting frosts; but it has never before been suspected that Lake Michigan, for instance, impresses upon the climatic character of a broad region, an influence which is truly comparable with that exerted by the great oceans. That such is the fact will become apparent when we turn our attention, for a few moments, to the charts.*

We take first into consideration the chart or set of curves for July. Each of these curves—that for 73°, for instance—passes through all the places having the same mean temperature for the month of July. The mean July temperature for several places along each curve, has been determined from good observations continued through a series of years; and the July means for the places between the principal ones, along the curve, are reasonably assumed to be the same as those of the principal places.

Turning our attention, then, to the curves, or isothermal lines for July, we are at once impressed by the magnitude of the deflections of the isothermals in passing the great lakes. These deflections are toward the south, in consequence of the cooling influence of the lakes. In the presence of that influence one must pass to a more southern latitude to find the same degree of warmth as exists in the regions removed more or less from the influence. In the lower peninsula of Michigan, the lines all form loops opening southward, showing that the mean temperature of July, in the interior, is much higher than along the lake borders. And yet, within the peninsula of Michigan, the isothermals do not attain so high a northern limit as in the continental region west of Lake Superior. The isotherm of 70°, for instance, first appears within the limits of the chart in the latitude of 48°, in the valley of the Red River of the North. Passing southeastward and eastward to the valley of the Menominee river, it comes within the influence of Lake Michigan, and bends directly southward through Green Bay and Milwaukie to latitude 42° 40', and thence trends northward to Traverse City, in latitude 44° 40'. Here it is deflected southward again, under the influence of Lake Huron, and, passing Saginaw and Sanilac, finally bends north-eastward to attain its normal position, striking Penetanguishene on Georgian Bay of Lake Huron. West of Lake Michigan, this isotherm sweeps across a latitudinal belt

* We think it will be conceded that the present writer was foremost in bringing into notice these great climatic facts. The conclusions of this paper were first foreshadowed in a *Report on the Grand Traverse Region* in 1866, and a paper read, the same year, at the Buffalo Meeting of the American Association for the Advancement of Science, entitled "*The Fruit Belt of Michigan.*" The subject was followed up in a carefully elaborated memoir on *The Isothermals of the Lake Region* read at the Troy Meeting of the Association, in 1870. This paper was appended to the writer's *Report on the Progress of the State Geological Survey*, 1870; and an abstract was published in the *Journal of the Austrian Society for Meteorology*, at Vienna, Vol. VII, p. 321, et seq.

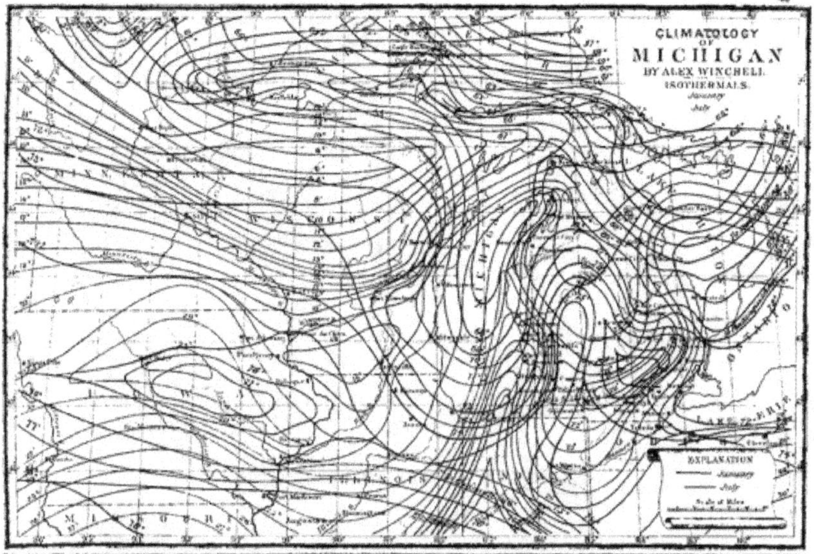

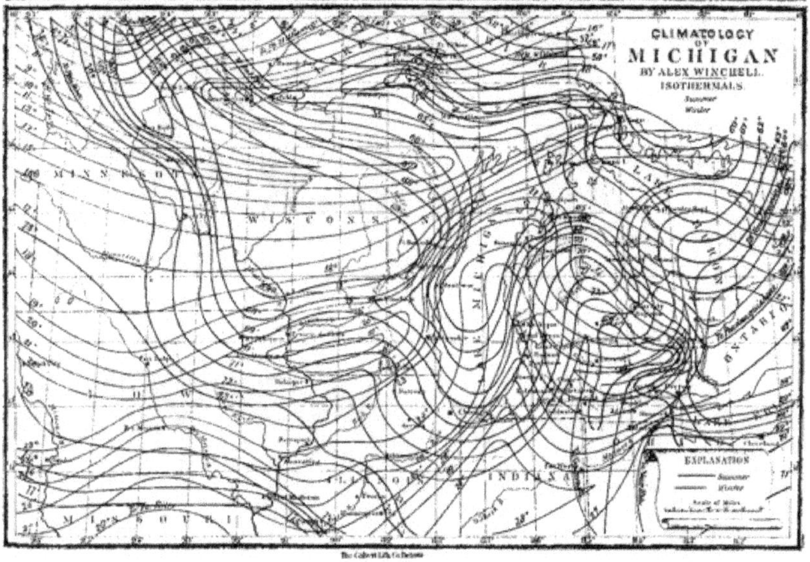

The Calvert Lith. Co. Detroit

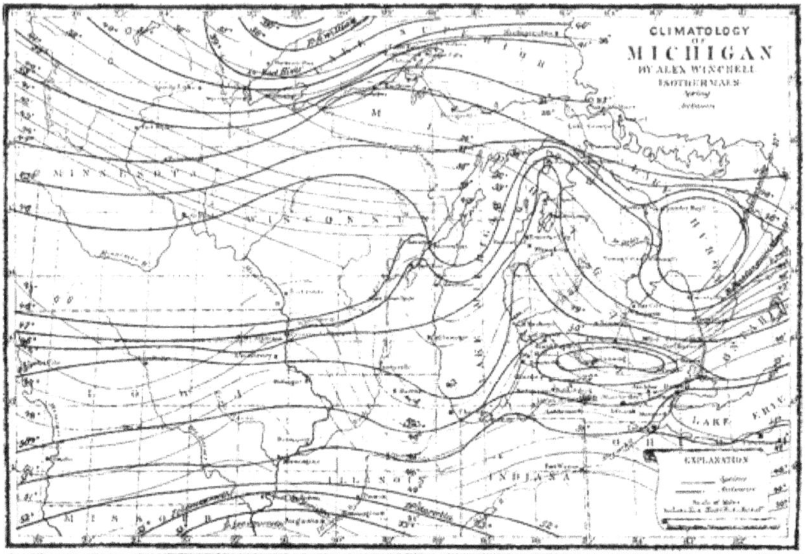
CLIMATOLOGY
OF
MICHIGAN
BY ALEX WINCHELL
ISOTHERMALS
MINNESOTA
WISCONSIN
IOWA
ILLINOIS
INDIANA
MISSOURI
LAKE ERIE
EXPLANATION

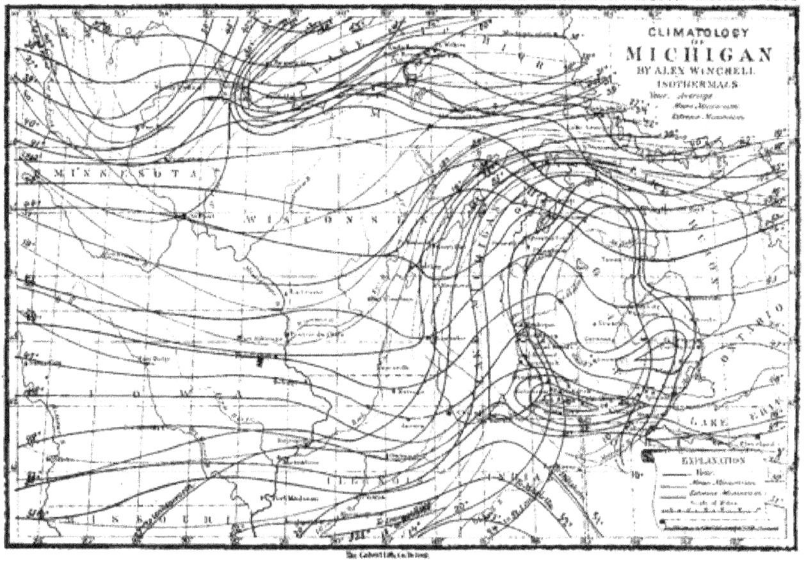
CLIMATOLOGY
OF
MICHIGAN
BY ALEX WINCHELL
ISOTHERMALS
Year. Average
MINNESOTA
WISCONSIN
IOWA
ILLINOIS
MISSOURI
ONTARIO
LAKE ERIE
EXPLANATION

of five and a half degrees. Within the peninsula of Michigan, it is deflected first northward two degrees, and then southward one and a half degrees.

Similar deflections are experienced by the isotherms between 67° and 72°. The isotherms of 73°, 74°, and 75° appear to escape much of the influence of Lake Huron. The isotherm of 74° divides in southern Michigan—one branch passing eastward through northern Ohio and the other through central Indiana and southern Ohio. The state of Ohio, consequently, constitutes an area of uniform temperature in July, which is identical with the mean temperature of central Michigan to the limit of four and a half degrees of latitude, or 300 miles, further north.

An area in the southeastern part of the peninsula of Michigan seems to be an area of cold; since the temperature is two or three degrees colder than it is on either side. There exists a region in this part of the State which is topographically elevated about 300 feet above the general level of the peninsula. It is the region of outcrop of the sandstones of the Marshall Group, but it is not entirely coincident with this area of cold. An area of warmth seems to be indicated in northern Iowa.

It will be observed that the cooling effect of Lake Michigan is somewhat greater on the west side than on the east. Not only are the isotherms deflected from a higher latitude on the west side, but they likewise attain a somewhat lower latitude. The lowest deflection of the curve of 75°, for instance, is at Ottawa, Ill., to the west of the meridian of the lake. The curves of 71° and 72° are also somewhat more southern on the west side than on the east. This circumstance is undoubtedly accounted for by the slight preponderance, during July, of winds from the east of the meridian. Thus, at Chicago, this preponderance is as 60 : 33=1.82; at Milwaukie, as 47 : 36=1.30. But at Milwaukie and further north, northerly and even northwesterly winds feel the influence of Green Bay.

Contrasting with these results those represented on the isothermal chart for January, we are at once struck with these phenomena: 1st, the great deflection of the isothermal lines; 2d, their northward deflection; and 3d, the exertion of an excessive amount of lake influence upon the east side. All this is illustrated by tracing the isotherm of 22°. Coming within the limits of the chart a few miles southwest of Omaha, it pursues an undulating course eastward to Ottawa, in Illinois, when it bends abruptly northward, passing west of Chicago, and east of Milwaukie, to Northport, at the mouth of Grand Traverse Bay, whence it bends southward to Corunna, in the middle of the lower peninsula of Michigan, and northward again to Thunder Bay Island of Lake Huron, and thence east to Penetanguishene on Georgian Bay. The isotherm of 23° reaches almost as far north; but, in crossing the peninsula of Michigan, it strikes southward into northern Indiana and Ohio, thence northward again almost to Thunder Bay Island. The sinuosities of this isotherm spread over a belt of four and one half degrees, or 300 miles in width. In other words, the influence of the lakes is such that the mean temperature of January at Northport and Thunder Bay Island is identical with that of Omaha, Peoria, Chicago and Fort Wayne. The January temperature of Mackinac and Marquette is the same as that of Green Bay and Fort Winnebago.

An island of cold is again indicated in the southeastern part of the peninsula of Michigan. In this case, its form and position correspond quite exactly with a region of elevation. The area in northern Iowa which, in July, is an island of warmth, appears to be in January, an island of cold. A similar one exists in the elevated region of southern Wisconsin, while a remarkable axis of cold stretches through northern Wisconsin and Minnesota. The axis is not entirely coincident with the crest of the ridge dividing the tributaries of Lake Superior from those of the Mississippi; since the warming influence of Lake Superior crowds it about 60 miles southward.

One of the most striking phenomena exhibited by the chart for January, is the excess of the warming influence along the eastern side of Lake Michigan. The isotherm of 23½° strikes from Chicago directly to Northport, almost at the opposite end of the lake. The contrast in January temperature between the opposite shores of the lake is, for the northern half, four degrees, and for the southern, six degrees. This circumstance is due to the fact that the prevailing winds of the region, during January, and indeed during the entire winter, come from the west and southwest, and are at the same time, the coldest winds. The precise ratios of all the winds from the east and the west of the meridian, in January, are, at Chicago, according to eleven years' observations, as 72 : 5=14.4; at Milwaukie, for thirteen years, as 60 : 18=3.33; at Manitowoc, for eleven years, as 67 : 11=6.09. These results embody all January winds, except those directly from the north or south. Thus the winds from the west of the meridian are greater in amount as well as severity. The reason why the excess of warming influence on the east side is greater toward the south than toward the north is evidently because north, and even northwest, winds coming from Green Bay, add their warming effect to that of Lake Michigan, in all the region north of Milwaukie.

The isothermal charts for the summer and winter contrast in the same way as those for July and January, though the contrast is naturally less marked. From the summer chart we perceive that the isothermal of 72° makes its advent upon the northern limit of the chart, and disappears upon its southern limit, only 12° of longitude further east. Coming from the Winnipeg country, it passes near Dubuque and Ottawa, thence into the centre of the peninsula of Michigan. Sweeping around this region, it strikes directly south to Germantown and Portsmouth in Ohio. The summer temperature of the Winnipeg region and of central Michigan, is identical with that of northern Illinois and southern Ohio. Areas of cold exist in southern Michigan and northern Minnesota; and large areas of uniform temperature in Wisconsin, Indiana and Ohio.

The excess of cooling influence upon the west side of the lake, during the entire summer, is quite noticeable. The isothermals, in approaching the Lake Superior region, make an angle of 45° with the meridian; and, under the influence of Lake Michigan, they become quite parallel with the meridian. It does not appear that, in the Lake Superior region, any excess of winds from that lake exists; but, in the vicinity of Lake Michigan, such excess is well established. At Chicago, the winds from the lake are to those from the land, during summer, as 151 : 119=1.27; at Milwaukie, the lake winds are to the land winds as 142 : 104=1.27; at Manitowoc, the lake winds are to the land winds as 153 : 123=1.24.

From the winter chart we notice that the isotherm of 24° undulates over a breadth of more than 200 miles. Other isotherms are similarly situated. The mean winter climate of Mackinac is 20°; and is identical with that of Green Bay, Fort Winnebago and Fort Dodge.

The excess of the warming influence on the east side of Lake Michigan is most apparent. The winter mean of Chicago is 24½°, while that of New Buffalo, in the same latitude, is 28°. The winter mean of Milwaukie is 22°, while that of its vis-a-vis, Grand Haven, is 26°. The winter mean of Fort Howard is 20° and of Appleton, 19°; while that of Traverse City, farther north than either, is 23½°. These contrasts illustrate again the effect of the prevalence, during the cold season, of winds from the west of the meridian.

As to the isothermals for the spring and autumn, it might be expected that they would suffer little deflection under the influence of the lakes. Comparatively speaking, this is the case; but it will be noticed, nevertheless, that a marked cooling influence is exerted in the spring; since the isotherm of 43°, for instance, is deflected southward one hundred and fifty miles. It is worthy of remark, at the same time, that the maximum deflection takes place on the west side of Lake Michigan. On the east side, the deflection of the same isotherm amounts to no more than twenty miles. In general, we find the mean spring temperature of the eastern side of Lake Michigan to be about three degrees higher than the mean spring temperature of the western side. As this excess is accumulated in April and May,—especially in May—it is at once apparent that the circumstance has a most important bearing upon the growth of spring crops on the opposite sides of the lake. The effect is such that the temperature of Grand Haven, March 15, is equal to that of Milwaukie, March 21; that of Grand Haven, April 16, is equal to that of Milwaukie, April 24; that of Grand Haven, May 15, is equal to that of

Milwaukie, May 28. These contrasts relate to *mean* temperatures. They show that vegetation on the east side secures a start of six to thirteen days. Add to this, protection from *exceptional* cold, in the form of spring frosts, and, to this, the effects of a drier and lighter soil, and we get a clear and demonstrative explanation of the difference of the agricultural and pomological products of the opposite sides of the lake.

This contrast of temperatures in spring is explained, as before, by the predominance, during the cold month of March, of winds from the west of the meridian, and, during the warmer months of April and May, of winds from the east of the meridian. Thus, at Manitowoc, in March, the winds from the west of the meridian are to those from the east, as 43 : 24=1.8; at Milwaukie, they are as 44 : 32=1.4; at Chicago, as 57 : 20=2.85. On the contrary, the preponderance of winds from the east of the meridian, during May, is, at Manitowoc, as 37 : 26=1.42; at Milwaukie, as 62 : 24=2.58; and in April, as 52 : 33=1.6. At Chicago, including north winds, which are here lake winds, the ratio of lake and land winds, in May, is as 44 : 40=1.1.

In autumn, the resultant of the lake influences on the west side is almost zero; while, on the east of Lake Michigan, a warming effect is experienced, amounting, along the southern half of the lake, to one or two degrees, and, along the northern half of the lake, to three or four degrees. This, as before, is caused by a preponderance, during each of the autumn months, of winds from the west of the meridian. This preponderance is shown, for Chicago, by the ratio of 151 : 70=2.16; for Milwaukie, by the ratio of 147 : 94=1.56, and for Manitowoc, by the ratio of 160 : 60=2.67.

The advantages thus secured to vegetation along the east side of the lake are not less in autumn than in spring. These singular facts depend upon a shifting of the prevalent winds at the end of the cold season, toward the close of March, and again at the end of the mild season near the close of November. An investigation of the monthly means on the opposite sides of the lake, during autumn, shows that the temperature attained at Milwaukie, October 15, is not reached at Grand Haven until October 20. The Milwaukie temperature of November 15 is only reached at Grand Haven, November 23. Comparing Chicago and New Buffalo, we find the Chicago temperature of September 15 is the same as the New Buffalo temperature of September 21. The October and November temperatures seem to be nearly coïncident. These comparisons show that the warm season is lengthened on the east side, about six to eight days in the autumn. This, added to the time gained in the spring, makes the growing season, on the east side of Lake Michigan, from twelve to twenty-one days longer than on the west side—to say nothing about exemption from unseasonable frosts and a much warmer constitution of the soil upon the east side.

Turning our attention, now, to the chart of isothermals for the year, we might anticipate that the warming and cooling influences of the lakes would exactly neutralize each other, so that the isothermals would experience no deflection. We find, however, that on the western side the resultant influence is slightly cooling, and on the eastern side, decidedly warming. The resultant of these two influences gives a final resultant of a warming character exerted upon the eastern side. This final resultant has a value of one-half to two degrees. In other words, Lake Michigan elevates the mean annual temperature of the contiguous region nearly two degrees above the norm. This results, of course, from the fact that the mean temperature of the lake waters is higher than that of the land. This excess must be considerably greater than the resultant warming influence upon the land. Its explanation is a curious and interesting subject of inquiry. It cannot be caused, as in the case of the Gulf Stream, by great currents moving from tropical regions. Nor can we attribute it to a large volume of river water poured into the lake from regions lying to the southward. Some more occult cause operates to raise the mean temperature of the lake above the normal temperature of the land. Some suggestions as to the nature of that cause have been offered by the writer on a former occasion, but it would be foreign to our purpose to introduce the discussion in this place.

In studying the influence of the great lakes upon the climate of the contiguous regions, we should especially note its presence under circumstances of exceptional cold or heat upon the land. For the purpose of illustrating these relations, we have constructed two isothermal charts for minimum temperatures. One of these is a chart for *mean minima*, and the other a chart for *extreme minima*. By the "mean minimum" of a locality, is meant the *average* of the yearly minima for a series of years; and by the "extreme minimum," the *lowest point* attained during that series of years. These charts present results which are truly striking. The isotherms in the vicinity of lakes Huron and Michigan, trend literally north and south. In the chart of mean minima, the isotherm of -15° strikes from Mackinac through Manitowoc, Milwaukie, and New Buffalo, to Fort Riley, in Kansas, near the parallel of 39°. Here is a deflection over nearly seven degrees of latitude, or about 480 miles in a straight line. The meaning of this is, that the most excessive cold at Mackinac, for a period of 28 years, is not, on the average greater than at Fort Riley, 480 miles further south. It is one degree less than at Chicago for a term of eleven years. By a glance at the chart of extreme minima, we perceive, that the lowest point reached at Mackinac is but two degrees lower than the extreme minimum of St. Louis. Extreme weather of Chicago is twelve degrees colder than at New Buffalo. The lowest extreme of Milwaukie is fourteen degrees below the extreme minimum of Grand Haven, while the extreme of Fort Howard is twenty degrees below that of Northport. In general, while the mean minimum along the west side of Lake Michigan is -16°; that along the east side is -6°; while the extreme minimum on the west side is -22° to -30°, that of the east side is -10° to -16°.

It is proper to direct attention to the important bearing of these additional facts upon the results of soil-cultivation. It will be remembered that it is not the severity of the winter mean, but that of the winter *extremes* which conditions the immunity of exotic plants from destructive *frost*. One killing freeze is as fatal as thirty. That one killing freeze is as likely to occur at Fort Riley, or Leavenworth, or Peoria, or even at St. Louis, as at Mackinac. The whole east shore of Lake Michigan is 15° to 20° more secure than any of the places just named. As grapes and peach trees require for their destruction, a temperature of -20°, it is apparent that peach orchards and vineyards are perfectly secure along the whole extent of the eastern shore of Lake Michigan.*

The *rationale* of these climatic effects is not difficult to discover. It lies in the comparatively low capacity of watery surfaces for absorbing and radiating heat. The mean temperature of the land, in the middle latitude of Lake Michigan, is about $44\frac{1}{2}^{\circ}$, and that of the lake, a few degrees higher. In July, the temperature of the land rises to 74° while that of the lake is not above 51° or 52°. This difference is partly due to the fact that upon the land the heat from the solar rays is accumulated near the surface, while upon the water it is disseminated through the whole mass, at least to a considerable extent, by the action of waves and currents. In January, the mean temperature of the land sinks to 19°, while that of the water does not, probably fall below 40°. The atmosphere in contact with the water must partake, to some extent, of the temperature of the water, and, when moving from the water to the land, must transfer to the land, some portion of the heat or cold proper to the lake. The effect is a tendency to equalize the land temperatures in summer and winter. This tendency is most distinctly felt in case of extreme weather. On occasion of our coldest weather, the wind blows generally from the southwest, and, passing diagonally over lake Michigan for a distance of 100 to 200 miles must necessarily experience a great degree of amelioration.

In this connection, it is worth while to point out the fact that the arcuation of the longitudinal axis of Lake Michigan is such that a southwest wind striking the Grand Traverse region, must have passed over a much greater breadth of lake-surface than the same wind, in striking the region of St. Joseph; and hence the amelioration of winter extremes must be more marked in the

* This statement refers only to exemption from winter-killing. As the northern portions of this belt enjoy a smaller aggregate of summer warmth than the southern, another climatic condition enters to determine the actual productiveness of different portions of the belt, and to affect the comparison between the whole belt and regions further south in Illinois and Missouri.

former region than in the latter. It is further obvious that in the rare case of absolute calm or a southerly wind at a time of extreme cold, no portion of the peninsula would experience the warming influence of the lake.

The foregoing generalizations from the numerical data of the science of meteorology are abundantly confirmed by the results of the attempts made during a few years past to introduce the cultivation of peaches, grapes and other fruits along the entire belt from St. Joseph to Grand Traverse Bay. These results are so much a success that it is now generally acknowledged that scarcely a superior fruit-producing region exists within the United States.

The influence of the sea in equalizing temperatures has long been understood. The immunity from unseasonable frosts secured by bodies of fresh water to localities in their immediate vicinity, has also been universally observed; but the fact that inland lakes, of the size of Lake Michigan, exert an ameliorating agency quite comparable with that of the Atlantic Ocean, is something which has only been brought to light by recent thorough discussions of a wide range of meteorological data. On general principles, it has, indeed, been asserted by Professor Henry and by Blodget, and, at an earlier period, by Humboldt, that the great lakes of North America must exert some influence in deflecting the isothermal lines; but when we come to examine any of the charts which have been published to represent existing knowledge or conceptions, we fail to detect any marked inflection of these lines in passing the region of the great lakes. In fact, the thermometric observations from the fifty-five meteorological stations in Michigan have not heretofore been employed in tracing out the remarkable tortuosities of the isothermals of the lower peninsula of Michigan. These discoveries are destined to take their place among the most interesting phenomena of climatological science.*

We do not deem it expedient to extend this paper by the introduction of barometrical and psychrometrical results; but the distribution of rain and snow is a climatic element of such paramount economical importance that we think a summarized table may be acceptable. We have, accordingly, selected from our voluminous records of results the following condensed view of the aqueous precipitation at a series of representative localities.

Precipitation of Rain and Snow.

LOCALITY.	[illegible]	[illegible]	[illegible]	[illegible]	SPRING. Mean. Inches.	SPRING. Mean. Ratio.	SPRING. Min. Inches.	SUMMER. Mean. Inches.	SUMMER. Mean. Ratio.	SUMMER. Min. Inches.	AUTUMN. Mean. Inches.	AUTUMN. Mean. Ratio.	AUTUMN. Min. Inches.	WINTER. Mean. Inches.	WINTER. Mean. Ratio.	WINTER. Min. Inches.	YEAR. Mean. Inches.	YEAR. Min. Inches.
Copper Falls	[illegible]	[illegible]	[illegible]	[illegible]	[illegible]	[illegible]	[illegible]	[illegible]	[illegible]	[illegible]	[illegible]	[illegible]	[illegible]	[illegible]	[illegible]	[illegible]	[illegible]	[illegible]
Ontonagon	[illegible]	[illegible]	[illegible]	[illegible]	[illegible]	[illegible]	[illegible]	[illegible]	[illegible]	[illegible]	[illegible]	[illegible]	[illegible]	[illegible]	[illegible]	[illegible]	[illegible]	[illegible]
Marquette	[illegible]	[illegible]	[illegible]	[illegible]	[illegible]	[illegible]	[illegible]	[illegible]	[illegible]	[illegible]	[illegible]	[illegible]	[illegible]	[illegible]	[illegible]	[illegible]	[illegible]	[illegible]
Sault Ste. Marie	[illegible]	[illegible]	[illegible]	[illegible]	[illegible]	[illegible]	[illegible]	[illegible]	[illegible]	[illegible]	[illegible]	[illegible]	[illegible]	[illegible]	[illegible]	[illegible]	[illegible]	[illegible]
Mackinac	[illegible]	[illegible]	[illegible]	[illegible]	[illegible]	[illegible]	[illegible]	[illegible]	[illegible]	[illegible]	[illegible]	[illegible]	[illegible]	[illegible]	[illegible]	[illegible]	[illegible]	[illegible]
[illegible]	[illegible]	[illegible]	[illegible]	[illegible]				[illegible]			[illegible]			[illegible]				
Thunder Bay I.	[illegible]	[illegible]	[illegible]	[illegible]	[illegible]	[illegible]	[illegible]	[illegible]	[illegible]	[illegible]	[illegible]	[illegible]	[illegible]	[illegible]	[illegible]	[illegible]	[illegible]	[illegible]
Traverse City	[illegible]	[illegible]	[illegible]	[illegible]	[illegible]	[illegible]	[illegible]	[illegible]	[illegible]	[illegible]	[illegible]	[illegible]	[illegible]	[illegible]	[illegible]	[illegible]	[illegible]	[illegible]
Grand Haven	[illegible]	[illegible]	[illegible]	[illegible]	[illegible]	[illegible]	[illegible]	[illegible]	[illegible]	[illegible]	[illegible]	[illegible]	[illegible]	[illegible]	[illegible]	[illegible]	[illegible]	[illegible]
[illegible]	[illegible]	[illegible]	[illegible]	[illegible]			[illegible]	[illegible]		[illegible]	[illegible]		[illegible]			[illegible]		[illegible]
Grand Rapids	[illegible]	[illegible]	[illegible]	[illegible]	[illegible]	[illegible]	[illegible]	[illegible]	[illegible]	[illegible]	[illegible]	[illegible]	[illegible]	[illegible]	[illegible]		[illegible]	[illegible]
Port Gratiot	[illegible]	[illegible]	[illegible]	[illegible]	[illegible]	[illegible]	[illegible]	[illegible]	[illegible]	[illegible]	[illegible]	[illegible]	[illegible]	[illegible]	[illegible]	[illegible]	[illegible]	[illegible]
Holland	[illegible]	[illegible]	[illegible]	[illegible]	[illegible]	[illegible]	[illegible]	[illegible]	[illegible]	[illegible]	[illegible]	[illegible]	[illegible]	[illegible]	[illegible]	[illegible]	[illegible]	[illegible]
Lansing	[illegible]	[illegible]	[illegible]	[illegible]	[illegible]	[illegible]	[illegible]	[illegible]	[illegible]	[illegible]	[illegible]	[illegible]	[illegible]	[illegible]	[illegible]	[illegible]	[illegible]	[illegible]
Battle Creek	[illegible]	[illegible]	[illegible]	[illegible]	[illegible]	[illegible]	[illegible]	[illegible]	[illegible]	[illegible]	[illegible]	[illegible]	[illegible]	[illegible]	[illegible]	[illegible]	[illegible]	[illegible]
Detroit	[illegible]	[illegible]	[illegible]	[illegible]	[illegible]	[illegible]	[illegible]	[illegible]	[illegible]	[illegible]	[illegible]	[illegible]	[illegible]	[illegible]	[illegible]	[illegible]	[illegible]	[illegible]
Ann Arbor	[illegible]	[illegible]	[illegible]	[illegible]	[illegible]	[illegible]	[illegible]	[illegible]	[illegible]	[illegible]	[illegible]	[illegible]	[illegible]	[illegible]	[illegible]	[illegible]	[illegible]	[illegible]
[illegible]*	[illegible]	[illegible]	[illegible]	[illegible]	[illegible]	[illegible]	[illegible]	[illegible]	[illegible]	[illegible]	[illegible]	[illegible]	[illegible]	[illegible]	[illegible]	[illegible]	[illegible]	[illegible]
Monroe	[illegible]	[illegible]	[illegible]	[illegible]	[illegible]	[illegible]	[illegible]	[illegible]	[illegible]	[illegible]	[illegible]	[illegible]	[illegible]	[illegible]	[illegible]	[illegible]	[illegible]	[illegible]

* [illegible]

This Table is based on observations extended, generally, to the year 1870, inclusive. Since the results were worked out, the volume of *Tables and Results of the Precipitation in Rain and Snow, in the United States*, compiled and discussed by Charles A. Schott of the U. S. Coast Survey, has been published by the Smithsonian Institution. Some slight discrepancies with our determinations may, undoubtedly, be attributed to the fact that Mr. Schott's data do not, generally, extend beyond 1866 or 1867. This Report, like everything which emanates from Mr. Schott's hands, is a masterly work. The country is deeply indebted to the Smithsonian Institution for meteorological data and discussions unsurpassed in volume and value by the productions of any country.

The mean annual precipitation over the whole State is 31 inches; in the Upper Peninsula, 30 inches, and in the Lower, 32 inches. This is about the average for Wisconsin, Minnesota, Iowa, Nebraska and Kansas. In the states south and east of Michigan, the annual fall of rain and snow reaches 40 to 44 inches. Further south, and along the Atlantic border, it rises still higher. The total precipitation throughout the lake-region sustains no discoverable relation to the great lakes. Aside from the varying influence of the great current of moisture from the Gulf of Mexico, the precipitation seems to vary with the topography and surface of the country. It is singular, however, that, in this State, the four localities receiving the lowest mean annual precipitation, are situated upon the lake shores. These are Tawas, Ontonagon, Mackinac, and Grand Haven. On the contrary, however, two other localities, Copper Falls and Holland, situated in close proximity to the lakes, are exceeded only by Grand Rapids.

The mode of distribution of the precipitation through the year is a question which has an important bearing on the ability of a region to sustain an agricultural industry. The Table referred to has columns headed "Ratio," in which is placed, for each season, the ratio of the precipitation for that season to the whole annual precipitation at the same place. These ratios are expressed in the form of percentages. From these percentages we have calculated the following generalized Table.

DISTRIBUTION OF PRECIPITATION THROUGH THE SEASONS.
(In percentages of Total Precipitation.)

	Spring.	Summer.	Autumn.	Winter.
Upper Peninsula,	19	27	28.8	23
Lower Peninsula,	21.8	28.7	27.3	19.1
Whole State,	25.8	28.3	27.7	20

In the State at large, we have, as appears, considerably less precipitation during winter than during any other season. The Lower Peninsula presents this deficiency to a marked extent, while, in the Upper Peninsula, the spring is the period of minimum precipitation, though Copper Falls has a marked winter excess. In the whole State, and in the Lower Peninsula, the summer season is marked by the greatest amount of rain; in the Upper Peninsula, the autumn. In the Lower Peninsula the three seasons of vegetable growth together receive nearly 82 per cent. of the whole precipitation. That is, the rain-fall, during the growing months, is as great as in other states having a total precipitation of 35 inches distributed equally through the seasons.

The liability of a region to occasional excessive droughts is not indicated by the total mean annual precipitation, nor, indeed, by the mean seasonal precipitation. An occasional prolonged and destructive period of dryness may occur without materially disturbing the annual or seasonal means. We have, accordingly, selected from the annual and seasonal means for a series of years, the ones which are lowest for each locality, and introduced them in our Table, in the columns headed "minima." From the column of minima for the year, we observe that the extreme minimum at Sault Ste. Marie is 12.11 inches, which is only 40 per cent. of the annual amount, and at Mackinac it is only 48 per cent. of the amount at that place. These numbers represent years of extreme scantiness of rain and snow. Had we the data, it would probably appear that the year 1871 was a year of remarkable dryness throughout the State. Generally, the extreme minimum of annual precipitation does not fall excessively below the normal annual mean. At Detroit, it is 60 per cent. of the annual mean; at Lansing, 81 per cent.; at Ann Arbor and Monroe, 82 per cent.; at Ontonagon, 83 per cent.; at Tawas, 84 per cent.; at Grand Haven, 87 per cent.; at Grand Rapids, 92 per cent., and at Marquette and Holland, 93 per cent., showing a remarkably uniform distribution through a series of years.

The extreme minima of the seasons exhibit a much greater departure from the normal seasonal means. For instance, in spring, the extreme minimum precipitation at Mack-

* The foregoing general results were embodied in a popular paper published (with reduced isothermal charts for July and January) in Harper's Magazine for July, 1871. This paper, with the charts, has been reproduced in *Der Michigan Wegweiser*, in Hamburg, and also in the *Zeitschrift der österreichischen Gesellschaft für Meteorologie* in Vienna, Vol. viii, p. 49, *et seq.* (February 1, 1872.) It seems a suggestive commentary on the intelligence of American state governments that, while these results, though thus meagerly set forth, possess such interest as to be published and republished at home and abroad, by newspaper and magazine managers, emigration agencies, learned societies, medical journals and horticultural associations, the public authorities of Michigan have neither instigated, aided nor endorsed their publication; but, incredible as it may seem, have actually declined, with expressions of derision, to publish them to their own citizens and the world. [See Michigan Legislative Proceedings, March and April, 1871.]

inac is only 33 per cent. of the norm; at Sault Ste. Marie, 34 per cent.; at Marquette, 43; at Ontonagon, 50; at Battle Creek and Ann Arbor, 54; at Detroit, 55; at Monroe, 56; at Grand Rapids, 60; at Thunder Bay I., 61; at Lansing, 81; at Holland, 86 per cent. Thus extreme dryness in spring is less severe in the lower peninsula than in the upper.

In summer, the extreme minimum precipitation at Mackinac is 34 per cent. of the norm; at Tawas, 38 per cent; at Sault Ste. Marie, 39; at Detroit, 41; at Marquette, 45; at Battle Creek and Ann Arbor, 52; at Lansing and Grand Rapids, 58; at Monroe, 62; at Ontonagon, Holland and Flint, 68; at Grand Haven, 90 per cent. This means that the liability to extreme dryness throughout the summer is greater at Tawas, Sault Ste. Marie, Detroit and Marquette than at the other places; and that at Grand Haven, the normal supply is never diminished more than one tenth. The trustworthiness of these generalizations, however, is only in proportion to the length of the period of observations at the several places.

In autumn, the extreme minimum of precipitation at Mackinac is only 22 per cent. of the normal precipitation for that season; at Tawas, it is 38 per cent.; at Marquette, 39; at Lansing, 40; at Detroit, 43; at Monroe, 47; at Battle Creek, 51; at Sault Ste. Marie, 52; at Grand Haven, 53; at Grand Rapids 60; at Flint, 67; at Ann Arbor, 71; at Ontonagon, 75; and at Holland, 97 per cent. of the norm.

In winter, the extreme minimum precipitation at Detroit is 31 per cent. of the normal amount; at Mackinac, it is 38 per cent.; at Sault Ste. Marie, 49; at Monroe, 56; at Ann Arbor, 60; at Battle Creek, 62; at Marquette, 64; at Ontonagon, 66; at Lansing, 69; at Tawas, 74; at Grand Haven, 76; at Holland, 90 per cent.

From the foregoing generalizations, it appears that the northern localities experience a somewhat greater liability to dryness in all the seasons. It must be borne in mind, however, that the percentages given are percentages of the seasonal means at the several localities. But this mean may be comparatively low. Thus, when we state extreme winter dryness at Ann Arbor as 60 per cent of the normal precipitation, it will be remembered that the normal precipitation, in winter, is only 15 per cent of the whole annual precipitation.

It is apparent that the seasonal minima are more excessive than the annual minima. It follows from this, that a deficiency of precipitation in one season is followed, within twelve months, by an excess in another season. This accords with popular belief.*

We append, finally, a condensed Table of the Winds of the State. The numbers in the columns denote the number of tri-daily observations, in each season and during the year, at which the wind, at the several localities, was from the directions indicated at the heads of the columns. Thus, at Ontonagon, in the spring, as the average result of three years' observations, the wind was found from the north 39 times, from the northeast, 45 times, and so on. The column headed "Ca" denotes the number of times a calm prevailed. Some observers report no calm—deciding always that there exists some determinable movement of the air, however slight. Hence the blanks in this column. Many interesting generalizations might be based upon the Table, some of which have already been presented in connection with the discussion of isothermals, but we forbear to extend this paper.

The foregoing popularized abstract of meteorological results is but a meagre exhibit of the amount of information in our possession, but the presentation is probably sufficiently full for the present purpose.

* The foregoing results are liable to be changed by further observations—the most so, at localities where the series of observations has not extended over a number of years. Of all the results, the extreme minima are most liable to undergo change. It will be noticed that the minima given are generally most extreme at those localities where the series of observations is most extended.

WINDS.

SPRING.

	N	NE	E	SE	S	SW	W	NW	Ca
Ontonagon	[illegible]	[illegible]	[illegible]	[illegible]	[illegible]	[illegible]	[illegible]	[illegible]	[illegible]
Marquette	[illegible]	[illegible]	[illegible]	[illegible]	[illegible]	[illegible]	[illegible]	[illegible]	[illegible]
Sault Ste. Marie	[illegible]	[illegible]	[illegible]	[illegible]	[illegible]	[illegible]	[illegible]	[illegible]	[illegible]
Mackinac	[illegible]	[illegible]	[illegible]	[illegible]	[illegible]	[illegible]	[illegible]	[illegible]	[illegible]
St. James	[illegible]	[illegible]	[illegible]	[illegible]	[illegible]	[illegible]	[illegible]	[illegible]	[illegible]
Thunder Bay I.	[illegible]	[illegible]	[illegible]	[illegible]	[illegible]	[illegible]	[illegible]	[illegible]	[illegible]
Tawas City	[illegible]	[illegible]	[illegible]	[illegible]	[illegible]	[illegible]	[illegible]	[illegible]	[illegible]
[illegible]	[illegible]	[illegible]	[illegible]	[illegible]	[illegible]	[illegible]	[illegible]	[illegible]	[illegible]
Grand Haven	[illegible]	[illegible]	[illegible]	[illegible]	[illegible]	[illegible]	[illegible]	[illegible]	[illegible]
Flint	[illegible]	[illegible]	[illegible]	[illegible]	[illegible]	[illegible]	[illegible]	[illegible]	[illegible]
Grand Rapids	[illegible]	[illegible]	[illegible]	[illegible]	[illegible]	[illegible]	[illegible]	[illegible]	[illegible]
Fort Gratiot	[illegible]	[illegible]	[illegible]	[illegible]	[illegible]	[illegible]	[illegible]	[illegible]	[illegible]
Port Huron	[illegible]	[illegible]	[illegible]	[illegible]	[illegible]	[illegible]	[illegible]	[illegible]	[illegible]
Lansing	[illegible]	[illegible]	[illegible]	[illegible]	[illegible]	[illegible]	[illegible]	[illegible]	[illegible]
[illegible]	[illegible]	[illegible]	[illegible]	[illegible]	[illegible]	[illegible]	[illegible]	[illegible]	[illegible]
Battle Creek	[illegible]	[illegible]	[illegible]	[illegible]	[illegible]	[illegible]	[illegible]	[illegible]	[illegible]
Detroit	[illegible]	[illegible]	[illegible]	[illegible]	[illegible]	[illegible]	[illegible]	[illegible]	[illegible]
Ann Arbor	[illegible]	[illegible]	[illegible]	[illegible]	[illegible]	[illegible]	[illegible]	[illegible]	[illegible]
Monroe	[illegible]	[illegible]	[illegible]	[illegible]	[illegible]	[illegible]	[illegible]	[illegible]	[illegible]

SUMMER.

	N	NE	E	SE	S	SW	W	NW	Ca
Ontonagon	[illegible]	[illegible]	[illegible]	[illegible]	[illegible]	[illegible]	[illegible]	[illegible]	[illegible]
Marquette	[illegible]	[illegible]	[illegible]	[illegible]	[illegible]	[illegible]	[illegible]	[illegible]	[illegible]
Sault Ste. Marie	[illegible]	[illegible]	[illegible]	[illegible]	[illegible]	[illegible]	[illegible]	[illegible]	[illegible]
Mackinac	[illegible]	[illegible]	[illegible]	[illegible]	[illegible]	[illegible]	[illegible]	[illegible]	[illegible]
St. James	[illegible]	[illegible]	[illegible]	[illegible]	[illegible]	[illegible]	[illegible]	[illegible]	[illegible]
Thunder Bay I.	[illegible]	[illegible]	[illegible]	[illegible]	[illegible]	[illegible]	[illegible]	[illegible]	[illegible]
Tawas City	[illegible]	[illegible]	[illegible]	[illegible]	[illegible]	[illegible]	[illegible]	[illegible]	[illegible]
[illegible]	[illegible]	[illegible]	[illegible]	[illegible]	[illegible]	[illegible]	[illegible]	[illegible]	[illegible]
Grand Haven	[illegible]	[illegible]	[illegible]	[illegible]	[illegible]	[illegible]	[illegible]	[illegible]	[illegible]
Flint	[illegible]	[illegible]	[illegible]	[illegible]	[illegible]	[illegible]	[illegible]	[illegible]	[illegible]
Grand Rapids	[illegible]	[illegible]	[illegible]	[illegible]	[illegible]	[illegible]	[illegible]	[illegible]	[illegible]
Fort Gratiot	[illegible]	[illegible]	[illegible]	[illegible]	[illegible]	[illegible]	[illegible]	[illegible]	[illegible]
Port Huron	[illegible]	[illegible]	[illegible]	[illegible]	[illegible]	[illegible]	[illegible]	[illegible]	[illegible]
Lansing	[illegible]	[illegible]	[illegible]	[illegible]	[illegible]	[illegible]	[illegible]	[illegible]	[illegible]
[illegible]	[illegible]	[illegible]	[illegible]	[illegible]	[illegible]	[illegible]	[illegible]	[illegible]	[illegible]
Battle Creek	[illegible]	[illegible]	[illegible]	[illegible]	[illegible]	[illegible]	[illegible]	[illegible]	[illegible]
Detroit	[illegible]	[illegible]	[illegible]	[illegible]	[illegible]	[illegible]	[illegible]	[illegible]	[illegible]
Ann Arbor	[illegible]	[illegible]	[illegible]	[illegible]	[illegible]	[illegible]	[illegible]	[illegible]	[illegible]
Monroe	[illegible]	[illegible]	[illegible]	[illegible]	[illegible]	[illegible]	[illegible]	[illegible]	[illegible]

AUTUMN.

	N	NE	E	SE	S	SW	W	NW	Ca
Ontonagon	[illegible]	[illegible]	[illegible]	[illegible]	[illegible]	[illegible]	[illegible]	[illegible]	[illegible]
Marquette	[illegible]	[illegible]	[illegible]	[illegible]	[illegible]	[illegible]	[illegible]	[illegible]	[illegible]
Sault Ste. Marie	[illegible]	[illegible]	[illegible]	[illegible]	[illegible]	[illegible]	[illegible]	[illegible]	[illegible]
Mackinac	[illegible]	[illegible]	[illegible]	[illegible]	[illegible]	[illegible]	[illegible]	[illegible]	[illegible]
St. James	[illegible]	[illegible]	[illegible]	[illegible]	[illegible]	[illegible]	[illegible]	[illegible]	[illegible]
Thunder Bay I.	[illegible]	[illegible]	[illegible]	[illegible]	[illegible]	[illegible]	[illegible]	[illegible]	[illegible]
Tawas City	[illegible]	[illegible]	[illegible]	[illegible]	[illegible]	[illegible]	[illegible]	[illegible]	[illegible]
[illegible]	[illegible]	[illegible]	[illegible]	[illegible]	[illegible]	[illegible]	[illegible]	[illegible]	[illegible]
Grand Haven	[illegible]	[illegible]	[illegible]	[illegible]	[illegible]	[illegible]	[illegible]	[illegible]	[illegible]
Flint	[illegible]	[illegible]	[illegible]	[illegible]	[illegible]	[illegible]	[illegible]	[illegible]	[illegible]
Grand Rapids	[illegible]	[illegible]	[illegible]	[illegible]	[illegible]	[illegible]	[illegible]	[illegible]	[illegible]
Fort Gratiot	[illegible]	[illegible]	[illegible]	[illegible]	[illegible]	[illegible]	[illegible]	[illegible]	[illegible]
Port Huron	[illegible]	[illegible]	[illegible]	[illegible]	[illegible]	[illegible]	[illegible]	[illegible]	[illegible]
Lansing	[illegible]	[illegible]	[illegible]	[illegible]	[illegible]	[illegible]	[illegible]	[illegible]	[illegible]
[illegible]	[illegible]	[illegible]	[illegible]	[illegible]	[illegible]	[illegible]	[illegible]	[illegible]	[illegible]
Battle Creek	[illegible]	[illegible]	[illegible]	[illegible]	[illegible]	[illegible]	[illegible]	[illegible]	[illegible]
Detroit	[illegible]	[illegible]	[illegible]	[illegible]	[illegible]	[illegible]	[illegible]	[illegible]	[illegible]
Ann Arbor	[illegible]	[illegible]	[illegible]	[illegible]	[illegible]	[illegible]	[illegible]	[illegible]	[illegible]
Monroe	[illegible]	[illegible]	[illegible]	[illegible]	[illegible]	[illegible]	[illegible]	[illegible]	[illegible]

WINTER.

	N	NE	E	SE	S	SW	W	NW	Ca
Ontonagon	[illegible]	[illegible]	[illegible]	[illegible]	[illegible]	[illegible]	[illegible]	[illegible]	[illegible]
Marquette	[illegible]	[illegible]	[illegible]	[illegible]	[illegible]	[illegible]	[illegible]	[illegible]	[illegible]
Sault Ste. Marie	[illegible]	[illegible]	[illegible]	[illegible]	[illegible]	[illegible]	[illegible]	[illegible]	[illegible]
Mackinac	[illegible]	[illegible]	[illegible]	[illegible]	[illegible]	[illegible]	[illegible]	[illegible]	[illegible]
St. James	[illegible]	[illegible]	[illegible]	[illegible]	[illegible]	[illegible]	[illegible]	[illegible]	[illegible]
Thunder Bay I.	[illegible]	[illegible]	[illegible]	[illegible]	[illegible]	[illegible]	[illegible]	[illegible]	[illegible]
Tawas City	[illegible]	[illegible]	[illegible]	[illegible]	[illegible]	[illegible]	[illegible]	[illegible]	[illegible]
[illegible]	[illegible]	[illegible]	[illegible]	[illegible]	[illegible]	[illegible]	[illegible]	[illegible]	[illegible]
Grand Haven	[illegible]	[illegible]	[illegible]	[illegible]	[illegible]	[illegible]	[illegible]	[illegible]	[illegible]
Flint	[illegible]	[illegible]	[illegible]	[illegible]	[illegible]	[illegible]	[illegible]	[illegible]	[illegible]
Grand Rapids	[illegible]	[illegible]	[illegible]	[illegible]	[illegible]	[illegible]	[illegible]	[illegible]	[illegible]
Fort Gratiot	[illegible]	[illegible]	[illegible]	[illegible]	[illegible]	[illegible]	[illegible]	[illegible]	[illegible]
Port Huron	[illegible]	[illegible]	[illegible]	[illegible]	[illegible]	[illegible]	[illegible]	[illegible]	[illegible]
Lansing	[illegible]	[illegible]	[illegible]	[illegible]	[illegible]	[illegible]	[illegible]	[illegible]	[illegible]
[illegible]	[illegible]	[illegible]	[illegible]	[illegible]	[illegible]	[illegible]	[illegible]	[illegible]	[illegible]
Battle Creek	[illegible]	[illegible]	[illegible]	[illegible]	[illegible]	[illegible]	[illegible]	[illegible]	[illegible]
Detroit	[illegible]	[illegible]	[illegible]	[illegible]	[illegible]	[illegible]	[illegible]	[illegible]	[illegible]
Ann Arbor	[illegible]	[illegible]	[illegible]	[illegible]	[illegible]	[illegible]	[illegible]	[illegible]	[illegible]
Monroe	[illegible]	[illegible]	[illegible]	[illegible]	[illegible]	[illegible]	[illegible]	[illegible]	[illegible]

YEAR.

	N	NE	E	SE	S	SW	W	NW	Ca
Ontonagon	[illegible]	[illegible]	[illegible]	[illegible]	[illegible]	[illegible]	[illegible]	[illegible]	[illegible]
Marquette	[illegible]	[illegible]	[illegible]	[illegible]	[illegible]	[illegible]	[illegible]	[illegible]	[illegible]
Sault Ste. Marie	[illegible]	[illegible]	[illegible]	[illegible]	[illegible]	[illegible]	[illegible]	[illegible]	[illegible]
Mackinac	[illegible]	[illegible]	[illegible]	[illegible]	[illegible]	[illegible]	[illegible]	[illegible]	[illegible]
St. James	[illegible]	[illegible]	[illegible]	[illegible]	[illegible]	[illegible]	[illegible]	[illegible]	[illegible]
Thunder Bay I.	[illegible]	[illegible]	[illegible]	[illegible]	[illegible]	[illegible]	[illegible]	[illegible]	[illegible]
Tawas City	[illegible]	[illegible]	[illegible]	[illegible]	[illegible]	[illegible]	[illegible]	[illegible]	[illegible]
[illegible]	[illegible]	[illegible]	[illegible]	[illegible]	[illegible]	[illegible]	[illegible]	[illegible]	[illegible]
Grand Haven	[illegible]	[illegible]	[illegible]	[illegible]	[illegible]	[illegible]	[illegible]	[illegible]	[illegible]
Flint	[illegible]	[illegible]	[illegible]	[illegible]	[illegible]	[illegible]	[illegible]	[illegible]	[illegible]
Grand Rapids	[illegible]	[illegible]	[illegible]	[illegible]	[illegible]	[illegible]	[illegible]	[illegible]	[illegible]
Fort Gratiot	[illegible]	[illegible]	[illegible]	[illegible]	[illegible]	[illegible]	[illegible]	[illegible]	[illegible]
Port Huron	[illegible]	[illegible]	[illegible]	[illegible]	[illegible]	[illegible]	[illegible]	[illegible]	[illegible]
Lansing	[illegible]	[illegible]	[illegible]	[illegible]	[illegible]	[illegible]	[illegible]	[illegible]	[illegible]
[illegible]	[illegible]	[illegible]	[illegible]	[illegible]	[illegible]	[illegible]	[illegible]	[illegible]	[illegible]
Battle Creek	[illegible]	[illegible]	[illegible]	[illegible]	[illegible]	[illegible]	[illegible]	[illegible]	[illegible]
Detroit	[illegible]	[illegible]	[illegible]	[illegible]	[illegible]	[illegible]	[illegible]	[illegible]	[illegible]
Ann Arbor	[illegible]	[illegible]	[illegible]	[illegible]	[illegible]	[illegible]	[illegible]	[illegible]	[illegible]
Monroe	[illegible]	[illegible]	[illegible]	[illegible]	[illegible]	[illegible]	[illegible]	[illegible]	[illegible]

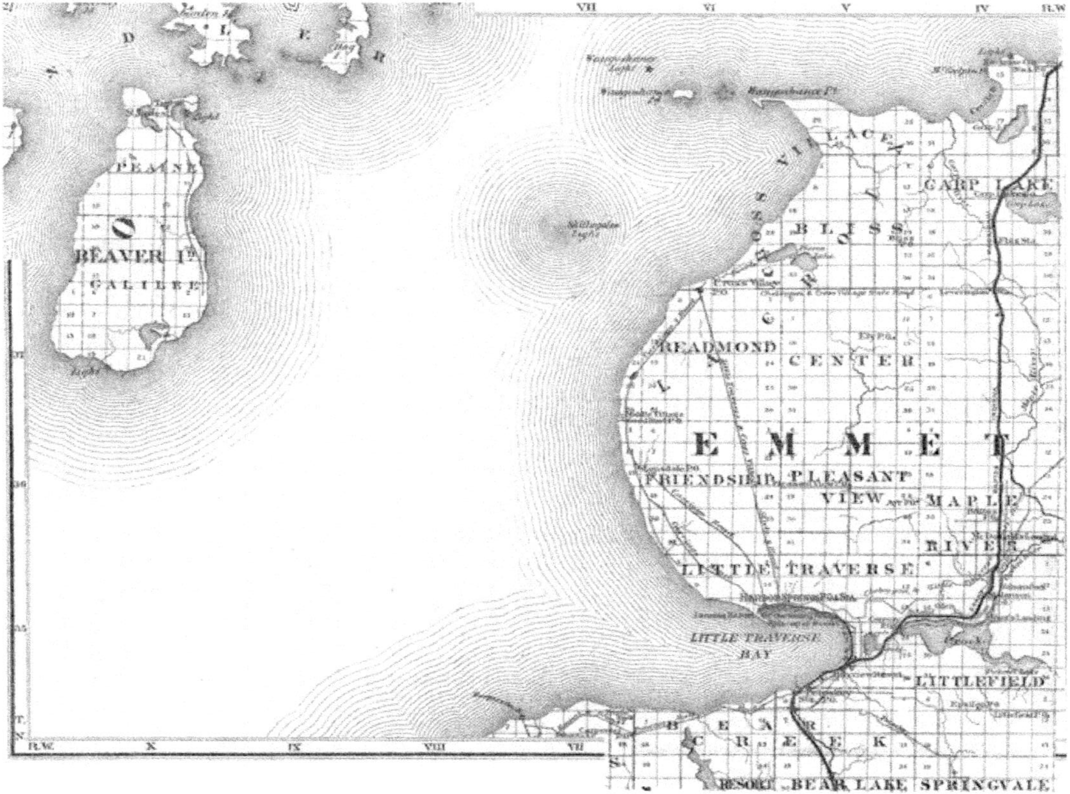

EMMET
BEAVER I^D.
PEAINE
GALILEE
BLISS
CARP LAKE
READMOND
CENTER
FRIENDSHIP
PLEASANT VIEW
MAPLE RIVER
LITTLE TRAVERSE
LITTLE TRAVERSE BAY
LITTLEFIELD
BEAR CREEK
RESORT
BEAR LAKE
SPRINGVALE

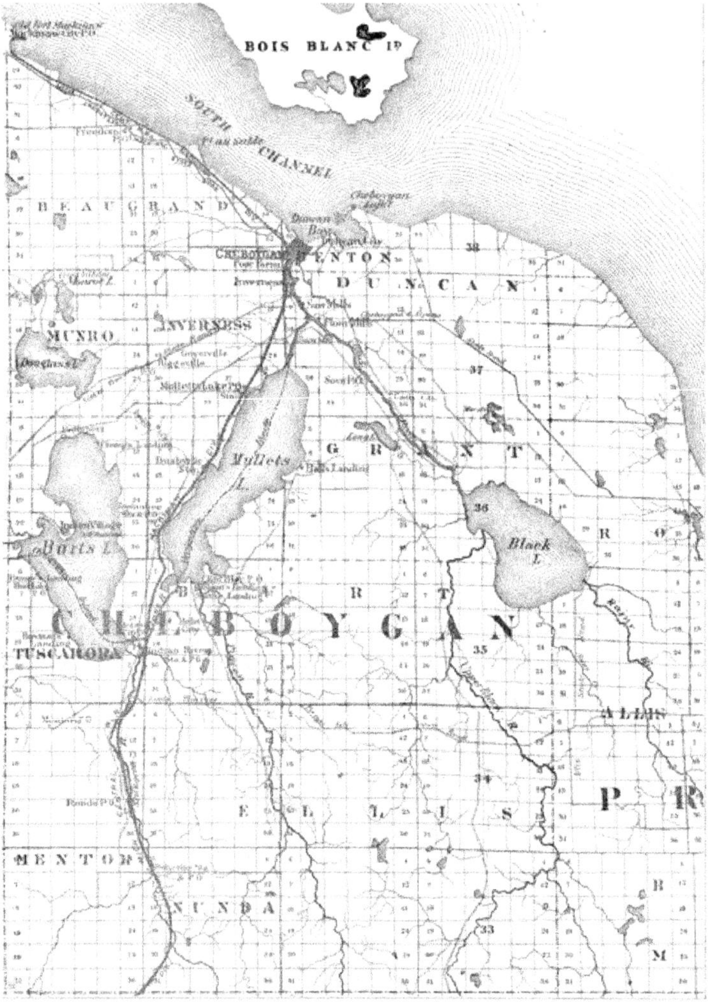
BOIS BLANC I?
SOUTH CHANNEL
B E A U G R A N D
CHEBOYGAN
BENTON
D U N C A N
INVERNESS
MUNRO
Mullets L.
G R A N T
38
37
36
Black L.
Burts L.
TUSCARORA
C H E B O Y G A N
35
34
E L L I S
M E N T O R
N U N D A
33
P R

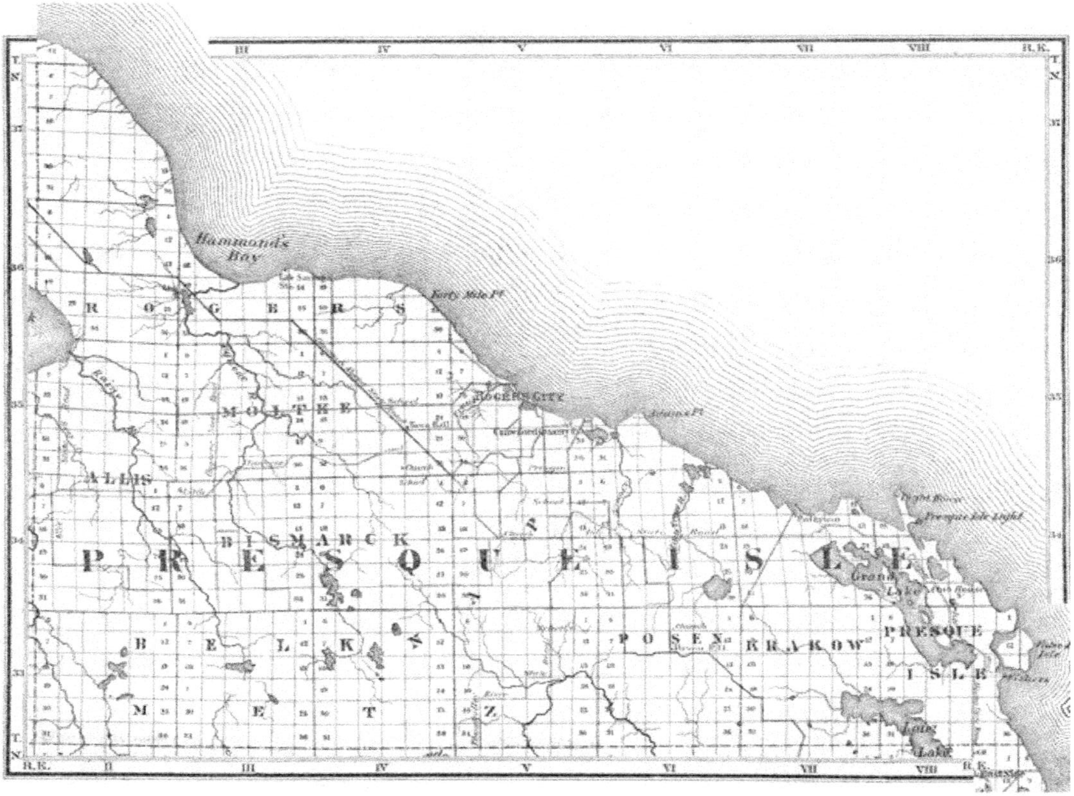

PRESQUE ISLE
ROGERS
MOLTKE
ALLIS
BISMARCK
BELKNAP
METZ
POSEN
KRAKOW
PRESQUE ISLE
Hammond's Bay
Forty Mile Pt.
ROGERS CITY
Adams Pt.
Grand Lake
Long Lake
Presque Isle Light

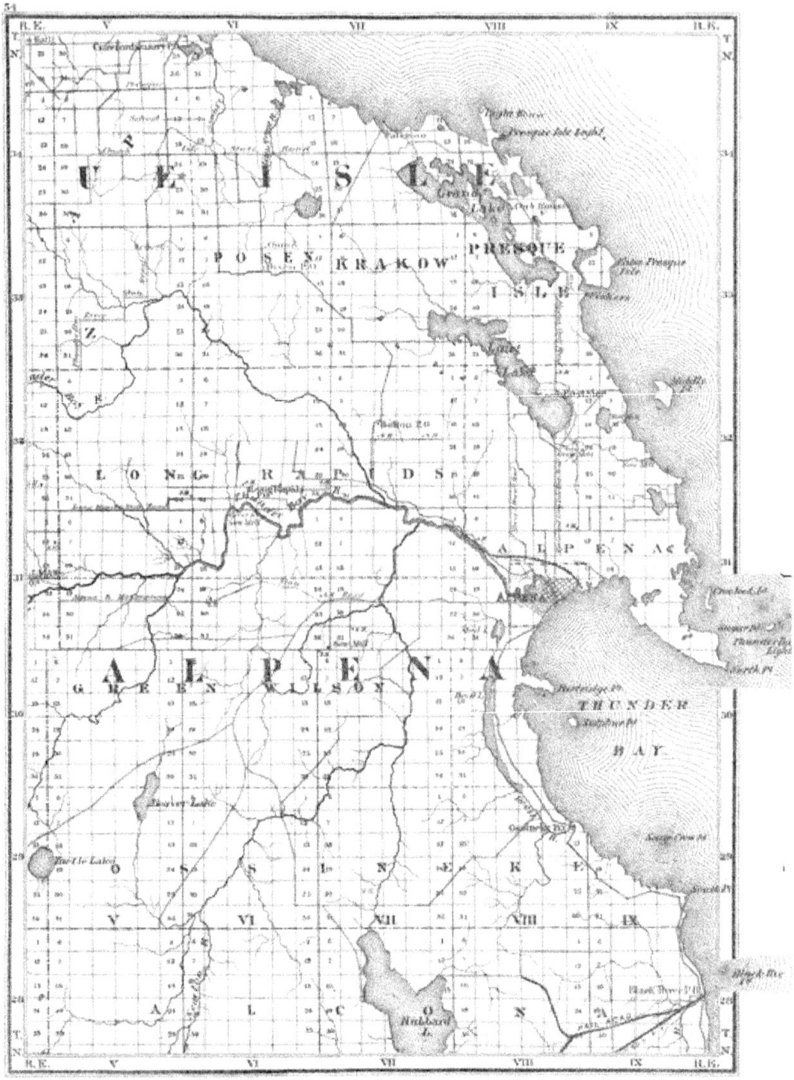
R.E.
V
VI
VII
VIII
IX
R.E.
T.
N.
PRESQUE ISLE
Grand Lake
POSEN
KRAKOW
PRESQUE
ISLE
Long Lake
LONG RAPIDS
ALPENA
ALPENA
GREEN
WILSON
THUNDER
BAY
Beaver Lake
OSSINEKE
ALCONA
Hubbard L.

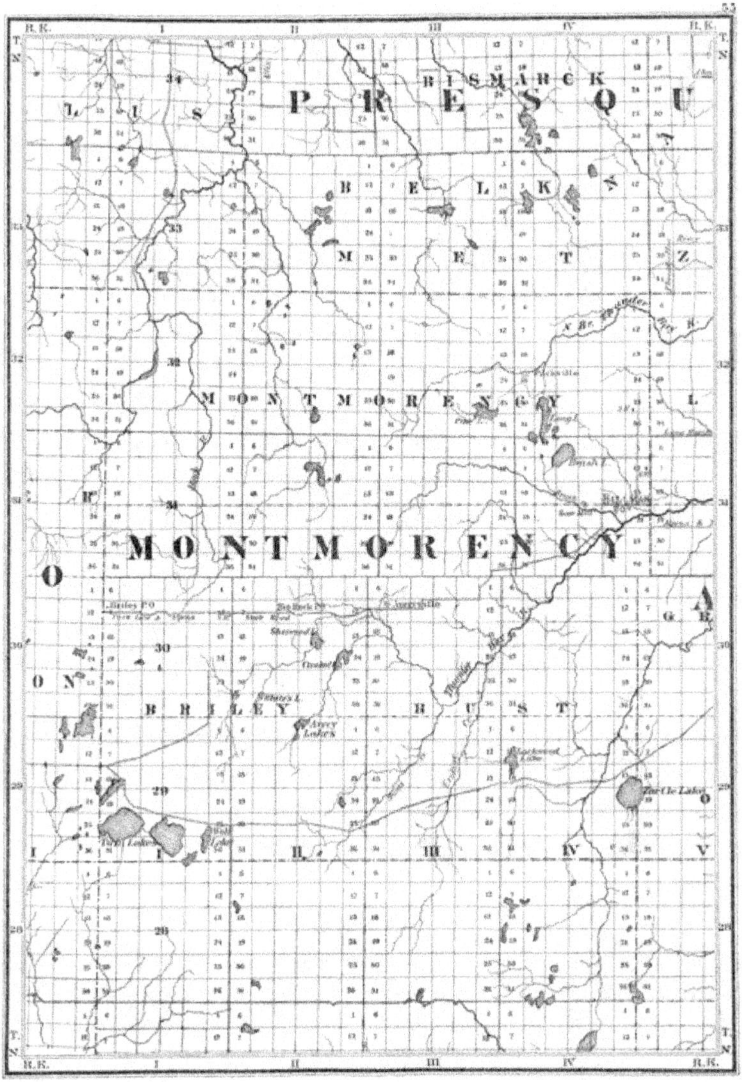

R. K.
I
II
III
IV
T. N.
BISMARCK
P R E S Q U
B E L K N
M E T Z
M O N T M O R E N C Y
MONTMORENCY
B R I L E Y
R U S T
Briley P.O.
Atlanta
Avery Lakes
Turtle Lake
Twin Lakes
Lockwood Lake
Thunder Bay R.
N. Br. Thunder Bay R.
Sherwood L.
Crooked L.
34
33
32
31
30
29
28
O
O N
A
G
O
V

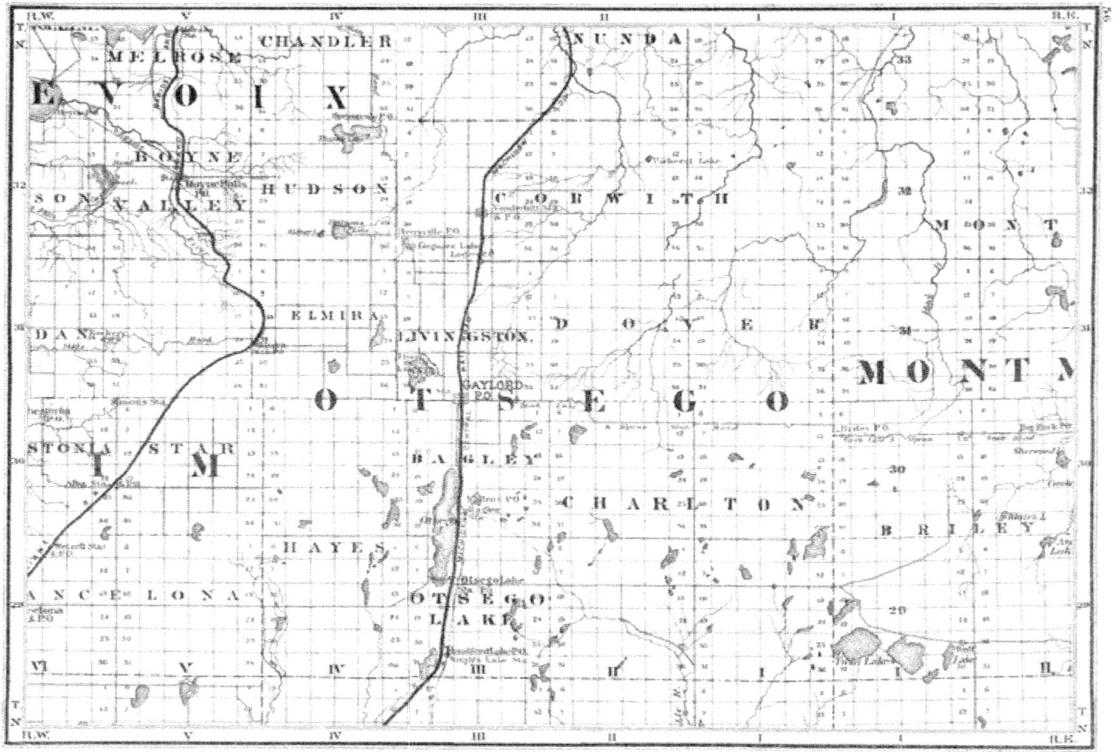

E V O I X
MELROSE
CHANDLER
NUNDA
BOYNE
HUDSON
SON VALLEY
CORWITH
ELMIRA
LIVINGSTON
DAN
DOVER
MONT
MONTM
O T S E G O
GAYLORD P.O.
STONIA
STAR
I M
BAGLEY
CHARLTON
BRILEY
HAYES
ANCELONA
OTSEGO LAKE
R.W.
R.E.

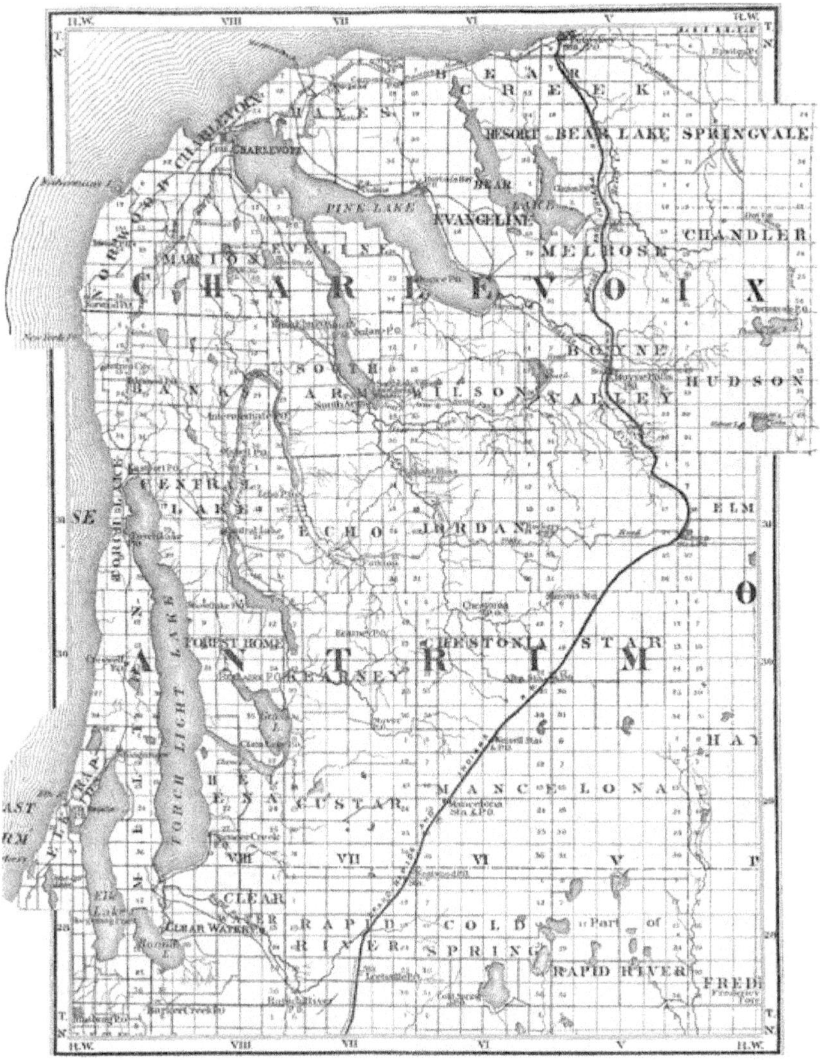
CHARLEVOIX
ANTRIM
BEAR CREEK
HAYES
RESORT
BEAR LAKE
SPRINGVALE
PINE LAKE
EVANGELINE
MELROSE
CHANDLER
MARION
EVELINE
BOYNE
HUDSON
SOUTH ARM
WILSON
BOYNE VALLEY
BANKS
CENTRAL LAKE
ECHO
JORDAN
ELM
FOREST HOME
CHESTONIA
STAR
KEARNEY
MANCELONA
CUSTAR
HELENA
TORCH LIGHT LAKE
CLEAR WATER
RAPID RIVER
COLD SPRING
Part of
RAPID RIVER
FRED
VIII
VII
VI
V
R.W.

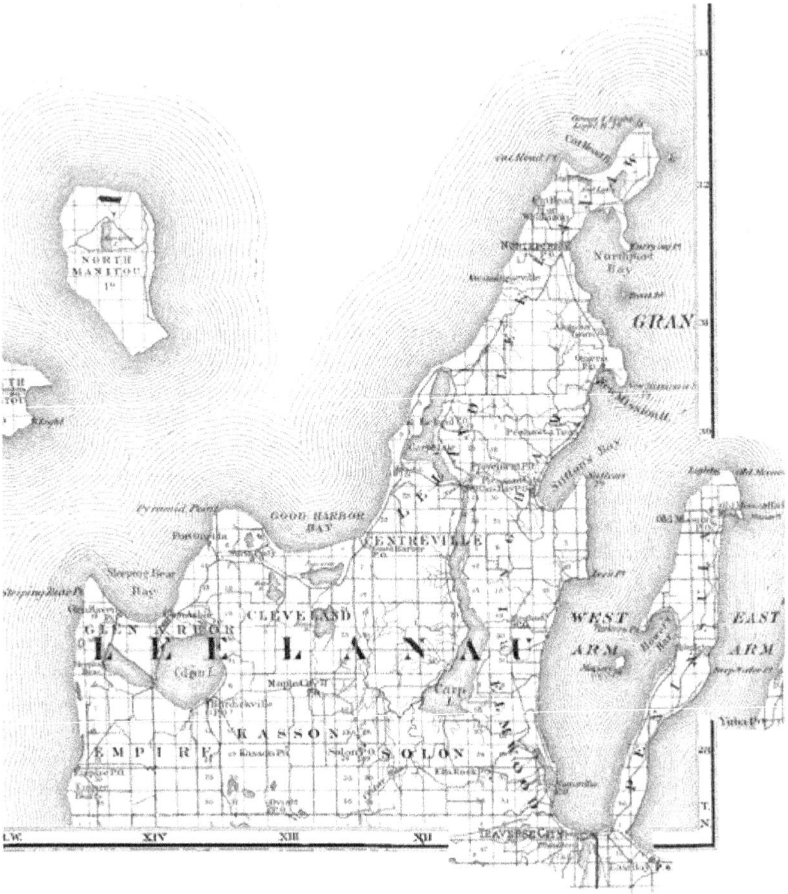
NORTH
MANITOU
GOOD HARBOR
BAY
CENTREVILLE
Sleeping Bear
Bay
CLEVELAND
GLEN ARBOR
LEE LANAU
KASSON
EMPIRE
SOLON
WEST
ARM
EAST
ARM
Northport
Bay
GRAN
XIV
XIII
XII

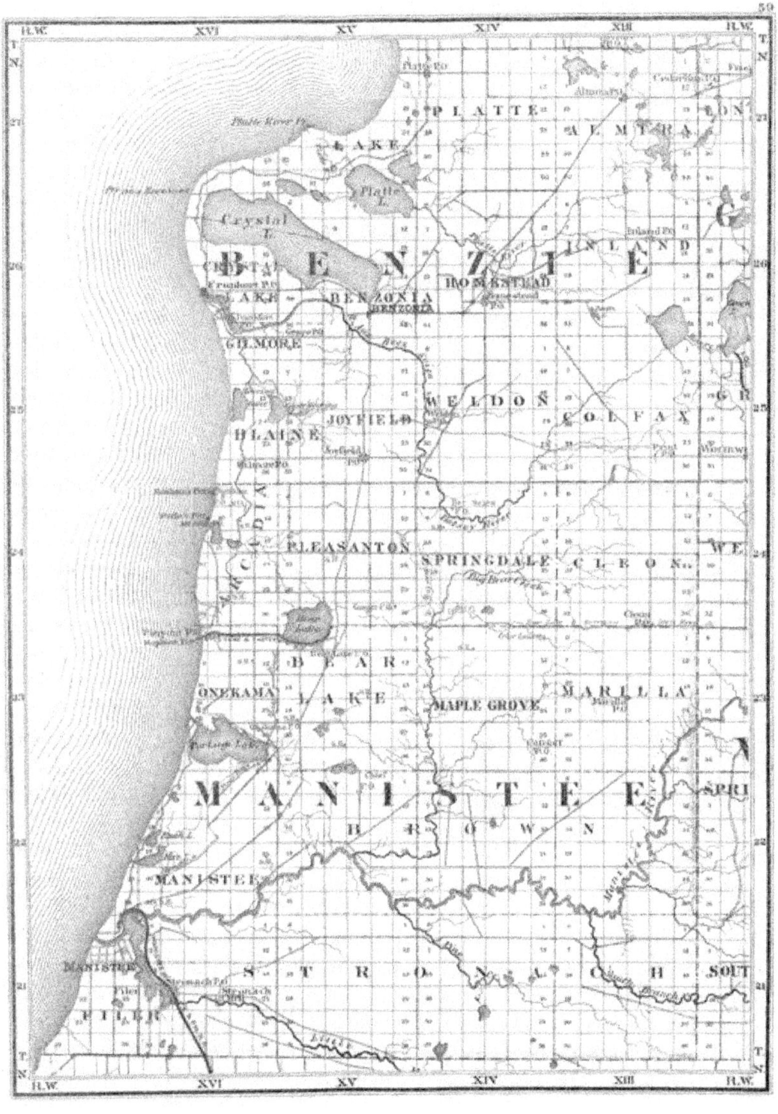
R.W.
XVI
XV
XIV
XIII
T.
N.
27
26
25
24
23
22
21
PLATTE
LAKE
ALMIRA
Crystal L.
Platte L.
B E N Z I E
INLAND
HOMESTEAD
BENZONIA
GILMORE
WELDON
JOYFIELD
BLAINE
COLFAX
ARCADIA
PLEASANTON
SPRINGDALE
CLEON
BEAR LAKE
ONEKAMA
MAPLE GROVE
MARILLA
M A N I S T E E
BROWN
MANISTEE
STRONACH
FILER

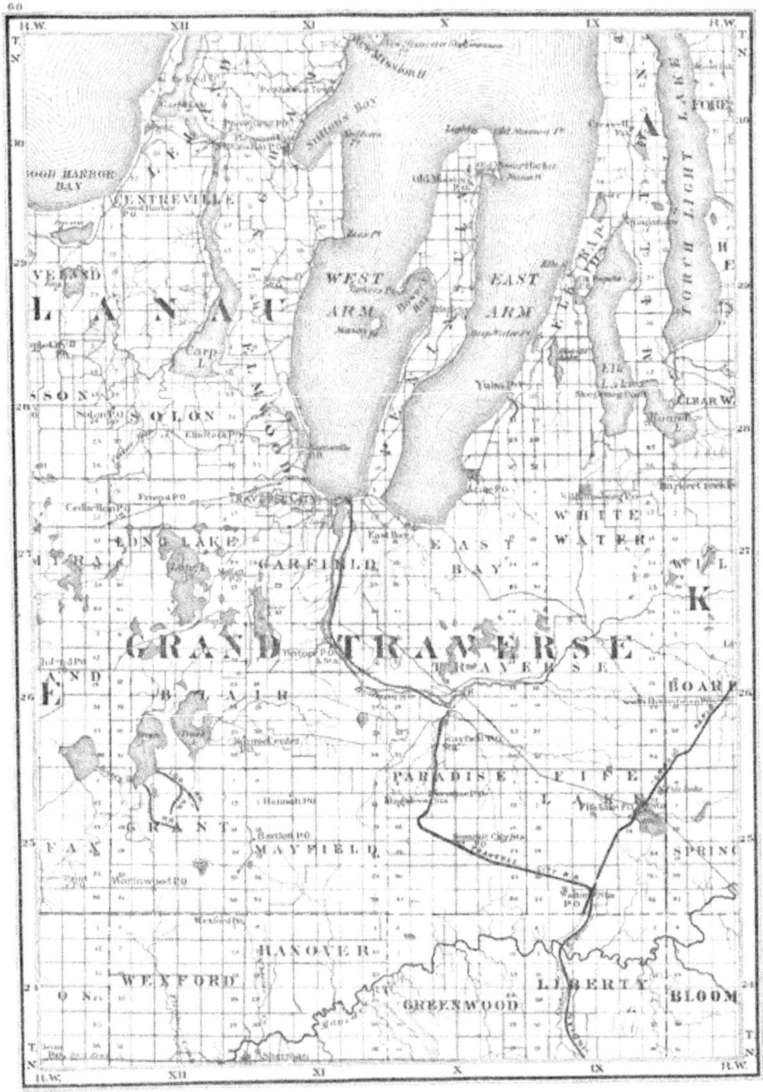
R.W.
XII
XI
X
IX
GOOD HARBOR BAY
CENTREVILLE
WEST ARM
EAST ARM
TORCH LIGHT LAKE
Carp L.
Elk Lake
SOLON
LONG LAKE
GARFIELD
EAST BAY
WHITE WATER
GRAND TRAVERSE
BLAIR
PARADISE
FIFE LAKE
GRANT
MAYFIELD
HANOVER
WEXFORD
GREENWOOD
LIBERTY
BLOOM
SPRING
BOARD
CLEAR W.

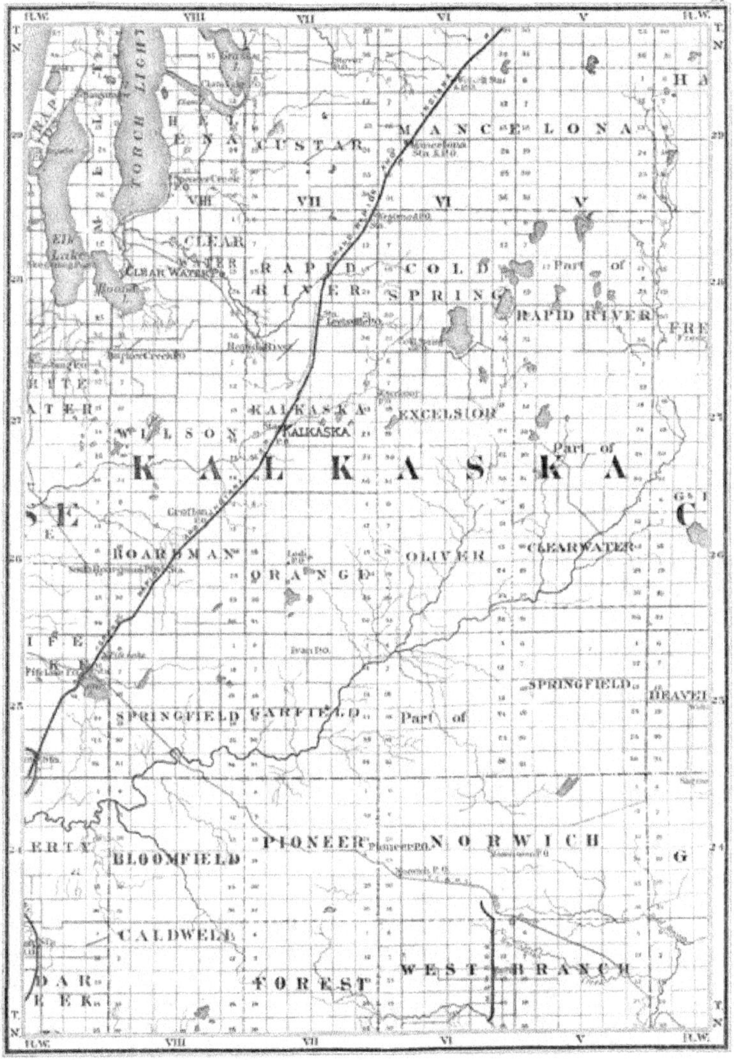
R.W.
VIII
VII
VI
V
TORCH LIGHT
Elk Lake
HELENA
CUSTAR
MANCELONA
CLEAR WATER
RAPID RIVER
COLD SPRINGS
Part of
RAPID RIVER
KALKASKA
EXCELSIOR
WILSON
KALKASKA
BOARDMAN
ORANGE
OLIVER
CLEARWATER
SPRINGFIELD
GARFIELD
SPRINGFIELD
PIONEER
NORWICH
BLOOMFIELD
CALDWELL
FOREST
WEST BRANCH

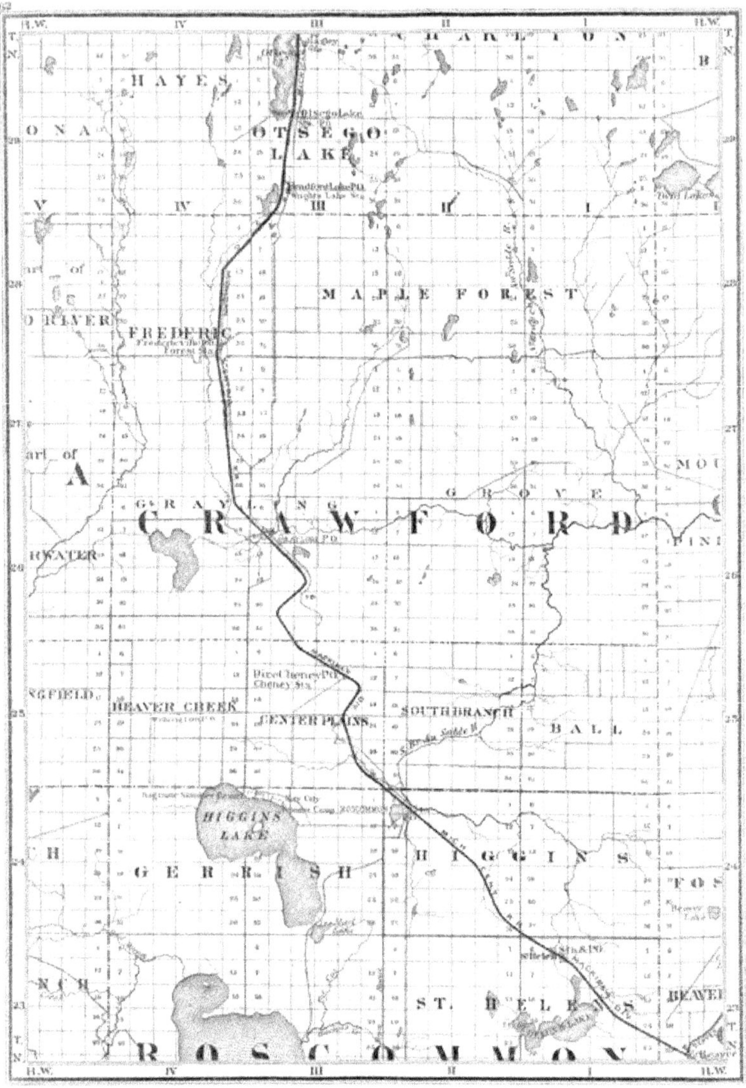
CRAWFORD
ROSCOMMON
HAYES
OTSEGO LAKE
CHARLTON
MAPLE FOREST
FREDERIC
GRAYLING
GROVE
BEAVER CREEK
CENTER PLAINS
SOUTH BRANCH
BALL
HIGGINS LAKE
GERRISH
HIGGINS
ST. HELENS
R.W.
IV
III
II
I
T.
N.

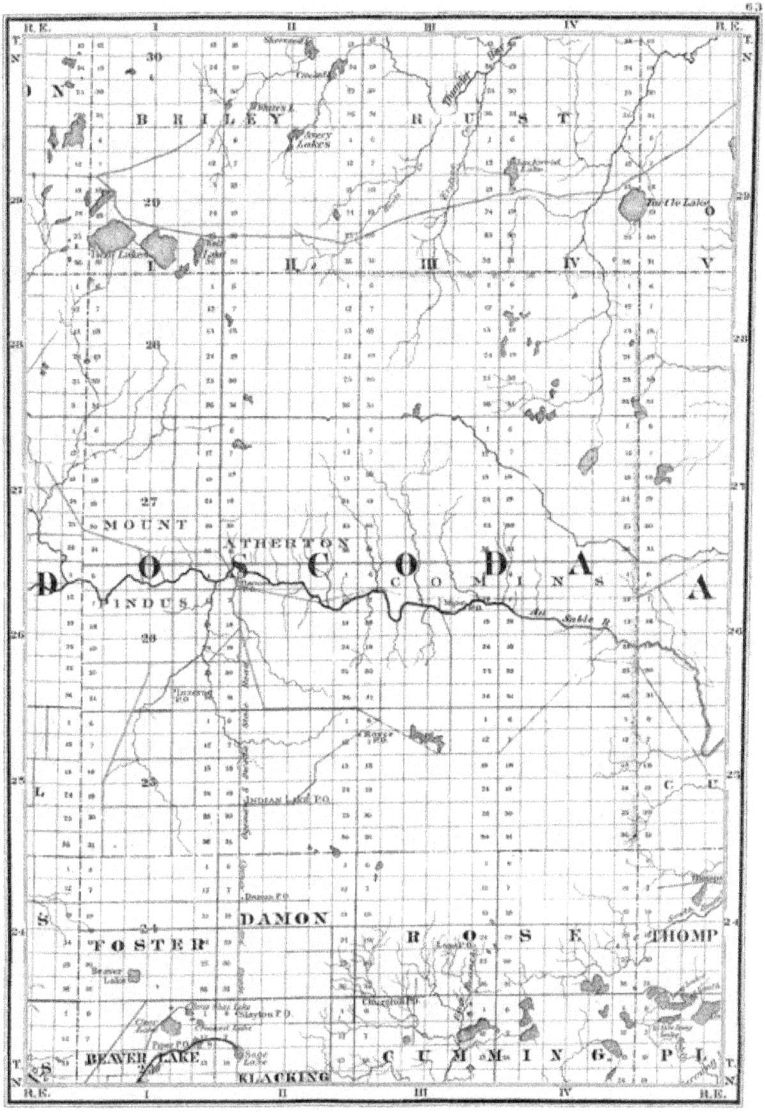
R.E.
I
II
III
IV
T.
N
30
29
28
27
26
25
24
BRILEY
RUST
MOUNT
ATHERTON
OSCODA
COMINS
INDUS
Au Sable R.
Turtle Lake
INDIAN LAKE P.O.
Damon P.O.
DAMON
FOSTER
Beaver Lake
ROSE
THOMP
BEAVER LAKE
KLACKING
CUMMING
Clayton P.O.

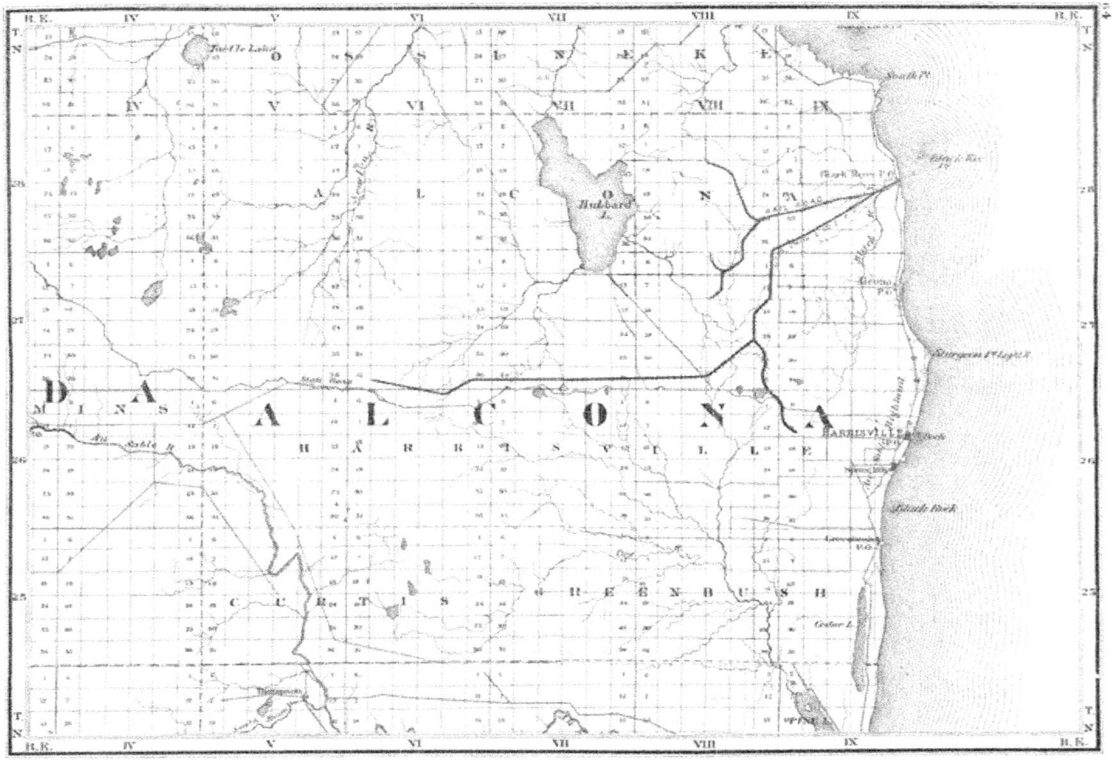
ALCONA
OSSINEKE
HARRISVILLE
GREENBUSH
CURTIS
MINS
Hubbard L.
Turtle Lake
Au Sable R.
HARRISVILLE
Sturgeon Pt.
Black Rock
Cedar L.
Pine L.
State Road
South Pt.
R. E.
T. N.
IV
V
VI
VII
VIII
IX
25
26
27
28

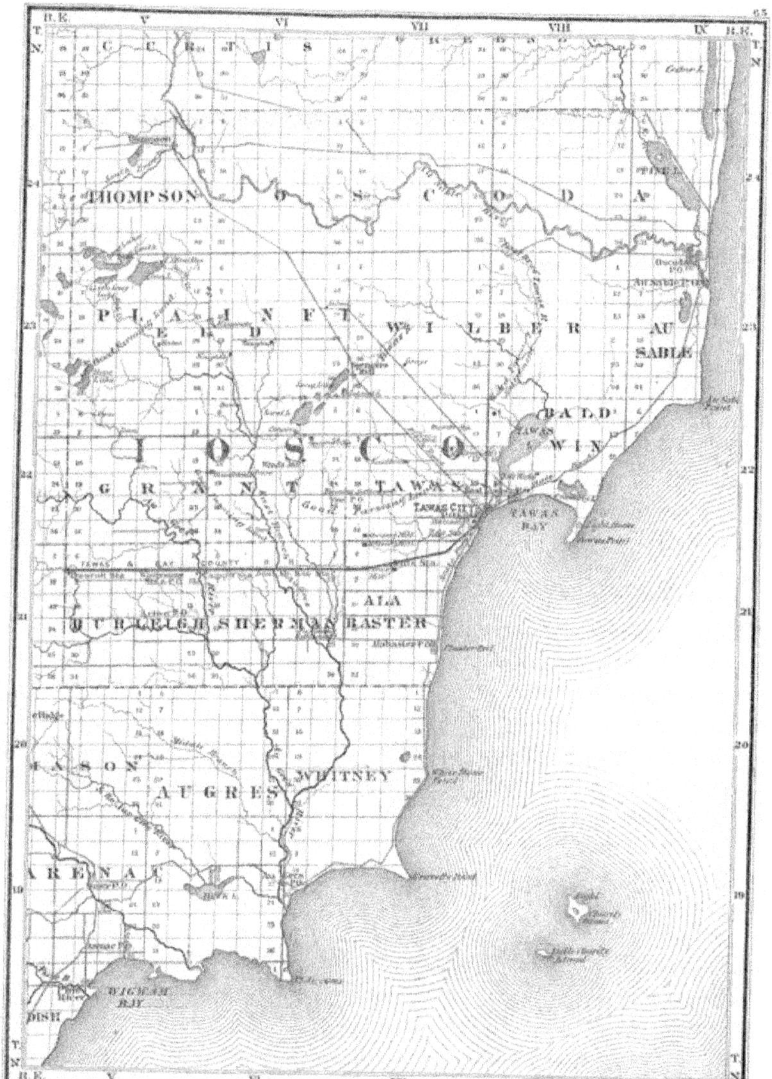
R.E.
V
VI
VII
VIII
IX
R.E.
T.
N.
C U R T I S
THOMPSON
O S C O D A
P L A I N F I E L D
W I L B E R
AU SABLE
BALD WIN
I O S C O
G R A N T
T A W A S
TAWAS CITY
TAWAS BAY
ALA BASTER
BURLEIGH
SHERMAN
WHITNEY
M A S O N
A U G R E S
A R E N A C
WIGWAM BAY
24
23
22
21
20
19

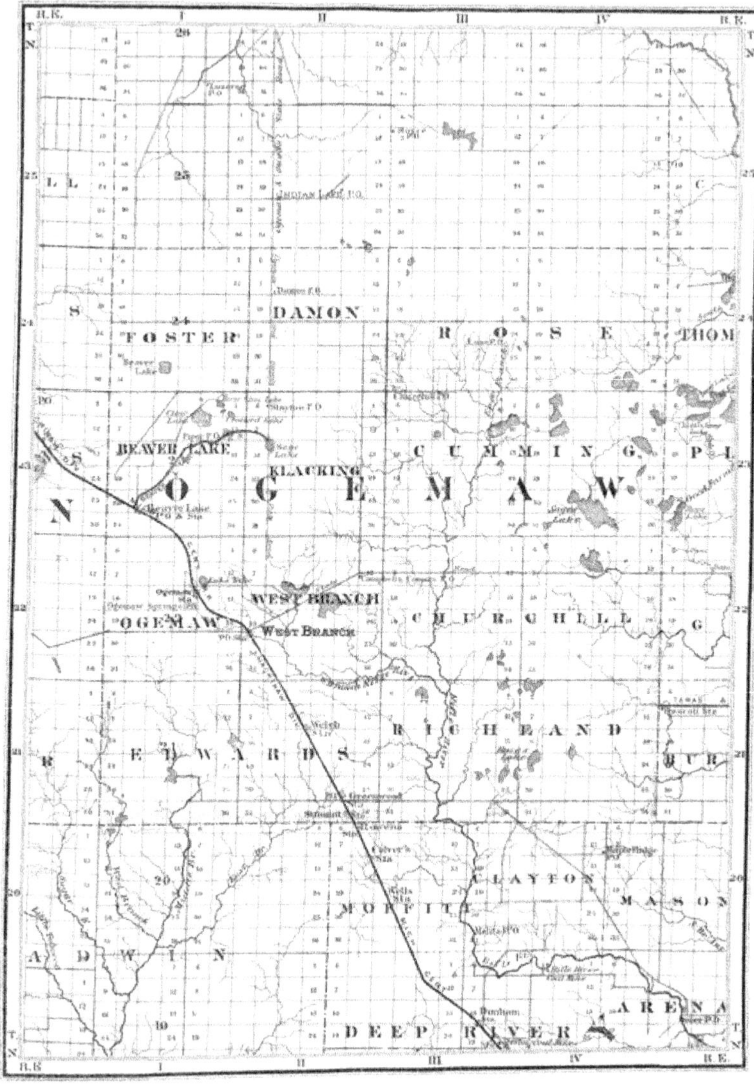
OGEMAW
FOSTER
DAMON
ROSE
THOM
BEAVER LAKE
KLACKING
CUMMING
WEST BRANCH
OGEMAW
West Branch
CHURCHILL
EDWARDS
RICHLAND
CLAYTON
MASON
DEEP RIVER
ARENA
Indian Lake P.O.
Damon P.O.

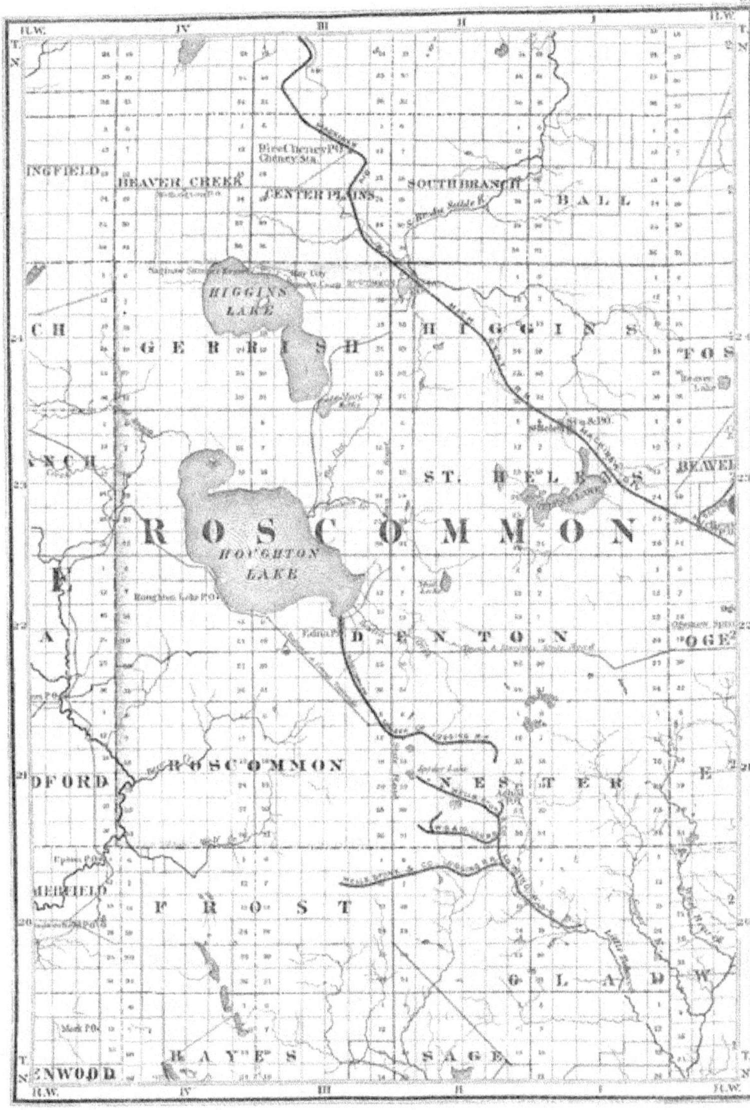
R.W.
IV
III
II
I
T.
N.
BEAVER CREEK
CENTER PLAINS
SOUTH BRANCH
BALL
HIGGINS LAKE
GERRISH
HIGGINS
ST. HELEN
ROSCOMMON
HOUGHTON LAKE
Houghton Lake P.O.
DENTON
ROSCOMMON
NESTER
FROST
GLADW
SAGE
Spider Lake
24
23
22
21
20

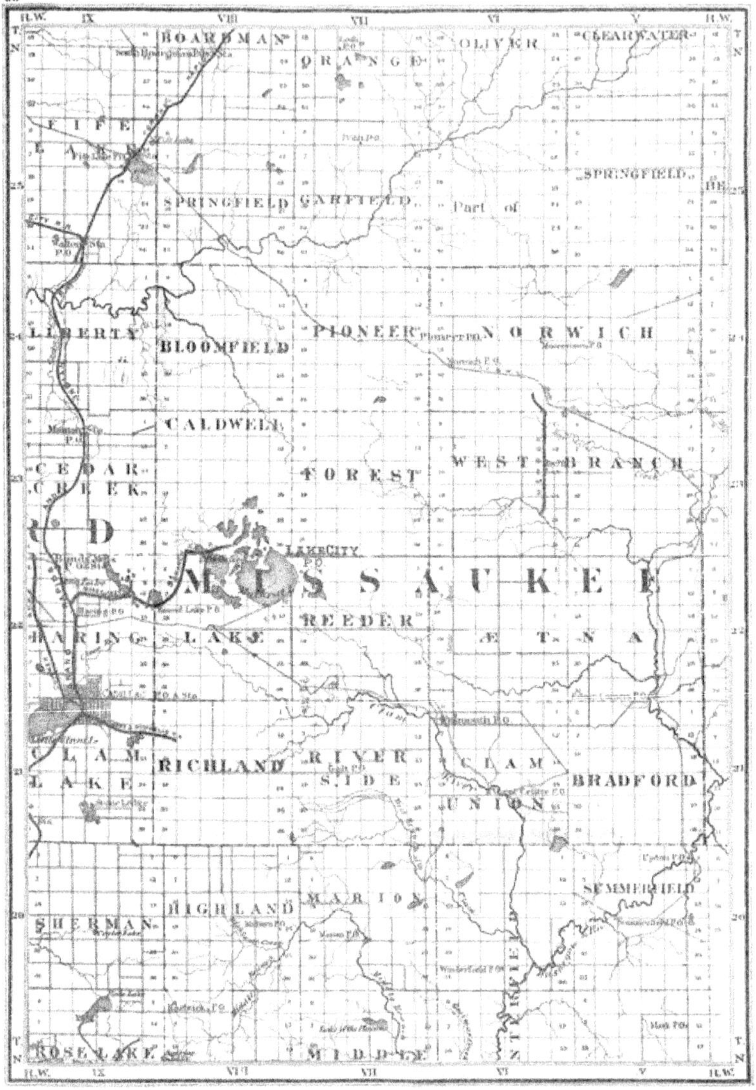
R.W.
IX
VIII
VII
VI
V
T.N.
BOARDMAN
ORANGE
OLIVER
CLEARWATER
FIFE LAKE
SPRINGFIELD
GARFIELD
Part of
SPRINGFIELD
LIBERTY
BLOOMFIELD
PIONEER
NORWICH
CALDWELL
CEDAR CREEK
FOREST
WEST BRANCH
MISSAUKEE
LAKE CITY
REEDER
HARING
LAKE
ÆTNA
CLAM LAKE
RICHLAND
RIVER SIDE
CLAM UNION
BRADFORD
SUMMERFIELD
SHERMAN
HIGHLAND
MARION
ROSE LAKE
MIDDLE

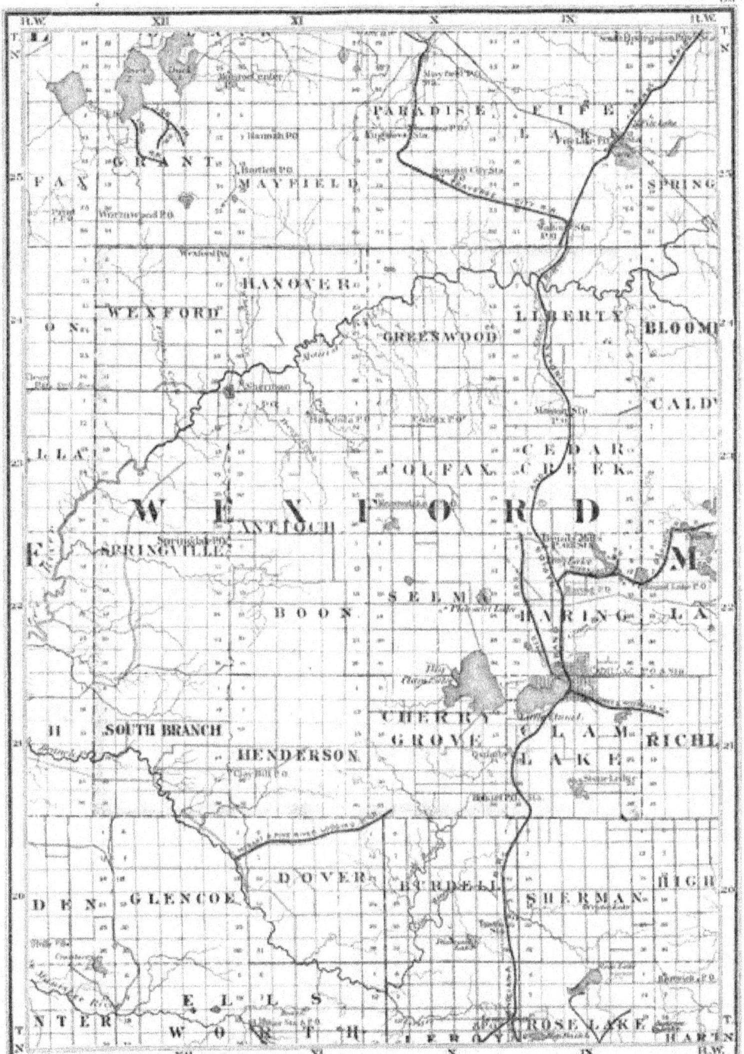
R.W.
XII
XI
X
IX
PARADISE
FIFE
LAKE
GRANT
MAYFIELD
SPRING
HANOVER
WEXFORD
LIBERTY
GREENWOOD
BLOOM
CALD
CEDAR
CREEK
COLFAX
W E X F O R D
ANTIOCH
SPRINGVILLE
SELMA
BOON
HARING
CHERRY
GROVE
CLAM
LAKE
RICH
SOUTH BRANCH
HENDERSON
DOVER
BURDELL
SHERMAN
HIGH
GLENCOE
ELLS
WORTH
LEROY
ROSE LAKE
HART
T.
N.

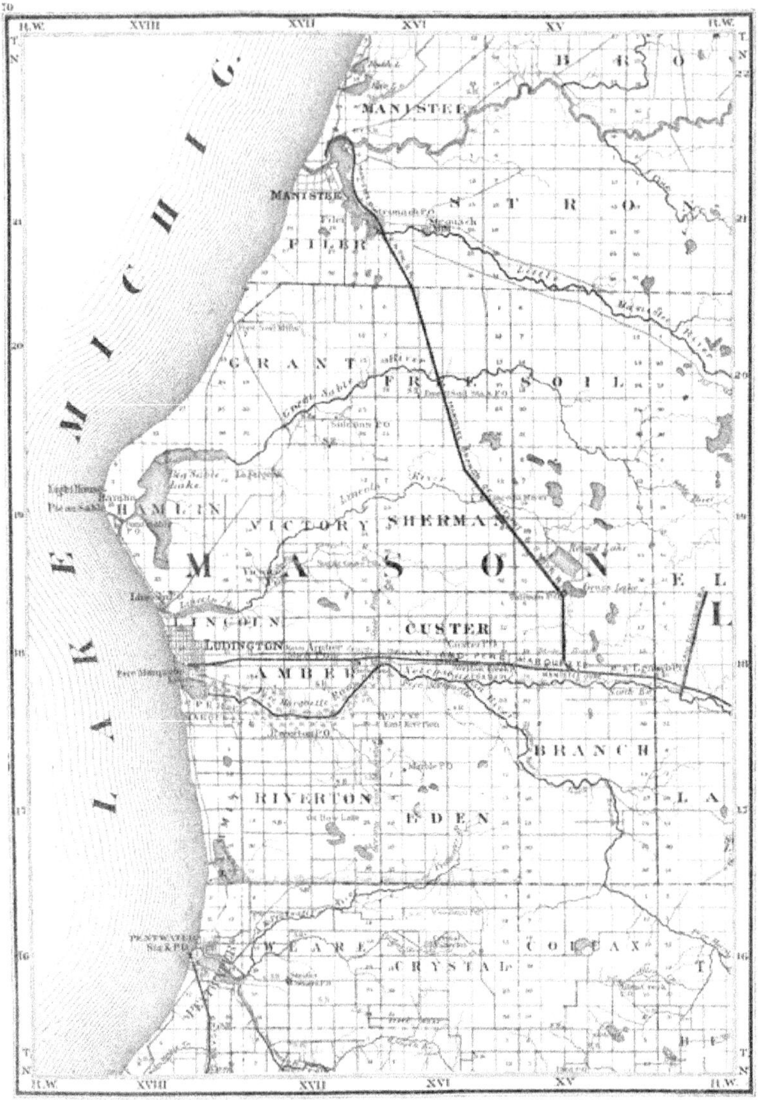
R.W.
XVIII
XVII
XVI
XV
R.W.
T.
N.
22
21
20
19
18
17
16
LAKE MICHIGAN
MANISTEE
FILER
GRANT
FREE SOIL
HAMLIN
VICTORY
SHERMAN
MASON
LINCOLN
CUSTER
LUDINGTON
AMBER
BRANCH
RIVERTON
EDEN
WEARE
CRYSTAL
COLFAX
PENTWATER

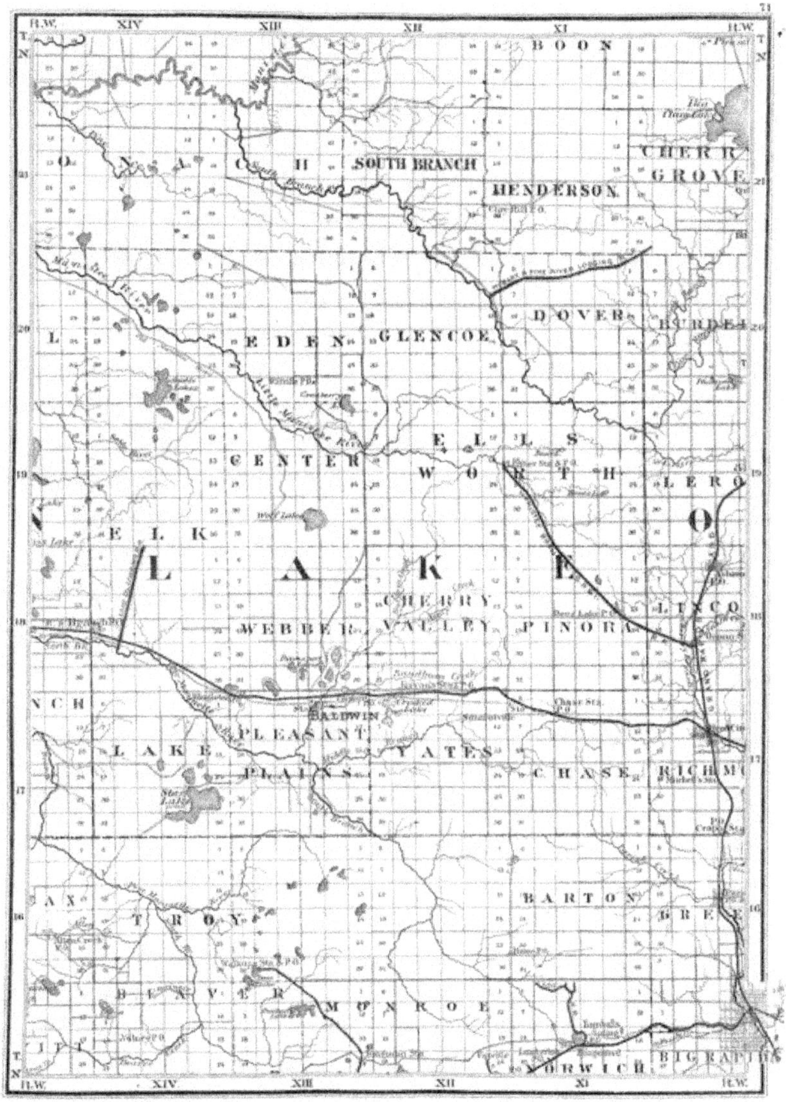
R.W.
XIV
XIII
XII
XI
BOON
SOUTH BRANCH
HENDERSON
CHERR
GROVE
DOVER
EDEN
GLENCOE
ELLS
WORTH
CENTER
ELK
LAKE
CHERRY
VALLEY
WEBBER
PINORA
BALDWIN
PLEASANT
PLAINS
YATES
CHASE
BARTON
TROY
BEAVER
MONROE
NORWICH

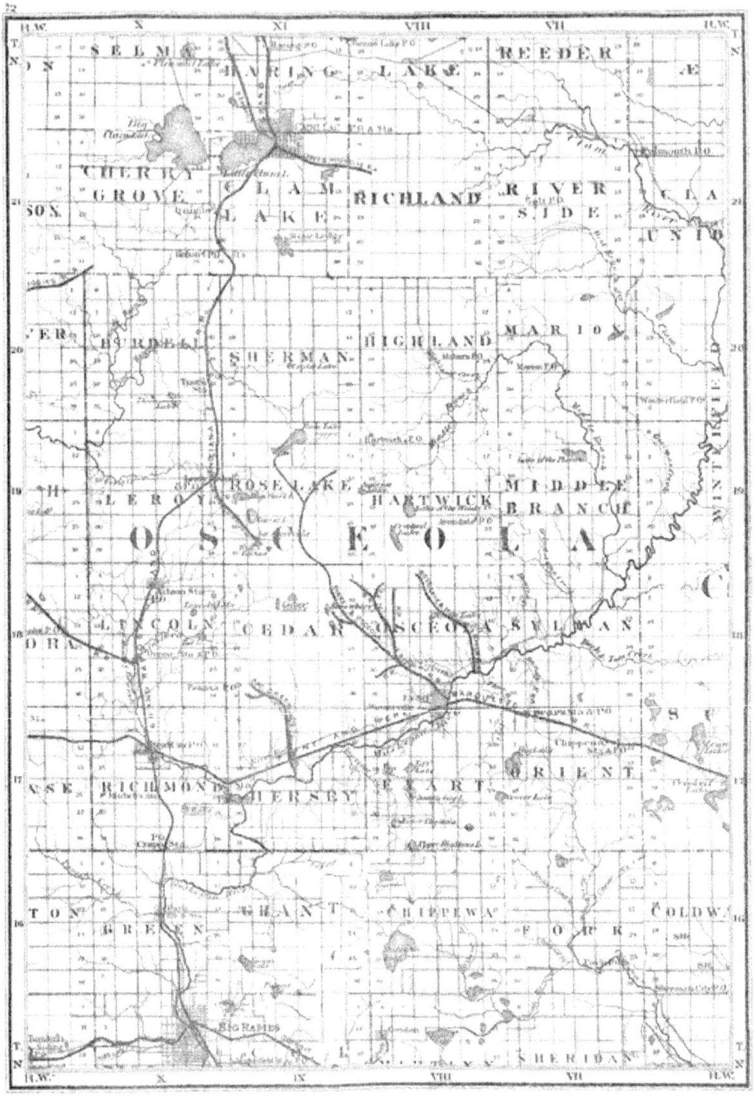
REEDER
HARING
CHERRY GROVE
CLAM LAKE
RICHLAND
RIVER SIDE
BURDELL
SHERMAN
HIGHLAND
MARION
LEROY
ROSE LAKE
HARTWICK
MIDDLE BRANCH
OSCEOLA
LINCOLN
CEDAR
SYLVAN
RICHMOND
HERSEY
EVART
ORIENT
GREEN
GRANT
CHIPPEWA
FORK
BIG RAPIDS
SHERIDAN

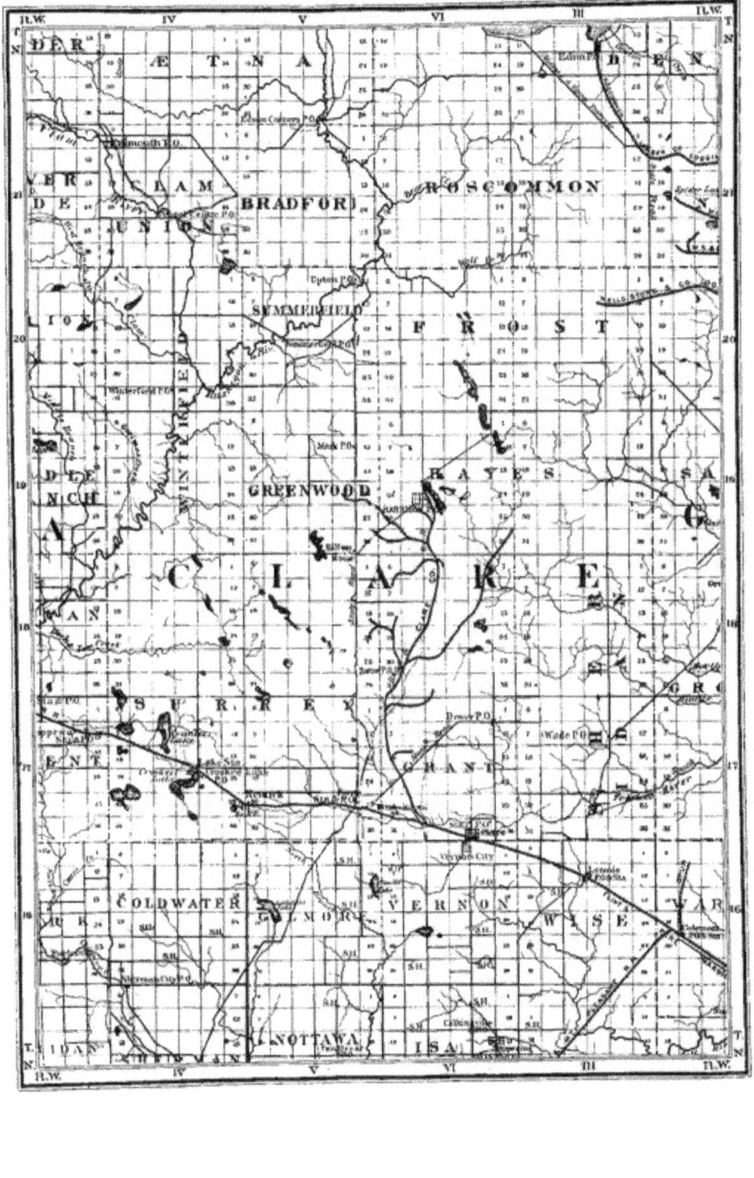

R.W.
IV
V
VI
III
R.W.
T.
N.
ROSCOMMON
BRADFORD
UNION
SUMMERFIELD
FROST
GREENWOOD
HAYES
WINTERFIELD
CLARE
SURREY
GRANT
COLDWATER
GILMORE
VERNON
WISE
NOTTAWA
Vernon City
21
20
19
18
17
16

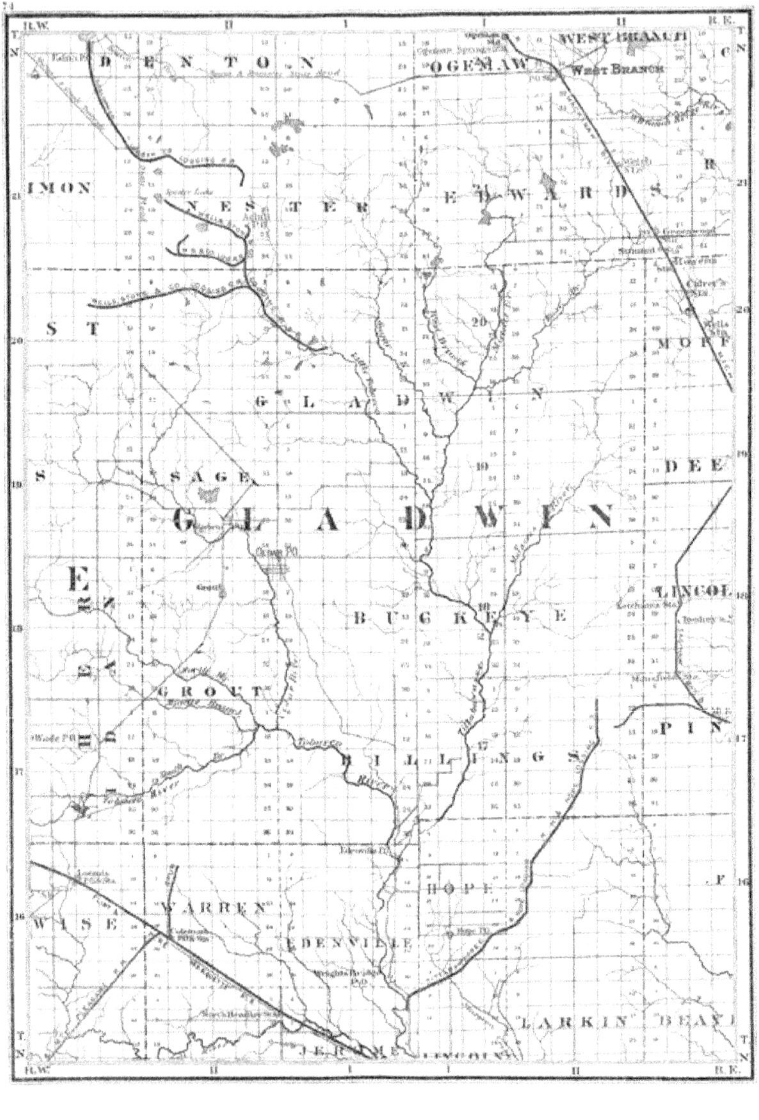
R.W.
R.E.
DENTON
OGEMAW
WEST BRANCH
West Branch
IMON
NESTER
EDWARDS
ST
GLADWIN
SAGE
S
GLADWIN
MOFF
DEE
LINCOL
BUCKEYE
GROUT
BILLINGS
PIN
HOPE
WARREN
WISE
EDENVILLE
LARKIN
JEROME
T.
N.
21
20
19
18
17
16

WIGWAM BAY
SAGINAW
BAY

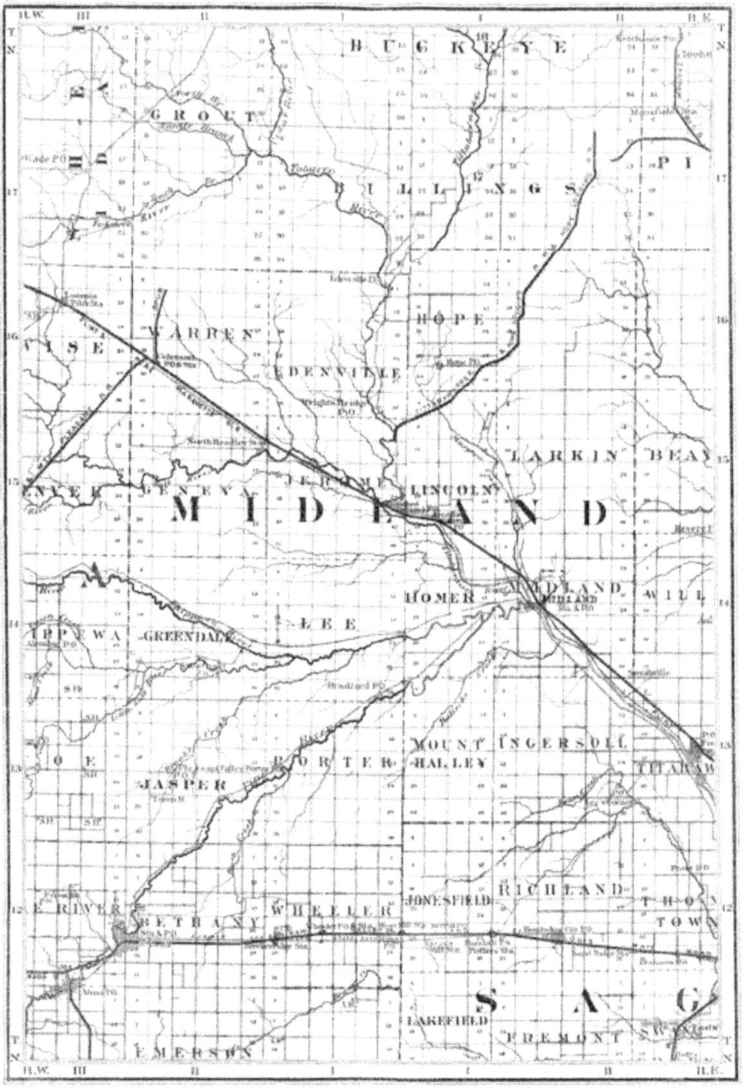
BUCKEYE
GROUT
BILLINGS
HOPE
WARREN
EDENVILLE
LARKIN
GENEVA
JEROME
LINCOLN
MIDLAND
HOMER
LEE
GREENDALE
PORTER
JASPER
JONESFIELD
RICHLAND
WHEELER
BETHANY
LAKEFIELD
FREMONT
EMERSON

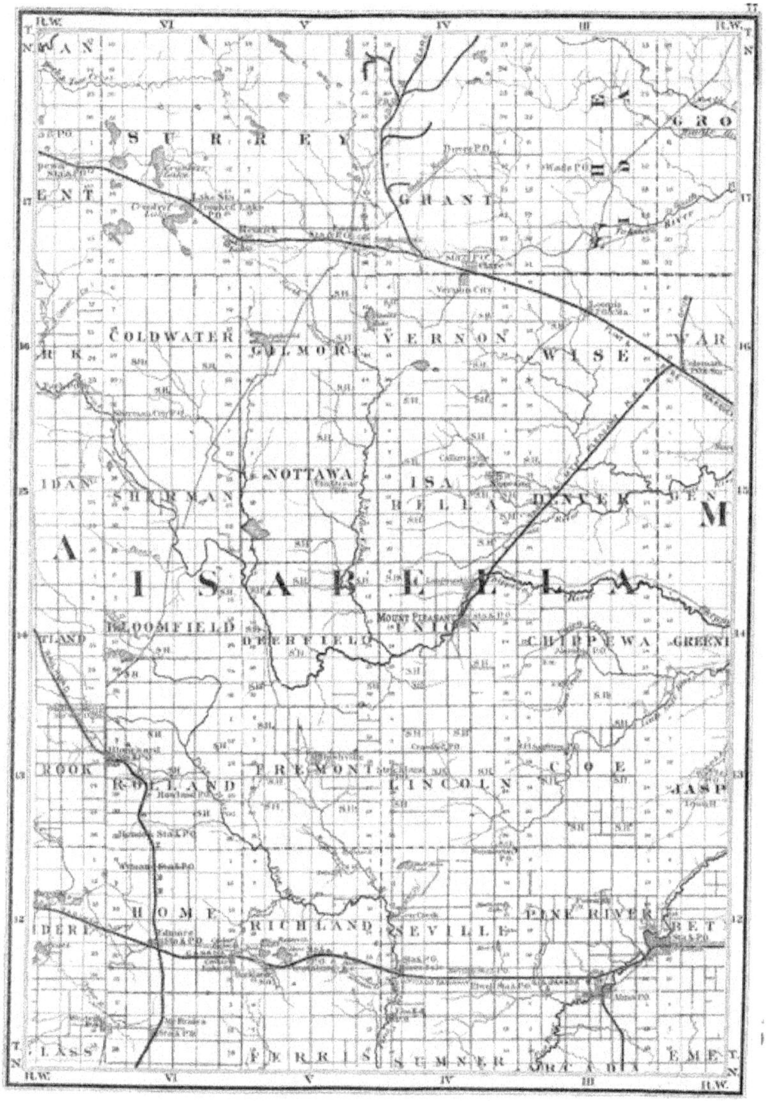

R.W.
VI
V
IV
III
SURREY
GRANT
COLDWATER
GILMORE
VERNON
WISE
NOTTAWA
ISA BELLA
DENVER
SHERMAN
M
A
ISABELLA
MOUNT PLEASANT
BLOOMFIELD
DEERFIELD
UNION
CHIPPEWA
FREMONT
LINCOLN
COE
ROLLAND
HOME
RICHLAND
NEVILLE
PINE RIVER
FERRIS
SUMNER
17
16
15
14
13
12

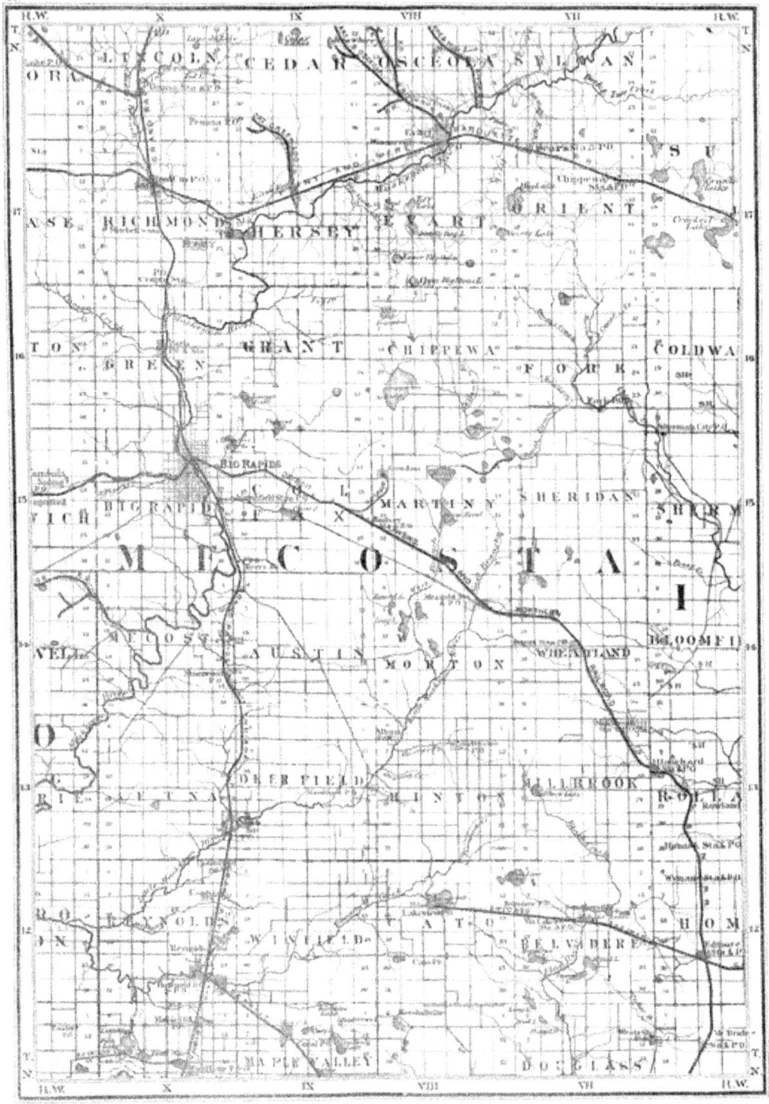
R.W.
X
IX
VIII
VII
T.
N.
LINCOLN
CEDAR
OSCEOLA
SYLVAN
ORIENT
RICHMOND
HERSEY
EVART
GRANT
CHIPPEWA
GREEN
FORK
COLDWA
BIG RAPIDS
COLFAX
MARTINY
SHERIDAN
M E C O S T A
AUSTIN
MORTON
WHEATLAND
BLOOMFI
DEERFIELD
HINTON
MILLBROOK
ETNA
ROLLA
REYNOLDS
WINFIELD
CATO
BELVADERE
HOM
MAPLE VALLEY
DOUGLASS
17
16
15
14
13
12

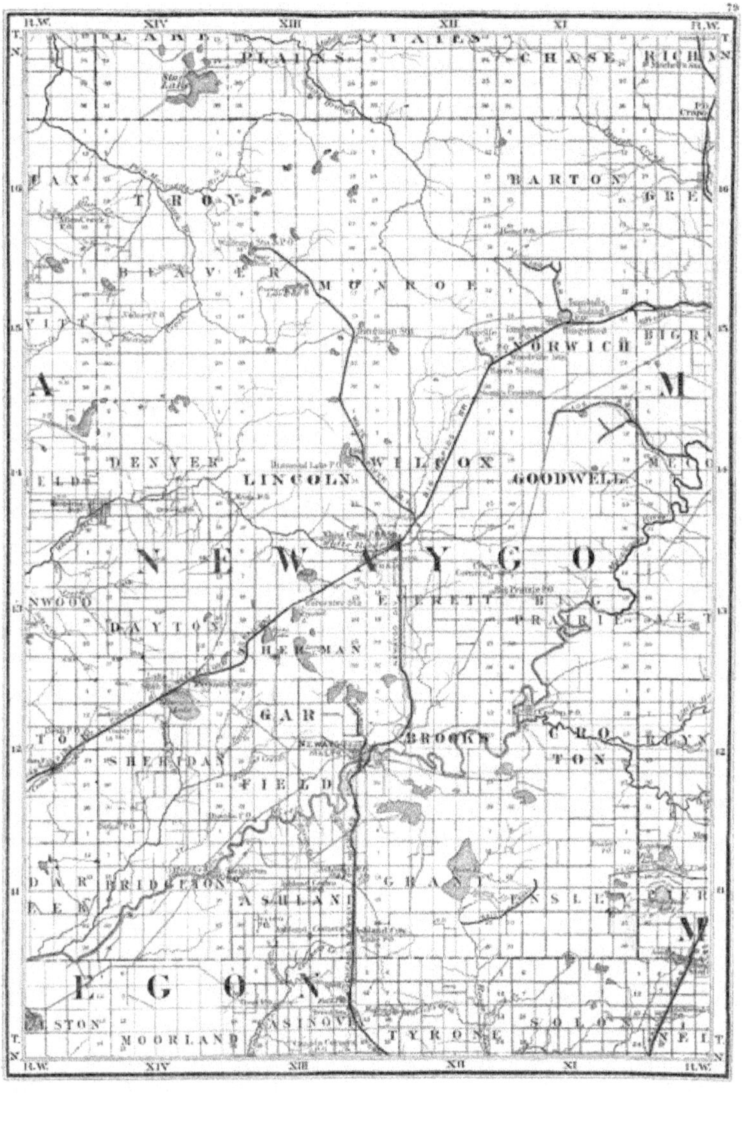
R.W.
XIV
XIII
XII
XI
T.
N.
PLAINS
CHASE
TROY
BARTON
BEAVER
MONROE
NORWICH
DENVER
LINCOLN
WILCOX
GOODWELL
N E W A Y G O
EVERETT
DAYTON
SHERMAN
GAR
FIELD
BROOKS
CRO
TON
SHERIDAN
BRIDGETON
ASHLAND
GRANT
E G O N
MOORLAND
TYRONE
SOLON

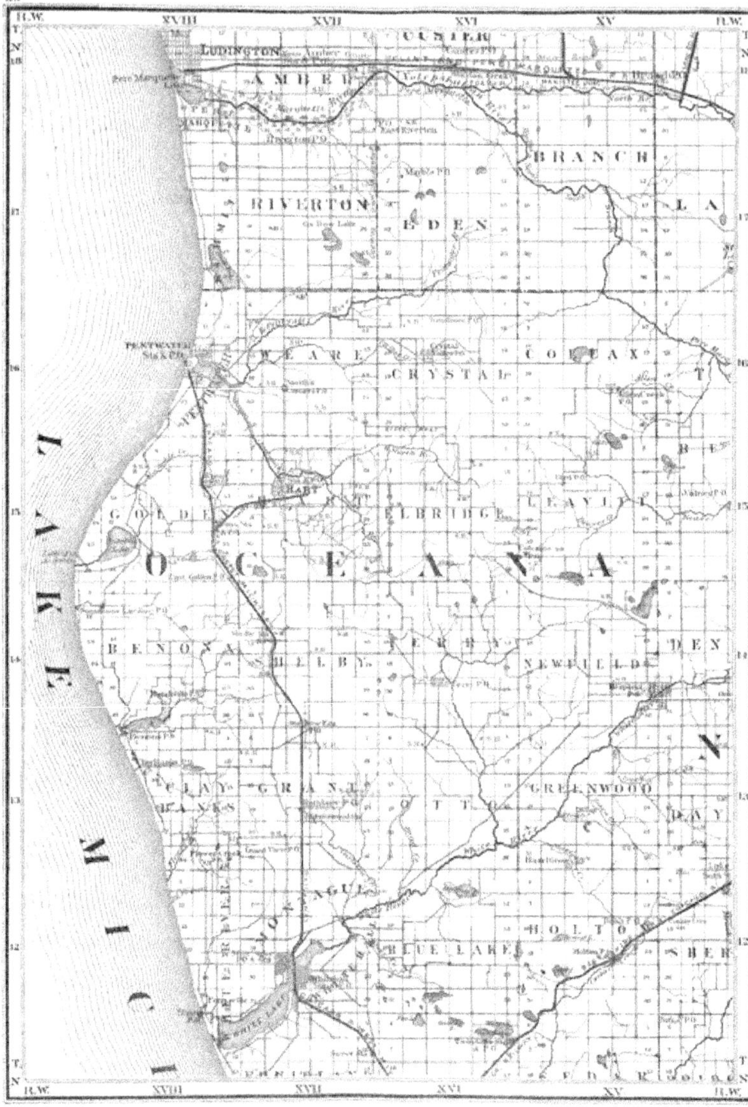
R.W.
XVIII
XVII
XVI
XV
R.W.
T.
N.
18
17
16
15
14
13
12
LUDINGTON
CUSTER
AMBER
RIVERTON
EDEN
BRANCH
WEARE
CRYSTAL
COLFAX
PENTWATER
ELBRIDGE
GOLDEN
O C E A N A
BENONA
SHELBY
NEWFIELD
GREENWOOD
CLAY BANKS
GRANT
OTTO
MONTAGUE
BLUE LAKE
HOLTON
L A K E M I C H I

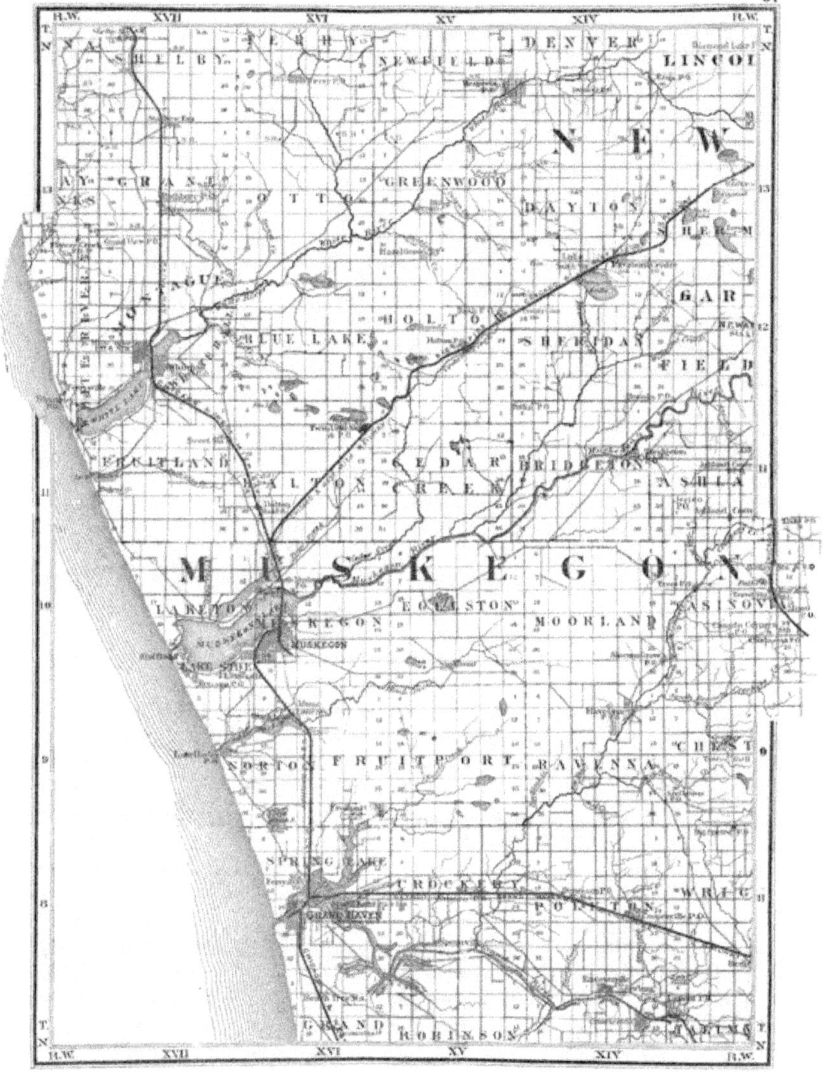
R.W.
XVII
XVI
XV
XIV
T.
N.
SHELBY
NEWFIELD
DENVER
NEW
GRANT
OTTO
GREENWOOD
DAYTON
MONTAGUE
HOLTON
BLUE LAKE
SHERIDAN
FRUITLAND
DALTON
CEDAR
CREEK
BRIDGETON
MUSKEGON
LAKETON
EGLESTON
MOORLAND
NORTON
FRUITPORT
RAVENNA
SPRING LAKE
CROCKERY
POLKTON
GRAND HAVEN
ROBINSON

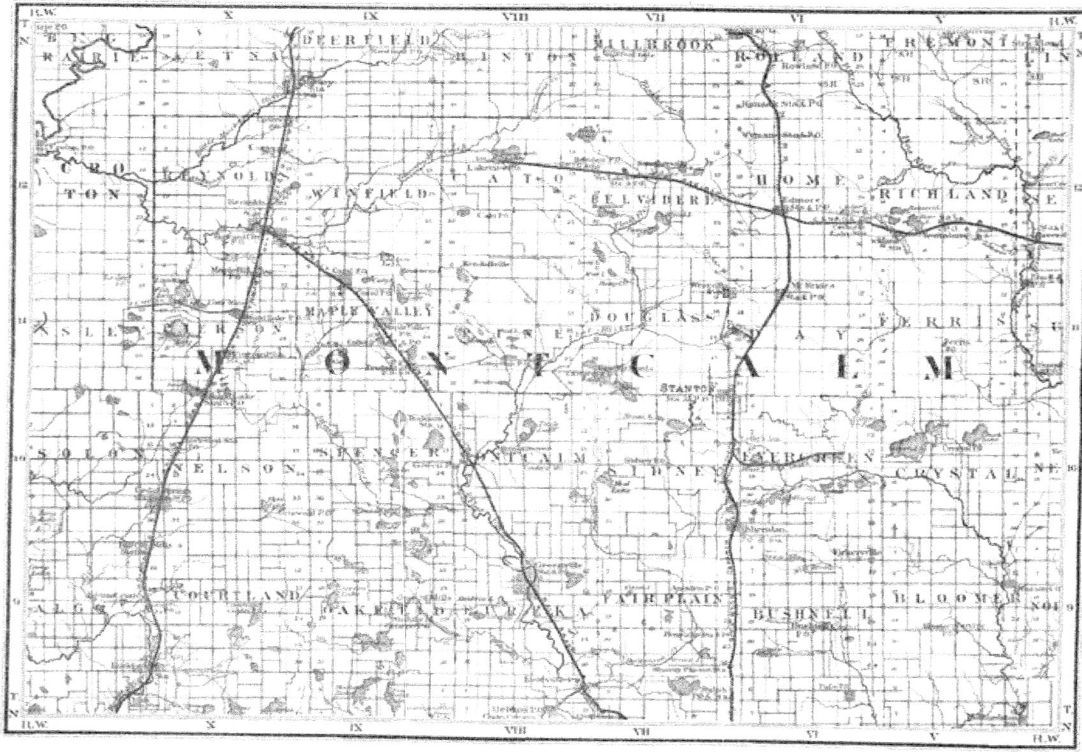
MONTCALM
DEERFIELD
AETNA
PINE
BINTON
HILLBROOK
ROLLAND
FREMONT
HOME
RICHLAND
WINFIELD
CATO
BELVIDERE
MAPLE VALLEY
DOUGLASS
DAY
FERRIS
STANTON
SOLON
NELSON
SPENCER
MONTCALM
SIDNEY
EVERGREEN
CRYSTAL
COURTLAND
OAKFIELD
EUREKA
FAIRPLAIN
BUSHNELL
BLOOMER
TON
R.W.
X
IX
VIII
VII
VI
V

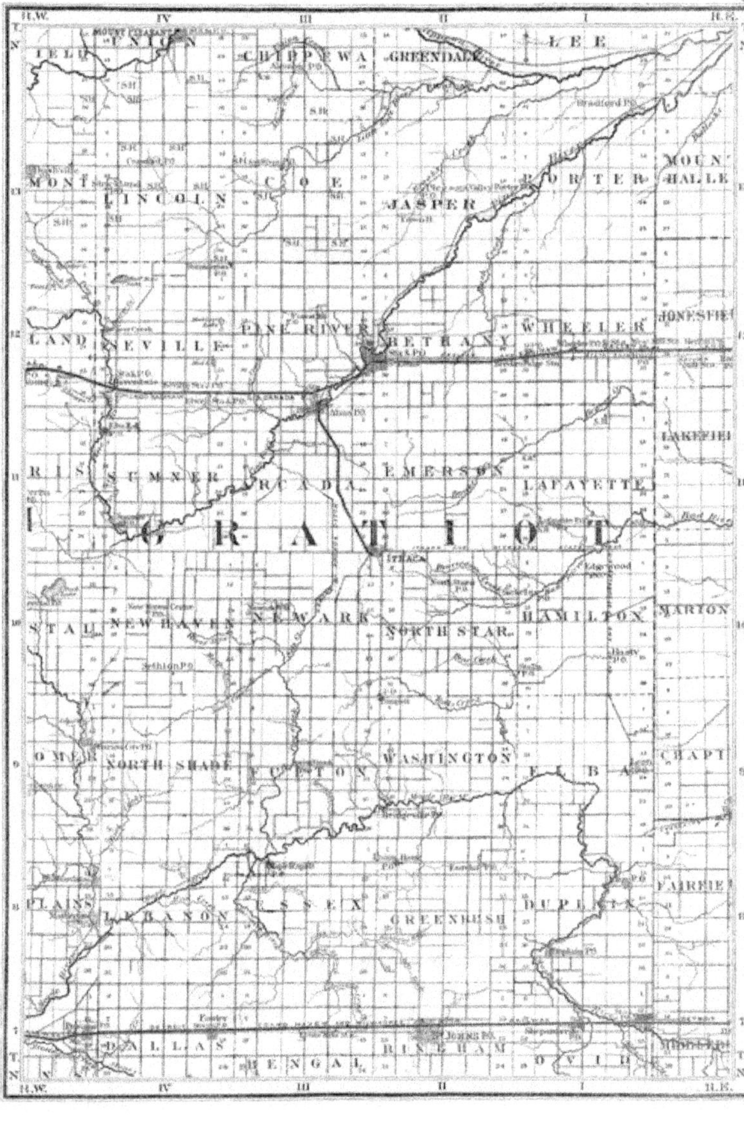
G R A T I O T
CHIPPEWA
GREENDALE
LEE
UNION
C O E
LINCOLN
JASPER
PORTER
PINE RIVER
BETHANY
WHEELER
NEVILLE
SUMNER
ARCADA
EMERSON
LAFAYETTE
NEWHAVEN
NEWARK
NORTH STAR
HAMILTON
MARION
NORTH SHADE
FULTON
WASHINGTON
ELBA
LEBANON
ESSEX
GREENBUSH
DUPLAIN
DALLAS
BENGAL
BINGHAM
OVID
ITHACA
R.W.
R.E.
IV
III
II
I

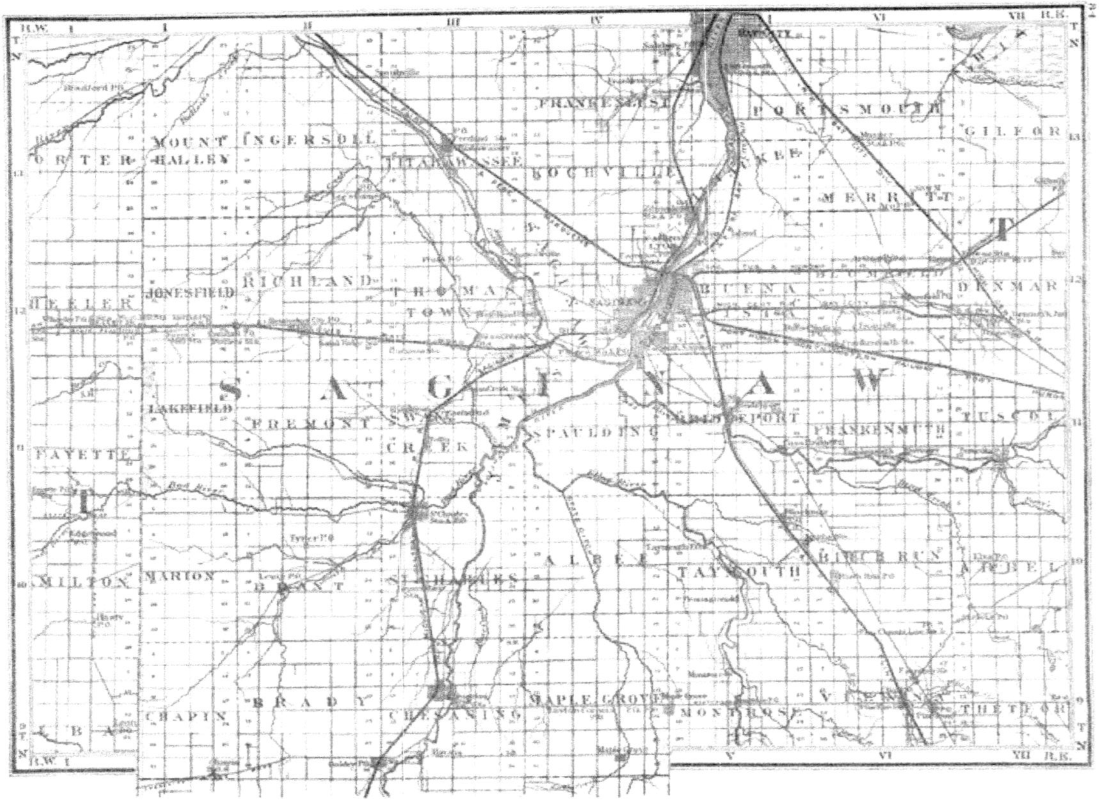
S A G I N A W
MOUNT
HALLEY
INGERSOLL
TITTABAWASSEE
FRANKENLUST
PORTSMOUTH
GILFORD
ZILWAUKEE
KOCHVILLE
MERRITT
JONESFIELD
RICHLAND
THOMAS
TOWN
BUENA VISTA
BLUMFIELD
DENMARK
LAKEFIELD
FREMONT
SWAN CREEK
SPAULDING
BRIDGEPORT
FRANKENMUTH
TUSCOLA
FAYETTE
MILTON
MARION
BRANT
ST. CHARLES
ALBEE
TAYMOUTH
BIRCH RUN
ARBELA
CHAPIN
BRADY
CHESANING
MAPLE GROVE
MONTROSE
VIENNA
THETFORD
BAY CITY
R.W.
R.E.
T
N

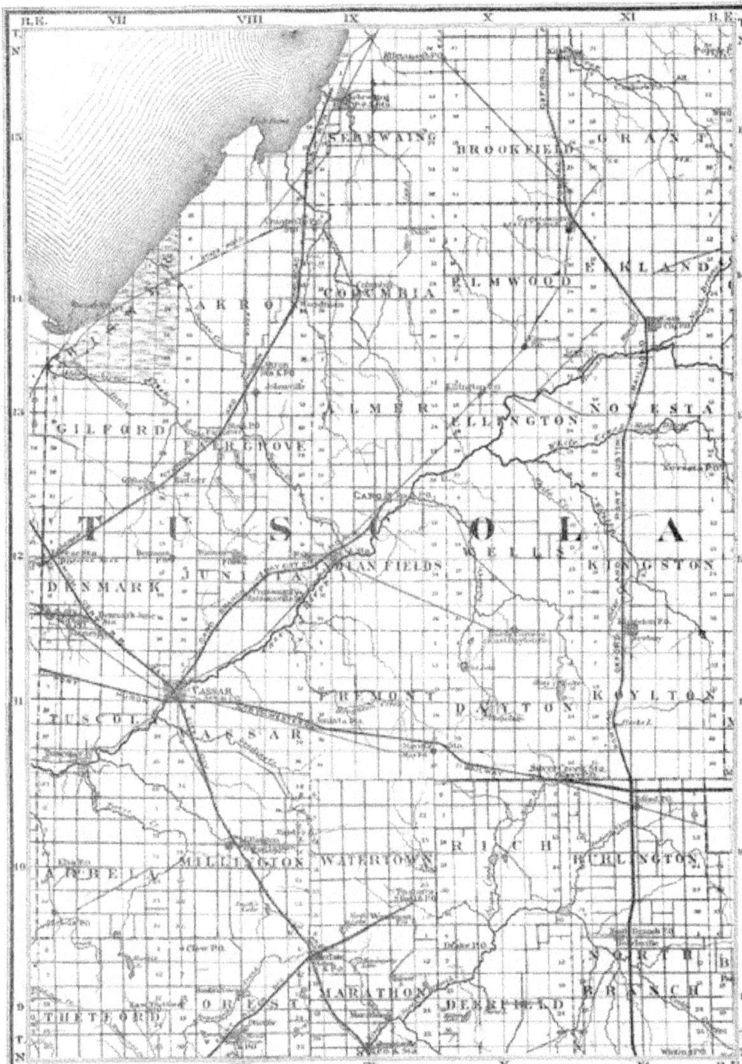
R.E.
VII
VIII
IX
X
XI
R.E.
T.
N
15
14
13
12
11
10
9
T
N
TUSCOLA
SEBEWAING
BROOKFIELD
GRANT
ELKLAND
ELMWOOD
COLUMBIA
AKRON
ALMER
ELLINGTON
NOVESTA
GILFORD
FAIRGROVE
WELLS
KINGSTON
DENMARK
JUNIATA
INDIANFIELDS
VASSAR
FREMONT
DAYTON
KOYLTON
TUSCOLA
RICH
BURLINGTON
MILLINGTON
WATERTOWN
ARBELA
NORTH
BRANCH
MARATHON
DEERFIELD
FOREST
THETFORD
Novesta P.O.
Caro
Clear P.O.

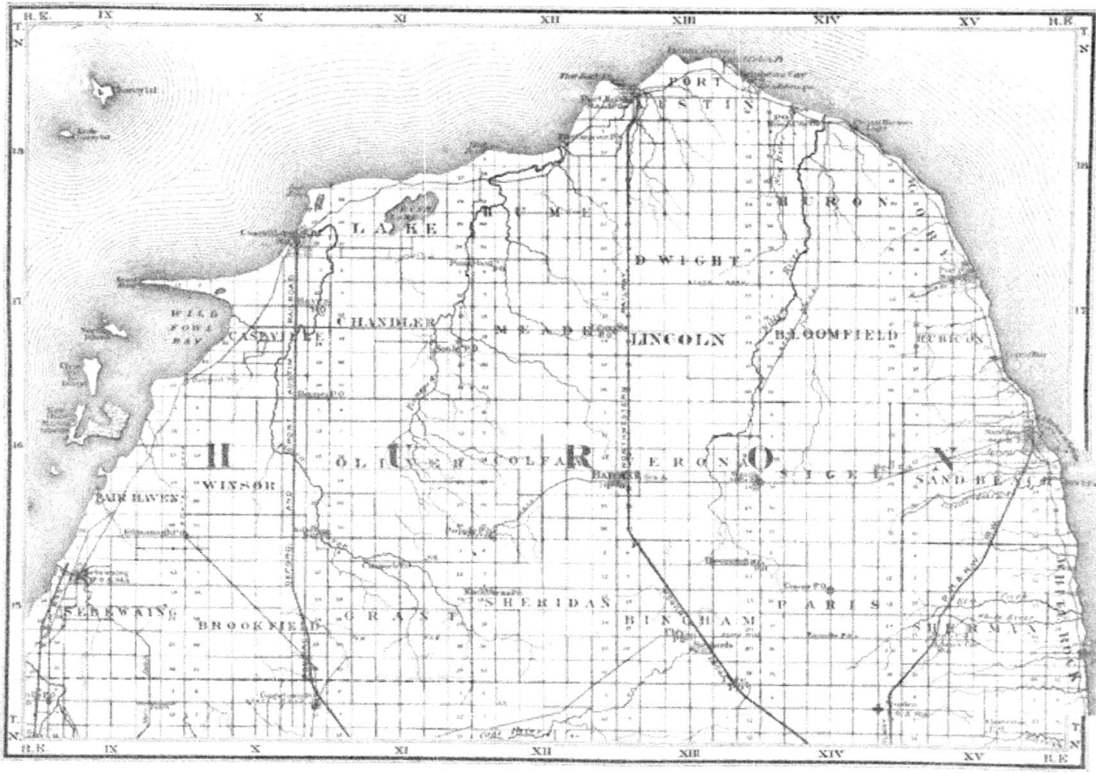
HURON
PORT AUSTIN
HUME
LAKE
DWIGHT
CHANDLER
MEADE
LINCOLN
BLOOMFIELD
HURON
GORE
WILD FOWL BAY
CASEVILLE
WINSOR
OLIVER
COLFAX
VERONA
SIGEL
SAND BEACH
FAIR HAVEN
SEBEWAING
BROOKFIELD
GRANT
SHERIDAN
BINGHAM
PARIS
SHERMAN
RUBICON
WHITE ROCK
R.E.
IX
X
XI
XII
XIII
XIV
XV
T.
N.
18
17
16
15

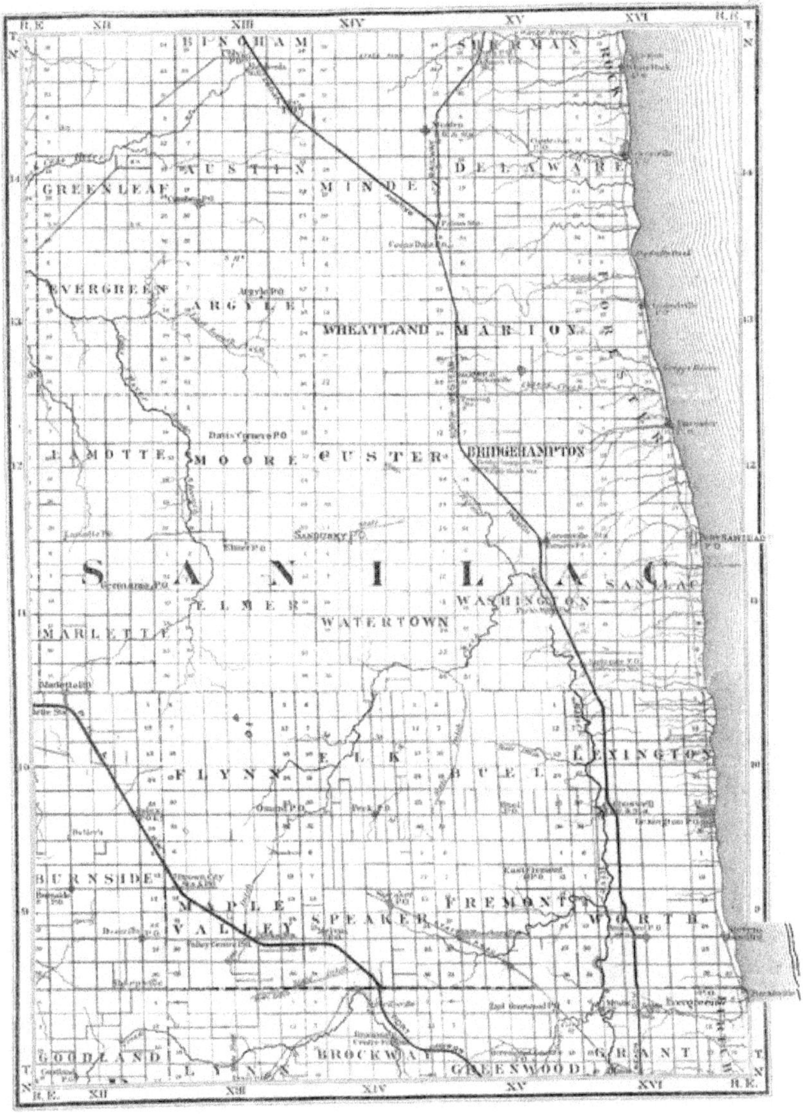
R.E.
XII
XIII
XIV
XV
XVI
T.
N.
BINGHAM
SHERMAN
AUSTIN
MINDEN
DELAWARE
GREENLEAF
EVERGREEN
ARGYLE
WHEATLAND
MARION
LAMOTTE
MOORE
CUSTER
BRIDGEHAMPTON
SANILAC
ELMER
WASHINGTON
WATERTOWN
MARLETTE
FLYNN
ELK
BUEL
LEXINGTON
BURNSIDE
MAPLE
VALLEY
SPEAKER
FREMONT
WORTH
GOODLAND
LYNN
BROCKWAY
GREENWOOD
GRANT
14
13
12
11
10
9

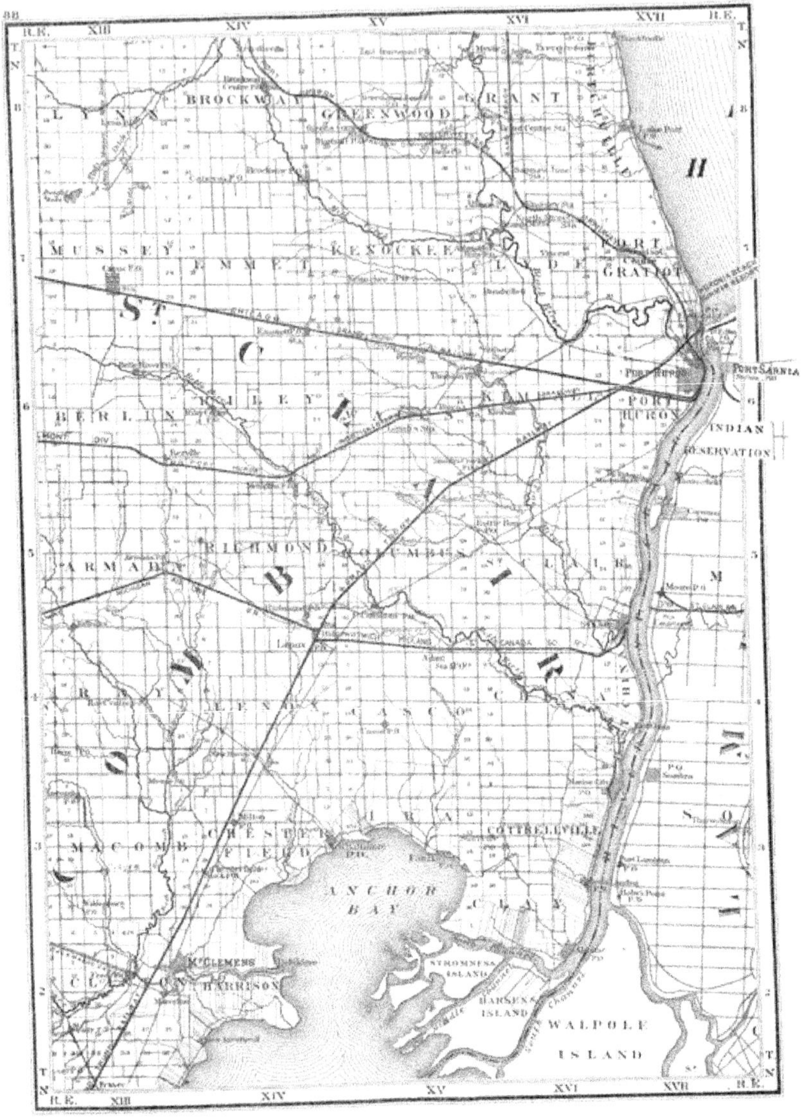
R.E.
XIII
XIV
XV
XVI
XVII
T
N
BROCKWAY
GREENWOOD
GRANT
LYNN
MUSSEY
EMMET
KENOCKEE
CLYDE
PORT GRATIOT
PORT SARNIA
PORT HURON
INDIAN RESERVATION
BERLIN
RILEY
RICHMOND
COLUMBUS
ARMADA
CASCO
IRA
CHESTERFIELD
MACOMB
COTTRELLVILLE
ANCHOR BAY
CLAY
MT CLEMENS
HARRISON
STROMNESS ISLAND
HARSENS ISLAND
WALPOLE ISLAND

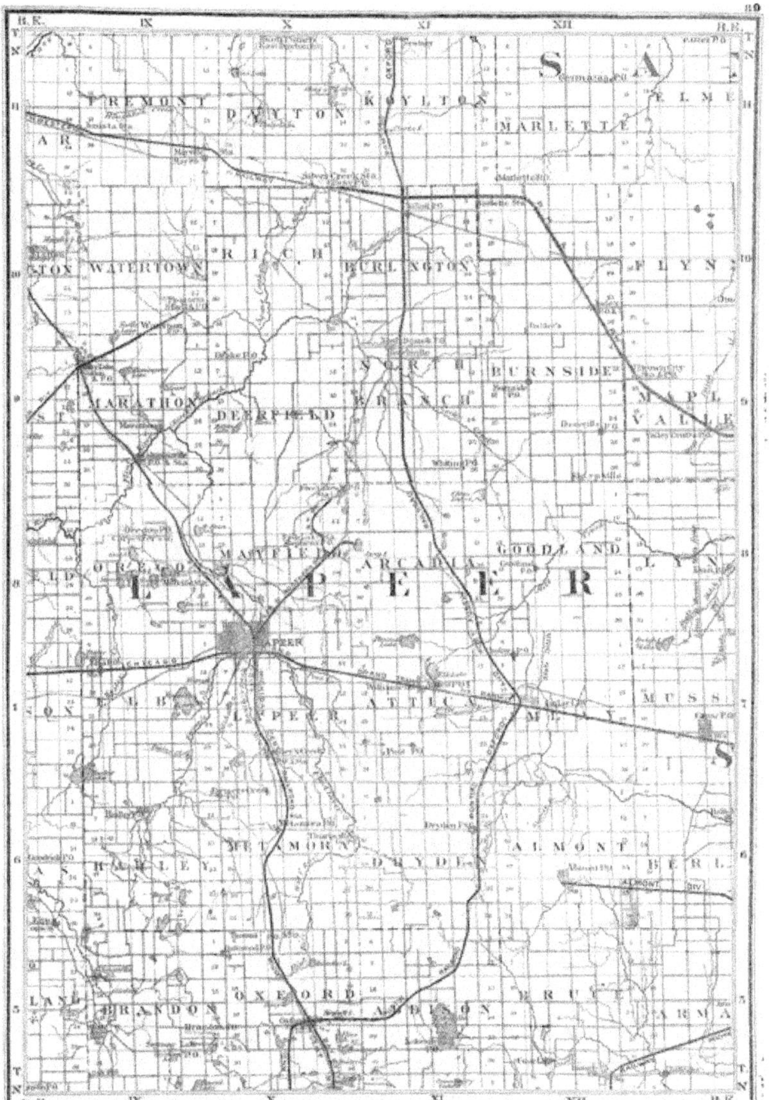
LAPEER
FREMONT
DAYTON
KOYLTON
MARLETTE
RICH
BURLINGTON
WATERTOWN
FLYNN
NORTH BRANCH
BURNSIDE
MARATHON
DEERFIELD
MAYFIELD
ARCADIA
GOODLAND
OREGON
ELBA
LAPEER
ATTICA
METAMORA
DRYDEN
ALMONT
HADLEY
OXFORD
ADDISON
BRANDON
BRUCE
ARMADA
IX
X
XI
XII
R.E.
T.N.

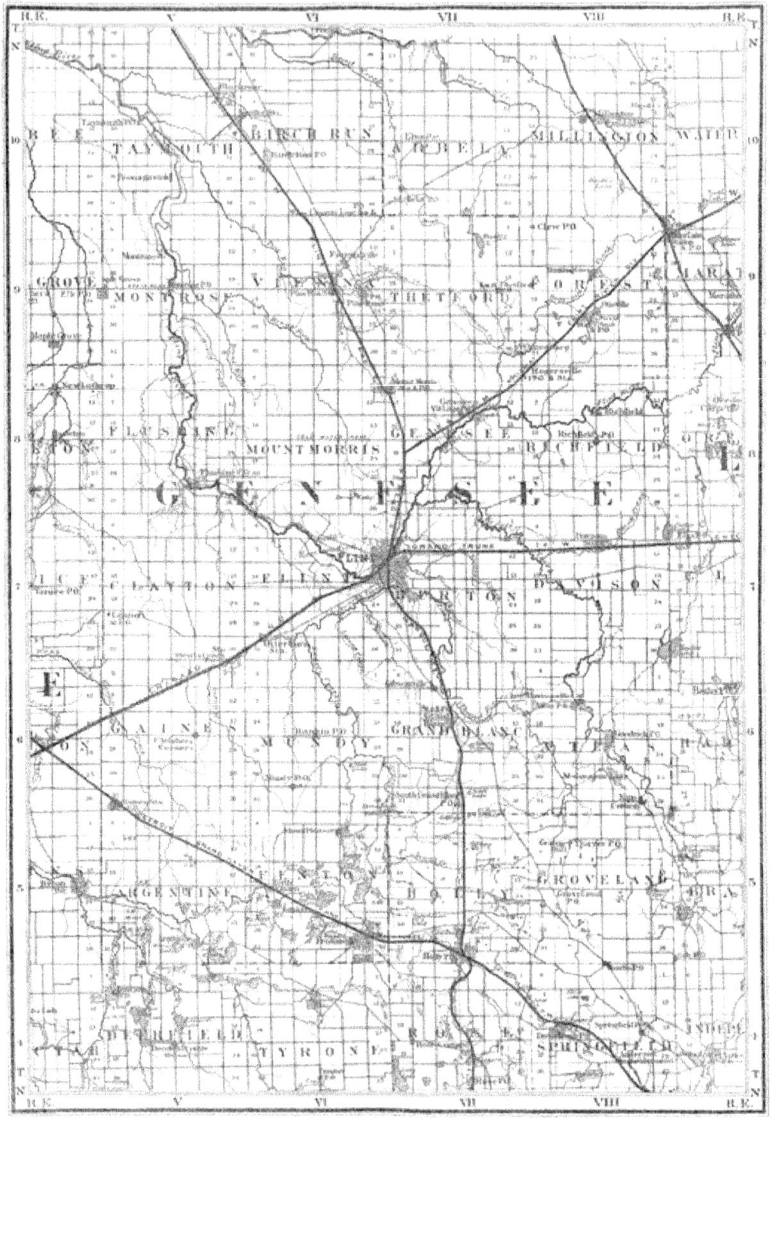
GENESEE
TAYMOUTH
BIRCH RUN
VIENNA
THETFORD
MONTROSE
MOUNT MORRIS
RICHFIELD
CLAYTON
FLINT
BURTON
MUNDY
GRAND BLANC
ARGENTINE
GROVELAND
TYRONE
SPRINGFIELD

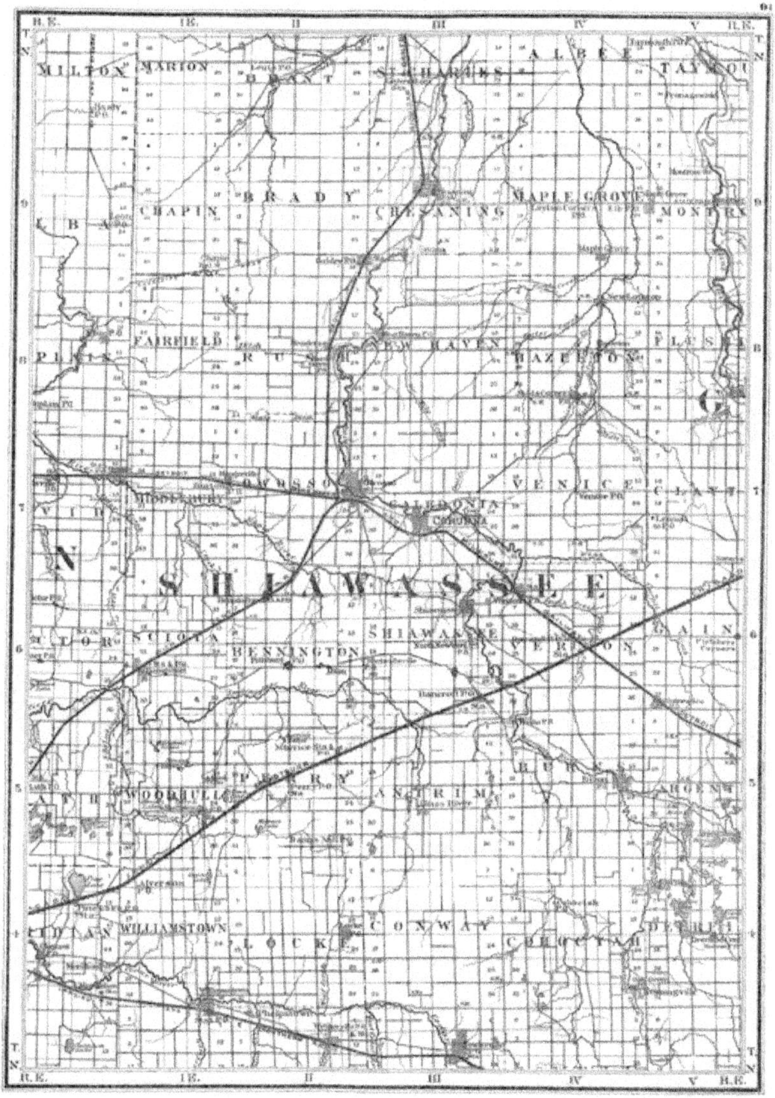

MILTON
MARION
BRANT
ST. CHARLES
BRADY
CHAPIN
CHESANING
MAPLE GROVE
FAIRFIELD
RUSH
NEW HAVEN
HAZELTON
OWOSSO
MIDDLEBURY
CALEDONIA
CORUNNA
VENICE
SHIAWASSEE
SCIOTA
BENNINGTON
VERNON
PERRY
WOODHULL
ANTRIM
WILLIAMSTOWN
LOCKE
CONWAY
COHOCTAH

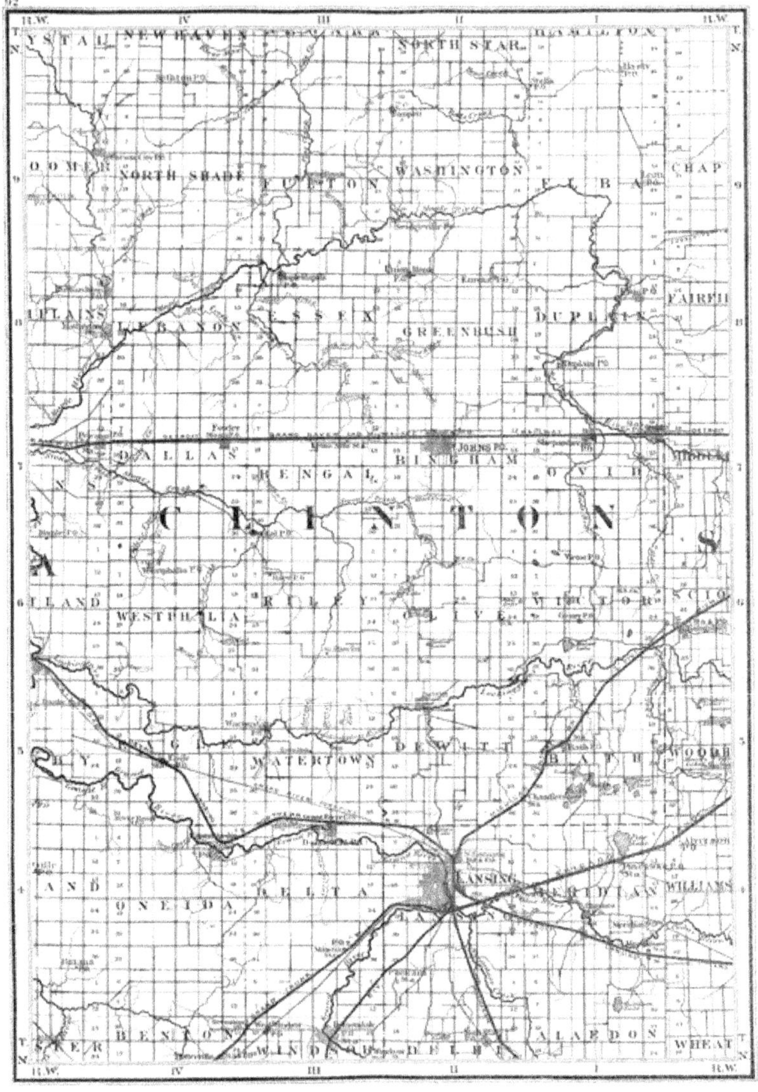
R.W.
IV
III
II
I
NORTH STAR
NORTH SHADE
WASHINGTON
LEBANON
GREENBUSH
DALLAS
BINGHAM
C L I N T O N
WESTPHALIA
WATERTOWN
LANSING
ONEIDA
WILLIAMS
WHEAT

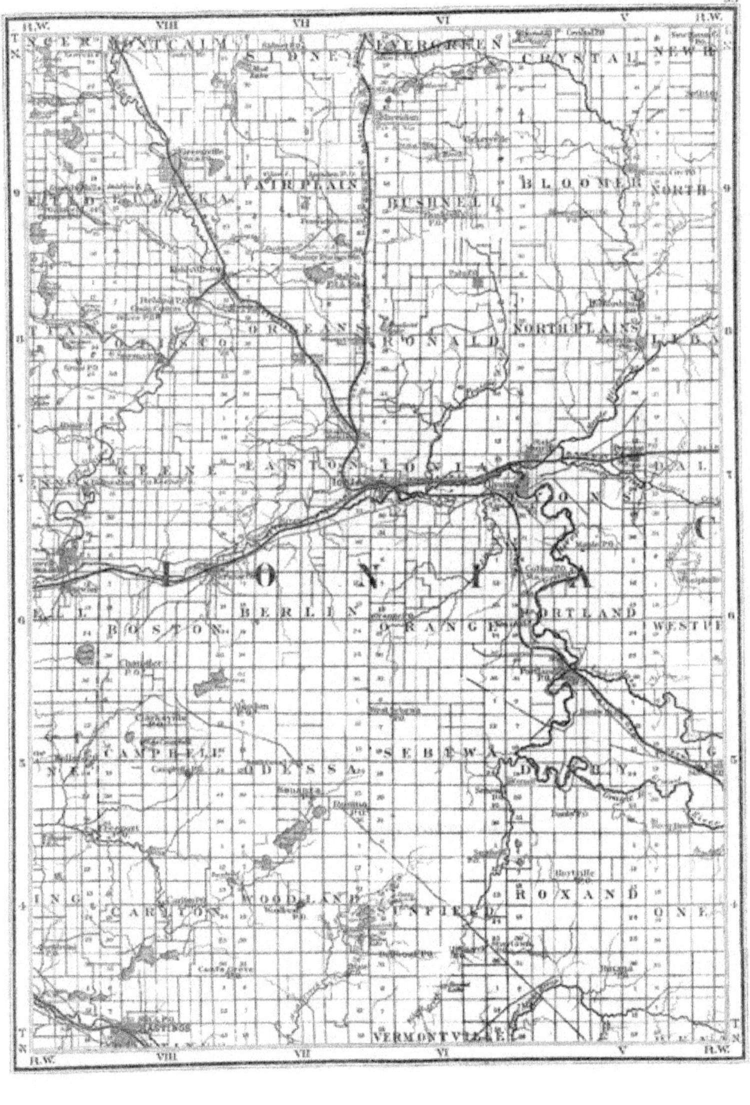
R.W.
VIII
VII
VI
V
R.W.
MONTCALM
SIDNEY
EVERGREEN
CRYSTAL
FAIRPLAIN
BUSHNELL
BLOOMER
NORTH
ORLEANS
RONALD
NORTHPLAINS
KEENE
EASTON
IONIA
I O N I A
BERLIN
BOSTON
ORANGE
PORTLAND
CAMPBELL
ODESSA
SEBEWA
WOODLAND
SUNFIELD
ROXAND
CARLTON
VERMONTVILLE
HASTINGS

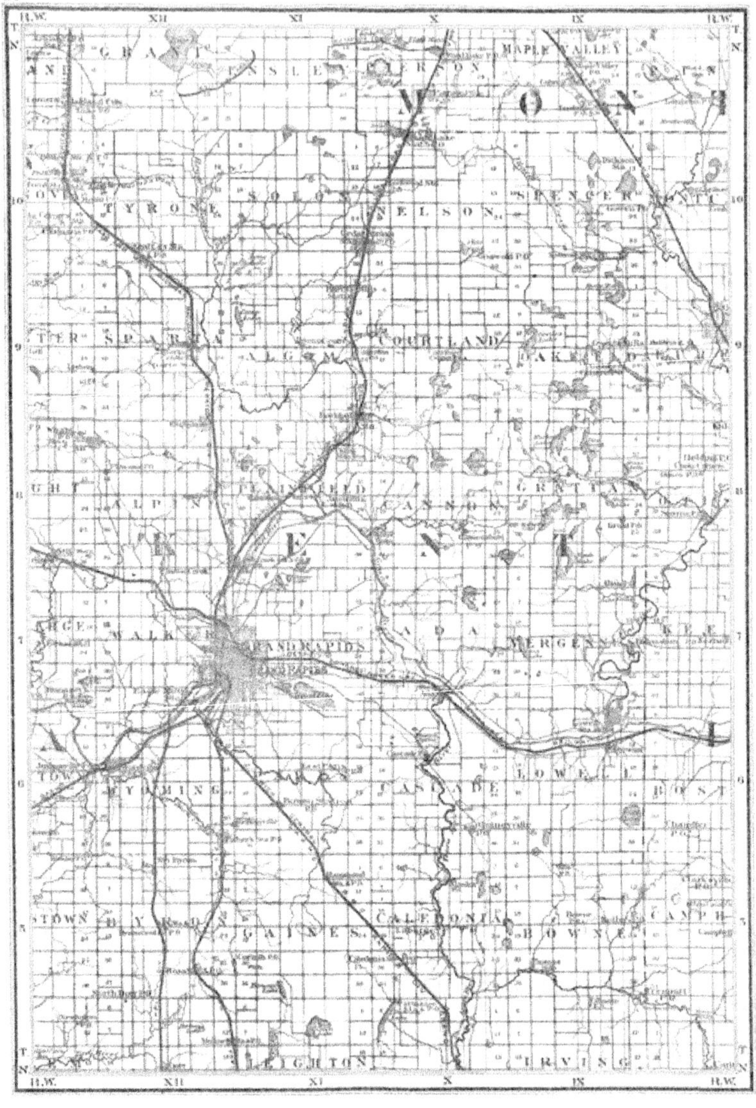
R.W.
XII
XI
X
IX
R.W.
T.
N.
10
9
8
7
6
5
GRANT
MAPLE VALLEY
TYRONE
NELSON
SPARTA
COURTLAND
ALPINE
CANNON
WALKER
GRAND RAPIDS
ADA
WYOMING
CASCADE
LOWELL
CALEDONIA
LEIGHTON
IRVING

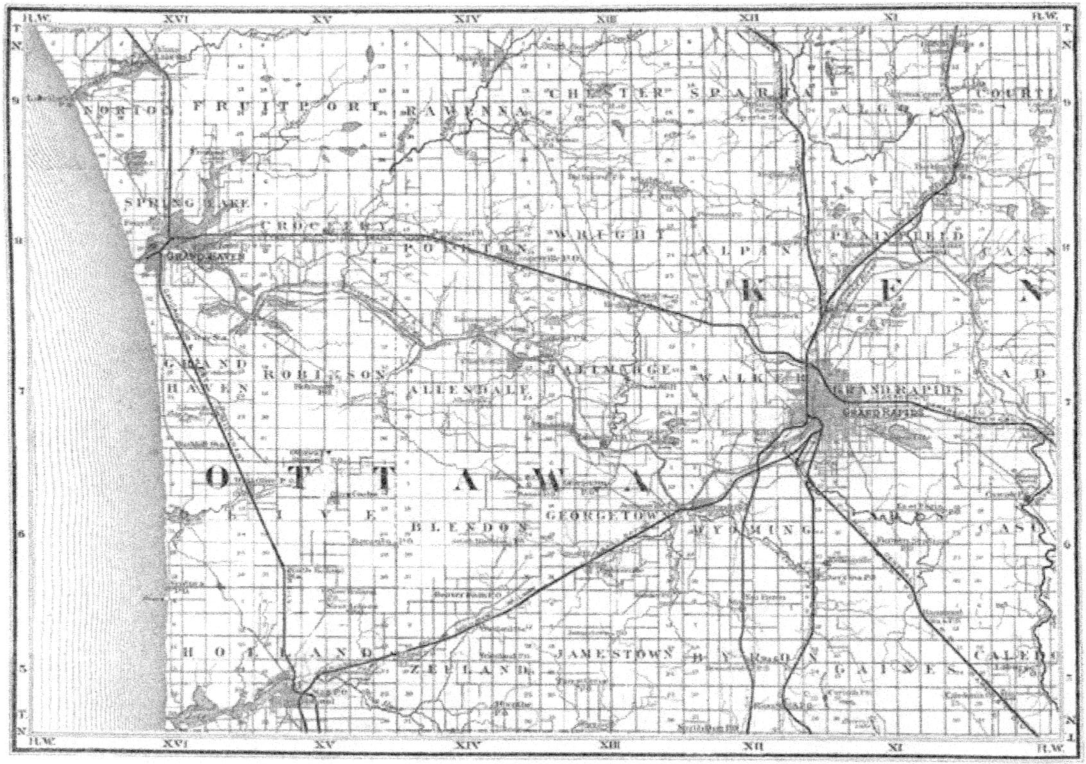
R.W.
XVI
XV
XIV
XIII
XII
XI
T.
N.
9
8
7
6
5
NORTON
FRUITPORT
RAVENNA
CHESTER
SPARTA
ALGOMA
COURTL
SPRING LAKE
CROCKERY
POLKTON
WRIGHT
ALPINE
PLAINFIELD
CANN
GRAND HAVEN
K
E
N
GRAND
HAVEN
ROBINSON
ALLENDALE
TALLMADGE
WALKER
GRAND RAPIDS
O
T
T
A
W
A
OLIVE
BLENDON
GEORGETOWN
WYOMING
CASC
HOLLAND
ZEELAND
JAMESTOWN
BYRON
GAINES
CALED

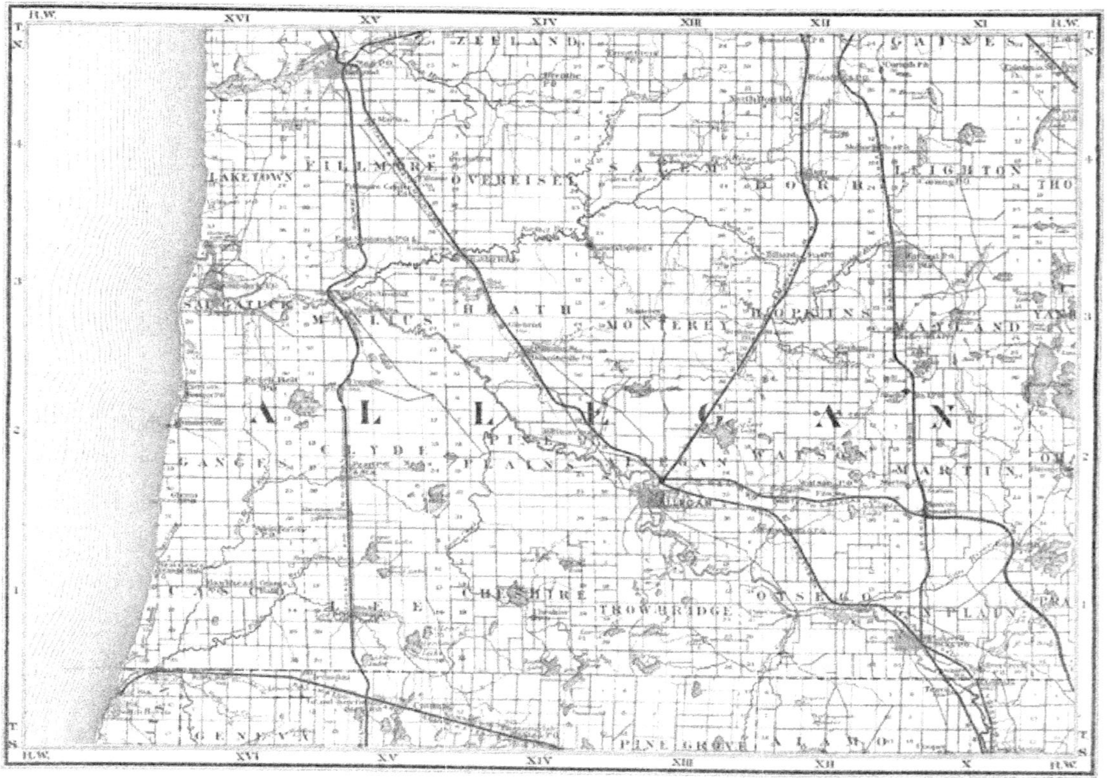
R.W.
XVI
XV
XIV
XIII
XII
XI
X
T.
N.
S.
4
3
2
1
ZEELAND
GAINES
FILLMORE
SALEM
DORR
LEIGHTON
THO
LAKETOWN
MANLIUS
HEATH
MONTEREY
HOPKINS
WAYLAND
ALLEGAN
CLYDE
WATSON
MARTIN
GANGES
LEE
CHESHIRE
TROWBRIDGE
OTSEGO
GENEVA
PINE GROVE
ALAMO

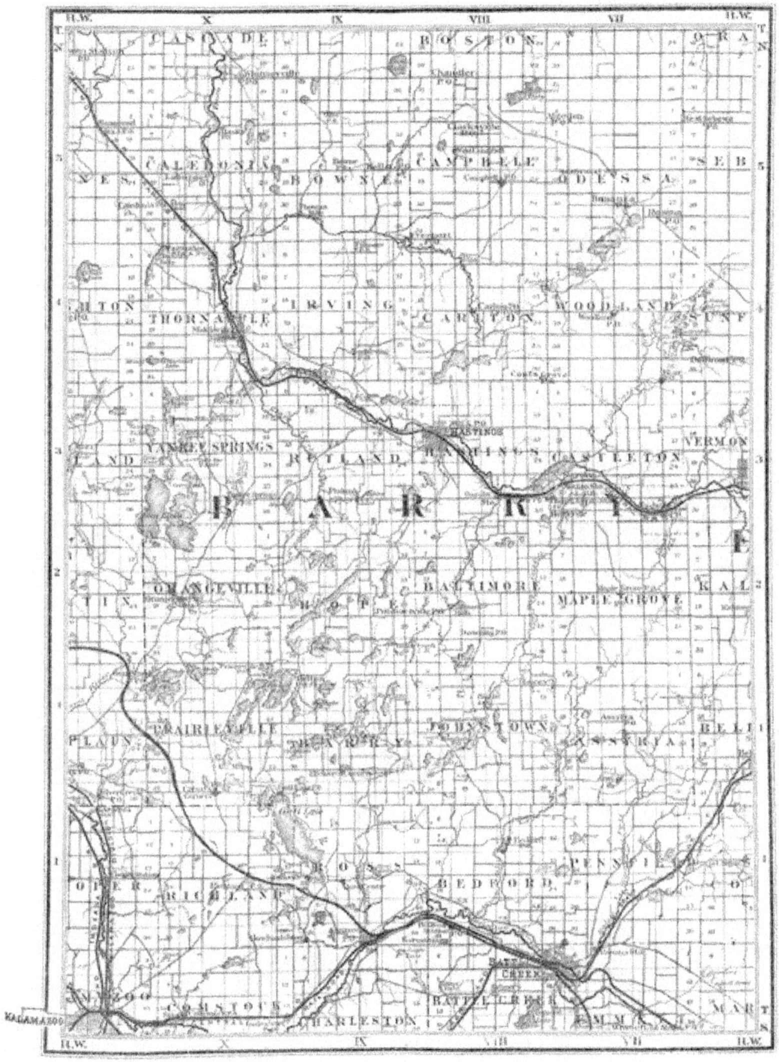
CASCADE
BOSTON
CALEDONIA
BOWNE
CAMPBELL
ODESSA
THORNAPPLE
IRVING
CARLTON
WOODLAND
YANKEE SPRINGS
RUTLAND
HASTINGS
CASTLETON
VERMON
B A R R Y
ORANGEVILLE
HOPE
BALTIMORE
MAPLE GROVE
PRAIRIEVILLE
BARRY
JOHNSTOWN
ASSYRIA
ROSS
BEDFORD
PENNFIELD
RICHLAND
COMSTOCK
CHARLESTON
BATTLE CREEK
EMMETT
KALAMAZOO
R.W.
X
IX
VIII
VII
T.
N.
S.

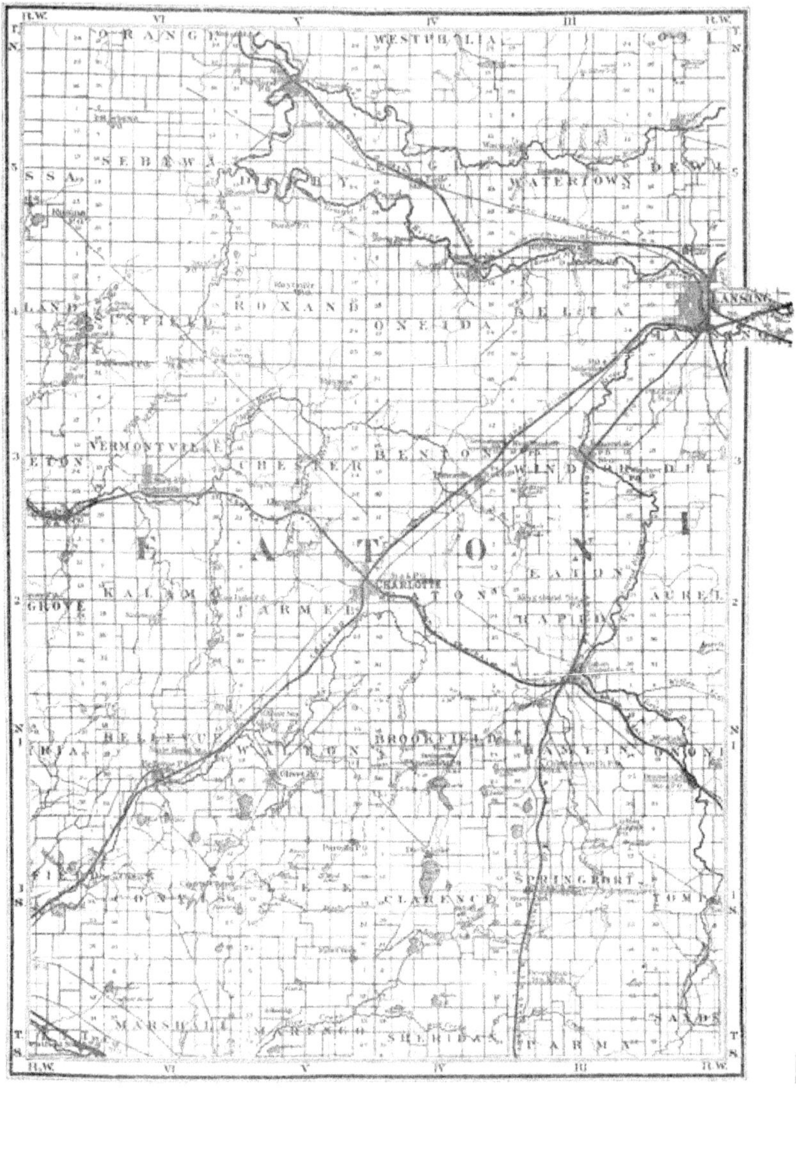
R.W.
VI
V
IV
III
R.W.
ORANGE
WESTPHALIA
SEBEWA
WATERTOWN
ROXAND
ONEIDA
DELTA
LANSING
VERMONTVILLE
CHESTER
BENTON
EATON
CHARLOTTE
CARMEL
GROVE
BELLEVUE
BROOKFIELD
SPRINGPORT
CLARENCE
MARSHALL
SHERIDAN
PARMA
R.W.
VI
V
IV
III
R.W.

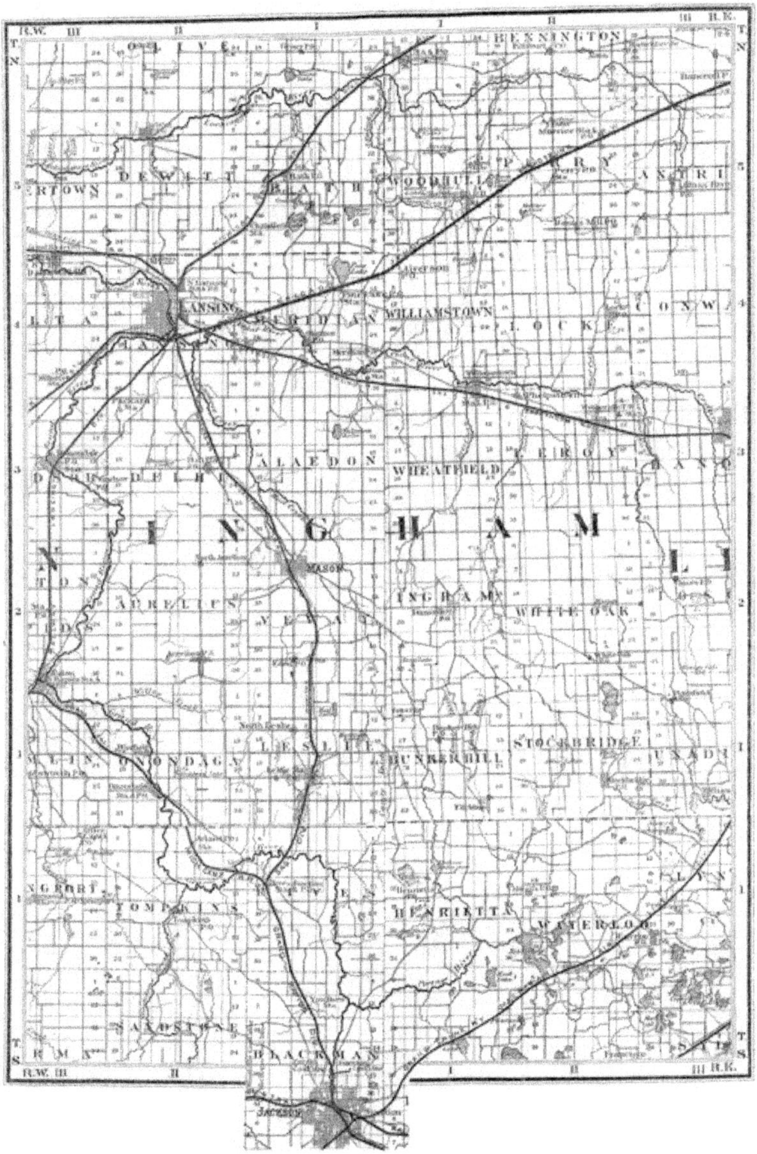
BENNINGTON
DEWITT
BATH
WOODHULL
LANSING
MERIDIAN
WILLIAMSTOWN
LOCKE
ALAEDON
WHEATFIELD
DELHI
I N G H A M
MASON
AURELIUS
INGHAM
WHITE OAK
LESLIE
ONONDAGA
BUNKERHILL
STOCKBRIDGE
TOMPKINS
HENRIETTA
WATERLOO
SANDSTONE
BLACKMAN
JACKSON

LIVINGSTON
CONWAY
TYRONE
ANTRIM
MUNDY
IOSCO
MARION
BRIGHTON
PUTNAM
WEBSTER
DEXTER
NORTHFIELD
LIMA

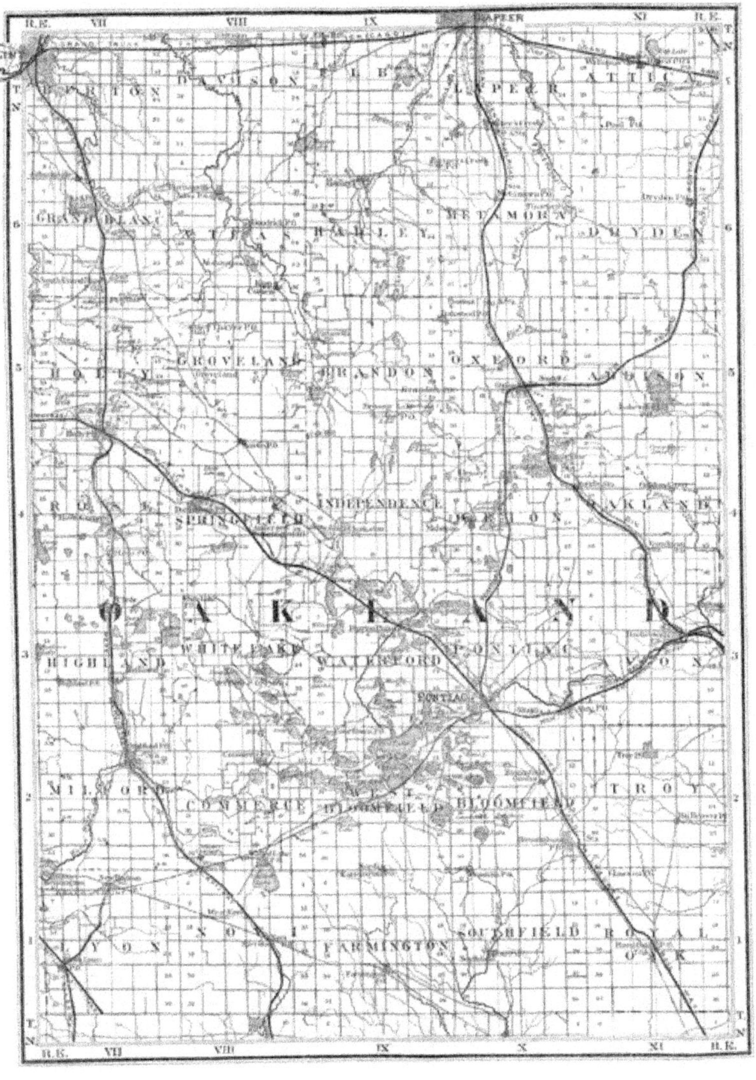
OAKLAND
DAVISON
LAPEER
ATTICA
GRAND BLANC
METAMORA
DRYDEN
HOLLY
GROVELAND
BRANDON
OXFORD
ADDISON
INDEPENDENCE
SPRINGFIELD
ORION
HIGHLAND
WHITE LAKE
WATERFORD
PONTIAC
MILFORD
COMMERCE
WEST BLOOMFIELD
BLOOMFIELD
TROY
LYON
NOVI
FARMINGTON
SOUTHFIELD
ROYAL OAK

L A K
S T C L A

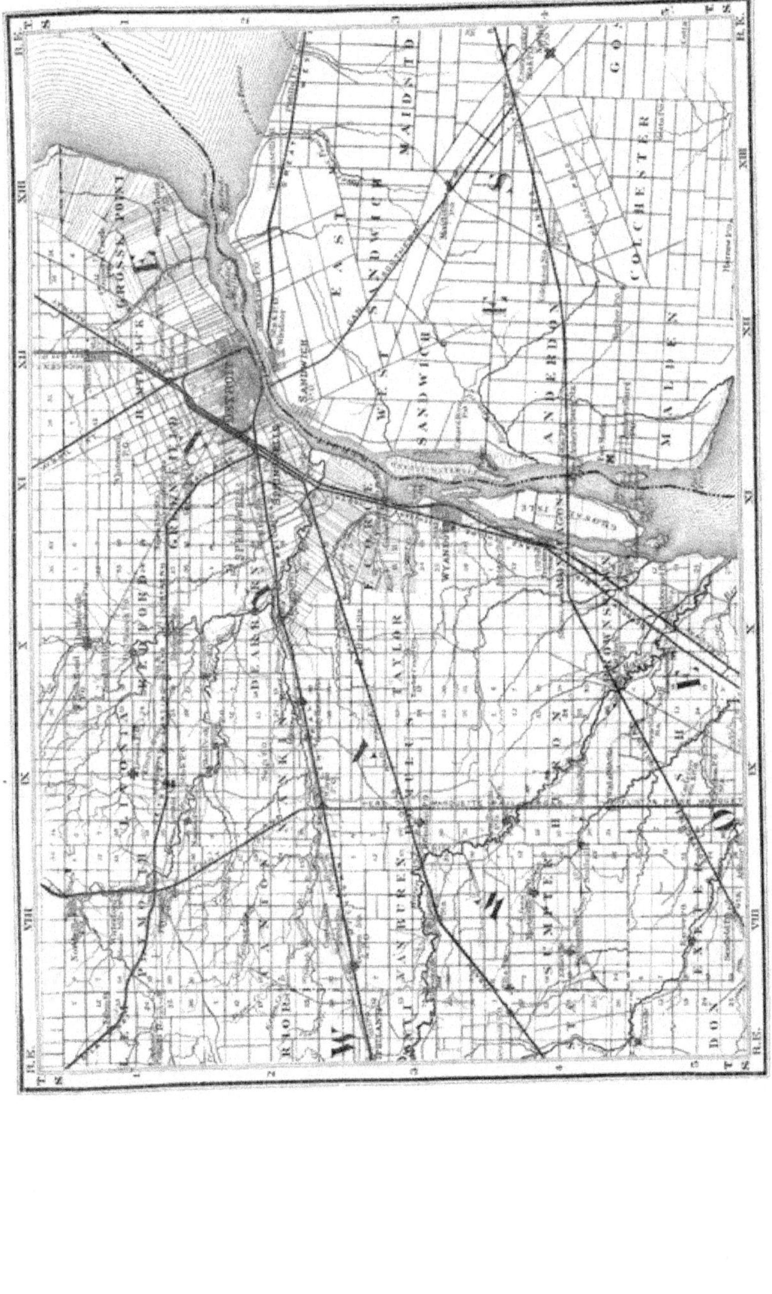
GROSSE POINT
EAST
SANDWICH
MAIDSTONE
COLCHESTER
WEST
SANDWICH
ANDERDON
MALDEN
TAYLOR
VAN BUREN
DEARBORN
SUMPTER
NANKIN
CANTON
LIVONIA
REDFORD
GREENFIELD
BROWNSTOWN

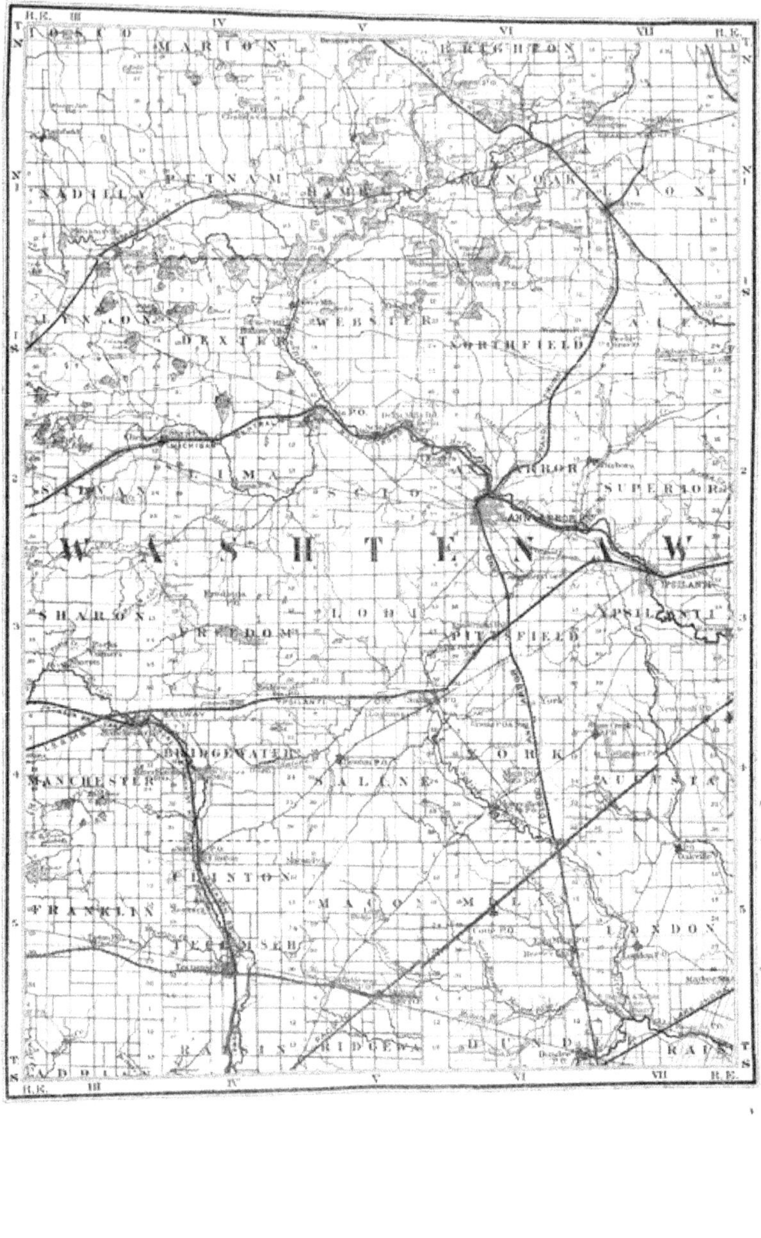
R.E. III
IV
V
VI
VII
R.E.
MARION
BRIGHTON
PUTNAM
LYON
DEXTER
WEBSTER
NORTHFIELD
LIMA
SCIO
ANN ARBOR
SUPERIOR
W A S H T E N A W
SHARON
LODI
PITTSFIELD
YPSILANTI
BRIDGEWATER
MANCHESTER
SALINE
YORK
AUGUSTA
CLINTON
FRANKLIN
MACON
LONDON
TECUMSEH
RAISIN
DUNDEE

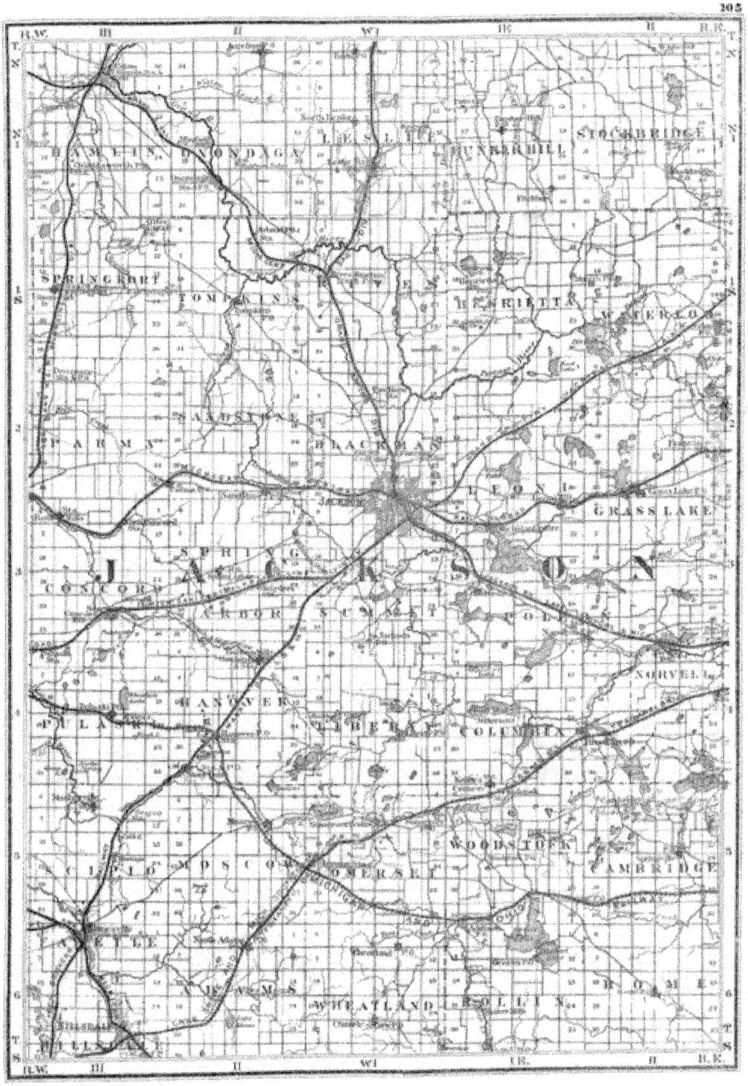
JACKSON
LESLIE
STOCKBRIDGE
HAMLIN
SPRINGPORT
TOMPKINS
HENRIETTA
SANDSTONE
BLACKMAN
PARMA
GRASS LAKE
SPRING
ARBOR
SUMMIT
CONCORD
HANOVER
COLUMBIA
WOODSTOCK
CAMBRIDGE
MOSCOW
WHEATLAND
ROME
R.W.
R.E.

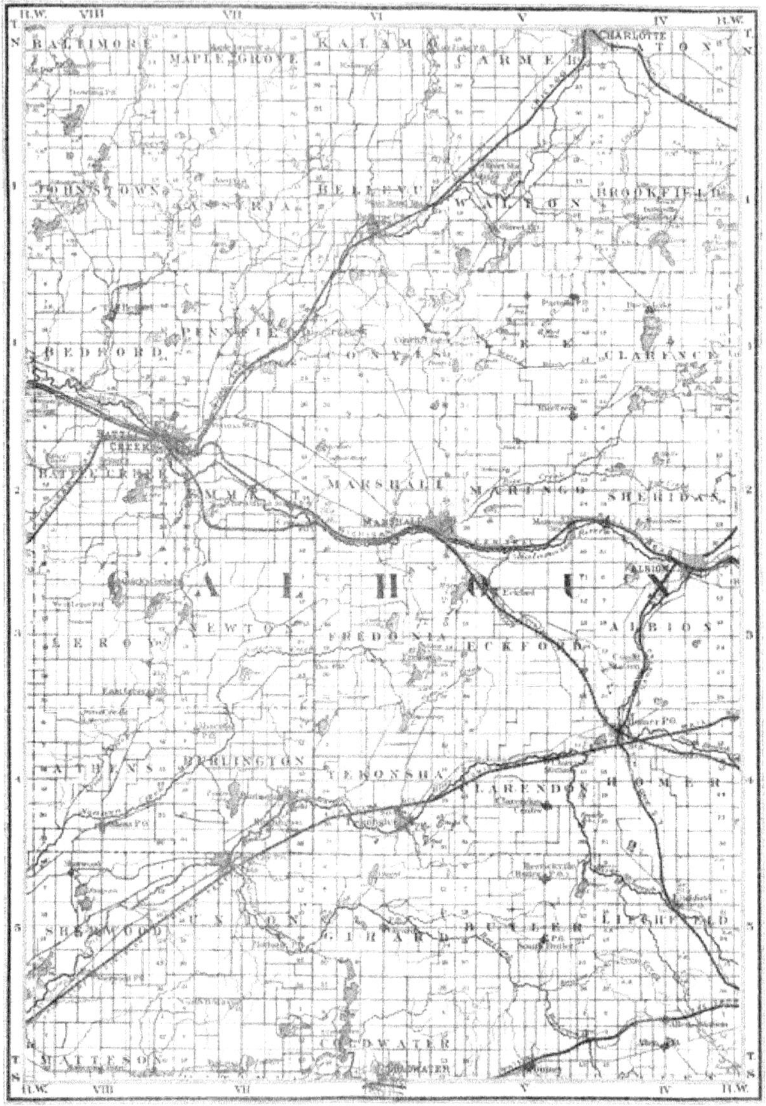
R.W.
VIII
VII
VI
V
IV
R.W.
T.
N
CHARLOTTE
BALTIMORE
MAPLE GROVE
KALAMO
CARMEL
EATON
JOHNSTOWN
ASSYRIA
BELLEVUE
WALTON
BROOKFIELD
BEDFORD
CONVIS
CLARENCE
BATTLE CREEK
MARSHALL
MARENGO
SHERIDAN
ALBION
NEWTON
FREDONIA
ECKFORD
ALBION
BURLINGTON
TEKONSHA
HOMER
LITCHFIELD
COLDWATER
T.
S

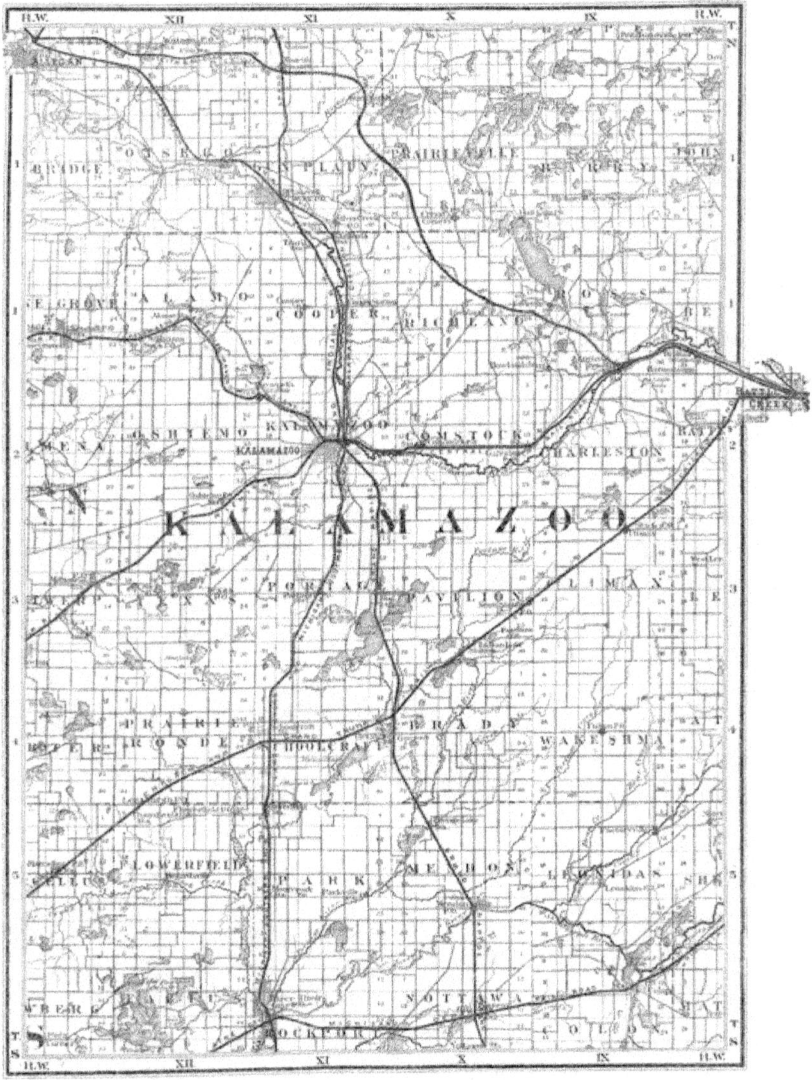

R.W.
XII
XI
X
IX
K A L A M A Z O O
OSHTEMO
KALAMAZOO
COMSTOCK
CHARLESTON
RICHLAND
COOPER
ALAMO
PORTAGE
PAVILION
TEXAS
PRAIRIE
RONDE
BRADY
WAKESHMA
PARK
LEONIDAS
NOTTAWA
PRAIRIEVILLE
BARRY

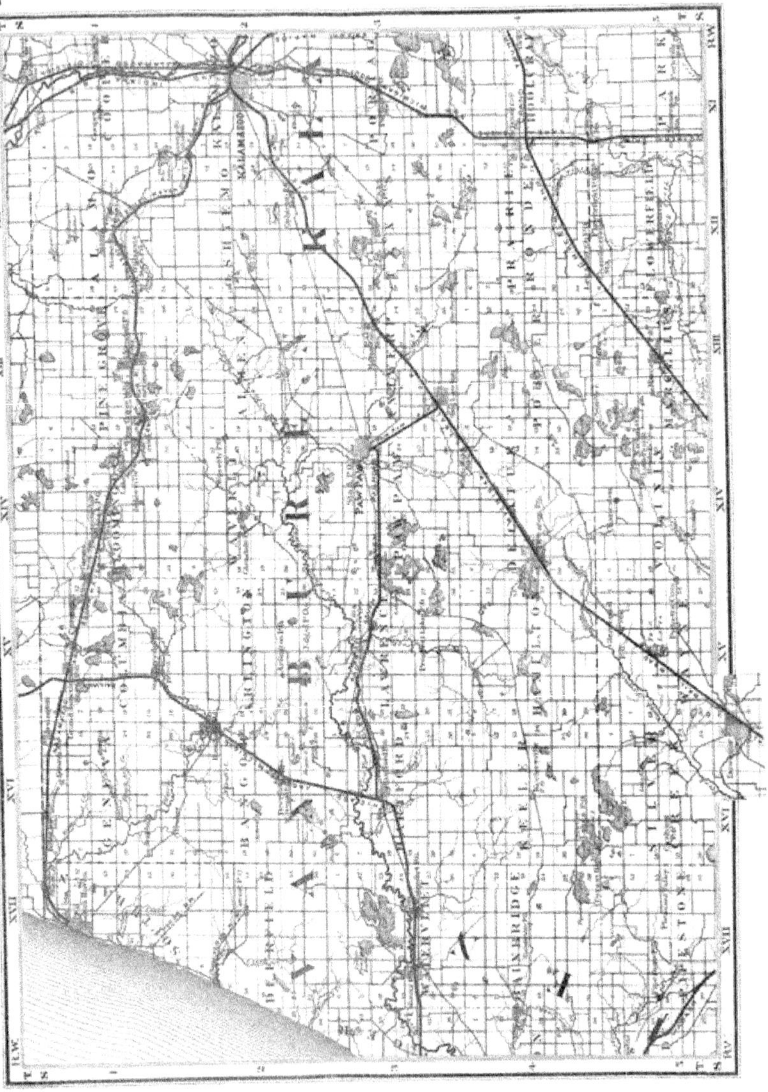
KALAMAZOO
PAW PAW
PINE GROVE
FLOWERFIELD
BAINBRIDGE

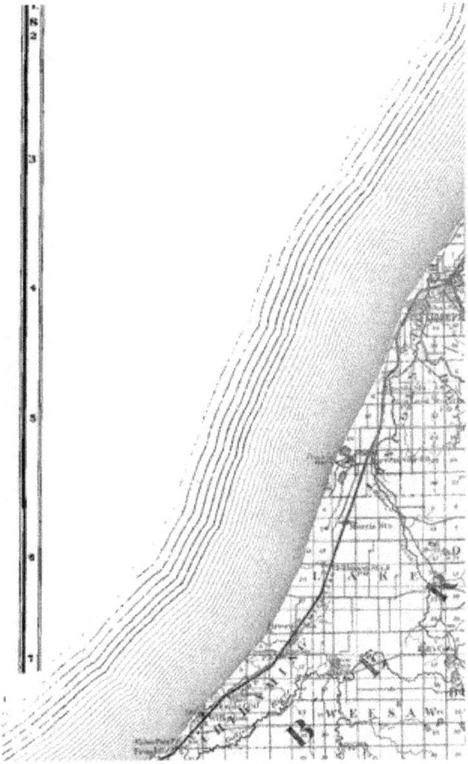

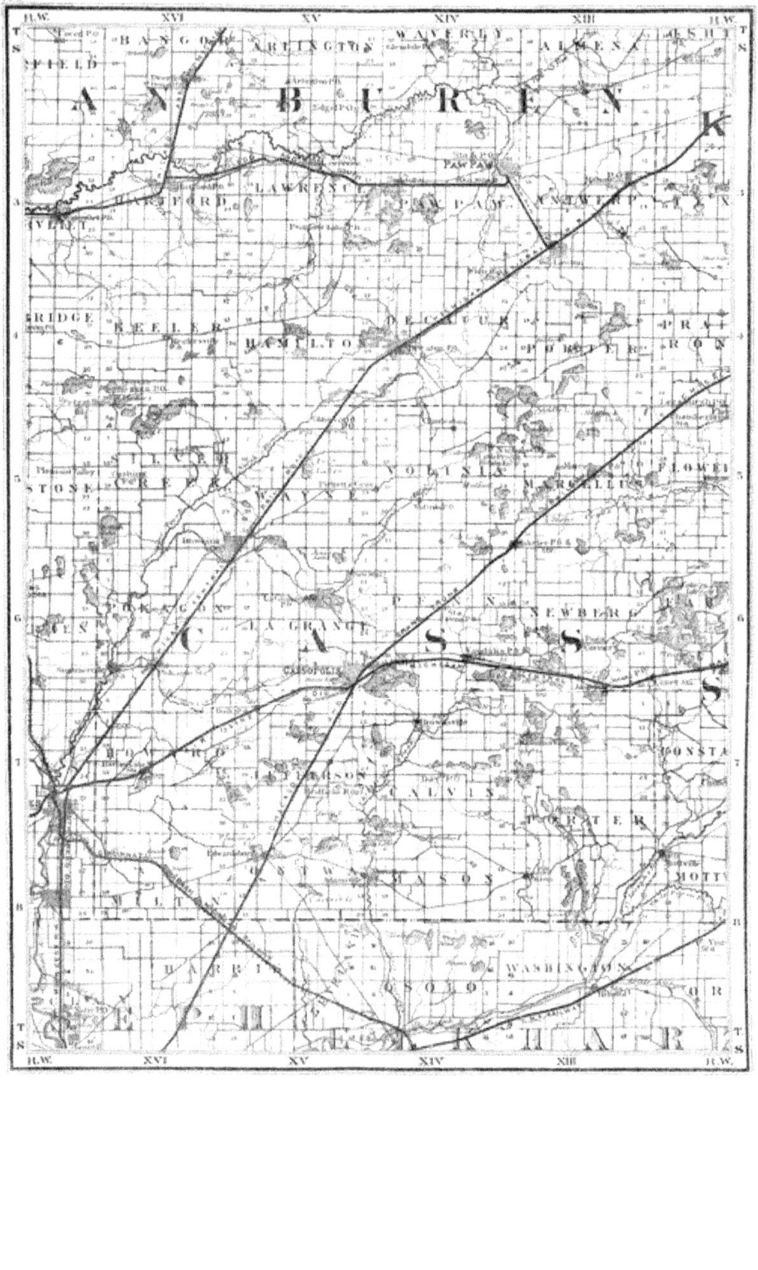
R.W.
XVI
XV
XIV
XIII
T
S
BANGOR
ARLINGTON
WAVERLY
ALMENA
LAWRENCE
HARTFORD
PAW PAW
ANTWERP
KEELER
HAMILTON
DECATUR
PORTER
SILVER CREEK
WAYNE
VOLINIA
MARCELLUS
POKAGON
LA GRANGE
PENN
NEWBERG
CASSOPOLIS
HOWARD
JEFFERSON
CALVIN
PORTER
MASON
MILTON
WASHINGTON

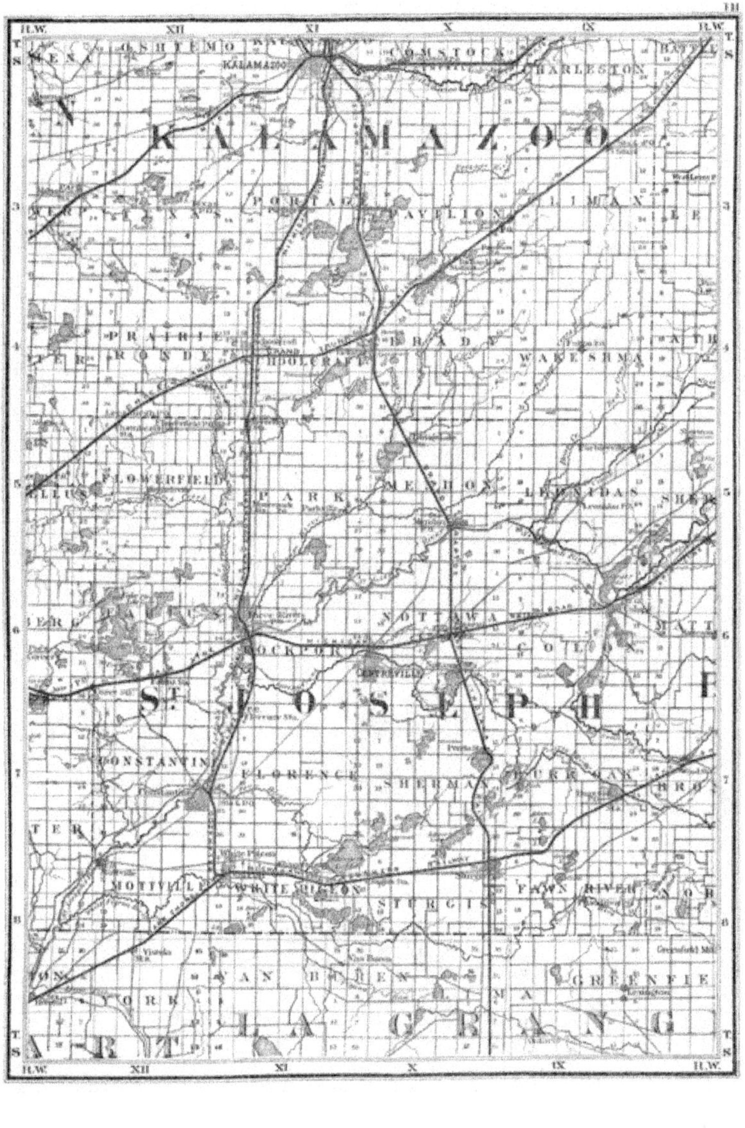
R.W.
XII
XI
X
IX
OSHTEMO
COMSTOCK
KALAMAZOO
CHARLESTON
K A L A M A Z O O
PORTAGE
PAVILION
CLIMAX
TEXAS
PRAIRIE
RONDE
SCHOOLCRAFT
BRADY
WAKESHMA
FLOWERFIELD
PARK
MENDON
LEONIDAS
NOTTAWA
COLON
LOCKPORT
CENTREVILLE
ST. J O S E P H
CONSTANTINE
FLORENCE
SHERMAN
MOTTVILLE
WHITE PIGEON
STURGIS
FAWN RIVER
VAN BUREN
YORK
LIMA
GREENFIELD
L A G R A N G
T.
S.
3
4
5
6
7
8

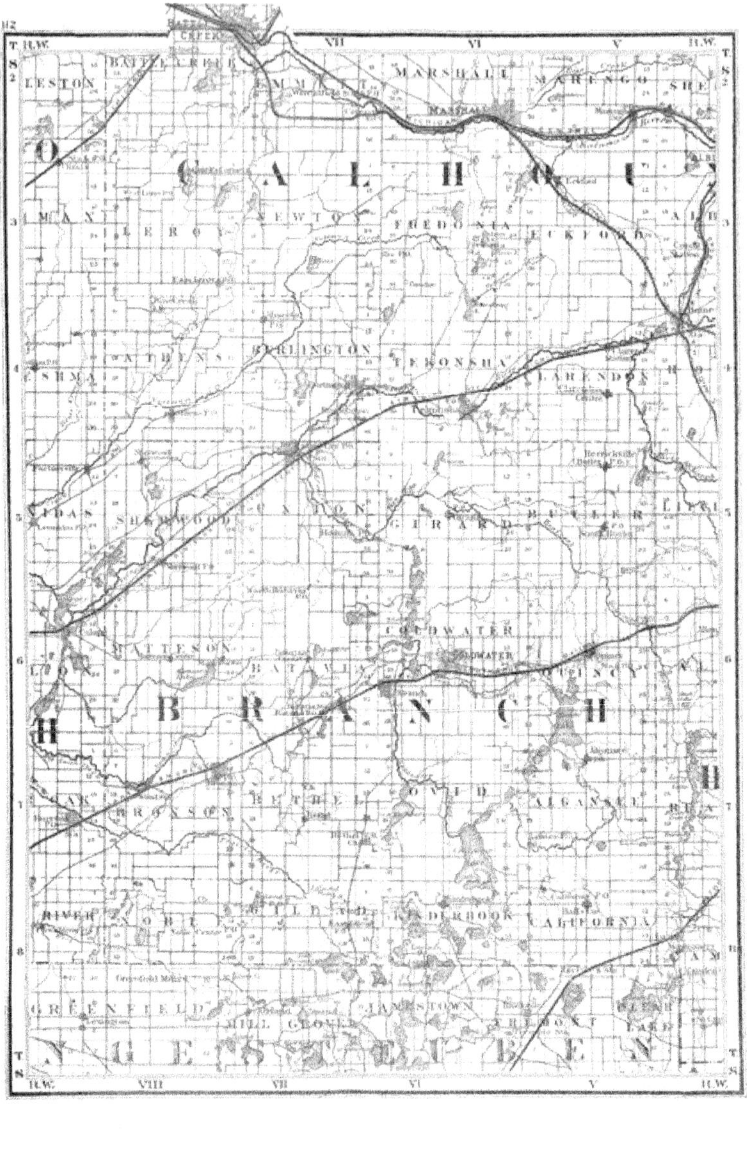

BATTLE CREEK
R.W.
VIII
VII
VI
V
MARSHALL
MARENGO
EMMETT
C A L H O U N
NEWTON
LE ROY
FREDONIA
ECKFORD
BURLINGTON
ATHENS
TEKONSHA
CLARENDON
SHERWOOD
UNION
GIRARD
BUTLER
MATTESON
COLDWATER
BATAVIA
QUINCY
B R A N C H
BRONSON
BETHEL
OVID
ALGANSEE
GILEAD
KINDERHOOK
CALIFORNIA
GREENFIELD
MILL GROVE
JAMESTOWN
FREMONT
S T E U B E N

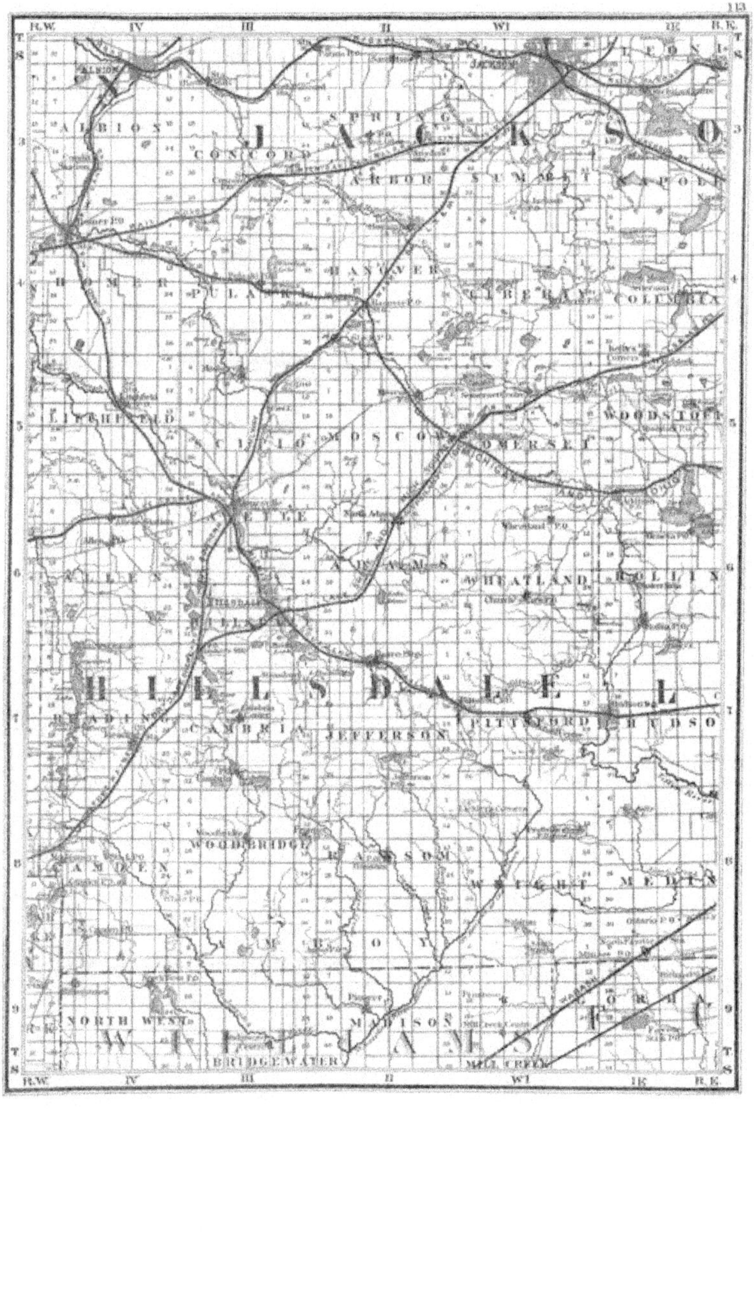
R.W.
IV
III
II
WI
IE
R.E.
T.
S.
3
4
5
6
7
8
9
ALBION
SPRING
J A C K S O
LEONI
CONCORD
ARBOR
SUMMIT
NAPOLE
HOMER
PULASKI
HANOVER
LIBERTY
COLUMBIA
LITCHFIELD
SCIPIO
MOSCOW
SOMERSET
WOODSTOCK
FAYETTE
ADAMS
WHEATLAND
ROLLIN
ALLEN
HILLSDALE
H I L L S D A L E
L
READING
CAMBRIA
JEFFERSON
PITTSFORD
HUDSO
WOODBRIDGE
RANSOM
CAMDEN
WRIGHT
MEDINA
AMBOY
NORTH WEST
MADISON
W I L L I A M S
BRIDGEWATER
MILL CREEK
GORHA

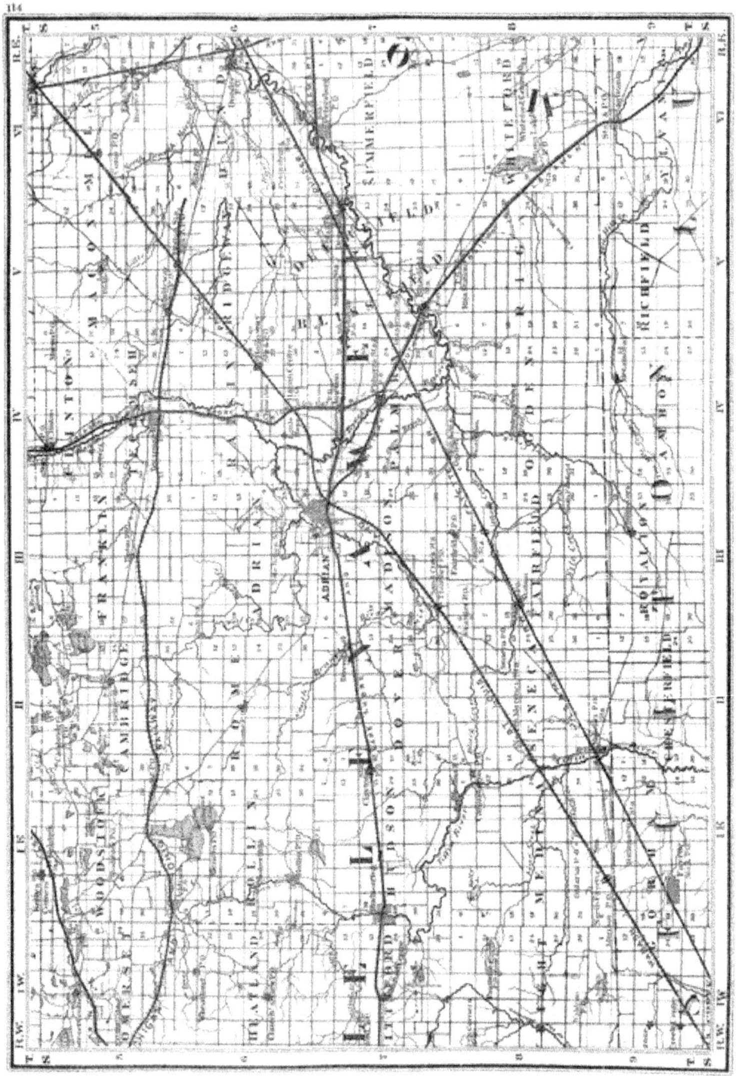
ADRIAN
MADISON
DOVER
HUDSON
SENECA
FAIRFIELD
RICHFIELD
CAMBRIDGE
WOODSTOCK
FRANKLIN
SUMMERFIELD
WHITEFORD
CLINTON
MACON

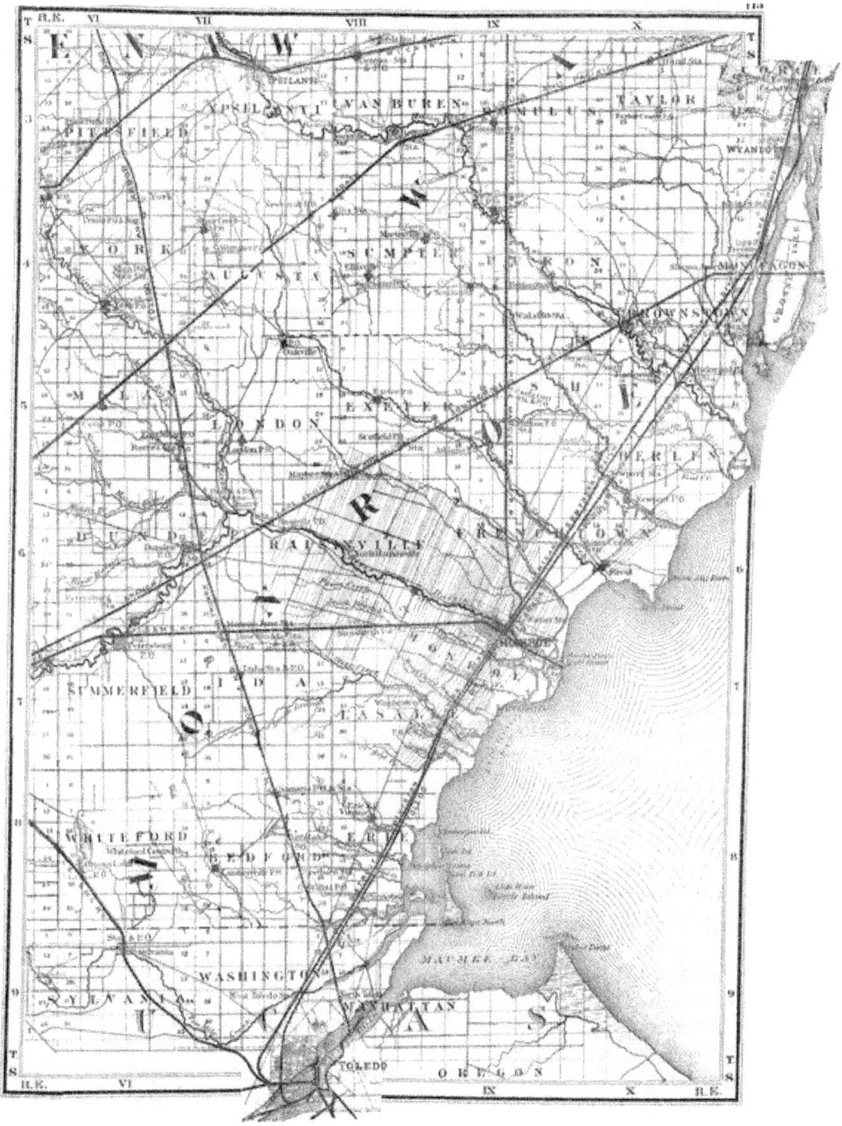

YPSILANTI
VAN BUREN
TAYLOR
PITTSFIELD
WYANDOTTE
YORK
AUGUSTA
LONDON
EXETER
RAISINVILLE
SUMMERFIELD
LASALLE
WHITEFORD
BEDFORD
ERIE
WASHINGTON
MANHATTAN
TOLEDO
OREGON
MAUMEE BAY

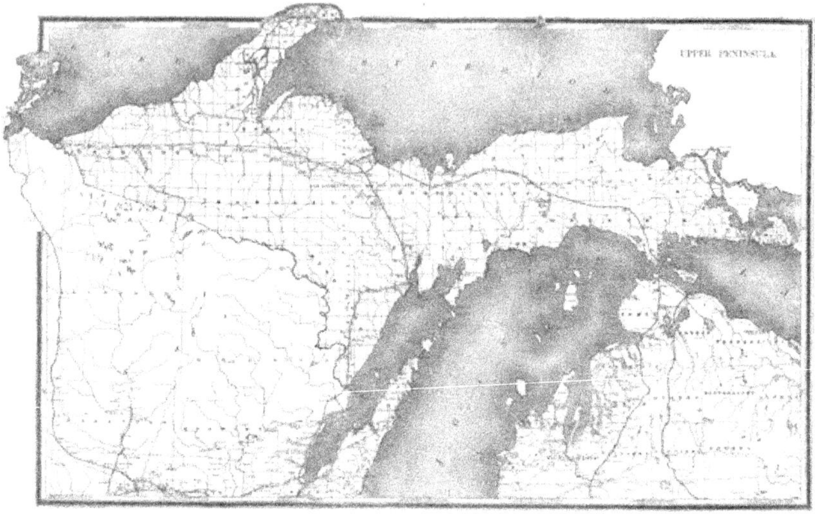
UPPER PENINSULA

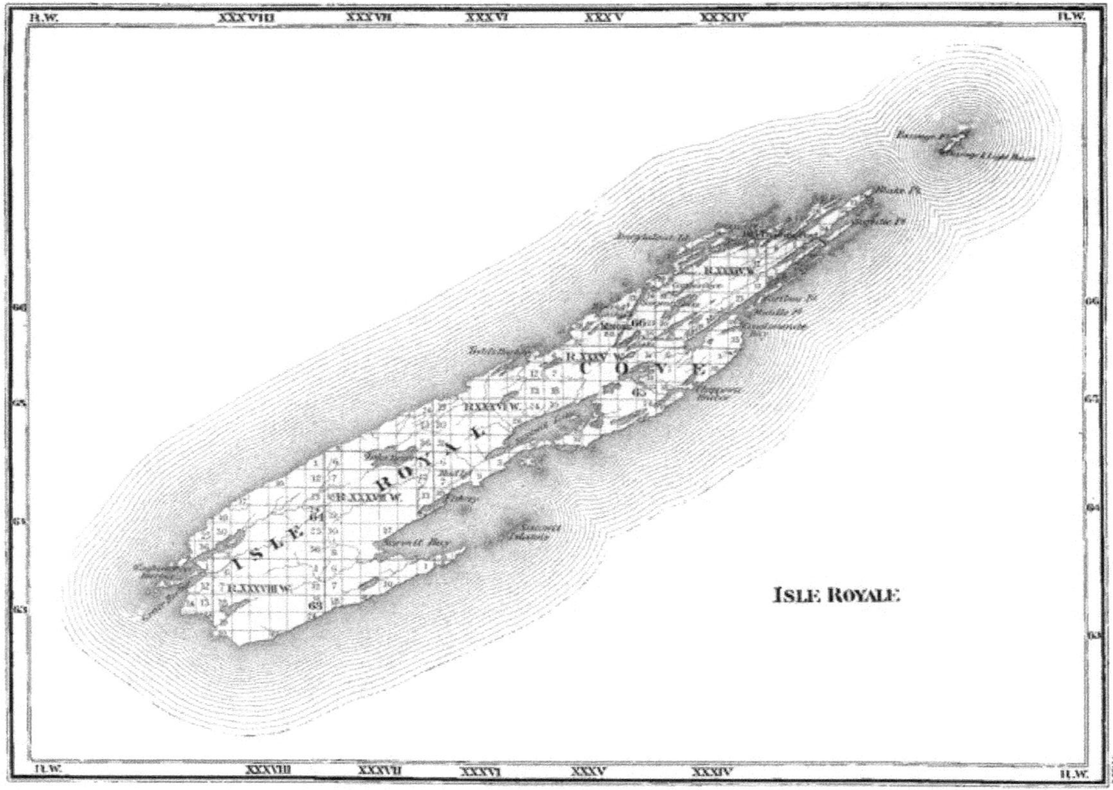
ISLE ROYALE
ISLE ROYAL
COVE
R.W.
XXXVIII
XXXVII
XXXVI
XXXV
XXXIV
R.XXXVIII W.
R.XXXVII W.
R.XXXVI W.
R.XXXV W.
Siskowit Bay
63
64
65
66
67

113A

O N T O N A G O N

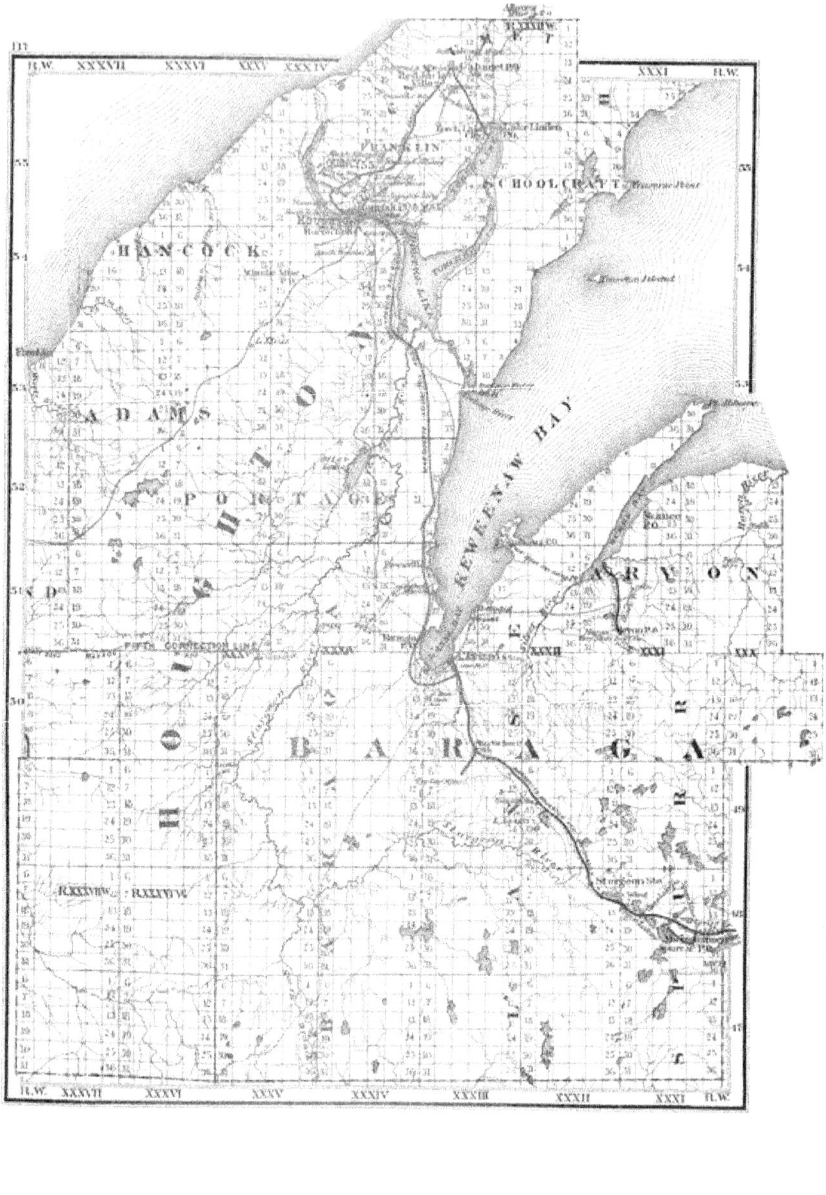
R.W.
XXXVII
XXXVI
XXXV
XXXIV
XXXI
HANCOCK
ADAMS
PORTAGE
FRANKLIN
SCHOOLCRAFT
KEWEENAW BAY
HOUGHTON
BARAGA
ARVON
FIFTH CORRECTION LINE
Lake Linden
R.XXXVIII W.
R.XXXVII W.
XXXIII
XXXII

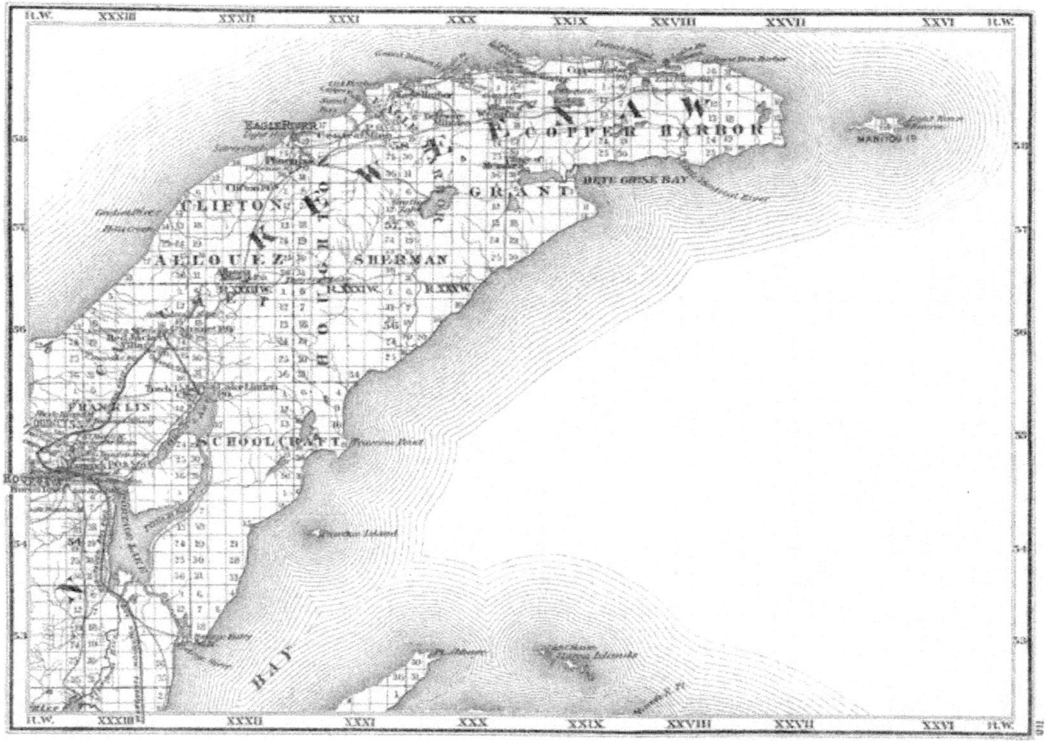

KEWEENAW
HOUGHTON
COPPER HARBOR
GRANT
CLIFTON
ALLOUEZ
SHERMAN
FRANKLIN
SCHOOLCRAFT
PORTAGE LAKE
DEVIL GRISE BAY
BAY
MANITOU IS
EAGLE RIVER
R.W.
XXXIII
XXXII
XXXI
XXX
XXIX
XXVIII
XXVII
XXVI
58
57
56
55
54
53

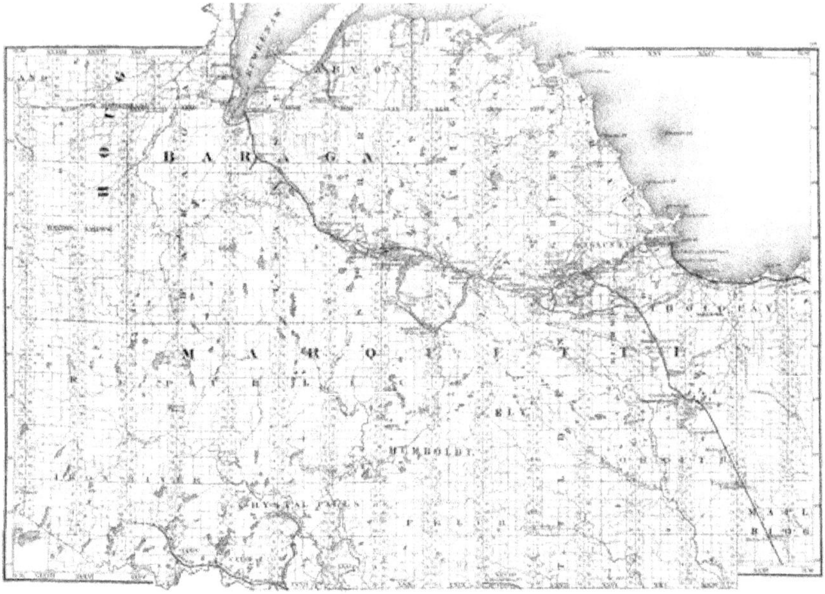
B A R A G A
HUMBOLDT

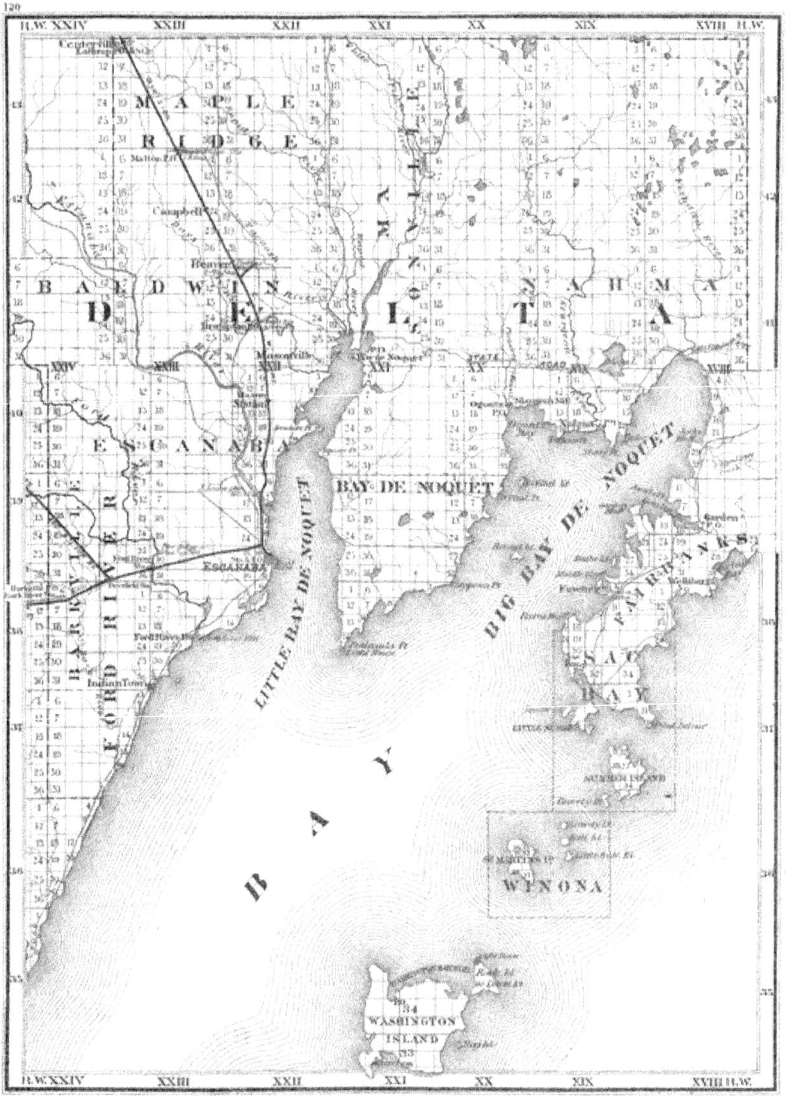
R.W. XXIV
XXIII
XXII
XXI
XX
XIX
XVIII R.W.
MAPLE
RIDGE
BALDWIN
DELTA
NAHMA
ESCANABA
BAY DE NOQUET
BIG BAY DE NOQUET
LITTLE BAY DE NOQUET
FORD RIVER
BARK RIVER
FAIRBANKS
SAC
BAY
WINONA
SUMMER ISLAND
WASHINGTON
ISLAND
BAY
Escanaba
R.W. XXIV
XXIII
XXII
XXI
XX
XIX
XVIII R.W.

MENOMINEE RANGE IRON MINES.

NAME OF MINE	SECTION	TOWNSHIP	RANGE	NAME OF PRESIDENT	P. O. ADDRESS	NAME OF SEC. OR AGENT	P. O. ADDRESS
Acme Mine	30	T. 43 N.	R. 32 W.			S. D. Hollister, Manager	Crystal Falls, Mich.
Alpha Mine	18	T. 43 N.	R. 32 W.			Capt. Schwartz, Sup't	Crystal Falls, Mich.
Breen Mine	33	T. 39 N.	R. 28 W.	E. S. Ingalls	Menominee, Mich.		
Briar Hill Mine	9	T. 34 N.	R. 30 W.	John Stambaugh	Youngstown, Ohio.	M. C. Davidson, Sup't	Norway, Mich.
Curry Mine	9	T. 34 N.	R. 30 W.	J. H. Outhwaite	Cleveland, Ohio.		
Cyclops Mine	5	T. 39 N.	R. 29 W.	Powell Stackhouse	Johnstown, Pa.		
Chapin Mine	30	T. 40 N.	R. 30 W.			C. H. Cady, Agent	Iron Mountain, Mich.
Crystal Falls Mine	20	T. 43 N.	R. 32 W.			J. H. Elmore, Sup't	Crystal Falls, Mich.
Chicagon Lake Mine	36	T. 43 N.	R. 34 W.			Henry Roberts, Agent	Iron River, Mich.
Dulphi Mine	14	T. 43 N.	R. 32 W.	George D. Smith	Florence, Wis.		
Fairbank Mine	31	T. 43 N.	R. 32 W.			J. H. Elmore, Agent	Crystal Falls, Mich.
Garfield Mine	13	T. 39 N.	R. 30 W.			J. E. Case, Agent	Vulcan, Mich.
Great Western Mine	21	T. 43 N.	R. 32 W.			S. D. Hollister, Sec. & Treas.	Crystal Falls, Mich.
Hewitt Mine	31	T. 40 N.	R. 30 W.			H. Tucker, Agent	Iron Mountain, Mich.
Indiana Mine	27	T. 40 N.	R. 32 W.	John Traverse	Chicago, Ill.		
Iron River Mine	25 & 26	T. 43 N.	R. 35 W.	John Stambaugh	Youngstown, Ohio.		
Keel Ridge Mine	20	T. 40 N.	R. 30 W.			J. T. Jones, Agent	Iron Mountain, Mich.
Ludington Mine	30	T. 40 N.	R. 31 W.	George E. Stockbridge	Iron Mountain, Mich.		
Mastodon Mine	18	T. 43 N.	R. 33 W.	Edward Breitung	Negaunee, Mich.		
Manhattan Mine	15	T. 42 N.	R. 33 W.	Edward Breitung	Negaunee, Mich.		
Norway Mine	5	T. 39 N.	R. 29 W.	Powell Stackhouse	Johnstown, Pa.		
Nanaimo Mine	36	T. 43 N.	R. 32 W.	John S. McDonald	Milwaukee, Wis.	Thomas Lenmore, Agent	Iron River Mich.
Perkins Mine	4	T. 39 N.	R. 29 W.	Samuel Mitchell	Somerville, Mich.	John Perkins, Agent	Norway, Mich.
Paint River Mine	20	T. 43 N.	R. 32 W.	Max Wineman	Chicago, Ill.	C. T. Roberts, Agent	Crystal Falls, Mich.
Quinnesec Mine	36	T. 40 N.	R. 30 W.	Powell Stackhouse	Johnstown, Pa.		
Quincy Mine	19	T. 43 N.	R. 32 W.			Joe Ames, Manager	Crystal Falls, Mich.
Union Mine	N. W. ¼ 21, S. W. ¼ 20	T. 43 N.	R. 32 W.	A. B. Meeker	Chicago, Ill.	George Lyon, Agent	Chicago, Ill.
Youngstown Mine	19	T. 43 N.	R. 32 W.	John Stambaugh	Youngstown, Ohio.	F. P. Mills, Agent	Crystal Falls, Mich.

FELCH MOUNTAIN RANGE IRON MINES.

Calumet Mine	3	T. 41 N.	R. 28 W.	A. B. Cornell	Youngstown, Ohio.	J. R. Wood, Agent	Metropolitan, Mich.
Hecla Mine	9	T. 41 N.	R. 28 W.	Edward Breitung	Negaunee, Mich.		
Metropolitan Mine	22	T. 42 N.	R. 28 W.	J. P. Burt	Cleveland, Ohio.	Jefferson Day, Agent	Metropolitan, Mich.
North Western Mine	29	T. 42 N.	R. 28 W.	W. D. Rees	Marquette, Mich.		

GOLD AND SILVER MINES.

Ropes Gold and Silver Mine	29	T. 48 N.	R. 27 W.	J. Ropes	Ishpeming, Mich.		

COPPER MINES—KEWEENAW CO., MICH.

Ash Bed Mine	14	T. 58 N.	R. 31 W.	William C. Coffin	Boston, Mass.	M. A. Delano, Agent	Phoenix, Mich.
Allouez Mine	21	T. 57 N.	R. 32 W.	William C. Stuart	New York, N. Y.	Frederick Smith, Agent	Allouez, Mich.
Conglomerate Mine	12	T. 58 N.	R. 30 W.	H. C. Davis	Philadelphia, Pa.	Charles H. Palmer, Agent	Delaware, Mich.
Central Mine	23	T. 58 N.	R. 30 W.	George A. Hoyt	New York, N. Y.	James Dunstan, Agent	Central Mine, Mich.
Copper Falls Mine	14	T. 58 N.	R. 31 W.	David Nevins	Boston, Mass.	B. F. Emerson, Agent	Copper Falls, Mich.
Cliff Mine	36	T. 58 N.	R. 32 W.	M. H. Simpson	Boston, Mass.	D. D. Brockway, Agent	Clifton, Mich.
Madison Mine	19	T. 58 N.	R. 30 W.	Charles Le Sier	Detroit, Mich.	Joseph Sewell, Agent	Hancock, Mich.
Phoenix Mine	26	T. 58 N.	R. 32 W.	William P. Nunn	Boston, Mass.	M. A. Delano, Agent	Phoenix, Mich.
Seneca Mine	33	T. 57 N.	R. 32 W.	J. W. Clark	Boston, Mass.	John Daniels, Agent	Opechee, Mich.
St. Clair Mine	36	T. 58 N.	R. 32 W.	John Brooks	Boston, Mass.	M. A. Delano, Agent	Phoenix, Mich.

COPPER MINES—HOUGHTON COUNTY.

Atlantic Mine	S. ¼ 4, N. ¼ 9	T. 54 N.	R. 34 W.	Joseph E. Gay	New York, N. Y.	William Tonkin, Agent	Houghton, Mich.
Centennial Mine	13	T. 56 N.	R. 33 W.	S. L. Smith	Lansing, Mich.	J. Hall, Agent	Houghton, Mich.
Calumet & Hecla Mine	S.E. ¼ 14, N.E. ¼ 23	T. 56 N.	R. 33 W.	Alexander Agassiz	Boston, Mass.	J. N. Wright, Agent	Calumet, Mich.
Concord Mine	12	T. 55 N.	R. 33 W.			D. L. Demmon, Sec. & Treas.	Boston, Mass.
Douglas Mine	26	T. 55 N.	R. 33 W.			D. L. Demmon, Sec. & Treas.	Boston, Mass.
Dorchester Mine	18	T. 55 N.	R. 33 W.			D. L. Demmon, Sec. & Treas.	Boston, Mass.
Franklin Mine	34	T. 55 N.	R. 34 W.			D. L. Demmon, Sec. & Treas.	Boston, Mass.
Grand Portage Mine	25	T. 54 N.	R. 34 W.	Joseph Worden	Hancock, Mich.		
Highland Mine	20	T. 55 N.	R. 33 W.	T. W. Edwards	Houghton, Mich.		
Hancock Mine	26	T. 55 N.	R. 34 W.	Ed. Ryan	Hancock, Mich.		
Huron Mine	S. ¼ 1 & 3	T. 54 N.	R. 34 W.			J. Vivian, Agent	Hancock, Mich.
Isle Royale Mine						Graham Pope, Agent	Houghton, Mich.
Kearsarge Mine	6	T. 56 N.	R. 32 W.	J. D. Clark	Boston, Mass.	R. R. Goodell, Agent	Houghton, Mich.
Mesnard Mine	24	T. 55 N.	R. 33 W.			D. L. Demmon, Sec. & Treas.	Boston, Mass.
Osceola Mine	26 N. ¼ 27	T. 55 N.	R. 33 W.	James D. Clark	Boston, Mass.	John Daniels, Agent	Opechee, Mich.
Peninsula Mine	24	T. 55 N.	R. 33 W.	Charles Fargo	New York, N. Y.	C. M. Wheeler, Agent	Houghton, Mich.
Pontiac Mine	25	T. 55 N.	R. 33 W.			Capt. J. Vivian, Agent	Houghton, Mich.
Pewabic Mine	20	T. 55 N.	R. 34 W.	D. L. Demmon, Sec. & Treas.	Boston, Mass.	J. Vivian, Agent	Hancock, Mich.
Quincy Mine	26	T. 55 N.	R. 34 W.	T. F. Mason	New York, N. Y.	Frank White, Agent	Hancock, Mich.
St. Mary's Mine	15	T. 55 N.	R. 33 W.			Frederick Beck, Sec. & Treas.	Boston, Mass.
Sheldon & Columbian Mine	26	T. 54 N.	R. 34 W.			Graham Pope, Agent	Houghton, Mich.
Tamarack Mine	14	T. 56 N.	R. 33 W.	J. D. Clark	Boston, Mass.	John Daniels, Agent	Opechee, Mich.
Tecumseh Mine	27	T. 56 N.	R. 33 W.			Charles H. Palmer Agent	Delaware, Mich.
Wolverine Mine	7	T. 56 N.	R. 32 W.	T. W. Edwards	Houghton, Mich.	R. Uren, Agent	Houghton, Mich.

COPPER MINES—ONTONAGON COUNTY.

Adventure Mine	32	T. 51 N.	R. 38 W.	Thomas F. Mason	New York, N. Y.		
Aztec Mine	21	T. 51 N.	R. 37 W.			Aaron Page, Sec. & Treas.	Boston, Mass.
Belt Mines				Earl Dunboyne	London, Eng.	Oscar Brand, Agent	Greenland, Mich.
Evergreen Bluff Mine	6	T. 50 N.	R. 39 W.			F. W. Capen, Sec. & Treas.	New York, N. Y.
Flintsteel Mine	13	T. 50 N.	R. 38 W.			Walter Ferguson, Sec. & Treas.	New York, N. Y.
Hazewood Mine	16	T. 51 N.	R. 37 W.			James R. Young, Sec. & Treas.	New York, N. Y.
Hilton Mine	36	T. 51 N.	R. 39 W.	Thomas F. Mason	New York, N. Y.	S. B. Harris, Agent	Greenland, Mich.
Indiana Mine	31	T. 51 N.	R. 37 W.			James M. Mills, Sec. & Treas.	New York, N. Y.
Knowlton Mine	1	T. 50 N.	R. 39 W.			F. W. Capen, Sec. & Treas.	New York, N. Y.
Lake Superior Mine	18	T. 50 N.	R. 39 W.			D. L. Demmon, Sec. & Treas.	Boston, Mass.
Mass Mine	6	T. 50 N.	R. 38 W.	C. G. Hussey	Pittsburgh, Pa.	John Cayneeret, Agent	Greenland, Mich.
Merimac Mine	24	T. 51 N.	R. 39 W.	J. G. Hussey	Philadelphia, Pa.		
Minnesota Mine	15	T. 50 N.	R. 39 W.	George D. Pond	New York, N. Y.	T. D. James, Agent	Rockland, Mich.
National Mine	15	T. 50 N.	R. 39 W.			Ed. Parnell, Agent	Rockland, Mich.
Norwich Mine	12	T. 49 N.	R. 41 W.			T. Meads, Agent	Ontonagon, Mich.
Nonesuch Mine	S. ¼ 1, N. ¼ 12	T. 50 N.	R. 43 W.			S. H. Harrison, Gen'l Manager	Nonesuch, Mich.
Ogima Mine	8	T. 50 N.	R. 39 W.			Samuel Cooper, Sec. & Treas.	New York, N. Y.
Rockland Mine	15	T. 50 N.	R. 39 W.			Ed. Parnell, Agent	Rockland, Mich.
Ridge Mine	25	T. 51 N.	R. 38 W.	T. F. Mason	New York, N. Y.	S. B. Harris, Agent	Greenland, Mich.
Superior Mine	4	T. 50 N.	R. 39 W.			D. L. Demmon, Sec. & Treas.	Boston, Mass.
Toltec Mine	26	T. 51 N.	R. 38 W.			Joseph Vila, Sec. & Treas.	Boston, Mass.
Victoria Mine	22	T. 51 N.	R. 40 W.	A. W. Coffin	Boston, Mass.	T. Hooper, Agent	Rockland, Mich.
White Pine Mine	8	T. 50 N.	R. 42 W.			T. Hooper, Agent	Rockland, Mich.

Concluded on page 121A.

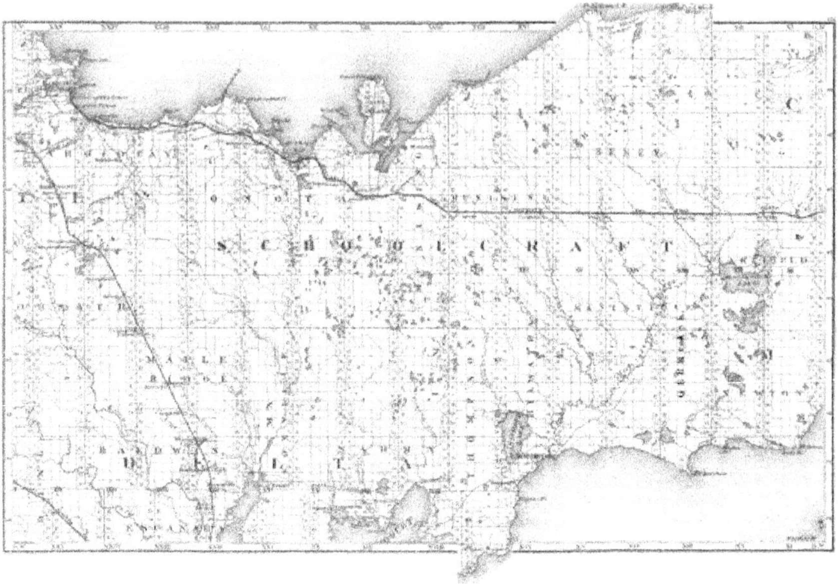
S C H O O L C R A F T
D E L T A

Continued from page 120A.

SLATE MINES—BARAGA COUNTY.

Name of Mine.	Section.	Township.	Range.	Name of President.	P. O. Address.	Name of Sec. or Agent.	P. O. Address.
Huron Bay Slate Quarries	33	T. 51 N.	R. 31 W.	W. D. Thompson	Jackson, Mich.	Thomas Hooper, Agent	L. Anse, Mich.

IRON MINES—MARQUETTE COUNTY.

Name of Mine.	Section.	Township.	Range.	Name of President.	P. O. Address.	Name of Sec. or Agent.	P. O. Address.
Argyle Mine	11	T. 47 N.	R. 29 W.	Don M. Dickinson	Detroit, Mich.		
Barnum Mine	N. ¼ 9, N. ¼ 10	T. 47 N.	R. 27 W.	William H. Barnum	Lime Rock, Conn.	William Sedgwick, Sup't	Ishpeming, Mich.
Breitung Mine	32	T. 48 N.	R. 27 W.			C. M. Wheeler, Gen'l Manager	Marquette, Mich.
Bay State Mine	9	T. 47 N.	R. 26 W.			Wm. J. Allen, Gen'l Manager	Negaunee, Mich.
Beaufort Mine	32	T. 48 N.	R. 31 W.			Solomon Curry, Agent	Ishpeming, Mich.
Boston Mine	32	T. 48 N.	R. 26 W.			F. A. Wright, Agent	Marquette, Mich.
Cleveland Mine	3, 8, 10, 11	T. 47 N.	R. 27 W.	S. L. Mather	Cleveland, Ohio.	Jay C. Morse, Agent	Marquette, Mich.
Cambria Mine	S. E. ¼ 33, W. ½ 36	T. 48 N.	R. 27 W.			A. W. Maitland, Gen'l Manager	Negaunee, Mich.
Cleveland Hematite	9	T. 47 N.	R. 27 W.	S. L. Mather	Cleveland, Ohio.		
Chicago Mine	7	T. 47 N.	R. 26 W.	J. F. Stevens	Negaunee, Mich.		
Clancy Mine	32	T. 47 N.	R. 26 W.	John Clancy	Grand Rapids, Mich.		
Columbia Mine	6	T. 46 N.	R. 25 W.			C. M. Wicker, Agent	Marquette, Mich.
Champion Mine	31	T. 48 N.	R. 29 W.			A. Kidder, Agent	Marquette, Mich.
Cheshire Mine	13	T. 45 N.	R. 25 W.	J. J. Pierce	Pittsburg, Pa.		
Detroit Mine	3	T. 47 N.	R. 27 W.	John P. Newbury	Detroit, Mich.		
Dalliba Mine	28	T. 48 N.	R. 29 W.	James H. Dalliba	Cleveland, Ohio.		
Dexter Mine	5	T. 47 N.	R. 28 W.	J. C. Morse	Cleveland, Ohio.		
Day Mine	8	T. 47 N.	R. 28 W.	Alexander H. Day	Detroit, Mich.		
East Champion	32	T. 48 N.	R. 29 W.	F. B. Spear	Marquette, Mich.	C. T. Hampson, Agent	Champion, Mich.
Edna Mine	7	T. 47 N.	R. 27 W.	I. C. Lewis	Negaunee, Mich.	J. M. Gannon, Sec.	Negaunee, Mich.
Erie Mine	28	T. 47 N.	R. 30 W.	E. H. Wright	Republic, Mich.	E. H. Wright, Manager	Republic, Mich.
Forest City Mine	33	T. 48 N.	R. 27 W.	C. A. Otis	Cleveland, Ohio.		
Foster Mine	23	T. 47 N.	R. 27 W.	William H. Barnum	Lime Rock, Conn.	A. W. Maitland, Agent	Negaunee, Mich.
Goodrich Mine	10	T. 47 N.	R. 27 W.			Henry Davis, Sup't	Ishpeming, Mich.
Grand Rapids Mine	28	T. 47 N.	R. 26 W.	J. I. Whitefield	Grand Rapids, Mich.		
Humboldt Mine	11	T. 47 N.	R. 29 W.			J. B. Maas, Agent	Humboldt, Mich.
Jackson Mine	1	T. 47 N.	R. 27 W.			Henry Merry, Agent	Negaunee, Mich.
Jim Pascoe Mine	30	T. 48 N.	R. 28 W.			A. Kidder, Agent	Marquette, Mich.
Lake Superior Iron Mine	9 & 10	T. 47 N.	R. 27 W.	Jos. S. Fay	Boston, Mass.	C. H. Hall, Agent	Ishpeming, Mich.
Lake Angeline Mine	15	T. 47 N.	R. 27 W.	John Outhwaite	Cleveland, Ohio.	A. Kidder, Agent	Marquette, Mich.
Lowthian Mine	20	T. 47 N.	R. 27 W.	Joseph P. Fay	Boston, Mass.	C. H. Hall, Agent	Ishpeming, Mich.
Laxey Mine	20	T. 47 N.	R. 26 W.	J. Q. Adams	Negaunee, Mich.		
McComber Mine	7	T. 47 N.	R. 26 W.			J. C. Foley, Agent	Negaunee, Mich.
Milwaukee Mine	7	T. 47 N.	R. 26 W.			J. C. Foley, Agent	Negaunee, Mich.
Mitchell Mine	21	T. 47 N.	R. 27 W.	E. O. St. Clair	Ishpeming, Mich.	George A. St. Clair, Sup't	Ishpeming, Mich.
Moylan Mine	33	T. 47 N.	R. 26 W.	W. F. Swift	Ishpeming, Mich.		
Marine Mine	30	T. 48 N.	R. 31 W.			Jim Pascoe, Agent	Champion, Mich.
Menard Mine	30	T. 48 N.	R. 29 W.	A. M. Byers	Pittsburgh, Pa.		
Michigamme Mine	29	T. 48 N.	R. 30 W.	William H. Barnum	Lime Rock, Conn.	J. C. Fowle, Agent	Michigamme, Mich.
Magnetic Mine	20	T. 47 N.	R. 30 W.			S. Peck, Agent	Marquette, Mich.
New York Mine	8	T. 47 N.	R. 27 W.	Samuel J. Tilden	New York, N. Y.		
Negaunee Concentration Co.	1	T. 47 N.	R. 27 W.			W. K. Allen, Sup't	Negaunee, Mich.
New York Hematite Mine	7	T. 47 N.	R. 26 W.			J. C. Foley, Agent	Negaunee, Mich.
National Mine	16	T. 47 N.	R. 27 W.	Samuel Mitchell	Ishpeming, Mich.		
New England Mine	20	T. 47 N.	R. 27 W.			C. H. Hall, Agent	Ishpeming, Mich.
Northampton Mine	30	T. 48 N.	R. 29 W.			A. Kidder, Agent	Marquette, Mich.
Pendill Mine	5	T. 47 N.	R. 26 W.			Hiram Burt, Agent	Marquette, Mich.
Pittsburgh & L. S. Mine	30	T. 47 N.	R. 26 W.			Joseph Kirkpatrick, Agent	Palmer, Mich.
Portland Mine	32	T. 48 N.	R. 31 W.	G. N. Northrop	Marquette, Mich.		
Rolling Mill Mine	7	T. 47 N.	R. 27 W.	Luther Beecher	Detroit, Mich.		
Republic Mine	7	T. 47 N.	R. 29 W.			David Morgan, Agent	Republic, Mich.
Star Mine	8	T. 47 N.	R. 26 W.	J. B. Maas	Negaunee, Mich.		
Section 12 Mine	12	T. 47 N.	R. 27 W.	Wm. H. Barnum	Lime Rock, Conn.	A. W. Maitland, Agent	Negaunee, Mich.
Salisbury Mine	18	T. 47 N.	R. 27 W.	Wm. H. Barnum	Lime Rock, Conn.	A. W. Maitland, Agent	Negaunee, Mich.
Saginaw Mine	19	T. 47 N.	R. 27 W.	Henry Chisholm	Chicago, Ill.	Samuel Mitchell, Agent	Stoneville, Mich.
Section 16 Mine	16	T. 47 N.	R. 27 W.	Henry Chisholm		Samuel Mitchell, Agent	Ishpeming, Mich.
Sterling Mine	30	T. 48 N.	R. 28 W.			G. W. Reed, Agent	Clarksburgh, Mich.
St. Lawrence Mine	3	T. 47 N.	R. 27 W.	A. B. Cornell	Youngstown, O.	J. R. Wood, Agent	Ishpeming, Mich.
Swanzy Mine	18	T. 45 N.	R. 26 W.	J. J. Pigeon	Pittsburgh, Pa.	A. P. Wood, Agent	Cheshire, Mich.
Stewart Mine	30	T. 48 N.	R. 31 W.				
Titan Mine	21	T. 48 N.	R. 31 W.			Solomon Curry, Agent	Michigamme, Mich.
Valley City Mine	6	T. 47 N.	R. 26 W.			G. F. Case, Agent	Negaunee, Mich.
Wheeling Mine	7	T. 47 N.	R. 26 W.	Daniel McGarry	Cleveland, Ohio.	J. C. Foley, Agent	Negaunee, Mich.
Winthrop Hematite Co.	21	T. 47 N.	R. 27 W.	E. O. St. Clair	Ishpeming, Mich.	Geo. A. St. Clair, Sup't	Ishpeming, Mich.
Wheat Mine	29	T. 47 N.	R. 26 W.	Daniel McGarry	Cleveland, Ohio.	J. T. Hayes, Agent	Negaunee, Mich.
Wick Mine	35	T. 46 N.	R. 27 W.	Daniel McGarry	Cleveland, Ohio.	J. T. Hayes, Agent	Negaunee, Mich.
Webster Mine	36	T. 48 N.	R. 31 W.	G. J. Northrop	Marquette, Mich.	E. B. Palmer, Sec. & Treas.	Marquette, Mich.
Wetmore Mine	28	T. 48 N.	R. 31 W.			Ed. Wetmore, Agent	Marquette, Mich.
West Republic	7	T. 46 N.	R. 29 W.	E. G. St. Clair	Ishpeming, Mich.	J. O. St. Clair, Sup't	Republic, Mich.

IRON MINES—BARAGA COUNTY.

Name of Mine.	Section.	Township.	Range.	Name of President.	P. O. Address.	Name of Sec. or Agent.	P. O. Address.
Spurr Mine	34	T. 48 N.	R. 31 W.	H. G. Pulling	Detroit, Mich.	W. D. Davis, Sup't	Spurr, Mich.
Taylor Mine	9	T. 49 N.	R. 32 W.	S. L. Mather	Cleveland, Ohio.	Henry E. Warner, Agent	Marquette, Mich.

MAP OF THE
CITY OF DETROIT
DETROIT

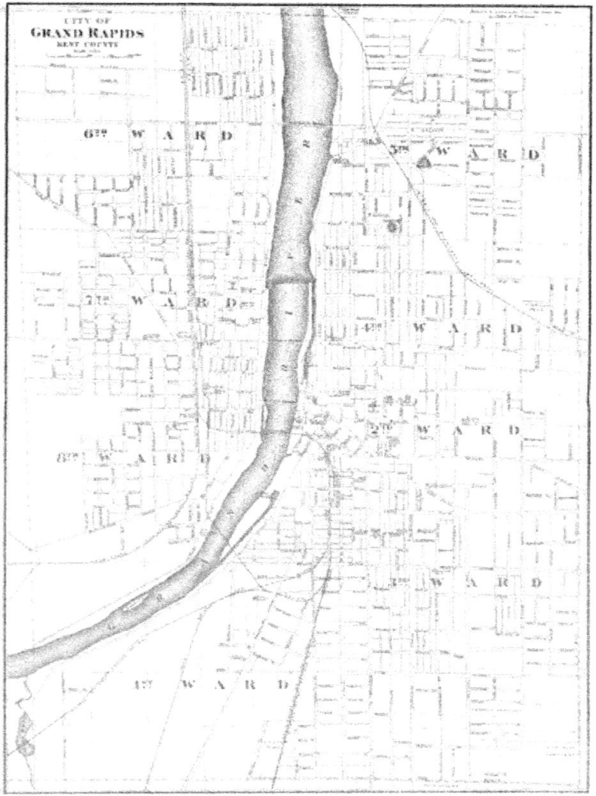
CITY OF
GRAND RAPIDS
KENT COUNTY
6TH WARD
5TH WARD
7TH WARD
4TH WARD
2ND WARD
8TH WARD
3RD WARD
1ST WARD

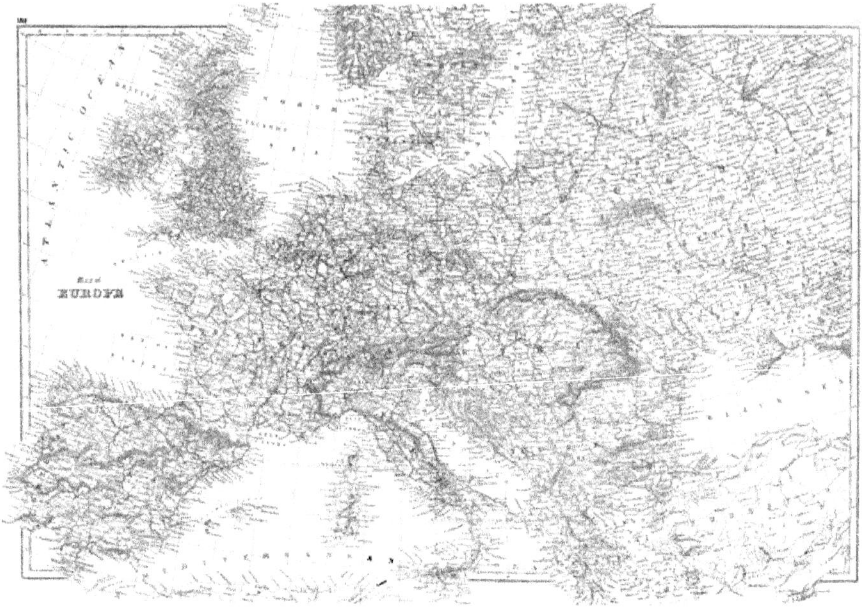
Map of
EUROPE

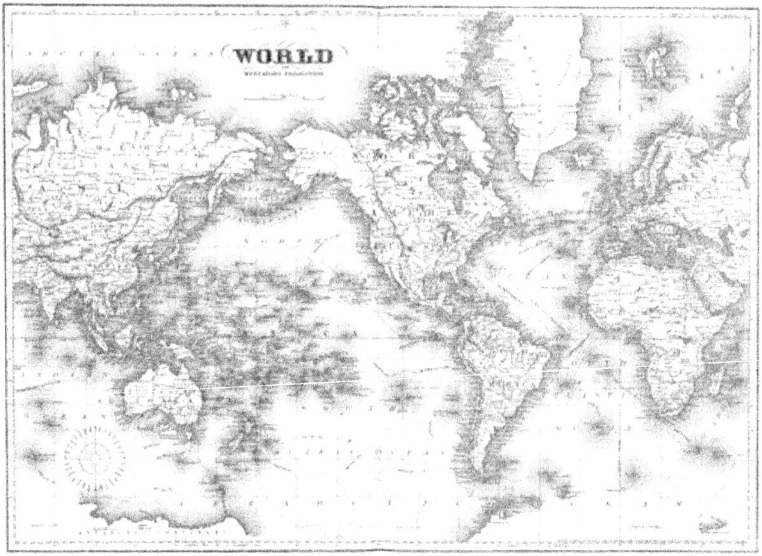
WORLD

MAP
SHOWING THE
Congressional
Districts
OF
MICHIGAN,
January 1st 1883.
LAKE SUPERIOR
LAKE MICHIGAN
LAKE HURON
LAKE ERIE
ILLINOIS
INDIANA
OHIO
ONTONAGON
MARQUETTE
SCHOOLCRAFT
CHIPPEWA
MACKINAC
DELTA
MENOMINEE
HOUGHTON
BARAGA
SAGINAW B.
HURON
SAGINAW

MAP
SHOWING THE
Judicial Circuits
OF
MICHIGAN,
January 1st 1883.
LAKE SUPERIOR
LAKE MICHIGAN
LAKE HURON
LAKE ERIE
INDIANA
OHIO
ONTONAGON
MARQUETTE
SCHOOLCRAFT
CHIPPEWA
MACKINAC
DELTA
MENOMINEE
HOUGHTON
BARAGA
SAGINAW B.
HURON
SAGINAW

MAP
SHOWING THE
Senatorial
Districts
OF
MICHIGAN,
January 1st 1883.
NOTE.
LAKE SUPERIOR
LAKE MICHIGAN
LAKE HURON
LAKE ERIE
ONTONAGON
MARQUETTE
SCHOOLCRAFT
CHIPPEWA
MACKINAC
DELTA
MENOMINEE
GREEN BAY
ILLINOIS
INDIANA
OHIO

MAP
SHOWING THE
Representative Districts
OF
MICHIGAN,
January 1st 1883.
LAKE SUPERIOR
LAKE MICHIGAN
LAKE HURON
LAKE ERIE
ONTONAGON
MARQUETTE
SCHOOLCRAFT
CHIPPEWA
MACKINAC
DELTA
MENOMINEE
GREEN BAY
INDIANA
OHIO

HISTORICAL SKETCH OF MICHIGAN RAILROADS.

BY RAY HADDOCK, ESQ.

INTRODUCTORY.

IT has been thought by certain ethical philosophers that the great material improvements which form such a marked characteristic of the age are typical of intellectual and moral advancement. We greatly fear that this view is one that is all too flattering to our race, for the material achievements referred to may well be characterized as wonderful. It is problematical if our higher advancement for the past half century can even be said to keep pace with the progress of science and the arts, and the latter, great as it is, must "pale its ineffectual fires" before the great improvements that have been made in the modes and means of travel and transportation. To realize the full extent, the "form and pressure," of this mighty revolution, it is only necessary to revert for a moment to the insufficient and uncomfortable modes in vogue one or two generations ago.

It is an interesting fact that the expediency, not to say the necessity, of connecting the East and West by means of artificial water communication first suggested itself to Washington as long ago as when he accompanied Gen. Braddock on his ill-starred expedition to what was then one of the outposts of civilization in the new world. A canal from the Chesapeake to the Ohio then suggested itself to his mind, a gigantic project, upon which would have hinged thousands of other great improvements. It is true that it was fated that in other localities should be inaugurated the great progressive triumphs which loomed before the prophetic eye of the Father of his Country, but this diversion none the less revealed his prescience and wisdom, and the possession of that marvelous executive talent which was destined, a few years later, to marshal the raw recruit into the veteran, call up munitions of war as if out of the earth, and lay broad and deep the foundations of a mighty empire.

It is not essential to our present purpose that we give in detail the history of the great improvements which have resulted in binding all of the various divisions of the country together in such an immense and intricate network of railways. It is certainly a most gratifying reflection that this result is no more than a fair index of the general prosperity, and affords a striking exposition of present and latent wealth. Without this prosperity and this wealth it could not have been accomplished. One or two decades since it was thought by many of our prudent business men that a sufficient number of railways had been constructed to meet the wants of the country for many years to come, yet the work has constantly progressed, and is still progressing. A prominent feature is the tendency to the accumulation of the stocks of the most important and valuable Roads in few hands. So rapidly has construction progressed that it is extremely doubtful if this class of monopolists have as large a proportionate interest under their immediate control as was the case a few years ago; but the fact remains that most of the new ones referred to, as well as those which are likely to be built, must be tributary, in a certain sense, to those mammoth corporations, and the fact is regarded by many as foreboding evil to the true interest of the country, if not to the principles of equality and popular rights. At the same time, there are many who attach no unhappy significance whatever to the phenomenal development. Their ideas concerning the matter are that the immense wealth of the parties referred to could not, in all probability, be invested and used in any other way less prejudicially to the interests of the country at large than it now is; that, although they may own the Roads, they cannot manage and work them; and that, inasmuch as no one is compelled to patronize their Roads, they are, after all, no more independent of the people than the people are of them. The tendency to consolidation is another growing feature of the times. The advantages of this policy under favoring circumstances are too obvious to require comment.

The pleasing fact has been developed within a comparatively few years that all the available surplus capital of the country need not necessarily center at the sea-board, and the various important cities throughout the land are rapidly becoming great financial centers. The commercial metropolis of Michigan is experiencing the beneficent influence of this modern development; in fact it has been, in her case, illustrated in a most striking and peculiar manner, for in view of a certain era in monetary affairs it seems like the sun of prosperity beaming with full effulgence upon the darkness of the past. For many years succeeding the memorable "wild cat" era, the popular prejudice against banks continued so strong that all of Detroit's varied interests languished for want of adequate banking capital, and the growth and development of the city was greatly retarded. The statement of the bare fact that for the entire decade from 1860 to 1870 not a foot of new railway penetrated the city, will suggest its own commentary upon the character and extent of this depression. From the effects of the great evil referred to, as well as from those of other drawbacks, the "City of the Straits" has recovered and has now girded herself anew for the race of enterprise and prosperity.

In all of our early railroad building eastern or foreign capital was depended on, and without it no important enterprise could by any possibility have been carried forward. All this is, in a measure, changed, and within a few years important railways have been built solely with home capital.

In the accompanying sketch it has not been thought necessary to allude particularly to the character of the equipment or the quality of the machinery and other essentials necessary to constitute first-class railways. It is universally understood and admitted that as regards these essentials the railways of Michigan will compare favorably with any in the country. Many of the most desirable improvements looking to safety and convenience are those which our leading Roads have been the first to introduce. All replacements are being made with steel rails, and in a short time no other kind will be in use upon any of our first class Roads.

DEVELOPMENT OF RAILWAY ENTERPRISE—THE INITIAL PROJECTS.

The history of Michigan railways may well be called identical with the history of the material advancement of the State, so far as relates to the Lower Peninsula, inasmuch as its real progress, its gigantic strides to wealth and greatness, date from their inception. Immigration was at its height during the period extending from 1830 to 1837. A large proportion was from Western New York, an element belonging mainly to the New England stock, and the maxims of thrift and enterprise came with it. The practical application of these maxims began to take shape in stupendous enterprises, even before Michigan emerged from the chrysalis condition of a territory. The name of these projects was legion, most of them being of an utopian character whose most important results consisted of fastening upon our then population an enormous load of indebtedness. This constitutes the first of two epochs in our history, comprising the era of wild speculation and "internal improvement" so vividly remembered by the comparatively few of the old citizens of the West who still survive, and in view of the great results which our pioneers hoped for, taken in connection with the insignificant means at their command, these too ambitious speculations may be regarded as eminently typical of that remarkable era. Of the numerous projects belonging to this period only three enterprises of any importance assumed substantial form and shape, namely, the Detroit and St. Joseph (the old corporate name of the Michigan Central) the Michigan Southern, and the Detroit and Pontine (which was ultimately merged in the Detroit and Milwaukee).

In 1830 the population of Detroit numbered 2,200 souls. The citizens of that day, consisting, almost without exception, of young and middle-aged men, were proverbially enterprising to a degree more than commensurate with their financial ability. If the public interests required any work to be done there were no capitalists to rely upon. Some few of the landed proprietors were comparatively well off, but those who were regarded as the wealthiest as a general rule had the least ready money, their possessions consisting of lands, and the necessity of borrowing money to pay their taxes being oftener the rule than the exception. The community could boast of two or three banking institutions, powerful affairs for those days, having more capital than could be conveniently used at home and considerable of their surplus currency was loaned to Ohio customers. There was comparatively little difficulty in borrowing money, and very naturally almost everybody was in debt. Thus situated, with no important trade with the outer world except in the single item of furs, when we remember that, poor as Detroit was, it was rich compared with the settlements elsewhere in the Territory, something like a true idea may be formed as to the ability of Michigan to prosecute great works of internal improvement.

It was not until the keels of countless merchantmen had vexed the waters of the bays and inlets of our Lower Peninsula, bearing away the rich spoils of our frontier forests, that our lumbermen began to work their way inward from the shore, a process that gradually became a matter of necessity as the supply began to show signs of diminution. By slow degrees the plow followed the paraphernalia of the mill, and in due time the important truth was revealed that the "pine barrens," which according to tradition constituted a large share of our Peninsula, were merely mythical so far as the term referred to the character of the soil. The choicest pine timber proved to be invariably interspersed with beech, maple and other hardwoods, growing mostly upon handsome rolling lands, with an arable and productive soil. The settlement of the North began in earnest; State roads were constructed; lands became valuable for farming purposes and the country began to feel the effect of the land grants that had been made by Congress in aid of railroads. These grants proved, indeed, the *coup de grace* in enhancing the value of lands along the line of the proposed Roads. They were granted in alternate sections, and a demand sprang up at advanced rates for the unappropriated sections, which, in turn, reacted upon and enhanced the value of the grants. The first specific grant by Congress for railroad purposes was made to the Illinois Central in 1850, but the first grant in aid of Michigan roads was not made until 1856. The grants were made to the State direct, and the conditions were imposed in detail by legislative enactment. The progress in railroad building being slow, the effect in enhancing the value of the lands was naturally on a corresponding scale.

MICHIGAN CENTRAL RAILROAD.

The financial condition of the city and Territory was as above described when the Detroit and St. Joseph Railroad Company was incorporated by the "Legislative Council of the Territory of Michigan." The act was consummated on the 29th June, 1832, and named twenty-one corporators under the name of Commissioners, all of whom are now deceased. Among these were included the names of John Biddle, John R. Williams, DeGarmo Jones and other prominent citizens. By the terms of the charter the State reserved the right to purchase the Road at a price not exceeding its original cost and fourteen per cent interest.

This initiatory step, destined to lead to great results in paving the way for a through line between the East and West, was due in a certain degree to the necessities of the case as well as to enterprise and public spirit. There were at the time four thoroughfares leading into Detroit: The Chicago, Grand River, Fort Gratiot and Saginaw or Pontiac, all of which had been built by government. They were all constructed upon a clay soil and were well nigh impassable for a considerable portion of the year; hence the necessity for iron outlets. The Detroit and St. Joseph Road was at the outset a strictly local enterprise, and probably not a dollar of the original stock was taken at the East. Every one in Detroit who had a hundred dollars at command, present or prospective, subscribed, and upon this subscription, with what little could be obtained along the line, the work was commenced. Within two years from the date of the act of incorporation the construction proceeded between Detroit and Ypsilanti, under the presidency of Major John Biddle. The civil engineer in charge was Col. John M. Berrien, then Lieut. Berrien, an officer in the regular army detached for civil service—a not uncommon proceeding, the valuable aid of army officers being frequently called into requisition in laying out roads and furnishing drawings of harbors and "paper cities." East of Ypsilanti the forest was almost entirely unbroken, and was so dense that it was with the greatest difficulty the surveying party could run a line. Notwithstanding this and countless other drawbacks, the construction progressed at a fair rate for that period, when every needed appliance was procured with great difficulty. The Albany and Schenectady Railroad (then Mohawk and Hudson—now a link in the chain of the New York Central), less than seventeen miles in length, the first Railroad built north of Pennsylvania, had been running only about a year when the Detroit and St. Joseph Railroad Company was chartered, and it must not be forgotten that Michigan was then but a Territory!

The construction of the Road progressed as rapidly as could be expected until Michigan was formally admitted into the Union as a State, in February, 1837. By this time the subject of internal improvements by the State had begun to be agitated to a considerable extent, and an act was passed and approved March 20, 1837, entitled "An act to provide for the construction of certain works of public improvement and for other purposes." This act provided for the purchase of the Detroit and St. Joseph Railroad in accordance with the stipulations of the charter, and, under its provisions, the Road passed into the possession of the State. This was after about $30,000 had been expended toward building the section between Detroit and Ypsilanti, and in purchasing the right of way beyond the last named point. Laws were passed by which a loan of $5,000,000 was to be effected for the purpose of inaugurating a system of internal improvement, and thus carrying out the popular idea. Somewhere between two and three millions was brought into service by means of the loan thus authorized, but by the great crash of 1837 the corporators who had taken the loan became insolvent, and the State was left financially powerless.

Upon the purchase of the Road by the State, the name was changed to the Michigan Central, and it became part and parcel of the famous plan of crossing the State by three parallel lines, namely, the Northern, having its eastern terminus at Port Huron, the Central, terminating at Detroit, and the Southern, at Monroe. By way of relieving the monotony attaching to so many land routes, a canal was projected from Clinton River to the Kalamazoo, upon which a large sum was expended before it was abandoned. The Northern Road, after being graded for some distance west of Port Huron, was abandoned after the expenditure of a large sum for the right of way, grubbing and grading. The late Hon. James B. Hunt was the Acting Commissioner of the Northern route, Gen. Levi S. Humphrey, of Monroe, holding the same position in reference to the Southern, the works being in charge of a general Board of Internal Improvements. The first Acting Commissioner of Internal Improvements was Col. David C. McKinstry, father of Commodore J. P. McKinstry.

To convey a correct idea of the character of the railroads of that day, we ought to state that up to this time, and for several years subsequently, the old-fashioned "strap rail" was the kind used. The rails, after a little wear, easily became displaced, the projecting ends being what were too familiarly known as "snake heads." The T rail had been introduced upon Eastern roads, but the idea of its possession did not even enter into the thoughts of our pioneers of internal improvement. It was, in fact, the very cheapness of railroads that served as a powerful incentive to men of small means to undertake their construction. Even the strap rail was at times a luxury, the supply being eked out in case of emergency by the substitution of wooden material. The rolling stock was mostly of a character in keeping with that of the track. The cars were small, divided into three compartments, but entirely innocent of any of the "modern improvements," and having doors through the sides. The first cars in use were built in Troy, but their manufacture was soon commenced here. The first passenger car of Detroit make was christened the *Lady Mason*, in honor of the wife of the Hon. Stevens T. Mason, Governor of the State.

The State built the Road as far west as Kalamazoo, but her reputation for railroad management was constantly on the descending scale. The Internal Improvement warrants sunk as low as forty cents to the dollar, there being no funds with which to meet them. The rails were rapidly wearing out, and the State was so new and so poor that it had no credit to purchase iron, or even to buy the spikes required to fasten down the "snake-heads," to say nothing of a further extension of the track. The affairs of the Road were in such a strait that it would have stopped entirely, but for the interposition of Governor Barry, who advanced $7,000 in money from his individual means, and became personally responsible for $30,000 more. In this condition of affairs the Legislature of 1846 assembled. Amongst the earliest proceedings, Judge Hand, the sole representative from Detroit in the House, moved a resolution for the appointment of a committee to consider the expediency of providing for the sale of the public works. This was carried, and a bill authorizing the sale was about being reported, when Mr. J. W. Brooks, of Boston, came forward as the representative of a number of eastern capitalists, and made a tender for the purchase of the Road. Negotiations were at once entered into, the result of which was that the present charter was drawn up and reported, conditioned for the payment of $2,000,000 as purchase money, and after a protracted struggle, the required two-thirds of each House was obtained, and the bill became a law. Previous to this time it is asserted that so large a sum as $100,000 had never been brought into the Western country from the East for investment in any one enterprise. Yet this act of incorporation contemplated the expenditure of from $6,000,000 to $8,000,000, of which half a million had to be paid before the State would relinquish possession. The Company were required to complete the Road to Lake Michigan with T rail of not less than sixty pounds to the yard—a very heavy rail for those days—and it was also stipulated that all the old Road should be relaid with similar rail. The Company were authorized to change the western terminus to any point in the State on Lake Michigan, and they were subsequently allowed to change it to Chicago. The line was completed in 1852. The carrying out of the provisions of the charter and the gradual change in equipment and outfit until the Road has become second to none in the country, if in the world, are matters upon which it is unnecessary to dwell at length. In the staunch construction of its cars, the excellence of its machinery and the superior character of its equipment, it has long been regarded as a model Road, while at the same it has always had the benefit of wise and prudent management. This has been signally manifested in the exhibition of that far-seeing wisdom which properly appreciates the importance of liberality and fairness in dealings with shippers and customers generally. The adherence to this principle has given the Central a popularity unsurpassed by that enjoyed by any similar corporation in any country. The line passes through a region which is, for the most part, famed for its fertility and natural beauty. Upon the main line are located the thriving and beautiful cities of Ypsilanti, Ann Arbor, Jackson, Marshall, Battle Creek, Kalamazoo, Niles and many fine places of less note, some of which have been called into existence by this great thoroughfare.

The "Michigan Air Line" was projected as a short line from Chicago to Buffalo, and was intended to run across the State from Chicago, striking the St. Clair River just above the town of St. Clair. The Michigan Central, which aided in building so much of this line as lies between Jackson and Niles, and furnished almost the entire capital with which it was built, finally made it a feeder for Detroit and the Central. Cassopolis, Three Rivers, Union City, Centreville, Homer and other thriving towns are located on this line, and it passes through as fine and productive region as any in Michigan. This Road, which was completed in 1871, is, in point of construction, equal to any in the West, and shortens the distance between Detroit and Chicago about 15 miles. Distance from Jackson to South Bend, 111 miles.

The South Bend division extends from the city of Niles to South Bend, a distance of 11 miles, about half the line being in Michigan. C. B. Bush, Division Superintendent, Jackson.

The freight traffic has increased so largely during the past few years that important innovations have been rendered necessary in terminal facilities in Detroit. Within the past year the Company has purchased, at an immense cost, nearly fifty acres of land in immediate proximity to the car-shops, and about 14 miles of new track have already been laid in the yards.

H. B. Ledyard, Detroit, is General Manager; D. A. Waterman, Auditor; J. E. Griffith, Cashier; main office, Detroit.

O. W. Ruggles, Chicago, General Passenger Agent; A. Grier, Chicago, General Freight Agent.

Distance from Detroit to Chicago, 284 miles (including 14 miles on track of Illinois Central); total length of line now operated, including Canada Southern, 1,450 miles; total length of Michigan lines, 1,035 miles; total income, 1881, $8,234,331.62; total operating expenses and taxes, 1881, $6,782,095.90.

A number of important Roads are operated and controlled by the Michigan Central, some of which owe their existence to its direct outlay or its influence, while others have come under its control through leases or some arrangement having the practical effect of a lease. These are as follows:

JACKSON, LANSING AND SAGINAW, AND MACKINAC DIVISIONS.

These very important connections now form the Saginaw and Mackinac divisions of the Michigan Central. The line extends from Jackson, via Lansing, the seat of government, to the Straits of Mackinac, a distance of 295 miles, passing through Saginaw, West Bay City, Gaylord and a number of other rapidly growing towns, and opening up a most important region with resources hitherto undeveloped. At the Straits it connects by a ferriage of five miles with the Detroit, Mackinac and Marquette Railroad of the Upper Peninsula. The section between West Bay City and Mackinac is of inestimable importance as practically a segment via the Mackinac and Marquette Road of the Northern Pacific. By way of the Detroit and Bay City Road, another division of the Michigan Central, the traffic of this great national thoroughfare will, when the links shall all have been completed, be brought direct to Detroit.

The Jackson, Lansing and Saginaw Road is now completed from Otsego Lake to the Straits of Mackinac, via Cheboygan, a distance of about 63 miles. The business of this final extension has exceeded the most sanguine anticipations, and the prospect is peculiarly flattering, especially in view of the rapid development of the important and interesting region penetrated by the Road. From 1877 to 1881, both inclusive, there was realized by the sale of lands and timber—the fruits of the government land grant—$2,000,000.

This Road was the first ever aided by the Michigan Central, a movement inaugurated nearly twenty years ago. When commenced, there was no thought of carrying the line as far as Saginaw, but upon its completion to Lansing, the idea was conceived of extending it to the former place. There lay in the way between Lansing and Owosso a segment of the old "Ramshorn Road," a familiar name for an old-time Road, whose corporate name was the Amboy, Lansing and Traverse Bay Railroad, the popular designation conveying a fair idea of the sinuous direction of the line. Amboy, the southern terminus of this once prospectively important thoroughfare, was a place of small consequence, commercial or otherwise, and the strongest incentive connected with the inception of the enterprise was to get possession of the rich land grant consequent upon its inauguration and progress. The Jackson, Lansing and Saginaw Company purchased this segment, with all its valuable franchises, under the authority of an act of the Legislature, made it "part and parcel" of their line, and carried it in triumph across the Saginaw valley to the Straits of Mackinac. Without the "sinews of war" obtained by means of the above grant, the initiative of this inestimably important enterprise, upon which has hinged the development of the vast resources of northern Michigan and the perfecting of the chain of the Northern Pacific, would not have been taken, at least not so early by many years as it has been. This route will control almost the entire traffic from Marquette during the protracted period of the year at which navigation is closed, constituting as it does the most direct route. The distance between Marquette and Detroit is shorter by 240 miles than by the old route via Chicago.

It is a coincidence worthy to be added, that the projected southern segment of the "Ramshorn," extending from Lansing to the main line of the Michigan Southern, has been carried forward to completion as a branch (Lansing Division) of the Lake Shore and Michigan Southern, the original rival of the Central. W. A Vaughan, Division Superintendent, Bay City.

GRAND RIVER VALLEY ROAD.

This Road, forming another great branch and feeder of the Central, was chartered in 1846, and finished in 1870. It is 94 miles in length, running from Rives Junction, near Jackson, to Grand Rapids, intersecting the Detroit, Grand Haven and Milwaukee Road, and connecting, by means of the latter, with the Chicago and West Michigan Road, (formerly known as the Chicago and Michigan Lake Shore), which runs from New Buffalo to Pentwater. It runs through the county seats of Eaton and Barry counties, tapping a fertile and to some extent heavily timbered region, and has done and is still doing well, although it did not have the benefit of a land grant. Like the Jackson, Lansing and Saginaw, it was undertaken by the citizens of Jackson, but they finally applied to the Central for help, without which its construction would have proved a herculean task. The governing consideration of the Michigan Central interest in taking hold of it was to control the traffic and bring it to Detroit, instead of allowing it to contribute toward building up business centers in other States. Amos Root, President, Jackson; E. W. Barber, Secretary and Treasurer, Charlotte; C. B Bush, Division Superintendent, Jackson.

KALAMAZOO AND SOUTH HAVEN ROAD.

This is another Road whose capital is chiefly owned by the Michigan Central. The latter company has also guaranteed its bonds, and obtained a lease of the Road, which is an important feeder of itself, 40 miles in length, and important also as affording an eligible connection with another Road in the same interest, the Chicago and West Michigan, the traffic of which it brings to Kalamazoo. It traverses a region partly timbered but being rapidly converted into productive farms. It was opened for business from Kalamazoo to South Haven, January 2, 1871. C. B. Bush, Division Superintendent, Jackson.

DETROIT AND BAY CITY ROAD.

This important Road, which has already been incidentally referred to as constituting part of a direct line to Mackinac, completes the category of the important enterprises which have been aided by the Michigan Central. Its length from Detroit to Bay City is about 108 miles, passing through a very rich agricultural region, while the trade in lumber and salt contributes very materially to swell its traffic. The Road owes its existence to the remarkable public spirit of the people along the line, that of Bay City being by no means the least conspicuous. It was opened for business from Detroit to Caro July 22, 1878, and to East Saginaw Jan. 5, 1879. Branches have been constructed as follows: Lapeer to Five Lakes, about 9 miles; Vassar to Caro, about 13 miles; Denmark Junction to East Saginaw, about 17 miles. W. A. Vaughan, Division Superintendent, Bay City.

From April 1, 1881, the Michigan Central Company leased the Detroit and Bay City Road, and assumed its debts; for which Michigan Central fifty year Five per cent. bonds, secured by a first mortgage on Bay City property, were issued to the amount of $3,576,000. There also remain outstanding 424 bonds of the original issue of the Detroit and Bay City Company, which, prior to the sale of the property in February, 1881, were secured by a first mortgage thereon, and also by the guarantee of the Michigan Central Company, but which, since the sale, hold no lien upon the property, and are valuable only for the guarantee above mentioned. They are, however, exchangeable for 424 bonds of the new issue, which are held for that purpose, and when so exchanged will increase the present issue to $4,000,000.

CANADA SOUTHERN.

The main line of this Road extends from the International Bridge, opposite Buffalo, to Detroit river, 230 miles, and the length of the Detroit and Toledo division is 56 miles. There is also a branch from St. Clair to Ridgeway. Total length in Canada, 330 miles; in Michigan, 66 miles; in Ohio, 9 miles. The enterprise is one that was long agitated in Canada, and was finally carried forward to a successful issue mainly by the enterprise and persistence of one or two individuals, especially W. A. Thompson. Early last season, an arrangement was concluded with the Michigan Central, by which it has passed under the control and management of the latter for the period of 21 years. By the terms of this agreement, the Canada Southern is to issue second mortgage Five per cent. bonds to the amount of $6,000,000, which sum is mainly to be used in making certain important improvements, which are specifically set forth. The Michigan Central agrees to work the Canada Southern's lines as if they were its own, pay the taxes on its property, the interest on its bonds, and to forward over it all the traffic it can control, which can be reached by it or by its connections, and to foster its present interchange of business with its Southwestern connections. From the sum total of gross earnings, there shall be paid, first, the cost of maintenance and operation; second, the fixed charges (interest and rentals) of both companies; and the balance shall be divided in the proportion of two-thirds to the Central, and one-third to the Southern. Quintennial conferences are also provided for to re-adjust the division of the surplus, should equity require a re-adjustment.

This arrangement will no doubt prove profitable to the Canada Southern, in that it thereby secures an interest in the earnings of one of the great transit channels of the continent, while at the same time it will no doubt also prove a good one for the Central in securing an eastern connection strictly under its own control, which it has never before had. The Toledo connection, affording direct communication with the South, is also an important one in some of its aspects. From the character of the country along the main line of the Canada Southern, even a fair local traffic cannot be expected for the present, but everything in the shape of gain in this regard will add to what is, even as it now stands, a favorable outlook. E. P. Murray, Superintendent Canada Division, St. Thomas.

LAKE SHORE AND MICHIGAN SOUTHERN RAILWAY.

The same committee in the Legislature (in 1846), that reported a bill providing for the sale of the Central, also framed a similar enactment for the sale of the Southern, which, as heretofore stated, was a twin project with the Central. The charter as originally granted was from Monroe to Lake Michigan. Subsequently it became a desideratum with the stockholders to have the terminus at Toledo, and they adopted measures that finally resulted in the perpetual lease of the Erie and Kalamazoo Road, whose indebtedness was assumed by the Southern to the extent of the amount of aid which had been afforded by the State. Previous to offering the Road for sale, the State had expended towards its construction $1,100,000. Of this work, 18 miles, laid with strap rail, were opened from Monroe to Petersburg in 1839; 15 miles from Petersburg to Adrian in 1840; and 33 miles from Adrian to Hillsdale in 1843. The President, Mr. Charles Noble, effected its purchase on behalf of himself and colleagues, who were mostly citizens of Monroe, and the public spirit displayed by them is worthy the highest praise. The Messrs. Litchfield, who subsequently figured so extensively in the history of the Road, then owned little or none of the stock. The price paid to the State was $500,000 for the whole Road, so far as completed, with the materials, right of way, etc., including also the Tecumseh branch, from Adrian to Manchester, which had been already built to Tecumseh, together with the franchises of the Palmyra and Jacksonburgh Road, now known as the Jackson division of the Southern. The Road, in default of payment, which was by instalments, was to revert to the State. The route to be followed was from the city of Monroe, through the towns of Petersburg, Adrian, Hillsdale, Jonesville and Coldwater, to Lake Michigan. No other east and west road was to be chartered to commence within 25 miles of Monroe, or to run within 20 miles of the line of the Southern. The Northern Indiana Railroad was chartered by the State of Indiana 1835, under the name of the Buffalo and Mississippi Railroad Company. The organization of this company was perfected in 1837, and the Road was put under contract, but operations were suspended in 1838 owing to the embarrassments entailed by the great financial revulsion. In 1847 a new board was formed, of which J. W. Brooks and W. B. Ogden were members, but the work of construction progressed slowly, and in 1849 the work passed under the control of the purchasers of the Michigan Southern, who then decided to make Chicago, instead of New Buffalo, the terminus. As soon as this determination was adopted, the construction of the Road was pushed forward in earnest, and it was completed in May, 1852, reaching Chicago in advance of the Michigan Central; distance, 243 miles. This result was due largely to the enterprise and energy of the Messrs. Litchfield, with whom the company had in a fortunate hour formed a contract for its construction. These gentlemen were dismayed by no disasters, and baffled by no obstacles.

The line of the Southern, as already intimated, began at Monroe, but the lease of the Erie and Kalamazoo Road, extending from Toledo to Adrian, 33 miles, afforded a direct through route via the last named points. The lease, which was perpetual, was effected in 1849. This branch, which was opened in 1837, was built with strap rail, and was at first operated by horse power. We may note parenthetically that "strap rail" and "horse power" were very familiar terms in those days, especially the former. On the 20th June, 1837, the first locomotive was placed on the Road. In 1838 the Palmyra and Jacksonburgh Road (Jackson branch, a private enterprise built in the interest of the Erie and Kalamazoo Company), was opened to Tecumseh, 13 miles. In 1844 it was sold to the State for $22,000, and was finally included in the State's transfer to the Michigan Southern Railroad Company, the purchasers subsequently completing it to Jackson.

The final completion of the Southern (in 1852) to Chicago, caused a wonderful sensation in business circles at the East. For a season, the enterprise completely overshadowed in the public mind that of the Central, which, for the time being, seemed to lag behind. It was only the more sagacious and watchful who were posted concerning the progress of this great innovation in the transportation facilities of the country. The obstacles to the building of long railway lines, especially in the West, were of such grave character, that the public generally seemed passively to entertain the belief that the thing was impossible, and when it was ascertained that a railway had actually been completed from Lake Erie to Lake Michigan—then regarded as located in the Far West—it seemed like the realization of one of the stories of the Arabian Nights. One wonder followed another, and the success of the enterprise and the enthusiasm the event occasioned led at an early day to the undertaking of the Air Line Railroad of Indiana, by which the distance between Toledo and Chicago was considerably shortened, and also to the establishment of a line of first class passenger steamers running to Buffalo, and the construction of a line of railroad between Toledo and Detroit, a connection placing the last named city in direct communication with the main line both via Toledo and via the Monroe and Adrian division. In the meantime the stock exhibited unparalleled fluctuations, at times attaining an almost fabulous value, and at others, under the influence of financial revulsions, becoming familiarized to the atmosphere circling about zero.

The Detroit and Toledo Railroad Company was chartered in 1856, and the work was vigorously prosecuted, the line being finished in 1857. The Michigan Southern obtained a perpetual lease, and the operations of the Road are included in the reports of the main line. This enterprise was aided by subscriptions in Detroit and Toledo, as well as at other points on the line. For many years it not only afforded the only direct means of railroad communication between Detroit and the South, but it was, and yet is, very frequently resorted to by Detroit merchants as a channel for the shipment of produce to the eastern and southeastern markets, especially to Pittsburgh, Philadelphia, Baltimore, etc.

In 1855, an act was passed authorizing the consolidation of the Michigan Southern and Northern Indiana Roads. By consolidation with Roads beyond the limits of the State, the Southern has become a gigantic corporation, the length of the main line and the different divisions aggregating in 1882 1178 miles. Like that of the Central, the building of the original line was attended with great difficulties, and the parallel is nobly maintained so far as concerns equipment and general management. The country which it traverses is famed for its beauty and productiveness.

The "Lake Shore and Michigan Southern Railway Company" was formed by consolidation in 1869 of the following companies: 1. Michigan Southern and Northern Indiana,—Chicago to Toledo, with branches. 2. Cleveland and Toledo,—Toledo to Cleveland. 3. Cleveland, Painesville and Ashtabula,—Cleveland to Erie. 4. Buffalo and Erie,—Erie to Buffalo.

John Newell is General Manager; E. D. Worcester, Secretary and Treasurer, New York; W. P. Johnson, General Passenger Agent, Chicago; George H. Vaillant, General Freight Agent, Cleveland.

LANSING DIVISION.

This division, which was opened in 1872, is wholly owned by the Lake Shore and Michigan Southern. It was originally known as the "Northern Central Michigan," and extends from Jonesville, on the main line, to North Lansing, a distance of 61 miles. It traverses a remarkably wealthy region, in which are located Homer, Albion, Eaton Rapids, and other prosperous towns, and succeeded to the franchises of the old Amboy, Lansing and Traverse Bay, or "Ramshorn" Road. The old company built a road from Lansing to Owosso, but it was constructed in primitive style. Financial difficulties arose, and, in September, 1864, the Hon. C. C. Trowbridge was appointed Receiver, who remained in possession about two years. The Road was managed under the direction of Mr. Trowbridge by the Superintendent of the D. & M. Road, and the rolling stock necessary to its proper working was supplied by that Road. The Receivership was, of course, only temporary, and, near the close of 1866, the Road was sold.

FORT WAYNE BRANCH.

This corporation represents a consolidation, formed in 1869, of interests under the name of the Fort Wayne, Jackson and Saginaw, Jackson, Fort Wayne and Cincinnati, and the Fort Wayne, Jackson and Saginaw Railroads. The length is 100 miles, and the Road was completed about the close of 1870. It affords direct communication with the heart of the rich and prosperous State of Indiana, a connection which could not prove otherwise than desirable. It forms, with the Jackson, Lansing and Saginaw Road, a great route for lumber between Northern Michigan and Cincinnati, Louisville and other points on the Ohio river. President, Samuel Sloan, New York; Secretary and Treasurer, R. G. Rolston, New York; Superintendent, M. D. Woodford, Jackson; General Freight and Ticket Agent, H. Bromley, Jackson.

JACKSON BRANCH.

This division extends from the city of Adrian, on the main line, to Jackson, a distance of 46 miles, and morning and afternoon express trains are run. The line passes through Tecumseh, Manchester and Napoleon, and has a fine farming region tributary to it. The Road is part of the old "Erie and Kalamazoo" project. It was partially opened in 1838.

DETROIT DIVISION.

See sketch of the main line.

KALAMAZOO DIVISION.

The Kalamazoo Division, familiarly known as "Gardner's Road," was built by piecemeal, having been commenced by Ransom Gardner, Esq., about the year 1866, without any clearly defined reference to the points that are now its termini. The Southern Road had had for several years a "strap" road from White Pigeon to Three Rivers, and the Company agreed that if Mr. Gardner would relay it, they would give him a lease of it, as a link in a project of his own, namely, the construction of a road from Three Rivers north to Schoolcraft, the latter point being the outlet of a rich prairie region. This arrangement was concluded, and the Road was extended to Schoolcraft, after which another corporation was formed by Mr. Gardner and his friends, to build from that point to Kalamazoo, which project was finally carried forward to completion, and at the last named point Mr. Gardner rested. He ultimately succeeded in carrying the Road to Grand Rapids, having been enabled to dispose of the bonds by means of a stipulated traffic arrangement with the Michigan Central, which corporation was desirous of obtaining an outlet to Grand Rapids. The Road, however, finally passed into the hands of the Michigan Southern, and the Central built the Grand River Valley Road, as already stated. Mr. Gardner also built a branch of his Road from Allegan to Holland, which was ultimately extended to Muskegon (known as the Chicago and West Michigan Road). The "Continental Improvement Company" (an association nearly identical in interest with the Pennsylvania Central), obtained control of all this line beyond Allegan, and built a Road from that place to Monteith, on the Grand Rapids and Indiana Road.

ADRIAN AND MONROE DIVISION.

This division is substantially part of the main line, Adrian being the point of divergence for the lines respectively to Toledo on the southeast, and Monroe and Detroit on the east and northeast. Distance from Adrian to Monroe, 33 miles; Adrian to Toledo, 33 miles; Monroe to Detroit, 40 miles.

YPSILANTI BRANCH.

This branch extends from Ypsilanti to Banker's, on the Fort Wayne Road, four miles southwest of Hillsdale, a distance of 65 miles. It traverses a productive region, and has junctions with the Michigan Central, the Toledo, Ann Arbor and Grand Trunk, with the Jackson branch of the Southern, and with the Fort Wayne Road. Saline, Manchester, Brooklyn, and several other flourishing towns are located on its line.

FAYETTE BRANCH.

This branch extends from Adrian to Fayette, Ohio, a distance of 32 miles. The length of the line in Michigan is 38 miles. One express train is run daily. This Road affords substantially an air line from Detroit to Fayette.

DUNDEE BRANCH.

This branch extends from Detroit to Adrian, and accommodates a number of thriving communities, that would otherwise be deprived of a convenient outlet by rail. Distance, 47 miles.

DETROIT, GRAND HAVEN AND MILWAUKEE RAILWAY.

The day upon which the iron horse first woke the echoes of the wilderness skirting the farther limits of this important thoroughfare, ushered in a triumph for the real live business men of Detroit, such as any class of men would have just cause to be proud of. It is due in a large measure to their exertions that the great work was consummated. True, the original capital stock was swamped, with hardly a struggle; but if the amount had been fifty times greater, the substantial benefit accruing to the city and State would be a most ample compensation.

Probably the history of no railroad is replete with more grotesque incidents, or has been marked by more financial perturbations than that of the old Detroit and Pontiac Road, the initial project of the line. At an early period in the history of Detroit, it became a desideratum to establish railroad connection with the rich agricultural region of Oakland county, whose milling facilities were already in a fair stage of development. A charter was obtained of the Territorial Legislature on the 7th March, 1834, and the capital stock fixed at $100,000. Messrs. Alfred Williams and Sherman Stevens, of Pontiac, were the principal stockholders and managers, their control continuing until 1840, during which period their financial operations, if they could be presented in full, would make a most racy chapter. The building of the Road in the meantime made slow progress, banking enterprises engaging the principal attention of its managers. It was finally completed to Birmingham in 1839, and in September of that year the late Hon. Henry J. Buckley, conductor, or agent, as it was then termed, put forth his advertisement in the papers for two trips a day to Birmingham, the cars running in connection with "post coaches" to Pontiac and Flint, together with a semi-weekly line to Grand River. The introduction of steam was regarded as a notable event, the cars, during the period for which Royal Oak had been the terminus, having been run by horse power. In 1840, parties in Syracuse, N. Y., having claims upon the Road, procured its sale under an execution. It was bid in by Gurdon Williams, of Detroit, and Giles Williams and Dean Richmond, of Buffalo, but was soon afterward transferred to other parties in Syracuse. It was finally completed to Pontiac in 1843. The Road was subsequently leased by the Syracuse owners for ten years to Gurdon Williams, who was to pay a graduated amount of rental, averaging about $10,000 a year. In 1848, before the expiration of the lease, steps were taken to rescue the Road from the slough of despond into which it had been sunk by a heavy load of indebtedness, which finally resulted in its coming into the possession of a company headed by H. N. Walker, Esq., and that eminent but ultimately unfortunate financier, N. P. Stewart. Mr. Walker, who was elected President, negotiated bonds of the Company for a sufficient amount to relay the track. The accession of this company was the turning point in the fortunes of the Road. The laughable anecdotes of its early days, in which "snake-heads" and hair-breadth escapes are among the leading staples, would fill a respectably sized volume.

On the 3d April, 1848, a charter was obtained by the "Oakland and Ottawa Railroad Company." The Company was poor; its bonds were negotiated with difficulty, and it was only by the most strenuous exertions that any progress was made. In 1852, work was commenced, and in 1853 Mr. Walker went to Europe in the interest of the Road, where he purchased 2,600 tons of iron, being sufficient to lay the track to Fentonville.

The "Detroit and Pontiac" and "Oakland and Ottawa" Railroads were consolidated on the 18th February, 1855, under the name of the Detroit and Milwaukee Railway. In July of that year Mr. Walker made a second trip to Europe, where he negotiated the Company's bonds to the amount of $1,250,000. Subsequently Mr. W. visited Europe for the third time, during which visit an arrangement was made with the Great Western Railway Company, which was calculated to put an end to financial embarrassment. The mortgage was closed in 1860, and a reorganization was effected under the name of the Detroit and Milwaukee Railroad. The interest on the bonds in default was funded in bonds, and the interest on other indebtedness in preferred stock. In November, 1873, default was made in the payment of interest on the bonds and the Road passed into the hands of a receiver April 10, 1875, and was sold September 4, 1878, to the bondholders, who placed its management under the Great Western Railway Company of Canada. By the transfer last year of the Great Western to the Grand Trunk, the latter corporation took charge of the Road, which is now known as the Detroit, Grand Haven and Milwaukee Railway.

It may be added, as a curious fact, that, while those who were early engaged in pushing forward the building of this Road made perhaps, greater sacrifices to promote the land grant policy than were made by any other interest in the country, the Road was ultimately deprived of all aid in the way of a grant. The Road was completed only by the most herculean efforts, but all these great sacrifices have been requited in the immense influence it has exerted in aiding the development of the country.

The staunch propellers "Michigan" and "Wisconsin," both doubly bottomed with iron, form a daily line between Grand Haven and Milwaukee. Upon the first opening of the Road, two elegant steamships, built for the purpose, were placed on the line, but that description of craft was found not so well adapted to the trade as that which has now been brought into requisition. If experience may be called the best teacher, it may be regarded as a settled fact, that the screw possesses decided advantages over wooden buckets in waters where rough seas are more nearly the rule than the exception. W. J. Morgan, Superintendent, Detroit; James H. Muir, Secretary, Detroit; G. McDonald, Through Freight Agent, Milwaukee.

GRAND TRUNK RAILWAY.

No little sensation was produced among the citizens of Detroit when, in 1858, it was authoritatively stated that the parties controlling this famous Canadian thoroughfare, running from Portland, Quebec and Montreal to Sarnia, had decided to extend the line to this point. The intelligence was at first thought almost too good to be true, especially as it was proposed to carry forward the project to completion wholly upon the responsibility of the Grand Trunk interest, without regard to subscriptions on the part of those whose interest could but be materially promoted by its consummation. The right of way was secured as soon as practicable, and the cars came into Detroit in the Fall of 1859. This division has proved of substantial benefit to a section of the State not otherwise accommodated, and, with its connections, has been of incalculable value to the merchants and shippers of Detroit, not only in affording a competing route to the seaboard, but in enabling them to reach with their surplus commodities all the various leading points in New England, to which they had previously had no convenient access.

This enterprise proved the precursor of others of even far greater importance, so far as concerns the State at large. The capitalists and managers connected with the Road seem to have become enamored of the peculiar advantages possessed by Michigan in affording eligible routes for transportation between all the important markets, as well as with the character of our soil, which furnishes so abundantly the leading products which contribute to swell the earnings of railways. They have completed several projects which, aside from their commercial and otherwise material importance, will tend to link the two countries in bonds of enduring brotherhood.

In addition to the divisions elsewhere noted, an enterprise is in contemplation, which, if carried out, will give Detroit a new Railway line, making the city a terminal point of the Chicago and Grand Trunk Railway conjointly with Port Huron. Surveyors are now on the line to mark out a Road from Detroit to South Lyon, to connect with the Air Line, having also in view a connection between the western terminus of the latter and the main line at or near Battle Creek. Another surveying party is on the west portion of the proposed line to determine the most feasible route from Battle Creek to connect with the Air Line at or near Jackson. The plan, as above intimated, contemplates the securing of a direct line between Detroit and Chicago, via South Lyon, Jackson and Battle Creek.

The Grand Trunk management have been quite fortunate in securing the services, as Solicitor in this State, of the Hon. E. W. Meddaugh, a gentleman whose untiring energy in promoting interests entrusted to his care is paralleled by his native ability and ample legal attainments.

The aggregate length of lines controlled by the Grand Trunk is 2,889 miles, which will be increased by the Air Line extension from Pontiac to Jackson, which is all under contract.

The Great Western Railway of Canada passed under the management of the Grand Trunk January 1, 1883, and is now operated as a part of the Grand Trunk system. The Company have for some years past been substituting new steel rails for the old iron, and the Road is now, in all its appointments, one of the most substantial and best equipped on the continent, and the route is a favorite one between the East and the West. Detroit to Suspension Bridge, 229 miles; London to Sarnia, 61 miles; London to Port Stanley, 24 miles.

Distances on main line of Grand Trunk—Detroit to Fort Gratiot, 62 miles; Detroit to Portland, 861 miles; Detroit to Montreal, 564 miles; Detroit to Quebec, 736 miles; Montreal to Riviere du Loup, 172 miles; Montreal to Rouse's Point, 50 miles.

General offices Montreal. Joseph Hickson, Gen. Manager; A. J. Read, Private Secretary; Wm. Wainwright, Assistant Gen. Manager; John Main, Assistant Gen. Freight Agent, Detroit; W. J. Spicer, Superintendent; E. J. Pierce, Gen. Passenger and Ticket Agent, Detroit. Great Western Division. Thomas Tandy, Gen. Freight Agent, Detroit.

CHICAGO AND GRAND TRUNK RAILWAY.

The route of this Road is from Chicago to Port Huron, traversing the rich counties of Kalamazoo, Calhoun, Eaton, Ingham, Shiawassee, Genesee, Lapeer and St. Clair. Distance, 332 miles. The company was formed by the consolidation of the Port Huron and Lake Michigan Railroad, Port Huron to Flint, opened December, 1871, and the Peninsular Railway, Lansing to South Bend, opened 1872. These companies were consolidated in August, 1873, as the Chicago and Lake Huron Railroad Company, and the road of the latter was extended to Valparaiso. The track between Flint and Lansing was built in 1876 by the Chicago and Northeastern Railroad Company. The extension from Valparaiso to Chicago was built by the Northwestern Grand Trunk Railway Company, and opened February 8, 1880. The consolidation of all the companies was made April 8, 1880. The track crosses the routes of quite a number of the most important Roads in the State, and touches many flourishing towns, including Cassopolis, Schoolcraft, Battle Creek, Vicksburg, Olivet, Charlotte, Lansing, Flint and Lapeer. The building of the section formerly known as the Peninsular Railway was undertaken about 15 years ago by Mr. Dibble, of Battle Creek, who displayed no small degree of energy in securing municipal aid and disposing of bonds to some extent in the European market. The section between Lansing and Flint was first known as the "Michigan Midland," and was regarded with longing eyes by Mr. Dibble as the possible means of working out an eastern connection.

The section known as the Port Huron and Lake Michigan Road was projected as long ago as 1836, constituting one of the three pet schemes of crossing the State heretofore referred to. At that time a line was marked out all the way to Grand Rapids, and a few miles were graded, but owing to the great financial embarrassments of 1837, the scheme fell through. In 1841 the Port Huron and Lake Michigan Railroad Company was formed, but its progress was confined to locating the line and obtaining the right of way. In 1856 the Port Huron and Milwaukee Railroad Company was organized, the line located, and a considerable sum expended, but the property was sold under its mortgage in 1864, and the company dissolved. In 1865 the property and franchises came into the possession of the Lake Huron and Michigan Company. Joseph Hickson, President, Montreal; S. R. Callaway, General Manager, Chicago; G. B. Reeve, Traffic Manager, Chicago; C. Percy, Secretary and Treasurer, Port Huron.

MICHIGAN AIR LINE BRANCH.

The line of this branch is from Ridgeway, on the main line, to the city of Jackson. The cars have been running for some time between Ridgeway and Pontiac, 36 miles, and the remainder of the line is all under contract and will be completed at once. The route is through a very productive region. Rochester, Romeo and Armada are on the section already completed. At Wixon the Road will cross the Flint and Pere Marquette Road; at South Lyon it will form a junction with the Detroit, Lansing and Northern, and also with the Toledo, Ann Arbor and Grand Trunk.

DETROIT, GRAND HAVEN AND MILWAUKEE DIVISION.

See Detroit, Grand Haven and Milwaukee Railway.

DETROIT, LANSING AND NORTHERN RAILROAD.

The Detroit, Lansing and Lake Michigan Road, an important channel in the railway system of Detroit and of the State, was completed in the Fall of 1871 to Howard City, at the junction with the Grand Rapids and Indiana Road. The project was consummated through the consolidation of three companies. The first was that of the Detroit and Howell with the Howell and Lansing, the latter, however, being organized in the interest of the Detroit and Howell. The next was that of the Detroit, Howell and Lansing with the Ionia and Lansing, which took place in April 1871. The Hon. James F. Joy, then President of the Michigan Central, first aided in raising the money to build the section from Lansing through Ionia to Greenville, some 56 miles in length. The parties who had it in charge became embarrassed, and Mr. Joy was obliged to take charge of it in order to save those who had invested in it from loss, and, in order to make it valuable, took up the Detroit and Howell project—an enterprise which had failed—with the view of extending the Road to Detroit, and from Greenville northwest to Lake Michigan. The parties above referred to had put in a large amount of capital, which would have been hopelessly sunk but for this last consolidation. Among the prominent men who espoused the cause of the Detroit and Howell Road, T. T. Lyon, Esq., the eminent fruit grower and horticulturist, deserves honorable mention. His ability and zeal in the good cause deserved a better fate.

In the year 1873, the Ionia, Stanton and Northern Railroad Company was formed to build a branch of this road from Ionia to Stanton. This branch was completed, and the two organizations, viz., The Detroit, Lansing and Lake Michigan Company and the Ionia, Stanton and Northern Company were consolidated under the name of the former company, during that year.

In the year 1876, default having been made in the payment of interest due on the bonds of the Detroit, Lansing and Lake Michigan Company, its entire property was sold under a decree of the Circuit Court of the United States for the Eastern District of Michigan, and was purchased in the interests of the bondholders by Messrs. Geo. O. Shattuck and J. Lewis Stackpole of Boston, December 27, 1877. The purchasers of this property filed articles of association changing the name of the Road to the one now borne by it, viz., The Detroit, Lansing and Northern Railroad Company.

In the year 1877, the Stanton Branch was extended from Stanton to McBride's, and in 1878 from McBride's to Blanchard, and in 1879 and '80 from Blanchard to Big Rapids.

This Road is now in a prosperous condition, promptly paying its obligations and improving its plant. Its great importance to Detroit and the State is a point universally conceded. The present mileage is: Main line, Detroit to Howard, 160.6; Stanton Branch, Stanton Junction to Big Rapids, 63.3; Belding Branch, Kiddville to Belding, 1.6: total, 225.5. The Company managing this Road also operate the Saginaw Valley and St. Louis Railroad, running from Alma through St. Louis, in Gratiot county, to Saginaw. With the last named Road connections are made with an independent line running due east and west, known as the Chicago, Saginaw and Canada Road, running from St. Louis through Alma and Edmore, on the Stanton branch, to Lakeview, a point having no other outlet by rail. The Chicago, Saginaw and Canada line is 38 miles. Alpheus Hardy, President, Boston; John B. Mulliken, General Manager, Detroit; Thomas M. Fish, Superintendent, Ionia; W. A. Carpenter, Gen. Freight and Passenger Agent, Detroit.

FLINT AND PERE MARQUETTE RAILROAD.

This is another of the great arteries in the system of the Peninsular State, and owes its inception and existence to the combined influence of a land grant and the enormous lumber trade of the region tributary to it. It has already been of inestimable value in stimulating the settlement and drawing out the resources of Northern Michigan. The Road was commenced at East Saginaw in 1862 and built to Flint, and in the Fall of 1866 the construction of the second division was commenced, running from the east bank of the Saginaw River, at East Saginaw, 26½ miles, to Averill's, on the Tittabawassee River, six and one-half miles west of Midland. Twenty miles were laid, ballasted and opened for traffic on the 1st of December, 1867. On the 24th of April, 1868, a lease was effected of the Flint and Holly Railroad—17 miles in length—for the term of 100 years. The latter Road had been opened for traffic in November, 1864. In December, 1868, a lease of the Bay City and East Saginaw Railroad was executed. The work on the main line has been steadily pushed forward. At the close of 1869, 77 miles were opened; in January, 1870, 20 additional miles were brought into use, and in 1874 the Road was completed to Ludington, on Lake Michigan. Distance from Monroe to Ludington, 253 miles.

Branches have been constructed as follows: Bay City to East Saginaw, 12½ miles; Mt. Pleasant to Coleman, 15 miles; Flint to Fostoria, 20 miles; East Saginaw Junction to South Saginaw, 4 miles; Coleman toward Cedar, 3½ miles. Another branch, starting in from the Atwood mill, on the Harrison branch, six miles long, is now under contract and will soon be completed. The Company is also constructing a branch track from Wingleton, four and a half miles south of Star Lake. Most of these branches are designed exclusively for the accommodation of the lumber trade. Total length of line operated, 318 miles.

The Holly, Wayne and Monroe Road, built in 1871, has been consolidated with the Flint and Pere Marquette, giving the latter a Toledo connection.

The Company has recently built two elegant steel-plated propellers, named respectively "Flint and Pere Marquette No. 1," and "Flint and Pere Marquette No. 2," which were added to the line in September, 1882, making daily trips between Ludington and Milwaukee, thus putting under one management the entire route between the last named point and Monroe. These steamers will run both summer and winter, one of them taking her departure from Ludington every night, excepting Sunday, and from Milwaukee every night excepting Saturday. No. 1 is under charge of Capt. James B. Muir, and No. 2 is commanded by Capt. John Duddleson, two of the most experienced navigators on Lake Michigan. The Company has a fine warehouse and elevator at Ludington, and first class docks in South Water street, Milwaukee, convenient to the business part of the city. The business in Milwaukee is in charge of Mr. A. Patriarch, who is the general western agent. Under the admirable arrangements of the Company throughout, the facilities offered for transportation to and from the west and southwest cannot be surpassed.

In 1879 and '80, a Road was built by this Company, but under a distinct organization, called the Saginaw and Clare County Railroad, from Harrison Junction, 53 miles west of Saginaw River, northerly to Harrison, a distance of 15¼ miles. In 1879, a Road (narrow gauge) was built from Coleman, 40 miles west of Saginaw River, to Mount Pleasant, in Isabella Co., a distance of 15 miles. This was bought by the Flint and Pere Marquette Company in 1880. In 1881 the Manistee Railroad Company was organized, the stock being owned by the Flint and Pere Marquette, and a Road was built of steel rails from Manistee Junction, 18 miles east of Ludington, to Manistee, a distance of 25¼ miles.

At the close of 1881, this Company had the following mileage: Monroe to Ludington, 253.31 miles; East Saginaw to Bay City, 12.35 miles; Coleman to Mt. Pleasant, 15.0+ miles; South Saginaw Branch, 3.94 miles; Harrison Branch (Clare Co.), 15.50 miles; Otter Lake Branch, 19.51 miles; Manistee Railroad, 25.53 miles; Sidings, 111.28 miles; Total, 456.45 miles.

The main line, Monroe to Ludington, and the Bay City Branch are laid with steel rails, as is also the Manistee Road. General offices, East Saginaw. H. C. Potter, General Manager and Treasurer; D. Edwards, Assistant General Manager; Sanford Keeler, Superintendent; W. F. Potter, Superintendent Eastern Division; M. V. Meredith, Superintendent Western Division.

SAGINAW VALLEY AND ST. LOUIS RAILROAD.

The Saginaw Valley and St. Louis Railroad Company was organized in 1871, with L. H. Eastman, President, and D. H. Jerome, Secretary.

The Company obtained no land grants or bonuses, but sold stock and issued bonds for the construction of the Road. The work of construction was pushed forward vigorously, and on the first of January, 1873, the Road was opened for traffic between the Saginaws and St. Louis, a distance of 35 miles. In

June, 1879, the Road was leased to The Detroit, Lansing and Northern Railroad Company, but it is operated as an independent Road, though by the same general management, and in the Fall of 1878 the Road was further extended four miles to Alma, making the length of the line 39 miles.

The Company have quite recently extended the Road from Alma to Ithaca, the county seat of Gratiot county, a distance of 7 miles.

This line, starting from East Saginaw, passes through Saginaw City, Titabawassee Junction, Swan Creek, Graham's, Sand Ridge, Hemlock, Porter's, Meridian, Wheeler's and Breckenridge to St. Louis, the location of the celebrated magnetic and mineral springs.

Distances—East Saginaw to Alma, 39 miles; Alma to Ithaca, under construction, 7 miles; length of siding, 3 miles. J. B. Mulliken, General Manager, Detroit; N. W. Merrill, Superintendent, Saginaw.

CHICAGO AND WEST MICHIGAN RAILWAY.

This Road—formerly known as the "Chicago and Michigan Lake Shore Railroad"—is an important one in many points of view. It traverses the whole of one of the most celebrated fruit belts in the United States, while its traffic in that great staple of the State, lumber—and especially of the very interesting region penetrated by it—is very large. Its trains make close connection with those of the Michigan Central, making it practically very nearly the same as a Detroit Road. Probably very few railway companies have, from first to last, been indoctrinated more completely with the "go ahead" principle and idea, than that which has controlled this section of the great Michigan system. To crown all, the importance of its ramifications is illustrated by a rather extraordinary profile. Its northernmost section, commencing at Pentwater, on Lake Michigan, passes through the counties of Oceana, Muskegon, Ottawa, Allegan, Van Buren and Berrien to New Buffalo on the Michigan Central, having Chicago as the chief objective point via the latter Road. Quite recently a north and south extension has been built from New Buffalo to La Crosse, Indiana, through La Porte. Eastward from this main line there is another, parallel with its northern section but at a sufficient distance from it to allow free scope for both, extending from Grand Rapids nearly due north to White Cloud, near the center of Newaygo county, whence there is an extension to Big Rapids. These various interests under one management, were attained through consolidation. From a point near Newaygo to Big Rapids the line fairly represents a segment of a semicircle, while on the other, the east, side of Big Rapids, a corresponding projection is made by the Detroit, Lansing and Northern, so that taken together a semicircle is formed, the bases being at points near Stanton on the Detroit, Lansing and Northern and Newaygo on the Lake Shore, Big Rapids being the arc. The contour which these Roads conspire to present, gives the Big Rapids railway system rather a novel appearance on the map. The consolidation of the Grand Haven and the Grand Rapids, Newaygo and Lake Shore Railroad was effected October 1, 1881. The distances on the main line and branches are as follows: Pentwater to New Buffalo, 170 miles; New Buffalo to La Porte (new extension), 15 miles; La Porte to La Crosse, Ind., 23 miles; total main line, 208 miles. Branches—Allegan: Holland to Allegan, 23 miles. Grand Rapids: Holland Junction to Grand Rapids, 24¼ miles. Newaygo: Grand Rapids to White Cloud, 47 miles. Big Rapids: Junction on main line to Big Rapids, 51 miles. Woodville: Woodville to Muskegon River, 13 miles. Hart: Mears to Hart, 3 miles. White River R. R.: Junction to end of track, 5 miles. Crooked Lake: White Cloud to Crooked Lake, 13 miles.

The main line north of Grand Haven, constitutes, with the Grand River Valley Road, a direct line from Detroit to the western coast of the State, trains leaving daily from the Michigan Central depot. The Chicago and Michigan Lake Shore Road was consolidated October 23, 1872, with the Muskegon and Big Rapids Road. The Road was opened for business from New Buffalo to St. Joseph, February 1, 1870; St. Joseph to Grand Junction, February 28, 1871; Grand Junction to Montague, July 1, 1871; Montague to Pentwater, January 1, 1872; Holland to Grand Rapids, January 1, 1872; Muskegon to Big Rapids, July 21, 1873; Mears to Hart, July 1, 1880.

Within the past year the Company have assumed control of the Grand Haven Road, running from Allegan to Muskegon, 57 miles. General offices Muskegon. George C. Kimball, General Manager; C. Harris, Superintendent; George McNutt, Division Superintendent Northern Division; E. W. Bliss, Superintendent Southern Division, Holland; A. M. Nichols, General Freight and Passenger Agent, Grand Rapids.

GRAND RAPIDS AND INDIANA RAILROAD.

This is a most important channel from a number of considerations, especially in view of its great length, the immense natural wealth of the vast region tributary to it, and from its connections, having the Straits of Mackinac as its northern terminus, and tapping the Grand River Valley with its network of railways and its rich stores of lumber, plaster and other leading commodities, for which it has opened a market in the rich State of Indiana, the principal outlet to the East being via Fort Wayne and Pittsburgh. Its financial history has been a checkered one. There were heavy losses from various causes, including inefficient management at the outset, quarrels with contractors, the failure of financial agents, and a great many other things that were anything but pleasant or profitable.

In 1852 and 1853, the "Fort Wayne and Southern Railroad Company" made such advances toward the construction of a railroad from Louisville to Fort Wayne as seemed to insure its completion. The President of that company made propositions that led to the organization of the Grand Rapids and Indiana Railroad Company in 1854. The proposed southern terminus was Hartford City, running north to the Michigan State line in the direction of Grand Rapids. The Grand Rapids and Southern Railroad Company was organized in 1854, and the two were consolidated under the present name. In 1855 the southern terminus was changed to Fort Wayne, and the same year application was made for a land grant, which was obtained in 1856, followed by another in 1864, the whole amount granted aggregating 1,160,382 acres. In June, 1857, the company was consolidated with two other organizations, the "Grand Rapids and Mackinaw," and the "Grand Rapids and Fort Wayne" Companies, the name of Grand Rapids and Indiana Railroad Company being retained by the new organization. Early in 1857, the company organized three full corps of engineers, one to operate direct from Grand Rapids to Grand Traverse Bay, the second west of that, nearer the Lake, and the other as direct from Grand Rapids to Little Traverse Bay, and thence to the Straits, as was practicable. On the data thus acquired, the present line was located. Owing to the embarrassments to which we have referred, the Company asked for and obtained numerous extensions in order to enable it to take advantage of the terms of the land grants, the time being finally extended to June 3, 1874. In 1869, the Continental Improvement Company (organized for this specific purpose) took the contract to build the Road for the full length, from Fort Wayne to Little Traverse, 50 miles beyond Traverse City, in all 330 miles. Owing to the guarantee of the construction bonds by the Pennsylvania Central, they became of par value.

The Road is now finally completed to the Straits of Mackinac, to which point it was extended in 1882. The distances are as follows: Fort Wayne to Mackinac City, 368 miles; Mackinac City to Cincinnati, 460 miles. Branches in Michigan: Monteith to Allegan: from Orono, completed, 12 miles to Luther, and projected to Manistee; from a point above Cadillac, 5 miles toward Lake City; from Walton to Traverse City; from Petoskey to Harbor Springs. The more important stations on the line are Petoskey, Cadillac, Reed City, Big Rapids, Grand Rapids, Plainwell, Kalamazoo and Sturgis.

It was this Road that the late lamented Hon. William A. Howard was so long connected with in the capacity of land commissioner. Mr. H.'s labors largely contributed toward inaugurating the prosperous condition of affairs experienced by the Road in these piping times of peace, which presents such a vivid contrast to old-time troubles.

The Traverse City Branch, as stated above, extends from Walton Junction, on the main line, to Traverse City, 26 miles. Organized October 30, 1871, the Road was opened December 1872. The branch is operated by the Company controlling the main line under temporary lease since December 1, 1873; rental net earnings. Total income for 1881, $28,203; total operating expenses and taxes, $26,107. The net earning under the lease for the first seven years, aggregated $54,038. Perry Hannah, President, Traverse City.

W. O. Hughart, President and Land Commissioner, Grand Rapids; A. B. Leet, Gen. Freight and Passenger Agent, ditto; J. M. Methany, Superintendent Northern Division, ditto; D. Darwin Hughes, Gen. Solicitor.

PORT HURON AND NORTHWESTERN RAILWAY.

This is a modern institution, the company having been organized in March, 1878, and the work begun in October of the same year. Everything connected with the construction has been pushed forward with great vigor, and the ramifications of the Road indicate its importance, and point to a lucrative business in the near future, as well as a very large one ultimately. The financial showing is a very satisfactory one even at the present time. It is essentially a Port Huron institution, and its inception and completion reflect the greatest credit upon that enterprising young city. The entire capital stock is owned either in Port Huron, on the lines of the various divisions, or elsewhere in Michigan.

The East Saginaw Division extends to the city of that name, 91 miles, passing through Marlette, Clifford, Mayville, Vassar, Frankenmouth, etc., and forming a junction with the Detroit and Bay City Road.

The Sand Beach Division extends to the port of that name, 70 miles, passing through Jeddo, Amadore, Croswell, Anderson, Palms, Minden, etc.

The Almont Division extends to the enterprising town of that name, 34 miles, passing through Memphis and a number of other growing towns.

The Port Austin Division extends from Minden on the Sand Beach Division to the well-known lake port of Port Austin, 31 miles from Minden. Distance from Port Huron to Port Austin, 87 miles. Aggregate of lines operated, 226 miles. Henry McMorran, Gen. Manager; J. R. Wadsworth, Supt.; C. C. Jenkins, Gen. Passenger Agent. General Offices, Port Huron.

WABASH, ST. LOUIS AND PACIFIC RAILWAY.

Previous to January, 1880, the "Wabash Railway," which served as the substructure of what has become one of the very grandest railway organizations on the Western continent, extended from Toledo to St. Louis, Hannibal, Quincy and Keokuk, with a branch from Logansport to Butler, Ind., having a total length of 782 miles. On the 1st January, 1880, it was consolidated with a number of Missouri lines, which swelled the total mileage to 1,551 miles, making it of decided importance as a St. Louis institution, and its headquarters were established in that city. In 1881 a line was completed from Logansport to Detroit, placing the latter city in direct correspondence with this stupendous organization, which has now a total length of 3,629 miles, being the third largest mileage of any railway company in the world. This important connection was accomplished through the completion of the "Detroit and Butler Railroad," being an extension of the Logansport and Butler Division to Detroit, 113 miles, and the purchase of the Indianapolis, Peru and Chicago Railroad, the line of which is from Indianapolis to Michigan City. Distance from Detroit to Logansport, 214 miles; Detroit to Indianapolis, 276 miles. The Indianapolis, Peru and Chicago Road crosses the Toledo line at Peru and the Detroit line at Denver, Indiana, forming the most direct routes between Indianapolis, Fort Wayne and the lake termini by about 60 miles. It will be remembered that even so far as the Indianapolis connection alone was concerned, the "live" business men of Detroit have long thought such a connection desirable, not more on account of the large and healthy home trade wielded by that city, than for its almost interminable railway system, penetrating every section of the West and Southwest whose traffic is of any object whatever. This consideration alone was of such grave moment that the far-seeing, enterprising and ambitious managers of the Wabash system could but indulge in well-founded congratulations upon the connection.

But this is only one of a hundred favorable points which might be adverted to. The "lines" of the Wabash have truly fallen in pleasant places. It controls the general railway traffic of the great Mid-West, a region which for productiveness cannot possibly be surpassed by any of similar geographical proportions either in the old world or the new. It is stated on the authority of returns of statistics to government that the number of bushels of wheat and corn harvested in 1880 in the six States through which the Road extends, was 1,310,125,363, equal to 60 per cent. of the entire production of the United States of that year, and 250,000,000 bushels more than the whole country produced in 1870. And this in addition to the vast stores of countless other agricultural products, as well as minerals, lumber, coal, etc.

It is a tradition that the founders of this remarkable Railway system aimed at the outset to make Detroit its lake terminus, but that they were in a manner repulsed. How this could have been possible needs no elucidation, in view of the anti-progressive maxims which well nigh bore sway in Detroit at that period. This tradition, if not founded in fact—and there is too good cause for the belief that it is—was for years like a hideous dream to the real wide-awake, progressive element of the population of the "City of Straits" who have done so much toward placing her in the proud position which she now holds. The action of a generation ago cannot be recalled, but it can do no harm to recall the fact that Detroit sorely needed the connection at the period referred to, possibly more than she needs it even now. There was a large demand all over the Canadian peninsula for Indian corn, for the supply of which the city was, from her peculiar geographical position, the natural mart, but from the circumscribed railway connection with the great corn-producing region this trade was in few hands, and was not a tithe of what it ought to have been; in fact it was merely of a retail character, a status which it held for many years. In the meantime immense stocks of this product were handled at Toledo—which had no home market worth speaking of—the trade of that city therein being practically as regular and almost as beneficent as the rising and setting of the sun, and she was thus enriched and built up at the expense of Detroit. No other single item of traffic has contributed so largely toward giving prosperity to Toledo, with the single exception perhaps of wheat, and it is exceedingly doubtful even if that constitutes an exception. The Wabash is an immense carrier of this leading product.

But a new and better era has dawned. The management found it an actual necessit to come to Detroit, a very potent consideration, but by no means the only one, being that connected with the unrivalled shipping advantages and harbor facilities possessed by Detroit, while at the same time the importance of tapping the railway system of that city, with its vast stores of lumber, minerals, salt, plaster and other merchantable commodities must also have had its due weight. That the connection, so long postponed, has finally been found necessary, suggests of itself a commentary exceedingly flattering to the pride of Detroit. But it is one of mutual advantage, and it would be paying Detroit a sorry compliment indeed to suppose that so far as she is concerned it is one regarding which there is a lack of appreciation. It is many long years since an event equally auspicious to her fortunes has transpired. Including the Wabash, the city of Detroit, if behind some others in the number of her railways, is now behind none others, New York and Chicago alone excepted, in the IMPORTANCE of the great thoroughfares connecting with her or making her a terminal point.

The following from a recent writer is quite appropriate, but not more appropriate than truthful: "At Peru connection is made with the train from Indianapolis to Detroit, and through cars from St. Louis are transferred to this line and passengers given an opportunity of continuing their journey via this route. The ride over this route is a most pleasant one, as the road passes through some of the finest agricultural sections in the great States of Indiana, Ohio and Michigan. The principal towns on the line are Auburn, Butler, Adrian and Milan, when Detroit, the Queen City of the Lakes is reached, and the traveler has several attractive routes from which to select as he continues his eastward journey. The monotony of a long rail ride can be most agreeably relieved by taking passage on one of the palatial steamers to Cleveland or Buffalo, or the water voyage may be continued even to Toronto, Montreal and Quebec, making the tour of the world-renowned St. Lawrence River and Thousand Islands. Detroit has a population of a hundred and forty thousand, and is celebrated for its broad, well-paved avenues, magnificent business blocks and public buildings and elegant residences, all combining to make it what it is generally conceded to be—the handsomest city in the west."

In April, 1883, the Missouri Pacific Railway effected a lease of the entire Wabash system, but the latter will be operated without important change as to the business generally. By this lease the mileage of the Missouri Pacific is increased to 9,522 miles, being by far the grandest railway organization in in the world. Robert Andrews, General Superintendent, St. Louis; G. W. Stevens, Division Superintendent, Fort Wayne; E. C. Murphy, Division Superintendent, Indianapolis; M. Knight, General Freight Agent, St. Louis; H. C. Townsend, General Passenger Ticket Agent, St. Louis; Frank E. Snow, General Agent Detroit Division, Detroit.

CHICAGO, SAGINAW AND CANADA RAILROAD.

This is a short but paying Road, of which Gen. Daniel E. Sickles is President. The line is from St. Louis to Lakeview, 38 miles. It was opened from St. Louis to Riverdale, Aug. 15, 1875; to Cedar Lake, Dec. 1, 1875; to Edmore, Oct. 1, 1878, to Lakeview, Aug. 1, 1879. Aggregate length of tracks, 41½ miles. The direction of the Road is due east and west, and it is practically a continuation of the Saginaw Valley and St. Louis Road. Its net earnings for 1879 were $189,177 out of a business amounting in the aggregate to $472,078. The connections at Saginaw and at Edmore—junction of the Lansing Road—are such as to afford ready communication with all quarters.

John A. Elwell, Lessee and Gen. Manager; James T. Hall, Superintendent; C. F. Hatch, Gen. Freight Agent. General Offices in St. Louis.

TOLEDO, ANN ARBOR AND GRAND TRUNK RAILROAD.

This is a Toledo enterprise, formed by the consolidation, Oct. 16, 1878, of the Toledo and Ann Arbor Railroad — 47 miles in length, completed August 1, 1880—and the Toledo, Ann Arbor and Northeastern Railroad. The main object in view by the consolidation was to tap the Grand Trunk system for the benefit of the Toledo interest, the objective point being Pontiac, whither the Grand Trunk Air Line had been carried from Ridgeway on the main line. The Toledo project has been completed to South Lyon, which practically concludes its work of construction, the Air Line, from Pontiac to Jackson, via South Lyon, being now all under contract, and partly constructed. Notwithstanding the title of the Company, there is no actual partnership or "arrangement" with the Grand Trunk interest. Distance from Toledo to South Lyon 61 miles; to Pontiac, 84 miles; to Ridgeway, 120 miles; to Fort Gratiot, 148 miles. There was already a *soi-disant* connection between Toledo and the Grand Trunk at Detroit. J. M. Ashley, President and Gen. Manager; W. H. Bennett, Gen. Agent. Office, Toledo.

CINCINNATI, WABASH AND MICHIGAN RAILWAY.

This Road is one of the modern institutions called into existence mainly by the growing local traffic of the productive State of Indiana, the connection having been until 1882 between Anderson, Indiana—a point of divergence for lines respectively to Indianapolis and Cincinnati—and Elkhart, a distance of 121 miles. In 1882, the Road achieved a lake terminus by an extension to Benton Harbor, 44 miles from Elkhart, making the entire line from Anderson to Benton Harbor 165 miles. The present corporation was formed by a consolidation in June, 1881, of the Warsaw, Goshen and White Pigeon Road with the Grand Rapids, Wabash and Cincinnati, and the Road was opened from Anderson to Elkhart about the 1st June, 1881. By the terms of reorganization, the capital stock was fixed at $4,000,000. No wonderful degree of prosperity has thus far attended the fortunes of the Road, yet the prospect is quite encouraging. The net earnings were in 1880 22 per cent. upon $230,838 of gross receipts. All earnings after current expenses were absorbed in new construction and equipment. The recent extension, it is hardly necessary to add, is quite an important one to the enterprising and prosperous lake port constituting the terminus. J. H. Wade, President, Cleveland; Norman Beckley, General Manager, Elkhart; O. W. Lamport, Superintendent, Wabash, Ind.; Owen Rice, General Agent, Elkhart.

SAGINAW BAY AND NORTHWESTERN RAILROAD.

This Road was constructed solely for the accommodation of the lumber traffic. It extends from Pinconning, on Saginaw Bay, in Bay county, westward nearly to the line of Gladwin, with north and south branches near its western terminus. Total length, 30 miles; from Pinconning to Ogden, 20 miles; one mixed train each day. The total income for 1881 was $165,765; operating expenses and taxes, $118,883. The stock is all owned by domestic holders. General offices at Pinconning. W. S. Gerrish, President and Gen. Manager, Muskegon; Charles Moore, Superintendent; F. T. Lillotte, Auditor and Gen. Freight Agent.

SAGINAW, TUSCOLA AND HURON RAILROAD.

This is a new Road, extending from East Saginaw to Sebewaing, a distance of 37 miles, via Reese, Gilford and Unionville. By its construction communication is opened between the Saginaws and the Huron peninsula, the want of which has been felt from an early stage of the development of the large traffic in coarse freights of all this region. There is some prospect of an extension beyond Sebewaing. Four trains are run daily, leaving from the depot of the Flint and Pere Marquette. General offices, East Saginaw; W. L. Webber, President; E. C. Judd, Secretary and Treasurer; C. S. McMillan, Sup't.

DETROIT, BAY CITY AND ALPENA RAILROAD.

The Company recently organized for the construction of this Road represent one out of three or four very important interests which have, as it were, sprung at a single bound into prominence, the others being referred to under their appropriate heads. Simultaneously with the formation of the Company, they effected the purchase of the Tawas and Bay County Railroad, a concern that had seemed certain of wielding a fine local traffic, but one that had not in view the important objective points in contemplation by the new Company. The completed Road to which we refer extends from a point 9½ miles east of Wells station on the Mackinac division of the Michigan Central, to East Tawas, to which point the Road was carried from Tawas during the year 1882. Distance from the present southwestern terminus to Tawas, 26 miles; to East Tawas, 28 miles. The old Company had also 12 miles of branches. It will probably be extended to Alpena via Au Sable, Harrisville and Black River making the entire line about 100 miles in length. It will thus be seen that the Road will touch nearly all the really important ports on Lake Huron, points which have hitherto been deprived of the inestimable advantages of railway connection, and the innovation will signally illustrate the importance of such connection in the impetus that will be given to all branches of business along the shore of the lake.

An Alpena connection was a project had in serious contemplation by the Michigan Central interest from an early stage of the development of that interest in this interesting quarter of the State, but from some cause the connection has been deferred. Alpena may now properly receive the congratulations of her sister cities. The Central Company have finally, at quite a recent period, had a corps of surveyors prospecting for a line from Beaver Lake (on their Mackinac division) to Alpena, and the owners of the Central have the report of that corps in their hands awaiting their determination, but the completion of the Detroit, Bay City and Alpena Road would seem to obviate the necessity of the Beaver Lake project, inasmuch as the two would practically stand in nearly the light of parallel lines.

The newly organized Company have some very peculiar advantages in their line. Superadded to its eligibility as a channel for coarse freights generally, and the choice pine lumber region tapped by it—of which commodity a quarter of a million is handled daily, even now—it passes for the most part through a fine agricultural region, suggestive of a rapidly growing traffic. The great Tawas salt region—the best in the State—and the renowned plaster beds of Alabaster, will also combine to swell the business of the Road. All this, in addition to the prospect regarding through traffic by extending the lines to the important points above referred to.

The Company have ample capital, and their facilities in connection with all departments of railway building and equipment are fully equal to those enjoyed by any other company, and they have also the advantage of a thorough acquaintance with all the minutiæ of lumbering operations. They are among those employing home capital exclusively.

There is no reasonable doubt that the gap of 9¾ miles necessary to effect a junction with the Mackinac division will be built up without unnecessary delay. The Road is a narrow gauge, but all the appointments are made with reference to a change of gauge without delay whenever circumstances render such a step necessary. Heavy steel rails are being laid, and the ties are adapted to all the requirements of the standard gauge. Gen. R. A. Alger, President; John S. Newberry, Secretary and Treasurer.

PONTIAC, OXFORD AND PORT AUSTIN RAILWAY.

This is the corporate name of a Road now (April, 1883), in process of construction, but the northern terminus has been changed to Caseville, another Lake Huron port, to which place it will soon be finished. If the Road should not be extended to Port Austin, a change in the name of the corporation will naturally be made, to correspond with its actual line. The enterprise is one of those whose inception and consummation have been unheralded. The capital stock is $1,-600,000, held by Eastern operators. The Road is well built, and is of the standard gauge. The enterprise appears to be one of an essentially speculative character, the easy gradients and well-known productiveness of the country penetrated by it being strong incentives. There are rumors that the Road will constitute part of a line between Alpena and Detroit—from the former port to Caseville by steamer—but the probabilities favor the belief that it is at least doubtful if such a project has as yet been seriously entertained by the builders and owners. Nevertheless, the idea is suggestive of the ample field open to enterprise in connection with steam transportation through the remarkable configuration of Michigan. By a close connection, the trip between Alpena and Detroit by lake and rail could be made in about ten hours, possibly in less time.

MICHIGAN AND OHIO RAILROAD.

The formation of this Company and rapid progress of the work is a superaddition to the numberless significant signs of the latent material wealth of the State. But yesterday there was no such line of railway as the Michigan and Ohio, but it is now an accomplished fact. The estimated line—from Toledo to Allegan—is 154 miles long, and its course is through one of the most productive regions of the State, the importance and value of which will be most materially enhanced by its construction. Among the important places on the line may be named Tecumseh, Hanover, Homer, Marshall, Ceresco, Battle Creek, Augusta and Monteith. The development of the system has caused considerable sensation in the city of Marshall, a place of remarkable beauty, situated in a fine region, but which of late years has been outstripped by many of her sister cities, a supervention which has occasioned a somewhat despondent feeling. The revival of the hopes of the place is owing in part to rumors of the building of an important branch after the completion of the main line, the prospective work being no less than a line to the Straits of Mackinac, by utilizing an old road-bed, having on its line Olivet, Vermontville, Muir, Hubbardston, Carson City, etc. This seems too gigantic a project to be undertaken at this particular time, or for many years hence, but it cannot be denied that the Company have a plentiful stock of enterprise and energy. The work is also being done every way in most unexceptionable style. The Road will pass through the counties of Monroe, Lenawee, Hillsdale, the southwest corner of Jackson, Calhoun, Kalamazoo, the southwest corner of Barry, and Allegan.

MINOR ROADS.

Hobart and Manistee River Railroad.—This is a lumber Road, about 9¼ miles in length, connecting Muskegon River with Hobart, on the Grand Rapids and Indiana Road. It was opened September 1, 1879. Income for 1881, $29,772; operating expenses and taxes, $31,919. General offices, Manistee. John Canfield, President; H. W. Marsh, Superintendent.

Michigan Midland and Canada Railway.—This Road belongs to the Canada Southern, and was leased, together with all the lines of the latter corporation, to the Michigan Central. It extends from the city of St Clair to Ridgeway, the junction of the Grand Trunk main line and air line. Distance, about 14½ miles. Income for 1881, $5,725; total expenses, $6,555. W. P. Taylor, Buffalo, General Superintendent; E. P. Murray, Division Superintendent; O. W. Ruggles, Chicago, General Passenger Agent.

Lake George and Muskegon River Railroad.—This Road was built for the purpose of concentrating the lumber around Lake George upon the line of Muskegon river, to facilitate its transportation. The distance from Lake George to the Muskegon is 7½ miles, and branches to various lumber camps increase the total to over 21 miles. Aggregate earnings for 1881, $70,320; total operating expenses and taxes, $86,355. President, N. L. Gerrish, Muskegon; General Superintendent, M. J. Borland, Muskegon.

Toledo and South Haven Railroad.—This Road, which was opened in October, 1877, is thirteen miles long, extending from Lawton, on the Michigan Central, to Lawrence, passing through Paw Paw. All of these places are in the rich agricultural county of Van Buren. The Road appears to have been built without any definite plan of connection with the termini named in its title, at least so far as Toledo is concerned, the Road being a feeder of the Central. It is operated with the "Paw Paw Railroad" (Paw Paw to Lawrence), and four trains are run daily. Total income, 1881, $6,673; total operating expenses and taxes, $5,373. General offices, Lawton. John F. Wolfe, Centreville, President; John Ibling, Lawton, Superintendent.

Muskegon River and Rose Lake Railroad.—This is another of the roads devoted exclusively to the facilitating of lumbering operations. It is 7 miles long, extending from the Muskegon to Rose Lake, and was opened December 28, 1878. Earnings, $9,669; expenses, $9,058. E. Eldred, President, Chicago; B. Dalzell, Superintendent, Evart. Principal office, Chicago.

Lake County Railroad.—This is a lumber Road, six miles long, extending from Elk, on the northwest quarter of section 29, to sections 5 and 7. Running expenses, $15,714; income, $21,714.

St. Joseph Valley Railroad.—This Road is 10 miles long, extending from Buchanan, on the Michigan Central, to Berrien Springs, the county seat of Berrien county, and was opened September 1, 1881. William R. Rough, President and Superintendent, Buchanan. Income, 1881, $1,266; expenses, $4,026.

Buckley and Douglas Railroad.—This is a new forest Road, built in 1881, at a cost of $45,619. Edward Buckley, President and General Manager, Manistee. Earnings, 1881, $6,372; expenses, $2,636.

Pierport and Bear Lake Railroad.—A lumber Road about five miles long has been built between the above-named points, on the shore of Lake Michigan, in Manistee county.

A Houghton Lake Logging Road will soon be finished from that point to section 25 township 22 R. 2 west; distance 8 miles. The party interested will float 200 million feet.

Gauges.—All, or nearly all, of the principal roads are of standard gauge—4 feet 8½ inches—excepting the Grand Rapids and Indiana, which (save the Allegan branch), is

4 feet 9; and excepting also the Port Huron and Northwestern, which is run advantageously upon less than standard gauge, and the Detroit, Bay City and Alpena.

The minor Roads, whereof a brief description is above presented, are nearly all of narrow gauge, and most of them are constructed and used exclusively for logging purposes.

The above lists comprise all of the Roads wholly or partially completed belonging to the Lower Peninsular system—at least all within the actual limits of the State.

PROJECTS—THE PROSPECT FOR THE COMING SEASON.

Rumors and in some cases pretty well authenticated reports are rife concerning new projects, some of them relating to proposed extensions of important lines already built, and others to new routes; local interest and local pride having of course much to do with those of the last-named class. Three important organizations have come very prominently before the public quite suddenly; at least suddenly so far as the successful consummation of their work is concerned. We allude, of course, to the Michigan and Ohio, the Detroit, Bay City and Alpena, and the Pontiac, Oxford and Port Austin Roads. Still another might no doubt properly be added to this particular category, for it is now almost morally certain that a new and very important Road will in due time be in successful operation between Detroit and Chicago, under the auspices of the Grand Trunk management. This line will run upon the Air Line between South Lyon and Jackson, thence upon a newly constructed line to Battle Creek, striking at the latter point the main line to Chicago. To inaugurate this great route it is only necessary to fill up the gaps between Detroit and South Lyon and between Jackson and Battle Creek, to which end a large corps of surveyors have been for some time at work on each section. One cause for the belief that the work is certain to be consummated, but not the only one, is found in the recent transfer of the Great Western Railway of Canada to the Grand Trunk, which transfer involves the necessity of providing an adequate feeder for the Great Western, and while this process will draw considerable from the other main line via Port Huron, it will also draw more or less from other interests—a potent consideration in view of the fact that comparatively so little steel is required to complete the connection. Including the important interests to which we have referred, together with the line between Pontiac and Jackson, which will soon be completed, the estimate of the Deputy Railroad Commissioner of the State that 600 miles of new lines will be constructed within the ensuing season is to all appearances strictly within bounds.

A new division of the Michigan Central from Beaver Lake to Alpena, 75 miles, is among the possibilities, the survey having been completed.

The Grand Trunk system appears to be growing in popularity. There are rumors of various connections, and in some instances bonuses are being offered. Notwithstanding these rumors there are no plans matured—and probably none even partially so—excepting so far as has been stated.

The Chicago and West Michigan Railway Company are surveying a route from White Cloud, Newaygo county, to Traverse City for an extension through Lake, Wexford and Grand Traverse counties, on a line almost due north. If built, the proposed line will pass within 12 or 14 miles of Cadillac, and the people of the latter place are moving in the matter of having it made an objective point. There is choice pine enough almost anywhere in this region, to constitute a paying freight traffic.

It is positively stated that the Chicago and West Michigan Railway Company will at an early day push forward their Road to Traverse City and the people of Charlevoix are hopeful of its ultimate extension thither. They have also an eye on a connection with the Grand Rapids and Indiana. A branch from this Road to Ironton is said to be seriously contemplated.

The Toledo, Ann Arbor and Grand Trunk has passed into the hands of the "Garrison interest," and there is some talk of extensions that would give employment to quite a gang of laborers. These rumors should, however, be received with a few grains of allowance.

It is fair to presume that the new Ohio and Michigan will be the means of stimulating some few enterprises in the way of securing connections with its line. Independent of all this there are other projects dependent upon "numerous" contingencies, some of which will in the nature of things prove failures, while others may possibly be pushed forward under encouraging auspices.

NORTHERN PACIFIC RAILWAY.

Ever since the contemplation under anything like flattering auspices of this great enterprise, it has very naturally been regarded as one of peculiar local interest by the people of both the peninsulas of Michigan, but for a number of years its actual connection with the system of the State has been a matter somewhat tinged with poetic license. This is now succeeded by something a little more substantial. The line has been finished eastward up to Superior, Wisconsin, and the driving of the last spike connecting it with Puget Sound, will be the signal for carrying it forward to the Michigan State line, to which the land grant of the Company runs, and in two or three years at farthest the Road will be completed for the whole distance from Puget Sound to Marquette, whence, as the reader is aware, an extension is already in successful operation to Detroit. That the City of the Straits is soon to be in close communication by rail with this stupendous thoroughfare, with all its mineral wealth, its grand romantic scenery and wondrous beauty, its majestic mountains, its marvelous geysers, and, what is of more worth even than all these, its golden promise as the great trans-continental artery of the world's richest traffic, is well calculated to produce inspiring emotions in the minds of our people. Beside all these great features, we should not overlook the wonderful results that must flow from the opening up of the resources of the immense region skirting this great Road. It will be almost like bringing to our doors the overflowing wealth of a new continent, and its influence is something that baffles all calculation. It is thought by men of mature judgment, that in a few years the amount of grain seeking an outlet at Duluth will exceed that now received at Chicago, that marvel of grain-receiving marts. But this is only one of many remarkable features the development of which is of such decided promise in connection with this subject. A field for enterprise will be opened whose limits are beyond the prophetic ken of the wisest. The building of the eastern section has given a new impetus to our Lake Superior steamboat interest, the business of which had previously been confined to pleasure travel and the freighting of minerals and supply of mining wants.

The Company was chartered by act of Congress approved July 2, 1864, and received a grant of 20 sections to the mile in the States, and 40 sections to the mile in the territories. Construction was commenced in 1869, and the Road was opened from Duluth to Bismarck, 450 miles, in 1873. The Company, guided by that liberal-minded and public spirited but unfortunate financier, Jay Cooke, made default in interest on the bonds in January, 1874; the works were placed in the hands of a receiver in April, and were sold August 12, 1875, to a new company organized in the interest of the stockholders and creditors of the old. The share capital of the Company at the time of foreclosure was a hundred million dollars; funded debt, $30,625,320, upon which was due interest to the amount of $400 on each bond, making a total of about $43,000,000. Up to that time there had been expended $21,358,418 in the construction and equipment of 450 miles in Minnesota and Dakota, and 105 in Washington Territory. By the terms of reorganization the amount of capital stock remained unchanged, of which $51,000,000 was to be preferred, and $49,000,000 common, and the funded debt and interest were to be converted into preferred stock. As the bonds of the old Company were convertible into the lands of the Company, the same option was continued to the holders of the preferred stock; such right however, being restricted to the lands of the Company in Minnesota and Dakota. A considerable amount of the preferred stock has been so converted and canceled. The preferred stock is entitled to dividends at the rate of 8 per cent. non-cumulative, before anything is paid on the common. Some idea of the prospect ultimately may be formed from the fact that the net earnings thus far have ranged from 20 to 40 per cent. upon the gross receipts. On the 1st January, 1881, the Company executed a mortgage on its entire property, including lands, to secure bonds to the amount of $25,000 per mile of line authorized by the charter—2,000 miles.

The sales of the Company's lands have been on a large scale, and the region along the entire line is being rapidly settled, but from its vast extent, generations must elapse before the country becomes thickly populated. The influence of these events upon the entire Lake Superior region can hardly fail to effect a complete revolution in its general status, especially in all that relates to its commerce, manufactures, and material interests generally. With the immense stocks of wheat seeking an outlet through Duluth, the breadstuffs problem must in the very nature of things have great prominence, and there are numerous points, especially within the limits of our own State, where peculiar advantages are enjoyed for the manufacture of flour. Minnesota and Wisconsin have hitherto enjoyed almost a complete monopoly of the trade in choice spring wheat flour, which has always been a very important branch of the breadstuffs trade, for the simple reason that bakers are compelled to use it almost exclusively whatever the cost, but which has latterly become of even far greater importance from its new acceptation as choice family flour under the "roller process." Recent developments prove that the Upper Peninsula is more than likely to attain prominence in the production of spring wheat, its soil being well adapted to its growth, and premiums having already been awarded at the Michigan State Fair to Upper Peninsula exhibitors. The development of such an important branch of industry will contribute very materially to infuse life and vigor into other channels of enterprise. Under the most ordinary circumstances that can possibly supervene, the carrying trade must be large, but there are the very best reasons for the belief that its proportions will be colossal—Lake Superior being not only the largest body of fresh water on the globe, but also the purest, most romantic and every way the most interesting, and possessing illimitable sources of wealth, especially in its minerals, it would be indeed remarkable if it were to fail in the exemplification of a large and steady advancement even under ordinary circumstances, and without any extraordinary developments tending to a great and rapid expansion, such as are now in progress.

The route of the Northern Pacific is shorter by 700 miles of land carriage than any other, and even this immense advantage is paralleled by others. Despite the fact of its comparatively high latitude, it passes through a milder region than the line of the Central Pacific, owing to isothermal influences, hence as one of its advantages the difficulties arising from snows in winter will be much less than those to which the latter route is subjected. The climatic phenomenon referred to was one familiar to all the army officers and explorers in old times, and was made of record by many of them. It was noted as one of the facts bearing upon this point that the bison and other animals regularly migrated northward to the vicinity of the line under consideration on the approach of winter, by reason of the greater mildness of the climate.

The shrewdest observers of the varying courses of the great trade routes of the world have long pretty generally concurred in the belief that the chief line of carriage for the Asiatic trade must ultimately be by the Northern Pacific. The reasons for this belief are too numerous to permit extended reference, but we will advert to a few of them in addition to those existing in the facts already stated, particularly in the short land carriage and extraordinary climatic advantages. Even if the familiar maxim that "God's highways are better than man's" were to be effectually exploded, this route would still loom up defiantly over all rival routes. Nature seldom or never performs great achievements in vain, and one of her greatest achievements bearing upon the question of commercial transit was the formation of Puget Sound, which for capacity and all other desirable features has no parallel in the world, presenting as it does a system of commodious and beautiful inlets capable of accommodating all the navies of the world with the best anchorage. Another point well worth adverting to is that this line is much nearer than any other to the great track of vessels navigating the Pacific. Even when hailing from ports on this continent far to the south, they run on this line from causes well understood by all experienced navigators.

The rate of progress that is being made in the construction of the Road is every way encouraging. A gap of barely 200 miles is all that remains to be filled up, which is well towards the western section, Bozeman being the name of the station at the eastern end of the gap. The progress of the work has been retarded by the digging of two tunnels under the mountains, to which part of the working force has necessarily been diverted. At the present vigorous rate of progress it is confidently expected that the line will be finished during the ensuing autumn. The tunnels will not be allowed to impede the passage of trains, as temporary tracks are being laid over the mountains. Freight rates from both Duluth and St. Paul have been given since about the middle of March, 1883. Trains are also running between the gap and the western terminus. The distance from Duluth to Bozeman is 1,033 miles; from St. Paul, 1,055 miles; Duluth to Portland, 1,889 miles.

DETROIT, MACKINAC AND MARQUETTE RAILROAD.

The Company that carried forward this important enterprise to successful completion was organized September 3, 1879. The survey was commenced October 10 of the same year; the grading of the first section was begun January 26, 1880; was finished July 24, 1880, and it was accepted by the State August 27, 1880. The entire line, extending from Marquette to St. Ignace, was finally completed in December, 1881. Distance, 150 miles.

Between St. Ignace and Marquette, across the Straits, the run is made by steamer in about forty minutes. Distance from Mackinac City to Bay City, 182 miles; Bay City to Detroit 108 miles. Total length of line from Detroit to Marquette, exclusive of the passage across the Straits, 440 miles.

From the period at which the development of Michigan was commenced in earnest, marvel has followed marvel in almost panoramic succession. Through the incompetency and general worthlessness of government surveyors, and from a number of other causes, a very erroneous impression early obtained with regard to the character of the soil generally of the northern portion of the Upper Peninsula, and the agricultural possibilities of that region were ignored and neglected, to the infinite disadvantage of immigrants and settlers, as was afterward too clearly demonstrated. There was, however, such inestimable latent wealth in the lumber and timber resources of all that region, that capital was drawn thither magnetically for investment. This movement led to the partial settlement of the region in question, operators in most cases basing their calculations upon merely a temporary residence; but soon it was found, by accident as it were, that the soil so generally regarded as intrinsically valueless and capable of producing so little, was in fact capable of producing everything, at least everything that can be produced in the temperate zone. This discovery was no partial development, but was the same in all quarters, and has lent an entirely new phase to the status of Michigan.

Three decades agone, the State was traversed from east to west by two great iron thoroughfares, passing through a region of country then, as now, justly famed for its fertility and natural beauty, while the north was a howling wilderness, whose echoes, excepting so far as the enterprising lumberman had made inroads, were wakened only by the hunter and trapper. The scene has changed as by magic; the north is demonstrating its capability of vieing with the older settled portion of the State in the products of its exuberant soil, while there are strong indications that in certain fields of material progress it will bear off the palm, even aside from the consideration of the peculiar great resources in which it holds supremacy. Casting the eye over the northern part of the Peninsula to the great inland sea that throbs against its western border, we find from thence half a dozen thoroughfares that have all been opened within a few years. Extending the vision from this remarkable contour in another direction over an immense region enclosing the very heart of our great commonwealth, a region peerless in all the elements of inherent wealth, we find that what a few years ago were lonely wilds are now threaded by talismanic lines representing railway routes, some of which have quite recently been completed, while others are in process of completion, the main trunk extending to the Straits of Mackinac, where in due time, it will meet the great highway of the world that is destined to connect the Great Lakes with Puget Sound.

Even after the long-existing delusion as to the character of the soil of so large a proportion of the Lower Peninsula had been dispelled, a vague idea of the same kind prevailed concerning the Upper Peninsula; but no doubt much more definite data regarding the matter would have been early elicited but for the great mineral wealth constituting the leading physical characteristic of that region, which had the effect of diverting public attention from the character of its soil. It is more than probable, nay, it is quite certain, that if it were a mere sterile waste, agriculturally speaking, the great inducements held out for building the Road would nevertheless have secured its completion. Although in times past comparatively little has been said concerning the agricultural capacities of the Upper Peninsula, they are now fully ascertained to be of a character that must insure the conversion at no distant day of almost the entire country into productive farms, especially when we take into consideration the easy accessibility of the country to immigrants compared with other sections where lands are obtainable at similar rates, as well as its convenience to market. The character of the climate holds out still another inducement, and a very great one. Owing to its being almost entirely surrounded by large bodies of water, the temperature is much more equable as well as much milder than any other locality in the same latitude on the continent. As a general rule the mercury indicates a milder temperature in winter than is observable at numerous points southward, while the atmosphere is so dry and exhilarating that the weather is really milder than is indicated by thermometrical representation. Miasmal diseases are practically unknown. Under such a phenomenally favorable state of things; with a productive soil; among communities advancing with rapid strides in all the elements constituting the highest Christian civilization; and with a population fairly bristling with the noble spirit of enterprise, it is worse than folly for immigrants to give the preference to far-away regions where suffering from the severity of the weather in winter is more frequently the rule than the exception, and at such great distance from market that grain and other produce are worth very little when the labor of production has been performed. These considerations and those of similar purport are beginning to exert their due influence, and quite recently we have accounts of the return of immigrants from Manitoba and other sections, who say, and with good reason, that there is no other country like Michigan.

In proof of the adaptability of the soil to the choicer descriptions of cereals, we may cite the fact that the first and second premiums for spring wheat and the first premium for winter wheat were awarded at the Michigan State Fair in 1881 to exhibitors in Chippewa county. Barley and all other coarse grains can be successfully cultivated, and a Detroit house of world-wide distinction as seedsmen, are authority for the statement, that as regards some descriptions of seeds they give the preference for their own use to the Lake Superior products over those grown anywhere else. One fact of very peculiar significance is presented in the magnificent quality of the Indian corn produced here, inasmuch as all experienced agriculturists are well aware of the utter impossibility of growing even a fair quality of this product on inferior soil in a high latitude. Many years ago, before the question of raising cereals in this quarter seemed to receive any attention whatever, the quality and size of the potato product excited universal surprise, and it was sought for with great avidity by consumers in Detroit and elsewhere. To give one striking illustration of the character of the soil, it may be stated that in one particular field, where potatoes had been planted for 30 years consecutively, the yield was 200 bushels to the acre, and of the most superior quality. The marshes are admirably adapted to grazing, and as the plants are well protected by the snow in winter, feed is afforded at a comparatively early period in the spring. Waste lands are literally unknown.

Under such a state of things touching agricultural prospects, and with lands easily obtained, in view of the ceaseless rush for farming lands, and the rapid filling up of the Great West, it requires no remarkable prescience to be able to foretell in a great measure the future of the Lake Superior region, and to see that a healthy traffic is in store for the new Road. In this case it may be truly said that history repeats itself. It is more than likely to be a repetition of the glowing story of the Lower Peninsula, a story that recounts within a *few* brief years of the making of thousands of colossal fortunes, and the upbuilding of myriads of happy homes.

The heart of the attractive region whose capacities we have faintly described—say the beautiful and prosperous city of Marquette, for example—is only about 20 hours' travel by the Detroit, Mackinac and Marquette Road, from the centrally located city of Detroit, the commercial metropolis of the great State of Michigan.

We invite attention to the statements elsewhere concerning the minerals of this region, particularly to the statistics of its products, etc., etc.

Still another point is that which relates to pine and hardwood lumber, a subject which is of momentous importance in many different points of view. The hitherto accessible supplies of pine are being rapidly thinned out, and even now the bulk of the supply of this vastly important commodity is enclosed within the limits of the Upper Peninsula, a fact whose prominence must constantly become more and more marked in the future. Pine land speculators have their eyes on this reserve, and in a few years at most the bulk of its manufacture, so long constituting an overtopping department of the industrial enterprise of the State, will be transferred to the North. The subject of hardwood lumber is one that is, at least prospectively considered, of equal importance. Several valuable varieties are produced in such profusion that the most prodigal disposition of them hardly occasions remark. Yet these descriptions are all in good demand in the Eastern markets for a variety of manufacturing purposes, and in the very nature of things this demand must rapidly increase. These woods are so desirable that even if they were not wanted in our domestic markets, their values would be affected to only a very slight extent, if at all, as they can be shipped to Europe at average transportation rates at a fair profit. By an enlargement of the Canadian canals that would admit of the passage of vessels of 600 to 1,000 tons, this branch of trade would at once become far more lucrative than anything at present known in the way of lake or ocean freighting.

Beside the immense stores of iron and copper which are practically inexhaustible, the Upper Peninsula comprises many other sources of latent wealth, especially in its deposits of marble, choice clays, porphyry, etc., etc. There may almost be said to be mountains of the last-named commodity, which will at some day be accessible under circumstances that must make it used largely for building purposes. In this field it will equal if not surpass any material used for that purpose in the world.

So many encouraging and attractive features are presented by this most interesting region in a material point of view that we are prone to lose sight of its wonderful beauty and countless romantic features, which in any other country would be constantly heralded. The resort is a favorite one for tourists and a visit never fails to beget a desire to repeat the journey and become more familiarized with its characteristic features.

The considerations to which brief reference has been made are of themselves amply sufficient to demonstrate the great importance of the Detroit, Mackinac and Marquette Railroad. There is another cardinal point, that in reference to it as a prospective link in the chain of the Northern Pacific system, which is of such momentous import that nothing like justice could be done consistently with the legitimate scope of our work. That the final completion of this great line in all its parts will be reached in the near future is known to be a foregone conclusion by even the most listless observers of the progress of the great railway enterprises of the country.

Even if, as most people seem to suppose, one fork of the Northern Pacific will diverge across St. Mary's River, and reach the Atlantic seaboard via Montreal, this diversion, even if it becomes a fixed fact, will exert little if any appreciable influence to the prejudice of the line via Detroit. With a city equipped like the City of the Straits with one of the most magnificent systems of land and water carriage in the world; with able and ambitious representatives in every department and field; with a population that will then be verging toward a quarter of a million; the metropolis of a State, or rather empire, of two millions, it stands to reason that she will seek to command, and *will* command, the lion's share of the general traffic of this great route. Then, again, the rapidly developing resources of the Upper Peninsula must also be thrown into the scale.

General offices at Detroit. James McMillan, President; Francis Palms, Vice President; Hugh McMillan, Secretary and Treasurer. D. McCool, General Superintendent, Marquette; Frank Milligan, General Freight and Passenger Agent, Marquette. W. O. Strong, Land Commissioner, Detroit.

CHICAGO AND NORTHWESTERN RAILWAY.

This was the earliest constructed of the Upper Peninsula railway lines, having been opened in 1864 under the name of the Peninsular Railroad, at which period it extended from Escanaba to a junction with the Marquette and Ontonagon Railroad, a distance of 71 miles. It was purchased during the autumn of the same year by the Northwestern, by the payment of $2,000,000 in stock, half of which was preferred. The line is now from Marquette and Negaunee a little east of south to Escanaba on the Little Bay de Noquet, 73 miles from Marquette, thence across Menominee River, the State line, to the Lake Michigan ports. From Marquette to the Menominee, 137 miles; Marquette to Chicago, 401 miles. Total length of the Road and branches in Michigan about 250 miles. The dates of opening various portions of the Road are as follows: Escanaba to Negaunee, 62 miles, 1864; Negaunee to Lake Angeline, 6 miles, 1870; Marinette to Escanaba, 64.65 miles, 1872; Menominee River Junction to Quinnesec, 24.71 miles, 1877; Quinnesec to Menominee River, 15.04 miles, 1880; Crystal Falls extension, 5.22 miles, 1881; from Deerfield northwest, 5.20 miles, 1881. From branches to mines, 39.80 miles, various dates.

The Road has a number of branches leading to the iron mines in the vicinity of its line, the most important of which is one extending from the main line in Menominee county, and passing northwesterly to Crystal Falls, where it taps the rich mining Menominee district. Another branch, recently built, leaves the main line near Escanaba, running northwest to Theodore village in the Felch mountains. There is also an extension from its Crystal Falls branch to Iron River. Still another branch is in progress, extending from Ishpeming to the Champion mine.

For about 17 years this Road afforded the only means of reaching the upper country by rail, and the only means of winter travel, aside from the now traditional "dog trains" which call to mind all too vividly days and nights of suffering, privation and peril. Although there have now been more direct routes established, this line will long be held in kindly remembrance by those whose business relations have compelled them to avail themselves of its facilities during the long season of the imprisonment in the chains of the Ice King of our upper lake ports. The prodigious strength of the "Northwestern" interest is a matter upon which it is unnecessary to dilate. Of all the stocks forming the sport of the money-changers, its own has the loftiest range as to market values, and the length of lines controlled by it exceed those of any other combination on the continent, with the single exception of the Missouri Pacific. Such a gigantic corporation, that has thrown out its iron arms into an important part of our State, is capable of making its influence felt more sensibly than ever, even when for so large a portion of the year it was the only anchor of the important mining, commercial and marine interests of the great Lake Superior region. It will be by no means devoid of local interest to name a few of the Detroit houses that were largely interested in the Lake Superior trade at the period referred to, particularly Moore, Foote & Co., Buckley & Co., Capt. E. B. Ward, Capt. Eber Ward, Brady & Co., J. T. Whiting & Co., Sheldon McKnight, John Hutchings, S. F. Hodge, Allan Shelden & Co.—of which Z. Chandler was a member—G. & R. McMillan, Beatty & Fitzsimmons, John J. Bagley, C. H. Buhl & Ducharme, and the Hon. C. C. Trowbridge, and no doubt a few others might properly be added.

Four daily trains are in operation on this division. W. B. Lindsley, Superintendent, Escanaba.

MARQUETTE, HOUGHTON AND ONTONAGON RAILROAD.

This important Road is 63 miles in length, extending from Marquette to L'Anse, at the head of Keweenaw Bay, and at the entrance of that rich and most interesting region, the Keweenaw peninsula, passing through the iron districts of Marquette and Baraga counties. The principal points on the line are Negaunee, Ishpeming, Humboldt, Champion, and Michigamme. The Road was opened from Marquette to Ishpeming in 1857; from Ishpeming to Champion in 1865; from Champion to L'Anse in 1872. There are quite a number of branches aggregating 26 miles, all of them rather too short for topographical delineation. Total earnings for 1881, $893,639; expenses, $459,883.

The Company was formed by the consolidation, in 1872, of the Marquette and Ontonagon, chartered February 9, 1857, and the Houghton and Ontonagon, chartered January 17, 1870. The original project contemplated an extension from L'Anse to Ontonagon direct, but possibly this may be slightly modified. The land grant of the Marquette, Houghton and Ontonagon extends from L'Anse to Ontonagon, but the Ontonagon and Brulé River Company having completed twenty miles of their Road from Ontonagon southeasterly, the Marquette, Houghton and Ontonagon Company regard a part of the Brulé River Road as too nearly parallel with their own line, and are soliciting legislative interposition to effect a change in their grant to lands southward instead of westerly, and if successful they propose to form a junction with the Brulé River Road and run to Ontonagon on the line of the latter. It is certainly to be hoped that anything calculated to facilitate the enterprises of this interesting region and develop its resources either in a strictly local sense, or in their relation to interests of great public concern, will not be found lacking so far as those interests may be promoted by proper legislation, but the issue in this case will come to some determination before this meets the eye of the reader.

The division between L'Anse and Houghton is in process of completion, and will doubtless be finished by October, 1883. Geo. Higginson, President, Boston; S. Schoch, General Manager, Marquette.

ONTONAGON AND BRULÉ RIVER RAILROAD.

The movements of the Company that have inaugurated this enterprise have attracted no little interest in the Lake Superior region, the more especially from the fact that it is intended to divert business from the system of our own State for the benefit of foreign interests. The objective point does not yet seem to be settled precisely, although the line will very naturally find its way to Green Bay and Milwaukee. Its construction was commenced in 1881, and 20 miles of rail were laid leading south from Ontonagon, but since 1882 nothing of consequence has been done. It is probable, however, that the work is now being prosecuted on the southern section, and it is stated upon pretty good authority that the entire line will be completed at no distant day. The late Jesse Hoyt was the soul of the project, but his death will make no material difference in its progress.

MINERAL RANGE RAILROAD.

This road is 12¾ miles in length, extending from Hancock, on Portage Lake, opposite Houghton, to Calumet. It was opened for business in October, 1873. It is located in the richest mineral section in the Upper Peninsula, and the richest copper region probably in the world, and its business has been satisfactory. Total income in 1881, $117,956. Total operating expenses and taxes, $81,037. Total liabilities, $437,298. Three daily trains are run.

Charles E. Holland, President and Superintendent; C. A. Wright, Secretary and Treasurer; W. H. Carr, General Agent. General offices, Hancock.

HECLA AND TORCH LAKE RAILROAD.

This is another short mining Road, its length being only four miles; opened in October, 1868. The running expenses of the line have generally been in excess of its income. It operates an incline seven-eighths of a mile in length and has in use a steam tow boat and other appliances furnished by the Calumet and Hecla Mining Company. This Company make good any deficit in the receipts of the Road as an equivalent for the transportation of their copper rock to their stamp mills at Torch Lake. Alexander Agassiz, President, Boston; General Manager, W. A. Childs, Calumet.

PROJECTS.

The effect of the prospective completion of the Northern Pacific, with other demonstrations hinging somewhat on that most important event, is beginning to be apparent in the outcropping of a number of railway enterprises, although as yet comparatively few of these have been matured. There are the best reasons for believing that in a few years, at farthest, a number of new Roads will be pushed forward under the stimulus referred to. One of the recent projects seems now so well matured as to amount to a fixed fact. This is the extension of the Wisconsin and Michigan Railroad to a junction with the Ontonagon and Brulé River Road, a blending of interests which will make them practically one Road, extending from Ontonagon to a connection with the Wisconsin system running through Green Bay, Milwaukee, etc.

The Chicago, Milwaukee and St. Paul Railroad Company are now making vigorous efforts to penetrate the great mineral and timber regions of Michigan. They are pushing the construction north to the State line, and thence east to the Menominee range, and to this end have lately purchased 70 miles of steel rail, and have 250 choppers at work clearing lands in order that the rails may be laid early this season from Antigo, a town that has recently sprung up. This will carry the Road 25 miles into Michigan.

The Road from L'Anse to Houghton will soon be built, the State having provided liberally for its construction in the way of land grants.

There is some talk of an extension of the Chicago and Northwestern through Manistique to St. Ignace, keeping as nearly as practicable along the southern shore of the Peninsula. This would be an auspicious movement for the important interests along the Straits and west of that point.

The Milwaukee, Lake Shore and Western Railroad Company have, it is said, perfected arrangements for an important extension from the present terminus of their line in Northern Wisconsin into the Upper Peninsula of this State, running westward to the southern end of Lake Agogebic and thence to the Montreal River. Over 100 miles of this line will be in Michigan.

One or two other projects are mentioned of considerable magnitude, too great, perhaps, for the indulgence of any very ardent hopes of their inauguration at present. Taken altogether, the prospect in the Upper Peninsula is quite flattering.

The "post coaches" of the past would not be considered an elegant or luxurious means of travel from the standpoint of the present day, and yet there are now infinitely more lines of railway than there were of the old-fashioned stage routes thirty years ago. And still the great work of construction shows no marked signs of diminution.

GENERAL STATISTICS.

From the tenth annual report of the State Commissioner of Railroads, covering the year ending 31st Dec., 1881, it appears that the total railway mileage in the State on that date was 4,232 miles against 3,828 miles on Dec. 31, 1880. In 1881, 441.43 miles were constructed, and 128 miles were abandoned by consolidation. Of double tracks there are 338 miles, and of sidings 1,744 miles.

Between December 31, 1881, and October 1, 1882, 272 miles were added.

The capital stock of all the Roads in the State on Dec. 31, 1881, was $239,505,423, an increase of $78,325,102. This heavy addition is attributable to the Chicago and Northwestern, the Detroit, Mackinac and Marquette and the Wabash, St. Louis and Pacific. A considerable part of this is to be credited to Roads lying partly outside of the State.

The funded debt of these Roads is $245,907,462, and their floating debt $32,593,149.

The year's revenue of these Roads from transportation was $76,322,484, and from other sources, $280,207.

Their expenses were as follows:

Maintenance of way	$13,383,456
Maintenance motive power and cars	6,589,479
Conducting transportation	24,539,340
General expenses and taxes	3,636,244
Interest on funded debt	13,625,475
Interest on floating debts	318,670
Rentals paid	3,963,201
Other disbursements	3,343,979

In addition to the above the dividend-paying Roads paid dividends to the amount of $9,055,250.

Nine Roads in the State failed to realize sufficient income to pay their ordinary operating expenses, viz.:

Companies	Amount of deficiency.
Chicago and Canada Southern	$3,051.46
Chicago, Detroit and Canada Grand Trunk Junction	80,499.87
Ypsilanti branch of Lake Shore Railway	1,924.88
Michigan Midland and Canada	952.79
St. Joseph Valley	9,534.32
Toledo, Canada Southern and Detroit	21,690.90
Hecla and Torch Lake	23,789.15
[illegible] and Manistee River	2,147.90
Lake George and Muskegon River	16,986.82
Total deficiency, nine Roads	$160,545.57

The earnings of Michigan Railroads were as follows:

From passengers	$18,473,190.71
From express	1,304,591.17
From mails	1,596,051.28
From freight	52,269,701.03
Miscellaneous	309,421.69
Unclassified	178,985.00
Total earnings	$72,146,845.48

The earnings of these companies per mile of road was $6,558 against $8,731 in the previous year, and per train mile their earnings were $1.52 against $1.64 in 1880.

Ten railroads having lines in the State paid dividends as follows

Chicago and Northwestern, 7 per cent. on preferred stock, 6 per cent. on common	$3,439,189 00
Chicago and West Michigan Railroad, $2.50 per share on 18,499 shares	152,372 50
Detroit, Grand Haven and Milwaukee, 3 per cent. for 1880, 4 per cent. 1881, 6 months	105,000 00
Detroit, Lansing and Northern, 7 per cent. on preferred stock	165,331 00
Flint and Pere Marquette, 3½ per cent.	227,300 00
Fort Wayne and Jackson, 3½ per cent.	80,479 00
Lake Shore and Michigan Southern, 8 per cent.	3,957,680 00
Michigan Central, 2½ per cent.	468,455 15
Mineral Range, 13 per cent.	11,236 50
Wabash, St. Louis and Pacific, 6 per cent. on preferred stock	1,030,948 50
Total	$9,655,250 65

The surplus earnings of a number of the Roads were expended in improvements, etc.

The number of highways crossed by railways in the State is reported at 4,714. Of these 4,425 are at grade without either gates or flagmen, 132 are at grade with gates and flagmen, 91 are over the railways and 66 are under them.

There are 889 railway stations in the State and 19,166 persons employed on the railways, being an average of one station for every 4.78 miles of road, and nearly five employes for every mile of railroad in the State.

The equipment of the several railways in the State at the close of 1881 was reported as follows.

Locomotives of all grades	2,379
Passenger cars	979
Express and baggage cars	481
Freight cars, box	38,598
Stock cars	5,090
Platform cars	17,069
Ore cars	8,471
Conductors' way cars	1,199
All other cars	896
Total cars	71,143

The Railroad Commissioner states that this is an increase of 66 per cent. in motive power and of 60 per cent. in cars over the report of the previous year.

During the year 18,914,933 passengers and 37,779,856 tons of freight were transported.

Of the total freight carried, 17¾ per cent. was grain, 18¾ per cent. was lumber and forest products, 11 per cent. was coal, 9 per cent. ore, and 5 per cent. live animals.

In 1874 there were 1,932,955,796 tons of freight carried one mile at a charge of 1.37 cents per mile.

Last year 5,747,847,621 tons were carried one mile at an average charge of 92.100 of a cent per mile. If the charge of 1874 had been maintained in 1881, and the same number of tons had been carried by the roads, it would have added $25,865,314 to their receipts. This reduction, therefore, saved transportation of freight over $25,000,000 in a single year.

The taxes assessed against the railways for the years 1877 to 1881 inclusive are stated as follows:

1877	$435,789 80
1878	450,654 00
1879	443,299 00
1880	501,518 34
1881	576,906 00

OUTLETS CONNECTING THE SEA-BOARD WITH THE SYSTEM OF THE GREAT WEST.

Among the other claims of Michigan to pre-eminence, it is a fact beyond all cavil, that no other State in the Union, and no other similar extent of territory on the globe, is traversed by so many trunk lines of railway. No other State does an equal part in the great carrying trade *between the East and the West.*

Nearly all the trunk lines, both eastward and westward, find an outlet through our State. The Chicago and Northwestern, the Chicago and Pacific, the Chicago, Burlington and Quincy, the Chicago and Iowa and all the other lines belonging to the great system of western railways, find an outlet in whole or in part over the Chicago and Grand Trunk, the Flint and Pere Marquette, the Detroit, Grand Haven and Milwaukee, the Wabash, St. Louis and Pacific, the Michigan Central, or the Michigan Southern and Lake Shore. The Chicago and Grand Trunk makes connection at Port Huron with the Grand Trunk system of Canada, and takes passengers and freight to Canadian ports and the East via Buffalo, as well as to the sea shore via Quebec and the River St Lawrence in summer and via Portland in winter. The Michigan Central, the Detroit, Lansing and Northern, the Flint and Pere Marquette, the Detroit, Grand Haven and Milwaukee, the Wabash, St. Louis and Pacific, and the lines, connecting Detroit with Bay City, Mackinac and Marquette, together with several minor lines and divisions, all make connection at Detroit for the sea shore and the various Eastern points via the Grand Trunk of Canada, the Canada Southern division of the Michigan Central, or the Great Western division of the Grand Trunk. These Roads deliver their passengers and freight at Buffalo at Suspension Bridge to the New York Central and Hudson River, the New York, Lake Erie and Western, or the Lake Shore division of the Rome, Watertown and Ogdensburg.

For years past there has been A GROWING NEED OF GREATER CARRYING FACILITIES BETWEEN THE GREAT LAKES AND THE SEABOARD. The existing Trunk Lines from the Atlantic seaboard to the West were opened nearly thirty years ago. Within these thirty years the population west of Buffalo has increased from five and a half millions to upwards of NINETEEN MILLIONS, or nearly three hundred per cent., and the miles of railway from about six thousand to nearly FIFTY THREE THOUSAND, or over seven hundred per cent. Yet during the period of all these mighty changes no additional trunk line has been built to bring to New York the traffic of these additional thirteen and a half millions of people and nearly fifty thousand miles of railway. Existing lines have been compelled to greatly increase their track facilities and equipment, but this increase has proved utterly inadequate to meet the demand for transportation facilities. Recourse has been had, when occasion demanded, to the Erie canal, and, despite this slow means of transportation, an immense amount of freight has been transferred from our trunk lines to the tow boats at Buffalo and not unfrequently at a ruinous cost to the owners of the cargoes, a fluctuating market being liable at all times to cancel anticipated profits before the property reaches New York. This has notably been the case when the Ice King has closed canal navigation too early for the sanguine anticipations of shippers or receivers, involving the locking up of millions of bushels of grain between Buffalo and tide water. In numerous unfortunate cases of the kind to which we have just referred the easiest way out of the dilemma seemed to be to procure teams and haul the ill-starred freight to the nearest shipping station on the New York Central and Hudson River Railroad; but upon making application for forwarding facilities to the officials of that Road the unwelcome intelligence was communicated that no such freight could be accepted, as the Road was taxed to its full capacity to transport the freight from its own and connecting lines.

Needed facilities are happily at hand, and the great railroad event of the year will be the opening for traffic of

NEW YORK, WEST SHORE AND BUFFALO RAILROAD

Upon a thoughtful survey of the whole ground we think the intelligent reader will at once conclude that with the single exception of the completion of the Northern Pacific, no similar event that has transpired within a quarter of a century is invested with half the interest that centers in the opening of the great commercial channel we are now considering.

The route is from Weehawken, opposite the city of New York, along the west shore of the Hudson river to Athens and Albany, thence through the Mohawk Valley to Utica, Syracuse, Rochester and Buffalo. The principal up town ferry connecting the Road with New York city will run to the foot of Forty-second street, and convenient down town ferry connections are provided, large and swift boats with iron hulls having been built for this special service.

The main line—double track from New York to Buffalo—is 425 miles in length, seventeen miles shorter than the route of the New York Central and Hudson River. There is a single lateral track from Coeymans to Albany, 13 miles, and another from Middletown to Cornwall, 25 miles.

The physical features of this great triumph in Railway enterprise are well stated by Civil Engineer Robert E. O'Brien, who has investigated the work on behalf of a syndicate interested in the securities, reporting as follows: The road-bed and track are made as near perfect as engineering science can make them. Standard plans based upon the best experience and practice have been adopted for all the work and structures, thereby absolutely insuring the best mode of construction. The cuts and embankments are made of unusual width (two feet wider than other Roads in the State) so that the tracks can be placed at the maximum distance apart—thirteen feet from center to center—and, where possible, the surplus excavation has been utilized in widening the embankments, affording extra siding and storage room for contingent use. The masonry is of a massive character and is constructed in the most thorough manner.

The bridging is of iron, proportioned to carry locomotives of eighty-five tons weight, being fifty per cent. stronger than the bridging used on competing roads. The track is being laid with sixty-seven pound steel rails, particular care being taken with the joints. The ballast is of stone laid on a sub-ballast of gravel.

So far as concerns gradients, a more favorable showing could hardly exist if the geographical configuration of the greater part of the country traversed had been planned purposely for its accommodation. One-third of the entire route is level. The prevailing maximum grade is twenty feet to the mile going east—the course of the great bulk of the traffic—and thirty feet to the mile going west. For a very short distance only is this limit exceeded, while the New York Central has to overcome grades of 86 feet, the New York, Lake Erie and Western 60 feet, the Pennsylvania 95 feet, and the Baltimore and Ohio 116 feet to the mile. When it is borne in mind that it requires double the power to haul a given weight up a grade of 26 feet that is required on a level track some idea may be formed of the immense traffic the "West Shore" will be capable of conducting. Eighty per cent. of the Road is on a straight line. The maximum curves are four degrees, and only on 28 miles does the curvature exceed two degrees.

It is extremely doubtful if a single feature can be called to mind in which this great thoroughfare will not be pre-eminent. Not an inconsiderable one is that which exists in the fact that its construction has been that of AN ENTIRETY instead of by piecemeal, insuring perfect symmetry.

The easy grades, light curves, new motive power, steel rails, fine equipment and road-bed—as nearly perfect as scientific experience and liberal expenditure can ensure—will enable the "West Shore Line" to compete successfully not only for the common carrying trade, but also for the first class tourist travel to and from West Point, the Catskills, Albany, Saratoga, Lake George, the Adirondacks, Montreal, and all other resorts. While it is, of course, reasonable to presume that the Road will divert to itself a share of the traffic hitherto monopolized by other routes, it must in the very nature of things call up an immense volume of trade yet unknown to the Railway interest. For this the route is eminently favorable, traversing as it does not only the opposite side of the Hudson river from its prominent rival, but also the opposite side of the rich valley of the Mohawk, while the great interests of Western New York are still in process of development and the Great West continues to multiply its giant resources, pouring out toward the eastern markets and seaboard a freight traffic whose equal in volume and multiform character the world has never seen. In view of the large profits known to have accrued for the benefit of the eastward channels already in operation, truly the capitalists interested in the "West Shore" Line may be congratulated.

The entire line will be completed by about Jan. 1, 1884.

The officers are as follows: President, Horace Porter; Gen. Manager, Charles Paine; Traffic Manager, W. P. Robinson; Ass't. Gen. Supt, J. F. Childs; Gen. Pass. Agt., Henry Monett; Ass't. Gen. Freight Agent, B. H. Bull.

THE NEW YORK, ONTARIO AND WESTERN RAILWAY.

This company was organized in 1880 as the successor of the New York and Oswego Midland Railroad company whose line of road ran through the State of New York, from the city of Oswego, on Lake Ontario, to Middletown, and consisted, with its branches, of 345 miles of main tracks.

Should the enlargement of the Welland Canal, now in progress by the Canadian Government, prove as great a success in diverting a portion of the Lake traffic now terminating at Buffalo, to Lake Ontario as its projectors anticipate, Oswego will become a formidable *competitor of Buffalo* as a terminal lake port, and the New York, Ontario and Western Railway will become an important factor in the carrying trade between the East and the West.

The Road is well prepared to meet this contingency, as it now possesses ample terminal yards and dock fronts in Oswego harbor, and forms by its connection with the West Shore Railway, an extension of the low grade system to Oswego as well as Buffalo.

GENERAL MATTERS.

The United States, a recent authority says, has 115,000 miles, or one-half of the railroad mileage of the entire world, four-fifths of which has been built in the last twenty-five years. The securities issued and existing to build these roads exceed $100 per capita of the nation. The earnings now aggregate over $800,000,000 per annum; the expenses, mainly for wages, over $500,000,000; and the construction of new lines and extensions, about $500,000,000. This property, with its receipts and expenditures, is in the hands of some 1,200 corporations. The entire manufacturing interests of the country in 1879 employed 2,538,400 operatives at an average salary of $350. At the same salary the railroads must have employed in 1882 a million operatives.

[In the preparation of our article we have been greatly aided by references to Henry V. Poor's admirable Railway "Manual;" also by information kindly furnished by the recent accomplished incumbents respectively of the offices of State Commissioner of Immigration and Deputy Commissioner, Col. F. Morley and Charles K. Backus, Esq.]

Commissioner Williams, referring to the legislation of the State taxing the railroads, says:

"I believe that the system of taxation for railroads prescribed by the general laws of this State is the best that has been adopted by any State or country. It is simple in its character, not open to fraud, readily determined, and in fact is the best mode of fixing the true value of the corporate property. A railroad that earns nothing is of no value except to take up, and the more it earns the greater its value, and the greater its rate of taxation under our system. It is practically an income tax, which is recognized to be the most just of all systems of taxation, when it does not open the doors to fraud or perjury and does not require a large corps of officers to assess and collect it. The power to prescribe the system of accounts to be used by our railroad corporations and to investigate the books when necessary, leaves little or no room for irregularities, and the mode of assessment and collection is certain and inexpensive. In short, the entire moneys derived from railroads are collected without additional expense to the State. It has, then, all the equities of the income system of taxation, without the frauds, perjuries and expense incident thereto."

REMINISCENT.

The Baltimore and Ohio Railroad was the pioneer Railroad of the United States. The Company was chartered in 1827 and the work of construction was begun the following year on the National Anniversary, the venerable Charles Carroll of Carrollton being the leading participator in the ceremonies. Upon this memorable occasion Mr. Carroll said: "I consider this among the most important acts of my life, second only to the signing of the Declaration of Independence, if even second to that." In the fall of 1829 the laying of the rails within the city of Baltimore was begun. The enthusiasm of the leading business men of the city was indescribable. The next Railway construction worthy of note was upon the South Carolina Railroad, begun in 1830 and opened for traffic in 1833 for its entire length—135 miles. At that time it was the longest continuous line of Railroad in the world. The construction of the "Mohawk and Hudson," subsequently Albany and Schenectady (now a part of the New York Central), was commenced in 1830, and the Road was opened in 1831, distance 17 miles. A portion of the Camden and Amboy (14 miles) was built in 1830. The Saratoga and Schenectady Road, 21½ miles, was opened in 1832. The Roads above named were the only Railroads in the United States at the period of the charter by the "Legislative Council of the Territory of Michigan" of the Detroit and St. Joseph Railroad Company. The Cayuga and Susquehanna, 34 miles long, connecting the Susquehanna River with Cayuga Lake, was opened in 1834; the Rensselaer and Saratoga, 25 miles, in 1835; and the Philadelphia and Columbia, 82 miles, and the Portage Railroad, 36 miles, in 1834. The last-named Road constituted part of the Pennsylvania system of public works. The first Roads built in the West were the Little Miami, running north from Cincinnati, and the north part of the line now connecting Sandusky, on Lake Erie, with Cincinnati. The first land grant of importance was that for the benefit of the Illinois Central, in 1850.

The first locomotive used in the United States was of English make. The first built in this country was made at the West Point Foundry Works in New York in 1830. It was named "The Best Friend of Charleston," and was built for the South Carolina Road, then in process of construction.

DETROIT AS A RAILWAY CENTRE —CONCLUSION.

While Chicago is confessedly the greatest railway centre on the American continent, and probably in the world, the second place must be assigned to New York, not so much by reason of the number of Roads terminating there, as from their importance—from the magnitude of the systems of which they are an integral part. By a corresponding classification, Detroit can claim the third rank, and the justness of the claim may be very clearly demonstrated. The cities of St. Louis, Cincinnati, Indianapolis, Philadelphia, Boston, Toledo and Detroit have a very nearly equal number of lines, Detroit being surpassed in this respect by one or two of those named, but she has decidedly a more favorable showing than either of the others in the importance of the routes making her a terminal point, taken as a whole. In considering the question of importance, a number of points have to be included, one very material one being that which relates to the various routes as primary channels for the transportation of grain and general produce. Let us glance at the system of Detroit: 1. The Michigan Central. 2. The Lake Shore and Michigan Southern main line via Adrian. 3. The Detroit and Toledo. 4. The Wabash, St. Louis and Pacific. 5. The Grand Trunk. 6. The Detroit, Grand Haven and Milwaukee. 7. The Detroit, Lansing and Northern. 8. The Detroit, Mackinac and Marquette. 9. The Great Western of Canada. 10. The Canada Southern. 11. The Flint and Pere Marquette. 12. Detroit and Toledo (Central Division). 13. Grand River Valley. 14. Michigan Central Air Line. 15. Detroit and Hillsdale. No competitor for the third rank can claim as belonging to its system five such important Roads—especially important as grain-receiving channels—as the Central, the Southern, the Wabash, the Grand Haven and Milwaukee, and the Lansing and the Northern. We may add that no other city on the continent save New York and Chicago has two such great Roads as the Central and the Southern. True, by the lease of the Canada Southern, Toledo is touched by a branch of the Central from Detroit, but the connection is not an important one in the sense we have illustrated, for not a barrel of flour or a bushel of grain would naturally be forwarded between Detroit and Toledo, except in the event of a famine or local scarcity. The opening of the projected Road between Detroit and Chicago by the Grand Trunk interest will add one more to the great channels of Detroit. The steamboat lines of Detroit constitute still another great feature. The number of first-class passenger steamers making her a terminal point exceed those of any other three ports combined upon the chain of the Great Lakes.

The future seems to present an especially inviting aspect for the great arteries of traffic and travel, and in the absence of any grave trouble, such as would flow from the failure of crops, they will be abundantly able in the future, as in the past, to lend their mighty influence to the good work of aiding in the development of the resources of the country. It is estimated that in even the great and productive State of Illinois, situated in the very heart of the country, less than one-fourth of its area has yet been brought under cultivation. In view of such a state of things, and when in connection therewith we glance at the vast States and territories the development of whose resources has yet hardly begun, we may form some faint idea of the immense traffic yet in store for our Railways. The lumber trade, although the maximum has now been reached, is still a heavy item. The predictions of even the most sagacious men connected with this great trade have happily proved at fault. Twenty-five years ago the very respectable authorities referred to concurred in the opinion that by this time the trade would be virtually a thing of the past, yet the evil day has not yet arrived, the production having shown a large and steady increase from the time of these predictions down to the present day.

The Roads, in their build and equipment, have nobly kept pace with the marvelous progress of the country; their steel rails, palatial coaches and model equipment and enginery being eminently worthy the commerce of the Mighty West. The pathway of the Iron Horse has led over the ghastly skeletons of scores of "foreclosures" and "second mortgages," but his course is still onward, the tirelessness of his sinews being equaled only by the grandeur of his mission. Freight and passengers may come and freight and passengers may go, but he goes on forever.

DETROIT, April, 1883.

LIST OF

CITIES, TOWNS AND VILLAGES IN MICHIGAN,

STATING MEANS OF ACCESS, APPROXIMATE NUMBERS OF POPULATION, ETC.

CENSUS OF 1880.

EXPLANATION.

Names of County Seats are given in full-faced type, thus,—**Adrian.** If a City, the word City is added. Cities which are not County Seats in small caps thus,—BATTLE CREEK. P. O. denotes Post Office. Money Order Post Office, thus—**P. O.** R. R. Sta. denotes Railroad Station. Tel. Sta., Telegraph Station. Ldg. Landing. In the second column will be found the abbreviated name of the most accessible Railroad, or the full name of the nearest Lake or navigable River, in case there is no railroad within convenient distance. The third column gives the nearest Railroad Station or Landing with the distance in miles (m.) The fourth column gives the Township and Range, in which the place is located, and the fifth column the County. The sixth column the estimated population. The seventh column indicates the page where the place will be found in the Atlas. Names of Railroads are abbreviated as follows:

Chicago & Grand Trunk Railroad	Chic. & G. T. R. R.	Michigan Central Railroad	M. C. R. R.
Chicago & North Western Railroad	Chic. & N. W. R. R.	Michigan & Ohio Railroad	Mich. & Ohio R. R.
Chicago, Saginaw & Canada Railroad	Chic., S. & C. R. R.	Mineral Range Railroad	M. R. R. R.
Chicago & West Michigan Railroad	Chic. & W. M. R. R.	Paw Paw, Toledo & South Haven Railroad	P. P., To. & S. Haven R. R.
Cincinnati, Wabash & Michigan Railroad	Cin., Wab. & Mich. R. R.	Pontiac, Oxford & Port Austin Railroad	P., O. & P. A. R. R.
Detroit, Grand Haven & Milwaukee Railroad	Det., Gr. H. & Mil. R. R.	Port Huron & North Western Railroad	P. H. & N. W. R. R.
Detroit, Lansing & Northern Railroad	Det., Lan. & Nor. R. R.	Saginaw & Mt. Pleasant Railroad	Sag. & Mt. P. R. R.
Detroit, Mackinac & Marquette Railroad	Det., Mack. & Mar. R. R.	Saginaw Bay & North Western Railroad	Sag. Bay & N. W. R. R.
Flint & Pere Marquette Railroad	F. & P. M. R. R.	Saginaw & Clare Co. Railroad	S. & C. C. R. R.
Grand Rapids & Indiana Railroad	Gr. R. & I. R. R.	Saginaw, Tuscola & Huron Railroad	S., T. & H. R. R.
Grand Trunk Railroad	Gr. T. R. R.	Saginaw Valley & St. Louis Railroad	Sag. Val. & St. L. R. R.
Lake Shore & Michigan Southern Railroad	L. S. & M. S. R. R.	Tawas & Bay County Railroad	T. & B. C. R. R.
Marquette, Houghton & Ontonagon Railroad	M., H. & O. R. R.	Toledo, Ann Arbor & Grand Trunk Railroad	To., A. Arbor & Gr. T. R. R.
Menominee River Railroad	Men. R. R. R.	Wabash, St. Louis & Pacific Railroad	Wab., St. L. & Pac. R. R.

NAME OF VILLAGE.	RAILROAD, LAKE, OR RIVER.	Nearest Sta. or Landing.	TOWNSHIP.	COUNTY.	Pop.	Page
Acme, P. O.	G. R. & I. R. R. (T. C. Br.)	Traverse City, 7 m.	T. 28 N., R. 10 W.	Gr. Traverse	75	60
Almira, P. O.	G. R. & I. R. R. (T. C. Br.)	Traverse City, 12 m.	T. 27 N., R. 12 W.	Benzie	30	50
Arcadia, P. O.	F. & P. M. R. R. (Man. Div.)	Manistee, 18 m.	T. 24 N., R. 16 W.	Manistee		50
Alvar	Chic. & W. Mich. R. R.	Muskegon, 7 m.	T. 10 N., R. 15 W.	Muskegon	25	81
Allen Creek, P. O.	Chic. & W. Mich. R. R.	Pentwater, 18 m.	T. 16 N., R. 15 W.	Oceana	200	80
Amsden, P. O.	Det. L. & N. R. R. (Sag. Div.)	Fenwick, 4 m.	T. 9 N., R. 7 W.	Montcalm	150	82
Ashland and R. R. Sta. O. P.	Chic. & W. Mich. R. R. (N. Div.)		T. 11 N., R. 13 W.	Newaygo	300	79
Ashland Centre, P. O.	Chic. & W. Mich. R. R. (N. Div.)	Ashland, 2 m.	T. 11 N., R. 13 W.	Newaygo		79
Ashland Corners	Chic. & W. Mich. R. R. (N. Div.)	Lake, 2 m.	T. 11 N., R. 13 W.	Newaygo		79
Akron P. O. and R. R. Sta.	S. T. & H. R. R.		T. 13 N., R. 8 E.	Tuscola	50	85
Arbela, P. O.	F. & P. M. R. R.	Clio, 5 m.	T. 10 N., R. 7 E.	Tuscola	50	85
Arthur, P. O.	M. C. R. R. (B. C. Div.)	Reese, 3 m.	T. 12 N., R. 6 E.	Saginaw		84
Aetna, P. O.	Chic. & W. Mich. R. R.	White Cloud, 8 m.	T. 14 N., R. 13 W.	Newaygo	200	79
Alleyton, P. O. and R. R. and Tel. Sta.	Chic. & W. Mich. R. R.		T. 13 N., R. 12 W.	Newaygo	300	79
Alma, P. O. and R. R. and Tel. Sta.	Chic. S. & C. R. R.		T. 12 N., R. 3 W.	Gratiot	800	83
Adair P. O. and R. R. Sta.	M. C. R. R. (M. M. & C. So. Div.)		T. 4 N., R. 15 E.	St. Clair	50	88
Algonac, P. O. and Tel. Sta.	M. C. R. R. (M. M. Div.) & St. Clair River	St. Clair, 12 m.	T. 2 N., R. 16 E.	St. Clair	800	88
Almont, P. O. and R. R. and Tel. Sta.	P. H. & N. W. R. R. (Almont Div.)		T. 6 N., R. 12 E.	Lapeer	800	89
Attica, P. O. and R. R. and Tel. Sta.	Chic. & Gr. T. R. R.		T. 7 N., R. 11 E.	Lapeer	400	89
Argentine, P. O.	Det. Gr. H. & Mil. R. R.	Fentonville, 7 m.	T. 5 N., R. 5 E.	Genesee	130	90
Argyle, P. O.	P. H. & N. W. R. R.	Deckerville, 12 m.	T. 13 N., R. 13 E.	Sanilac	40	87
Applegate P. O. and R. R. Sta.	P. H. & N. W. R. R.		T. 11 N., R. 15 E.	Sanilac	200	87
Amadore, P. O. and R. R. and Tel. Sta.	P. H. & N. W. R. R.		T. 9 N., R. 16 E.	Sanilac	150	87
Atlas, P. O.	F. & P. M. R. R.	Grand Blanc, 5 m.	T. 6 N., R. 7 E.	Genesee	120	90
Atkins, P. O.	P. H. & N. W. R. R.	Kingsley, 1 m.	T. 7 N., R. 16 E.	St. Clair		88
Altona, P. O.	Det. Lan. & Nor. R. R.	Mecosta, 9 m.	T. 16 N., R. 8 W.	Mecosta	200	78
Alcona, P. O.	Lake Huron	Alpena, 27 m.	T. 27 N., R. 9 E.	Alcona	250	64
Au Sable, P. O. and Tel. Sta.	Lake Huron	Tawas City, 14 m.	T. 23 N., R. 9 E.	Iosco	3,200	65
Acton, P. O.	M. C. R. R. (Mac. Div.)	Sterling, 16 m.	T. 21 N., R. 5 E.	Iosco		65
Alabaster, P. O. and Tel. Sta.	Tawas & Bay County R. R.	Tawas City, 5 m.	T. 21 N., R. 7 E.	Iosco	300	65
Allouez Mine, P. O. and Tel. Sta.	Lake Superior	Eagle River, 9 m.	T. 57 N., R. 32 W.	Keweenaw		118
Atlantic Mine, P. O.	M. H. & O. R. R.	Houghton, 4 m.	T. 54 N., R. 34 W.	Houghton	1,400	117
Arvon, P. O.	M. H. & O. R. R.	L'Anse, 12 m.	T. 51 N., R. 31 W.	Baraga	400	117
Ayr, P. O.	G. R. & I. R. R.	Brutus, 4 m.	T. 36 N., R. 5 W.	Emmet	45	34
Alanson, P. O. and R. R. Sta.	Gr. R. I. & Mack. R. R.		T. 35 N., R. 4 W.	Emmet	100	31
Alpena, P. O., Tel. Sta. and Landing	Lake Huron		T. 31 N., R. 8 E.	Alpena	6,000	34
Au Train, P. O. and R. R. Sta.	Det. M. & M. R. R.		T. 47 N., R. 20 W.	Schoolcraft		121
Anna River, R. R. Sta.	Det. M. & M. R. R.		T. 46 N., R. 19 W.	Schoolcraft		121
Averyville	M. C. R. R.	Gaylord, 25 m.	T. 30 N., R. 3 E.	Montmorency		55
Algoma Town	G. R. & I. R. R. (T. C. Br.)	Traverse City, 26 m.	T. 31 N., R. 11 W.	Leelanaw		58
Alba, P. O. and R. R. Sta.	G. R. & I. R. R.		T. 30 N., R. 6 W.	Antrim	200	57
Atlanta, P. O.	M. C. R. R. (Mack. Div.)	Gaylord, 28 m.	T. 30 N., R. 2 E.	Montmorency		55
Avondale, P. O.	F. & P. M. R. R.	Sears, 10 m.	T. 19 N., R. 8 W.	Osceola		73
Ashton, P. O. and R. R. and Tel. Sta.	G. R. & I. R. R.		T. 18 N., R. 10 W.	Osceola	90	73
Antrim City	G. R. & I. R. R. Lake Mich.	Boyne Falls, 27 m.	T. 32 N., R. 9 W.	Antrim	65	57
Atwood, P. O.	G. R. & I. R. R. Lake Mich.	Boyne Falls, 25 m.	T. 32 N., R. 9 W.	Antrim	250	57
Arro	G. R. & I. R. R.	Boyne Falls, 16 m.	T. 33 N., R. 7 W.	Charlevoix		57
Advance, P. O.	G. R. & I. R. R.	Boyne Falls, 11 m.	T. 32 N., R. 6 W.	Charlevoix	200	57
Amber, P. O. and R. R. and Tel. Sta.	F. & P. M. R. R.		T. 18 N., R. 17 W.	Mason	150	70
Ashill, P. O.	M. C. R. R. (Mack. Div.)	Ogemaw, 20 m.	T. 21 N., R. 2 W.	Roscommon		67
Alcoutie, P. O.	F. & P. M. R. R. (Mt. P. Div.)	Mt. Pleasant, 6 m.	T. 14 N., R. 6 W.	Isabella	100	77
Averill, P. O. and R. R. and Tel. Sta.	F. & P. M. R. R.		T. 15 N., R. 1 E.	Midland	130	76

LIST OF CITIES, TOWNS, ETC.

NAME OF VILLAGE.	RAILROAD, LAKE, OR RIVER.	Nearest Sta. or Landing	TOWNSHIP.	COUNTY.	Pop.	Page
*Arkona, P. O.	G. R. & I. R. R.	Alba, 10 m.	T. 29 N., R. 7 W.	Antrim		53
Agate Harbor, Landing	Lake Superior		T. 58 N., R. 29 W.	Keweenaw		118
Addison, P. O. and R. R. Sta.	Mich. & Ohio R. R.		T. 6 S., R. 1 E.	Lenawee	500	114
Adrian, P. O. and R. R. and Tel. Sta.	L. S. & M. S., Wab. St. L. & Pac. R. R.		T. 7 S., R. 3 E.	Lenawee	10,000	114
Amboy, P. O.	Wab. St. L. & Pac. R. R.	North Fayette, 14 m.	T. 8 S., R. 2 W.	Hillsdale	100	113
Allen's, R. R. Sta.	L. S. & M. S. R. R.		T. 6 S., R. 4 W.	Hillsdale		113
Allen, P. O. and Tel. Sta.	L. S. & M. S. R. R.	Allens Sta., 1 m.	T. 6 S., R. 4 W.	Hillsdale	400	113
Auburn, R. R. Sta. (Amy P. O.)	Gr. T. R. R. (M. Air Line Br.)		T. 3 N., R. 10 E.	Oakland		101
Austin, P. O.	Det. Gr. H. & Mil. R. R.	Davisburgh, 4 m.	T. 4 N., R. 8 E.	Oakland	800	101
Anderson Settlement	Det. Gr. H. & Mil. R. R.	Davisburgh, 3 m.	T. 4 N., R. 8 E.	Oakland		101
Amy, P. O. and R. R. Sta.	Gr. T. R. R. (M. Air Line Br.)		T. 3 N., R. 10 E.	Oakland	80	101
Alton, P. O.	Det. Gr. H. & Mil. R. R.	Lowell, 7 m.	T. 7 N., R. 9 W.	Kent	80	94
Ada, P. O. and R. R. and Tel. Sta.	Det. Gr. H. & Mil. R. R.		T. 7 N., R. 10 W.	Kent	450	94
Alto, P. O.	D. G. H. & M. R. R.	Lowell, 7 m.	T. 5 N., R. 9 W.	Kent		94
Alaska, P. O.	M. C. R. R. (Gr. R. Div.)	Caledonia, 5 m.	T. 5 N., R. 10 W.	Kent	200	94
Algoma Centre	Gr. R. & I. R. R.	Rockford, 4 m.	T. 9 N., R. 11 W.	Kent	25	94
Alpine, P. O. and R. R. and Tel. Sta.	Chic. & W. Mich. (Newaygo Div.)		T. 8 N., R. 12 W.	Kent	100	94
Austerlitz, P. O.	Gr. R. & I. R. R.	Belmont, 2 m.	T. 8 N., R. 11 W.	Kent	80	94
Ann Arbor, P. O. and R. R. and Tel. Sta.	M. C. R. R., Toledo, A. Arbor & Gr. T.		T. 2 S., R. 6 E.	Washtenaw	9,500	104
Arland, P. O. and R. R. Sta.	M. C. R. R. (Gr. R. Div.)		T. 1 S., R. 2 W.	Jackson	20	105
Abscota, P. O.	M. C. R. R. (Air Line Div.)	Union City, 6 m.	T. 4 S., R. 7 W.	Calhoun	25	106
Athens, P. O.	M. C. R. R. (Air Line Div.)	Union City, 7 m.	T. 4 S., R. 8 W.	Calhoun	400	106
Albion, P. O. and R. R. and Tel. Sta.	M. C., L. S. & M. S. R. R. (Lan. Div.)		T. 3 S., R. 4 W.	Calhoun	4,000	106
Algansee, P. O.	L. S. & M. S. R. R.	Quincy, 5 m.	T. 7 S., R. 5 W.	Branch	80	112
Aurelius, P. O.	M. C. R. R. (Sag. Div.)	Eden, 5 m.	T. 2 N., R. 2 W.	Ingham	250	99
Armada, P. O. and R. R. and Tel. Sta.	Gr. T. R. R. (Mich. Air Line Br.)		T. 5 N., R. 14 E.	Macomb	700	102
Arlington, P. O.	Chic. & W. Mich. R. R.	Deerfield, 5 m.	T. 2 S., R. 15 W.	Van Buren	25	108
Alverson, P. O.	Chic. & Gr. T. R. R.	Pine Lake, 4 m.	T. 4 N., R. 1 E.	Ingham		99
Avery, P. O. and R. R. Sta.	M. C. R. R.		T. 8 S., R. 19 W.	Berrien	50	109
Almena, P. O.	M. C. R. R.	Mattawan, 6 m.	T. 2 S., R. 13 W.	Van Buren	115	108
Adamsville, P. O.	Chic. & Gr. T. R. R.	Edwardsburgh, 5 m.	T. 8 S., R. 15 W.	Cass	200	110
Austin, R. R. Sta.	Gr. R. & I. R. R.		T. 3 S., R. 11 W.	Kalamazoo		107
Andersonville	Chic. & Gr. T. R. R.		T. 7 S., R. 15 W.	Cass		110
Alamo, P. O. and R. R. Sta.	M. C. R. R. (Kal. Div.)		T. 1 S., R. 12 W.	Kalamazoo	50	107
Argenta, R. R. Sta.	L. S. & M. S. R. R. (Kal. Div.)		T. 1 S., R. 11 W.	Kalamazoo		107
Augusta, P. O. and R. R. and Tel. Sta.	Gr. R. & I., (M. & A. Div.) M. C. R. R.		T. 1 S., R. 9 W.	Kalamazoo		107
Allendale, P. O.	Det. Gr. H. & Mil. R. R.	Coopersville, 9 m.	T. 7 N., R. 14 W.	Ottawa	200	95
Ainger, P. O. (Olivet Sta.)	Chic. & Gr. T. R. R.		T. 1 N., R. 5 W.	Eaton	200	98
Abronia, P. O. and R. R. Sta.	L. S. & M. S. R. R. (Kal. Div.)		T. 2 N., R. 12 W.	Allegan	150	96
Allegan, P. O. and R. R. and Tel. Sta.	M. & O., L. S. & M. S. (Kal. Div.), G. R. & I. (M. & A. Div.)		T. 2 N., R. 13 W.	Allegan	2,500	96
Argenta, R. R. Sta.	G. R. & I. R. R.		T. 1 N., R. 11 W.	Allegan		96
Assyria, P. O.	Chic. & Gr. T. R. R.	Bellevue, 8 m.	T. 1 N., R. 7 W.	Barry	100	97
Alton	Chic. & Gr. T. R. R.	Morrice, 5 m.	T. 6 N., R. 2 E.	Shiawassee		93
Algodon, P. O.	Det. Gr. H. & Mil. R. R.	Saranac, 8 m.	T. 5 N., R. 7 W.	Ionia	50	115
Athlone, P. O.	F. & P. M. R. R.	Grafton, 8 m.	T. 5 S., R. 9 E.	Monroe	200	75
Au Gres, P. O. and Tel. Sta.	Saginaw Bay, M. C. R. R. (M. Div.)	Standish, 17 m.	T. 19 N., R. 7 E.	Arenac	300	75
Arenac, P. O. and Tel. Sta.	Saginaw Bay, M. C. R. R. (M. Div.)	Standish, 7 m.	T. 19 N., R. 5 E.	Arenac	75	75
Auburn, P. O.	M. C. R. R.	Kaw Kawlin, 8 m.	T. 14 N., R. 3 E.	Bay	200	75
Arn, P. O. & R. R. Sta.	M. C. R. R. (B. C. Div.)		T. 13 N., R. 6 E.	Bay	50	96
*Advent City		Allegan, 5 m.	T. 3 N., R. 18 W.	Allegan	30	70
*Albion Mines	M. H. & O. R. R.	Greenwood Sta., 5 m.		Marquette		119
*Allens	M. C. R. R. (Gr. R. Div.)	Chester, 2 m.	T. 3 N., R. 5 W.	Eaton	20	98
Allenville, R. R. Sta.	D., M. & M. R. R.		T. 42 N., R. 5 W.	Mackinac		122
*Amity		Kalkaska, 6 m.		Kalkaska		61
*Anchorville Landing	Lake St. Clair, Gr. T. R. R.	New Haven, 7 m.	T. 3 N., R. 15 E.	St. Clair	400	88
*Argyle			T. 11 N., R. 15 E.	Sanilac		87
*Arkdale, P. O.				Lapeer		89
*Ashley				Kent		94
*Aral, P. O.				Benzie		60
Adams Corners, (Ruth P. O.) Sta.	P. H. & N. W. R. R.		T. 15 N., R. 15 E.	Huron		86
Anderson, R. R. Sta.	P. H. & N. W. R. R. (Branch Div.)		T. 11 N., R. 16 E.	Sanilac		87
Abbotsford, (Beley P. O.)	P. H. & N. W. R. R.	Kingsly Sta., 2½ m.	T. 7 N., R. 16 E.	St. Clair		88
Black River, P. O. and Tel. Sta.	Lake Huron	Alpena, 23 m.	T. 28 N., R. 9 E.	Alcona	400	64
Bay Mills	Lake Superior	St. Ignace, 60 m.	T. 47 N., R. 2 W.	Chippewa	200	123
Bravers, R. R. Sta.	Chic. & N. W. R. R.		T. 41 N., R. 22 W.	Delta	45	120
Brampton, P. O. and R. R. Sta.	Chic. & N. W. R. R.		T. 41 N., R. 22 W.	Delta	225	120
Barkville, P. O. and R. R. Sta.	Chic. & N. W. R. R.		T. 39 N., R. 24 W.	Delta	30	120
Bark River, Tel. Sta.	Chic. & N. W. R. R.		T. 38 N., R. 24 W.	Delta		120
Bay-de-Noquet, P. O.	Chic. & N. W. R. R.	Brampton, 9 m.	T. 41 N., R. 21 W.	Delta	250	120
Baraga, P. O. and R. R. Sta.	M. H. & O. R. R.		T. 51 N., R. 33 W.	Baraga	250	117
Bushville, R. R. Sta.	M. C. R. R. (Mack. Div.)		T. 36 N., R. 2 W.	Cheboygan		52
Burt Lake, P. O.	M. C. R. R. (Mack. Div.)	Indian River, 7 m.	T. 35 N., R. 3 W.	Cheboygan		52
Bowman's Landing	M. C. R. R. (Mack. Div.)	Indian River, 4 m.	T. 35 N., R. 3 W.	Cheboygan		52
Bells Landing	Mullet's Lake	Cheboygan, 11 m.	T. 36 N., R. 1 W.	Cheboygan		52
Bliss, P. O.	G. R., I. & Mack. R. R.	Flag Sta., 4 m.	T. 38 N., R. 5 W.	Emmet		51
Brutus, P. O. and R. R. Sta.	G. R., I. & Mack. R. R.		T. 35 N., R. 4 W.	Emmet	100	51
Bayview, R. R. Sta.	G. R. & I. R. R.		T. 35 N., R. 5 W.	Emmet	50	51
Bolton, P. O.	Lake Huron	Alpena Landing, 11 m.	T. 31 N., R. 8 E.	Alpena	250	54
Beaufort	M. H. & O. R. R.	Michigamme, 2 m.	T. 48 N., R. 31 W.	Baraga		117
Briley, P. O.	M. C. R. R.	Gaylord, 15 m.	T. 30 N., R. 1 E.	Montmorency		55
Big Rock, P. O.	M. C. R. R.	Gaylord, 25 m.	T. 30 N., R. 2 E.	Montmorency		55
Bodickville, P. O.	G. R. & I. R. R. (T. C. Br.)	Traverse City, 20 m.	T. 28 N., R. 13 W.	Leelanaw	50	58
Bingham, P. O.	G. R. & I. R. R. (T. C. Br.)	Traverse City, 10 m.	T. 29 N., R. 11 W.	Leelanaw	200	58
Bellaire, P. O. and Tel. Sta.	G. R. & I. R. R.	Alba, 14 m.	T. 30 N., R. 8 W.	Antrim	200	58
Berryville, P. O.	M. C. R. R.	Vanderbilt, 5 m.	T. 32 N., R. 3 W.	Otsego	80	56
Bagley, R. R. Sta.	M. C. R. R.		T. 30 N., R. 3 W.	Otsego	85	56
Bradford Lake, P. O.	M. C. R. R.	Wright's Lake, ½ m.	T. 29 N., R. 3 W.	Otsego	80	56
Branch, P. O. and R. R. Sta.	F. & P. M. R. R.		T. 18 N., R. 14 W.	Lake		71
Baldwin, P. O. and R. R. and Tel. Sta.	F. & P. M. R. R.		T. 17 N., R. 13 W.	Lake	500	71
Bergma, P. O.	G. R. & I. R. R.	Petoskey, 10 m.	T. 34 N., R. 7 W.	Charlevoix	25	57
Boyne, P. O.	G. R. & I. R. R.	Boyne Falls, 5 m.	T. 33 N., R. 6 W.	Charlevoix	500	57
Boyne Falls, P. O. and R. R. and Tel. Sta.	G. R. & I. R. R.		T. 32 N., R. 5 W.	Charlevoix	50	57
Bagley, P. O. and R. R. Sta.	Chic. & N. W. R. R.		T. 37 N., R. 30 W.	Menominee	300	124
Beacon, P. O. and Tel. Sta.	M. H. & O. R. R.	Champion, 1 m.	T. 48 N., R. 29 W.	Marquette	2,000	119
Brace, R. R. Sta.	M. H. & O. R. R.		T. 48 N., R. 28 W.	Marquette		119
Branch, P. O. and R. R. and Tel. Sta.	F. & P. M. R. R.		T. 18 N., R. 15 W.	Mason		70
Benkela, P. O.	G. R. & I. R. R.	Manton, 11 m.	T. 23 N., R. 11 W.	Wexford	50	69
Bond's Mills, P. O. and R. R. Sta.	G. R. & I. R. R.		T. 22 N., R. 9 W.	Wexford	150	69
Blanchard, P. O. and R. R. Sta.	Det., Lan. & Nor. R. R.		T. 13 N., R. 6 W.	Isabella	200	77
Bradford, P. O.	F. & P. M. R. R.	Midland, 7 m.	T. 14 N., R. 1 W.	Midland	25	76
Beitner, P. O. and R. R. and Tel. Sta.	G. R. & I. R. R. (T. C. Br.)		T. 26 N., R. 11 W.	Gr. Traverse		60
Bartlett, P. O.	G. R. & I. R. R. (T. C. Br.)	Kingsley's Sta., 10 m.	T. 25 N., R. 11 W.	Gr. Traverse		60

☞ Names marked with a star (*) will not be found on the Maps.

NAME OF VILLAGE.	RAILROAD, LAKE, OR RIVER.	Nearest Sta. or Landing.	TOWNSHIP.	COUNTY.	Pop.	Page
Beaver Lake, P. O. and R. R. Sta.	M. C. R. R. (Mack. Div.)		T. 22 N., R. 1 E.	Ogemaw	80	60
Bear Lake, P. O., and Tel. Sta.	F. & P. M. R. R. (Man. Div.)	Manistee, 18 m.	T. 23 N., R. 15 W.	Manistee	600	59
Barker Creek, P. O.	G. R. & I. R. R.	Kalkaska, 9 m.	T. 27 N., R. 8 W.	Kalkaska		61
Benzonia, P. O. and Tel. Sta.	F. & P. M. R. R. (Man. Div.)	Manistee, 31 m.	T. 26 N., R. 15 W.	Benzie	150	59
Burnham, P. O.	Lake Michigan	Manistee, 20 m.	T. 24 N., R. 16 W.	Manistee	200	59
Bec Scies	F. & P. M. R. R. (Man. Div.)	Manistee, 28 m.	T. 24 N., R. 14 W.	Manistee		59
Benona, P. O.	Chic. & W. Mich. R. R., Lake Michigan	New Era, 8 m.	T. 14 N., R. 18 W.	Oceana	250	90
Bluffton, P. O.	Chic. & W. Mich. R. R., Lake Michigan	Muskegon, 4 m.	T. 10 N., R. 17 W.	Muskegon	600	81
Bailey, P. O. and R. R. Sta.	Chic. & W. Mich. R. R.		T. 10 N., R. 13 W.	Muskegon	400	81
Black Lake, P. O. and R. R. Sta.	Chic. & W. Mich. R. R.		T. 9 N., R. 16 W.	Muskegon		81
Bird, P. O.	Chic. & W. Mich. R. R.	Mears, 13 m.	T. 15 N., R. 15 W.	Oceana	50	90
Bloomer Center, P. O.	Det. L. & Nor. R. R. (Sag. Div.)	Fenwick, 9 m.	T. 9 N., R. 5 W.	Montcalm	25	82
Bushnell Centre, P. O.	Det. L. & Nor. R. R. (Sag. Div.)	Fenwick, 3 m.	T. 9 N., R. 6 W.	Montcalm		82
Bridgeton, P. O.	Chic. & W. Mich. R. R. (N. Div.)	Ashland, 6 m.	T. 11 N., R. 14 W.	Newaygo	75	79
Belvidere, P. O. and R. R. Sta.	Chic. S. & C. R. R.		T. 12 N., R. 7 W.	Montcalm	250	82
Bad Axe, P. O. and R. R. Sta.	P. H. & N. W. R. R.		T. 16 N., R. 13 E.	Huron	500	86
Bloomington, P. O.	P. H. & N. W. R. R.	Bad Axe, 9 m.	T. 15 N., R. 14 E.	Huron		86
Brooks, R. R. Sta.	M. C. R. R. (J., L. & S. Div.)		T. 14 N., R. 5 E.	Saginaw		84
Blumfield, P. O.	M. C. R. R. (B. C. Div.)	Reese, 4 m.	T. 12 N., R. 6 E.	Saginaw	100	84
Buena Vista, P. O.	P. H. & N. W. R. R.	Frankenmuth, 1 m.	T. 12 N., R. 6 E.	Saginaw	50	84
Bridgeport, P. O. and R. R. and Tel. Sta.	F. & P. M. R. R.		T. 11 N., R. 5 E.	Saginaw	300	84
Blectmar, P. O. and R. R. Sta.	F. & P. M. R. R.		T. 10 N., R. 5 E.	Saginaw	150	84
Birch Run, P. O. and R. R. and Tel. Sta.	F. & P. M. R. R.		T. 10 N., R. 6 E.	Saginaw	200	84
Big Prairie, P. O.	Chic. & W. Mich. R. R.	White Cloud, 8 m.	T. 13 N., R. 11 W.	Newaygo	60	79
Brooks, P. O.	Chic. & W. Mich. R. R. (N. Div.)	Newaygo, 5 m.	T. 12 N., R. 12 W.	Newaygo		79
Bridgeville, P. O.	Det. Gr. H. & Mil. R. R.	St. Johns, 10 m.	T. 9 N., R. 2 W.	Gratiot	100	83
Bayport, P. O. and Tel. Sta.	Saginaw Bay	Caseville, 7 m.	T. 17 N., R. 10 E.	Huron	25	86
Berne, P. O.	P. O. & P. A. R. R.	Caseville, 8 m.	T. 16 N., R. 11 E.	Huron		86
Beaver Creek	Chic. S. & C. R. R.	Riverdale, 3 m.	T. 12 N., R. 4 W.	Gratiot	25	83
Breckenridge, P. O. and R. R. and Tel. Sta.	Sag. Valley & St. Louis R. R.		T. 12 N., R. 1 W.	Gratiot	450	83
Burnside, P. O.	P. H. & N. W. R. R.	Brown City, 4 m.	T. 9 N., R. 12 E.	Lapeer	125	89
Butler's	P. H. & N. W. R. R.	Imlay, 4 m.	T. 10 N., R. 12 E.	Lapeer		89
Bridgehampton, P. O. (Wilber Road R. R. Sta.)	P. H. & N. W. R. R.		T. 12 N., R. 15 E.	Sanilac		87
Brown City, P. O. and R. R. Sta.	P. H. & N. W. R. R.		T. 9 N., R. 13 E.	Sanilac	125	87
Beal, P. O.	P. H. & N. W. R. R.	Croswell, 5 m.	T. 10 N., R. 15 E.	Sanilac		87
Brockway Centre, P. O. and R. R. Sta.	P. H. & N. W. R. R.		T. 8 N., R. 14 E.	St. Clair	300	88
Brockway, P. O.	Chic. & Gr. T. R. R.	Emmett, 6 m.	T. 8 N., R. 14 E.	St. Clair	250	88
Burtchville	Lake Huron	Jeddo, 3 m.	T. 8 N., R. 17 E.	St. Clair		88
Blaine, P. O. (Grant Centre Sta.)	P. H. & N. W. R. R.		T. 8 N., R. 16 E.	St. Clair	500	88
Beard's Mills	P. H. & N. W. R. R.	Kingsley, 1½ m.	T. 7 N., R. 16 E.	St. Clair		88
Bendville	P. H. & N. W. R. R.	Port Huron, 8 m.	T. 7 N., R. 16 E.	St. Clair		88
Belle River, P. O.	Chic. & Gr. T. R. R.	Capac, 4 m.	T. 6 N., R. 13 E.	St. Clair	50	88
Berville, P. O. and R. R. Sta.	P. H. & N. W. R. R.		T. 6 N., R. 13 E.	St. Clair	75	88
Berea, R. R. Sta.	P. H. & N. W. R. R.		T. 6 N., R. 16 E.	St. Clair		88
Blair, P. O.	M. C. R. R. (Gr. R. Div.)	Nashville, 4 m.	T. 4 N., R. 7 W.	Barry		97
Barryville	M. C. R. R. (Gr. R. Div.)	Morgan, 2 m.	T. 3 N., R. 7 W.	Barry	15	97
Bowen's Mills, P. O.	M. C. R. R. (Gr. R. Div.)	Middleville, 7 m.	T. 3 N., R. 10 W.	Barry	50	97
Byers, P. O. and R. R. Sta.	G. R. & I. R. R.		T. 15 N., R. 9 W.	Mecosta	100	78
Big Rapids, P. O. and R. R. and Tel. Sta.	Det. Lan. & Nor. R. R., F. & P. M. R. R.		T. 15 N., R. 10 W.	Mecosta	5,000	78
Bradford, P. O.	Sag. Val. & St. L. R. R.	St. Louis 14 m.	T. 14 N., R. 1 W.	Midland		70
Blissfield, P. O., and R. R. and Tel. Sta.	L. S. & M. S. R. R.		T. 7 S., R. 5 E.	Lenawee	1,200	114
Bankers, P. O., and R. R. and Tel. Sta.	L. S. & M. S. (Ft. Wayne Branch)		T. 7 S., R. 3 W.	Hillsdale	100	113
Balch, P.O., and R. R. Sta.	Wab. St. L. & Pac. R. R.		T. 6 S., R. 5 E.	Lenawee	100	114
Britton, R. R. Sta.	Wab. St. L. & Pac. R. R.		T. 6 S., R. 5 E.	Lenawee	100	114
Burr Oak, P.O., and R. R. and Tel. Sta.	L. S. & M. S. R. R.		T. 7 S., R. 9 W.	St. Joseph	900	111
Big Beaver, P. O.	Det. Gr. H. & Mil. R. R.	Royal Oak, 5 m.	T. 2 N., R. 11 E.	Oakland	250	101
Bloomfield Centre	Det. Gr. H. & Mil. R. R.	Birmingham, 3 m.	T. 2 N., R. 10 E.	Oakland	20	101
Birmingham, P. O., and R. R. and Tel. Sta.	Det. Gr. H. & Mil. R. R.		T. 2 N., R. 10 E.	Oakland	800	101
Brandon, P. O.	M. C. R. R. (B. C. Div.)	Oxford, 4 m.	T. 5 N., R. 9 E.	Oakland		101
Bengal, P. O.	Det. Gr. H. & Mil. R. R.	Fowler, 5 m.	T. 7 N., R. 3 W.	Clinton		92
Bath, P. O., and R. R. and Tel. Sta.	M. C. R. R. (Sag. Div.)		T. 5 N., R. 1 W.	Clinton	320	92
Byron Centre, P. O., and R. R. and Tel. Sta.	L. S. & M. S. (Kal. Div.)		T. 5 N., R. 12 W.	Kent	300	94
Bowen Station, P. O.	M. C. R. R. (Gr. R. Div.)		T. 6 N., R. 11 W.	Kent	100	94
Bowne, P. O.	M. C. R. R. (Gr. R. Div.)	Caledonia, 9 m.	T. 5 N., R. 9 W.	Kent	100	94
Borets Mills R. R. Sta.	Gr. R. & I. R. R.		T. 9 N., R. 11 W.	Kent	50	94
Belmont, P. O., and R. R. and Tel. Sta.	Gr. R. & I. R. R.		T. 8 N., R. 11 W.	Kent	65	94
Buena Vista	Gr. R. & I. R. R.	Belmont, 5 m.	T. 8 N., R. 10 W.	Kent		94
Bridgewater, P. O., and R. R. Sta.	L. S. & M. S. (Ypsilanti Div.)		T. 4 S., R. 4 E.	Washtenaw	100	104
Benton, P. O.	L. S. & M. S. R. R.	Saline, 4 m.	T. 4 S., R. 5 E.	Washtenaw	40	104
Baldwin Mills, R. R. Sta.	L. S. & M. S. (Ft. Wayne Br.)		T. 4 S., R. 2 W.	Jackson		105
Brooklyn, P. O., and R. R. and Tel. Sta.	L. S. & M. S. (Ypsilanti Br.)		T. 4 S., R. 1 E.	Jackson	600	105
Birkett, P. O.	M. C. R. R.	Dexter, 4 m.	T. 1 S., R. 4 E.	Washtenaw	60	104
Brookville	Det. Lan. & Nor. R. R.	Salem, 3 m.	T. 1 S., R. 7 E.	Washtenaw		104
Bath Mills, R. R. and Tel. Sta.	M. C. R. R.		T. 3 S., R. 3 W.	Jackson		105
Belleville, P. O. and R. R. and Tel. Sta.	Wab. St. L. & Pac. R. R.		T. 3 S., R. 8 E.	Wayne	500	103
Belden, P. O. and R. R. and Tel. Sta.	F. & P. M. R. R.		T. 4 S., R. 9 E.	Wayne	350	103
Burlington, P. O.	M. C. R. R. (Air Line Div.)	Burlington Sta., 2 m.	T. 4 S., R. 7 W.	Calhoun	325	106
Burlington, R. R. Sta.	M. C. R. R. (Air Line Div.)		T. 4 S., R. 7 W.	Calhoun	400	106
Beech, P. O. and R. R. Sta.	Det. Lan. & Nor. R. R.		T. 1 S., R. 10 E.	Wayne	350	103
Bell Branch, P. O.	Det. Lan. & Nor. R. R.	Bedford, 2 m.	T. 1 S., R. 10 E.	Wayne	75	103
Bedford, P. O.	Chic. Gr. T., M. C. R. R.	Battle Creek, 6 m.	T. 1 S., R. 8 W.	Calhoun	200	106
Bedford, P. O. and R. R. and Tel. Sta.	M. C. R. R.		T. 1 S., R. 8 W.	Calhoun	205	106
Battle Creek, P. O. and R. R. and Tel. Sta.	Chic. & Gr. T., M. C., M. & O. R. R.		T. 2 S., R. 8 W.	Calhoun	11,000	106
Batavia, P. O. and R. R. Sta.	L. S. & M. S. R. R.		T. 6 S., R. 7 W.	Branch	100	112
Batavia Centre	L. S. & M. S. R. R.	Batavia, 4 m.	T. 6 S., R. 7 W.	Branch		112
Butler, P. O.	M. C. R. R. (Air Line Br.)	Clarendon, 5 m.	T. 5 S., R. 5 W.	Branch	100	112
Bethel, P. O.	L. S. & M. S. R. R.	Branch, 6 m.	T. 7 S., R. 7 W.	Branch	75	112
Branch, P. O. and R. R. Sta.	L. S. & M. S. R. R.		T. 6 S., R. 7 W.	Branch		112
Bronson, P. O. and R. R. and Tel. Sta.	L. S. & M. S. R. R.		T. 7 S., R. 8 W.	Branch	1,000	112
Brighton, P. O. and R. R. and Tel. Sta.	Det. Lan. & Nor. R. R.		T. 2 N., R. 6 E.	Livingston	1,000	100
Belvidere	Gr. T. R. R., Lake St. Clair	Mt. Clemens, 3 m.	T. 2 N., R. 14 E.	Macomb		102
Bunker Hill, P. O.	M. C. R. R. (Sag. Div.)	Leslie, 6 m.	T. 1 N., R. 1 E.	Ingham	100	91
Bangor, P. O. and R. R. and Tel. Sta.	Chic. & W. Mich. R. R.		T. 2 S., R. 16 W.	Van Buren	1,600	108
Berlamont, P. O. and R. R. Sta.	M. C. R. R. (Kal. & S. Haven Div.)		T. 1 S., R. 14 W.	Van Buren	150	108
Bloomingdale, P. O. and R. R. Sta.	M. C. R. R. (Kal. & S. Haven Div.)		T. 1 S., R. 14 W.	Van Buren	450	108
Breedsville, P. O. and R. R. and Tel. Sta.	Chic. & W. Mich. R. R.		T. 1 S., R. 15 W.	Van Buren	500	108
Bridgman, P. O. and R. R. and Tel. Sta.	Chic. & W. Mich. R. R.		T. 6 S., R. 19 W.	Berrien	100	109
Brown's Sta.	Chic. & W. Mich. R. R.		T. 6 S., R. 20 W.	Berrien		109
Berrien Springs, P. O. and R. R. and Tel. Sta.	M. C. (St. Joseph Val. Br.)		T. 6 S., R. 17 W.	Berrien	800	109
Bakertown	M. C. R. R.	Buchanan, 3 m.	T. 8 S., R. 18 W.	Berrien		109
Bertrand, P. O. and R. R. and Tel. Sta.	M. C. R. R. (South Bend Div.)		T. 8 S., R. 17 W.	Berrien	200	109
Buchanan, P. O. and R. R. and Tel. Sta.	M. C. R. R.		T. 7 S., R. 18 W.	Berrien	2,000	109

LIST OF CITIES, TOWNS, ETC.

NAME OF VILLAGE.	RAILROAD, LAKE, OR RIVER.	Nearest Sta. or Landing	TOWNSHIP.	COUNTY.	Pop.	Page
Berrien Centre P. O. and R. R. and Tel. Sta	Cin. Wab. & Mich. R. R		T. 6 S., R. 17 W.	Berrien	50	109
Brownsville P. O	M. C., (Air Line Div.) Chic. & Gr. T.	Cassopolis, 4 m	T. 7 S., R. 14 W.	Cass	100	110
Bainbridge, P.O	Chic. & W. Mich., Cin. Wab. & Mich	Benton Harbor, 6 m	T. 4 S., R. 18 W.	Berrien	150	109
Benton Harbor, P.O. and R.R. and Tel. Sta.(Ldg)	Chic. & W. Mich., Cin. Wab. & Mich. (Lake Mich.)		T. 4 S., R. 19 W.	Berrien	2,500	109
Barron Lake, R. R. Sta	M. C. R. R. (Air Line Div.)		T. 7 S., R. 16 W.	Cass		110
Brownell's, R. R. Sta	M. C. R. R. (Kal. Div.)		T. 3 S., R. 11 W.	Kalamazoo		107
Beaver Dam, P. O	Chic. & W. Mich. (Gr. R. Div.)	Vriesland, 2 m	T. 7 N., R. 14 W.	Ottawa	30	95
Bauer, P. O	Chic. & W. Mich. (Gr. R. Div.)	Grandville, 7 m	T. 6 N., R. 13 W.	Ottawa	250	95
Blendon, P. O	Chic. & W. Mich. (Gr. R. Div.)	Grandville, 8 m	T. 6 N., R. 14 W.	Ottawa	40	95
Blendon Ldg	Chic. & W. Mich. (Gr. R. Div.)	Grandville, 7 m	T. 7 N., R. 13 W.	Ottawa		95
Berlin, P. O. and R. R. and Tel. Sta	Det. Gr. H. & Mil. R. R		T. 7 N., R. 13 W.	Ottawa	800	95
*Bass River, P. O		Grand Haven, 14 m		Ottawa		95
Big Spring, P. O	Det. Gr. H. & Mil. R. R	Berlin, 6 m	T. 8 N., R. 13 W.	Ottawa	125	95
Beach Tree, R. R. Sta	Chic. & W. Mich. R. R		T. 7 N., R. 16 W.	Ottawa		95
Bockhill, R. R. Sta	Chic. & W. Mich. R. R		T. 7 N., R. 16 W.	Ottawa		95
Borculo, P. O	Chic. and W. Mich. (Gr. R. Div.)	Zeeland, 5 m	T. 6 N., R. 15 W.	Ottawa		95
Bismarck, P. O	M. C. R. R	Vermontville, 7 m	T. 4 N., R. 6 W.	Eaton	200	98
Bellevue, P. O. and R. R. and Tel. Sta	Chic. & Gr. T. R. R		T. 1 N., R. 6 W.	Eaton	1,000	98
Brookfield, P. O	M. C. R. R., L. S. & M. S	Eaton Rapids, 8 m	T. 1 N., R. 4 W.	Eaton	150	98
Black River, R. R. Sta	Chic. & W. Mich. R. R		T. 1 N., R. 15 W.	Allegan		96
Burnip's Corners, P. O	L. S. & M. S. R. R. (Kal. Div.)	Dorr, 6 m	T. 4 N., R. 13 W.	Allegan	100	96
Bradley, P. O. and R. R. Sta	Gr. R. & I. R. R		T. 3 N., R. 11 W.	Allegan	200	96
Baltimore Mills	M. C. R. R. (Gr. R. Div.)	Hastings, 8 m	T. 2 N., R. 8 W.	Barry	150	97
Banfield, P. O	M. C. R. R	Battle Creek, 12 m	T. 1 N., R. 8 W.	Barry		97
Bravo, P. O. and R. R. Sta	Chic. & W. Mich. R. R		T. 2 N., R. 15 W.	Allegan	200	96
Burton, P. O. and R. R. Sta	Det. Gr. H. & Mil. R. R		T. 7 N., R. 1 E.	Shiawassee	100	91
Bennington, P. O. and R. R. and Tel. Sta	M. C. R. R. (Sag. Div.)		T. 6 N., R. 2 E.	Shiawassee	200	91
Bancroft, P. O. and R. R. and Tel. Sta	Chic. & Gr. T. R. R		T. 6 N., R. 3 E.	Shiawassee	700	91
Burns, P. O	Chic. & Gr. T. R. R	Bancroft, 2 m	T. 5 N., R. 4 E.	Shiawassee	50	91
Byron, P. O	Det. Gr. H. & Mil. R. R	Gaines, 5 m	T. 5 N., R. 4 E.	Shiawassee	300	91
Boston, P. O	Det. Gr. H. & Mil. R. R	Saranac, 12 m	T. 5 N., R. 7 W.	Ionia	100	93
Belding, P. O. and Tel. Sta	Det. Lan. & Nor. R. R	Kiddville, 2 m	T. 8 N., R. 8 W.	Ionia	800	93
Bryan Hill, R. R. Sta	L. S. & M. S. R. R. (Dundee Br.)		T. 5 S., R. 9 E.	Monroe		115
Brest	M. C. R. R. (Toledo Div.)	Stony Creek, 2 m	T. 6 S., R. 10 E.	Monroe	180	115
Banks, P. O	M. C. R. R	West Bay City, 2 m	T. 14 N., R. 5 E.	Bay		75
Bay City, P. O. and R. R. and Tel. Sta. (Ldg)	M. C. R.R. (B. C. Div.) Sag. River, F. & P. M. R. R		T. 14 N., R. 5 E.	Bay	28,000	75
*Bell Mountain		Pontiac, 5 m	T. 3 N., R. 10 E.	Oakland		101
*Barnard	Gr. R. & I. R. R	Charlevoix, 6 m	T. 33 N., R. 8 W.	Charlevoix	40	57
*Barton	Chic. & W. Mich. R. R	Hungerford, (near)	T. 16 N., R. 11 W.	Newaygo	20	79
*Bay Siding	C. & N. W. R. R	Escanaba, 5 m	T. 40 N., R. 22 W.	Delta		120
*Bay Springs	Pine Lake	Boyne Falls, 6 m	T. 33 N., R. 6 W.	Charlevoix		57
*Bear River		Petoskey, 5 m	T. 35 N., R. 5 W.	Emmet		51
*Beaver	C. & N. W. R. R			Marquette		119
*Beaver				Newaygo	25	79
*Belsay	Chic. & Gr. T. R. R	Flint, 4 m	T. 7 N., R. 7 E.	Genesee		90
*Boney Lake		Traverse City, 8 m	T. 26 N., R. 11 W.	Gr. Traverse	20	60
*Big Rapids Junction, Tel. Sta	Chic. & W. M. R. R		T. 10 N., R. 16 W.	Muskegon		81
*Birch Creek	Chic. & N. W. R. R	Menominee, 7 m	T. 33 N., R. 27 W.	Menominee		124
*Bloomington				Sanilac		87
*Blooming Valley	Chic. & W. M. R. R	Shelby, 3 m	T. 14 N., R. 18 W.	Oceana		80
*Blue Lake	Chic. & W. M. (B. R. Br.)	Holton, 6 m	T. 12 N., R. 16 W.	Muskegon	20	81
*Bostwick Lake	Gr. R. & I. R. R	Belmont, 9 m	T. 8 N., R. 10 W.	Kent	25	94
*Boynton Village		Port Huron, 3 m	T. 6 N., R. 17 E.	St. Clair		89
*Bradley	M. C. R. R. (S. Div.)			Saginaw		84
*Brown	Chic. & N. W. (M. R. Br.)			Menominee		124
*Bross, P. O		Carson City, 5 m	T. 9 N., R. 4 W.	Gratiot		88
*Brick Tavern	Det. Gr. H. & Mil. R. R	Berlin, 4 m	T. 8 N., R. 12 W.	Kent		94
*Bristol			R. 6 W.	Isabella	20	77
*Brooklyn				Macomb	50	102
*Broomfield	F. & P. M. R. R	Farwell, 15 m	T. 14 N., R. 6 W.	Isabella		77
*Brown				Manistee	30	59
*Brown's Dale	M. C. R. R. (M. Div.)	Gaylord, 10 m	T. 32 N., R. 3 W.	Otsego	50	56
*Bohemian, P. O				Ontonagon		119
*Bannister, P. O				Gratiot		88
*Bailey, Tel. Sta			T. 18 N.	Clare		73
Beachville (North Branch P. O.)	P. O. & P. A. R. R	Lapeer, 14 m	T. 9 N., R. 11 E.	Lapeer		89
Camp 2, R. R. Sta	Tawas & Bay County R. R		T. 21 N., R. 6 E.	Iosco		65
Church's Ldg	St. Mary's River	Sault St. Marie, 13 m	T. 46 N., R. 3 E.	Chippewa		123
Carltonville	St. Mary's River		T. 47 N., R. 3 E.	Chippewa		123
Copper Falls Mine, P. O	Lake Superior	Eagle Harbor, 2 m	T. 58 N., R. 31 W.	Keweenaw	300	118
Central Mine, P. O	Lake Superior	Eagle Harbor, 4 m	T. 58 N., R. 31 W.	Keweenaw	1,300	118
Clifton, P. O	Lake Superior	Eagle River, 3 m	T. 57 N., R. 32 W.	Keweenaw	350	118
Campbell, R. R. Sta	Chic. & N. W. R. R		T. 42 N., R. 23 W.	Delta		120
Calumet, P. O. and R. R. and Tel. Sta	Mineral Range, R. R		T. 56 N., R. 33 W.	Houghton	8,000	117
Cliff's Siding	M. H. & O. R. R		T. 48 N., R. 32 W.	Baraga		117
Cheboygan, P. O. and R. R. and Tel. Sta. (Ldg)	M. C. R. R. (Mack. Div.)		T. 38 N., R. 1 W.	Cheboygan	4,000	52
Crump's Landing	M. C. R. R. (Mack. Div.)	Mullett Lake, 7 m	T. 36 N., R. 3 W.	Cheboygan		52
Crawford Quarry, P. O. and Tel. Sta	Lake Huron		T. 35 N., R. 5 E.	Presque Isle	125	53
Cross Village, P. O	G. R. I. & Mack. R. R	Harbor Springs, 14 m	T. 38 N., R. 6 W.	Emmet	600	51
Carp Lake, P. O. and R. R. Sta	G. R. I. & Mack. R. R		T. 38 N., R. 4 W.	Emmet		51
Conway, P. O. and R. R. Sta	G. R. I. & Mack. R. R		T. 35 N., R. 5 W.	Emmet	50	51
Creighton, R. R. Sta	Det. M. & M. R. R		T. 46 N., R. 16 W.	Schoolcraft		122
Cathead	G. R. & I. R. R. (T. C. Br.)	Traverse City, 33 m	T. 32 N., R. 11 W.	Leelanaw	25	58
Central Lake, P. O	Lake Michigan		T. 31 N., R. 8 W.	Antrim	60	57
Creswell, P. O	G. R. & I. R. R	Westwood, 20 m	T. 30 N., R. 9 W.	Antrim	25	57
Clam Lake, P. O	G. R. & I. R. R	Wetzel, 10 m	T. 29 N., R. 7 W.	Antrim	100	57
Chestonia, P. O	G. R. & I. R. R	Alba, 5 m	T. 30 N., R. 6 W.	Antrim		57
Crapo, P. O. and R. R. Sta	G. R. & I. R. R		T. 17 N., R. 10 W.	Osceola	50	72
Clare, P. O. and R. R. and Tel. Sta	F. & P. M. R. R		T. 17 N., R. 4 W.	Clare	200	73
Chippewa, P. O. and R. R. and Tel. Sta	F. & P. M. R. R		T. 17 N., R. 7 W.	Osceola	100	72
Cedar, P. O	F. & P. M. R. R	Loomis, 18 m	T. 19 N., R. 2 W.	Gladwin	40	74
Chase, P. O. and R. R. and Tel. Sta	F. & P. M. R. R		T. 17 N., R. 11 W.	Lake	400	71
Crooked Lake, P. O	F. & P. M. R. R	Lake, ½ m	T. 17 N., R. 4 W.	Clare	75	73
Champion, P. O. and R. R. and Tel. Sta	M. H. & O. R. R		T. 48 N., R. 29 W.	Marquette	600	119
Carpenter, P. O	G. R. & I. R. R	Petoskey, 8 m	T. 34 N., R. 7 W.	Charlevoix		57
Charlevoix, P. O. and Tel. Sta	G. R. & I. R. R., Lake Mich	Petoskey, 10 m	T. 34 N., R. 8 W.	Charlevoix	1,200	57
Clarion, P. O	G. R. & I. R. R	Melrose, 2 m	T. 33 N., R. 5 W.	Charlevoix	80	57
Cedar Forks, P. O	Chic. & N. W. R. R	Stephenson, 12 m	T. 35 N., R. 30 W.	Menominee	300	124
Carbondale, P. O	Chic. & N. W. R. R		T. 34 N., R. 27 W.	Menominee	400	124
Clarksburg, P. O. and R. R. and Tel. Sta	M. H. & O. R. R		T. 47 N., R. 29 W.	Marquette	500	119
Custer, P. O. and R. R. and Tel. Sta	F. & P. M. R. R		T. 18 N., R. 16 W.	Mason	150	70
Colfax, P. O	G. R. & I. R. R	Manton, 5 m	T. 23 N., R. 10 W.	Wexford	50	69

☞ Names marked with a star (*) will not be found on the Maps.

NAME OF VILLAGE.	RAILROAD, LAKE, OR RIVER.	Nearest Sta. or Landing	TOWNSHIP.	COUNTY.	Pop.	Page
Cadillac, P. O. and R. R. and Tel. Sta	G. R. & I. R. R		T. 21&22N., R. 9 W.	Wexford	3,500	69
Clay Hill, P. O.	G. R. & I. R. R	Hobart, 14 m	T. 21 N., R. 11 W.	Wexford		69
Calkinsville, P. O.	F. & P. M. R. R.	Clare, 8 m	T. 15 N., R. 4 W.	Isabella	45	77
Crawford, P. O.	F. & P. M. R. R. (Mt. P. Div.)	Mount Pleasant, 6 m	T. 13 N., R. 4 W.	Isabella	50	77
Chocolay, R. R. Sta	Det. M. & M. R. R		T. 47 N., R. 24 W.	Marquette	75	119
Cheshire Junc., R. R. and Tel. Sta. (Forsyth P.O.)	Chic. & N. W. R. R.		T. 45 N., R. 25 W.	Marquette		119
Crystal Falls, P. O. and R. R. Sta	Menominee River R. R. (Crystal Falls Br.)		T. 43 N., R. 32 W.	Marquette	1,000	119
Coleman, P. O. and R. R. Sta	F. & P. M. R. R.		T. 16 N., R. 2 W.	Midland	300	76
Copper Harbor Ldg., P. O. and Tel. Sta	Lake Superior		T. 58 N., R. 28 W.	Keweenaw	200	118
Cedar Run, P. O	G. R. & I. R. R. (T. C. Br.)	Traverse City, 9 m	T. 27 N., R. 12 W.	Gr. Traverse	20	60
Churchill, P. O.	M. C. R. R. (Mack. Div.)	West Branch, 10 m	T. 23 N., R. 2 E.	Ogemaw	70	66
Campbell's Corners, P. O	M. C. R. R. (Mack. Div.)	West Branch, 5 m	T. 22 N., R. 2 E.	Ogemaw		66
Cleon, P. O.	F. & P. M. (Man. Div.)	Manistee, 20 m	T. 24 N., R. 13 W.	Manistee		59
Congre, P. O.	F. & P. M. R. R. (Man. Div.)	Manistee, 22 m	T. 24 N., R. 14 W.	Manistee		59
Chief, P. O	F. & P. M. R. R. (Man. Div.)	Manistee, 12 m	T. 22 N., R. 15 W.	Manistee		59
Clear Water, P. O	G. R. & I. R. R	Leetsville, 6 m	T. 28 N., R. 8 W.	Kalkaska	150	61
Cold Spring, P. O	G. R. & I. R. R	Leetsville, 5 m	T. 28 N., R. 6 W.	Kalkaska		61
Crofton, P. O. and R. R. Sta	G. R. & I. R. R.		T. 26 N., R. 8 W.	Kalkaska	130	61
Cheney, R. R. and Tel. Sta	M. C. R. R		T. 25 N., R. 3 W.	Crawford		62
Clay Banks, P. O	Chic. & W. Mich., Lake Mich	Montague, 14 m	T. 13 N., R. 18 W.	Oceana	30	80
Cliff, R. R. Sta	Chic. & W. Mich. R. R		T. 11 N., R. 16 W.	Muskegon		81
Canada Corners, P. O. and R. R. Sta	Chic. & W. Mich. R. R		T. 10 N., R. 13 W.	Muskegon	65	81
Casnovia, P. O. and R. R. and Tel. Sta	Chic. & W. Mich. R. R		T. 10 N., R. 13 W.	Muskegon	250	81
Crystal Valley, P. O	Chic. & W. Mich. R. R	Pentwater, 10 m	T. 16 N., R. 16 W.	Oceana	150	80
Cob-moo-sa, P. O.	Chic. & W. Mich. R. R	Mears, 15 m	T. 15 N., R. 16 W.	Oceana	100	80
Coral, P. O. and R. R. and Tel. Sta	Det. L. & N. R. R		T. 11 N., R. 9 W.	Montcalm	200	82
Colwell, P. O. and R. R. and Tel. Sta	Det. L. & N. R. R		T. 11 N., R. 9 W.	Montcalm	150	82
Crosby's Mill	Det. L. & N. R. R	Greenville, 4 m	T. 10 N., R. 8 W.	Montcalm		82
Colby, R. R. and Tel. Sta	Det. L. & N. (Sag. Div.)		T. 10 N., R. 7 W.	Montcalm	150	82
Crystal, P. O	Det. L. & N. (Sag. Div.)	Sheridan, 13 m	T. 10 N., R. 5 W.	Montcalm	200	82
Croton, P. O.	Chic. & W. Mich. (N. Div.)	Newaygo, 10 m	T. 12 N., R. 11 W.	Newaygo	200	79
Cooper, R. R. Sta	G. R. & I. R. R		T. 12 N., R. 10 W.	Montcalm		82
Cato, P. O.	Chic. S. & C. R. R.	Lakeview, 2 m	T. 12 N., R. 8 W.	Montcalm	125	82
Cedar Lake, R. R. and Tel. Sta	Chic. S. & C. R. R.		T. 12 N., R. 6 W.	Montcalm	250	82
Carson City, P. O.	Det. L. & N. (Sag. Div.)	Fenwick, 13 m	T. 9 N., R. 5 W.	Montcalm	720	82
Cranow, P. O	P. H. & N. W. R. R	Adams, 6 m	T. 15 N., R. 14 E.	Huron	60	86
Columbia, P. O.	S. T. & H. R. R	Akron, 7 m	T. 14 N., R. 9 E.	Tuscola		85
Cass City, P. O. and R. R. Sta	P. O. & P. A. R. R		T. 14 N., R. 11 E.	Tuscola	500	85
Caro, P. O. and R. R. and Tel. Sta	M. C. (B. C. Div.)		T. 13 N., R. 9 E.	Tuscola	2,000	85
Crossman, P. O.	M. C. (B. C. Div.)	Wahjamega, 2 m	T. 12 N., R. 8 E.	Tuscola		85
Crow Island	F. & P. M. R. R	East Saginaw, 2 m	T. 12 N., R. 5 E.	Saginaw		84
Carrollton, P. O. and R. R. and Tel. Sta	M. C. (Sag. Div.)		T. 12 N., R. 5 E.	Saginaw	850	84
Chesaning, P. O. and R. R. Sta	M. C. (Sag. Div.)		T. 9 N., R. 3 E.	Saginaw	1,200	84
Chapin, P. O	M. C. (Sag. Div.)	Oakley, 7 m	T. 9 N., R. 1 E.	Saginaw		84
Cass Bridge, P. O.	F. & P. M. R. R	Bridgeport, 2 m	T. 11 N., R. 5 E.	Saginaw		84
County Line, P. O. and R. R. Sta	F. & P. M. R. R.		T. 10 N., R. 6 E.	Saginaw	200	84
County Line, R. R. Sta	Chic. & W. Mich. R. R		T. 12 N., R. 14 W.	Newaygo		79
Caseville, P. O. and R. R. and Tel. Sta	P. O. & P. A., Lake Huron		T. 17 N., R. 10 E.	Huron	800	86
Canboro, P. O	P. O. & P. A. R. R.	Gagetown, 9 m	T. 15 N., R. 9 E.	Huron	25	86
Columbus, P. O	Gr. T. R. R	Ridgeway, 4 m	T. 4 N., R. 15 E.	St. Clair	110	88
Casco, P. O	Gr. T. R. R	Ridgeway, 6 m	T. 4 N., R. 15 E.	St. Clair	800	88
Clifford, P. O. and R. R. and Tel. Sta	P. H. & N. W. R. R		T. 10 N., R. 11 E.	Lapeer	150	89
Columbiaville, P. O. and R. R. and Tel. Sta	M. C. (B. C. Div.)		T. 9 N., R. 9 E.	Lapeer	400	89
Cumber, P. O	P. H. & N. W. R. R	Minden City, 18 m	T. 14 N., R. 13 E.	Sanilac	70	87
Cedar Dale, P. O. and R. R. Sta	P. H. & N. W. R. R		T. 14 N., R. 14 E.	Sanilac	200	87
Charlestown, P. O	P. H. & N. W. R. R	Minden City, 5 m	T. 14 N., R. 15 E.	Sanilac	50	87
Carsonville, P. O. and R. R. and Tel. Sta	P. H. & N. W. R. R		T. 12 N., R. 15 E.	Sanilac	150	87
Croswell, P. O. and R. R. and Tel. Sta	P. H. & N. W. R. R		T. 10 N., R. 16 E.	Sanilac	600	87
Clio (Pine Run), P. O. and R. R. Sta	F. & P. M. R. R.		T. 9 N., R. 6 E.	Genesee	500	90
Clew, P. O.	F. & P. M. (F. R. Div.)	Otisville, 5 m	T. 9 N., R. 7 E.	Genesee		90
Capac, P. O. and R. R. and Tel. Sta	Chic. & Gr. T. R. R.		T. 7 N., R. 13 E.	St. Clair	600	88
Caroon, P. O.	Chic. & Gr. T. R. R	Emmett, 9 m	T. 8 N., R. 14 E.	St. Clair	250	88
Carlton Centre, P. O	M. C. R. R. (Gr. R. Div.)	Hastings, 7 m	T. 4 N., R. 8 W.	Barry	100	97
Cressey's Corners, P. O.	M. & O. R. R	Richland, 4 m	T. 1 N., R. 10 W.	Barry	200	97
Coaldon	Det. Lan. & Nor. R. R		T. 15 N., R. 8 W.	Mecosta		78
Clayton, P. O. and R. R. and Tel. Sta	L. S. & M. S. R. R		T. 7 S., R. 2 E.	Lenawee	600	114
Chase's R. R. Sta.	L. S. & M. S. (Jackson Br.)		T. 6 S., R. 4 E.	Lenawee		114
Corbus, R. R. Sta	L. S. & M. S. (Dundee Br.)		T. 7 S., R. 5 E.	Lenawee		114
Church's Corners, P. O	L. S. & M. S. R. R	Hudson, 8 m	T. 6 S., R. 1 W.	Hillsdale	100	113
Camden, P. O.	L. S. & M. S. (Ft. Wayne Br.)	Montgomery, 4 m	T. 8 S., R. 4 W.	Hillsdale	400	113
Canandaigua, P. O	Wab. St. L. & Pac. R. R	North Morenci, 8 m	T. 8 S., R. 2 E.	Lenawee	200	114
Cambria Mills, P. O.	L. S. & M. S. R. R	Reading, 6 m	T. 7 S., R. 3 W.	Hillsdale	400	113
Cambria Centre	L. S. & M. S. R. R	Hillsdale, 5 m	T. 7 S., R. 3 W.	Hillsdale		113
Centreville, P. O. and R. R. and Tel. Sta	M. C. R. R. (Air Line Div.)		T. 6 S., R. 10 W.	St. Joseph	900	111
Constantine, P. O. and R. R. and Tel. Sta	L. S. & M. S. R. R		T. 7 S., R. 12 W.	St. Joseph	1,600	111
Cory, P. O. and R. R. Sta	M. C. R. R. (Air Line Div.)		T. 6 S., R. 12 W.	St. Joseph		111
Cambridge, P. O	L. S. & M. S. (Ypsilanti Br.)	Brooklyn, 8 m	T. 5 S., R. 2 E.	Lenawee	200	114
Clinton, P. O. and R. R. and Tel. Sta	L. S. & M. S. (Jackson Br.)		T. 5 S., R. 4 E.	Lenawee	1,000	114
Chamberlains, R. R. Sta	Chic. & Gr. T. R. R.		T. 5 S., R. 12 W.	St. Joseph		111
Colon, P. O. and R. R. and Tel. Sta	M. C. R. R. (Air Line Div.)		T. 6 S., R. 9 W.	St. Joseph	425	111
Clawson, P. O.	Det. Gr. H. & Mil. R. R	Royal Oak, 3 m	T. 1 N., R. 11 E.	Oakland		101
Clyde, P. O. and R. R. and Tel. Sta	F. & P. M. R. R		T. 3 N., R. 7 E.	Oakland	100	101
Commerce, P. O	F. & P. M. R. R	Milford, 6 m	T. 2 N., R. 8 E.	Oakland	350	101
Clarkston, P. O. and R. R. and Tel. Sta	Det. Gr. H. & Mil. R. R	Clarkston Sta., 2 m	T. 4 N., R. 9 E.	Oakland	400	101
Clintonville	Det. Gr. H. & Mil. R. R	Drayton Plains, 2 m	T. 3 N., R. 9 E.	Oakland	77	101
Chandlers R. R. Sta.	M. C. R. R. (Sag. Div.)		T. 5 N., R. 1 W.	Clinton		92
*Corkin, P. O.				Clinton		92
Casnovia, P. O. and R. R. Sta	Chic. & W. Mich. R. R. (Newaygo Div.)		T. 10 N., R. 12 W.	Kent	850	94
Corinth, P. O	Gr. R. & I. R. R	Ross, 2 m	T. 5 N., R. 12 W.	Kent	100	94
Cascade, P. O.	Det. Gr. H. & Mil. R. R	Ada, 4 m	T. 6 N., R. 10 W.	Kent	120	94
Caledonia, P. O. and R. R. and Tel. Sta	M. C. R. R. (Gr. R. Div.)		T. 5 N., R. 10 W.	Kent	500	94
Cedar Springs, P. O. and R. R. and Tel. Sta	Gr. R. & I. R. R		T. 10 N., R. 11 W.	Kent	1,300	94
Courtland Centre, P. O	Gr. R. & I. R. R	Rockford, 6 m	T. 9 N., R. 10 W.	Kent		94
Childs' Mills, R. R. Sta	Gr. R. & I. R. R		T. 8 N., R. 11 W.	Kent		94
Cannonsburg, P. O	Det. Gr. H. & Mil. R. R	Ada, 9 m	T. 8 N., R. 10 W.	Kent	200	94
*Chauncey, P. O.				Kent		94
Carpenter's Corners	L. S. & M. S. (Ypsilanti Div.)	Ypsilanti, 4 m	T. 3 S., R. 6 E.	Washtenaw		104
Concord, P. O. and R. R. and Tel. Sta	M. C. R. R. (Air Line Div.)		T. 3 S., R. 3 W.	Jackson	600	105
Chelsea, P. O. and R. R. and Tel. Sta	M. C. R. R		T. 2 S., R. 3 E.	Washtenaw	1,400	104
Connors Creek, P. O	M. C. R. R. (B. C. Div.)	Norris, 4 m	T. 1 S., R. 12 E.	Wayne	800	108
Canton, P. O.	M. C. R. R	Swords Sta., 1 m	T. 2 S., R. 8 E.	Wayne		108
County House, R. R. Sta	M. C. R. R		T. 2 S., R. 9 E.	Wayne		108

☞ Names marked with a star (*) will not be found on the Maps.

LIST OF CITIES, TOWNS, ETC.

NAME OF VILLAGE.	RAILROAD, LAKE, OR RIVER.	Nearest Sta. or Landing	TOWNSHIP.	COUNTY.	Pop.	Page
*Calon, P. O.				Calhoun		106
Convis	Chic. & Gr. T. R. R.	Madison, 8 m	T. 1 S., R. 6 W.	Calhoun		106
Convis Centre	M. C. R. R.	Marshall, 9 m	T. 1 S., R. 6 W.	Calhoun	50	106
Condit, R. R. Sta	L. S. & M. S. R. R.		T. 3 S., R. 4 W.	Calhoun		106
Clarendon, R. R. Sta	M. C. R. R. (Air Line Div.)		T. 4 S., R. 5 W.	Calhoun	50	106
Clarendon Centre	M. C. R. R. (Air Line Div.)	Clarendon Sta., 2 m	T. 4 S., R. 5 W.	Calhoun	45	106
Ceresco, P. O. and R. R. and Tel. Sta	M. C. R. R.		T. 2 S., R. 7 W.	Calhoun	600	106
Coldwater, P. O. and R. R. Sta	L. S. & M. S. R. R.		T. 6 S., R. 6 W.	Branch	5,000	112
California, P. O.	Fort Wayne & Jackson R. R.	Ray, 3 m	T. 8 S., R. 5 W.	Branch	250	112
Cohoctah, P. O.	Det. Lan. & Nor. R. R.	Howell, 12 m	T. 4 N., R. 4 E.	Livingston	75	100
Chemungville, (Oak Grove P. O.)	Det. Lan. & Nor. R. R.	Howell, 8 m	T. 4 N., R. 4 E.	Livingston		100
Chubb's Corners, P. O.	Det. Lan. & Nor. R. R.	Brighton, 9 m	T. 2 N., R. 4 E.	Livingston	150	100
Centre Line, P. O. and R. R. Sta	M. C. R. R. (B. C. Div.)		T. 1 N., R. 12 E.	Macomb	200	102
Cady, P. O.	Gr. T. R. R.	Mt. Clemens, 5 m	T. 2 N., R. 13 E.	Macomb	200	102
Chesterfield, P. O. and R. R. and Tel. Sta	Gr. T. R. R.		T. 3 N., R. 14 E.	Macomb	50	102
Cusic Lake	Gr. T. R. R. (Mich. Air Line Br.)	Romeo, 3 m	T. 5 N., R. 12 E.	Macomb		102
College Farm, R. R. Sta	Det. Lan. & Nor. R. R.		T. 4 N., R. 2 W.	Ingham		99
Covert, P. O.	Chic. & W. Mich. R. R.	Deerfield, 6 m	T. 2 S., R. 17 W.	Van Buren	250	108
Columbia, R. R. Sta	M. C. R. R. (Kal. & S. Haven Div.)		T. 1 S., R. 15 W.	Van Buren	37	108
Chickaming, R. R. Sta	Chic. & W. Mich. R. R.		T. 7 S., R. 20 W.	Berrien		109
Calvin, P. O.	M. C. R. R. (Air Line Div.)	Vandalia, 7 m	T. 7 S., R. 14 W.	Cass	500	110
Christian	Chic. & Gr. T. R. R.	Edwardsburgh, 5 m	T. 8 S., R. 15 W.	Cass		110
Corey, P. O. and R. R. and Tel. Sta	M. C. R. R. (Air Line Div.)		T. 6 S., R. 13 W.	Cass	50	110
Coloma, P. O. and R. R. and Tel. Sta	Chic. & W. Mich. R. R.		T. 3 S., R. 17 W.	Berrien	300	109
Climax, P. O. and R. R. and Tel. Sta	Chic. & Gr. T. R. R.		T. 3 S., R. 9 W.	Kalamazoo	250	107
Cushing, P. O.	M. C. R. R.	Dowagiac, 7 m	T. 5 S., R. 16 W.	Cass		110
Charleston	M. C. R. R.	Decatur, 4 m	T. 5 S., R. 14 W.	Cass		110
Cassopolis, P. O. and R. R. and Tel. Sta	M. C. (Air Line Div.), Chic. & Gr. T.		T. 6 S., R. 15 W.	Cass	1,100	110
Cooper, P. O.	L. S. & M. S. R. R.	Cooper Sta., 2 m	T. 1 S., R. 11 W.	Kalamazoo	200	107
Cooper, R. R. Sta	L. S. & M. S. R. R. (Kal. Div.)		T. 1 S., R. 11 W.	Kalamazoo	151	107
Comstock, P. O. and R. R. and Tel. Sta	M. C. R. R.		T. 2 S., R. 10 W.	Kalamazoo	300	107
Charleston	Det. Gr. H. & Mil. R. R.	Coopersville, 6 m	T. 7 N., R. 14 W.	Ottawa		95
Charlesworth, P. O. and R. R. Sta	L. S. & M. S. R. R. (Lan. Div.)		T. 1 N., R. 3 W.	Eaton	30	98
Coopersville, P. O. and R. R. and Tel. Sta	Det. Gr. H. & Mil. R. R.		T. 8 N., R. 14 W.	Ottawa	800	95
Chester, P. O. and R. R. Sta	M. C. R. R.		T. 3 N., R. 5 W.	Eaton	70	98
Carlisle, P. O.	M. C., Chic. & Gr. T. R. R.	Charlotte, 6 m	T. 2 N., R. 6 W.	Eaton	120	98
Charlotte, P. O. and R. R. and Tel. Sta	M. C., Chic. & Gr. T. R. R.		T. 2 N., R. 5 W.	Eaton	3,000	98
Cheshire, P. O.	M. & O. R. R., L. S. & M. S. (Kal. Div.)	Allegan, 10 m	T. 1 N., R. 14 W.	Allegan		98
Corning, P. O.	Gr. R. & I. R. R.	Wayland, 5 m	T. 4 N., R. 11 W.	Allegan		98
Cedar Creek, P. O.	M. C. R. R. (Gr. R. Div.)	Hastings, 11 m	T. 2 N., R. 9 W.	Barry	300	97
Coats Grove, P. O.	M. C. R. R. (Gr. R. Div.)	Hastings, 7 m	T. 4 N., R. 8 W.	Barry	175	97
Corunna, P. O. and R. R. and Tel. Sta	Det. Gr. H. & Mil. R. R.		T. 7 N., R. 3 E.	Shiawassee	1,500	91
Collins, P. O. and R. R. Sta	Det. Lan. & Nor. R. R.		T. 6 N., R. 5 W.	Ionia	100	94
Chandler, P. O.	Det. Gr. H. & Mil. R. R.	Saranac, 6 m	T. 6 N., R. 8 W.	Ionia		94
Clarksville, P. O.	Det. Gr. H. & Mil. R. R.	Saranac, 8 m	T. 5 N., R. 8 W.	Ionia	100	94
Campbell	Det. Gr. H. & Mil. R. R.	Saranac, 6 m	T. 5 N., R. 8 W.	Ionia	185	94
Cook's Corners, (Belding P. O.)	Det. L. & Nor. R. R.	Kiddville, 2 m	T. 8 N., R. 8 W.	Ionia	100	94
Chadwick, P. O. and R. R. Sta	Det. Lan. & Nor. R. R.		T. 8 N., R. 7 W.	Ionia	120	94
Cone, P. O. and R. R. Sta	Wab. St. L. & Pac. R. R.		T. 5 S., R. 6 E.	Monroe	150	115
Carleton, P. O. and R. R. and Tel. Sta	F. & P. M., L. S. & M. S.		T. 5 S., R. 9 E.	Monroe	500	115
Culver's R. R. Sta	M. C. R. R. (Mack. Div.)		T. 20 N., R. 3 E.	Arenac	125	75
*Cooley, P. O.				Huron		86
*Campbell's Corners			T. 5 N., R. 9 E.	Oakland		101
*Carney, P. O.	Chic. & W. M. R. R.			Menominee		124
*Carp				Leelanaw	30	58
*Carp, R. R. Sta	M. H. & O. R. R.	Marquette, 11 m		Marquette		119
*Carpenter		Petoskey, 6 m	T. 34 N., R. 6 W.	Emmet		51
Cascade Junction	Chic. N. W. & M. H. & O. R. R.		T. 47 N., R. 26 W.	Marquette		119
*Catholic Mission	Keweenaw Bay			Baraga		117
*Chandler	L. S. & M. S. (Det. Div.)		T. 3 S., R. 10 E.	Wayne		103
*Chapple Corners		Ludington, 12 m	T. 19 N., R. 17 W.	Mason	30	70
*Chicago Junction	Det. Lan. & Nor. & Chic. & Gr. T.			Ingham		99
*China	St. Clair River	St. Clair, 3 m	T. 4 N., R. 17 E.	St. Clair		88
*Chippewa Lake	F. & P. M. R. R.	Evart, 15 m	T. 16 N., R. 8 W.	Mecosta	25	78
*Clayton			T. 7 N., R. 8 E.	Genesee		90
*Clinton Junction	M. C. R. R.	Vermontville, 9 m	T. 4 N., R. 6 W.	Eaton		98
*Clyde, R. R. Sta	Chic. & W. M. R. R.		T. 2 N., R. 15 W.	Allegan		98
*Clyde Mills		Port Huron, 5 m	T. 6 N., R. 16 E.	St. Clair		88
*Collinsville	Lake Superior			Marquette		119
*Columbia	L. S. & M. S. R. R.	Brooklyn, 3 m	T. 4 S., R. 1 E.	Jackson	25	105
*Comins				Oscoda		63
Carpenter's, R. R. Sta. (Oregon P. O.)	M. C. (B. C. Div.)		T. 8 N., R. 9 E.	Lapeer		89
Donaldson, P. O.	St. Mary's River	Sault St. Marie, 13 m	T. 45 N., R. 1 W.	Chippewa		123
Detour Ldg., P. O.	Detour Passage		T. 42 N., R. 4 E.	Chippewa	300	124
Drummond Ldg., P. O.	Drummond's Isle		T. 42 N., R. 5 E.	Chippewa		124
Delaware Mine, P. O. and Tel. Sta	Lake Superior	Eagle Harbor, 4 m	T. 58 N., R. 30 W.	Keweenaw	1,000	118
Deerfield, R. R. Sta	Chic. & N. W. R. R.		T. 38 N., R. 23 W.	Delta		120
Duncan City, Tel. Sta	M. C. R. R. (Mack. Div.)	Cheboygan, 2 m	T. 38 N., R. 1 W.	Cheboygan	250	32
Deerton, R. R. Sta	Det. M. & M. R. R.		T. 47 N., R. 22 W.	Schoolcraft		121
Driggs, R. R. Sta	Det. M. & M. R. R.		T. 46 N., R. 15 W.	Schoolcraft		121
Deer Lake, P. O. and R. R. Sta	Gr. R. & I. R. R.		T. 18 N., R. 11 W.	Lake		71
Dover, P. O.	F. & P. M. R. R.	Clare, 6 m	T. 17 N., R. 6 W.	Clare	50	73
Dot, P. O.	Gr. R. & I. R. R.	Melrose, 6 m	T. 33 N., R. 4 W.	Charlevoix		57
De Longhary, P. O.	Chic. & N. W. R. R.		T. 39 N., R. 25 W.	Menominee	300	124
Daggetts, P. O. and R. R. Sta	Chic. & N. W. R. R.		T. 35 N., R. 26 W.	Menominee	450	124
Dutch Settlers	Det. M. & M. R. R.		T. 42 N., R. 24 W.	Marquette		119
Dushville, P. O.	Det. Lan. & Nor. R. R.	Blanchard, 9 m	T. 13 N., R. 5 W.	Isabella	150	77
Damon, P. O.	M. C. R. R. (Mack. Div.)	Beaver Lake, 13 m	T. 24 N., R. 2 E.	Ogemaw		66
Dash, P. O. and R. R. Sta	Chic. & W. Mich. (B. R. Br.)		T. 12 N., R. 15 W.	Muskegon		84
Dalton, P. O. and R. R. Sta	Chic. & W. Mich. R. R.		T. 11 N., R. 16 W.	Muskegon	25	84
Denmark, P. O. and Tel. Sta	M. C. R. R.	Reese, 5 m	T. 12 N., R. 7 E.	Tuscola	100	85
Dingman, R. R. Sta	Chic. & W. Mich. (W. Riv. Br.)		T. 15 N., R. 13 W.	Newaygo		79
Diamond Lake, P. O. and R. R. Sta	Chic. & W. Mich. (W. Riv. Br.)		T. 14 N., R. 13 W.	Newaygo		79
Dryden, P. O. and R. R. Sta	P. O. & P. A. R. R.		T. 6 N., R. 11 E.	Lapeer	300	89
Drake, P. O.	F. & P. M. (P. H. Div.)	Fostoria, 4 m	T. 9 N., R. 10 E.	Lapeer		89
Deanville, P. O.	P. H. & N. W. R. R.	Brown City, 3 m	T. 9 N., R. 12 E.	Lapeer	150	89
Deckerville, P. O. and R. R. Sta	P. H. & N. W. R. R.		T. 13 N., R. 15 E.	Sanilac	275	87
Downing, P. O. and R. R. and Tel. Sta	P. H. & N. W. R. R.		T. 12 N., R. 15 E.	Sanilac		87
Davis Corners, P. O.	P. H. & N. W. R. R.	Wilbur Road, 11 m	T. 12 N., R. 13 E.	Sanilac	200	87
Davison, P. O. and R. R. and Tel. Sta	Chic. & Gr. T. R. R.		T. 7 N., R. 8 E.	Genesee	300	90
Delton, P. O.	M. C. R. R.	Augusta, 14 m	T. 1 N., R. 9 W.	Barry	100	97
Dushville, P. O.	Det. Lan. & Nor. R. R.	Blanchard, 11 m	T. 13 N., R. 5 W.	Isabella	150	77

☞ Names marked with a star (*) will not be found on the Maps.

LIST OF CITIES, TOWNS, ETC.

NAME OF VILLAGE.	RAILROAD, LAKE, OR RIVER.	Nearest Sta. or Landing	TOWNSHIP.	COUNTY.	Pop.	Page
Dover, R. R. Sta	L. S. & M. S. R. R		T. 7 S., R. 2 E.	Lenawee		114
Deerfield, P. O. and R. R. and Tel. Sta	L. S. & M. S. R. R		T. 7 S., R. 5 E.	Lenawee	800	114
Douglas, R. R. Sta	L. S. & M. S. R. R		T. 8 S., R. 10 W.	St. Joseph		111
Drayton Plains, P. O. and R. R. and Tel. Sta	Det. Gr. H. & Mil. R. R		T. 3 N., R. 9 E.	Oakland	300	101
Davisburg, P. O. and R. R. and Tel. Sta	Det. Gr. H. & Mil. R. R		T. 4 N., R. 8 E.	Oakland	300	101
Duplain, P. O	Det. Gr. H. & Mil. R. R	Shepardsville, 4 m	T. 8 N., R. 1 W.	Clinton	150	92
DeWitt, P. O.		Lansing, 7 m	T. 5 N., R. 2 W.	Clinton	400	92
Dutton, P. O. and R. R. and Tel. Sta	M. C. R. R. (Gr. R. Div.)		T. 5 N., R. 11 W.	Kent		94
Dickson, R. R. Sta	Det. Lan. & Nor. R. R		T. 10 N., R. 9 W.	Kent		94
Dixboro	Gr. T., M. C. R. R	Ann Arbor, 4 m	T. 2 S., R. 7 E.	Washtenaw		104
Dexter, P. O. and R. R. and Tel. Sta	M. C. R. R		T. 2 S., R. 5 E.	Washtenaw	1,300	104
Dover Mills	M. C. R. R	Dexter, 3 m	T. 1 S., R. 1 E.	Washtenaw		104
Delhi Mills, P. O. and Tel. Sta	M. C. R. R	Delhi Sta., 1 m	T. 2 S., R. 5 E.	Washtenaw	180	104
Delhi, R. R. Sta	M. C. R. R		T. 2 S., R. 5 E.	Washtenaw		104
Devereaux, P. O. and R. R. and Tel. Sta	L. S. & M. S. (Lan. Div.)		T. 2 S., R. 3 W.	Jackson	200	105
Detroit City, P. O. and R. R. and Tel. Sta. (Ldg.)	Det. Gr. H. & Mil., M. C., L. S. & M. S., Gr. T. Det. Lan. & Nor., P. M., Wab. St. L. & Pac. (Det. River)		T. 2 S., R. 12 E.	Wayne	100000	103
Delray, P. O		Detroit, 4 m	T. 2 S., R. 11 E.	Wayne	400	103
Dearborn, P. O. and R. R. and Tel. Sta	M. C. R. R		T. 2 S., R. 10 E.	Wayne	600	103
Denton, P. O. and R. R. and Tel. Sta	M. C. R. R		T. 3 S., R. 8 E.	Wayne	250	108
Detroit Junction, Tel. Sta			T. 2 S., R. 11 E.	Wayne	600	108
DuBoisville (Bedford P. O.)	Det. L. & Nor. R. R	Bedford, 4 m	T. 1 S., R. 10 E.	Wayne		103
Duck Lake, P. O	M. C. R. R	Albion, 11 m	T. 1 S., R. 4 W.	Calhoun	50	106
Deer Creek, P. O	Det. Lan. & Nor. R. R	Howell, 13 m	T. 4 N., R. 3 E.	Livingston	75	100
Deerfield Centre, (Madison P. O.)	Det. Lan. & Nor. R. R	Howell, 12 m	T. 4 N., R. 5 E.	Livingston	100	100
Davis, P. O	Gr. T. R. R. (Mich. Air Line Br.)	Washington, 4 m	T. 4 N., R. 13 E.	Macomb	150	102
Disco, P. O	Gr. T. R. R. (Mich. Air Line Div.)	Washington, 3 m	T. 3 N., R. 12 E.	Macomb	130	102
Decatur, P. O. and R. R. and Tel. Sta	M. C. R. R		T. 4 S., R. 14 W.	Van Buren	1,000	108
Dansville, P. O	M. C. R. R. (Sag. Div.)	Mason, 7 m	T. 2 N., R. 1 E.	Ingham	500	99
Deerfield, R. R. Sta. (McDonald P. O.)	Chic. & W. Mich. R. R		T. 2 S., R. 16 W.	Van Buren	200	108
Dayton, P. O. and R. R. Sta	M. C. R. R		T. 8 S., R. 18 W.	Berrien	300	109
Day, P. O	M. C. (Air Line Div.), Chic. & Gr. T.	Cassopolis, 8 m	T. 7 S., R. 14 W.	Cass	30	110
Dowagiac, P. O. and R. R. and Tel. Sta	M. C. R. R		T. 5 S., R. 16 W.	Cass	2,800	110
Dailey, P. O. and R. R. and Tel. Sta	M. C. R. R. (Air Line Div.		T. 7 S., R. 15 W.	Cass	85	110
Drenthe, P. O	Chic. & W. Mich. R. R	Zeeland, 6 m	T. 5 N., R. 14 W.	Ottawa	600	95
Dennison, P. O. and R. R. Sta	Det. Gr. H. & Mil. R. R		T. 8 N., R. 14 W.	Ottawa	20	95
Delta, P. O. and R. R. and Tel. Sta	Det. Lan. & Nor. R. R		T. 4 N., R. 3 W.	Eaton	200	98
Dellwood, P. O	M. C. R. R	Vermontville, 5 m	T. 4 N., R. 6 W.	Eaton		98
Dulcurville	M. C. R. R. L. S. & M. S	Eaton Rapids, 7 m	T. 1 N., R. 4 W.	Eaton		98
Dimondale, P. O. and R. R. and Tel. Sta	L. S. & M. S. (Lan. Div.)		T. 3 N., R. 3 W.	Eaton	300	98
Dunningville, P. O. (Dunning Sta.)	Chic. & W. Mich. R. R		T. 2 N., R. 14 W.	Allegan	100	96
Diamond Springs, P. O	Chic. & W. Mich. R. R	Dunning, 7 m	T. 4 N., R. 13 W.	Allegan	100	96
Dorr, P. O. and R. R. and Tel. Sta	L. S. & M. S. R. R. (Kal. Div.)		T. 4 N., R. 12 W.	Allegan	300	96
Dowling, P. O	M. C. R. R. (Gr. R. Div.)	Hastings, 11 m	T. 2 N., R. 8 W.	Barry	75	97
Douglas, P. O	Chic. & W. Mich. R. R	Fennville, 7 m	T. 3 N., R. 16 W.	Allegan	700	96
Durand P. O. and R. R. and Tel. Sta	Det. Gr. H. & Mil. R. R. & C. & G. T. R'y.		T. 6 N., R. 4 E.	Shiawassee	300	91
Danby, R. R. Sta	Det. Lan. & Nor. R. R		T. 5 N., R. 5 W.	Ionia		93
Danby, P. O	Det. Lan. & Nor. R. R	Portland, 6 m	T. 5 N., R. 5 W.	Ionia	200	93
Dundee, P. O. and R. R. and Tel. Sta	To. A. Arbor & G. T., L. S. & M. S		T. 6 S., R. 7 E.	Monroe	1,300	115
Dunham, R. R. and Tel. Sta	M. C. R. R. (Mack. Div.)		T. 19 N., R. 4 E.	Arenac	71	75
Deep River, P. O. and R. R. Sta	M. C. R. R. (Mack. Div.)		T. 19 N., R. 4 E.	Arenac	125	75
*Dawson, R. R. Sta	Chic. & Gr. T. R. R		T. 7 N., R. 6 E.	Genesee		90
Day's River, and R. R. and Tel. Sta	Chic. & N. W. R. R	Escanaba, 13 m	T. 41 N., R. 22 W.	Delta		120
Dean's Mills	Det. Lan. & Nor. (Stanton Br.)	Sheridan, 4 m	T. 9 N., R. 8 W.	Montcalm		82
*Decorah	Gr. R. & I. R. R	Howard City, 4 m	T. 12 N., R. 9 W.	Montcalm		82
*Doctor Bridge		Grout, 2 m	T. 19 N., R. 2 W.	Gladwin		74
*Delwin, R. R. Sta	F. & P. M. R. R. (Mt. P. Div.)		T. 15 N., R. 3 W.	Isabella		77
*Denmark, R. R. Sta	Det. Lan. & Nor. R. R			Montcalm		82
Denver, P. O	Chic. & W. Mich. R. R	Fremont Centre, 8 m	T. 14 N., R. 14 W.	Newaygo	50	79
*Delwin, P. O. and R. R. Sta	F. & P. M. (Mt. P. Div.)			Isabella		77
*Devil's Lake	Chic. & W. Mich. R. R	Fremont Centre, 3 m	T. 13 N., R. 14 W.	Newaygo	75	79
*Diver	M. C. R. R. (M. Div.)	Wolverine Sta., 7 m		Cheboygan		52
*Dorr R. R. Sta	F. & P. M. R. R		T. 16 N., R. 2 W.	Midland		76
*Driggs, R. R. Sta	Det. M. & M. R. R			Chippewa		123
*Dressel, R. R. Sta	F. & P. M. R. R		T. 12 N., R. 4 E.	Saginaw		84
Denmark Junction	M. C. R. R. (B. C. Div.)		T. 12 N., R. 7 E.	Saginaw		84
Davisonville (Atlas P. O.)	F. & P. M. R. R	Grand Blanc, 7 m	T. 6 N., R. 8 E.	Genesee		90
Dunning, R. R. Sta. (Dunningville P. O.)	C. & W. M. R. R		T. 2 N., R. 14 W.	Allegan		96
East Tawas, P. O. and Tel Sta	Lake Huron	Tawas City, 1 m	T. 22 N., R. 8 E.	Iosco	1,400	65
Eagle Harbor Ldg., P. O. and Tel. Sta	Lake Superior		T. 58 N., R. 30 W.	Keweenaw	200	118
Eagle River Ldg., P. O. and Tel. Sta	Lake Superior		T. 58 N., R. 31 W.	Keweenaw	450	118
Escanaba, P. O. and R. R. and Tel. Sta	Chic. & N. W. R. R		T. 39 N., R. 22 W.	Delta	4,500	120
Ely, P. O	G. R. I. & Mack. R. R	Leverington, 6 m	T. 37 N., R. 5 W.	Emmet		51
Epsilon, P. O	G. R. & I. R. R	Petoskey, 8 m	T. 34 N., R. 4 W.	Emmet		51
East Side	Lake Huron	Alpena Ldg., 9 m	T. 32 N., R. 9 E.	Alpena	314	54
Empire, P. O	G. R. & I. R. R. (T. C. Br.)	Traverse City, 25 m	T. 28 N., R. 14 W.	Leelanaw	200	58
Elm Rock, P. O	G. R. & I. R. R. (T. C. Br.)	Traverse City, 6 m	T. 28 N., R. 12 W.	Leelanaw		58
Echo, P. O	G. R. & I. R. R	Elmira, 19 m	T. 31 N., R. 7 W.	Antrim	50	57
Elk Rapids, P. O. and Tel. Sta	G. R. & I. R. R	Westwood, 27 m	T. 29 N., R. 9 W.	Antrim	1,000	57
Elmira, P. O. and R. R. and Tel. Sta	M. C. R. R		T. 31 N., R. 4 W.	Otsego	25	56
Evart, P. O. and R. R. and Tel. Sta	F. & P. M. R. R		T. 18 N., R. 8 W.	Osceola	1,400	72
East Jordan, P. O. and Tel. Sta	G. R. & I. R. R	Boyne Falls, 11 m	T. 32 N., R. 7 W.	Charlevoix	500	57
Eastport, P. O	G. R. & I. R. R. (Lake Mich.)	Boyne Falls, 30 m	T. 31 N., R. 9 W.	Antrim	100	57
English, P. O. and R. R. Sta	Chic. & N. W. R. R		T. 38 N., R. 28 W.	Menominee	180	124
East Riverton, P. O	F. & P. M. R. R	Scottville, 2 m	T. 18 N., R. 18 W.	Mason	225	70
Edna, P. O	M. C. R. R. (Mack Div.)	St. Helens, 10 m	T. 22 N., R. 2 W.	Roscommon	125	67
Eben Corners, P. O	G. R. & I. R. R	Cadillac, 25 m	T. 22 N., R. 5 W.	Missaukee		68
Eagle Mills, P. O. and Tel. Sta	M. H. & O. R. R		T. 48 N., R. 26 W.	Marquette	125	119
Edenville, P. O	F. & P. M. R. R	Sanford, 11 m	T. 15 N., R. 1 W.	Midland	175	76
*Egypt, P. O				Mason		70
*East Lake, P. O				Manistee		59
*Ellisville	F. & P. M. R. R. (Mt. P. Br.)	Mount Pleasant, 10 m	T. 16 N., R. 4 W.	Isabella		77
East Bay	G. R. & I. R. R. (T. C. Br.)	Traverse City, 3 m	T. 27 N., R. 10 W.	Gd. Traverse	40	60
Excelsior, P. O	G. R. & I. R. R	Kalkaska, 5 m	T. 27 N., R. 6 W.	Kalkaska		61
East Golden, P. O. and R. R. Sta	Chic. & W. Mich. R. R		T. 15 N., R. 18 W.	Oceana	40	80
Ensley, P. O	G. R. & I. R. R	Maple Hill, 5 m	T. 11 N., R. 11 W.	Newaygo	200	79
Edmore, P. O. and R. R. and Tel. Sta	Det. Lan. & N., C. S. & C. R. R		T. 12 N., R. 6 W.	Montcalm	1,000	82
Elmwood, P. O	P. O. & P. A. R. R	Cass City, 6 m	T. 14 N., R. 10 E.	Tuscola	50	85
Ellington, P. O	M. C. (B. C. Div.)	Caro, 6 m	T. 13 N., R. 10 E.	Tuscola	75	85
East Dayton, P. O	M. C. (B. C. Div.)	Wahjamega, 7 m	T. 11 N., R. 10 E.	Tuscola	125	85
Easy, P. O. and R. R. Sta	P. H. & N. W. R. R		T. 11 N., R. 10 E.	Tuscola		85

☞ Names marked with a star (*) will not be found on the Maps.

NAME OF VILLAGE.	RAILROAD, LAKE, OR RIVER.	Nearest Sta. or Landing	TOWNSHIP.	COUNTY.	Pop.	Page
Elva, P. O.	M. C. (B. C. Div.)	Millington, 8 m.	T. 10 N., R. 7 E.	Tuscola	80	85
Eastwood, P. O. and R. R. Sta.	M. C. (Sag. Div.)		T. 11 N., R. 3 E.	Saginaw	150	84
Elk, P. O.	M. C. (Sag. Div.)	Chesaning, 10 m.	T. 9 N., R. 4 E.	Saginaw	100	84
East Saginaw, P. O. and R. R. and Tel. Sta.	M. C., P. H. & N. W., F. & P. M. S. Val. & St. L.		T. 12 N., R. 5 E.	Saginaw	25,000	84
Elba, P. O. and R. R. and Tel. Sta.	Chic. & Gr. T. R. R.		T. 7 N., R. 9 E.	Lapeer	150	89
Elwell, P. O. and R. R. Sta.	Chic. S. & C. R. R.		T. 12 N., R. 4 W.	Gratiot	100	83
Elm Hall, P. O.	Chic. S. & C. R. R.	Riverdale, 2 m.	T. 11 N., R. 4 W.	Gratiot	300	83
Edgewood, P. O.	S. Val. & St. L. R. R.	Wheeler, 10 m.	T. 10 N., R. 1 W.	Gratiot	50	83
East China	M. C. (M. & M. Div.) St. Clair River	St. Clair, 4 m.	T. 4 N., R. 17 E.	St. Clair		88
Elmer, P. O.	P. H. & N. W. R. R.	Carsonville, 13 m.	T. 11 N., R. 13 E.	Sanilac	50	87
East Thetford, P. O.	F. & P. M. (F. R. Div.)	Otisville, 4 m.	T. 9 N., R. 7 E.	Genesee	270	90
East Fremont, P. O.	P. H. & N. W. R. R.	Croswell, 6 m.	T. 9 N., R. 15 E.	Sanilac		87
East Greenwood, P. O.	P. H. & N. W. R. R.	Jeddo, 3½ m.	T. 8 N., R. 15 E.	St. Clair		88
Evergreen, P. O.	P. H. & N. W. R. R.	Jeddo, 3 m.	T. 8 N., R. 16 E.	St. Clair		88
Emmett, P. O. and R. R. and Tel. Sta.	Chic. & Gr. T. R. R.		T. 7 N., R. 14 E.	St. Clair	300	88
Edenville, P. O.	F. & P. M. R. R.	Sanford, 10 m.	T. 16 N., R. 1 W.	Midland	173	76
Eureka, P. O.	Det. Gr. H. & Mil. R. R.	St. Johns, 8 m.	T. 8 N., R. 2 W.	Clinton	200	92
Elsie, P. O.	Det. Gr. H. & Mil. R. R.	Ovid, 6 m.	T. 8 N., R. 1 W.	Clinton	300	92
Eagle, P. O. and R. R. and Tel. Sta.	Det. Lan. & Nor. R. R.		T. 5 N., R. 4 W.	Clinton	200	92
Eagle Mills, R. R. Sta.	L. S. & M. S. R. R. (Kal. Div.)		T. 7 N., R. 12 W.	Kent		94
East Paris, P. O.	M. C. R. R. (Gr. R. Div.)	Bowen, 4 m.	T. 6 N., R. 11 W.	Kent		94
Edgerton, P. O. and R. R. Sta.	Gr. R. & I. R. R.		T. 9 N., R. 11 W.	Kent	250	94
Englishville, P. O. and R. R. and Tel. Sta.	Chic. & W. Mich. (Newaygo Div.)		T. 8 N., R. 12 W.	Kent	200	94
East Springport, P. O.	L. S. & M. S. (Lan. Div.)	Springport, 5 m.	T. 1 S., R. 3 W.	Jackson		105
Eldred, R. R. Sta.	L. S. & M. S. (Jackson Br.)		T. 3 S., R. 1 E.	Jackson		105
Ellisville	Wab. St. L. & Pac. R. R.	Willis, 5 m.	T. 4 S., R. 8 E.	Wayne		103
Ecorse, P. O. and R. R. and Tel. Sta. (Ldg.)	L. S. & M. S. (Det. River)		T. 3 S., R. 11 E.	Wayne	400	103
Ellis, P. O.	M. C. R. R.	Coresco, 7 m.	T. 3 S., R. 6 W.	Calhoun		106
Elm, P. O. and R. R. Sta.	Det. Lan. & Nor. R. R.		T. 1 S., R. 9 E.	Wayne	50	103
Eckford	M. C., Mich. & Ohio R. R.	Marshall, 8 m.	T. 3 S., R. 5 W.	Calhoun		106
East Leroy, P. O.	M. C. (Air Line Div.)	Union City, 9 m.	T. 3 S., R. 8 W.	Calhoun		106
Eden, P. O. and R. R. and Tel. Sta.	M. C. R. R. (Sag. Div.)		T. 2 N., R. 1 W.	Ingham	100	99
Edgel, P. O.	Paw Paw, Toledo & S. Haven R. R.	Lawrence, 5 m.	T. 2 S., R. 15 W.	Van Buren		108
Eau Claire, P. O. and R. R. Sta.	Cin. Wab. & Mich. R. R.		T. 5 S., R. 17 W.	Berrien	100	109
Edwardsburgh, P. O. and R. R. and Tel. Sta.	Chic. & Gr. T. R. R.		T. 8 S., R. 15 W.	Cass	600	110
Eastmanville, P. O.	Det. Gr. H. & Mil. R. R.	Coopersville, 4 m.	T. 7 N., R. 14 W.	Ottawa	400	95
Eaton Rapids, P. O. and R. R. and Tel. Sta.	L. S. & M. S. (Lan. Div.) M. C.		T. 1 N., R. 3 W.	Eaton	2,000	98
East Saugatuck, P. O. and R. R. Sta.	Chic. & W. Mich. R. R.		T. 3 N., R. 15 W.	Allegan	300	96
Erie, P. O. and R. R. Sta.	L. S. & M. S. R. R. (Det. Div.)		T. 8 S., R. 8 E.	Monroe	300	115
East Milan (Reeves), P. O. and R. R. and Tel. Sta.	To. A. Arbor & Gr. T. R. R.		T. 5 S., R. 7 E.	Monroe	200	115
Exeter, P. O.	L. S. & M. S. (Dundee Br.)	Scofield, 3 m.	T. 5 S., R. 8 E.	Monroe		115
Epoufette, (Ldg.) P. O.	Lake Mich., Det. M. & M. R. R.	St. Ignace, 22 m.	T. 42 N., R. 7 W.	Mackinac		122
Essexville, P. O.	M. C. R. R. (B. C. Div.)	Bay City, 1 m.	T. 14 N., R. 5 E.	Bay	1,500	75
Eddy's, R. R. Sta.	M. C. R. R. (M. Div.)		T. 18 N., R. 4 E.	Arenac		75
Eagle Lake	Det. Gr. H. & Mil. R. R.	Clarkston Sta., 7 m.	T. 5 N., R. 9 E.	Oakland		101
*Englestown			T. 30 N., R. 11 W.	Leelanaw		58
East Gilead	L. S. & M. S. R. R.	Bronson, 10 m.	T. 8 S., R. 7 W.	Branch	60	112
*East Nankin	M. C. R. R.	Inkster, 4 m.	T. 2 S.	Wayne		103
*Easton	Det. Lan. & Nor., Det. Gr. H. & Mil.	Ionia, 5 m.	T. 7 N., R. 7 W.	Ionia		93
*East Raisinville	L. S. & M. S. R. R.	Monroe, 4 m.	T. 6 S., R. 8 E.	Monroe		115
Elgin	Gr. R. & I. R. R.	Kalkaska, 19 m.	T. 29 N., R. 8 W.	Antrim		57
*Elkland	M. C. P. H. & N. W. R. R.	Vassar, 38 m.	T. 14 N., R. 11 E.	Tuscola		85
*Elm Creek	Chic. & Gr. T., M. C. (B. C. Div.)	Lapeer, 10 m.	T. 9 N., R. 10 E.	Lapeer		89
*Elmira	M. C. R. R.	Charlotte, 10 m.	T. 1 N., R. 6 W.	Eaton		98
*Embo	Gr. R. & I. R. R.	Petoskey, 11 m.	T. 34 N., R. 11 W.	Charlevoix		57
*Essex	Det. Gr. H. & Mil. R. R.	St. Johns, 7 m.	T. 8 N., R. 3 W.	Clinton		92
Eata, P. O.	M. C. R. R. (Sag. Div.)	St. Charles, 9 m.	T. 10 N., R. 2 E.	Saginaw		84
Ford River, P. O.	Chic. & N. W. R. R.	Escanaba, 4 m.	T. 38 N., R. 23 W.	Delta	300	120
Fayette, P. O. (Ldg.)	Chic. & N. W. (Big Bay de Noquet)	Brampton, 40 m.	T. 38 N., R. 19 W.	Delta	300	120
Fewsville, R. R. Sta.	M. H. & O. R. R.		T. 51 N., R. 33 W.	Baraga		117
Flag, R. R. Sta.	G. R. I. & Mack. R. R.		T. 38 N., R. 4 W.	Emmet		51
Freedom, P. O. and R. R. Sta.	M. C. R. R. (Mack. Div.)		T. 39 N., R. 3 W.	Cheboygan	100	61
Finkton, P. O.	G. R. & I. R. R.	Elmira, 14 m.	T. 31 N., R. 7 W.	Antrim		57
Forman, P. O. & R. R. Sta.	F. & P. M. R. R.		T. 17 N., R. 13 W.	Lake	300	71
Farwell, P. O. and R. R. and Tel. Sta.	F. & P. M. R. R.		T. 17 N., R. 5 W.	Clare	800	72
Free Soil, P. O. and R. R. Sta.	F. & P. M. R. R. (M. Div.)		T. 20 N., R. 16 W.	Mason	400	70
Falmouth, P. O.	G. R. & I. R. R.	Cadillac, 19 m.	T. 21 N., R. 6 W.	Missaukee	100	68
Forsyth, P. O. and R. R. Sta.	Chic. & N. W. R. R.		T. 45 N., R. 25 W.	Marquette	150	119
*Frelingville, P. O.				Osceola		72
Friend, P. O.	Gr. R. & I. R. R. (T. C. Br.)	Traverse City, 6 m.	T. 27 N., R. 12 W.	Gr. Traverse		60
Fife Lake, P. O. and R. R. and Tel. Sta.	G. R. & I. R. R.		T. 25 N., R. 9 W.	Gr. Traverse	700	60
Filer City, Tel. Sta.	F. & P. M. R. R. (Man. Div.)	Stronach, 1 m.	T. 21 N., R. 16 W.	Manistee	558	59
Fredericville, P. O. and R. R. Sta.	M. C. R. R.		T. 28 N., R. 4 W.	Crawford	150	62
Forest, R. R. Sta. (Fredericville P. O.)	M. C. R. R.		T. 28 N., R. 4 W.	Crawford		62
Frankfort, P. O. and Tel. Sta.	G. R. & I. R. R. (T. C. Br.)	Traverse City, 35 m.	T. 26 N., R. 16 W.	Benzie	2,000	59
Flower Creek, P. O.	Chic. & W. Mich. R. R.	Montague, 7 m.	T. 13 N., R. 18 W.	Oceana		80
Ferry, P. O.	Chic. & W. Mich. R. R.	New Era, 7 m.	T. 14 N., R. 16 W.	Oceana	150	80
Fruitport, P. O. and Tel. Sta.	Det. Gr. H. & Mil., Chic. & W. Mich. R. R.	Grand Haven, 4 m.	T. 9 N., R. 16 W.	Muskegon	600	81
Fenwick, P. O. and R. R. Sta.	Det. L. & N. (Sag. Div.)		T. 9 N., R. 7 W.	Montcalm	50	82
Ferryville	Chic. & W. Mich., Lake Mich.	Montague, 4 m.	T. 12 N., R. 17 W.	Muskegon		81
Ferris, P. O.	Chic. S. & C. R. R.	Vestaburg, 5 m.	T. 11 N., R. 5 W.	Montcalm	100	82
Filion, P. O. and R. R. Sta.	P. H. & N. W. R. R.		T. 17 N., R. 12 E.	Huron		86
Fair grove, P. O. and R. R. Sta.	S. T. & H. R. R.		T. 13 N., R. 8 E.	Tuscola	80	85
Fostoria, P. O. and R. R. Sta.	F. & P. M. (F. R. Div.)		T. 10 N., R. 9 E.	Tuscola	100	85
Frankenlust	M. C. (Sag. Div.)	Bay City, 5 m.	T. 14 N., R. 4 E.	Saginaw	300	84
Freeland, P. O. and R. R. and Tel. Sta.	F. & P. M. R. R.		T. 13 N., R. 3 E.	Saginaw	270	84
Frost, P. O.	S. Val. & St. L. R. R.	Swan Creek, 5 m.	T. 12 N., R. 3 E.	Saginaw		84
Frankenmuth, R. R. Sta.	P. H. & N. W. R. R.		T. 12 N., R. 6 E.	Saginaw		84
Frankenmuth, P. O.	F. & P. M. R. R.	Bridgeport, 6 m.	T. 11 N., R. 6 E.	Saginaw	350	84
Forville, R. R. Sta.	Chic. & W. Mich. (B. R. Br.)		T. 15 N., R. 12 W.	Newaygo		79
Fremont Centre, P. O. and R. R. and Tel. Sta.	Chic. & W. Mich. R. R.		T. 12 N., R. 14 W.	Newaygo	1,200	79
Forest Bay	Lake Huron	Sand Beach, 3 m.	T. 17 N., R. 15 E.	Huron		86
Farmers' Creek, P. O.	M. C. (B. C. Div.)	Metamora, 3 m.	T. 6 N., R. 10 E.	Lapeer	100	89
Forest Hill, P. O.	Det. L. & N. (Sag. Div.)	Alma, 5 m.	T. 12 N., R. 3 W.	Gratiot		83
Fargo, P. O.	P. H. & N. W. (Sag. Div.)	Saginaw Junct., 4 m.	T. 6 N., R. 15 E.	St. Clair	50	88
Fair Haven, P. O. and Tel. Sta.	Gr. T. R. R.	Chesterfield, 17 m.	T. 3 N., R. 15 E.	St. Clair	500	88
Five Lakes, P. O. and R. R. and Tel. Sta.	M. C. (B. C. Div.)		T. 8 N., R. 10 E.	Lapeer	250	89
Fentonville, P. O. and R. R. and Tel. Sta.	Det. Gr. H. & Mil. R. R.		T. 5 N., R. 6 E.	Genesee	2,500	90
Flint, P. O. and R. R. and Tel. Sta.	F. & P. M., Chic. & Gr. T. R. R.		T. 7 N., R. 7 E.	Genesee	9,500	90
Farrandville	F. & P. M. R. R.	Clio, 1 m.	T. 9 N., R. 6 E.	Genesee	65	90
Flushing, P. O.	F. & P. M. R. R., Chic. & Gr. T.	Flint, 7 m.	T. 8 N., R. 5 E.	Genesee	850	90
Fletcher's Corners	Chic. & Gr. T. R. R.	Swartz Creek, 4 m.	T. 6 N., R. 5 E.	Genesee		90

☞ Names marked with a star (*) will not be found on the Maps.

NAME OF VILLAGE.	RAILROAD, LAKE, OR RIVER.	Nearest Sta. or Landing	TOWNSHIP.	COUNTY.	Pop.	Page
Forester, P. O. and Tel. Sta	Lake Huron	Bridgehampton, 9 m	T. 12 N., R. 16 E.	Sanilac	250	87
Forestville, P. O. and Tel. Sta	Lake Huron	Minden City, 9 m	T. 14 N., R. 16 E.	Sanilac	300	87
Fort Gratiot, P. O. and R. R. and Tel. Sta	Gr. T., P. H. & N. W. R. R		T. 7 N., R. 17 E.	St. Clair	1,800	88
Fillmore, P. O. and Tel. Sta	M. C. R. R. (Gr. R. Div.)	Middleville, 9 m	T. 4 N., R. 9 W.	Barry	150	97
Freeport, P. O	M. C. R. R. (Gr. R. Div.)	Hastings, 9 m	T. 4 N., R. 9 W.	Barry	300	97
Fork, P. O	F. & P. M. R. R	Chippewa, 11 m	T. 16 N., R. 7 W.	Mecosta		78
Frontier, P. O	L. S. & M. S. R. R	Hillsdale, 10 m	T. 9 S., R. 4 W.	Hillsdale	200	113
Fairfield, P. O	L. S. & M. S. (Fayette Br.)	Jasper, 2 m	T. 8 S., R. 3 E.	Lenawee	300	114
Florence, P. O. and R. R. Sta	L. S. & M. S. R. R		T. 7 S., R. 11 W.	St. Joseph		111
Fabius, R. R. Sta	M. C. R. R. (Air Line Div.)		T. 6 S., R. 12 W.	St. Joseph		111
Flowerfield, P. O. and Tel. Sta	L. S. & M. S. R. R	Flowerfield Sta., 1 m	T. 5 S., R. 12 W.	St. Joseph	200	111
Flowerfield, Tel. Sta	L. S. & M. S. R. R		T. 5 S., R. 11 W.	St. Joseph	200	111
Factoryville	M. C. R. R. (Air Line Div.)	Colon, 8 m	T. 5 S., R. 9 W.	St. Joseph		111
Fawn River, P. O	L. S. & M. S. Gr. R. & I. R. R	Sturgis, 6 m	T. 8 S., R. 9 W.	St. Joseph	110	111
Franklin, P. O	Det. Gr. H. & Mil. R. R	Birmingham, 3 m	T. 1 N., R. 10 E.	Oakland	200	101
Farmington, P. O	F. & P. M. R. R	Novi, 5 m	T. 1 N., R. 9 E.	Oakland	700	101
Four Towns, P. O	D. G. H. & M. R. R	Pontiac, 7 m	T. 2 N., R. 9 E.	Oakland	225	101
Fowler, P. O. and R. R. and Tel. Sta	Det. Gr. H. & Mil. R. R		T. 7 N., R. 4 W.	Clinton	320	92
Fallasburg, P. O	Det. Gr. H. & Mil. R. R	Lowell, 5 m	T. 7 N., R. 9 W.	Kent	100	94
Fisher's, P. O. and R. R. Sta	Gr. R. & I. R. R		T. 6 N., R. 12 W.	Kent	75	94
Fredonia, P. O	L. S. & M. S. R. R	Bridgewater, 6 m	T. 3 S., R. 4 E.	Washtenaw	60	104
Foster's, R. R. Sta	M. C. R. R		T. 2 S., R. 6 E.	Washtenaw		104
Francisco, P. O. and R. R. and Tel. Sta	M. C. R. R		T. 2 S., R. 2 E.	Jackson		105
Flat Rock, P. O. and R. R. and Tel. Sta	L. S. & M. S. R. R		T. 4 S., R. 10 E.	Wayne	700	103
Fredonia	M. C. R. R. (Air Line Div.)	Tekonsha, 6 m	T. 4 S., R. 6 W.	Calhoun		106
Fowlerville, P. O. and R. R. and Tel. Sta	Det. Lan. & Nor. R. R		T. 3 N., R. 3 E.	Livingston	1,200	100
Fleming, R. R. Sta	Det. Lan. & Nor. R. R		T. 3 N., R. 4 E.	Livingston	180	100
Fleming, P. O	Det. Lan. & Nor. R. R	Fleming Sta., 1m	T. 3 N., R. 4 E.	Livingston		100
Frederick	Gr. T. R. R	Mt. Clemens, 2 m	T. 2 N., R. 13 E.	Macomb		102
Fraser, P. O	Gr. T. R. R	Fraser Sta., 1 m	T. 1 N., R. 13 E.	Macomb		102
Fraser, R. R. and Tel. Sta	Gr. T. R. R		T. 1 N., R. 13 E.	Macomb		102
Fitchburg, P. O	M. C. R. R. (Sag. Div.)	Leslie, 8 m	T. 1 N., R. 1 E.	Ingham	100	99
Felts, P. O	M. C. R. R. (Sag. Div.)	Leslie, 5 m	T. 1 N., R. 1 E.	Ingham		99
Forest Hall, R. R. Sta	Chic. & Gr. T. R. R		T. 6 S., R. 15 W.	Cass		110
Forest Home	Chic. & W. Mich	Watervliet, 11 m	T. 4 S., R. 16 W.	Van Buren		109
Fulton, P. O	Gr. R. & I., Chic. & Gr. T. R. R	Vicksburg, 9 m	T. 4 S., R. 9 W.	Kalamazoo	150	107
Forest Mill	Det. Gr. H. & Mil. R. R	Berlin, 3½ m	T. 7 N., R. 13 W.	Ottawa		95
Fennessy, P. O	Chic. & W. Mich. R. R	Grandville, 4 m	T. 7 N., R. 13 W.	Ottawa		95
Forest Grove, P. O	Chic. & W. Mich. R. R	Hudsonville, 6 m	T. 5 N., R. 13 W.	Ottawa		95
Ferrysburg, P. O. and R. R. and Tel. Sta	Chic. & W. Mich. R. R		T. 8 N., R. 16 W.	Ottawa	450	95
Fillmore Centre, P. O	Chic. & W. Mich. R. R		T. 4 N., R. 15 W.	Allegan	200	98
Fillmore, R. R. Sta	Chic. & W. Mich. R. R		T. 4 N., R. 15 W.	Allegan	180	98
Fennville, P. O. and R. R. and Tel. Sta	Chic. & W. Mich. R. R		T. 3 N., R. 15 W.	Allegan	200	98
Fisk, R. R. Sta	M. & O. R. R		T. 2 N., R. 12 W.	Allegan		98
*Fairview	Chic. & W. M. R. R	Pentwater, 7 m	T. 17 N., R. 18 W.	Mason		70
*Falcon, R. R. Sta	P. H. & N. W. R. R		T. 10 N., R. 10 E.	Sanilac	200	87
*False Presque Isle	Lake Huron		T. 30 N., R. 9 E.	Presque Isle	30	53
*Fergus, P. O				Saginaw		84
*Fitchville				Antrim		57
*Flat Rock		Escanaba, 4 m	T. 39 N., R. 22 W.	Delta		120
*Forest City	Chic. & W. M. R. R	Fremont Centre, 4 m	T. 13 N., R. 15 W.	Oceana		80
*Franklin	M. R. R. R			Houghton		117
*Fremont	Gr. T. R. R	Bancroft, 2 m	T. 6 N., R. 3 E.	Shiawassee	200	91
*Fritz Corners	M. C. R. R	Dearborn, 4 m	T. 3 S., R. 10 E.	Wayne		103
*Faith, P. O				Crawford		62
Farmers, P. O	P. H. & N. W. R. R		T. 11 N., R. 15 E.	Sanilac		87
Fish Lake, (Stephen's P. O) R. R. Sta	M. C. R. R. (L. & N. Br.)		T. 8 N., R. 10 E.	Lapeer		89
Greenwood, P. O. and R. R. Sta	M. C. (M. Div.)		T. 21 N., R. 2 E.	Ogemaw	100	60
Greenbush, P. O. and Tel. Sta	Lake Huron	Alpena, 30 m	T. 25 N., R. 9 E.	Alcona	500	54
Garden, P. O	Chic. & N. W. R. R	Brampton, 38 m	T. 39 N., R. 18 W.	Delta	800	120
Guyerville	M. C. R. R. (Mack. Div.)	Cheboygan, 7 m	T. 37 N., R. 2 W.	Cheboygan		52
Good Hart, P. O	Gr. R. & I. R. R	Harbor Springs, 10 m	T. 37 N., R. 6 W.	Emmet		51
Greenland, P. O. and Tel. Sta	Lake Superior	Ontonagon, 11 m	T. 51 N., R. 38 W.	Ontonagon	1,000	118
Galilee	Lake Michigan		T. 37 N., R. 10 W.	Emmet		51
*Grand Marias, P. O				Schoolcraft		121
Good Harbor, P. O	G. R. & I. R. R. (T. C. Br.)	Traverse City, 24 m	T. 30 N., R. 12 W.	Leelanaw	200	58
Glen Haven, P. O. and Tel. Sta	G. R. & I. R. R. (T. C. Br.)	Traverse City, 33 m	T. 29 N., R. 14 W.	Leelanaw	60	58
Glen Arbor, P. O	G. R. & I. R. R. (T. C. Br.)	Traverse City, 30 m	T. 29 N., R. 14 W.	Leelanaw	100	58
Gaylord, P. O. and R. R. and Tel. Sta	M. C. R. R		T. 31 N., R. 3 W.	Otsego	900	56
Gladwin, P. O	F. & P. M. R. R	Loomis, 18 m	T. 19 N., R. 2 W.	Gladwin	60	74
Grout	F. & P. M. R. R	Loomis, 14 m	T. 18 N., R. 2 W.	Gladwin		74
Greenwood, Tel. Sta	M. H. & O. R. R		T. 47 N., R. 27 W.	Marquette		119
Goose Lake, R. R. Sta	Chic. & N. W. R. R		T. 47 N., R. 26 W.	Marquette		119
Galt, P. O	G. R. & I. R. R	Cadillac, 15 m	T. 21 N., R. 7 W.	Missaukee		68
*Gills Pier, P. O				Leelanaw		58
Grayling, P. O. and R. R. and Tel. Sta	M. C. R. R		T. 26 N., R. 3 W.	Crawford	500	62
Grace, P. O	F. & P. M. R. R. (Man. Div.)	Manistee, 20 m	T. 26 N., R. 15 W.	Benzie	100	59
Gilmore, P. O	F. & P. M. R. R. (Man. Div.)	Manistee, 22 m	T. 25 N., R. 15 W.	Benzie	250	59
Grand View, P. O	Chic. & W. Mich. R. R	Montague, 6 m	T. 13 N., R. 17 W.	Oceana		80
Gowen, P. O. and R. R. and Tel. Sta	Det. L. & N. R. R		T. 10 N., R. 8 W.	Montcalm	300	82
Greenville, P. O. and R. R. and Tel. Sta	Det. L. & N. R. R		T. 9 N., R. 8 W.	Montcalm	3,200	82
Gagetown, P. O. and R. R. Sta	P. O. & P. A. R. R		T. 14 N., R. 11 E.	Tuscola	250	85
Gilford, P. O. and R. R. Sta	S. T. & H. R. R		T. 13 N., R. 7 E.	Tuscola	125	85
Graham, R. R. Sta	S. Val. & St. L. R. R		T. 12 N., R. 3 E.	Saginaw		84
Groveton, R. R. Sta	M. C. (Sag. Div.)		T. 10 N., R. 3 E.	Saginaw		84
Grindstone City, P. O. Ldg., and Tel. Sta	Lake Huron	Port Austin, 5 m	T. 18 N., R. 13 E.	Huron	600	86
Goodland, P. O	Gr. T. R. R	Imlay City, 6 m	T. 8 N., R. 12 E.	Lapeer		89
Germania, P. O	P. H. & N. W. R. R	Marlette, 8 m	T. 11 N., R. 12 E.	Sanilac	30	87
Genesee Village, P. O. and R. R. Sta	F. & P. M. (F. R. Div.)		T. 8 N., R. 7 E.	Genesee	100	90
Goodrich, P. O	F. & P. M. R. R	Grand Blanc, 7 m	T. 6 N., R. 8 E.	Genesee	250	90
Gibsonville	F. & P. M. R. R	Grand Blanc, 2 m	T. 6 N., R. 7 E.	Genesee		90
Grand Blanc, P. O. and R. R. and Tel. Sta	F. & P. M. R. R		T. 6 N., R. 7 E.	Genesee	250	90
Gaines, P. O. and R. R. and Tel. Sta	Det. Gr. H. & Mil. R. R		T. 6 N., R. 5 E.	Genesee	300	90
Greenwood Centre, P. O	P. H. & N. W. R. R	Hartsuff, 8 m	T. 8 N., R. 15 E.	St. Clair		88
Goodells, P. O. and R. R. Sta	Chic. & Gr. T. R. R		T. 6 N., R. 15 E.	St. Clair	225	88
Gratiot Centre, R. R. Sta	P. H. & N. W. R. R		T. 7 N., R. 17 E.	St. Clair		88
Gull Lake, P. O	M. C. R. R	Augusta, 11 m	T. 1 N., R. 10 W.	Barry	51	97
Geneva, P. O	Mich. & Ohio R. R	Addison, 4 m	T. 6 S., R. 1 E.	Lenawee	100	114
Grosvenor, R. R. and Tel. Sta	L. S. & M. S. R. R. (Fayette Br.)		T. 7 S., R. 4 E.	Lenawee		114
Granger, P. O	Wab. St. L. & Pac. R. R	Sand Creek, 2 m	T. 8 S., R. 3 E.	Lenawee		114
Grange Hall	F. & P. M., Det. Gr. H. & Mil	Holly, 5 m	T. 5 N., R. 8 E.	Oakland		101
Groveland, P. O	F. & P. M., Det. Gr. H. & Mil	Holly, 6 m	T. 5 N., R. 8 E.	Oakland		101

☞ Names marked with a star (*) will not be found on the Maps.

NAME OF VILLAGE.	RAILROAD, LAKE, OR RIVER.	Nearest Sta. or Landing	TOWNSHIP.	COUNTY.	Pop.	Page
Goodison P. O. and R. R. Sta	M. C. R. R. (B. D. Div.)		T. 4 N., R. 11 E.	Oakland	30	101
Grand River City, R. R. Sta	Det. Lan. & Nor. R. R		T. 5 N., R. 3 W.	Clinton		92
Geary, P. O	M. C. R. R. (Sag. Div.)	Laingsburg, 5 m	T. 6 N., R. 1 W.	Clinton		92
Grattan, P. O	Det. Gr. H. & Mil. R. R	Lowell, 14 m	T. 8 N., R. 9 W.	Kent	150	94
Grant, P. O. and Tel. Sta	Det. Gr. H. & Mil. R. R	Lowell, 11 m	T. 8 N., R. 9 W.	Kent		94
Grand Rapids City, **P.O.** and R. R. and Tel. Sta.	Det. Gr. H. & Mil. R. R., G. R. & I. R. R		T. 7 N., R. 11 W.	Kent	40,000	94
	M. C., L. S. & M. S					
	Chic. & W. Mich. R. R					
Grandville, P. O. and R. R. and Tel. Sta	Chic. & W. Mich. (Gr. R. Div.)		T. 6 N., R. 12 W.	Kent	800	94
Griswold, P. O	Gr. R. & I. R. R	Cedar Springs, 8 m	T. 10 N., R. 9 W.	Kent	50	94
Gould's Mills	Det. Lan. & Nor. R. R	Greenville, 6 m	T. 9 N., R. 9 W.	Kent		94
Geddes, P. O. and R. R. and Tel. Sta	M. C. R. R		T. 2 S., R. 6 E.	Washtenaw		104
Grass Lake, **P. O.** and R. R. and Tel. Sta	M. C. R. R		T. 2 S., R. 2 E.	Jackson	800	105
Grosse Point, P. O	Lake St. Clair	Detroit, 8 m	T. 1 S., R. 13 E.	Wayne	200	103
Grand Point Village	L. S. & M. S. R. R	Ecorse, 1 m	T. 3 S., R. 11 E.	Wayne		103
Gibraltar, P. O. and R. R. Sta	M. C. R. R. (Toledo Div.)		T. 5 S., R. 10 E.	Wayne	350	103
Grosse Isle, P. O. and R. R. and Tel. Sta	M. C. R. R. (Det. River)		T. 4 S., R. 11 E.	Wayne	850	103
Greenfield, R. R. Sta	Det. Lan. & Nor. R. R		T. 1 S., R. 11 E.	Wayne		103
Greenfield, P. O	Det. Lan. & Nor. R. R	Greenfield Sta., 2 m	T. 1 S., R. 11 E.	Wayne	100	103
Girard, P. O	M. C. R. R. (Air Line Div.)	Tekonsha, 5 m	T. 5 S., R. 6 W.	Branch	200	112
Gilead, P. O	L. S. & M. S. R. R	Bronson, 8 m	T. 8 S., R. 7 W.	Branch	350	112
Genoa, R. R. Sta	Det. Lan. & Nor. R. R		T. 2 N., R. 5 E.	Livingston	75	100
Genoa, P. O	Det. Lan. & Nor. R. R	Genoa, 1 m	T. 2 N., R. 5 E.	Livingston		100
Green Oak, P. O. and R. R. Sta	Det. Lan. & Nor. R. R		T. 1 N., R. 6 E.	Livingston	40	100
Geneva, (Lovington P. O.) R. R. Sta	M. C. R. R. (Kal. & S. Haven Div.)		T. 1 S., R. 16 W.	Van Buren	105	108
Grand Junction, P. O. and R. R. and Tel. Sta	M. C. R. R. (Kal. & S. Haven Div.)		T. 1 S., R. 15 W.	Van Buren	200	108
	Chic. & W. Mich. R. R					
Gobleville, P. O	M. C. (Kal. & S. Haven Div.)	Goble, 1 m	T. 1 S., R. 14 W.	Van Buren	400	108
Goble, R. R. and Tel. Sta	M. C. (Kal. & S. Haven Div.)		T. 1 S., R. 14 W.	Van Buren	100	108
Glendale, P. O	M. C. (Kal. & S. Haven Div.)	Bloomingdale, 6 m	T. 2 S., R. 14 W.	Van Buren	100	108
Galien, P. O. and R. R. and Tel. Sta	M. C. R. R		T. 8 S., R. 19 W.	Berrien	500	109
Glen Lord, P. O	Chic. & W. Mich. R. R	Lincoln, 2 m	T. 5 S., R. 19 W.	Berrien		109
Glenwood, P. O. and R. R. and Tel. Sta	M. C. R. R		T. 5 S., R. 15 W.	Cass	125	110
Galesburg, **P. O.** and R. R. and Tel. Sta	M. C. R. R		T. 2 S., R. 10 W.	Kalamazoo	800	107
Georgetown, P. O	Chic. & W. Mich. (Gr. R. Div.)	Grandville, 5 m	T. 6 N., R. 13 W.	Ottawa	151	85
Grand Haven, City, Ldg., **P. O.** R. R. Tel. Sta.	Det. Gr. H. & Mil., Chic. & W. Mich. (Lake Mich.		T. 8 N., R. 16 W.	Ottawa	5,000	85
Grand Ledge, **P. O.** and R. R. and Tel. Sta	Det. Lan. & Nor. R. R		T. 4 N., R. 4 W.	Eaton	1,800	88
Grange Hall, P. O	Chic. & W. Mich. R. R	Hoppertown, 8 m	T. 1 N., R. 16 W.	Allegan		95
Gilchrist, R. R. Sta	Chic. & W. Mich. R. R		T. 3 N., R. 14 W.	Allegan		95
Gun Marsh, P. O. and R. R. Sta	M. & O. R. R		T. 1 N., R. 11 W.	Allegan	50	95
Graafschap, P. O	Chic. & W. Mich. R. R	Holland, 4 m	T. 4 N., R. 15 W.	Allegan	100	95
Gibson, P. O	Chic. & W. Mich. R. R	East Saugatuck, 7 m	T. 4 N., R. 16 W.	Allegan	150	95
Ganges, P. O	Chic. & W. Mich. R. R	Fennville, 6 m	T. 2 N., R. 16 W.	Allegan	60	95
Glenn, P. O	Chic. & W. Mich. R. R	Sherman, 7 m	T. 2 N., R. 16 W.	Allegan	50	95
Glass River, P. O	Chic. & Gr. T. R. R	Perry, 7 m	T. 5 N., R. 3 E.	Shiawassee	30	91
Grafton, P. O. and R. R. Sta	F. & P. M. R. R		T. 5 S., R. 9 E.	Monroe	300	115
Gilchrist, P. O., Ldg	Lake Mich. Det. M. & M. R. R	St. Ignace, 31 m	T. 43 N., R. 8 W.	Mackinac		122
*Glencoe	M. C. R. R. (Mack. Div.)	Pinconning, 10 m	T. 17 N., R. 3 E.	Bay	150	75
*Gainesville, R. R. Sta	Gr. R. & I. R. R		T. 5 N., R. 12 W.	Kent		94
*Garfield	Gr. R. & I. R. R	Cadillac, 8 m	T. 21 N., R. 8 W.	Missaukee		68
*Gibbs	Det. Lan. & Nor. R. R	Portland, 3 m	T. 6 N., R. 6 W.	Ionia		89
*Gifford	M. C. R. R. (Sag. Div.)	Mason, 10 m	T. 2 N., R. 2 E.	Ingham		99
*Gleason, R. R. Sta	M. H. & O. R. R		T. 48 N., R. 30 W.	Marquette		119
*Goguac Lake		Battle Creek, 2 m	T. 1 S., R. 8 W.	Calhoun		106
*Golding	Chic. & W. M. R. R	Mears, 4 m	T. 15 N., R. 18 W.	Oceana		80
*Goodrich	M. H. & O. R. R			Marquette		92
*Gough		Mt. Pleasant, 5 m	T. 14 N., R. 5 W.	Isabella		77
*Grantville	Det. Lan. & Nor. R. R. (S. Br.)			Montcalm	125	82
*Grand Island	Lake Superior		T. 47 N., R. 19 W.	Schoolcraft	25	12
*Grand Rapids Junction	Chic. & W. M. R. R	Holland, 1 m	T. 5 N., R. 15 W.	Ottawa		85
*Grand Trunk Junction	Chic. & Gr. T. R. R			St. Clair		89
*Gratiot Road Siding	Det. Gr. H. & Mil. R. R	Detroit, 2 m	T. 1 S., R. 12 E.	Wayne		103
*Gravel Pit	Chic. & N. W. R. R			Menominee		124
*Gravel Run			T. 1 S., R. 5 E.	Washtenaw		104
*Gatesville, P. O				Chippewa		123
*Galloway, P. O				Saginaw		84
Grant Centre, (Blaine P. O.) R. R. Sta	P. H. & N. W. R. R		T. 8 N., R. 15 E.	St. Clair		58
Harmon, P. O	M. C. (M. Div.)	Roscommon, 27 m	T. 20 N., R. 2 E.	Oscoda		63
Harrisville, **P. O.** and Tel. Sta	Lake Huron	Alpena, 30 m. (Ldg.)	T. 26 N., R. 9 E.	Alcona	700	64
Hale, R. R. Sta	Tawas & Bay County		T. 22 N., R. 7 E.	Iosco		65
Hendrie, R. R. Sta	Det. M. & M. R. R		T. 45 N., R. 7 W.	Chippewa		122
Hermansville, P. O. and R. R. and Tel. Sta	Menominee River R. R		T. 38 N., R. 27 W.	Menominee	350	124
Hancock, **P. O.** and R. R. and Tel. Sta	Mineral Range R. R		T. 55 N., R. 34 W.	Houghton	3,000	117
Houghton, P. O. and R. R. and Tel. Sta	M. H. & O. R. R		T. 54 N., R. 34 W.	Houghton	2,500	117
Huron	M. H. & O. R. R	Houghton, 1 m	T. 54 N., R. 34 W.	Houghton		117
Harbor Springs, **P. O.** and R. R. and Tel. Sta	G. R. & I. R. R		T. 35 N., R. 6 W.	Emmet	1,000	51
Hersey, **P. O.** and R. R. and Tel. Sta	F. & P. M. R. R		T. 17 N., R. 9 W.	Osceola	500	72
Hillman, P. O	Lake Huron	Alpena, 24 m. (Ldg.)	T. 31 N., R. 4 E.	Montmorency	30	55
Hartwick, P. O	G. R. & I. R. R	Leroy, 10 m	T. 19 N., R. 8 W.	Osceola		72
Harrison, P. O. and R. R. and Tel. Sta	F. & P. M. R. R. (Sag. & Clare C. Br.)		T. 19 N., R. 4 W.	Clare	600	73
Hatton, P. O	F. & P. M. R. R. (Sag. & Clare County Div.)		T. 18 N., R. 4 W.	Clare		73
Hinkle's Mills, R. R. Sta	F. & P. M. R. R		T. 17 N., R. 6 W.	Clare		73
Horton's Bay, P. O	G. R. & I. R. R	Melrose, 10 m	T. 33 N., R. 6 W.	Charlevoix	25	57
Humboldt, P. O. and R. R. Sta	M. H. & O. R		T. 47 N., R. 29 W.	Marquette	900	119
Houghton Lake, P. O	M. C. R. R. (Mack. Div.)	St. Helens, 22 m	T. 22 N., R. 4 W.	Roscommon	125	67
Haring, P. O. and R. R. Sta	G. R. & I. R. R		T. 22 N., R. 9 W.	Wexford		69
Hobart, P. O. and R. R. Sta	G. R. & I. R. R		T. 24 N., R. 9 W.	Wexford	60	69
Harvey, P. O. (Chocolay Sta.)	Det. M. & M. R. R	Chocolay, 1 m	T. 47 N., R. 24 W.	Marquette	126	119
Helena, R. R. Sta	Chic. & N. W. R. R		T. 44 N., R. 24 W.	Marquette		119
Hope, P. O	F. & P. M. R. R	Averill, 6 m	T. 16 N., R. 1 E.	Midland		76
Hannah, P. O	G. R. & I. (T. C. Br.)	Kingsleys Sta., 6 m	T. 25 N., R. 11 W.	Gr. Traverse	60	60
Homestead, P. O	G. R. & I. (T. C. Br.)	Traverse City, 23 m	T. 26 N., R. 14 W.	Benzie		59
Hesperia, **P. O.**	Chic. & W. Mich. (B. R. Br.)	White Cloud, 13 m	T. 14 N., R. 15 W.	Ocea. & Newgo.	600	81
Hazel Grove	Chic. & W. Mich. R. R	Whitehall, 14 m	T. 13 N., R. 15 W.	Oceana	50	80
Hart, P. O. and R. R. and Tel. Sta	Chic. & W. Mich. (H. Br.)		T. 15 N., R. 17 W.	Oceana	1,000	80
Holton, P. O. and R. R. and Tel. Sta	Chic. & W. Mich. (B. R. Br.)		T. 12 N., R. 15 W.	Muskegon	300	81
Howard City, **P. O.** and R. R. and Tel. Sta	G. R. & I., Det. L. & N		T. 12 N., R. 10 W.	Montcalm	1,200	82
Hemlock City, P. O. and R. R. and Tel. Sta	S. Val. & St. L. R. R		T. 12 N., R. 2 E.	Saginaw	250	84
Havana	M. C. R. R. (Sag. Div.)	Oakley, 2 m	T. 9 N., R. 3 E.	Saginaw		84
Holzinger	F. & P. M. R. R	Bridgeport, 7 m	T. 11 N., R. 6 E.	Saginaw		84
Home, P. O	Chic. & W. Mich. (B. R. Br.)	Hungerford, 5 m	T. 16 N., R. 11 W.	Newaygo		79
Hungerford, P. O. and R. R. and Tel. Sta	Chic. & W. Mich. (B. R. Br.)		T. 15 N., R. 11 W.	Newaygo	450	79

☞ Names marked with a star (*) will not be found on the Maps.

NAME OF VILLAGE.	RAILROAD, LAKE, OR RIVER.	Nearest Sta. or Landing	TOWNSHIP.	COUNTY.	Pop.	Page
Huron City, P. O. and Tel. Sta	Lake Huron	Port Austin, 6 m.	T. 18 N., R. 14 E.	Huron	100	86
Hayes, P. O	P. O. & P. A. R. R	Caseville, 3 m	T. 17 N., R. 10 E.	Huron	100	86
Hunters Creek, P. O. and R. R. and Tel. Sta.	M. C. R. R. (B. C. Div.)		T. 7 N., R. 10 E.	Lapeer	100	89
Hadley, P. O.	M. C. R. R. (B. C. Div.)	Metamora, 7 m	T. 6 N., R. 9 E.	Lapeer	350	89
Husly, P. O	S. V. & St. L. R. R	Wheeler, 18 m	T. 10 N., R. 1 W.	Gratiot	50	83
Huntington	F. & P. M. (F. R. Div.)	Otisville, 2 m	T. 9 N., R. 8 E.	Genesee		90
Hartsuff P. O. (Green's Corners), R. R. Sta	P. H. & N. W. R. R		T. 8 N., R. 15 E.	St. Clair	100	88
Huronia Beach, (Summer Resort)	Lake Huron	Fort Gratiot, 1 m	T. 7 N., R. 17 E.	St. Clair		88
Hastings, P. O. and R. R. and Tel. Sta	M. C. R. R. (Gr. R. Div.)		T. 3 N., R. 8 W.	Barry	2,700	97
Hickory Corners, P. O	M. C. R. R	Augusta, 8 m	T. 1 N., R. 9 W.	Barry	150	97
Hope, P. O	F. & P. M. R. R	Averill's Sta., 7 m	T. 16 N., R. 1 E.	Midland		78
Hudson, P. O. and R. R. and Tel. Sta	L. S. & M. S. R. R		T. 7 S., R. 1 E.	Lenawee	2,000	114
Holloway, P. O. and R. R. and Tel. Sta	Wab. St. L. & Pac. R. R		T. 6 S., R. 4 E.	Lenawee	80	114
Hillsdale, P. O. and R. R. and Tel. Sta	L. S. & M. S. R. R.		T. 6 S., R. 3 W.	Hillsdale	3,000	118
Holly, P. O. and R. R. and Tel. Sta	Det. Gr. H. & Mil., F. & P. M		T. 5 N., R. 7 E.	Oakland	1,500	101
Highland, P. O	F. & P. M. R. R	Highland Sta., 7 m	T. 3 N., R. 7 E.	Oakland	100	101
Highland, R. R. and Tel. Sta	F. & P. M. R. R.		T. 3 N., R. 7 E.	Oakland	250	101
Howardsville, P. O	L. S. & M. S. R. R	Mottville, 6 m	T. 5 S., R. 12 W.	St. Joseph	250	113
Horton, P. O.	L. S. & M. S. (Ft. Wayne Br.)	Dexter, 5 m	T. 4 S., R. 2 W.	Jackson	350	105
Hudson Mills, (Birkett P. O)	M. C. R. R		T. 1 S., R. 4 E.	Washtenaw		104
Henrietta, P. O	M. C. R. R	Rives Junction, 6 m	T. 1 S., R. 1 E.	Jackson		105
Hanover, P. O. and R. R. and Tel. Sta	L. S. & M. S. (Ft. Wayne Br.) Ohio & Mich		T. 4 S., R. 2 W.	Jackson	400	105
Hoffman's, R. R. Sta	M. C. R. R		T. 2 S., R. 8 E.	Wayne		108
Hand, P. O. and Tel. Sta	Wab. St. L. & Pac. R. R		T. 3 S., R. 10 E.	Wayne		103
Homer, P. O. and R. R. and Tel. Sta	L. S. & M. S. (Lan. Div.) Ohio & Mich		T. 4 S., R. 4 W.	Calhoun	600	106
Harmonia	M. C. R. R	Bedford, 1 m	T. 1 S., R. 8 W.	Calhoun		106
Helmer's, R. R. Sta	Chic. & Gr. T. R. R		T. 2 S., R. 8 W.	Calhoun		109
Hodunk, P. O.	M. C. R. R. (Air Line Div.)	Union City, 5 m	T. 5 S., R. 7 W.	Branch	80	112
Herrickville (Butler P. O.)	M. C. R. R. (Air Line Div.)	Clarendon, 5 m	T. 5 S., R. 5 W.	Branch		112
Hall's Corner	L. S. & M. S. (Ft. Wayne & Jackson Br.)	Bay, 3 m	T. 8 S., R. 5 W.	Branch		112
Howell, P. O. and R. R. and Tel. Sta	Det. Lan. & Nor. R. R		T. 3 N., R. 4 E.	Livingston	2,500	100
Hartland, P. O	Det. Lan. & Nor. R. R	Brighton, 11 m	T. 3 N., R. 6 E.	Livingston	200	100
Hamburg, P. O	Det. Lan. & Nor. R. R	Brighton, 6 m	T. 1 N., R. 5 E.	Livingston	100	100
Holt, P. O. and R. R. and Tel. Sta	M. C. R. R. (Sag. Div.)		T. 3 N., R. 2 W.	Ingham	300	99
Hartford, P. O. and R. R. and Tel. Sta	Chic. & W. Mich., Toledo & S. Haven		T. 3 S., R. 16 W.	Van Buren	1,100	108
Hooker	Chic. & W. Mich. R. R	Bangor, 4 m	T. 1 S., R. 16 W.	Van Buren		108
Hill's Corners, P. O.	M. C. R. R	Galien, 7 m	T. 7 S., R. 19 W.	Berrien	30	109
Hagar, P. O. and R. R. Sta	Chic. & W. Mich. R. R		T. 3 S., R. 18 W.	Berrien	30	109
Howlandsburg	M. C. R. R	Augusta, 3 m	T. 1 S., R. 9 W.	Kalamazoo	30	107
Holland, P. O. and R. R. and Tel. Sta	Chic. & W. Mich. R. R		T. 5 N., R. 15 W.	Ottawa	3,000	95
Hudsonville, P. O. and R. R. and Tel. Sta.	Chic. & W. Mich. R. R.		T. 6 N., R. 13 W.	Ottawa	2,000	95
Hanley, P. O	Chic. & W. Mich. R. R.	Grandville, 5 m	T. 5 N., R. 13 W.	Ottawa		95
Hoytville, P. O	Det. Lan. & Nor. R. R	Grand Ledge, 9 m	T. 4 N., R. 5 W.	Eaton	150	98
Hamilton, P. O. and R. R. and Tel. Sta	Chic. & W. Mich. R. R		T. 3 N., R. 14 W.	Allegan	350	90
Hilliards, P. O. and R. R. and Tel. Sta	L. S. & M. S. R. R. (Kal. Div.)		T. 3 N., R. 12 W.	Allegan	200	90
Hopkins, P. O. and R. R. and Tel. Sta	L. S. & M. S. R. R. (Kal. Div.)		T. 3 N., R. 12 W.	Allegan	250	90
Hopkins, P. O	Gr. R. & I. R. R	Bradley, 3 m	T. 3 N., R. 12 W.	Allegan	100	90
Hoppertown, R. R. Sta	Chic. & W. Mich. R. R		T. 1 N., R. 15 W.	Allegan	45	90
Hawkhead, P. O	Chic. & W. Mich. R. R	Hoppertown, 7 m	T. 1 N., R. 16 W.	Allegan	75	90
Henderson, P. O. and R. R. Sta	M. C. R. R. (Sag. Div.)		T. 8 N., R. 3 E.	Shiawassee	65	91
Hazel Green, P. O. and R. R. Sta	M. C. R. R. (Sag. Div.)		T. 8 N., R. 2 E.	Shiawassee		91
Hazelton, P. O	M. C. R. R. (Sag. Div.)	Henderson, 11 m	T. 8 N., R. 4 E.	Shiawassee	200	91
Hartwellville, P. O.	Chic. & Gr. T. R. R	Morrice, 3 m	T. 6 N., R. 3 E.	Shiawassee	45	91
Hawthorn, R. R. Sta	Toledo, A. Arbor & Gr. T. R. R		T. 8 S., R. 8 E.	Monroe		115
Hubbardston, P. O	Det. Gr. H. & Mil. R. R	Pewamo, 7 m	T. 8 N., R. 5 W.	Ionia	600	93
*Harbee	M. C. R. R. (M. Div.)	Pinconning, 8 m	T. 17 N., R. 3 E.	Bay		75
*Herr	Saginaw Bay	Standish, 5 m	T. 18 N., R. 5 E.	Arenac		75
*Hamlin (Point Sable P. O)	F. & P. M. R. R.	Ludington, 6 m	T. 19 N., R. 18 W.	Mason		70
*Hamlin	L. S. & M. S. (Dundee Br.)		T. 6 S., R. 7 E.	Monroe		115
*Hammers, (Flag Sta.)	Gr. R. & I. R. R		T. 34 N., R. 5 W.	Charlevoix		57
*Hansen	Chic. & W. M. R. R	Shelby, 8 m	T. 14 N., R. 18 W.	Oceana		80
*Harlows		Marquette, 2 m	T. 48 N., R. 25 W.	Marquette		119
*Harris Creek	M. C. R. R. (Gr. R. Div.)	Parmelee, 6 m	T. 5 N., R. 10 W.	Kent	65	94
*Harrison's, R. R. Sta	L. S. & M. S. (Ypsilanti Br.)		T. 3 S., R. 6 E.	Washtenaw	600	104
*Haywood Vale		Sand Beach, 6 m	T. 15 N., R. 15 E.	Huron		86
*Headland	F. & P. M. R. R	Evart, 9 m	T. 19 N., R. 8 W.	Osceola		72
*Hemmingway	Det. Lan. & Nor. (Stanton Br.)		T. 11 N., R. 6 W.	Montcalm		82
*Henderson				Wexford	25	69
*Henry's		Rives Junct., 4 m	T. 1 N.	Ingham		99
*Highway	M. R. R. R			Houghton		117
*Hopkins, R. R. Sta	M. C. (S. H. Div.)			Kalamazoo		107
*Hughart				Emmet		51
*Hubbard Lake, P. O				Alpena		54
*Hammond, R. R. Sta	M. C. R. R. (Gr. R. Div.)		T. 5 N., R. 11 W.	Kent	60	94
*Hamilton, R. R. Sta	Chic. & Gr. T. R. R.			Genesee	210	90
Hurd's Corners, (East Dayton P. O.)	P. O. & P. A. R. R	Kingston, 5 m	T. 12 N., R. 10 E.	Tuscola		85
Indian Lake, P. O	Mich. Cent. (M. Div.)	Beaver Lake, 20m	T. 25 N., R. 3 E.	Oscoda		63
Iron Mountain, P. O. and R. R. and Tel. Sta.	Chic. & Nor. W. (Menominee Br.)		T. 40 N., R. 30 W.	Menominee	50	126
Indian Town	Chic. & N. W. R. R	Escanaba, 8 m	T. 39 N., R. 23 W.	Delta		120
Inverness	M. C. R. R. (Mack. Div.)	Cheboygan, 2 m	T. 38 N., R. 1 W.	Cheboygan		52
Indian Village	M. C. R. R. (Mack. Div.)	Mullett Lake 14 m	T. 36 N., R. 3 W.	Cheboygan		52
Inland City, P. O	M. C. R. R. (Mack. Div.)	Indian River, 1 m	T. 35 N., R. 3 W.	Cheboygan		52
Indian River, P. O. and R. R. Sta	M. C. R. R. (Mack. Div.)		T. 35 N., R. 2 W.	Cheboygan	200	52
Ironton, P. O. and Tel. Sta	G. R. & I. R. R	Boyne Falls, 16 m	T. 33 N., R. 7 W.	Charlevoix		57
Ironwood, P. O	G. R. & I. R. R	Boyne Falls, 22 m	T. 32 N., R. 9 W.	Charlevoix		57
Intermediate, P. O.	G. R. & I. R. R., Lake Mich	Boyne Falls, 17 m	T. 32 N., R. 7 W.	Charlevoix		57
Ingalls, P. O	Chic. & N. W. R. R.		T. 35 N., R. 27 W.	Menominee	250	124
Ishpeming, P. O. and R. R. and Tel. Sta.	M. H. & O. R. R		T. 47 N., R. 27 W.	Marquette	8,000	119
Iron River, P. O. and R. R. and Tel. Sta	Men. R. R. R. (Iron River Br.)		T. 43 N., R. 35 W.	Marquette	800	119
Ivan, P. O	G. R. & I. R. R	Fife Lake, 10 m	T. 25 N., R. 7 W.	Kalkaska	150	61
Inland, P. O	G. R. & I. R. R. (T. C. Br.)	Traverse City, 14 m	T. 26 N., R. 13 W.	Benzie	300	59
Ithaca, P. O. and R. R. and Tel. Sta	C. S. & C. R. R	Alma, 8 m	T. 10 N., R. 3 W.	Gratiot	1,000	83
Indes, P. O. and R. R. Sta	P. H. & N. W. R. R		T. 10 N., R. 12 E.	Lapeer		89
Imlay, P. O.	Gr. T. R. R	Imlay City, 2 m	T. 7 N., R. 12 E.	Lapeer	150	89
Imlay City, P. O. and R. R. and Tel. Sta	Gr. T., P. O. & P. A. R. R		T. 7 N., R. 12 E.	Lapeer	1,000	89
Irving, P. O. and R. R. Sta	M. C. R. R. (Gr. R. Div.)		T. 4 N., R. 9 W.	Barry	20	97
Ingersoll, P. O. and R. R. Sta	Det. L. & Nor. R. R		T. 5 N., R. 3 W.	Clinton	50	92
Indian Creek		Grand Rapids, 6 m	T. 7 N., R. 12 W.	Kent		94
Inkster, P. O. and R. R. Sta	M. C. R. R		T. 2 S., R. 9 E.	Wayne	300	108
Iosco, P. O	Det. Lan. & Nor. R. R	Fowlerville, 8 m	T. 2 N., R. 3 E.	Livingston	100	100
Irvington, P. O. (Geneva Sta.)	M. C. (Kal. & S. Haven Div.)		T. 1 S., R. 16 W.	Van Buren	150	108
Indian Lake, R. R. Sta	Chic. & Gr. T. R. R		T. 3 S., R. 10 W.	Kalamazoo	75	107

☞ Names marked with a star (*) will not be found on the Maps.

NAME OF VILLAGE.	RAILROAD, LAKE, OR RIVER.	Nearest Sta. or Landing	TOWNSHIP.	COUNTY.	Pop.	Page
Ionia, P. O. and R. R. and Tel. Sta	Det. Lan. & Nor., Det. Gr. H. & Mil.		T. 7 N., R. 6 W.	Ionia	5,000	93
Ida, P. O. and R. R. and Tel. Sta	L. S. & M. S. R. R.		T. 7 S., R. 8 E.	Monroe	250	115
*Imperial Mills			T. 8 N., R. 10 W.	Kent		94
Island Mine	Lake Superior			Isle Royale		115
Isle Royale	Lake Superior			Isle Royale		115
*Iroquois, P. O.				Chippewa		128
*Idlewild, Tel. Sta				Genesee		90
Jeromeville, R. R. Sta	Det. M. & M. R. R.		T. 46 N., R. 17 W.	Schoolcraft		121
Joyfield, P. O.	F. & P. M. R. R. (Man. Div.)	Manistee, 23 m	T. 25 N., R. 15 W.	Benzie	100	39
Jericho, P. O.	Chic. & W. Mich. (N. Div.)	Lake, 4 m	T. 11 N., R. 13 W.	Newaygo		79
Juniata, P. O. and R. R. Sta	M. C. (B. C. Div.)		T. 12 N., R. 7 E.	Tuscola		85
Juniata, R. R. Sta	P. H. & N. W. R. R.		T. 11 N., R. 9 E.	Tuscola		85
Jeddo, P. O. and R. R. Sta	P. H. & N. W. R. R.		T. 8 N., R. 16 E.	St. Clair	150	88
Jonesville, P. O. and R. R. Sta	L. S. & M. S. R. R.		T. 6 S., R. 3 W.	Hillsdale	1,800	118
Jerome, P. O. and R. R. Sta	L. S. & M. S. R. R.		T. 5 S., R. 1 W.	Hillsdale	125	118
Jefferson, P. O.	L. S. & M. S. R. R.	Osseo, 5 m	T. 7 S., R. 2 W.	Hillsdale		118
Jasper, P. O. and R. R. and Tel. Sta	L. S. & M. S. R. R. (Fayette Br.)		T. 8 S., R. 5 E.	Lenawee	250	114
Jersey, P. O.	M. C. R. R. (B. C. Div.) P. O. & P. A. R. R.	Oxford, 6 m	T. 4 N., R. 10 E.	Oakland		101
Jackson, P. O. and R. R. and Tel. Sta	L. S. & M. S., M. C. R. R.		T. 3 S., R. 1 W.	Jackson	22,000	105
Jefferson	L. S. & M. S. (Ypsilanti Br.)	Brooklyn, 3 m	T. 4 S., R. 1 E.	Jackson	100	105
Junction, P. O. and R. R. Sta	M. C., Det. Lan. & Nor.		T. 2 S., R. 11 E.	Wayne		103
Junction	Gr. T. R. R.	Fraser, 2 m	T. 1 N., R. 13 E.	Macomb		102
Jericho	Chic. & W. Mich. R. R.	Bangor, 5 m	T. 1 S., R. 16 W.	Van Buren		108
Jones, P. O. and R. R. Sta	M. C. R. R. (Air Line Div.)		T. 6 S., R. 13 W.	Cass	175	110
Jenisonville, P. O. and R. R. Sta	Chic. & W. Mich. (Gr. R. Div.)		T. 6 N., R. 13 W.	Ottawa	200	95
Jamestown, P. O.	Chic. & W. Mich. R. R.	Hudsonville, 4 m	T. 5 N., R. 13 W.	Ottawa	100	95
Johnsville, P. O. and R. R. Sta	Chic. & W. Mich. R. R.		T. 7 N., R. 16 W.	Ottawa	100	95
Johnstown, P. O.	M. C. R. R.	Battle Creek, 15 m	T. 1 N., R. 8 W.	Barry	50	97
Judd's Corners, P. O.	Det. Gr. H. & Mil. R. R.	Corunna, 9 m	T. 8 N., R. 4 E.	Shiawassee	150	91
Jackson Junction	M. C., L. S. & M. S. R. R.		T. 3 S., R. 1 W.	Jackson		105
J. L. & S. Junction	Det. Gr. H. & M., M. C. (S. Div.)		T. 7 N., R. 2 E.	Shiawassee		91
Jacob City, P. O. and R. R. Sta	Det. Mack. & Mar. R. R.		T. 42 N., R. 4 W.	Mackinac	75	122
*Jeffersonville		Cassopolis, 4 m	T. 6 S., R. 15 W.	Cass		110
*Johnson, R. R. Sta	Det. Mack. & Mar. R. R.			Chippewa		122
Johnsville	Sag. Tus. & H. R. R.	Akron, 1 m	T. 13 N., R. 8 E.	Tuscola		85
*Junction	F. & P. M. (F. R. Div.)		T. 8 N., R. 7 E.	Genesee		90
*Jennings, P. O.				Missaukee		68
*Jenson, P. O.				Newaygo		79
Johnson, R. R. Sta	Det. Mack. & Mar. R. R.		T. 45 N., R. 5 W.	Mackinac		122
Koehler, Ldg., P. O.	M. C. R. R. (Mack. Div.)	Topinabee, 3 m	T. 35 N., R. 2 W.	Cheboygan	70	32
Kasson, P. O.	G. R. & I. R. R. (T. C. Br.)	Traverse City, 17 m	T. 28 N., R. 13 W.	Leelanaw	125	58
Kearney, P. O.	G. R. & I. R. R.	Alba, 12 m	T. 30 N., R. 7 W.	Antrim		57
Kloman, R. R. Sta	Chic. & N. W. R. R.		T. 38 N., R. 29 W.	Menominee		124
*Kewadin, P. O.				Antrim		57
Kingsley, R. R. and Tel. Sta	G. R. & I. (T. C. Br.)		T. 25 N., R. 10 W.	Gr. Traverse	200	60
Kalkaska, P. O. and R. R. and Tel. Sta	G. R. & I. R. R.		T. 27 N., R. 7 W.	Kalkaska	1,000	61
Kendallville	Det. L. & N. R. R.	Maple Valley, 6 m	T. 11 N., R. 8 W.	Montcalm		82
Kintnor, R. R. Sta	S. T. & H. R. R.		T. 13 N., R. 8 E.	Tuscola		85
Kingston, P. O. and R. R. Sta	P. O. & P. A. R. R.		T. 12 N., R. 11 E.	Tuscola	100	85
Kilmanagh, P. O.	S. T. & H. R. R.	Sebewaing, 5 m	T. 16 N., R. 10 E.	Huron	150	88
Kilkenny, P. O.	P. O. & P. A. R. R.	Gagetown, 7 m	T. 15 N., R. 10 E.	Huron		88
Kipp's Corners	F. & P. M. R. R.	Grand Blanc, 10 m	T. 6 N., R. 8 E.	Genesee		90
Kenockee, P. O.	Chic. & Gr. T. R. R.	Emmett, 6 m	T. 7 N., R. 13 E.	St. Clair	100	88
Kingsley P. O. and R. R. and Tel. Sta	P. H. & N. W. R. R.		T. 7 N., R. 16 E.	St. Clair		88
Kimball, R. R. Sta	P. H. & N. W. R. R.		T. 6 N., R. 16 E.	St. Clair		88
Klinger's Lake, P. O. and Tel. Sta	L. S. & M. S. R. R.		T. 8 S., R. 11 W.	St. Joseph		111
Kelley's Corners, P. O.	L. S. & M. S. (Ypsilanti Br.)	Woodstock, 1 m	T. 5 S., R. 1 E.	Lenawee	130	114
Kensington, P. O.	Det. Lan. & Nor., Tol. A. A. & Gr. T. R. R.	South Lyon, 4 m	T. 1 N., R. 7 E.	Oakland	60	101
Kelloggsville	Gr. R. & I. R. R.	Fisher's Sta., 1 m	T. 6 N., R. 12 W.	Kent		94
Keller, P. O.	M. C. R. R. (Gr. R. Div.)	Caledonia, 11 m	T. 5 N., R. 9 W.	Kent		94
Kent City, P. O. and R. R. and Tel. Sta	Chic. & W. Mich. (Newaygo Div.)		T. 10 N., R. 12 W.	Kent	400	94
Kinderhook, P. O.	L. S. & M. S. (Ft. Wayne & Jackson Br.)	Fremont, 8 m	T. 8 S., R. 6 W.	Branch		112
Keelersville, P. O.	M. C. R. R.	Decatur, 10 m	T. 4 S., R. 16 W.	Van Buren	200	108
Kibbie, P. O. and R. R. Sta	M. C. (Kal. & S. H. Div.)		T. 1 S., R. 16 W.	Van Buren	100	108
Kendall, P. O. and R. R. Sta	M. C. (Kal. & S. Haven Div.)		T. 1 S., R. 13 W.	Van Buren	200	108
Kalamazoo, P. O. and R. R. Sta	M. C., Gr. R. & I. R. R.		T. 2 S., R. 11 W.	Kalamazoo	16,000	107
Kingsland, P. O. and R. R. Sta	L. S. & M. S. (Lan. Div.)		T. 2 N., R. 3 W.	Eaton		99
Kalamo, P. O.	Chic. & Gr. T. R. R.	Bellevue, 7 m	T. 2 N., R. 6 W.	Eaton	140	99
Kellogg, R. R. Sta	M. & O. R. R.		T. 2 N., R. 12 W.	Allegan		96
Keene, P. O.	D. G. H. & M. R. R.	Saranac, 4½ m	T. 7 N., R. 8 W.	Ionia		93
Kenneth, R. R. Sta	Det. Lan. & Nor. R. R.		T. 6 N., R. 5 W.	Ionia		93
Kiddville, P. O. and R. R. Sta	Det. Lan. & Nor. R. R.		T. 8 N., R. 6 W.	Ionia	100	93
Ketcham's, R. R. Sta	Sag. Bay & N. W. R. R.		T. 18 N., R. 3 E.	Bay		75
Kawkawlin, P. O. and R. R. Sta	M. C. R. R. (Mack. Div.)		T. 14 N., R. 4 E.	Bay	300	75
*Kaska	Gr. R. & I. R. R.	Fife Lake, 9 m	T. 25 N., R. 7 W.	Kalkaska		61
*Kinneyville	M. C. R. R. (Gr. R. Div.)	Onondaga, 2 m	T. 1 N., R. 2 W.	Ingham		99
Luzerne, P. O.	M. C. (M. Div.)	Roscommon, 20 m	T. 26 N., R. 1 E.	Oscoda		63
Lathrop, P. O. and R. R. and Tel. Sta	Chic. & N. W. R. R.		T. 43 N., R. 23 W.	Delta	200	120
Lake Linden, P. O.	Mineral Range R. R.	Calumet, 5 m	T. 55 N., R. 32 W.	Houghton	2,700	117
L'Anse, P. O. and R. R. and Tel. Sta	M. H. & O. R. R.		T. 50 N., R. 33 W.	Baraga	1,200	117
Levering, R. R. and Tel. Sta	Gr. R. I. & Mack. R. R.		T. 37 N., R. 4 W.	Emmet		51
Lansdale, P. O.	G. R. & I. R. R.	Harbor Springs, 8 m	T. 36 N., R. 6 W.	Emmet		51
Littlefield, P. O.	G. R. & I. R. R.	Petoskey, 10 m	T. 34 N., R. 4 W.	Emmet		51
Long Rapids, P. O.	Lake Huron	Alpena Ldg., 13 m	T. 32 N., R. 6 E.	Alpena		54
Leland, P. O. and Tel. Sta	G. R. & I. R. R. (T. C. Br.)	Traverse City, 24 m	T. 30 N., R. 12 W.	Leelanaw	400	58
Logan, P. O.	M. C. R. R.	Vanderbilt, 3 m	T. 32 N., R. 3 W.	Otsego		56
Leroy, P. O. and R. R. and Tel. Sta	G. R. & I. R. R.		T. 19 N., R. 10 W.	Osceola	350	72
Luther, P. O. and R. R. Sta	G. R. & I. R. R.		T. 19 N., R. 12 W.	Lake	650	71
Lake, R. R. and Tel. Sta	F. & P. M. R. R.		T. 17 N., R. 4 W.	Clare		78
LaFarge	F. & P. M. R. R.	Ludington, 10 m	T. 19 N., R. 17 W.	Mason		70
Lincoln, P. O.	F. & P. M. R. R.	Ludington, 2 m	T. 18 N., R. 18 W.	Mason	125	70
Ludington, P. O. and R. R. and Tel. Sta	F. & P. M. R. R.		T. 18 N., R. 18 W.	Mason	6,000	70
Lincoln River	F. & P. M. R. R. (Man. Div.)		T. 19 N., R. 18 W.	Mason	81	70
Lake City, P. O.	G. R. & I. R. R.	Cadillac, 14 m	T. 22 N., R. 8 W.	Missaukee	150	68
Loomis, P. O. and R. R. and Tel. Sta	F. & P. M. R. R.		T. 16 N., R. 3 W.	Isabella	215	77
Longwood	F. & P. M. R. R. (Sag. & Mt. P. Div.)	Mount Pleasant, 2 m	T. 14 N., R. 4 W.	Isabella		77
Little Lake, R. R. Sta	Chic. & N. W. R. R.		T. 45 N., R. 24 W.	Marquette		119
Lee's Corners, P. O.	F. & P. M. R. R.	Freeland, 5 m	T. 13 N., R. 2 E.	Midland	80	70
Lane, P. O.	M. C. R. R. (Mack. Div.)	Beaver Lake, 22 m	T. 24 N., R. 3 E.	Ogemaw		65
Leetsville, P. O. and R. R. Sta	G. R. & I. R. R.		T. 28 N., R. 7 W.	Kalkaska	25	61
Lodi, P. O.	G. R. & I. R. R.	South Boardman, 5 m	T. 26 N., R. 7 W.	Kalkaska	50	61
Lake Side	Chic. & W. Mich. R. R.	Muskegon, 2 m	T. 10 N., R. 17 W.	Muskegon		81

☞ Names marked with a star (*) will not be found on the Maps.

NAME OF VILLAGE.	RAILROAD, LAKE, OR RIVER.	Nearest Sta. or Landing	TOWNSHIP.	COUNTY.	Pop.	Page
Lake Harbor, Ldg	Chic. & W. Mich., Lake Mich	Ferrysburg, 6 m	T. 9 N., R. 17 W.	Muskegon	350	81
Lake Switch, P. O. and R. R. Sta	Chic. & W. Mich. (N. Div.)		T. 12 N., R. 14 W.	Newaygo	200	79
Leathem, P. O				Menominee		124
Lakeview, P. O. and R. R. and Tel. Sta	Chic. S. & C. R. R		T. 12 N., R. 8 W.	Montcalm	850	82
Langston, P. O	Det. L. & N. R. R	Maple Valley, 7 m	T. 11 N., R. 8 W.	Montcalm	150	82
Lentz, P. O	M. C. (Sag. Div.)	St. Charles, 7 m	T. 10 N., R. 2 E.	Saginaw	50	84
Layton Corners, P. O	M. C. (Sag. Div.)	Chesaning, 7 m	T. 9 N., R. 4 E.	Saginaw	100	84
Lumberton, P. O. and R. R. and Tel. Sta	Chic. & W. Mich. (B. R. Br.)		T. 13 N., R. 11 W.	Newaygo	100	79
Lapeer, P. O. and R. R. and Tel. Sta	Chic. & Gr. T., M. C. (B. C. Div.)		T. 7 N., R. 10 E.	Lapeer	2,912	89
Lafayette, P. O	S. Val. & St. L. R. R	Breckenridge, 8 m	T. 11 N., R. 1 W.	Gratiot		83
Leon, P. O	Det. G. H. & Mil. R. R	Ovid, 10 m	T. 9 N., R. 1 W.	Gratiot	165	83
Linden, P. O. and Tel. Sta	Det. G. H. & Mil. R. R	North Linden, 1 m	T. 5 N., R. 6 E.	Genesee	800	90
Lamotte, P. O	P. H. & N. W. R. R	Marlette, 6 m	T. 12 N., R. 12 E.	Sanilac		87
Lexington, P. O. and Tel. Sta	P. H. & N. W., Lake Huron	Croswell, 4 m	T. 10 N., R. 16 E.	Sanilac	1,000	87
Lennon, P. O	Chic. & Gr. T. R. R	Swartz Creek, 6 m	T. 7 N., R. 5 E.	Genesee		90
Lynn, P. O	Chic. & Gr. T. R. R	Capac, 6 m	T. 8 N., R. 13 E.	St. Clair	40	88
Lake Port, P. O. and Tel. Sta	Lake Huron	Blaine, 5 m	T. 8 N., R. 17 E.	St. Clair	200	88
Lamb's, R. R. Sta	P. H. & N. W. R. R		T. 6 N., R. 15 E.	St. Clair	100	88
Loomis, P. O. and R. R. Sta	F. & P. M. R. R		T. 16 N., R. 3 W.	Isabella	400	77
Longwood	Sag. & Mt. Pleasant R. R	Mount Pleasant, 2 m	T. 14 N., R. 4 W.	Isabella		77
Lee's Corners, P. O	F. & P. M. R. R	Freeland, 6 m	T. 13 N., R. 2 E.	Midland		76
Little Hope		Adrian, 5 m	T. 6 S., R. 4 E.	Lenawee		114
Lenawee Junction, P. O. and Tel. Sta	L. S. & M. S. R. R		T. 7 S., R. 4 E.	Lenawee		114
Lyons	L. S. & M. S. R. R		T. 7 S., R. 5 E.	Lenawee		114
Litchfield, P. O. and R. R. and Tel. Sta	L. S. & M. S. (Lan. Div.)		T. 5 S., R. 4 W.	Hillsdale	600	113
Lickley's Corners, P. O	L. S. & M. S. R. R	Pittsford, 6 m	T. 8 S., R. 1 W.	Hillsdale	30	113
Lake Ridge, P. O	Wab. St. L. & Pac. R. R	Britton, 4 m	T. 5 S., R. 5 E.	Lenawee	70	114
Leonidas, P. O	M. C. R. R. (Air Line Div.)	Colon, 8 m	T. 5 S., R. 9 W.	St. Joseph	225	111
Lakeville, P. O	M. C. R. R. (B. C. Div.)	Orion, 6 m	T. 5 N., R. 11 E.	Oakland	180	101
Lyons' Mills, R. R. Sta	Det. Gr. H. & Mil. R. R		T. 7 N., R. 3 W.	Clinton		92
Lowell, P. O. and R. R. and Tel. Sta	Det. Gr. H. & Mil. R. R		T. 6 N., R. 9 W.	Kent	1,600	94
Leona, P. O				Missaukee		68
Labarge, P. O	M. C. R. R. (Gr. R. Div.)	Caledonia, 3 m	T. 5 N., R. 10 W.	Kent	75	94
Lockwood, P. O. and R. R. and Tel. Sta	Gr. R. & I. R. R		T. 10 N., R. 10 W.	Kent	125	94
Lima, P. O	M. C. R. R	Chelsea, 4 m	T. 2 S., R. 4 E.	Washtenaw	65	104
Logansport	L. S. & M. S. R. R	Saline, 2 m	T. 4 S., R. 5 E.	Washtenaw		104
Lapham's Corners	Det. Lan. & Nor. R. R	Salem, 3 m	T. 1 S., R. 7 E.	Washtenaw		104
Leoni, P. O. and R. R. and Tel. Sta	M. C. R. R		T. 3 S., R. 1 E.	Jackson	250	105
Liberty, P. O	L. S. & M. S. (Ypsilanti Br.)	Somerset, 4 m	T. 4 S., R. 1 W.	Jackson	100	105
Leesville, P. O		Detroit, 4 m	T. 1 S., R. 12 E.	Wayne	800	103
Livonia, P. O	Det. Lan. & Nor. R. R	Livonia Sta., 2 m	T. 1 S., R. 9 E.	Wayne	50	103
Livonia, R. R. Sta	Det. Lan. & Nor. R. R		T. 1 S., R. 9 E.	Wayne	55	103
Lester, P. O	L. S. & M. S. (Ft. Wayne & Jack. Br.)	Ray, 8 m	T. 7 S., R. 5 W.	Branch		112
Leslie, P. O. and R. R. and Tel. Sta	M. C. R. R. (Sag. Div.)		T. 1 N., R. 1 W.	Ingham	1,500	99
Lenox, P. O. (Ridgeway Sta.)	Chic. & Gr. T. R. R		T. 4 N., R. 14 E.	Macomb	200	102
Lawton, P. O. and R. R. and Tel. Sta	M. C. R. R., To. & S. Haven R. R., C. & G. T. R. R		T. 3 S., R. 13 W.	Van Buren	800	108
Lansing, City, P. O. and R. R. and Tel. Sta	Det. Lan. & Nor., M. C. (L. Div.)		T. 4 N., R. 2 W.	Ingham	8,500	99
	C. I. G. T. R. R., L. S. & M. S. (Lan. Div.)					
Locke, P. O	Det. Lan. & Nor. R. R	Webberville, 6 m	T. 3 N., R. 2 E.	Ingham	130	99
Lake Mills	M. C. (Kal. & S. Haven Div.)	Gobls, 1 m	T. 1 S., R. 14 W.	Van Buren		108
Lawrence, P. O. and R. R. Sta	Toledo & S. Haven R. R		T. 3 S., R. 15 W.	Van Buren	800	108
Lake Side, P. O. and R. R. and Tel. Sta	Chic. & W. Mich. R. R		T. 7 S., R. 20 W.	Berrien	150	109
Lincoln, R. R. Sta	Chic. & W. Mich. R. R		T. 5 S., R. 19 W.	Berrien		109
Little Prairie Ronde, P. O	Chic. & Gr. T. R. R	Marcellus, 5 m	T. 5 S., R. 14 W.	Cass	200	110
La Grange, P. O	M. C. (Air Line Div.) Chic. & Gr. T	Cassopolis, 5 m	T. 6 S., R. 15 W.	Cass	200	110
Leesburgh, P. O. and R. R. Sta	Chic. & Gr. T. R. R		T. 4 S., R. 12 W.	Kalamazoo	80	107
Lamont, P. O	Det. Gr. H. & Mil. R. R	Berlin, 6 m	T. 7 N., R. 13 W.	Ottawa	400	95
Lisbon, P. O	Chic. & W. Mich. (Newaygo Div.)	Sparta, 5 m	T. 9 N., R. 13 W.	Ottawa	200	95
Lee, P. O. and R. R. Sta	Chic. & W. Mich. R. R		T. 1 N., R. 15 W.	Allegan	100	96
Lacey, P. O	M. C. R. R. (Gr. R. Div.)	Morgan, 11 m	T. 1 N., R. 8 W.	Barry		97
Laingsburg, P. O. and R. R. and Tel. Sta	M. C. R. R. (Sag. Div.)		T. 6 N., R. 1 E.	Shiawassee	750	91
Lyons, P. O. and R. R. and Tel. Sta	Det. Lan. & Nor. R. R		T. 7 N., R. 5 W.	Ionia	800	93
La Salle, P. O. and R. R. and Tel. Sta	L. S. & M. S. R. R. (Det. Div.)		T. 7 S., R. 9 E.	Monroe	50	115
Little Lake, P. O. and R. R. Sta	Toledo, A. Arbor & Gr. T. R. R		T. 8 S., R. 8 E.	Monroe		115
Lambertville, P. O	Toledo, A. Arbor & Gr. T. R. R	Hawthorn, 3 m	T. 8 S., R. 7 E.	Monroe	100	115
London, P. O	Toledo, A. Arbor & Gr. T. R. R	East Milan, 3 m	T. 5 S., R. 7 E.	Monroe	50	115
Lulu, P. O. and R. R. Sta	Toledo, A. Arbor & Gr. T. R. R		T. 7 S., R. 7 E.	Monroe		115
Linwood, P. O. and R. R. Sta	M. C. R. R. (Mack. Div.)		T. 16 N., R. 4 E.	Bay	25	75
*La Carp		Ludington, 12 m	T. 19 N., R. 17 W.	Mason		70
*Lake Shore	Gr. & I. R. R	Mancelona, 10 m	T. 30 N., R. 7 W.	Antrim		57
*Leavitt				Oceana		80
*Leaton, R. R. Sta	Sag. & Mt. P. R. R		T. 15 N., R. 3 W.	Isabella	100	77
*Lebanon			T. 8 N., R. 4 W.	Clinton		92
*Lee Centre	M. C. R. R	Marshall, 10 m	T. 1 S.	Calhoun		100
*Leland	To. A. Arbor & Gr. T. R. R	Ann Arbor, 5 m	T. 2 N., R. 6 E.	Washtenaw		104
*Lester's Mills	C. & G. T. R. R	Capac, 4 m	T. 6 N., R. 13 E.	St. Clair		88
*Little Point Au Sable	Lake Michigan	Benona, 7 m	T. 15 N., R. 19 W.	Oceana		80
*Long Lake		Traverse City, 8 m	T. 27 N., R. 12 W.	Gr. Traverse		60
*McLane, P. O	Chic. & W. Mich. (B. R. Br.)	White Cloud, 5 m	T. 14 N., R. 13 W.	Newaygo		79
*Lockport, Tel. Sta				St. Joseph		111
Lake Ridge, P. O	Wab. St. L. & Pac. R. R	Britton, 4 m	T. 6 S., R. 5 E.	Lenawee		114
Mio, P. O	M. C. R. R. (M. Div.)	Roscommon, 35 m	T. 26 N., R. 3 E.	Oscoda	50	53
Mills, R. R. Sta	Tawas & Bay County R. R		T. 21 N., R. 7 E.	Iosco		65
McIvor, R. R. Sta	Tawas & Bay County R. R		T. 21 N., R. 6 E.	Iosco		65
Munuskong	Lake Superior		T. 47 N., R. 5 W.	Chippewa		123
McMillan, P. O. and R. R. Sta	Det. M. & M. R. R		T. 46 N., R. 11 W.	Chippewa		122
Mandan	Lake Superior	Copper Harbor, 11 m	T. 58 N., R. 29 W.	Keweenaw		118
Malton, P. O. and R. R. Sta	Chic. & N. W. R. R		T. 42 N., R. 23 W.	Delta	250	120
Masonville, R. R. Sta	Chic. & N. W. R. R		T. 41 N., R. 22 W.	Delta	140	120
Mason, R. R. Sta	Chic. & N. W. R. R		T. 40 N., R. 22 W.	Delta		120
Minong	Lake Superior		T. 65 N., R. 35 W.	Isle Royal		115
Michigamme, P. O. and Tel. Sta	M. H. & O. R. R		T. 48 N., R. 30 W.	Marquette	1,300	119
Mullett Lake, P. O. and R. R. Sta	M. C. (Mack. Div.)		T. 37 N., R. 2 W.	Cheboygan	60	52
Mentor, P. O	M. C. R. R. (Mack. Div.)	Indian River, 5 m	T. 34 N., R. 3 W.	Cheboygan		52
Mullet City	M. C. R. R. (Mack. Div.)	Indian River, 3 m	T. 35 N., R. 2 W.	Cheboygan		52
Mackinaw City, P. O. and R. R. and Tel. Sta	G. R. & I. & M. C. R. R		T. 39 N., R. 4 W.	Cheboygan	400	52
Manistique R. R. Sta	Det. M. & M. R. R		T. 46 N., R. 19 W.	Schoolcraft		121
Munising	Lake Superior	South Bay	T. 47 N., R. 18 W.	Schoolcraft	600	121
Manistique, P. O	Lake Michigan		T. 41 N., R. 15 W.	Schoolcraft	000	128
Maple City, P. O	G. R. & I. R. R. (T. C. Br.)	Traverse City, 16 m	T. 28 N., R. 12 W.	Leelanaw	50	58
Mount Bliss, P. O	G. R. & I. R. R	Elmira, 15 m	T. 34 N., R. 6 W.	Antrim	50	57
Mancelona, P. O. and R. R. and Tel. Sta	G. R. & I. R. R		T. 29 N., R. 6 W.	Antrim	500	57

☞ Names marked with a star (*) will not be found on the Maps.

LIST OF CITIES, TOWNS, ETC.

NAME OF VILLAGE.	RAILROAD, LAKE, OR RIVER.	Nearest Sta. or Landing.	TOWNSHIP.	COUNTY.	Pop.	Page
Middle Village, (See Good Hart P. O.)						
Mitchell's, R. R. Sta	G. R. & I. R. R.		T. 17 N., R. 10 W.	Osceola		72
Mellens, P. O.	M. C. R. R.	Bagley, 1 m	T. 30 N., R. 3 W.	Otsego		56
Milburn, P. O.	G. R. & I. R. R.	Tustin, 18 m	T. 20 N., R. 8 W.	Osceola		72
Marion, P. O.	G. R. & I. R. R.	Tustin, 21 m	T. 20 N., R. 7 W.	Osceola	500	72
Mark, P. O.	F. & P. M. R. R.	Farwell, 17 m	T. 19 N., R. 5 W.	Clare		73
Melrose, R. R. Sta	G. R. & I. R. R.		T. 33 N., R. 5 W.	Charlevoix		57
Mitchell, P. O.	G. R. & I. R. R., Lake Michigan	Boyne Falls, 25 m	T. 32 N., R. 8 W.	Charlevoix		57
Menominee, P. O. and R. R. and Tel. Sta	Chic. & N. W. R. R.		T. 31 N., R. 27 W.	Menominee	4,000	124
Marquette, P. O. and R. R. and Tel. Sta	M. H. & O., Det. M. & M., Lake Superior		T. 48 N., R. 25 W.	Marquette	5,500	119
Morgan, R. R. Sta	M. H. & O. R. R.		T. 48 N., R. 28 W.	Marquette	300	119
Marble, P. O.	F. & P. M. R. R.	Scottville, 5 m	T. 17 N., R. 16 W.	Mason		70
Meauwataka, P. O.	G. R. & I. R. R.	Boon's Mills, 8 m	T. 23 N., R. 9 W.	Wexford		69
Manton, P. O. and R. R. and Tel. Sta	G. R. & I. R. R.		T. 23 N., R. 9 W.	Wexford	400	69
Moorestown, P. O.	G. R. & I. R. R.	Fife Lake, 20 m	T. 24 N., R. 6 W.	Missaukee		68
Missaukee, R. R. Sta	G. R. & I. R. R.	Cadillac, 10 m	T. 22 N., R. 8 W.	Missaukee		68
Mount Pleasant, P. O. and R. R. and Tel. Sta	F. & P. M. R. R. (Mt. P. Div.)		T. 14 N., R. 4 W.	Isabella	1,500	77
Metropolitan, P. O.	Escanaba & Lake Superior R. R.		T. 42 N., R. 28 W.	Marquette	500	119
Midland, P. O. and R. R. and Tel. Sta	F. & P. M. R. R.		T. 14 N., R. 2 E.	Midland	2,000	76
Moffat, P. O.	G. R. & I. (T. C. Br.)	Traverse City, 6 m	T. 27 N., R. 11 W.	Gr. Traverse		60
Monroe Center, P. O.	G. R. & I. R. R. (T. C. Br.)	Traverse City, 12 m	T. 26 N., R. 12 W.	Gr. Traverse	200	60
Mayfield, P. O. and R. R. Sta	G. R. & I. R. R. (T. C. Br.)		T. 26 N., R. 10 W.	Gr. Traverse	100	60
Marilla, P. O.	F. & P. M. R. R. (Man. Div.)	Manistee, 28 m	T. 23 N., R. 13 W.	Manistee		50
Manistee, P. O. and R. R. and Tel. Sta	F. & P. M. R. R. (Man. Div.)		T. 21 N., R. 16 W.	Manistee	9,000	50
Mapleton, P. O.	G. R. & I. R. R. (T. C. Br.)	Traverse City, 10 m	T. 29 N., R. 10 W.	Gr. Traverse	150	60
Marshville, P. O.	Chic. & W. Mich. R. R.	New Era, 5 m	T. 14 N., R. 18 W.	Oceana	125	80
Muskegon, **P. O.** (Ldg.) and R. R. and Tel. Sta	Chic. & W. Mich., Muskegon Lake		T. 10 N., R. 16 W.	Muskegon	15,000	81
Moss Lake, R. R. and Tel. Sta	Chic. & W. Mich. R. R.		T. 9 N., R. 16 W.	Muskegon		81
Moon, P. O. and R. R. Sta	Chic. & W. Mich. R. R.		T. 10 N., R. 13 W.	Muskegon	100	81
Mears, P. O. and R. R. and Tel. Sta	Chic. & W. Mich. R. R.		T. 15 N., R. 18 W.	Oceana	300	80
Maple Valley, P. O. and R. R. and Tel. Sta	Det. L. & N. R. R.		T. 11 N., R. 9 W.	Montcalm	250	82
Maple Hill, P. O. and R. R. Sta	G. R. & I. R. R.		T. 11 N., R. 10 W.	Montcalm	100	82
Montague, **P. O.** and R. R. and Tel. Sta	Chic. & W. Mich. R. R.		T. 12 N., R. 17 W.	Muskegon	2,000	81
McBride, P. O. and R. R. and Tel. Sta	Det. L. & N. (Sag. Div.)		T. 11 N., R. 6 W.	Montcalm	300	82
May, **P. O.** and R. R. Sta	P. H. & N. W. R. R.		T. 11 N., R. 9 E.	Tuscola	400	85
Millington, **P. O.** and R. R. and Tel. Sta	M. C. (B. C. Div.)		T. 10 N., R. 8 E.	Tuscola	550	85
Merrill, P. O. and R. R. and Tel. Sta	Sag. Val. & St. L. R. R.	Oakley, 10 m	T. 12 N., R. 1 E.	Saginaw	150	84
Maple Grove	M. C. (Sag. Div.)		T. 9 N., R. 4 E.	Saginaw	45	84
Metamora, **P. O.** and R. R. and Tel. Sta	M. C. (B. C. Div.)		T. 6 N., R. 10 E.	Lapeer	250	89
Millville, R. R. Sta	M. C. (B. C. Div.)		T. 8 N., R. 9 E.	Lapeer	30	89
Marine City, **P. O.** and Tel. Sta	M. C. (Mich. & Midland Div.) St. Clair River	St. Clair, 8 m	T. 3 N., R. 17 E.	St. Clair	2,000	88
Marathon	M. C. (B. C. Div.)	Columbiaville, 1 m	T. 9 N., R. 9 E.	Lapeer		89
Mount Pleasant	Det. Gr. H. & Mil. R. R.	Fentonville, 4 m	T. 5 N., R. 6 E.	Genesee		90
Minden City, **P. O.** and R. R. and Tel. Sta	P. H. & N. W. R. R.		T. 14 N., R. 14 E.	Sanilac	500	87
Marlette, P. O. and R. R. Sta	P. H. & N. W. R. R.		T. 10 N., R. 12 E.	Sanilac	800	87
Montrose, P. O.	F. & P. M. R. R.	Clio, 7 m	T. 9 N., R. 5 E.	Genesee	60	90
Mount Morris, **P. O.** and R. R. and Tel. Sta	F. & P. M. R. R.		T. 8 N., R. 7 E.	Genesee	500	90
Mundy, P. O.	Det. Gr. H. & Mil. R. R.	North Linden, 4 m	T. 6 N., R. 6 E.	Genesee	40	90
Melvin, P. O.	P. H. & N. W. R. R.	Yorks, 3 m	T. 9 N., R. 14 E.	Sanilac	125	87
Merrillsville	P. H. & N. W. R. R.	Brockway Centre, 2 m	T. 8 N., R. 14 E.	St. Clair		88
Mystic	P. H. & N. W. R. R.	Jeddo, 1½ m	T. 8 N., R. 16 E.	St. Clair		88
Memphis, P. O. and R. R. and Tel. Sta	P. H. & N. W. R. R.		T. 6 N., R. 14 E.	Macomb	700	89
Marysville, P. O. and Tel. Sta	St. Clair River	Port Huron, 4 m	T. 6 N., R. 17 E.	St. Clair	270	88
Middleville, **P. O.** and R. R. and Tel. Sta	M. C. R. R. (Gr. R. Div.)		T. 4 N., R. 10 W.	Barry	720	97
Morgan, P. O. and R. R. Sta	M. C. R. R. (Gr. R. Div.)		T. 2 N., R. 7 W.	Barry	150	97
Milo	Gr. R. & I. R. R.	Plainwell, 11 m	T. 1 N., R. 10 W.	Barry		97
Marshfield, P. O. and R. R. and Tel. Sta	Det. Lan. & Nor. R. R.		T. 15 N., R. 9 W.	Mecosta		78
Morley, **P. O.** and R. R. and Tel. Sta	Gr. R. & I. R. R.		T. 13 N., R. 10 W.	Mecosta	400	78
Mecosta, P. O. and R. R. and Tel. Sta	Det. Lan. & Nor. R. R.		T. 14 N., R. 8 W.	Mecosta	500	78
Millbrook, **P. O.** and R. R. and Tel. Sta	Det. Lan. & Nor. R. R.		T. 15 N., R. 7 W.	Mecosta	300	78
Mount Pleasant, **P. O.** and R. R. and Tel. Sta	Sag. & Mt. Pleasant R. R.		T. 14 N., R. 4 W.	Isabella	1,115	77
Midland, **P. O.** and R. R. Sta	F. & P. M. R. R.		T. 14 N., R. 2 E.	Midland	1,300	76
Mosherville, P. O. and Tel. Sta	L. S. & M. S. (Ft. Wayne Br.)	Scipio, 1 m	T. 5 S., R. 3 W.	Hillsdale	100	113
Moscow, P. O. and R. R. Sta	L. S. & M. S. R. R.	Jerome, 3 m	T. 5 S., R. 2 W.	Hillsdale	400	113
Montgomery, P. O. and R. R. and Tel. Sta	L. S. & M. S. (Ft. Wayne Br.)		T. 8 S., R. 4 W.	Hillsdale	275	113
Morenci, **P. O.** and R. R. and Tel. Sta	L. S. & M. S. (Fayette Br.)		T. 8 S., R. 2 E.	Lenawee	1,400	114
Medina, P. O.	L. S. & M. S. R. R.	Clayton, 5 m	T. 8 S., R. 1 E.	Lenawee	220	114
Munson, P. O. (North Fayette Sta.)	Wab. St. L. & Pac. R. R.		T. 8 S., R. 1 E.	Lenawee	30	114
Mottville, P. O.	L. S. & M. S. R. R.	White Pigeon, 5 m	T. 8 S., R. 12 W.	St. Joseph	150	111
Macon, P. O.	L. S. & M. S. (Jackson Br.)	Tecumseh, 7 m	T. 5 S., R. 5 E.	Lenawee	200	114
Moorepark, P. O. and R. R. Sta	L. S. & M. S. R. R.		T. 5 S., R. 11 W.	St. Joseph	100	111
Mendon, **P. O.** and R. R. and Tel. Sta	Gr. R. & I. R. R.		T. 5 S., R. 10 W.	St. Joseph	1,000	111
Milford, **P. O.** and R. R. and Tel. Sta	F. & P. M. R. R.		T. 2 N., R. 7 E.	Oakland	1,600	101
Mahopac	Det. Gr. H. & Mil. R. R.	Pontiac, 7 m	T. 4 N., R. 10 E.	Oakland		101
Maple Rapids, **P. O.**	Det. Gr. H. & Mil. R. R.	Lyons Mills, 10 m	T. 8 N., R. 3 W.	Clinton	800	92
Mill Creek, P. O. and R. R. Sta	Gr. R. & I. R. R.		T. 8 N., R. 11 W.	Kent	51	94
Manchester, **P. O.** and R. R. and Tel. Sta	L. S. & M. S. (Jackson Br.)		T. 4 S., R. 3 E.	Washtenaw	1,500	104
*Milan, P. O. and Tel. Sta				Washtenaw	700	104
Munith, P. O.	M. C. R. R.	Grass Lake, 10 m	T. 1 S., R. 2 E.	Jackson		105
Michigan Centre, P. O. and R. R. Sta	M. C. R. R.		T. 3 S., R. 1 E.	Jackson		105
Martinsville, P. O.	F. & P. M. R. R.	New Boston, 4 m	T. 4 S., R. 8 E.	Wayne	150	103
Meads' Mills, P. O. and R. R. Sta	F. & P. M. R. R.		T. 1 S., R. 8 E.	Wayne	200	103
McKinstry's, R. R. Sta	Det. Lan. & Nor. R. R.		T. 1 S., R. 9 E.	Wayne		103
Madison, R. R. Sta	Chic. & Gr. T. R. R.		T. 1 S., R. 7 W.	Calhoun		106
Marengo, P. O. and R. R. and Tel. Sta	M. C. R. R.		T. 2 S., R. 5 W.	Calhoun	150	106
Marshall, P. O. and R. R. and Tel. Sta	M. C. R. R., Mich. & Ohio		T. 2 S., R. 6 W.	Calhoun	7,000	106
Mattison Centre	M. C. R. R. (Air Line Div.)	Sherwood, 4 m	T. 6 S., R. 8 W.	Branch		112
Mattison, P. O.	L. S. & M. S. R. R.	Bronson, 4 m	T. 6 S., R. 8 W.	Branch	50	112
Madison, P. O.	Det. Lan. & Nor. R. R.	Howell, 12 m	T. 4 N., R. 5 E.	Livingston	100	100
Meade, P. O.	Gr. T. R. R.	New Haven, 5 m	T. 3 N., R. 14 E.	Macomb	200	102
Macomb, P. O.	Gr. T. R. R. (Mich. Air Line Div.)	Washington, 6 m	T. 3 N., R. 13 E.	Macomb	150	102
Marosline	Gr. T. R. R.	Mt. Clemens, 1 m	T. 2 N., R. 13 E.	Macomb		102
Monroe, Junc. R. R. Sta	Tol. A. Arbor & Gr. T., L. S. & M. S.		T. 7 S., R. 7 E.	Monroe		115
Mt. Clemens, P. O. and R. R. and Tel. Sta	Gr. T. R. R.		T. 2 N., R. 13 E.	Macomb	3,000	102
Milton, P. O.	G. T. R. R.	Chesterfield, 3 m	T. 3 N., R. 14 E.	Macomb	200	102
Memphis, **P. O.** and R. R. and Tel. Sta	P. H. & N. W. (Almont Div.)		T. 5 N., R. 14 E.	Macomb	580	102
Mt. Vernon, P. O.	Gr. T. R. R. (Mich. Air Line Div.)	Washington, 4 m	T. 4 N., R. 12 E.	Macomb	125	102
Meridian, P. O.	Det. Lan. & Nor. R. R.	Meridian Sta., 2 m	T. 4 N., R. 1 W.	Ingham		99
Meridian, R. R. and Tel. Sta	Det. Lan. & Nor. R. R.		T. 4 N., R. 1 W.	Ingham	350	99
Mason, P. O. and R. R. and Tel. Sta	M. C. R. R. (Sag. Div.)		T. 2 N., R. 1 W.	Ingham	2,000	99
McDonald, P. O. (Deerfield R. R. Sta.)	Chic. & W. Mich. R. R.		T. 2 S., R. 16 W.	Van Buren	45	108
Mattawan, **P. O.** and R. R. and Tel. Sta	M. C. R. R.		T. 3 S., R. 13 W.	Van Buren	350	108

☞ Names marked with a star (*) will not be found on the Maps

NAME OF VILLAGE.	RAILROAD, LAKE, OR RIVER.	Nearest Sta. or Landing	TOWNSHIP.	COUNTY.	Pop.	Page
Morris, R. R. Sta	Chic. & W. Mich. R. R.		T. 6 S., R. 19 W.	Berrien		109
Millburg, P. O.	Chic. & W. Mich., Cin. Wab. & Mich	Benton Harbor, 6 m.	T. 4 S., R. 18 W.	Berrien	60	109
Marcellus, P. O. and R. R. and Tel. Sta	Chic. & Gr. T. R. R.		T. 5 S., R. 13 W.	Cass	700	110
Milletts, P. O. and R. R. Sta	Chic. & Gr. T. R. R		T. 4 N., R. 3 W.	Eaton	200	98
Manlius, R. R. Sta	Chic. & W. Mich. R. R.		T. 3 N., R. 15 W.	Allegan		90
Mill Grove, P. O. and R. R. Sta	Chic. & W. Mich. R. R.		T. 2 N., R. 14 W.	Allegan	200	90
May, R. R. Sta	Chic. & W. Mich. R. R.		T. 4 N., R. 15 W.	Allegan		90
Monterey, P. O	Chic. & W. Mich. R. R	Allegan, 7 m	T. 3 N., R. 13 W.	Allegan	200	95
Moline, P. O. and R. R. Sta	Gr. R. & I. R. R		T. 4 N., R. 12 W.	Allegan	200	90
Martin, P. O. and R. R. and Tel. Sta	Gr. R. & I. R. R		T. 2 N., R. 11 W.	Allegan	200	96
Monteith, P. O. and R. R. and Tel. Sta	Gr. R. & I. R. R., M. & O. R. R		T. 2 N., R. 11 W.	Allegan		96
Maple Grove, P. O. and Tel. Sta	M. C. (Gr. R. Div.)	Nashville, 6 m.	T. 2 N., R. 7 W.	Barry	50	97
Morrice, P. O. and R. R. and Tel. Sta	Chic. & Gr. T. R. R.		T. 5 N., R. 2 E.	Shiawassee	300	91
Maple, P. O	Det. Lan. & Nor. R. R	Portland, 5 m	T. 6 N., R. 5 W.	Ionia		93
Miriam, P. O				Ionia		93
Monroe, P. O. and R. R. and Tel. Sta	L. S. & M. S. (Det. Div.) Can. So. (Toledo Div.)		T. 7 S., R. 9 E.	Monroe	6,000	115
Matherton, P. O.	Det. Gr. H. & Mil. R. R.	Pewamo, 5 m	T. 8 N., R. 5 W.	Ionia	350	93
Muir, **P. O.** and R. R. and Tel. Sta.	Det. Gr. H. & Mil. R. R.		T. 7 N., R. 5 W.	Ionia	600	93
Maybee, P. O. and R. R. and Tel. Sta	L. S. & M. S. (Dundee Br.)		T. 5 S., R. 8 E.	Monroe	300	115
Moran, R. R. Sta	Det. Mack. & Mar. R. R		T. 42 N., R. 4 W.	Mackinac		122
Mackinac, **P. O.** and Tel. Sta	Straits of Mackinac	Mackinac City, 9 m	T. 40 N., R. 2 W.	Mackinac	750	122
Melita, P. O	M. C. R. R. (M. Div.)	Dunham, 4 m	T. 20 N., R. 4 E.	Arenac	150	75
Maple Ridge, P. O.	M. C. R. R. (M. Div.)	Dunham, 11 m	T. 20 N., R. 4 E.	Arenac	100	75
Mansfield, R. R. Sta	Sag. Bay & N. W. R. R		T. 17 N., R. 3 E.	Bay		75
Mt. Forest, R. R. Sta	Sag. Bay & N. W. R. R		T. 17 N., R. 3 E.	Bay		75
Michie, P. O. and R. R. Sta	M. C. R. R. (M. Div.)		T. 18 N., R. 4 E.	Bay	60	75
Munger, P. O. and R. R. Sta	M. C. R. R. (B. C. Div.)		T. 13 N., R. 6 E.	Bay	40	75
*Macon, R. R. Sta	To. A. Arbor & Gr. T. R. R			Monroe		115
*Main St. R. R. Sta	M. C. R. R. (S. B. Div.)		T. 7 S., R. 17 W.	Berrien		109
*Marion	Det. Lan. & Nor. R. R	Howell, 8 m	T. 2 N., R. 4 E.	Livingston		100
*Maple Range	Chic. & W. Mich. R. R.	Hart, 14 m	T. 14 N., R. 16 W.	Oceana		80
*Maplewood		Petoskey, 4 m	T. 35 N., R. 5 W.	Emmet		51
*Martiney		Big Rapids, 18 m	T. 15 N., R. 8 W.	Mecosta		78
*Meadville			T. 2 N., R. 1 E.	Ingham		99
*Meadville, R. R. Sta	M. C. R. R. (Gr. R. Div.)		T. 3 N., R. 7 W.	Barry		97
Methodist Mission	Keweenaw Bay	L'Anse, 4 m	T. 51 N., R. 33 W.	Baraga		117
*Micham	Grand Traverse Bay		R. 11 W.	Leelanaw		58
*Middleton			T. 2 N., R. 2 E.	Ingham		99
*Mill Creek				Muskegon		81
*Mineral Branch	Chic. & N. W.			Marquette		119
*Mineral Spring		Sand Lake, 7 m	T. 11 N., R. 11 W.	Newaygo		79
*Moore's	Chic. & Gr. T. R. R		T. 1 N.	Eaton		98
*Morganville			T. 8 S., R. 3 W.	Hillsdale		113
*Mossville		Petoskey, 9 m	T. 34 N., R. 4 W.	Emmet		51
*Mullison	Saginaw Bay		T. 20 N., R. 7 E.	Arenac		75
Mungerville (Burton P. O.)	Det. Gr. H. & Mil. R. R.	Owosso, 5 m	T. 7 N., R. 1 E.	Shiawassee		91
Newberry, P. O. and R. R. Sta	Det. M. & M. R. R		T. 46 N., R. 10 W.	Chippewa	1,000	122
Norway, **P. O.** and R. R. and Tel. Sta	Men. R. R. R.		T. 39 N., R. 29 W.	Menominee	2,000	124
Nahma, P. O.	Chic. & N. W. R. R	Brampton, 19 m	T. 40 N., R. 19 W.	Delta		120
Nonesuch, P. O	Lake Superior	Silver City, 5 m	T. 50 N., R. 43 W.	Ontonagon	400	115
Northport, **P. O.** and Tel. Sta	G. R. & I. R. R. (T. C. Br.)	Traverse City, 30 m	T. 31 N., R. 11 W.	Leelanaw	400	58
North Unity, P. O.	G. R. & I. R. R. (T. C. Br.)	Traverse City, 27 m	T. 29 N., R. 13 W.	Leelanaw		58
Norrisville, P. O	G. R. & I. R. R. (T. C. Br.)	Traverse City, 2 m	T. 28 N., R. 11 W.	Leelanaw		58
Norwood, P. O., Ldg., and Tel. Sta	G. R. & I. R. R	Petoskey, 32 m	T. 33 N., R. 9 W.	Charlevoix	200	57
Nadeau, P. O. and R. R. Sta	Chic. & N. W. R. R.		T. 37 N., R. 25 W.	Menominee	180	124
Negaunee, **P. O.** and R. R. and Tel. Sta	M. M. & O. R. R		T. 47 N., R. 26 W.	Marquette	5,000	119
Norwich, P. O	G. R. & I. R. R	Fife Lake, 14 m	T. 24 N., R. 6 W.	Missaukee	35	68
Nipposing	F. & P. M. R. R	Longwood, 4 m	T. 13 N., R. 4 W.	Isabella		77
Nana-i-mo	Men. R. R. R. (Iron River Br.)	Iron River, 1½ m	T. 43 N., R. 35 W.	Marquette		119
National Mine, P. O	M. H. & O. R. R	Negaunee, 4 m	T. 47 N., R. 27 W.	Marquette	600	118
North Bradley, R. R. and Tel. Sta	F. & P. M. R. R.		T. 15 N., R. 2 W.	Midland	200	78
New Era, P. O. and R. R. and Tel. Sta	Chic. & W. Mich. R. R		T. 14 N., R. 17 W.	Oceana	125	80
North Muskegon	Chic. & W. Mich. R. R	Muskegon, 4 m	T. 10 N., R. 16 W.	Muskegon	2,000	81
Newaygo, P. O. and R. R. and Tel. Sta	Chic. & W. Mich. (N. Div.)		T. 12 N., R. 12 W.	Newaygo	1,200	79
Novesta, P. O.	P. O. & P. A. R. R	Cass City, 9 m	T. 13 N., R. 11 E.	Tuscola		85
New Haven Centre, P. O.	C. S. & C. R. R.	Seville, 10 m	T. 10 N., R. 4 W.	Gratiot		88
Newark, P. O	C. S. & C. R. R	Ithaca, 7 m	T. 10 N., R. 3 W.	Gratiot	50	88
North Star, P. O	S. Val. & St. L. R. R	St. Louis, 12 m	T. 10 N., R. 2 W.	Gratiot		88
North Burns, P. O.	P. H. & N. W. R. R	Bad Axe, 8 m	T. 15 N., R. 13 E.	Huron		86
North Branch, P. O. and R. R. Sta	P. O. & P. A. R. R		T. 9 N., R. 11 E.	Lapeer	700	89
North Linden, R. R. Sta	Det. Gr. H. & Mil. R. R		T. 5 N., R. 6 E.	Genesee		90
North Street, R. R. Sta	P. H. & N. W. R. R		T. 7 N., R. 16 E.	St. Clair		88
North Irving, P. O	M. C. R. R. (Gr. R. Div.)	Irving, 3 m	T. 4 N., R. 9 W.	Barry		97
Nashville, P. O. and R. R. and Tel. Sta	M. C. R. R. (Gr. R. Div.)		T. 3 N., R. 7 W.	Barry	1,200	97
North Adams, **P. O.** and R. R. and Tel. Sta	L. S. & M. S. (Ypsilanti Br.)		T. 6 S., R. 2 W.	Hillsdale	425	113
North Morenci, P. O. and R. R. Sta	Wab. St. L. & Pac. R. R		T. 8 S., R. 2 E.	Lenawee		114
North Fayette, (Morenci P. O.) R. R. Sta	Wab. St. L. & Pac. R. R.		T. 8 S., R. 1 E.	Lenawee		114
Nottawa, P. O. and R. R. and Tel. Sta	Gr. R. & I. R. R		T. 6 S., R. 10 W.	St. Joseph	100	111
Newburg	L. S. & M. S. (Jackson Br.)	Tecumseh, 4 m	T. 5 S., R. 4 E.	Lenawee		114
New Hudson, P. O. and R. R. Sta	Gr. T. R. R. (Air Line Div.)	South Lyon, 5 m	T. 1 N., R. 7 E.	Oakland	250	101
North Farmington, P. O	Det. Gr. H. & Mil. R. R	Birmingham, 6 m	T. 1 N., R. 9 E.	Oakland	51	101
Novi, P. O. and R. R. and Tel. Sta	F. & P. M. R. R		T. 1 N., R. 8 E.	Oakland	250	101
North Byron, R. R. Sta	L. S. & M. S. (Kal. Div.)		T. 5 N., R. 12 W.	Kent		94
Newcomb, P. O. and R. R. Sta	Wab. St. L. & Pac. R. R		T. 4 S., R. 7 E.	Washtenaw		104
Nora, P. O. and R. R. Sta	To. A. Arbor & Gr. T. R. R.		T. 4 S., R. 6 E.	Washtenaw	35	104
Norvell, **P. O.** and R. R. and Tel. Sta	L. S. & M. S. (Jackson Br.)		T. 4 S., R. 3 E.	Jackson	150	105
Napoleon, **P. O.** and R. R. and Tel. Sta	L. S. & M. S. (Jackson Br.)		T. 3 S., R. 1 E.	Jackson	450	105
North Concord, R. R. Sta	M. C. R. R		T. 3 S., R. 3 W.	Jackson		105
Nankin, P. O	Det. Lan. & Nor. R. R	Livonia, 2 m	T. 1 S., R. 9 E.	Wayne	100	103
New Boston, P. O. and R. R. and Tel. Sta	F. & P. M. R. R		T. 4 S., R. 9 E.	Wayne	300	103
Northville, **P. O.** and R. R. and Tel. Sta	F. & P. M. R. R		T. 1 S., R. 8 E.	Wayne	1,000	103
Norris, P. O. and R. R. and Tel. Sta	M. C. R. R. (B. C. Div.)		T. 1 S., R. 12 E.	Wayne	200	103
North Batavia, P. O	L. S. & M. S. R. R	Branch, 7 m	T. 6 S., R. 7 W.	Branch	125	112
Noble Centre, P. O	L. S. & M. S. R. R	Bronson, 8 m	T. 8 S., R. 8 W.	Branch	20	112
New Haven, P. O. and R. R. and Tel. Sta	Gr. T. R. R		T. 4 N., R. 14 E.	Macomb	325	102
New Liverpool	Gr. T. R. R., Lake St. Clair	Mt. Clemens, 5 m	T. 2 N., R. 14 E.	Macomb		102
New Baltimore, **P. O.** and Tel. Sta	Gr. T. R. R	Chesterfield, 6 m	T. 3 N., R. 14 E.	Macomb	1,300	102
North Aurelius	M. C. R. R. (Sag. Div.)	Mason, 4 m	T. 2 N., R. 2 W.	Ingham		99
North Leslie	M. C. R. R. (Sag. Div.)	Leslie, 2 m	T. 1 N., R. 1 W.	Ingham		99
North Lansing, P. O. and R. R. and Tel. Sta	Det. Lan. & Nor., M. C. (Sag. Div.)		T. 4 N., R. 2 W.	Ingham		99
New Buffalo, P. O. and R. R. and Tel. Sta	Chic. & W. Mich., M. C. R. R.		T. 8 S., R. 21 W.	Berrien	1,000	109
New Troy, P. O.	Chic. & W. Mich. R. R.	Troy Sta., 2½ m	T. 7 S., R. 19 W.	Berrien	300	109

☞ Names marked with a star (*) will not be found on the Maps.

LIST OF CITIES, TOWNS, ETC.

NAME OF VILLAGE.	RAILROAD, LAKE, OR RIVER.	Nearest Sta. or Landing	TOWNSHIP.	COUNTY.	Pop.	Page
Niles, P. O. and R. R. and Tel. Sta.	M. C., Cin. Wab. & Mich. R. R.		T. 7 S., R. 17 W.	Berrien	5,000	108
Nicholsville	Chic. & Gr. T. R. R.	Marcellus, 6 m	T. 5 S., R. 14 W.	Cass		110
New Holland, P. O.	Chic. & W. Mich. R. R.	Holland, 5 m	T. 5 N., R. 15 W.	Ottawa	100	95
Noordeloos, P. O.	Chic. & W. Mich. R. R.	Holland, 5 m	T. 5 N., R. 15 W.	Ottawa		95
New Groningen, P. O. and R. R. Sta.	Chic. & W. Mich. R. R. (Gr. R. Div.)		T. 5 N., R. 15 W.	Ottawa	100	95
Nunica, P. O. and R. R. and Tel. Sta.	Det. Gr. H. & Mil. R. R.		T. 8 N., R. 15 W.	Ottawa	400	95
Newburg	Det. Gr. H. & Mil. R. R.	Coopersville, 3 m	T. 7 N., R. 14 W.	Ottawa		95
Newcomb, P. O. and R. R. and Tel. Sta.	Wab. St. L. & Pac. R. R.		T. 4 S., R. 7 E.	Washtenaw		104
North Holland, R. R. Sta.	Chic. & W. Mich. R. R.		T. 6 N., R. 15 W.	Ottawa	1,500	95
New Richmond, P. O. and R. R. and Tel. Sta.	Chic. & W. Mich. R. R.		T. 3 N., R. 15 W.	Allegan	50	96
Nash's Mill	Chic. & W. Mich. R. R.	Pearl, 2 m	T. 2 N., R. 15 W.	Allegan		96
North Dorr, P. O.	L. S. & M. S. R. R. (Kal. Div.)	Dorr, 5 m	T. 4 N., R. 12 W.	Allegan		96
New Salem, P. O.	L. S. & M. S. R. R. (Kal. Div.)	Dorr, 6 m	T. 4 N., R. 13 W.	Allegan	25	96
New Lothrop, P. O.	M. C. R. R. (Sag. Div.)	Henderson, 12 m	T. 8 N., R. 4 E.	Shiawassee	300	91
North Newburg, P. O.	Det. Gr. H. & Mil. R. R.	Durand, 4 m	T. 6 N., R. 3 E.	Shiawassee	200	91
Newport, P. O.		Newport Sta., 2 m	T. 5 S., R. 10 E.	Monroe	450	115
Newport, R. R. and Tel. Sta.	L. S. & M. S. (Det. Div.) Can. So. (To. Div.)		T. 5 S., R. 10 E.	Monroe	450	115
North Raisinville	L. S. & M. S. (Det. Div.)	Monroe, 8 m	T. 6 S., R. 8 E.	Monroe		116
Nortonville		Grand Haven, 3 m	T. 8 N., R. 16 W.	Ottawa		95
Naubinway, P. O., Ldg.	Lake Mich. Det. Mack. & Mar. R. R.	St. Ignace, 35 m	T. 43 N., R. 9 W.	Mackinac		122
*Nelson			T. 40 N., R. 10 W.	Chippewa		123
*Newberry, P. O. and R. R. Sta.	Det. Mack. & Mar. R. R.			Wayne		103
New	Lake Huron		T. 19 N., R. 14 E.	Huron		80
New York Mine		Ishpeming, 1 m	T. 47 N., R. 27 W.	Marquette		119
Nirvana P. O. and R. R. and Tel. Sta.	F. & P. M. R. R.		T. 18 N., R. 12 W.	Lake	300	71
Norwalk	F. & P. M. R. R.	Manistee, 11 m	T. 23 N., R. 15 W.	Manistee	50	50
Newberry, R. R. Sta. (Kingston P. O.)	P. O. & P. A. R. R.		T. 12 N., R. 11 E.	Tuscola		85
New London	Lake Huron	Port Sanilac, 2 m	T. 11 N., R. 16 E.	Sanilac		87
Oscoda, P. O. and Tel. Sta.	Au Sable River	Tawas City, 15 m	T. 23 N., R. 9 E.	Iosco	3,500	65
Ogontz, P. O.	Chic. & N. W. R. R.	Brampton, 17 m	T. 40 N., R. 20 W.	Delta		120
Opechee, P. O. and R. R. Sta.	Mineral Range R. R.		T. 56 N., R. 33 W.	Houghton	1,100	117
Osceola, R. R. Sta.	Mineral Range R. R.		T. 56 N., R. 33 W.	Houghton		117
Oden, P. O. and R. R. Sta.	Gr. R. I. & Mack. R. R.		T. 35 N., R. 4 W.	Emmet		51
Ossineke, P. O. and Tel. Sta.	Lake Huron	Alpena Ldg., 12 m	T. 30 N., R. 8 E.	Alpena	100	34
Ontonagon, P. O. and Tel. Sta.	Lake Superior		T. 52 N., R. 40 W.	Ontonagon	1,200	116
Onota, P. O. and R. R. Sta.	Det. Mack. & Mar. R. R.		T. 47 N., R. 22 W.	Schoolcraft		121
Onomineeville	G. R. & I. R. R. (T. C. Br.)	Traverse City, 20 m	T. 31 N., R. 11 W.	Leelanaw		58
Omena, P. O.	G. R. & I. R. R. (T. C. Br.)	Traverse City, 24 m	T. 31 N., R. 11 W.	Leelanaw	200	58
Oviatt, P. O.	G. R. & I. R. R. (T. C. Br.)	Traverse City, 15 m	T. 28 N., R. 13 W.	Leelanaw		58
Otsego Lake, P. O. and R. R. and Tel. Sta.	M. C. R. R.		T. 29 N., R. 3 W.	Otsego	250	56
Orono, P. O. and R. R. Sta.	G. R. & I. R. R.		T. 18 N., R. 10 W.	Osceola	250	72
Ogemaw Springs, P. O. and R. R. and Tel. Sta.	M. C. R. R. (Mack. Div.)		T. 22 N., R. 1 E.	Ogemaw	175	60
Onekama, P. O. and Tel. Sta.	F. & P. M. R. R. (Man. Div.)	Manistee, 14 m	T. 23 N., R. 15 W.	Manistee	200	50
Old Mission, P. O.	G. R. & I. R. R. (T. C. Br.)	Traverse City, 18 m	T. 30 N., R. 10 W.	Gr. Traverse	50	60
Oakley, P. O. and R. R. and Tel. Sta.	M. C. (Sag. Div.)		T. 9 N., R. 2 E.	Saginaw	400	84
Oregon, P. O. (Carpenters) and R. R. Sta.	M. C. (Bay C. Div.)		T. 8 N., R. 9 E.	Lapeer	50	89
Otter Lake, P. O. and R. R. and Tel. Sta.	M. C., F. & P. M. R. R.		T. 9 N., R. 9 E.	Lapeer	600	89
Otisville, P. O. and R. R. and Tel. Sta.	F. & P. M. (F. R. Div.)		T. 9 N., R. 8 E.	Genesee	400	90
Otterburn, R. R. Sta.	Chic. & Gr. T. R. R.		T. 7 N., R. 6 E.	Genesee		90
Omard, P. O.	P. H. & N. W. R. R.	Yorks, 6 m	T. 10 N., R. 13 E.	Sanilac		87
Orangeville Mills, P. O.	Gr. R. & I. R. R.	Monteith, 7 m	T. 2 N., R. 10 W.	Barry	500	97
Ogden Centre, P. O.	L. S. & M. S. (Fayette Br.)	Ogden, 4 m	T. 8 S., R. 4 E.	Lenawee		114
Osseo, P. O. and R. R. and Tel. Sta.	L. S. & M. S. R. R.		T. 7 S., R. 2 W.	Hillsdale	300	113
Ogden, P. O. and R. R. Sta.	L. S. & M. S. (Fayette Br.)		T. 8 S., R. 4 E.	Lenawee	100	114
Ontario, P. O.	Wab. St. L. & Pac. R. R.	North Fayette, 3 m	T. 8 S., R. 1 E.	Lenawee		114
Oxbow, P. O.	F. & P. M. R. R.	Milford, 9 m	T. 3 N., R. 8 E.	Oakland	50	101
Orchard Lake, P. O.	Gr. T. R. R. (M. Air Line Br.)	Pontiac, 4 m	T. 2 N., R. 9 E.	Oakland	100	101
Ortonville, P. O.	M. C. R. R. (B. C. Div.)	Oxford, 11 m	T. 5 N., R. 9 E.	Oakland	350	101
Oak Hill	Det. Gr. H. & Mil. R. R.	Davisburgh, 6 m	T. 5 N., R. 9 E.	Oakland		101
Oakwood, P. O.	M. C. R. R. (B. C. Div.)	Thomas, 2 m	T. 6 N., R. 10 E.	Oakland	200	101
Oxford, P. O. and R. R. and Tel. Sta.	M. C. (B. C. Div.) P. O. & P. A.		T. 5 N., R. 10 E.	Oakland	1,200	101
Orion, P. O. and R. R. and Tel. Sta.	M. C. R. R. (B. C. Div.)		T. 4 N., R. 10 E.	Oakland	600	101
Oakland, P. O.	M. C. R. R. (B. C. Div.)	Rudds, 4 m	T. 4 N., R. 11 E.	Oakland		101
Ovid, P. O. and R. R. and Tel. Sta.	Det. Gr. H. & Mil. R. R.		T. 7 N., R. 1 W.	Clinton	1,500	92
Oakfield Centre, P. O.	Det. Lan. & Nor. R. R.	Greenville, 7 m	T. 9 N., R. 9 W.	Kent	60	94
Over's Corners (Springport P. O.), R. R. Sta.	L. S. & M. S. (Lan. Div.)		T. 1 S., R. 3 W.	Jackson		106
Otter Creek, P. O.	M. C. R. R. (Gr. R. Div.)	Onondaga, 5 m	T. 1 S., R. 3 W.	Jackson	150	105
Oak, P. O. Redford R. R. Sta.	Det. Lan. & Nor. R. R.		T. 1 S., R. 10 E.	Wayne	150	103
Oak Grove, P. O.	Det. Lan. & Nor. R. R.	Howell, 8 m	T. 4 N., R. 4 E.	Livingston	100	100
Oceola Centre, P. O.	Det. Lan. & Nor. R. R.	Howell, 7 m	T. 3 N., R. 5 E.	Livingston		100
Onondaga, P. O. and R. R. and Tel. Sta.	M. C. R. R. (Gr. R. Div.)		T. 1 N., R. 2 W.	Ingham	350	99
Okemos, P. O. and R. R. and Tel. Sta.	Det. Lan. & Nor. R. R.		T. 4 N., R. 1 W.	Ingham	375	99
Oshtemo, P. O. and R. R. and Tel. Sta.	M. C. R. R.		T. 2 S., R. 12 W.	Kalamazoo	200	107
Omania, R. R. Sta.	Chic. & W. Mich. R. R.		T. 7 N., R. 16 W.	Ottawa		95
Ottawa, P. O.	Chic. & W. Mich. R. R.	West Olive, 4 m	T. 6 N., R. 15 W.	Ottawa	300	95
Olive Centre, P. O.	Chic. & W. Mich. R. R.	West Olive, 4 m	T. 6 N., R. 15 W.	Ottawa	250	95
Olivet (Ainger P. O.), R. R. and Tel. Sta.	Chic. & Gr. T. R. R.		T. 1 N., R. 5 W.	Eaton		98
Olivet, P. O. and Tel. Sta.	Chic. & Gr. T. R. R.	Olivet Sta., 2 m	T. 1 N., R. 5 W.	Eaton	600	98
Otsego, P. O. and R. R. Sta.	L. S. & M. S. R. R. (Kal. Div.)		T. 1 N., R. 12 W.	Allegan	1,100	96
Overisel, P. O.	Chic. & W. Mich. R. R.	Fillmore, 2 m	T. 4 N., R. 14 W.	Allegan	75	96
Owosso, P. O. and R. R. and Tel. Sta.	M. C. (Sag. Div.) Det. Gr. H. & Mil.		T. 7 N., R. 2 E.	Shiawassee	3,000	91
Orange, P. O.	Det. Lan. & Nor. R. R.	Portland, 10 m	T. 6 N., R. 6 W.	Ionia	80	93
Ottawa Lake, P. O. and R. R. and Tel. Sta.	L. S. & M. S. R. R.		T. 8 S., R. 6 E.	Monroe	200	115
Otisco, P. O.	Det. Lan. & Nor. R. R.	Chadwick, 5 m	T. 8 N., R. 8 W.	Ionia	125	93
Orleans, P. O. and R. R. and Tel. Sta.	Det. Lan. & Nor. R. R.		T. 8 N., R. 7 W.	Ionia	100	93
Oakville, P. O.	L. S. & M. S. R. R. (Dundee Br.)	Maybee, 7 m	T. 5 S., R. 8 E.	Monroe	60	115
Orville, P. O., Ldg.	Lake Michigan		T. 41 N., R. 11 W.	Mackinac		122
Omer, P. O.	M. C. R. R. (M. Div.)	Standish, 8 m	T. 19 N., R. 5 E.	Arenac	125	75
*Oakfield, (Centre P. O.)	Det. Lan. & Nor. R. R.	Greenville, 5 m	T. 9 N., R. 9 W.	Kent	60	94
*Odessa, P. O.				Oscoda		63
*Odessa Centre, (See South Cass P. O.)						
*Ogemaw		Tawas City, 8 m	T. 22 N., R. 6 E.	Iosco		65
*Ontonagon Junc.	M. H. & O. R. R.		T. 47 N., R. 27 W.	Marquette		119
*Ore Siding	Chic. & N. W. R. R.	Escanaba, 1 m	T. 39 N., R. 22 W.	Delta		120
*Otia, P. O. and R. R. and Tel. Sta.	Chic. & W. M. (W. R. Br.)		T. 15 N., R. 13 W.	Newaygo		70
*Ottawa Centre			T. 9 N., R. 13 W.	Ottawa		95
*Ottawa		Grand Haven, (near)		Ottawa	25	95
Prescott, R. R. Sta.	Tawas & Bay County		T. 21 N., R. 5 E.	Iosco		65
Pickford, P. O.	St. Mary's River	Sault St. Marie, 24 m	T. 43 N., R. 1 E.	Chippewa	100	123
Prentis Bay, P. O.	Lake Huron	Sault St. Marie, 42 m	T. 42 N., R. 2 E.	Chippewa	50	123
Phoenix, P. O. and Tel. Sta.	Lake Superior	Eagle River, 2 m	T. 58 N., R. 31 W.	Keweenaw	1,000	118
Pequaming, P. O.	M. H. & O. (Keweenaw Bay)	L'Anse, 7 m	T. 51 N., R. 32 W.	Baraga		117

☞ Names marked with a star (*) will not be found on the Maps.

NAME OF VILLAGE.	RAILROAD, LAKE, OR RIVER.	Nearest Sta. or Landing	TOWNSHIP.	COUNTY.	Pop.	Page
Pellsport	M. C. R. R. (Mack. Div.)	Mullett Lake, 8 m	T. 35 N., R. 3 W.	Cheboygan		52
Posen, P. O	Lake Huron	Rogers City, 10 m	T. 33 N., R. 6 E.	Presque Isle		53
Palermo	Lake Huron	Rogers City, 16 m	T. 34 N., R. 7 E.	Presque Isle		53
Pleasant View, P. O	G. R. & I. R. R	Harbor Springs, 10 m.	T. 36 N., R. 5 W.	Emmet	50	51
*Pellston, P. O			T. 36 N., R. 5 W.	Emmet		51
Petoskey, **P. O.** and R. R. and Tel. Sta	Gr. R. & I. R. R		T. 35 N., R. 5 W.	Emmet	3,000	51
Peshawba Town	Gr. R. & I. R. R. (T. C. Br.)	Traverse City, 25 m.	T. 30 N., R. 11 W.	Leelanaw		58
Provemont, P. O	Gr. R. & I. R. R. (T. C. Br.)	Traverse City, 22 m.	T. 30 N., R. 11 W.	Leelanaw	200	58
Pleasant City	Gr. R. & I. R. R. (T. C. Br.)	Traverse City, 20 m.	T. 30 N., R. 11 W.	Leelanaw		58
Port Oneida	Lake Michigan		T. 29 N., R. 13 W.	Leelanaw		58
Parkville	Lake Huron	Alpena Ldg., 32 m.	T. 32 N., R. 4 E.	Montmorency		55
Pennes, P. O	G. R. & I. R. R	Orono, 5 m	T. 18 N., R. 9 W.	Osceola		72
Powers, P. O. and R. R. Sta	Chic. & N. W. R. R		T. 38 N., R. 25 W.	Menominee	100	124
Palmer, P. O	M. H. & O. R. R	Negaunee, 4 m	T. 47 N., R. 26 W.	Marquette	900	119
Pioneer, P. O	Gr. R. & I. R. R	Fife Lake, 10 m.	T. 24 N., R. 8 W.	Missaukee		68
Plains, R. R. Sta	Chic. & N. W. R. R		T. 46 N., R. 25 W.	Marquette		110
Pleasant Valley, P. O	Sag. Val. & St. L. R. R	St. Louis, 8 m.	T. 13 N., R. 2 W.	Midland	60	70
Porter, P. O	Sag. Val. & St. L. R. R.	St. Louis, 10 m.	T. 13 N., R. 1 W.	Midland		70
Piper, P. O.	M. C. R. R. (Mack. Div., Beaver Lake Br.)	Beaver Lake, 6 m.	T. 23 N., R. 1 E.	Ogemaw	125	66
Pierport, P. O. and Tel. Sta	F. & P. M. (Man. Div.)	Manistee, 14 m	T. 23 N., R. 16 W.	Manistee	300	59
Pere Cheney, P. O	M. C. R. R	Cheney Sta., ½ m	T. 25 N., R. 3 W.	Crawford	51	62
Platte, P. O	Gr. R. & I. R. R. (T. C. Br.)	Traverse City, 21 m.	T. 27 N., R. 14 W.	Benzie	50	59
Print, P. O	Gr. R. & I. R. R. (T. C. Br.)	Traverse City, 25 m.	T. 25 N., R. 13 W.	Benzie		59
Pentwater, **P. O.** and R. R. and Tel. Sta	Chic. & W. Mich., Lake Mich		T. 16 N., R. 18 W.	Oceana	1,200	80
Pierson, **P. O.** and R. R. and Tel. Sta	Gr. R. & I. R. R		T. 11 N., R. 10 W.	Montcalm	400	82
Point Richards, P. O.	Det. Lan. & Nor. (S. Br.)	Stanton, 6 m	T. 11 N., R. 7 W.	Montcalm		82
Pinnebog, P. O	P. H. & N. W. R. R	Filion, 3 m	T. 17 N., R. 12 E.	Huron		86
Popple	P. H. & N. W. R. R	Bad Axe, 5 m	T. 15 N., R. 12 E.	Huron		86
Parisville, P. O	P. H. & N. W. R. R	Minden City, 4 m	T. 15 N., R. 14 E.	Huron	60	86
Paines, P. O. and R. R. and Tel. Sta	M. C. (Sag. Div.)		T. 12 N., R. 4 E.	Saginaw	150	84
Pecongowink	F. & P. M. R. R	Sadlie, 4 m.	T. 10 N., R. 5 E.	Saginaw		84
Pompeii, P. O.	Det. Gr. H. & Mil. R. R	St. Johns, 15 m	T. 9 N., R. 2 W.	Gratiot	150	93
Port Austin, **P. O.** (Ldg.) and R. R. and Tel. Sta.	P. H. & N. W., Lake Huron		T. 18 N., R. 13 E.	Huron	1,000	86
Port Hope, P. O. and Tel. Sta	Lake Huron		T. 17 N., R. 15 E.	Huron	500	86
Port Crescent, P. O. and Tel. Sta	Lake Huron	Port Austin, 8 m.	T. 18 N., R. 12 E.	Huron	350	86
Pool, P.	M. C. (B. C. Div.)	Hunter's Creek, 3 m	T. 7 N., R. 11 E.	Lapeer		89
Palms, R. R. and Tel. Sta.	P. H. & N. W. R. R		T. 14 N., R. 15 E.	Sanilac		87
Peck's Mills, R. R. Sta	P. H. & N. W. R. R		T. 11 N., R. 15 E.	Sanilac		87
Pine Run, P. O. and Tel. Sta	F. & P. M. R. R	Clio, 1 m	T. 9 N., R. 6 E.	Genesee	325	90
Port Sanilac, **P. O.** and Tel. Sta	Lake Huron	Carsonville, 7 m.	T. 12 N., R. 16 E.	Sanilac	500	87
Peck, P. O	P. H. & N. W. R. R.	Croswell, 10 m.	T. 10 N., R. 14 E.	Sanilac	400	87
Port Huron, P. O. (Ldg.) and R.R. and Tel. Sta.	P. H. & N. W., Gr. T., Chic. & Gr. T.		T. 6 N., R. 17 E.	St. Clair	12,000	88
Parmalee, P. O. and R. R. Sta.	M. C. R. R. (Gr. R. Div.)		T. 4 N., R. 10 W.	Barry		97
Podunk	M. C. R. R. (Gr. R. Div.)	Hastings, 6 m.	T. 3 N., R. 9 W.	Barry		97
Prairieville, P. O	Gr. R. & I. R. R	Plainwell, 12 m	T. 1 N., R. 10 W.	Barry	250	97
Pritchardville, P. O	M. C. R. R. (Gr. R. Div.)	Hastings, 10 m.	T. 2 N., R. 8 W.	Barry	75	97
Paris, P. O. and R. R. and Tel. Sta	Gr. R. & I. R. R		T. 16 N., R. 10 W.	Mecosta	350	78
Porter, P. O	Sag. Val. & St. L. R. R.	St. Louis, 10 m.	T. 13 N., R. 1 W.	Midland	50	70
Palmyra, P. O. and R. R. Sta	L. S. & M. S. R. R		T. 7 S., R. 4 E.	Lenawee	325	114
Pittsford, P. O. and R. R. and Tel. Sta	L. S. & M. S. R. R		T. 7 S., R. 1 W.	Hillsdale	400	113
Pittsford Centre	L. S. & M. S. R. R	Pittsford, 3 m	T. 7 S., R. 1 W.	Hillsdale		113
Prattville, P. O	L. S. & M. S. R. R	Hudson, 7 m	T. 8 S., R. 1 W.	Hillsdale	250	113
Parvin, R. R. Sta	Gr. R. & I. R. R		T. 7 S., R. 10 W.	St. Joseph		111
Pontiac, P. O. and R. R. and Tel. Sta	Det. Gr. H. & Mil. R. R		T. 3 N., R. 10 E.	Oakland	5,000	101
	P. O. & P. A., Gr. T. (Air Line Br.)					
Parkville, P. O	L. S. & M. S. R. R	Moorepark, 4 m	T. 5 S., R. 11 W.	St. Joseph	160	111
Portage Lake, R. R. Sta	Gr. R. & I. R. R		T. 5 S., R. 10 W.	St. Joseph		111
Pleasant, P. O	Chic. & W. Mich. (Newaygo Div.)	Alpine, 6 m	T. 9 N., R. 12 W.	Kent		94
Park's Corners	L. S. & M. S. (Jackson Br.)	Manchester, 5 m.	T. 3 S., R. 3 E.	Washtenaw		104
Pittsfield Junction	L. S. & M. S. Gr. T., (To. & A. Arbor Div.)		T. 3 S., R. 6 E.	Washtenaw		104
Pittsfield, P. O. and Tel. Sta		Pittsfield Junc., 2 m.	T. 3 S., R. 6 E.	Washtenaw		104
Pulaski, R. R. Sta	M. C. R. R. (Air Line Div.)		T. 4 S., R. 3 W.	Jackson	51	105
Pulaski, P. O	Mich. & Ohio R. R	Hanover, 3 m	T. 4 S., R. 3 W.	Jackson	50	105
Pardee Corners	Gr. T. R. R. (To. & A. Arbor Div.)	Worden, 1 m	T. 1 S., R. 7 E.	Washtenaw		104
Parma, **P. O.** and R. R. and Tel. Sta	M. C. R. R		T. 2 S., R. 2 W.	Jackson	600	105
Plymouth, **P. O.** and R. R. and Tel. Sta	Det. Lan. & Nor., F. & P. M		T. 1 S., R. 8 E.	Wayne	1,500	103
Perrinsville, P. O	Det. Lan. & Nor. R. R	Livonia, 3 m.	T. 2 S., R. 9 E.	Wayne	200	103
Pike's Peak	Det. Lan. & Nor. R. R	Livonia, 2 m.	T. 2 S., R. 9 E.	Wayne		103
Pine Creek, P. O	Chic. & Gr. T. R. R	Climax, 10 m	T. 4 S., R. 8 W.	Calhoun	100	106
Plank Road, P. O	Det. Lan. & Nor. R. R	Beech, 3 m	T. 1 S., R. 10 E.	Wayne	300	103
Partello, P. O	Chic. & Gr. T. R. R	Olivet, 8 m	T. 1 S., R. 5 W.	Calhoun	150	106
Penfield, R. R. Sta	Chic. & Gr. T. R. R		T. 1 S., R. 7 W.	Calhoun		106
Parshallville, P. O.	Det. Gr. H. & Mil. R. R	Fentonville, 10 m.	T. 4 N., R. 6 E.	Livingston	200	100
Plainfield, P. O	Det. Lan. & Nor. R. R	Fowlerville, 14 m	T. 1 N., R. 3 E.	Livingston	500	100
Pinckney, **P. O.** and Tel. Sta	M. C. R. R	Dexter, 10 m.	T. 1 N., R. 4 E.	Livingston	500	100
Pettysville, P. O.	Det. Lan. & Nor. R. R	Brighton, 9 m.	T. 1 N., R. 5 E.	Livingston	75	100
Peters	Gr. T. R. R.	Mt. Clemens, 6 m	T. 3 N., R. 13 E.	Macomb		102
Packard, R. R. Sta	L. S. & M. S. (Lan. Div.)		T. 3 N., R. 2 W.	Ingham		99
Prospect Lake, P. O	M. C. R. R	Decatur, 7 m.	T. 3 S., R. 15 W.	Van Buren	200	108
Pine Lake, P. O. and R. R. Sta	Chic. & Gr. T. R. R		T. 4 N., R. 1 W.	Ingham	54	99
Phelpstown	Det. Lan. & Nor. R. R.	Williamstown, 2 m.	T. 3 N., R. 2 E.	Ingham		99
Pine Grove Mills, P. O. and R. R. Sta	M. C. (Kal. & S. Haven Div.)		T. 1 S., R. 13 W.	Van Buren	140	108
Pine Grove, R. R. Sta	M. C. (Kal. & S. Haven Div.)		T. 1 S., R. 13 W.	Van Buren	50	108
Paw Paw, **P. O.** and R. R. and Tel. Sta	P. & F., To. & S. Haven R. R		T. 3 S., R. 14 W.	Van Buren	2,000	108
Pipestone, P. O	Cin. Wab. & Mich. R. R	Eau Claire, 4 m	T. 5 S., R. 17 W.	Berrien	125	109
Pleasant Valley	Cin. Wab. & Mich. R. R	Eau Claire, 6 m	T. 6 S., R. 17 W.	Berrien		109
Poe's Corner	M. C. R. R. (Air Line Div.)	Jones, 2 m	T. 6 S., R. 13 W.	Cass		110
Pavilion, P. O.	Chic. & Gr. T. R. R.	Scott Sta., 2 m	T. 3 S., R. 10 W.	Kalamazoo	300	107
Pickett's Corners	M. C. R. R	Dowagiac, 6 m	T. 5 S., R. 15 W.	Cass		110
Pokagon, P. O. and R. R. and Tel. Sta	M. C. R. R		T. 6 S., R. 16 W.	Cass	200	110
Penn, P. O. and R. R. Sta	Chic. & Gr. T. R. R		T. 6 S., R. 14 W.	Cass	200	110
Portage, P. O. and R. R. Sta	L. S. & M. S. R. R		T. 3 S., R. 11 W.	Kalamazoo	100	107
Potterville, P. O. and R. R. and Tel. Sta	Chic. & Gr. T. R. R		T. 3 N., R. 4 W.	Eaton	500	98
Pearl, P. O. and R. R. Sta	Chic. & W. Mich. R. R		T. 2 N., R. 15 W.	Allegan	100	96
Pine Creek	L. S. & M. S. R. R. (Kal. Div.)	Otsego, 3 m	T. 1 N., R. 12 W.	Allegan		96
Plainwell, **P. O.** and R. R. and Tel. Sta.	Gr. R. & I., L. S. & M. S. R. R. (Kal. Div.)		T. 1 N., R. 11 W.	Allegan	1,500	96
Peach Belt, P. O	Chic. & W. Mich. R. R	Fennville, 3 m	T. 2 N., R. 16 W.	Allegan	30	96
Plummerville	Chic. & W. Mich. R. R.	Pearl, 2 m	T. 2 N., R. 15 W.	Allegan		96
Pittsburgh, P. O.	Chic. & Gr. T. R. R	Morrice, 6 m	T. 6 N., R. 2 E.	Shiawassee	200	91
Perry, **P. O.** and R. R. and Tel. Sta	Chic. & Gr. T. R. R		T. 5 N., R. 2 E.	Shiawassee	300	91
Portland, **P. O.** and R. R. and Tel. Sta	Det. Lan. & Nor. R. R		T. 6 N., R. 5 W.	Ionia	1,000	93
Petersburg, **P. O.** and R. R. and Tel. Sta	L. S. & M. S. R. R		T. 7 S., R. 6 E.	Monroe	420	115

☞ Names marked with a star (*) will not be found on the Maps.

NAME OF VILLAGE.	RAILROAD, LAKE, OR RIVER.	Nearest Sta. or Landing	TOWNSHIP.	COUNTY.	Pop.	Page
Palo, P. O.	Det. Lan. & Nor. (Stanton Br.)	Shiloh, 5 m.	T. 8 N., R. 6 W.	Ionia	400	94
Pewamo, P. O. and R. R. and Tel. Sta.	Det. Gr. H. & Mil. R. R.		T. 7 N., R. 5 W.	Ionia	350	93
Petersburg, R. R. Sta.	L. S. & M. S. (Dundee Br.)		T. 6 S., R. 6 E.	Monroe	600	115
Paradise, P. O. and R. R. Sta.	G. R. & I. (T. C. Br.)		T. 25 N., R. 10 W.	Gr. Traverse	200	60
Pine River	Sag. Bay	Standish, 5 m.	T. 18 N., R. 5 E.	Arenac	97	75
Pinconning, P. O. and R. R. and Tel. Sta.	M. C. R. R. (Mack. Div.)		T. 17 N., R. 4 E.	Bay	400	75
Palms, R. R. Sta.	Det. Mack. & Mar. R. R.		T. 43 N., R. 5 W.	Mackinac		122
*Pearson				Newaygo		79
*Partridge	Chic. & N. W. R. R.			Marquette		110
*Patterson Mills	Det. Lan. & Nor. R. R.	Kiddville, 2 m.	T. 9 N., R. 8 W.	Montcalm		82
*Penn Yan		Lapeer, 5 m.	T. 8 N.	Lapeer		89
*Perkins	Chic. & N. W. R. R.			Delta		120
*Petrieville		Eaton Rapids, 2 m.	T. 2 N., R. 3 W.	Eaton		98
*Pigeon	Lake Michigan			Ottawa		95
*Pine Hill	P. H. & N. W. R. R.	Anderson, 5 m.	T. 11 N., R. 16 E.	Sanilac	75	87
*Pine Plains				Allegan		96
*Pine Ridge	Chic. & N. W. R. R.		T. 39 N., R. 22 W.	Delta		120
*Pleasant Lake			T. 1 S., R. 1 E.	Jackson	45	105
*Pleasant Ridge	L. S. & M. S. R. R.		T. 6 S., R. 5 W.	Branch		112
*Plum Creek				Monroe		115
*Point Sable		Ludington, 7 m.	T. 19 N., R. 18 W.	Mason	375	70
*Portage Entry	Keweenaw Bay		T. 53 N., R. 33 W.	Houghton		117
*Port Sheldon	Lake Mich., Chic. & W. M.	Johnsville, 3 m.	T. 6 N., R. 16 W.	Ottawa		95
*Port Sheldon	Lake Michigan	Muskegon, 5 m.	T. 10 N., R. 16 W.	Muskegon		91
*Pottersville	P. H. & N. W. R. R.	Amadore, 6 m.	T. 9 N., R. 15 E.	Sanilac		87
*Prairie	F. & P. M. R. R.	Grafton, 3 m.	T. 5 S., R. 9 E.	Monroe		115
*Prescott, P. O.				Ogemaw		66
Portsmouth, P. O. and R. R. and Tel. Sta.	F. & P. M. R. R.	Part of Bay City		Bay	3,500	75
Paines, P. O. and R. R. Sta.	Sag. Val. & St. L., M. C. R. R.		T. 12 N., R. 4 E.	Saginaw		84
Potters, (Randall P. O.) R. R. Sta.	Sag. Val. & St. L. R. R.		T. 12 N., R. 2 E.	Saginaw		84
Pine Run, (Clio P. O.) R. R. Sta.	F. & P. M. R. R.		T. 9 N., R. 6 E.	Genesee		90
Pier Cove	Lake Michigan		T. 2 N., R. 16 W.	Allegan		96
Quinnesec, P. O. and R. R. and Tel. Sta.	Chic. & N. W. (Menominee R. R.)		T. 40 N., R. 30 W.	Menominee	1,200	124
Quincy, R. R. and Tel. Sta.	Mineral Range R. R.	Hancock, 1 m.	T. 55 N., R. 34 W.	Houghton		117
Quimby, R. R. Sta.	Gr. R. & I. R. R.		T. 21 N., R. 9 W.	Wexford		69
Quimby, R. R. Sta.	M. C. R. R. (Gr. R. Div.)		T. 3 N., R. 8 W.	Barry		97
Quaker Mills	L. S. & M. S. R. R.	Hudson, 6 m.	T. 8 S., R. 1 E.	Lenawee		114
Quick's Corners	M. C., Chic. & Gr. T. R. R.	Battle Creek, 7 m.	T. 3 S., R. 8 W.	Calhoun		100
Quincy, P. O. and R. R. and Tel. Sta.	L. S. & M. S. R. R.		T. 6 S., R. 5 W.	Branch	1,800	112
Quinn		Mt. Clemens, 3 m.	T. 2 N., R. 13 E.	Macomb	50	102
Royce, P. O.	M. C. (M. Div.)	Beaver Lake, 23 m.	T. 25 N., R. 3 E.	Oscoda	15	63
Rapids	Hay Lake		T. 45 N., R. 2 E.	Chippewa		128
Red Jacket	Mineral Range R. R.	Calumet, 2 m.	T. 56 N., R. 33 W.	Houghton	2,140	117
Riggsville, P. O.	M. C. R. R. (Mack. Div.)	Cheboygan, 9 m.	T. 37 N., R. 2 W.	Cheboygan		52
Rondo, P. O. and R. R. Sta.	M. C. R. R. (Mack. Div.)		T. 34 N., R. 3 W.	Cheboygan		52
Rogers City, P. O. Ldg., and Tel. Sta.	Lake Huron		T. 35 N., R. 5 E.	Presque Isle	500	53
Rockland, P. O. and Tel. Sta.	Lake Superior	Ontonagon, 9 m.	T. 50 N., R. 39 W.	Ontonagon	330	116
Rock River Kilns, R. R. Sta.	Det. Mack. & Mar. R. R.		T. 47 N., R. 21 W.	Schoolcraft		121
Rockery, P. O.	Gr. R. & I. R. R.	Elmira, 7 m.	T. 31 N., R. 6 W.	Antrim		57
Reed City, P. O. and R. R. and Tel. Sta.	F. & P. M. R. R., Gr. R. & I.		T. 17 N., R. 10 W.	Osceola	1,500	72
Renwick	F. & P. M. R. R.	Farwell, 6 m.	T. 17 N., R. 5 W.	Clare		79
Rock Elm, P. O.	Gr. R. & I. R. R., Lake Mich.	Boyne Falls, 17 m.	T. 32 N., R. 7 W.	Charlevoix	125	57
Riverton, P. O.	F. & P. M. R. R.	Ludington, 6 m.	T. 18 N., R. 17 W.	Mason		70
Roscommon, P. O. and R. R. and Tel. Sta.	M. C. R. R. (Mack. Div.)		T. 24 N., R. 2 W.	Roscommon	800	67
Roy, P. O.	Gr. R. & I. R. R.	Cadillac, 30 m.	T. 23 N., R. 8 W.	Missaukee		68
Round Lake, P. O.	Gr. R. & I. R. R.	Cadillac, 6 m.	T. 22 N., R. 9 W.	Wexford		69
Republic, P. O. and Tel. Sta.	M. H. & O. R. R.	Humboldt, 7 m.	T. 46 N., R. 30 W.	Marquette	2,800	110
Rowland, P. O.	Det. Lan. & Nor. R. R.	Blanchard, 6 m.	T. 13 N., R. 6 W.	Isabella	45	77
Remick, P. O. and R. R. Sta.	Det. Lan. & Nor. R. R.		T. 13 N., R. 6 W.	Isabella		77
Rapid River	Gr. R. & I. R. R.	Leetsville, 3 m.	T. 28 N., R. 7 W.	Kalkaska		61
Rothbury, P. O. and R. R. Sta.	Chic. & W. Mich. R. R.		T. 13 N., R. 17 W.	Oceana		80
Ryerson, P. O.	Chic. & W. Mich. R. R.	Muskegon, 8 m.	T. 10 N., R. 17 W.	Muskegon		91
Readsville	Chic. & W. Mich. R. R.	Muskegon, 3 m.	T. 10 N., R. 16 W.	Muskegon		91
Ravenna, P. O.	Det. Gr. H. & Mil. R. R.	Coopersville, 10 m.	T. 9 N., R. 14 W.	Muskegon	200	91
Reynolds, R. R. Sta.	Gr. R. & I. R. R.		T. 12 N., R. 10 W.	Montcalm		82
Ruth (Adams' Corners), P. O. and R. R. Sta.	P. H. & N. W. R. R.		T. 15 N., R. 15 E.	Huron	150	86
Reese, P. O. and R. R. and Tel. Sta.	M. C., S. T. & H. R. R.		T. 12 N., R. 7 E.	Tuscola	400	85
Richville, P. O. and R. R. Sta.	M. C. (B. C. Div.)		T. 13 N., R. 7 E.	Tuscola	200	85
Randall, P. O. and R. R. Sta.	Sag. Val. & St. L. R. R.		T. 12 N., R. 2 E.	Saginaw	40	84
Ring, P. O. and R. R. Sta.	Sag. Val. & St. L. R. R.		T. 12 N., R. 1 W.	Gratiot	100	83
Rock Falls	Lake Huron	Sand Beach, 7 m.	T. 16 N., R. 16 E.	Huron		86
Riverdale, P. O. and R. R. and Tel. Sta.	Chic. S. & C. R. R.		T. 12 N., R. 4 W.	Gratiot	175	83
Rattle Run, P. O.	Gr. T. R. R.	Smith's Creek, 3 m.	T. 5 N., R. 16 E.	St. Clair	100	88
Roberts Landing, P. O.	M. C. (Mack. & Mar. Div.) St. Clair River	St. Clair, 10 m.	T. 3 N., R. 16 E.	St. Clair	90	88
Rogersville, P. O. and R. R. Sta.	F. & P. M. (P. R. Div.)		T. 8 N., R. 8 E.	Genesee	100	90
Richfield, P. O.	F. & P. M. (P. R. Div.)	Rogersville, 6 m.	T. 8 N., R. 8 E.	Genesee	100	90
Rankin, P. O.	F. & P. M. R. R.	Grand Blanc, 6 m.	T. 6 N., R. 6 E.	Genesee		90
Richmondville, P. O. and Tel. Sta.	Lake Huron	Deckerville, 10 m.	T. 13 N., R. 16 E.	Sanilac	300	87
Roseburg, P. O.	P. H. & N. W. R. R.	Amadore, 7 m.	T. 9 N., R. 15 E.	Sanilac	50	87
Ruby, P. O.	P. H. & N. W. R. R.	Kingsley, 2½ m.	T. 7 N., R. 16 E.	St. Clair	300	88
Riley Centre, P. O.	Chic. & Gr. T. R. R.	Emmett, 7 m.	T. 6 N., R. 14 E.	St. Clair	150	88
Rust, R. R. Sta.	Gr. R. & I. R. R.		T. 14 N., R. 10 W.	Mecosta		78
Rustford, P. O.	Gr. R. & I. R. R.	Morley, 6 m.	T. 13 N., R. 9 W.	Mecosta	50	78
Remus, P. O. and R. R. Sta.	Det. Lan. & Nor. R. R.		T. 14 N., R. 7 W.	Mecosta	150	78
Rodney, P. O. and R. R. and Tel. Sta.	Det. Lan. & Nor. R. R.		T. 15 N., R. 9 W.	Mecosta	200	78
Rowland, P. O.	Det. Lan. & Nor. R. R.	Blanchard, 5 m.	T. 13 N., R. 6 W.	Isabella	45	77
Rollin, P. O.	L. S. & M. S. R. R.	Hudson, 5 m.	T. 6 S., R. 1 E.	Lenawee	130	114
Rome, P. O.	L. S. & M. S. R. R.	Dover, 6 m.	T. 6 S., R. 2 E.	Lenawee	250	114
Raisin Centre, P. O. and R. R. Sta.	L. S. & M. S., Wab. St. L. & Pac.		T. 6 S., R. 4 E.	Lenawee	80	114
Riga, P. O. and R. R. and Tel. Sta.	L. S. & M. S. R. R.		T. 8 S., R. 5 E.	Lenawee	200	114
Ransom, P. O.	L. S. & M. S. R. R.	Osseo, 8 m.	T. 8 S., R. 2 W.	Hillsdale	250	113
Reading, P. O. and R. R. and Tel. Sta.	L. S. & M. S. (Ft. Wayne Br.)		T. 7 S., R. 4 W.	Hillsdale	900	113
Ridgeway, P. O. and Tel. Sta.	Wab. St. L. & Pac. R. R.	Britton, 2 m.	T. 5 S., R. 5 E.	Lenawee	300	114
Rose Corners	Det. Gr. H. & Mil., F. & P. M.	Holly, 5 m.	T. 4 N., R. 7 E.	Oakland		101
Royal Oak, P. O. and R. R. and Tel. Sta.	Det. Gr. H. & Mil. R. R.		T. 1 N., R. 11 E.	Oakland	450	101
Rose, P. O. and R. R. and Tel. Sta.	F. & P. M. R. R.		T. 4 N., R. 7 E.	Oakland	80	101
Reids, R. R. Sta.	M. C. R. R. (B. C. Div.)		T. 4 N., R. 10 E.	Oakland		101
Rochester, P. O. and R. R. and Tel. Sta.	M. C. (B. C. Div.) G. T. (Air Line Br.)		T. 3 N., R. 11 E.	Oakland	1,200	101
Riley, P. O.	Det. Gr. H. & Mil. R. R.	Lyons Mills, 8 m.	T. 6 N., R. 3 W.	Clinton		92
River Bend, P. O.	Det. Lan. & Nor. R. R.	Grand Ledge, 5 m.	T. 5 N., R. 4 W.	Clinton	150	92
*Ruston, P. O.				Clinton		92
Ross, P. O. and R. R. and Tel. Sta.	Gr. R. & I. R. R.		T. 5 N., R. 12 W.	Kent	75	94

☞ Names marked with a star (*) will not be found on the Maps.

NAME OF VILLAGE.	RAILROAD, LAKE, OR RIVER.	Nearest Sta. or Landing	TOWNSHIP.	COUNTY.	Pop.	Page
Rockford, P. O. and R. R. and Tel. Sta	Gr. R. & I. R. R		T. 9 N., R. 11 W.	Kent	900	94
River Raisin, P. O. and R. R. Sta	L. S. & M. S. (Jackson Br.)		T. 4 S., R. 4 E.	Washtenaw	50	104
Rives Junction, P. O. and R. R. and Tel. Sta	M. C. R. R. (Gr. R. & Sag. Div.)		T. 1 S., R. 1 W.	Jackson	80	105
Rawsonville, P. O	Wab. St. L. & Pac. R. R	Belleville, 3 m	T. 3 S., R. 8 E.	Wayne	150	103
Romulus, P. O. and R. R. and Tel. Sta	Wab. St. L. & Pac. R. R.		T. 3 S., R. 9 E.	Wayne	100	103
Rockwood, P. O. and R. R. and Tel. Sta	Can. So. (To. Div.)		T. 5 S., R. 10 E.	Wayne	800	103
Redford, P. O	Det. Lan. & Nor. R. R	Redford Sta., 4 m	T. 1 S., R. 10 E.	Wayne	131	103
Redford (Oak P. O.), R. R. Sta	Det. Lan. & Nor. R. R		T. 1 S., R. 10 E.	Wayne	200	103
Rice Creek	M. C. R. R	Marengo, 4 m	T. 1 S., R. 5 W.	Calhoun		100
Batz	Det. Lan. & Nor. R. R	Genoa, 1 m	T. 2 N., R. 5 E.	Livingston		100
Red Run Corners (Cady P. O.)	Gr. T. R. R	Mt. Clemens, 5 m	T. 2 N., R. 13 E.	Macomb		102
Roseville, P. O	Gr. T. R. R	Fraser, 4 m	T. 1 N., R. 13 E.	Macomb	400	102
Richmond, P. O.	Gr. T. R. R	Ridgeway, 1 m	T. 5 N., R. 14 E.	Macomb	1,200	102
Ridgeway (Lenox P. O.), R. R. Sta	Chic. & Gr. T. R. R		T. 4 N., R. 14 E.	Macomb	200	102
Romeo, P. O. and R. R. and Tel. Sta	Gr. T. R. R., Mich. (Air Line Br.)		T. 4 N., R. 12 E.	Macomb	2,000	102
Ray Centre, P. O	Gr. T. R. R	New Haven, 6 m	T. 4 N., R. 13 E.	Macomb	90	102
Redfield, P. O	M. C. (Air Line Div.) Chic. & Gr. T	Cassopolis, 4 m	T. 7 S., R. 15 W.	Cass	25	110
Riverside, P. O. and R. R. and Tel. Sta	Chic. & W. Mich. R. R		T. 3 S., R. 18 W.	Berrien	25	100
Royalton, P. O	Chic. & W. Mich. R. R	Lincoln, 3 m	T. 5 S., R. 19 W.	Berrien	73	100
Richland, P. O. and R. R. and Sta	Gr. R. & I. R. R. (M. & A. Div.)		T. 1 S., R. 10 W.	Kalamazoo	230	107
Ross Centre	M. C. R. R	Augusta, 3 m	T. 1 S., R. 9 W.	Kalamazoo		107
Robinson, P. O. and Tel. Sta	Det. Gr. H. & Mil., Chic. & W. Mich	Grand Haven, 8 m	T. 7 N., R. 15 W.	Ottawa	100	95
Roxana, P. O	M. C., Chic. & Gr. T. R. R	Charlotte, 8 m	T. 4 N., R. 5 W.	Eaton	60	98
Rabbit River, R. R. Sta	Chic. & W. Mich. R. R		T. 3 N., R. 14 W.	Allegan	850	96
Rann's Mill, P. O	Chic. & Gr. T. R. R	Morrice, 3 m	T. 5 N., R. 2 E.	Shiawassee		91
Rosina, P. O	Det. Lan. & Nor. R. R	Portland, 14 m	T. 5 N., R. 7 W.	Ionia		89
Reeve's (East Milan P. O.), R. R. Sta	To. & A. Arbor R. R		T. 5 S., R. 7 E.	Monroe		115
Raisinville, P. O. and R. R. Sta	L. S. & M. S. (Dundee Br.)		T. 6 S., R. 7 E.	Monroe	150	115
*Ransom	Chic. & Gr. T. R. R		T. 1 S., R. 7 W.	Calhoun		106
*Reeze	F. & P. M. R. R			Lake		71
*Renton	Chic. & Gr. T. R. R	Battle Creek, 6 m	R. 8 W.	Calhoun		106
*Riverside		Detroit, 3 m	T. 2 S., R. 11 E.	Wayne		103
*Ronald Centre	Det. Gr. H. & Mil. R. R	Ionia, 4 m	T. 7 N., R. 6 W.	Ionia		93
*Rogers	Chic. & Gr. T. R. R		T. 6 S., R. 14 W.	Cass		110
*Ross Centre	M. C. R. R	Augusta, 3 m		Calhoun		106
*Round Lake	L. S. & M. S. R. R	Burr Oak, 5 m	T. 7 S., R. 8 W.	Branch		112
*Rowena, R. R. Sta	M. C. R. R. (Mack. Div.)		T. 20 N., R. 3 E.	Arenac		75
*Russell's Mill, R. R. Sta	F. & P. M. R. R		T. 17 N., R. 11 W.	Lake	32	71
Rosey, P. O	M. C. R. R. (M. Div.)	Kawkawlin, 8 m	T. 15 N., R. 3 E.	Bay		75
Summit, R. R. and Tel. Sta	M. C. R. R. (M. Div.)		T. 21 N., R. 2 E.	Ogemaw	100	66
Spring Port	Lake Huron	Alpena, 35 m	T. 26 N., R. 9 E.	Alcona		64
Spencer's Mill	Tawas & Bay County	Tawas City, 5 m	T. 23 N., R. 7 E.	Iosco		65
Sault Ste. Marie Ldg., P. O. and Tel. Sta	St. Mary's River		T. 47 N., R. 1 E.	Chippewa	2,500	123
Stevensburgh, P. O	Lake Superior	Sault Ste. Marie, 9 m	T. 46 N., R. 1 W.	Chippewa	180	123
Sage, R. R. Sta	Det. Mack. & Mar. R. R		T. 46 N., R. 8 W.	Chippewa		122
Strongsville, P. O	Det. Mack. & Mar. R. R	St. Ignace, 32 m	T. 44 N., R. 7 W.	Chippewa		123
Stalwart, P. O	St. Mary's River	Sault Ste. Marie, 34 m	T. 43 N., R. 1 E.	Chippewa	50	123
Spalding, P. O. and R. R. and Tel. Sta	Chic. & N. W. R. R		T. 38 N., R. 25 W.	Menominee	500	124
Sac Bay	Chic. & N. W. R. R	Brampton, 47 m	T. 38 N., R. 19 W.	Delta	50	120
Skanee, P. O	M. H. & O. R. R	L'Anse, 17 m	T. 52 N., R. 31 W.	Baraga	130	117
Summit, R. R. Sta	M. H. & O. R. R		T. 49 N., R. 32 W.	Baraga		117
Sturgeon, R. R. Sta	M. H. & O. R. R		T. 48 N., R. 32 W.	Baraga		117
Soca, P. O	M. C. R. R. (Mack. Div.)	Cheboygan, 7 m	T. 37 N., R. 1 W.	Cheboygan		52
*Shaw, P. O				Presque Isle		53
Spurr Mine, R. R. Sta	M. H. & O. R. R	Michigamme, 1 m	T. 48 N., R. 31 W.	Baraga		117
Spurr Mt. P. O	M. H. & O. R. R	Michigamme, 1 m	T. 48 N., R. 31 W.	Baraga	250	117
Silver City	Lake Superior		T. 51 N., R. 42 W.	Ontonagon	25	116
Summit, R. R. Sta	Det. Mack. & Mar. R. R		T. 46 N., R. 20 W.	Schoolcraft		121
Seney, P. O. and R. R. Sta	Det. Mack. & Mar. R. R		T. 46 N., R. 13 W.	Schoolcraft		121
Sutton's Bay, P. O. and Tel. Sta	Gr. R. & I. R. R. (T. C. Br.)	Traverse City, 17 m	T. 30 N., R. 11 W.	Leelanaw	250	58
Solon, P. O	Gr. R. & I. R. R. (T. C. Br.)	Traverse City, 13 m	T. 28 N., R. 12 W.	Leelanaw	30	58
Snowflake, P. O	Gr. R. & I. R. R	Alba, 20 m	T. 30 N., R. 8 W.	Antrim	100	57
Stover, P. O	Gr. R. & I. R. R	Wetzell, 6 m	T. 30 N., R. 7 W.	Antrim	40	57
Simons, R. R. Sta	Gr. R. & I. R. R		T. 30 N., R. 5 W.	Antrim		57
Spencer Creek, P. O. and Tel. Sta	Gr. R. & I. R. R	Mancelona, 12 m	T. 29 N., R. 8 W.	Antrim	50	57
Sawyerville	Gr. R. & I. R. R	Leroy, 5 m	T. 19 N., R. 9 W.	Osceola		72
Sears, P. O. and R. R. and Tel. Sta	F. & P. M. R. R		T. 17 N., R. 7 W.	Osceola	200	72
Summitville, (Flag Sta.)	F. & P. M. R. R		T. 18 N., R. 11 W.	Lake		71
Summerfield, P. O	F. & P. M. R. R	Farwell, 21 m	T. 20 N., R. 5 W.	Clare		73
Springvale, P. O	Gr. R. & I. R. R	Boyne Falls, 11 m	T. 33 N., R. 4 W.	Charlevoix		57
Sedan, P. O	Gr. R. & I. R. R	Boyne Falls, 11 m	T. 32 N., R. 7 W.	Charlevoix	100	57
South Arm, P. O.	Gr. R. & I. R. R	Boyne Falls, 12 m	T. 32 N., R. 7 W.	Charlevoix	500	57
South Lake Village	Gr. R. & I. R. R	Boyne Falls, 11 m	T. 32 N., R. 7 W.	Charlevoix		57
Stephenson, P. O. and R. R. and Tel. Sta	Chic. & N. W. R. R		T. 35 N., R. 26 W.	Menominee	500	124
Stoneville, P. O	M. H. & O. R. R		T. 47 N., R. 27 W.	Marquette	600	119
Siddons, P. O.	F. & P. M. R. R. (Man. Div.)	Free Soil, 4 m	T. 20 N., R. 17 W.	Mason		70
Sugar Grove, P. O.	F. & P. M. R. R	Scottville, 4 m	T. 19 N., R. 16 W.	Mason		70
Scottville, P. O. and R. R. Sta	F. & P. M. R. R		T. 18 N., R. 17 W.	Mason	200	70
St. Helen, P. O. and R. R. and Tel. Sta	M. C. R. R. (Mack. Div.)		T. 23 N., R. 1 W.	Roscommon	400	67
Sherman, P. O	Gr. R. & I. R. R.	Manton, 10 m	T. 24 N., R. 11 W.	Wexford	403	69
Springdale, P. O	Gr. R. & I. R. R	Bond's Mills, 10 m	T. 22 N., R. 12 W.	Wexford	25	69
Sherman City, P. O	F. & P. M. R. R	Farwell, 12 m	T. 16 N., R. 6 W.	Isabella	115	77
Salt River, P. O.	F. & P. M. R. R. (Mt. Pleasant Div.)	Mount Pleasant, 7 m	T. 13 N., R. 3 W.	Isabella	194	77
Strickland, P. O.	Sag. Val. & St. L. R. R	Riverdale, 3 m	T. 13 N., R. 4 W.	Isabella		77
Sand River, R. R. Sta	Det. Mack. & Mar. R. R		T. 47 N., R. 23 W.	Marquette		118
Sands, P. O. and R. R. Sta	Chic. & N. W. R. R		T. 46 N., R. 25 W.	Marquette	130	119
Scooptown	Chic. & N. W. R. R.	Little Lake Sta., 4 m	T. 44 N., R. 24 W.	Marquette		119
Sanford, P. O. and R. R. and Tel. Sta	F. & P. M. R. R		T. 15 N., R. 1 W.	Midland	100	70
Stearns, P. O	Sag. Val. & St. L. R. R	St. Louis, 15 m	T. 14 N., R. 2 W.	Midland	30	70
Summit City, P. O. and R. R. Sta	Gr. R. & I. R. R. (T. C. Br.)		T. 25 N., R. 10 W.	Gr. Traverse	75	60
Slayton, P. O	M. C. R. R. (Mack. Div.)	Bourne Lake, 10 m	T. 23 N., R. 2 E.	Ogemaw	25	66
Stronach, P. O. and R. R. and Tel. Sta	F. & P. M. R. R. (Man. Div.)		T. 21 N., R. 16 W.	Manistee	120	50
Stronach Mill	F. & P. M. R. R. (Man. Div.)	Stronach, 2 m	T. 21 N., R. 16 W.	Manistee		50
South Boardman, P. O. and R. R. and Tel. Sta.	Gr. R. & I. R. R		T. 26 N., R. 8 W.	Kalkaska	40	61
South Frankfort, P. O	F. & P. M. R. R. (Man. Div.)	Manistee, 20 m	T. 26 N., R. 16 W.	Benzie	500	52
Sammons Landing, P. O	Chic. & W. Mich., Lake Mich	Shelby, 8 m	T. 14 N., R. 18 W.	Oceana		80
Shelby, P. O. and R. R. and Tel. Sta	Chic. & W. Mich. R. R		T. 14 N., R. 17 W.	Oceana	700	80
Sweet's, R. R. Sta	Chic. & W. Mich. R. R.		T. 11 N., R. 17 W.	Muskegon		81
Slocum's Grove, P. O	Chic. & W. Mich. R. R.	Canada Corners, 7 m	T. 10 N., R. 13 W.	Muskegon	100	81
Smith's Corners, P. O	Chic. & W. Mich. R. R.	Pentwater, 4 m	T. 16 N., R. 17 W.	Oceana	125	80
Sidney, P. O	Det. Lan. & Nor. R. R. (S. Div.)	Stanton, 5 m	T. 10 N., R. 7 W.	Montcalm	200	82
Sheridan, P. O. and R. R. and Tel. Sta	Det. Lan. & Nor. R. R. (S. Div.)		T. 10 N., R. 7 W.	Montcalm	700	82

☞ Names marked with a star (*) will not be found on the Maps.

LIST OF CITIES, TOWNS, ETC.

NAME OF VILLAGE.	RAILROAD, LAKE, OR RIVER.	Nearest Sta. or Landing	TOWNSHIP.	COUNTY.	Pop.	Page
Shanty Plains, R. R. Sta	Det. Lan. & Nor. R. R. (S. Div.)		T. 9 N., R. 7 W.	Montcalm		82
Stamp, P. O	Chic. & W. Mich., Lake Mich	Montague, 5 m	T. 12 N., R. 17 W.	Muskegon		83
Sitka, P. O	Chic. & W. Mich. (B. R. Br.)	Holton, 7 m	T. 11 N., R. 14 W.	Newaygo		79
Six Lakes, P. O. and R. R. and Tel. Sta	C. S. & C. R. R		T. 12 N., R. 7 W.	Montcalm	150	82
Summerville, R. R. Sta	C. S. & C. R. R		T. 12 N., R. 7 W.	Montcalm		82
Stanton, P. O. and R. R. and Tel. Sta	Det. Lan. & Nor. (S. Br.)		T. 11 N., R. 7 W.	Montcalm	2,500	82
Shepherds Mills, R. R. Sta	P. H. & N. W. R. R		T. 15 N., R. 13 E.	Huron		86
Sigel, P. O	P. H. & N. W. R. R	Sand Beach, 5 m	T. 16 N., R. 15 E.	Huron		86
Shattuckville	F. & P. M. R. R., M. C.	Saginaw, 6 m	T. 12 N., R. 3 E.	Saginaw	46	84
Sand Ridge, R. R. Sta	S. Val. & St. L. R. R		T. 12 N., R. 2 E.	Saginaw		84
Swan Creek, R. R. Sta	M. C. (Sag. Div.)		T. 11 N., R. 3 E.	Saginaw		84
Shinglestown, (Eastwood P. O.) R. R. Sta	M. C. (Sag. Div.)		T. 11 N., R. 3 E.	Saginaw		84
St. Charles, P. O. and R. R. and Tel. Sta	M. C. (Sag. Div.)		T. 10 N., R. 3 E.	Saginaw	700	84
Saginaw, P. O. and R. R. and Tel. Sta	M. C., F. & P. M., S. Val. & St. L.		T. 12 N., R. 4 E.	Saginaw	12,500	84
South Saginaw, P. O. and Tel. Sta	F. & P. M. R. R		T. 12 N., R. 4 E.	Saginaw	2,700	84
Smith's, R. R. Sta	F. & P. M. R. R		T. 10 N., R. 5 E.	Saginaw		84
Switch, R. R. Sta	Chic. & W. Mich. R. R		T. 12 N., R. 14 W.	Newaygo		79
Sethton, P. O	C. S. & C. R. R	Riverdale, 15 m	T. 10 N., R. 4 W.	Gratiot		83
Spring Brook, P. O	Det. Gr. H. & Mil. R. R	Fowler, 14 m	T. 9 N., R. 3 W.	Gratiot	25	83
Sickles, P. O	S. Val. & St. L. R. R	Breckenridge, 11 m	T. 10 N., R. 1 W.	Gratiot		83
Stella, P. O	Det. Gr. H. & Mil. R. R	St. Johns, 17 m	T. 10 N., R. 1 W.	Gratiot	31	83
Sand Beach, **P. O.**, Ldg. and R. R. and Tel. Sta	P. H. & N. W., Lake Huron		T. 16 N., R. 15 E.	Huron	1,200	86
Sebewaing, P. O., Ldg., and R. R. and Tel. Sta	S. T. & H. R. R., Sag. Bay		T. 15 N., R. 9 E.	Huron	700	86
Soule, P. O	P. H. & N. W. R. R	Filion, 8 m	T. 17 N., R. 11 E.	Huron		86
Summerton, P. O	Chic. S. & C. R. R	Seville, 6 m	T. 12 N., R. 4 W.	Gratiot	50	83
Seville, P. O. and R. R. Sta	Chic. S. & C. R. R.		T. 12 N., R. 4 W.	Gratiot	60	83
Sumner, P. O	Chic. S. & C. R. R	Riverdale, 6 m	T. 11 N., R. 4 W.	Gratiot	350	83
St. Louis, **P. O.** and R. R. and Tel. Sta	Chic. S. & C. R. R		T. 12 N., R. 3 W.	Gratiot	3,000	83
Starrville, P. O	M. C. R. R	Adair, 10 m	T. 3 N., R. 16 E.	St. Clair	150	88
Sharpville	P. H. & N. W. R. R	Brown City, 6 m	T. 9 N., R. 12 E.	Lapeer	30	89
Stephens (Fish Lake Sta.), P. O. and Tel. Sta	M. C. (B. C. Div.)		T. 8 N., R. 10 E.	Lapeer	1,700	89
Sandusky, P. O.	P. H. & N. W. R. R	Carsonville, 8 m	T. 11 N., R. 14 E.	Sanilac	150	87
Swartz Creek, P. O. and R. R. Sta	Chic. & Gr. T. R. R		T. 6 N., R. 5 E.	Genesee	180	90
South Gr. Blanc, P. O.	F. & P. M. R. R	Grand Blanc, 4 m	T. 6 N., R. 7 E.	Genesee	60	90
Stevens Landing	Lake Huron	Amadore, 4 m	T. 9 N., R. 17 E.	Sanilac		87
Speaker, P. O	P. H. & N. W. R. R	Amadore, 10 m	T. 9 N., R. 14 E.	Sanilac	125	87
Saginaw Junction, R. R. Sta	P. H. & N. W. R. R		T. 8 N., R. 16 E.	St. Clair		88
Sanborn, R. R. Sta	Chic. & Gr. T. R. R		T. 6 N., R. 16 E.	St. Clair		88
Smith's Creek, P. O. and R. R. and Tel. Sta	Gr. T. R. R		T. 6 N., R. 16 E.	St. Clair	250	88
St. Clair, **P. O.** and R. R. and Tel. Sta	M. C. R. R		T. 5 N., R. 17 E.	St. Clair	2,000	88
Sheridan, R. R. Sta	M. C. R. R. (Gr. R. Div.)		T. 3 N., R. 7 W.	Barry		97
Stanwood, P. O. and R. R. and Tel. Sta	Gr. R. & I. R. R		T. 14 N., R. 10 W.	Mecosta	300	78
Sylvester, P. O	Det. Lan. Nor. R. R	Mecosta, 8 m	T. 13 N., R. 8 W.	Mecosta	80	78
Sherman City, P. O	F. & P. M. R. R	Farwell, 14 m	T. 16 N., R. 6 W.	Isabella	200	77
Salt River, P. O	Chic. Sag. & Can. R. R	St. Louis, 11 m	T. 13 N., R. 3 W.	Isabella	105	77
Strickland, P. O	Chic. Sag. & Can. R. R	Riverdale, 8 m	T. 13 N., R. 4 W.	Isabella	200	77
Simon, R. R. Sta	L. S. & M. S. R. R		T. 7 S., R. 5 E.	Lenawee		114
Scipio, R. R. and Tel. Sta	L. S. & M. S. (Ft. Wayne Br.)		T. 5 S., R. 3 W.	Hillsdale		113
Somerset Centre, P. O. and R. R. Sta	L. S. & M. S. (Ypsilanti Br.)		T. 5 S., R. 1 W.	Hillsdale	200	113
Somerset P. O. and R. R. and Tel. Sta	L. S. & M. S. (Ypsilanti Br.)		T. 5 S., R. 1 W.	Hillsdale	100	113
South Wright	Wab. St. L. & Pac. R. R	North Fayette, 5 m	T. 8 S., R. 1 W.	Hillsdale		113
South Camden, P. O	L. S. & M. S. (Ft. Wayne Br.)	Montgomery, 4 m	T. 8 S., R. 4 W.	Hillsdale	40	113
South Fairfield, P. O	L. S. & M. S. (Fayette Br.)	Jasper, 4 m	T. 8 S., R. 3 E.	Lenawee		114
Sand Creek, (Thurber P. O.) R. R. and Tel. Sta	Wab. St. L. & Pac. R. R		T. 7 S., R. 3 E.	Lenawee		114
Seneca, P. O	L. S. & M. S. (Fayette Br.)	Weston, 4 m	T. 8 S., R. 2 E.	Lenawee		114
Steamburg	L. S. & M. S. R. R	Hillsdale, 4 m	T. 7 S., R. 3 W.	Hillsdale		113
Sturgis, **P. O.** and R. R. and Tel. Sta	L. S. & M. S., Gr. R. & I. R. R		T. 8 S., R. 10 W.	St. Joseph	2,500	111
Springville, P. O	L. S. & M. S. (Ypsilanti Br.)	Brooklyn, 6 m	T. 5 S., R. 2 E.	Lenawee	130	114
South Lyon, **P. O.** and R. R. and Tel. Sta	Det. Lan. & Nor., To. A. Arbor & Gr. R. R		T. 1 N., R. 7 E.	Oakland	600	101
Southfield, P. O	Det. Gr. H. & Mil. R. R	Royal Oak, 8 m	T. 1 N., R. 10 E.	Oakland	300	101
Straits Lake	F. & P. M. R. R	Pontiac, 8 m	T. 2 N., R. 9 E.	Oakland		101
Springfield, P. O	Det. Gr. H. & Mil. R. R	Davisburgh, 3 m	T. 4 N., R. 8 E.	Oakland	90	101
Seymour Lake, P. O	M. C. (B. C. Div.) P. O. & P. A.	Oxford, 6 m	T. 5 N., R. 9 E.	Oakland	200	101
Stony Creek	M. C. (B. C. Div.) Gr. T. (Air Line Br.)	Rochester, 2 m	T. 3 N., R. 11 E.	Oakland	100	101
Shepardsville, P. O. and R. R. and Tel. Sta	Det. Gr. H. & Mil. R. R		T. 7 N., R. 1 W.	Clinton	200	92
St. Johns, **P. O.** and R. R. and Tel. Sta	Det. Gr. H. & Mil. R. R		T. 7 N., R. 2 W.	Clinton	2,500	92
South Riley, P. O	Det. Lan. & Nor. R. R	Grand River City, 7 m	T. 6 N., R. 3 W.	Clinton	30	92
Segwun, R. R. Sta	Det. Gr. H. & Mil. R. R		T. 6 N., R. 9 W.	Kent		94
Sand Lake, P. O. and R. R. and Tel. Sta	Gr. R. & I. R. R		T. 10 N., R. 10 W.	Kent	600	94
Spencer Mills, P. O	Det. Lan. & Nor. R. R	Greenville, 7 m	T. 10 N., R. 9 W.	Kent	140	94
Sparta Centre, **P. O.** and R. R. and Tel. Sta	Chic. & W. Mich. (Newaygo Div.)		T. 9 N., R. 12 W.	Kent	800	94
Sparta, R. R. Sta	Chic. & W. Mich. (Newaygo Div.)		T. 9 N., R. 12 W.	Kent		94
Sylvan, P. O	M. C. R. R	Chelsea, 4 m	T. 2 S., R. 3 E.	Washtenaw	50	104
Sharon	L. S. & M. S. R. R	Manchester, 4 m	T. 3 S., R. 3 E.	Washtenaw	45	104
Stony Creek, P. O	To. A. Arbor & Gr. T. R. R	Nora, 3 m	T. 4 S., R. 7 E.	Washtenaw	60	104
Saline, **P. O.** and R. R. and Tel. Sta	L. S. & M. S. (Ypsilanti Div.)		T. 4 S., R. 5 E.	Washtenaw	1,100	104
Sandstone, P. O	M. C. R. R	Trumbull Sta., 1 m	T. 2 S., R. 2 W.	Jackson	80	105
Spring Arbor, P. O	M. C. R. R. (Air Line Div.)	Snyders Sta., 2 m	T. 3 S., R. 2 W.	Jackson	500	105
Stony Point, P. O. and R. R. and Tel. Sta	L. S. & M. S. (Ft. Wayne Br.)		T. 4 S., R. 2 W.	Jackson	70	105
Scio, P. O. and R. R. Sta	M. C. R. R		T. 2 S., R. 5 E.	Washtenaw	200	104
Salem, P. O. and R. R. and Tel. Sta	Det. Lan. & Nor. R. R		T. 1 S., R. 7 E.	Washtenaw	100	104
Springport, **P. O.** and R. R. and Tel. Sta	L. S. & M. S. (Lan. Div.)		T. 1 S., R. 3 W.	Jackson	450	105
South Jackson, P. O		Jackson, 7 m	T. 3 S., R. 1 W.	Jackson	125	105
Sheldons, R. R. Sta	M. C. R. R		T. 2 S., R. 8 E.	Wayne		108
Stark, P. O	Det. Lan. & Nor. R. R	Livonia, 1 m	T. 1 S., R. 9 E.	Wayne	25	108
Swift, P. O	M. C. R. R	Wayne, 3 m	T. 2 S., R. 9 E.	Wayne	50	108
Smithville	F. & P. M. R. R	Belden, 1 m	T. 4 S., R. 8 E.	Wayne		108
Sibley's Station	L. S. & M. S. R. R		T. 4 S., R. 11 E.	Wayne		108
Sand Hill, P. O	Det. Lan. & Nor. R. R	Redford, 3 m	T. 1 S., R. 10 E.	Wayne	50	108
Sherwood	M. C. R. R. (Air Line Div.)	Union City, 7 m	T. 5 S., R. 8 W.	Branch		112
Sherwood, **P. O.** and R. R. and Tel. Sta	M. C. R. R. (Air Line Div.)		T. 5 S., R. 8 W.	Branch	600	112
South Butler, P. O	L. S. & M. S. R. R	Quincy, 5 m	T. 5 S., R. 5 W.	Branch		112
Stockbridge, P. O.	Gr. T. R. R. (Air Line Div.)	Unadilla, 7 m	T. 1 N., R. 2 E.	Ingham	150	99
Selleck's	Gr. T. R. R. (Mich. Air Line Br.)	Romeo, 2 m	T. 5 N., R. 13 W.	Macomb		102
Sister Lakes, P. O	Chic. & W. Mich. R. R	Watervliet, 11 m	T. 4 S., R. 16 W.	Van Buren	300	109
South Haven, Ldg., **P. O.** and R. R. and Tel. Sta	Lake Mich., M. C. (Kal. & S. H. Div.)		T. 1 S., R. 17 W.	Van Buren	1,500	109
Stevensville, P. O. and R. R. and Tel. Sta	Chic. & W. Mich. R. R		T. 5 S., R. 19 W.	Berrien	250	109
Sawyer, P. O. (Troy Sta.)	Chic. & W. Mich. R. R		T. 7 S., R. 20 W.	Berrien	100	109
St. Joseph, **P. O.** (Ldg.) and R. R. and Tel. Sta	Chic. & W. Mich., Cin. Wab. & Mich., Lake Mich		T. 4 S., R. 19 W.	Berrien	2,000	109
Sodus, P. O. and R. R. Sta	Cin. Wab. & Mich. R. R		T. 5 S., R. 18 W.	Berrien		109
Scott's, P. O. and R. R. and Tel. Sta	Chic. & Gr. T. R. R		T. 3 S., R. 10 W.	Kalamazoo	150	107
Summerville, P. O	M. C. R. R	Pokagon, 2 m	T. 6 S., R. 16 W.	Cass	125	110

NAME OF VILLAGE.	RAILROAD, LAKE, OR RIVER.	Nearest Sta. or Landing	TOWNSHIP.	COUNTY.	Pop.	Page
Schoolcraft, P. O. and R. R. and Tel. Sta	L. S. & M. S. R. R		T. 4 S., R. 11 W.	Kalamazoo	1,000	107
South Blendon, P. O	Chic. & W. Mich. (Gr. R. Div.)	Hudsonville, 5 m	T. 6 N., R. 14 W.	Ottawa	300	95
Spoonville	Det. Gr. H. & Mil. R. R	Nunica, 3 m	T. 8 N., R. 15 W.	Ottawa	50	95
Spring Lake, P. O. and R. R. and Tel. Sta	Det. Gr. H. & Mil. R. R		T. 8 N., R. 16 W.	Ottawa	2,000	95
Six Corners, P. O	Det. Gr. H. & Mil. R. R	Coopersville, 7 m	T. 9 N., R. 13 W.	Ottawa	30	95
Sunfield, P. O	Det. Lan. & Nor. R. R	Grand Ledge, 13 m	T. 4 N., R. 6 W.	Eaton	100	98
Shaytown, P. O	M. C., Chic. & Gr. T. R. R	Vermontville, 8 m	T. 4 N., R. 6 W.	Eaton	75	98
Sevastapol, R. R. Sta	Chic. & Gr. T. R. R		T. 3 N., R. 3 W.	Eaton		98
State Road, R. R. Sta	Chic. & Gr. T. R. R		T. 1 N., R. 6 W.	Eaton		98
Spicerville	M. C., L. S. & M. S. R. R	Eaton Rapids, 2½ m	T. 1 N., R. 3 W.	Eaton	30	98
Salem Centre	L. S. & M. S. (Kal. Div.)	Dorr, 6 m	T. 4 N., R. 13 W.	Allegan		96
Shelbyville, P. O. and R. R. Sta	Gr. R. & I. R. R		T. 2 N., R. 11 W.	Allegan	100	96
Silver Creek, P. O	L. S. & M. S. (Kal. Div.)	Argenta, 1 m	T. 1 N., R. 11 W.	Allegan	50	96
Singapore	Chic. & W. Mich. R. R	New Richmond, 5 m	T. 3 N., R. 16 W.	Allegan		96
Saugatuck, P. O. and Tel. Sta	Chic. & W. Mich. R. R	New Richmond, 5 m	T. 3 N., R. 16 W.	Allegan	900	96
Sherman, P. O. and R. R. and Tel. Sta	Chic. & W. Mich. R. R		T. 2 N., R. 15 W.	Allegan	200	96
Spring Grove, P. O	Chic. & W. Mich. R. R	Hoppertown, 5 m	T. 1 N., R. 16 W.	Allegan	100	96
Shaftsburgh, P. O. and R. R. and Tel. Sta	Chic. & Gr. T. R. R		T. 5 N., R. 1 E.	Shiawassee	80	91
Shiawassee	Det. Gr. H. & Mil. R. R	Vernon, 2 m	T. 6 N., R. 3 E.	Shiawassee	100	91
Stanton Junction, R. R. and Tel. Sta	Det. Lan. & Nor. R. R		T. 7 N., R. 7 W.	Ionia		93
Saranac, P. O. and R. R. and Tel. Sta	Det. Gr. H. & Mil. R. R		T. 6 N., R. 8 W.	Ionia	900	93
South Cass, P. O	Det. Gr. H. & Mil. R. R	Saranac, 10 m	T. 5 N., R. 7 W.	Ionia	100	93
Sebewa, P. O	Det. Lan. & Nor. R. R	Portland, 7 m	T. 5 N., R. 6 W.	Ionia	150	93
Samaria, P. O. and R. R. and Tel. Sta	To. A. Arbor & Gr. T. R. R		T. 8 S., R. 7 E.	Monroe	50	115
Smyrna, P. O	Det. Lan. & Nor. R. R	Chadwick, 6 m	T. 8 N., R. 8 W.	Ionia	300	93
Shiloh, P. O. and R. R. and Tel. Sta	Det. Lan. & Nor. (Stanton Br.)		T. 8 N., R. 7 W.	Ionia	100	93
Scofield, P. O. and R. R. and Tel. Sta	L. S. & M. S. (Dundee Br.)		T. 5 S., R. 8 E.	Monroe	300	115
South Rockwood, P. O. and R. R. Sta	L. S. & M. S. (Det. Div.)		T. 5 S., R. 10 E.	Monroe	250	115
Stony Creek, R. R. Sta	M. C. R. R. (Toledo Div.)		T. 6 S., R. 10 E.	Monroe		115
Strasburgh, P. O. and R. R. Sta	L. S. & M. S. R. R		T. 7 S., R. 8 E.	Monroe	40	115
St. James, P. O	Lake Michigan	Harbor Springs, 30 m	T. 39 N., R. 10 W.	Manitou	400	51
*Sable Bridge				Mason		70
South Manitou	Lake Michigan		T. 30 N., R. 14 W.	Manitou	98	51
Saint Ignace, P. O. Ldg., and R. R. and Tel. Sta.	Det. Mack. & Mar. (Straits of Mackinac)		T. 40 N., R. 3 W.	Mackinac	3,000	122
*Seabrook, P. O				Mackinac		122
Sterling, P. O. and R. R. and Tel. Sta	M. C. R. R. (M. Div.)		T. 18 N., R. 4 E.	Arenac	250	75
Standish, P. O. and R. R. and Tel. Sta	M. C. R. R. (M. Div.)		T. 19 N., R. 4 E.	Arenac	400	75
Saganing, R. R. Sta	Bag Bay	Saganing Sta., 3 m	T. 18 N., R. 5 E.	Arenac	243	75
Saganing, R. R. Sta	M. C. R. R. (M. Div.)		T. 18 N., R. 4 E.	Arenac	125	75
St. Johns, R. R. Sta	Sag. Bay & N. W. R. R		T. 17 N., R. 3 E.	Bay		75
State Road, R. R. Sta	M. C. R. R. (M. Div.)		T. 16 N., R. 4 E.	Bay		75
Saltburg, P. O. and R. R. and Tel. Sta	M. C. R. R		T. 14 N., R. 5 E.	Bay		75
*Saddle Bag Siding	Det. Gr. H. & Mil. R. R		T. 7 N., R. 11 W.	Kent		94
*Saginaw Mine	M. H. & O. R. R			Marquette		119
*Sanders Fishery	Green Bay		R. 24 W.	Delta	20	120
*Sevillia				Calhoun		106
*Seitzville	S. T. & H. R. R	East Saginaw, 9 m	T. 12 N., R. 6 E.	Saginaw		84
*Seney	Det. Mack. & Mar. R. R			Chippewa		123
*Soule	To. A. Arbor & Gr. T. R. R		T. 7 N., R. 7 E.	Monroe		115
*Sibleys	M. C. R. R. (To. Div.)			Wayne		108
*Silver Creek	M. C. R. R	Dowagiac	T. 5 S., R. 16 W.	Cass		110
*Silver Lake	Gr. R. & I. R. R	Traverse City, 4 m	T. 27 N., R. 11 W.	Gr. Traverse		60
*Sharon Junction, Tel. Sta	L. S. & M. S. R. R. & M. C. R. R. (To. Div.)			Wayne		108
*Smithville, R. R. Sta	F. & P. M. R. R		T. 14 N., R. 2 E.	Midland		76
*Snow Prairie	L. S. & M. S. R. R	Bronson		Branch		112
Snyders, R. R. Sta	M. C. R. R. (Air Line Div.)		T. 3 S., R. 2 W.	Jackson		105
*South Boston	Det. Gr. H. & Mil. R. R	Saranac, 5 m	T. 6 N., R. 8 W.	Ionia		93
*South Henrietta		Jackson, 7 m	T. 2 N., R. 1 E.	Jackson		105
*South Lansing	L. S. & M. S. R. R		T. 4 N., R. 2 W.	Ingham		99
*Spinnings	M. C. R. R. (B. C. Div.)			Macomb	40	102
*Spring Mill	Lake Huron	Harrisville, 2 m	T. 26 N., R. 9 E.	Alcona		64
*Spring Mills	F. & P. M. R. R	Highland, 2 m	T. 3 N., R. 7 E.	Oakland	75	101
*Spring Station	Lake Michigan			Oceana		80
*Stambaugh, P. O. and Tel. Sta				Marquette		119
*Starkey's Pier	Lake Mich., F. & P. M. R. R	Manistee, 20 m		Manistee		59
*Stark's Corners	M. C. R. R	Dowagiac, 7 m	T. 5 S., R. 16 W.	Cass	50	110
*State Line	L. S. & M. S. (Ft. W. Br.)			Branch		112
*State Road	Chic. & Gr. T. R. R	Bellevue, 3 m	T. 1 S., R. 7 W.	Barry		97
*Stearns	F. & P. M. R. R			Lake		71
*Sugar Island	St. Mary's River			Chippewa	400	128
*Swedetown	M. R. R. R			Houghton		117
State Road Bridge	S. Val. & St. L. R. R	Saginaw, 4 m	T. 12 N., R. 4 E.	Saginaw		84
Silver Creek, (Ewy P. O.) R. R. Sta	P. H. & N. W. R. R		T. 10 N., R. 10 E.	Tuscola		85
Thompson	Tawas & Bay County	Tawas City, 17 m	T. 24 N., R. 5 E.	Iosco		65
Tawas City, P. O. and R. R. and Tel. Sta	Tawas & Bay County		T. 22 N., R. 7 E.	Iosco	1,500	65
Trout Lake, R. R. Sta	Det. Mack. & Mar. R. R		T. 44 N., R. 6 W.	Chippewa		122
Torch Lake City	Mineral Range R. R	Calumet, 4 m	T. 55 N., R. 32 W.	Houghton		117
Taylor Junction, R. R. Sta	M. H. & O. R. R		T. 50 N., R. 33 W.	Baraga		117
Three Lakes, R. R. Sta	M. H. & O. R. R		T. 48 N., R. 31 W.	Baraga		117
Trowbridge	M. C. R. R. (Mack. Div.)		T. 38 N., R. 2 E.	Cheboygan		52
Topinabee, P. O. and R. R. Sta	M. C. R. R. (Mack. Div.)		T. 36 N., R. 2 W.	Cheboygan	25	52
Town Hall	Lake Huron	Rogers City, 6 m	T. 35 N., R. 4 E.	Presque Isle		53
Thompson, P. O	Lake Michigan		T. 41 N., R. 16 W.	Schoolcraft		122
Torch Lake, P. O. and Tel. Sta	Lake Michigan		T. 31 N., R. 9 W.	Antrim	100	57
Tustin P. O. and R. R. and Tel. Sta	Gr. R. & I. R. R		T. 20 N., R. 10 W.	Osceola	400	72
Triple Rock	Gr. R. & I. R. R	Petoskey, 5 m	T. 34 N., R. 7 W.	Charlevoix		57
Thumb Lake, P. O	M. C. R. R	Vanderbilt, 7 m	T. 32 N., R. 4 W.	Charlevoix	25	57
Tilden	M. H. & O. R. R	Negaunee, 4 m	T. 47 N., R. 27 W.	Marquette		119
Tallman, P. O. and R. R. and Tel. Sta	F. & P. M. (M. Div.)		T. 18 N., R. 15 W.	Mason		70
Traverse City, P. O. and R. R. and Tel. Sta	Gr. R. & I. (T. C. Br.)		T. 27 N., R. 11 W.	Gr. Traverse	2,500	60
Trent, P. O	Chic. & W. Mich. R. R	Trent Sta., 3 m	T. 10 N., R. 14 W.	Muskegon	125	81
Trufant, P. O. and R. R. and Tel. Sta	Det. Lan. & Nor. R. R		T. 11 N., R. 9 W.	Montcalm	300	82
Twin Lake, P. O. and R. R. and Tel. Sta	Chic. & W. Mich. (B. R. Br.)		T. 11 N., R. 16 W.	Muskegon	100	81
Tuscola, P. O	M. C. R. R	Vassar, 5 m	T. 11 N., R. 7 E.	Tuscola	300	85
Tefft's, R. R. Sta	M. C. (Sag. Div.)		T. 11 N., R. 3 E.	Saginaw		84
Tyner, P. O	M. C. (Sag. Div.)	St. Charles, 6 m	T. 10 N., R. 2 E.	Saginaw	80	84
Trustville	P. H. & N. W. R. R	Frankenmuth, 2 m	T. 12 N., R. 6 E.	Saginaw	50	84
Taymouth, P. O	F. & P. M. R. R	Blackmar, 4 m	T. 10 N., R. 5 E.	Saginaw	50	84
Thornville, P. O	M. C. (B. C. Div.)	Metamora, 3 m	T. 6 N., R. 10 E.	Lapeer	250	89
Tyre, P. O	P. H. & N. W. R. R	Minden City, 7 m	T. 14 N., R. 13 E.	Sanilac	175	87
Thornton, P. O. and R. R. Sta	Chic. & Gr. T. R. R		T. 6 N., R. 16 E.	St. Clair	110	88
Thorn Apple, R. R. Sta	M. C. R. R. (Gr. R. Div.)		T. 3 N., R. 8 W.	Barry		97

☞ Names marked with a star (*) will not be found on the Maps.

NAME OF VILLAGE.	RAILROAD, LAKE, OR RIVER.	Nearest Sta. or Landing.	TOWNSHIP.	COUNTY.	Pop.	Page
Town H	Sag. Val. & St. L. R. R.	St. Louis, 6 m.	T. 13 N., R. 2 W.	Midland		76
Tecumseh, P. O. (Sand Creek Sta.)	Wab. St. L. & Pac. R. R.		T. 7 S., R. 3 E.	Lenawee	75	114
Tipton, P. O.	L. S. & M. S. (Jackson Br.)	Tecumseh, 6 m.	T. 5 S., R. 3 E.	Lenawee	75	114
Tecumseh, P. O. and R. R. and Tel. Sta.	L. S. & M. S. (Jackson Br.) Mich. & Ohio		T. 5 S., R. 4 E.	Lenawee	3,000	114
Three Rivers, P. O. and R. R. and Tel. Sta.	M. C. (Air Line Div.) L. S. & M. S.		T. 6 S., R. 11 W.	St. Joseph	2,225	111
Troy, P. O.	Gr. T. R. R. (Mich. Air Line Br.)	Amy, 5 m.	T. 2 N., R. 11 E.	Oakland	100	101
Thomas, P. O. and R. R. and Tel. Sta.	M. C. R. R. (D. C. Div.)		T. 5 N., R. 10 E.	Oakland	175	101
Thayer, P. O.	F. & P. M., Det. Gr. H. & Mil. R. R.	Holly, 8 m.	T. 5 N., R. 8 E.	Oakland		101
Town Hall	Det. Lan. & Nor. R. R.	Ingersoll, 4 m.	T. 5 N., R. 3 W.	Clinton		92
Thomas' Mills	M. C. R. R. (Gr. R. Div.)	Caledonia, 7 m.	T. 5 N., R. 9 W.	Kent		94
Tompkins, P. O.	M. C. R. R. (Gr. R. Div.)	River Junction, 5 m.	T. 1 S., R. 2 W.	Jackson	30	105
Trumbull, R. R. and Tel. Sta.	M. C. R. R.		T. 2 S., R. 2 W.	Jackson		105
Trenton, P. O. and R. R. and Tel. Sta.	L. S. & M. S., Detroit River		T. 4 S., R. 11 E.	Wayne	1,200	103
Taylor Centre, P. O.	Wab. St. L. & Pac. R. R.	Nand. 2 m.	T. 3 S., R. 10 E.	Wayne	80	103
Town Line, R. R. Sta.	Det. Lan. & Nor. R. R.		T. 1 S., R. 11 E.	Wayne		103
Tekonsha, P. O. and R. R. and Tel. Sta.	M. C. R. R. (Air Line Div.)		T. 4 S., R. 6 W.	Calhoun	600	106
Tyrone, P. O.	Det. Gr. H. & Mil. R. R.	Fentonville, 7 m.	T. 4 N., R. 6 E.	Livingston	30	100
Troy, (Sawyer P. O.) R. R. and Tel. Sta.	Chic. & W. Mich. R. R.		T. 7 S., R. 20 W.	Berrien		109
Town Line, R. R. Sta.	Chic. & W. Mich. R. R.		T. 8 S., R. 20 W.	Berrien		109
Three Oaks, P. O. and R. R. and Tel. Sta.	M. C. R. R.		T. 8 S., R. 20 W.	Berrien	400	109
Travis, R. R. Sta.	Gr. R. & I. R. R.		T. 1 S., R. 11 W.	Kalamazoo		107
Texas, P. O.	L. S. & M. S. R. R.	Portage, 5 m.	T. 3 S., R. 12 W.	Kalamazoo	150	107
Tallmadge, P. O.	Chic. & W. Mich. R. R.	Grand Rapids, 9 m.	T. 7 N., R. 13 W.	Ottawa	75	95
Town Hall	Chic. & W. Mich. (Newaygo Div.)	Sparta, 7 m.	T. 9 N., R. 13 E.	Ottawa		95
Toobey's, R. R. Sta.	Sag. Bay & N. W. R. R.		T. 18 N., R. 4 E.	Bay		75
Terry's, P. O. and R. R. Sta.	M. C. R. R. (M. Div.)		T. 15 N., R. 4 E.	Bay	30	75
*Tamarack	Gr. R. & I. R. R.	Congor, 6 m.	T. 12 N., R. 9 W.	Montcalm		82
*Torch Lake	Lake Superior			Keweenaw		118
*Troy Corners	Det. Gr. H. & Mil. R. R.	Birmingham, 5 m.	T. 2 N., R. 11 E.	Oakland		101
*Twelve Mile Siding	F. & P. M. R. R.	Flag Station		Mason		70
Trent Sta.	Chic. & W. Mich. R. R.		T. 10 N., R. 15 W.	Muskegon		81
Upton, P. O.	F. & P. M. R. R.	Farwell, 23 m.	T. 20 N., R. 5 W.	Clare	85	73
Undine, P. O.	Gr. R. & I. R. R.	Melrose, 14 m.	T. 34 N., R. 7 W.	Charlevoix		57
Underwood, P. O. and R. R. Sta.	Gr. R. & I. R. R.		T. 12 N., R. 10 W.	Montcalm		82
Ubly, P. O.	P. H. & N. W. R. R.	Bad Axe, 10 m.	T. 15 N., R. 13 E.	Huron	50	86
Unionville, P. O. and R. R. and Tel. Sta.	S. T. & H. R. R.		T. 14 N., R. 9 E.	Tuscola	500	85
Utley's Corners	Chic. & W. Mich. R. R.	White Cloud, 2 m.	T. 13 N., R. 11 W.	Newaygo		79
Union Home, P. O.	Det. Gr. H. & Mil. R. R.	St. Johns, 8 m.	T. 8 N., R. 2 W.	Clinton	30	92
Urania, P. O. and R. R. Sta.	To. A. Arbor & Gr. T. R. R.		T. 4 S., R. 6 E.	Washtenaw		104
Union City, P. O. and R. R. and Tel. Sta.	M. C. R. R. (Air Line Div.)		T. 5 S., R. 7 W.	Branch	1,500	112
Unadilla, P. O.	M. C. R. R.	Chelsea, 10 m.	T. 1 N., R. 3 E.	Livingston	225	100
Utica, P. O. and R. R. and Tel. Sta.	M. C. R. R. (B. C. Div.)		T. 3 N., R. 12 E.	Macomb	550	102
Union Pier, P. O. (Town Line Sta.)	Chic. & W. Mich. R. R.		T. 7 S., R. 20 W.	Berrien	200	109
Union, P. O.	Chic. & Gr. T. R. R.	Edwardsburgh, 11 m.	T. 8 S., R. 13 W.	Cass	150	110
Umatilla			T. 22 N., R. 11 W.	Wexford		69
Vine, P. O.	Tawas & Bay County	Tawas City, 5 m.	T. 22 N., R. 7 E.	Iosco		65
Vulcan, P. O. and R. R. and Tel. Sta.	Men. R. R. R.		T. 39 N., R. 29 W.	Menominee	1,500	124
Vanderbilt, P. O. and R. R. Sta.	M. C. R. R.		T. 32 N., R. 3 W.	Otsego	250	56
Victory, P. O.	F. & P. M. R. R.	Ludington, 6 m.	T. 19 N., R. 17 W.	Mason	100	70
Vogel Centre, P. O.	Gr. R. & I. R. R.	Cadillac, 22 m.	T. 21 N., R. 6 W.	Missaukee	200	68
Vernon City, R. R. Sta.	F. & P. M. R. R.		T. 10 N., R. 4 W.	Isabella	30	77
Van Decar, P. O.	F. & P. M. R. R. (Mt. Pleasant Br.)	Mt. Pleasant, 11 m.	T. 15 N., R. 5 W.	Isabella		77
Vickeryville, P. O.	Det. Lan. & Nor. R. R. (S. Br.)	Sheridan, 7 m.	T. 9 N., R. 6 W.	Montcalm	75	87
Vestaburg, P. O. and R. R. and Tel. Sta.	C. S. & C. R. R.		T. 12 N., R. 5 W.	Montcalm	300	82
Verona Mills, P. O.	P. H. & N. W. R. R.	Bad Axe 6 m.	T. 16 N., R. 14 E.	Huron	100	86
Vassar, P. O. and R. R. and Tel. Sta.	M. C., P. H. & N. W. R. R.		T. 11 N., R. 8 E.	Tuscola	2,000	85
Veru Flats, R. R. Sta.	M. C. (B. C. Div.)		T. 12 N., R. 5 E.	Saginaw		84
Volney, P. O.	Chic. & W. Mich. R. R.	Fremont, 18 m.	T. 15 N., R. 14 W.	Newaygo	70	79
Valley Centre, P. O. and R. R. Sta.	P. H. & N. W. R. R.		T. 9 N., R. 13 E.	Sanilac	50	87
Vincent	P. H. & N. W. R. R.	Gratiot Centre, 3 m.	T. 7 N., R. 16 E.	St. Clair		88
Van Decar, P. O.	F. & P. M. R. R.	Farwell, 13 m.	T. 15 N., R. 5 W.	Isabella	35	77
Victor, P. O.	Det. Gr. H. & Mil. R. R.	Shepherdsville, 5 m.	T. 6 N., R. 1 W.	Clinton	400	92
Van Horn, R. R. Sta.	M. C. R. R. (Gr. R. Div.)		T. 2 S., R. 1 W.	Jackson		105
Verona, R. R. Sta.	Chic. & Gr. T. R. R.		T. 2 S., R. 7 W.	Calhoun		106
Vandalia, P. O. and R. R. and Tel. Sta.	M. C. R. R. (Air Line Div.)		T. 6 S., R. 14 W.	Cass	450	110
Volinia, P. O.	Chic. & Gr. T. R. R.	Wakelee, 6 m.	T. 5 S., R. 14 W.	Cass	75	110
Vriesland, P. O.	Chic. & W. Mich. R. R.	Vriesland Sta., 2 m.	T. 5 N., R. 14 W.	Ottawa	350	95
Vriesland, R. R. Sta.	Chic. & W. Mich. R. R.		T. 5 N., R. 14 W.	Ottawa		95
Vicksburg, P. O. and R. R. and Tel. Sta.	Gr. R. & I. R. R.		T. 4 S., R. 11 W.	Kalamazoo	1,000	107
Venturn, P. O.	Lake Mich., Chic. & W. Mich.	Holland, 8 m.	T. 6 N., R. 16 W.	Ottawa	100	95
Vermontville, P. O. and R. R. and Tel. Sta.	M. C. R. R.		T. 3 N., R. 6 W.	Eaton	700	98
Venice, P. O.	Det. Gr. H. & Mil. R. R.	Durand, 6 m.	T. 7 N., R. 4 E.	Shiawassee		91
Vernon, P. O. and R. R. and Tel. Sta.	Det. Gr. H. & Mil. R. R.		T. 6 N., R. 4 E.	Shiawassee	500	91
Vienna, (Erie P. O.) R. R. and Tel. Sta.	L. S. & M. S. R. R. (Detroit Div.)		T. 8 S., R. 8 E.	Monroe		115
Vicksburg, (Marysville P. O.)	River St. Clair		T. 6 N., R. 17 E.	St. Clair		89
Whittemore, P. O. and R. R. Sta.	Tawas & Bay County		T. 21 N., R. 5 E.	Iosco	50	65
White Fish Pt., Lt. Ho. & P. O.	Lake Superior		T. 51 N., R. 5 W.	Chippewa	100	122
Wausaukee, P. O. and R. R. and Tel. Sta.	Men. R. R. R.		T. 39 N., R. 28 W.	Menominee	300	124
Wilson, P. O. and R. R. Sta.	Chic. & N. W. R. R.		T. 38 N., R. 25 W.	Menominee		124
Wellsburg	Chic. & N. W. R. R.	Brampton, 34 m.	T. 38 N., R. 18 W.	Delta		120
Wolverine, P. O. and R. R. Sta.	M. C. R. R. (Mack. Div.)		T. 33 N., R. 2 W.	Cheboygan	40	52
White Fish, R. R. Sta.	Det. Mack. & Mar. R. R.		T. 47 N., R. 22 W.	Schoolcraft		121
Wards, R. R. Sta.	Det. Mack. & Mar. R. R.		T. 47 N., R. 21 W.	Schoolcraft		121
Williams Ldg.	Lake Superior		T. 47 N., R. 19 W.	Schoolcraft		121
Weukamo	Gr. R. & I. R. R. (T. C. Br.)	Traverse City, 33 m.	T. 32 N., R. 11 W.	Leelanaw		58
Warpagamaw	Gr. R. & I. R. R.	Westward, 21 m.	T. 29 N., R. 9 W.	Antrim		37
Wetzell, P. O. and R. R. Sta.	Gr. R. & I. R. R.		T. 29 N., R. 6 W.	Antrim	120	57
Wright's Lake, R. R. and Tel. Sta.	M. C. R. R.		T. 29 N., R. 3 W.	Otsego		56
Wade	F. & P. M. R. R.	Leonia, 3 m.	T. 17 N., R. 4 W.	Clare	90	73
Winnerville	F. & P. M. R. R.	Evart	T. 17 N., R. 8 W.	Osceola		72
Wildville, P. O.	F. & P. M. R. R.	Baldwin, 15 m.	T. 20 N., R. 10 W.	Lake		71
Wingleton, P. O. and R. R. Sta.	F. & P. M. R. R.		T. 17 N., R. 14 W.	Lake	100	71
Winterfield, P. O.	F. & P. M. R. R.	Chippewa, 21 m.	T. 20 N., R. 4 W.	Clare		73
*Walloon				Charlevoix		57
Wallace, P. O. and R. R. and Tel. Sta.	Chic. & N. W. R. R.		T. 34 N., R. 27 W.	Menominee	350	124
Wexford, P. O.	Gr. R. & I. R. R.	Walton, 16 m.	T. 24 N., R. 14 W.	Wexford	70	69
Wright's Bridge, P. O.	F. & P. M. R. R.	Sanford, 4 m.	T. 16 N., R. 1 W.	Midland		76
Wyoming	Lake Superior	Copper Harbor, 10 m.	T. 58 N., R. 30 W.	Keweenaw		118
Wormwood, P. O.	Gr. R. & I. R. R. (T. C. Br.)	Summit City, 15 m.	T. 25 N., R. 12 W.	Gr. Traverse		60
Walton, P. O. and R. R. and Tel. Sta.	Gr. R. & I. R. R.		T. 25 N., R. 9 W.	Gr. Traverse	150	60
West Branch, P. O. and R. R. and Tel. Sta.	M. C. R. R. (Mack. Div.)		T. 22 N., R. 2 E.	Ogemaw	300	66
Welch, R. R. Sta.	M. C. R. R. (Mack. Div.)		T. 21 N., R. 2 E.	Ogemaw		66

☞ Names marked with a star (*) will not be found on the Maps.

NAME OF VILLAGE.	RAILROAD, LAKE, OR RIVER.	Nearest Sta. or Landing	TOWNSHIP.	COUNTY.	Pop.	Page
Westwood, P. O. and R. R. Sta	Gr. R. & I. R. R		T. 28 N., R. 7 W.	Kalkaska	100	61
Williamsburg, P. O. and Tel. Sta	Gr. R. & I. R. R. (T. C. Br.)	Traverse City, 11 m.	T. 27 N., R. 9 W.	Gr. Traverse	200	60
Wellington, P. O	M. C. R. R	Cheney Sta., 8 m	T. 25 N., R. 4 W.	Crawford		62
Weldon, P. O	F. & P. M. R. R. (Man. Div.)	Manistee, 20 m	T. 25 N., R. 14 W.	Benzie		59
Woodburn, P. O	Chic. & W. Mich. R. R	Pentwater, 13 m	T. 16 N., R. 16 W.	Oceana		80
Wood Lake, P. O. and R. R. Sta	Gr. R. & I. R. R		T. 11 N., R. 10 W.	Montcalm	150	82
Whitehall, P. O. and R. R. and Tel. Sta	Chic. & W. Mich. R. R		T. 12 N., R. 17 W.	Muskegon	2,500	81
Wyman, P. O. and R. R. and Tel. Sta	Det. Lan. & Nor. R. R. (S. Br.)		T. 12 N., R. 6 W.	Montcalm	200	82
Westville, P. O	Det. Lan. & Nor. R. R. (S. Br.)	McBride, 2 m	T. 11 N., R. 7 W.	Montcalm	300	82
Wisner, P. O	S. T. & H. R. R	Unionville, 8 m	T. 14 N., R. 7 E.	Tuscola	75	85
Wackman, R. R. Sta	S. T. & H. R. R		T. 14 N., R. 8 E.	Tuscola		85
Watrousville, P. O. and Tel. Sta	M. C. (B. C. Div.)	Watrousville, 1½ m	T. 12 N., R. 8 E.	Tuscola	250	85
Wahjamega, P. O. and R. R. and Tel. Sta	M. C. (B. C. Div.)		T. 12 N., R. 9 E.	Tuscola	100	85
West Mill (Merrill P. O.), R. R. Sta	S. Val. & St. L. R. R		T. 12 N., R. 1 E.	Saginaw	25	84
Walkup, P. O. and R. R. Sta	Chic. & W. Mich. (W. R. Br.)		T. 16 N., R. 13 W.	Newaygo		79
Woodville, R. R. and Tel. Sta	Chic. & W. Mich. (B. R. Br.)		T. 15 N., R. 11 W.	Newaygo	400	79
White Cloud, P. O. and R. R. and Tel. Sta	Chic. & W. Mich. R. R		T. 13 N., R. 12 W.	Newaygo	400	79
Worcester, R. R. Sta	Chic. & W. Mich. R. R		T. 13 N., R. 13 W.	Newaygo		79
White Rock, P. O. and Tel. Sta	Lake Huron	Adams Corners, 6½ m.	T. 15 N., R. 16 E.	Huron	300	86
Williamstown, (Attica Sta. and P. O.)	Chic. & Gr. T. R. R		T. 7 N., R. 11 E.	Lapeer		89
Wheeler, P. O. and R. R. Sta	Sag. Val. & St. L. R. R		T. 12 N., R. 1 W.	Gratiot	300	83
Whiting, P. O	P. O. & P. A. R. R	North Branch, 7 m	T. 9 N., R. 11 E.	Lapeer	20	89
Wilber Road (Bridgehampton P. O.), R. R. Sta	P. H. & N. W. R. R		T. 12 N., R. 15 E.	Sanilac		87
Whitesburg	F. & P. M. (P. H. Div.)	Rogersville, 1 m	T. 9 N., R. 7 E.	Genesee		90
Wales, P. O. and R. R. Sta	P. H. & N. W. R. R		T. 6 N., R. 15 E.	St. Clair	100	98
Woodland, P. O	M. C. R. R. (Gr. R. Div.)	Nashville, 10 m	T. 4 N., R. 7 W.	Barry	250	97
*West Millbrook, P. O				Mecosta		78
Wolf, P. O	L. S. & M. S. R. R	Adrian, 9 m	T. 6 S., R. 3 E.	Lenawee		114
Wellsville, P. O. and R. R. Sta	L. S. & M. S. R. R		T. 7 S., R. 5 E.	Lenawee	150	114
Wood, R. R. Sta	L. S. & M. S. R. R		T. 8 S., R. 3 E.	Lenawee		114
West Ogden	L. S. & M. S. (Fayette Br.)	Ogden, 2 m	T. 8 S., R. 4 E.	Lenawee		114
Wheatland, P. O	Mich. & Ohio R. R	Addison, 3 m	T. 6 S., R. 1 W.	Hillsdale	70	113
Waldron, P. O	Wab. St. L. & Pac. R. R	North Fayette, 6 m	T. 8 S., R. 1 W.	Hillsdale	250	113
White, P. O	L. S. & M. S. (Ft. Wayne Br.)	Montgomery, 7 m	T. 8 S., R. 4 W.	Hillsdale	75	113
Woodbridge	L. S. & M. S. (Ft. Wayne Br.)	Montgomery, 8 m	T. 8 S., R. 8 W.	Hillsdale		113
Weston, P. O. and R. R. and Tel. Sta	L. S. & M. S. (Fayette Br.)		T. 8 S., R. 3 E.	Lenawee	400	114
White Pigeon, P. O. and R. R. and Tel. Sta	L. S. & M. S. R. R		T. 8 S., R. 12 W.	St. Joseph	1,200	111
Woodstock, R. R. and Tel. Sta	L. S. & M. S. (Ypsilanti Br.)		T. 5 S., R. 1 E.	Lenawee		114
Woodstock, P. O	L. S. & M. S. (Ypsilanti Br.)	Woodstock Sta., 4 m	T. 5 S., R. 1 E.	Lenawee		114
Woodbridge, P. O. and R. R. Sta	Mich. & Ohio R. R		T. 5 S., R. 1 E.	Lenawee		114
West Novi, R. R. Sta	F. & P. M. R. R		T. 1 N., R. 8 E.	Oakland		101
Wasepi, P. O. and R. R. and Tel. Sta	Gr. R. & I. (M. C. Air Line Div.)		T. 6 S., R. 10 W.	St. Joseph	100	111
Walled Lake, P. O	F. & P. M. R. R	Wixom, 3 m	T. 2 N., R. 8 E.	Oakland	400	101
White Lake, P. O	Det. Gr. H. & Mil. R. R	Clyde, 3 m	T. 3 N., R. 8 E.	Oakland	75	101
Wixom, P. O. and R. R. and Tel. Sta	F. & P. M. R. R		T. 2 N., R. 8 E.	Oakland	150	101
Waterford, P. O. and R. R. and Tel. Sta	Det. Gr. H. & Mil. R. R		T. 3 N., R. 9 E.	Oakland	300	102
Westphalia, P. O	Det. Gr. H. & Mil. R. R	Fowler, 8 m	T. 6 N., R. 4 W.	Clinton	450	92
Wacousta, P. O	Det. Lan. & Nor. R. R	Eagle, 6 m	T. 5 N., R. 3 W.	Clinton	275	92
Whitneyville, P. O	Det. Gr. H. & Mil. R. R	Ada, 6 m	T. 6 N., R. 10 W.	Kent	100	94
Whittaker, P. O. and R. R. Sta	Wab. St. L. & Pac. R. R		T. 4 S., R. 7 E.	Washtenaw	100	104
Wilson, R. R. Sta	M. C. R. R		T. 3 S., R. 1 W.	Jackson		105
Worden, P. O. and R. R. Sta	Gr. T. R. R. (To. & A. Arbor Div.)		T. 1 S., R. 6 E.	Washtenaw		104
Whitmore Lake, P. O	Gr. T. R. R. (To. & A. Arbor Div.)	Worden, 3 m	T. 1 S., R. 6 E.	Washtenaw	150	104
Walsh, P. O	Gr. T. R. R. (To. & A. Arbor Div.)	Worden, 5 m	T. 1 S., R. 6 E.	Washtenaw	40	104
Webster, P. O	M. C. R. R	Delhi, 3 m	T. 1 S., R. 5 E.	Washtenaw		104
Waterloo, P. O	M. C. R. R	Francisco, 6 m	T. 1 S., R. 2 E.	Jackson	175	105
Wayne Junction	M. C., F. & P. M. R. R		T. 2 S., R. 9 E.	Wayne		103
Wayne, P. O. and R. R. and Tel. Sta	M. C. R. R		T. 2 S., R. 9 E.	Wayne	1,000	103
Wallaceville, P. O	Det. Lan. & Nor. R. R	Beech, 2 m	T. 2 S., R. 10 E.	Wayne		103
West End, P. O	M. C. R. R., Det. Lan. & Nor	Junction, 2 m	T. 2 S., R. 11 E.	Wayne		103
West Sumpter, P. O	F. & P. M. R. R	Belden, 5 m	T. 4 S., R. 8 E.	Wayne	80	103
Wyandotte, P. O., Ldg., and R. R. and Tel. Sta	L. S. & M. S. (Det. Div.) M. C., Detroit River		T. 3 S., R. 11 E.	Wayne	4,000	103
Waltz, P. O. and R. R. and Tel. Sta	F. & P. M. R. R		T. 4 S., R. 9 E.	Wayne	300	103
Waterford, R. R. Sta	F. & P. M. R. R		T. 1 S., R. 8 E.	Wayne		102
Whitewood, P. O	Det. Gr. H. & Mil. R. R	Detroit, 3 m	T. 1 S., R. 11 E.	Wayne	450	103
Wheatfield, P. O. and R. R. and Tel. Sta	M. C. R. R		T. 2 S., R. 7 W.	Calhoun		100
West Leroy, P. O	Chic. & Gr. T. R. R	Climax, 3 m	T. 3 S., R. 5 W.	Calhoun	80	100
Wood R. R. Sta	L. S. & M. S. R. R		T. 7 S., R. 8 W.	Branch		112
Williamsville	M. C. R. R	Chelsea, 11 m	T. 1 N., R. 3 E.	Livingston		100
Waldenburg, P. O	Gr. T. R. R	Mt. Clemens, 5 m	T. 4 N., R. 13 E.	Macomb	150	102
Warren, P. O. and R. R. and Tel. Sta	M. C. R. R. (B. C. Div.)		T. 1 N., R. 12 E.	Macomb	175	102
Winfield, P. O	M. C. R. R. (Gr. R. Div.)	Onondaga, 2 m	T. 1 N., R. 2 W.	Ingham	200	99
Webberville, P. O. and R. R. and Tel. Sta	Det. Lan. & Nor. R. R		T. 3 N., R. 2 E.	Ingham	550	99
White Oak, P. O	Det. Lan. & Nor. R. R	Webberville, 11 m	T. 2 N., R. 2 E.	Ingham	50	99
Washington, P. O. and R. R. Sta	Gr. T. R. R. (Mich. Air Line Br.)		T. 4 N., R. 12 E.	Macomb	225	102
White Oak, R. R. Sta	M. C. R. R		T. 4 S., R. 14 W.	Van Buren		108
Williamston, P. O. and R. R. and Tel. Sta	Det. Lan. & Nor. R. R		T. 4 N., R. 1 E.	Ingham	1,500	99
Waverly, P. O	M. C. (Kal. & S. H. Div.)	Gobleville, 4 m	T. 2 S., R. 14 W.	Van Buren	30	108
Wilkinson, R. R. Sta	Chic. & W. Mich. R. R		T. 7 S., R. 20 W.	Berrien	30	109
Williamsville, P. O	M. C. R. R. (Air Line Div.)	Jones, 3 m	T. 5 S., R. 13 W.	Cass	125	110
Watervliet, P. O. and R. R. and Tel. Sta	Chic. & W. Mich. R. R		T. 3 S., R. 17 W.	Berrien	250	109
Wakelee, P. O. and R. R. and Tel. Sta	Chic. & Gr. T. R. R		T. 5 S., R. 13 W.	Cass	200	110
Williams, P. O. and R. R. Sta	M. C. R. R. (Kal. Div.)		T. 1 S., R. 12 W.	Kalamazoo		107
Wright, P. O	Det. Gr. H. & Mil. R. R	Berlin, 6 m	T. 8 N., R. 13 W.	Ottawa		95
West Olive, P. O. and R. R. and Tel. Sta	Chic. & W. Mich. R. R		T. 6 N., R. 16 W.	Ottawa	30	95
West Windsor, P. O	Chic. & Gr. T. R. R	Sevastopol, 1 m	T. 3 N., R. 3 W.	Eaton	250	98
Windsor, P. O	L. S. & M. S. R. R. (Lan. Div.)	Dimondale, 2 m	T. 3 N., R. 3 W.	Eaton		98
West Casco, P. O	Chic. & W. Mich. R. R	Hoppertown, 8 m	T. 1 N., R. 16 W.	Allegan	70	96
Watson, P. O	M. & O. R. R	Fisk, 1 m	T. 2 N., R. 12 W.	Allegan	30	96
Wayland, P. O. and R. R. and Tel. Sta	Gr. R. & I. R. R		T. 3 N., R. 11 W.	Allegan	750	96
West Haven, P. O	M. C. R. R. (Sag. Div.)	Henderson, 2 m	T. 8 N., R. 3 E.	Shiawassee	175	91
West Campbell, P. O	Det. Gr. H. & Mil. R. R	Saranac, 10 m	T. 5 N., R. 8 W.	Ionia	300	93
West Sebewa, P. O	Det. Lan. & Nor. R. R	Portland, 9 m	T. 5 N., R. 6 W.	Ionia	125	93
Willits, P. O. and R. R. Sta	To. A. Arbor & Gr. T. R. R		T. 8 S., R. 8 E.	Monroe		115
Whiteford Centre, P. O	L. S. & M. S. R. R	Sylvania, 6 m	T. 8 S., R. 7 E.	Monroe	125	115
Ward's Corners, P. O. and R. R. Sta	Det. Lan. & Nor. (Stanton Br.)		T. 8 N., R. 7 W.	Ionia	80	93
Warner, R. R. Sta	L. S. & M. S. (Det. Div.)		T. 7 S., R. 9 E.	Monroe		115
Winchester	L. S. & M. S. (Det. Div.)	La Salle, 2 m	T. 7 S., R. 8 E.	Monroe		115
Wells, R. R. and Tel. Sta	M. C. R. R. (M. Div.)		T. 20 N., R. 8 E.	Arenac	70	75
White Feather, R. R. Sta	M. C. R. R. (M. Div.)		T. 17 N., R. 4 E.	Bay	120	75
*Wagars	Det. Lan. & No. (S. Br.)			Montcalm		82
*Warsaw				Lenawee		114

☞ Names marked with a star (*) will not be found on the Maps.

NAME OF VILLAGE.	RAILROAD, LAKE, OR RIVER.	Nearest Sta. or Landing	TOWNSHIP.	COUNTY.	Pop.	Page
Watkins	L. S. & M. S. R. R. (Ypsilanti Br.)		T. 4 S., R. 3 E.	Washtenaw		104
*Weare	Chic. & W. Mich. R. R.	Hart, 7 m.		Oceana		80
Weldon Creek, P. O. and R. R. Sta.	F. & P. M. R. R.		T. 8 N., R. 16 W.	Mason	152	70
*Wequetonsing	Gr. R. & I. R. R., Little Traverse Bay	Harbor Springs, 2 m.	T. 35 N.	Emmet		51
*West Berlin	Chic. & Gr. T. R. R.	Capac, 6 m.	T. 6 N., R. 13 E.	St. Clair		88
*West Geneva	M. C. R. R. (S. H. Div.)		T. 1 S., R. 16 W.	Van Buren		108
*West Summit	Gr. R. & I. R. R.			Wexford		99
*Wickware, P. O.				Sanilac		87
*Williams, P. O.		Midland, 3 m.	T. 14 N.	Midland		76
Willis, R. R. and Tel. Sta.	Wab. St. L. & Pac. R. R.		T. 4 S., R. 7 E.	Washtenaw		104
*Wings Junction, R. R. Sta.	F. & P. M. R. R.			Osceola		72
*Wiola				Isabella		77
*Wood				Monroe		115
*Wooster Hill				Newaygo		70
*Worth	M. C. R. R. (B. C. Div.)	Vassar, 7 m.		Tuscola		85
*Wright's				Ogemaw		66
West Bay City, P. O., Ldg., R. R. and Tel. Sta.	M. C. R. R. (Sag. Div.)		T. 14 N., R. 5 E.	Bay	8,500	75
Watrousville, R. R. Sta.	M. C. R. R. (B. C. Div.)		T. 12 N., R. 8 E.	Tuscola		85
Yuba, P. O.	Gr. R. & I. R. R. (T. C. Br.)	Traverse City, 11 m.	T. 28 N., R. 9 W.	Gr. Traverse	120	99
Yorks, (Valley Centre P. O.) R. R. Sta.	P. H. & N. W. R. R.		T. 9 N., R. 13 E.	Sanilac		87
Yankee Springs, P. O.	M. C. R. R. (Gr. R. Div.)	Hastings, 11 m.	T. 3 N., R. 10 W.	Barry		97
Ypsilanti, P. O. and R. R. and Tel. Sta.	M. C., L. S. & M. S. R. R.		T. 3 S., R. 7 E.	Washtenaw	5,500	104
York, P. O.	To. A. Arbor & Gr. T. R. R.	Nora, 7 m.	T. 4 S., R. 6 E.	Washtenaw	150	104
Yates, R. R. Sta.	M. C. R. R. (B. C. Div.)		T. 3 N., R. 12 E.	Macomb		109
Yorkville, P. O.	M. C. R. R.	Augusta, 3 m.	T. 1 S., R. 9 W.	Kalamazoo	200	107
Yates	M. C. R. R. (B. C. Div.)			Oakland		101
Zilwaukee, P. O. and R. R. and Tel. Sta.	M. C. (Sag. Div.) Saginaw River		T. 13 N., R. 5 E.	Saginaw	900	84
Zutphen, P. O.				Ottawa		95
Zeeland, P. O. and R. R. and Tel. Sta.	Chic. & W. Mich. (Gr. R. Div.)		T. 5 N., R. 14 W.	Ottawa	500	95

POSTAL CHANGES.—The Following Post Offices have been Established, Discontinued or Names Changed.

ESTABLISHED.

Aral ... Benzie
Arbona ... Antrim
Ashley ... Gratiot
Au Train ... Schoolcraft
Averill ... Midland
Ball ... Cheboygan
Bannister ... Gratiot
Barleson ... Chippewa
Bloomer ... Montcalm
Bohemian ... Ontonagon
Bellis ... Livingston
Cash ... Sanilac
Cedar River ... Menominee
Chapel ... Kent
Chauncey ... Kent
Chippewa Lake ... Mecosta
Clarendon ... Calhoun
Cooley ... Huron
Copley ... Lake
Corbin ... Clinton
Crosby ... Kent
Deford ... Tuscola
Dingman ... Newaygo
Dollarville ... Chippewa
Downington ... Sanilac
Dutton ... Kent
Eames ... Oakland
Eastlake ... Manistee
Egypt ... Mason
Ellsworth ... Antrim
Fairview ... Oscoda
Fergus ... Saginaw
Filer City ... Manistee
Elbridge ... Oceana
Fletcher ... Kalkaska
Flowler ... Schoolcraft
Forrester ... Sanilac
Fremont ... Newaygo
Frederickville ... Osceola
Fruit Ridge ... Lenawee
Galloway ... Saginaw
Gurley ... Barry
Gilbert ... Wexford
Gill's Pier ... Leelanaw
Godfrey ... Montmorency
Green Creek ... Muskegon
Gresham ... Eaton
Grove ... Newaygo
Haire ... Wexford
Hubbard Lake ... Alpena
Huron ... Huron
Jennings ... Missaukee
Juniata ... Tuscola
Ketcham ... Midland
Kellogg ... Allegan
Kewadin ... Antrim
Keystone ... Grand Traverse
Kimball ... St. Clair
King's Mill ... Lapeer
Kingsley ... Grand Traverse
Lamb ... St. Clair
Leathem ... Menominee
Levering ... Emmet
Lucas ... Missaukee
Mack City ... Oscoda
Markell ... Tuscola
Manhattan Mine ... Marquette
Mastodon ... Marquette
Meredith ... Clare
Minden City ... Sanilac
Mio (r. h.) ... Oscoda
Moran ... Mackinac
Munising ... Schoolcraft
Nacomi ... Berrien
Nelson ... Saginaw
Newtonville ... Baraga
North Morenci ... Lenawee
Olds ... Branch
Olney ... Shiawassee
Orchard Hill ... Alpena
Palmerville ... Newaygo
Putnam ... Missaukee
Rosedale ... Chippewa
Saganing ... Bay
Seney ... Schoolcraft
Smith ... St. Clair
South Allen ... Hillsdale
South Manistique ... Schoolcraft
Sutton ... Lenawee
Talbot ... Menominee
Tallmadge ... Ottawa
Thorp ... Wexford
Turin ... Marquette
Urban ... Sanilac
Verne ... Saginaw
Vincent ... Menominee
Walloon ... Charlevoix
Watersmeet ... Ontonagon
West Millbrook ... Mecosta
Whitney ... Menominee
Whiteville ... Isabella
Wilmot ... Tuscola

DISCONTINUED.

Acton, Ionia ... Mail to Maple Ridge
Bee Stine, Manistee ... Mail to Bear Lake
Benton, Washtenaw ... Mail to Saline
Colon, Calhoun ... Mail to Battle Creek
Comara, St. Clair ... Mail to Brockway
Cold Spring, Kalkaska ... Mail to Excelsior
East Golden, Oceana ... Mail to Mears
Edgel, Van Buren ... Mail to Lawrence
Elm Rock, Leelanaw ... Mail to Traverse City
Faith, Crawford ... Mail to Roscommon
Finnesay, Ottawa ... Mail to Grand Rapids
Gilchrist, Mackinac ... Mail to Epoufette
Iroquois, Chippewa ... Mail to Sault de Ste. Marie
Jensen, Newaygo ... Mail to Sand Lake
Kearney, Antrim ... Mail to Bellaire
Kilkenny, Huron ... Mail to Caseville
Logan, Otsego ... Mail to Vanderbilt
Lonsdale, Emmet ... Mail to Harbor Springs
Malton, Delta ... Mail to Lathrop
Marshfield, Mecosta ... Mail to Rodney
Mead's Mills, Wayne ... Mail to Northville
Mellows, Otsego ... Mail to Otsego Lake
Munising, Schoolcraft ... Mail to Au Train
Pt. Richards, Montcalm ... Mail to Stanton
Nair, Livingston ... Mail to Genoa
Ring, Gratiot ... Mail to Wheeler
Rustic, Clinton ... Mail to St. John's
Seabrook, Mackinac ... Mail to McMillan
Sedan, Charlevoix ... Mail to Advance
Seneca, Lenawee ... Mail to Morenci
Seville, Gratiot ... Mail to Elwell
Slayton, Ogemaw ... Mail to Churchill
Stephens, Lapeer ... Mail to Lapeer
Wade, Clare ... Mail to Clare
*Watertown, Tuscola ... Mail to Markell
Wellsville, Lake ... Mail to Baldwin

NAMES CHANGED.

Averill's Station, Midland ... To Averill
Bellaire, Grand Traverse ... To Keystone
Bloomer Centre, Montcalm ... To Bloomer
Bowen Station, Kent ... To Crosby
Cedar Fork, Menominee ... To Cedar River
Davis Corners, Sanilac ... To Urban
Forrester, Sanilac ... To Forrester
Fremont Center, Newaygo ... To Fremont
Grange, Lenawee ... To Fruit Ridge
Hammond, Kent ... To Dutton
Huron City, Huron ... To Huron
Jacob City, Mackinac ... To Moran
Minden, Sanilac ... To Minden City
Mio (r. h.), Oscoda ... To Mio (r. h.)
North Batavia, Branch ... To Olds
Otis, Newaygo ... To Dingman
Paradise, Grand Traverse ... To Kingsley
Roy, Missaukee ... To Putnam

☞ Names marked with a star (*) will not be found on the Maps.

BUSINESS CARDS
OF
PATRONS IN DETROIT.

ATTORNEYS.

Charles F. Barton,
Attorney at Law,
33 Newberry and McMillan Building.

C. A. Beardsley,
Lawyer,
Bank Block.

Brennan & Donnelly,
Attorneys at Law,
10 and 12 Telegraph Block.

Corliss & Andrus,
Attorneys,
N. E. Cor. of Jefferson Ave. and Griswold St.
John B Corliss, City Attorney.

Julian G. Dickinson,
Attorney at Law,
Newberry & McMillan Building.

Dickinson, Thurber & Hosmer,
Law Firm,
149 Jefferson Avenue.

D. C. Holbrook,
Lawyer,
27 Moffat Block.

Addison Mandell,
Attorney at Law,
Ex-Clerk C. C. U. S.

Sidney D. Miller, John H. Bissell, Fred T. Sibley,
Attorneys at Law,
Bank Chambers.

E. W. Meddaugh,
Lawyer,
6 Bank Block.

Wm. B. Moran. Henry D. Barnard. Fred T. Moran
Moran, Barnard & Moran,
Lawyers,
Campau Building.

Ward & Palmer,
Attorneys at Law.
Oldest Law Firm in City ; 42 Seitz Block.

Alfred Russell,
Lawyer,
Newberry & McMillan Building.

L. S. Trowbridge,
Lawyer,
Newberry & McMillan Building.

ASSESSOR.

John D. Standish.

BANKS.

American National Bank,
Newberry & McMillan Building,
A. H. Dey, President.
G. B. Sartwell, Cashier.

Commercial National Bank,
Corner Griswold and Larned Streets,
Hugh McMillan, President.
M. L. Williams, Cashier.

Detroit Savings Bank.
Thos. Ferguson, Vice President.
E. C. Bowman, Cashier.

David Preston & Co.
Bankers.
Campau Building.

First National Bank.
Corner Griswold St. and Jefferson Ave.
Emory Wendell, President.
L. E. Clark, Cashier.

A. Ives & Sons,
Bankers,
149 Jefferson Avenue.

Michigan Savings Bank,
Corner Griswold St. and Lafayette Ave.
George Peck, President.
Sam'l R. Mumford, Sec. and Treas.

The People's Savings Bank.
109 Griswold St.
Francis Palms, President.
M. W. O'Brien, Cashier.

Second National Bank.
N. P. Baldwin, Pres.
C. M. Davison, Cashier.

Wayne County Savings Bank,
32 Congress St. West.
Wm. B. Weston, President.
S. D. Elwood, Sec. and Treas.

BARRELS, HOOPS, ETC.

Burrell & Whitman,
Barrel Hoop Manufacturers,
Geo. S. Bingham, Supt.
Foot of McDougall Avenue.

BOOK BINDERS & STATIONERS.

Thorndike Nourse,
Wholesale and Retail Bookseller & Stationer,
Printer and Blank Book Manufacturer,
51 Larned Street West.

Jos C. Schuknecht,
Book Binder,
204 Woodward Avenue.

Richmond, Backus & Co.,
Manufacturers and Dealers in Blank Books and Stationery, Printers and Binders,
183 Jefferson Ave.

Boots and Shoes, Wholesale.

H. P. Baldwin, 2nd & Co.
Wholesale Boots and Shoes,
41 and 43 Woodward Ave.

A. C. McGraw & Co.
Wholesale Boots and Shoes,
128, 130 and 132 Jefferson Ave.

Pingree & Smith,
Wholesale Boots and Shoes,
Woodbridge St. West.

BRUSH MANUFACTURERS.

Detroit Patent Brush Co.,
Specialties in Horse, Scrub, Shoe and Stove Brushes.

BREWERIES.

Edward W. Voigt,
Brewer of Rheingold and Pilsen Beer,
Detroit, Michigan.

The Lion Brewing Co.,
Brewers and Maltsters,
Detroit, Mich.
B. Stroh, Pres't. J. Stroh, Secy.

CHEMISTS.

Parke, Davis & Co.
Manufacturing Chemists,
Cor. Atwater St. and McDougall Ave.
Detroit, New York & London, Eng.

Charles Wright & Co.
Manufact. Chemists,
15 Jefferson Ave.

CLOTHIERS.

Kauffman & Wolff,
Manufacturers and Dealers in Ready-Made Clothing,
122 Jefferson Avenue.

Heavenrich Bros.
Manufacturers of and Dealers in Ready Made Clothing.
139 & 141 Jefferson Ave. and 32 & 34 Woodbr.

Heineman, Butzel & Co.
Wholesale Clothiers,
142 and 144 Jefferson Ave.

Schloss Bros. & Co.
Manufacturers of and Dealers in Clothing and Gent's Furnishing Goods.

C. R. Mabley & Company.
Dealer in Clothing, Furnishing Goods, Hats, Caps, Boots and Shoes;
127 to 129 & 122 to 132 Woodward Ave.

Commissioner of Immigration.

H. W. Fairbank,
Ass't Commissioner of Immigration,
In charge of Office.

COMMISSION MERCHANTS.

Brady & Co.
Commission Merchants and Dealers in Mining and Lumber Camp Supplies,
Foot of Woodward Avenue.

COMMERCIAL AGENCIES.

Bradstreet's Imp. Mercantile Agcy.
9 Chamber of Commerce.
Chas. F. Beck, Supt.

R. G. Dun & Co. Mercantile Agency
88 and 90 Griswold Street,
Geo. Minchener, Manager.

Cracker & Biscuit Manufact'rs.

Lawrence Depew & Co.,
Manufacturers of Crackers and Biscuits
37 and 39 Woodward Ave.

Vail & Crane,
Cracker and Biscuit Manufacturers,
48 to 56 Woodbridge St. East.

CROCKERY AND GLASSWARE.

R. W. King.
Importer and Jobber of Crockery, Glassware, China, Lamps, etc.
103 Woodward Ave.

Chas. H. Werner,
Importer, Jobber and Dealer of Crockery, Glassware, Lamp Goods, Cutlery, Stoneware, Fancy Goods, &c.
196 and 198 Randolph Street.

Chas. S. Wetmore,
Importers and Dealers in Crockery, China Lamps, Gas Fixtures, etc.
100 Woodward Ave.

DRY GOODS,—Wholesale.

Allan Sheldon & Co.
Wholesale Dry Goods and Notions,
162 to 168 Jefferson Ave.

Edson, Moore & Co.
Wholesale Dry Goods,
194 to 202 Jefferson Avenue.

Newcomb, Endicott & Co.
Importers, Jobbers, and Retailers of Dry Goods,
197 to 150 Woodward Avenue.

S. Simon & Co.
Wholesale Dry Goods and Notions,
Manufacturers of Gent's Furnishing Goods,
179 and 192 Jefferson Avenue.

Taylor, Woolfenden & Co.
Importers, Jobbers and Retailers of Dry Goods,
165 & 167 Woodward Avenue.

DRUGGISTS,—Wholesale.

Farrand, Williams & Co.
Wholesale Druggists, Dealers in Paints, Oils, Etc.
11 to 17 Larned Street East.

T. H. Hinchman & Sons.
Wholesale Druggists and Grocers,
Importers of Druggists' Sundries, Etc.,
78 and 80 Jefferson Avenue.

Milburn & Williamson.
Wholesale and Retail Dealers in Druggists', Physicians' and Surgeons' Supplies,
81 Woodward Avenue.

John J. Dodds & Co.,
Wholesale Druggists, Dealers in Paints, Oils, Etc.,
51 and 53 Shelby Street.

FISH DEALERS, Wholesale.

Jas. Craig.
Wholesale Fish Dealer,
62 Atwater Street.

C. W. Gauthier.
Wholesale Dealer in Fish, Fresh, Frozen and Salt,
64 Atwater Street.

FRUITS, ETC.

Thos. Swan.
Fruit and Restaurant,
Cor. Woodward Ave. and Larned St.

FRUITS, ETC.—CONTINUED.

D. D. Mallory & Co.,
Wholesale Fruit and Oysters,
55 Jefferson Avenue.

FURNITURE.

Gray & Baffey,
Wholesale Upholsterers,
98, 100 and 102 Congress St.

N. & J. Flattery,
Furniture Dealers,
95 Woodward Avenue.

GLASS.

Wm. Reid,
Dealer in Window and Plate Glass.
12 and 14 Congress Street East,
73 and 75 Larned St. West.

GROCERS.

Beatty, Fitzsimons & Co.,
Wholesale Grocers,
45, 47 and 49 Woodward Avenue,
40 and 42 Griswold St.

B. F. Farrington & Co.,
Wholesale Grocers,
73 and 75 Jefferson Avenue.

Peter Henkel,
Wholesale Grocer and Pork Packer,
Randolph Street.

Johnson & Wheeler,
Wholesale Grocers,
102 and 104 Jefferson Avenue.

A. R. & W. F. Linn,
Wholesale Teas, Coffees, Spices, etc.
120 Jefferson Avenue.

G. & R. McMillan,
Grocers and Importers of Wines, etc.
131 Woodw. Ave. and 1, 3 & 5 Fort St. W.

GOVERNMENT OFFICES.

Geo. C. Codd,
Post Master.

George R. Woolfenden,
Ass't P. M.

HATS, CAPS AND FURS.

A. C. Bacon & Co.,
Wholesale Dealers in Hats, Caps, Straw Goods, Buffalo and Fancy Robes, Buck Gloves, Mittens, &c.
96 Jefferson Avenue.

F. Buhl & Co.,
Wholesale Hats, Caps and Furs,
148 Jefferson Avenue.

Henry A. Newland & Co.,
Wholesale Hats, Caps and Furs,
144 and 146 Jefferson Ave.

HARDWARE.

Black & Owen,
Wholesale Hardware,
Cor. Woodbridge and Wayne Streets.

Buhl, Sons & Co.,
Wholesale Hardware,
103 to 111 Woodbridge St. West.

Coulson & Morhous,
House Keepers' Palace,
178 Woodward Ave.

Ducharme Fletcher & Co.,
Wholesale Hardware,
63 to 69 Woodbridge St. West.

THOS. B. RAYL. W. W. SMITH.
T. B. Rayl & Co.
General & Fancy Hardware, Tools and Stoves.
114 Woodward Ave.

Standart Bros.,
Wholesale Hardware,
92, 94 and 96 Woodbridge St. West.

INSURANCE.

Detroit Fire and Marine Ins. Co.,
J. J. Clark, Sec.
90 Griswold St.

Imperial Life Insurance Society,
Mechanics' Block, Detroit.
Anson Waring, Sec'y.

Jno. L. McCloud,
Supreme Secretary Order Knights of Columbia,
Room 20 Walker Block.

S. L. Fuller,
Insurance Agent,
88 Griswold Street.

Jas. H. Garmey,
General Insurance,
115 Griswold St. (off. at end of hall.)

Fred Guenther,
General Insurance,
124 Griswold St.

A. G. Lindsay,
General Insurance Agent,
93 Griswold St.

Michigan Mutual Life Ins. Co.
O. R. Looker, Sec.
Cor. Jefferson Ave. and Griswold St.

J. A. Sexton,
Lumber and Insurance,
7 Lafayette Ave.

The Mutual Life Ins. Co. of N. Y.
F. S. Winston, President.
Assets over One Hundred Millions of Dollars.
Messrs. & Frothingham, Gen'l Agts for Michigan, Indiana, Ill's, Wis., Iowa & Minn.

Iron Dealers & Manufacturers.

Baker, Gray & Co.,
Wholesale Iron, Steel and Carriage Goods and Woodwork,
36 and 38 Woodward Avenue.

W. W. Collier & Co.,
Iron Merchants,
Foot of Wayne Street.

Detroit Steel Works,
Manufacturers of Steel,
Office No. 2 Moffat Block.

Eureka Iron Co.,
Office Newberry & McMillan Block,
Griswold Street.

Rohns & Scherer,
Dealers in Carriage Goods, Woodwork, Iron and Steel,
52 and 54 Congress St. East.

Wm. Fischer, Jr.,
Dealer in Watches, Jewelry, Clocks, etc.
236 Randolph St.

James Bostwick,
Junk Dealer, Sub-Marine Diving.
Highest Cash Price paid for Old Rope, Canvas, Brass, Copper, Lead, Zinc, Iron, Anchors, Chains, etc.

LUMBER DEALERS.

Alger, Smith & Co.,
Dealers in Long Pine Timber, Lumber and Pine Lands,
100 Griswold Street.

J. H. Bearns,
Dealer in Pine and Hardwood Lumber,
Yard, 553 Fort St. W., cor. 15th.

A. K. Hunton,
Wholesale Lumber Dealer,
88 Griswold Street.

Simon J. Murphy,
Lumber Dealer,
Off. 40 Moffat Block.

J. A. Sexton,
Lumber and Insurance,
7 Lafayette Ave.

Whitney & Stinchfield,
Lumber and Pine Lands,
5 Merrill Block.

LIQUOR DEALERS.

Frehheimer Bros.,
Herman C. Frehheimer.
Wholesale Liquor Dealers,
67 and 69 Jefferson Ave.

Robinson Bros.,
Distillers & Wholesale Liquor Dealers,
64 & 66 Congress St. East.

Julius Robinson,
Distiller and Wholesale Dealer in Wines and Liquors,
40 Woodward Avenue.

Webster & Doolittle,
Importers and Wholesale Dealers in Wines and Liquors,
74 Woodward Avenue.

LEATHER DEALERS.

Mumford, Foster & Co.,
Dealers in Leather and Shoe Findings;
16 Gratiot Ave.

Traugott Schmidt,
Dealer in Leather, Hides, Wool & Furs,
56 to 64 Croghan St.

LITHOGRAPHERS.

Thomas Calvert, Pres. G. H. Calvert, Sec. C. B. Calvert, Treas.
The Calvert Lithographing Co.,
Cor. Larned and Shelby Sts.

LIVERY STABLES, ETC.

Geo. Case,
Livery, Coupés and Coaches,
41 and 43 Congress Street, West.
(Open at all hours.)

Machinery & Farm Implements.

Woodford & Niles,
Manufacturers' Agents and Wholesale Dealers in Farm Machinery,
23 Woodward Ave.

G. S. Wormer & Sons,
Michigan Machinery Depot,
Machinery and Mill Supplies,
55, 57 & 59 Woodbridge St. W.

MANUFACTURERS.

Michigan Car Co.,
Office in Newberry & McMillan Bldg.,
James McMillan, President.
Hugh McMillan, Vice Pres. and Gen. Man.

Michigan Stove Co.
Manuf. Garland Stoves and Ranges,
THE WORLD'S BEST.
Detroit. Chicago. Buffalo.

Clough & Warren Organ Co.
Manuf. of The Only Reed Organs,
Having the PATENT TUBES, rendering the Tone equal to Pipe Organs.

Peninsular Car Works & Detroit Steam Forge,
Operating Car Works at Detroit and Adrian.

Detroit Mills,
Manufacturer Imperial Star Roller Patent, Starlight, Roller Process and French Bolt Family Flour.
John Clark, Prop. 144 & 146 Mich. Ave.

Allen Bros.,
Manufacturers of Picture Frames and Mats, Wholesale Dealers in Photograph Materials,
14 and 16 East Larned St.

Leonard Laurense & Co.,
Manufacturers of Picture Frames, Mouldings, Backing, &c.
57 and 59 Atwater St.

Hargreaves Manufacturing Co.,
Howard and 17th and 18th Sts.,
Picture Frames and Mouldings.
WM. S. WRIGHT, President.
FRANK F. WRIGHT, Manager.
L. N. BALDWIN, Sec'y and Treas.

Geo. Hargreaves,
Manufacturer and Proprietor of Valuable Patents.

Russell Wheel & Foundry Co.,
Manufact. of Car Wheels and Castings, Logging Cars and Car Trucks,
Foot of Walker St.

Detroit Safe Co.,
Manuf. of Steel Jamb, Fire Proof Safes, Burglar Proof Safes, &c
67 to 81 Fort St. E.

Leahoff Bros.,
Machine Mill Works, Mill Furnishers, and Manufacturers of Patent and General Machinery,
Cor. Chene and Grain St.

Leahoff Bros.,
Leahoff Mills, Manufacturers of Patent Flour by Wheat-ending System,
326 Russell Street.

The Singer Manufacturing Co.
153 Woodward Avenue.
W. R. Clark, Agt.

The Webster Manufacturing Co.
(Limited.)
Screen & Wind Engine Manufacturers,
51, 53, 55 & 57 Atwater St.

MARBLE AND STONE WORKS.

David Patterson,
Dealer in & Manuf. of all Descriptions of Granite Work, Monuments, &c
262 Woodward Ave.

MARBLE & STONE WORKS, CONTINUED.

Batchelder & Long,
Contractors and Dealers in Stone, Sewer Pipe and Drain Tile.
Cut Stone and Flagging a Specialty.
70 Atwater Street.

MILLINERY.

Rothchild & Hitting,
Wholesale Millinery,
117 and 119 Jefferson Avenue.

MUSIC.

F. J. Schwankovsky & Co's
Music House,
Pianos, Organs and Musical Merchandise, Wholesale and Retail,
23 Monroe Avenue, Opp. City Hall.

Roe Stephens Music Co.
Knabe Pianos, Behning, Bros. Mason & Hamlin and Ideal Organs. Publishers of "The Amphion."
184 and 186 Woodward Avenue.

J. P. Weiss,
Dealer in Superior Pianos, Organs and Musical Instruments of Every Description. Sheet Music and Music Books of American & Foreign Publications, 76 Woodward Ave.

NOTIONS—Wholesale.

Jacob Brown,
Wholesale Notions,
180 Jefferson Avenue.

Geo. Hadsell & Co.,
Wholesale Notions,
36 and 38 Jefferson Avenue.

NEWSPAPERS.

The Post & Tribune,
(Daily, Tri-Weekly and Weekly.)
Post & Tribune Co. Prop's,—James F. Joy, Pres.; Wm. H. Thompson, Mngr.; Lafayette Harter, Treas.

The Detroit Free Press,
(Daily, Tri-Weekly and Weekly.)
Detroit Free Press Co.,—Wm. E. Quinby, Pres.; Albert G. Boynton, V. Pres.; N. Eisenlord, Sec'y.

The Detroit Evening News,
(Daily.)
Evening News Association, Prop's,—James E. Scripps, Pres.; Geo. H. Scripps, Treas.

The Detroit Evening Journal,
(Daily.)
Lloyd Breese, Editor.

Chaff,
(Weekly.)
Lloyd Breese, Editor and Proprietor; Chas. Hull, Manager.

The Michigan Catholic,
Wm. H. Hughes, Ed. and Propr.

Michigan Christian Advocate,
(Weekly.)
Methodist Publishing Co., Proprietors. Rev. I. N. Elwood, Pres.; Rev. J. M. Arnold D. D., Ed.; Rev. J. H. Potts, Asso. Ed.

Michigan Christian Herald,
(Weekly.)
Luther H. Trowbridge, Ed. & Prop.

Michigan Farmer and State Journal of Agriculture,
Johnstone & Gibbons, Proprietors.

Michigan Good Templar,
Will W. Secord, Propr.

Michigan Journal & Herald,
(German Weekly.)
Pope & Coleman, Proprietors.

The Times Publishing Co.
A Live Daily. D. J. McDonald, Business Manager.

Detroit Every Saturday,
Send for Sample Copy.
Moore & Parker, Proprietors.

OILS.

John Greenslade,
Wholesale Dealer in Oils.
40 and 42 Jefferson Avenue.

Ingalls & Co.,
Wholesale Dealers in Oils,
46 Jefferson Avenue.

PAINTS AND OILS.

Boydell Bros.
Manufacturers of White Lead, Zinc, Putty and Colors. Also, Dealers in Brushes, Varnishes, and Painters' Materials.
18 Congress St. East.

Detroit White Lead Works,
Makers of White Lead, Zinc, Putty and Colors.
Office 97 Jefferson Avenue.
Fred D. Hinchman, Pres., Horace M. Dean, Vice Pres., Charles H. Stowell, Sec.

PHOTOGRAPHERS.

Hamilton's Art Gallery,
204 and 206 Woodward Avenue.
We make a specialty of fine Photographs; also portraits in Ink, Oil, Water and Crayon.

Wm. Marriatt,
Photographer,
131, 133 and 135 Woodward Ave.
City Hall Photograph Gallery.

Printers' Supplies.

John B. Price,
Printers' Supplies. Wholesale Paper Warehouse, 123 Jeff. Av. Agent for Farmer, Little & Co's Type; Chas. E. Johnson & Co's Printing Ink; Geo. Mather & Son's Printing Ink; Peerless, Cranston and Potter Presses, and Paper Cutters.

F. B Way,
Job Printer,
N. E. Cor Jeff. Ave. and Griswold St.

Publishers,—Books.

J. C. Chilton & Co.,
Book Publishers.
Latest Standard Subscription Books.

C. G. G. Paine,
Publisher of Standard Subscription Books. Good agents always wanted,
68 Seitz Block.

R. L. Polk & Co.,
Directory Publishers.
Ralph L. Polk. Jacob W. Weeks.
40 Larned Street.

Physicians and Surgeons.

Wm. Brodie,
Physician and Surgeon.

Albert Campau,
Physician.

Willard Chaney,
Physician.

Henry A. Cleland,
Physician.

J. DeCou,
Cancer Specialist.

E. R. Ellis,
Physician.

W. A. Fiole,
Physician.

O. Lang,
Physician.

C. C. Miller,
Physician.

E. E. Riepel,
Physician.

F. X. Spranger,
Physician.

C. C. Yemans,
Physician.

REAL ESTATE.

Newell Avery (Heirs),
Real Estate, Pine Lands, Lumber Dealers.
41 Moffat Block.

J. D. Baer & Son,
Real Estate.
141 Griswold Street.

William Congdon,
Real Estate,
145 Griswold Street.

J. S. Dewey,
Attorney, Real Estate, Pine and Hardwood Lands a specialty.
48 Moffat Block.

L. M. Curtis,
Real Estate,
105 Griswold Street.

D. J. Evans,
Real Estate and Loan Agency,
Pine and Farming Lands,
3 Mechanics' Block.

Geo. S. Frost & Co.,
Pine Lands, No. 11 Campau Block,
Cor. Griswold and Larned Sts.,
Geo. S. Frost. Chas. W. Noble.

Samuel A. Plumer,
Real Estate, Room 45 Moffat Block,
Money Loaned on Real Estate Security.
[illegible]

Feist Rothschild,
Real Estate. Dealer in Pine and Farming Lands,
77 Jefferson Avenue.

Wm. Foxen,
Real Estate,
118 Griswold Street.

Wm. Y. Hamlin,
Real Estate and Insurance,
43 Griswold Street.

Stephen Martin,
Real Estate,
35 Walker Block.

Chas. L. Ortman,
Real Estate,
Pine and Farming Lands,
149 Mechanics' Building.

Anthony Parent,
Real Estate,
100 Griswold Street.

David Parsons,
Real Estate,
Room 17 Telegraph Block.

F. G. Russell,
Law and Real Estate,
38 Moffat Block, Griswold St.

E. C. Skinner,
Real Estate and Investments on Mortgages.
Abstract Building.

Geo. W. Snover,
Real Estate,
103 Griswold Street.

Wm. Tait,
Real Estate,
12 Walker Block.

Wm. J. Waterman,
Real Estate Exchange,
Opposite P. O.

W. C. Yawkey,
Real Estate,
480 Second Avenue.
Pine and Farming Lands.

Railroads and Capitalist.

J. F. Joy,
Capitalist,
Office, 5 Telegraph Block.

Paw Paw & Toledo & South Haven.
[illegible]
General Offices,—Lawton, Mich.

Port Huron & Northwestern.
[illegible]
General Offices,—Port Huron.

Saginaw, Tuscola & Huron.
[illegible]
General Offices,—East Saginaw, Mich.

Toledo, Ann Arbor & Grand Trunk.
[illegible]

Wabash, St. Louis & Pacific.
General Offices,—St. Louis, Mo.
[illegible]

Pontiac, Oxford & Port Austin.
[illegible]

Chicago & Grand Trunk.
[illegible]

Chicago & West Michigan.
[illegible]

Cincinnati, Wabash & Michigan.
[illegible]

RAILROADS CONTINUED.

Detroit, Gr'd Haven & Milwaukee.

[illegible]

General Offices—Detroit, Mich.

Detroit, Lansing & Northern.

[illegible]

General Offices—Detroit, Mich.

Central Time—Am. Exp.

Detroit, Mackinac & Marquette.

[illegible]

Flint & Pere Marquette.

[illegible]

Grand Rapids & Indiana.

[illegible]

Grand Trunk R'y, General Officers.

[illegible]

Lake Shore & Mich. Southern.

[illegible]

Marquette, Houghton & Onton.

[illegible]

Mich. Cent. R'y, General Officers.

[illegible]

Miles Operated.

[illegible]

Michigan & Ohio.

[illegible]

Rubber Goods & Belting.

H. D. Edwards & Co.,
Dealers in Rubber goods, Leather Beltings, Mill Supplies and Ship Chandlery, 16, 18 and 20 Woodward Ave.

Seed Merchants & Florists.

Michigan Seed Co.,
Seed Merchants and Florists,
214 Woodward Ave.

Steam Boat Lines.

Star Line Steamers,
Foot of Shelby St.,
Geo. McMillan, Pres.; T. D. Carter, Secretary and Gen'l Manager.

TURKISH BATHS.

Geo. I. Betts,
[illegible]
274 Woodward Avenue.
Turkish, Roman, Russian and Electric Baths, [illegible]
Manager Ladies' Department.
(Separate Rooms for Ladies at all hours.)

Tobacco Manufacturers.

American Eagle Tobacco Works,
43 to 53 Woodbridge Street,
Chas. B. Hull, Treas. & Gen'l Man'gr.

Telegraph & Telephone Co.

Telegraph & Telephone Construction Co.,
W. A. Jackson, General Manager,
68 Griswold Street.

YEAST.

Union Yeast Company,
Manuf. of J. B. Stratton's Vegetable Dry Hop Yeast,
Grand River Avenue and [illegible] Street.

Waterloo Yeast Co.,
Manufs. of the only original Dry Hop Yeast
Factories,—Waterloo, N. Y.; Chicago, Ill.; Toronto, Ont., Detroit, Mich.;
47 Murray St. N. Y. City.

PORT HURON.

BANKS.

Commercial Bank,
Chas A. Ward, President.

DENTISTRY.

Jared Kibbee, M. D.,
Dentist,
Office over Tibbal's Drug Store.

HOTELS.

Pacific House,
J. D. Whitney, Proprietor.

LAWYERS.

A. E. Chadwick,
Attorney.

Chas. K. Dodge,
Attorney-at-Law.

E. G. Stevenson,
Attorney.

W. L. Jenks,
Attorney-at-Law.

Mitchell & Wellman,
Lawyers.

Thomas & Ivers,
Attorneys-at-Law.

MANUFACTURERS.

Brooks & Jenlyn,
Manufacturers and Dealers in Lumber,
Wholesale and Retail

NEWSPAPERS.

Port Huron Times Co.,
Daily and Weekly Times.

"The Mail,"
Y. Lew Kibets, Editor and Proprietor.

Tribune Publishing Co.
Publishers of Sunday and Weekly Tribune.
Albert H. Finn, Manager.

Williams Publishing Co.
Daily and Weekly Telegraph, and
"The Monthly Bee Hive."

REAL ESTATE.

Fraser Fish,
Abstracts, Real Estate and Insurance.

J. L. Paldi,
Surveyor,
Times Block, Pt. Huron.
Owner of Farming and Wild Lands.

Summer Resorts.

Huronia Beach,
A Private Family Summer Resort.
Cottages to rent. Weekly Board, $7.50.
Marcus Young, Propr., Port Huron.

BATTLE CREEK.

BANKS.

City Bank,
Nelson Eldred, President.

First National Bank,
V. P. Collier, President;
C. Wakelee, Vice President;
Wm. H. Skinner, Cashier.

CLERGY.

M. J. Dempsey,
Pastor of St. Philips Church.

LUMBER.

Mason, Rathburn & Co
Lumber Dealers,
Lath, Shingles, Posts, Etc.,
Office near Chic. & Gr. T. R. R. Depot.

Manufacturers.

Dress Reform Manufacturing Co.
Battle Creek, Mich.
Send for Illustrated Pamphlet
"How to Dress Healthfully." Mailed Free.
[illegible]

Medical Sanitariums.

Dr. Fairfield's Health Home,
A private Sanitarium, Equipped with every Convenience for Treating a limited Number of Patients.

The Medical & Surgical Sanitarium
A Medical Institution for the Treatment of Chronic Maladies and Surgical Cases of every description, unexcelled by any similar establishment in the United States, for the completeness of its Appointments and Facilities.

J. V. Spencer,
Physician,
Battle Creek.

PHOTOGRAPHERS.

J. F. Miller,
Photographer, No. 10 W. Main St.,
Fine Photographs a Specialty.
Battle Creek.

E. H. Perry & Son,
Photograph Artists,
Battle Creek.

PUBLISHERS.

Review & Herald,
Book and Job Printing, Electrotyping, Stereotyping, Book Binding, Paper Ruling, Etc.

J. E. White,
Subscription Book Publishers,
Parson's Hand Book of Forms.
Agents Wanted.
Battle Creek, Mich. & Kansas City, Mo.

JEWELER.

O. Davis,
Watchmaker, Jeweler and Optician, and Dealer in Watches, Clocks, Etc., 118 West Main St.

Threshing Machines.

The Case & Willard Thresher Co.
Manufacturers of the "Advance Thresher."

Nichols, Shepard & Co.
Makers of Vibrator Threshing Machinery, Portable and Traction Engines.
John Nichols, Pres.; David Shepard, Vice-Pres.; E. C. Nichols, Treas.

BAY CITY.

ARCHITECTS.

Pratt & Koeppe.
Leverett A. Pratt. Walter Koeppe.
Architects' and Superintendents' Office, Room No. 5, Bank Building, Center Street, Bay City, Mich.

ATTORNEYS.

Geo. P. Cobb,
Attorney,
Cor. Center and Saginaw Sts.

C. L. Collins,
Attorney at Law.

R. R. Taylor,
Attorney and Real Estate Dealer.

CITY OFFICERS.

T. A. Delzell,
Recorder,
Bay City.

H. C. Thompson,
Civil Engineer and Surveyor, and County Drain Commissioner. Of firm of Turner & Thompson.
Office, City Building, Saginaw Street.

FLOUR MILLS

McDonald & Shearer,
Flour Mills, Flour, Feed and Meal.

GROCERS.

Chas. Supe,
Wholesale Groceries and Provisions,
Cor. 3d and Adams St.

HOTELS.

Forest City House,
Bay City, Mich. Thomas Lawton, Propr.,
Cor. Washington Ave. and Sixth St.
[illegible]

INSURANCE.

John Drake,
Insurance Agent.
Central Block.

J. W. Knaggs,
Insurance.

Robert S. Pratt,
Insurance.

A. L. Stewart,
Real Estate and Insurance,
Cor. Center and Saginaw Streets.

Lumber Dealers & Manufrs.

C. H. Bradley,
Commission Lumber Dealer.

F. E. Bradley & Co.,
Manufacturers of Lumber, Shingles and Salt.

N. B. Bradley & Sons,
Lumber and Salt Manufacturers.

Dolsen, Chapin & Co.,
Lumber, Lath and Salt Manufacturers.

Eddy Bros' & Co.,
Manufacturers and Dealers in Lumber, Lath and Salt,
Cor. Water and Belinda Sts.

S. G. M. Gates,
Lumber Manufacturer.

J. R. Hall,
Manufacturer of Shingles, Heading, and Salt.

E. J. Hargrave & Son,
Manufacturers of Lumber and Lath.

Joseph D. Hucklns,
Dealer in Lumber, Logs, and Pine Lands.
Special Bills cut to Order.
N. E. Cor. Center & Washington Sts.,
Bay City, Mich.

McEwan Bros.,
Manufacturers of Lumber, Lath, Staves and Salt.

T. H. McGraw,
Lumber and Timber Dealer.

Miller & Lewis,
Wholesale and Retail Dealers in Lumber and Salt.

Mosher & Fisher,
West Bay City,
Wholesale Lumber and Timber Dealers.

Murphy & Dorr,
Manufacturers of Lumber and Salt.
Bay City.

Geo. C. Myers,
Manufacturer of Lumber, Lath, and Salt.

Pitts & Cranage,
Lumber and Salt Manufacturers.

C. H. Prescott,
Dealer in Farming Lands and Lumber.

John Welch,
Manufacturer and Dealer in Lumber.
Office at East Saginaw, opposite Bancroft House, & at Mill W. Bay City.

MANUFACTURERS.

Bousfield & Co.,
Manufacturers of Wooden Ware,
Pails, Tubs, etc.

Emery & Garland,
Exclusive Agents for Evart's Detachable Chain, and Manufacturers and Dealers in Saw Mill and Grain Elevator Machinery.
Bay City, Mich., & [illegible] Minneapolis, Minn.

McKinnon Manufacturing Co.
Bay City Steam Boiler Works.
Manfrs. of all kinds of Stationary, Marine and Locomotive Boilers.
J. D. McKinnon, Pres.

H. W. Simms,
Agent for Jackson Fire Clay Co., and Mafr. of Chapman's Magic Cough Cure,
Washington St., Munger Block.

The American Chemical Co.,
West Bay City.
Herman Frasch, Supt.; Chas. Morgan, Asst. Supt.;
J. B. Ketcham, Treas. & Gen'l Mangr.

Smalley Bros. & Co.
Manufacturers of Steam Engines, Mill and Salt Well Machinery; also Proprietors of Smalley & Co's Saw Mills at West Bay City. Manufacture all kinds of Lumber and Mill Stuff.

J. D. Jackson,
Pattern Maker at Smalley Bros. & Co's Machine Works.

PUBLISHERS.

Edwin T. Bennett,
Publisher and Proprietor Lumbermans' Gazette, and Tribune & Chronicle,
207 Center St.

REAL ESTATE.

C. M. Averill,
Dealer in Real Estate.

E. B. Denison,
Dealer in Real Estate.

Wm. McEwen,
Real Estate,
702 Center Street.

Frank Fitzhugh,
Dealer in Real Estate.

John H. Wilkins,
Abstract and Real Estate.

Shearer Bros.,
Successors to Jas. Shearer & Sons.
Real Estate and Land Dealers.
Office, 808 Adams St., Shearer Block.

Cheboygan.

ATTORNEYS.

Humphrey & Perkins,
Attorneys,
Watts S. Humphrey,
Edwin Z. Perkins.

CLERGY.

Peter J. Desmet,
Pastor of St. Mary's Church.

EDITORS.

Edward Forsyth,
Editor and Proprietor of the Cheboygan Democrat.

HOTELS.

Grand Central Hotel,
Offers Superb Accommodations for Tourists. Headquarters for Commercial Travelers. The Best Sample Rooms in Town. Fishing & Hunting Unsurpassed. J. M. French, Propr.

INSURANCE.

Wm. H. Daniels & Co.
Insurance, Real Estate, and Loan Agents.

MANUFACTURERS.

W. & A. McArthur,
[illegible]
Wm. McArthur, [illegible], Cheboygan, Mich.;
Arch. McArthur, [illegible], Chicago, Ill.

East Saginaw.

ATTORNEYS.

Frederick Anneke,
Attorney, Fire Insurance Agent, and Dealer in Real Estate.

Camp & Brooks,
Attorneys.

S. G. Higgins,
Attorney At Law.

H. H. Hoyt,
Law and Real Estate.

M. P. Smith & Co.
Law, Real Estate and Abstract Off.

Wm. S. Tennant,
Lawyer.

Wheeler & McKnight,
Attorneys.

W. L. Webber,
Solicitor and Land Commissioner of Flint & Pere Marquette R. R. Co.

BANKS.

First National Bank,
E. Judd, President;
Clarence L. Judd, Cashier.

Merchants' National Bank,
H. C. Potter, President;
Douglass Hoyt, Cashier.

Boots & Shoes.

C. S. Grant & Co.
Wholesale and Retail Boot & Shoe Dealers.

H. C. Potter,
General Manager of F. & P. M. R. R.

CLOTHING.

Heavenrich Bros. & Co.
Wholesale and Retail Clothing, Lumbermens' Supplies. Merchant Tailors.

FACTORIES.

John V. Chapman,
Patent Hoop and Box Factory.

Charles Lee,
Saw Mill, Planing Mill, and Sash, Door and Blind Factory.

Wm. B. Mershon,
Planing Mill and Box Factory.

HOTELS.

Goodrich House,
(Strictly Temperance.)
North Side of Michigan Avenue, Over Nos. 115 & 117. Terms $1 per day.
T. G. King, Proprietor.

HARDWARE.

Morley Bros.
Wholesale Hardware.

Lumber & Salt.

Eddy, Avery & Eddy,
Dealers in
Lumber and Salt.

C. K. Eddy & Son,
Manufacturers of Lumber and Salt.

C. W. Hill,
Lumber Manufacturer,
Office First National Bank Building.

Chas. Merrill & Co.
Manufacturers and Dealers in Lumber and Salt.

A. W. Morse,
Inspector of and Commission Dealer in Logs and Lumber, Pine and Hardwood.

James Patterson,
Manufacturer of Lumber and Salt.

D. F. Rose,
Commission Lumber Dealer.

John Welch,
Manufacturer of Norway and White Pine, Lumber
Office, E. Saginaw, Office & Mill W. Bay City.

Warner & Eastman,
Manufacturers and Dealers in Lumber, Salt and Shingles.

MANUFACTURERS.

Mayflower Mills,
Manufacturer of Flour and Feed.

Michigan Saw & File Works.
W. R. Burt, Pres.; R. B. McKnight, Sec'y; Sewell Avery, Treas.

R. Wildman,
Excelsior Steam Boiler Works.
Stationary, Marine and Locomotive Boilers of every description. Sheet Iron Work of all kinds. Repairing promptly done.

Nora Duggan,
Manufacturer of Shirts, Collars, Cuffs, and Underwear.

MUSIC.

C. M. Norris,
Dealer in Pianos, Organs and Music.

PHYSICIANS.

D. G. Sutherland,
Veterinary Surgeon. Graduate of Ontario Veterinary College.

H. Williams,
Physician.

PUBLISHERS.

Courier Company,
The Courier Job Printing, Binding & Paper House. Publishers of Daily and Weekly Courier & Evening Express.

REAL ESTATE.

Real Estate Exchange,
R. Z. Smith, Conveyancer and Notary Public, and Dealer in Farming Lands and City Property,
No. 2 Music Block, East Saginaw.

Rupp & Kerr,
Lands, Logs and Lumber.

J. D. Wilson,
Real Estate, Pine Lands a Specialty.

John J. Rupp,
East Saginaw Wood Works.
Wholesale and Retail Dealer in Carriage and Sleigh Beadings, Etc.

ANN ARBOR.

ATTORNEYS.

J. H. Morris,
Attorney and Counselor At Law.
Solicitor in Chancery,
Huron Street, Ann Arbor.

Mary E. Foster,
Attorney and Counselor At Law,
Box 1610 Ann Arbor.

Architects & Builders.

John S. Mann,
(Ann Arbor P. O.)
Architect and Builder,
Sec 12, Ann Arbor Tp. 10 Acres.

ARMY OFFICERS.

N. D. Badger,
Capt. U. S. Army, Retired.

BARBERS.

Paul Schall,
Shaving Parlors,
Ann Arbor.

CHEMISTS.

Eberbach & Son,
Chemists,
The only Depot in the West for C. P. Chemicals, Chemical Glass and Porcelain Ware.

CIVIL ENGINEERS.

J. B. Davis,
Civil Engineer.

CLOTHIERS.

J. T. Jacobs,
Clothier and Dealer in Hats, Caps, and Gents' Furnishing Goods,
27 and 29 Main St.

Contractors & Jobbers.

Edward Graff,
Contractor and Jobber of Mason Work.
South Liberty Street.

FARMERS.

E. W. Codington,
Ann Arbor P. O., Sec. 3 and 10, Pittsfield Tp., 130 acres.
Holstein Cattle, Poland China Swine and Plymouth Rock Fowls.

Wm. Dye,
Ann Arbor P. O., Northfield Tp., Section 31. 46 acres.

C. R. Gardner,
Ann Arbor P. O., (Gardener of Small Fruits.
Sec. 21, Ann Arbor Tp. 20 Acres.

John Geddes,
Farmer,
Ann Arbor P. O., Sec. 36, Ann Arbor Tp. 70 Acres.

Roswell Goodell,
Ann Arbor P. O., Sec. 17, Ann Arbor Tp. 50 Acres.

J. W. Hulbert,
General Farmer, Ann Arbor P. O., Sec. 31, Ann Arbor Tp. 60 Acres.

Chas. Malonba,
Farmer,
Ann Arbor P. O., Sec. 30, Ann Arbor Tp. 200 Acres.

Thomas LeCompte,
Ann Arbor P. O., Sec. 10, Ann Arbor Tp. 70 Acres.

Arthur S. Lyon,
Dealer in Stock and Raising of Produce, Ann Arbor P. O., Sec. 23, Scio Tp. 140 Acres.

E. A. Matteson,
Ann Arbor P. O., Secs. 13 and 24, Ann Arbor Tp. 175 Acres.

John C. Schenk,
Ann Arbor P. O., Sec. 19, Ann Arbor Tp. 41 Acres.
Building, Farming and Fruit Raising.

Mrs. L. Tichnor,
Ann Arbor P. O., Sec. 4, Ann Arbor Tp. 149 Acres.

L. F. Wade,
Ann Arbor P. O., Sec. 22, Ann Arbor Tp. 160 Acres.

J. D. Williams,
Ann Arbor P. O., Sec. 33, Ann Arbor Tp. 60 Acres.

GRAVE STONES.

Anton Eisele,
Dealer in Marble and Granite Monuments, Gravestones, Etc.

Sed James,
Manufacturer of Granite and Marble Monuments.

HOTELS.

Cook House,
E. H. Hudson, Proprietor.
Newly Furnished and heated by Steam.

MANUFACTURERS.

A. M. Bodwell,
Inventor and Manufacturer of the Tecumseh Windmills. Best made in the Market. Price of Mill and Derrick, put up in vicinity Ann Arbor, $70.00.

Luick & Bros.
Manufacturers and Dealers in Lumber, Sash, Doors, Blinds, Etc.,
Cor. North and Fifth Streets.

MEATS.

Henry Matthews,
Dealer in Fresh, Salt and Smoked Meats, Sausage, Lard, Tallow, &c.
Cash paid for all kinds of Poultry, Pelts, Hides, Tallow, &c.
West Huron St., Adjoining Sausage Factory.

SALOONS.

N. H. Drake,
Saloon,
70 East Huron Street.

Alfreus Gwinner,
Saloon and Restaurant,
5 Detroit St.

Teachers of Languages.

J. Brueckner,
Teacher of Languages,
Ann Arbor.

ALMA.

ATTORNEYS.

James B. Clark,
Attorney.

Francis Palmer,
Attorney At Law.

Marcus Pollasky,
Attorney At Law.
Money to loan on Real Estate.
Collections a Specialty.

HOTELS.

Dallas House,
George L. Spier, Proprietor.
Affords all the comforts of a first class house.
G. L. Spier also Prop. of Meat Market.

Manufacturers.

Geo. D. Barton & Co.
Manufacturers of Hardwood and Pine Lumber, Mouldings, Casing, Siding, Flooring, Lath, Shingles, Sash, Doors, Lime, Calcine and Building Paper.

S. C. Bliss,
Manufacturer of Staves, Heading, and Hoops.

J. W. Montigel & Co.
Manufacturers of all kinds of Steel Plows, Farming Implements, Carriages, Wagons, Sleighs, Etc.

NEWSPAPERS.

The Alma Record,
N. G. Davidson, Editor and Publisher. Published every Saturday Afternoon, at $1.00 per Year.

Saginaw City.

ATTORNEYS.

Hanchett & Stark,
Lawyers,
Merrill Block.

BANKS.

Citizens' National Bank,
D. Hardin, Pres.;
D. W. Briggs, Cashier.

First National Bank,
A. W. Wright, Pres.;
Wm. Powell, Cashier.

Book-keepers.

W. E. Ramsay,
Book-keeper.

GROCERS.

G. A. Alderton,
Wholesale Grocer.

Wells, Stone & Co.
Wholesale Grocers and Lumbermens' Supplies.

Lumber & Real Estate.

N. & A. Barnard,
Lumber, Lath and Shingles, Salt, Pine and Farming Lands.

Backus & Binder,
Salt and Lumber.

Gaylord & Fowler,
Insurance and Real Estate Agents.

J. H. Hill & Sons,
Lumber and Real Estate Agents.

Thomas Merrill,
Dealer in Pine Lands, Logs & Lumber.

J. K. Stevens,
Real Estate and Abstract Office.

Wright & Ketcham,
Dealer in General Merchandise, Pine, Hemlock, and Hardwood Lumber.

MANUFACTURERS.

John L. Jackson,
Manufr. of Steam Engines, Salt Well & Mill Machinery. Particular Attention given to repairing all kinds of Machinery.

D. Hardin & Co.
Manufacturers of Sash, Doors, Blinds, Flooring, Siding, Mouldings, and all kinds of Fancy Wood Work.

H. M. Hosmer,
Shingle Manufacturer.

G. F. Williams & Bros.
Manufacturers of and Wholesale and Retail Dealers in Lumber, Lath, Shingles, and Salt.

Grand Haven.

HOTELS.

Cutler House,
The most Popular Summer Resort in the West.
D. Cutler, Owner and Proprietor;
H. B. Irish, Manager.

LIVERY STABLES.

Cutler House,
Livery, Sale, and Boarding Stable,
Cor. 3d & Columbus Sts.,
Grand Haven, Slayton Bro's Props.
All Orders Promptly Attended.

Lumber & Lands.

Cutler & Savage,
Dealers in Lumber and Pine Lands, Spring Lake.

MILLERS.

Forest Brothers,
Millers and Dealers in Flour.

NEWSPAPERS.

Grand Haven Herald,
The only Republican Paper printed in English in Ottawa County.
Kedzie & Kedzie, Editors and Props.

Grand Rapids.

ATTORNEYS.

A. S. Hall,
Attorney At Law,
41 Monroe St.

Norris & Uhl,
Attorneys At Law,
79 & 81 Lyon Street.

Birney Hoyt,
Attorney At Law,
20 Powers' Opera House Block.

D. Darwin Hughes,
General Counsel Gr. R. & Ind. R. R.

Edward W. Withey,
Attorney At Law.

BREWERS.

Kusterer Brewing Co.
Manufacturers and Bottlers of Bohemian Export & Stock Lager Beer,
Cor. E. Bridge and Indiana Sts.

Frey Bros.
Proprietors of Cold Brook Brewing and Bottling Works.

BANKS.

City National Bank,
Thos. D. Gilbert, Pres.

Old National Bank,
Martin L. Sweet, Pres.;
J. M. Barnett, Vice-President.

Fourth National Bank,
A. B. Watson, President,
J. M. Wheeler, Cashier.

Grand Rapids National Bank,
Edwin F. Uhl, President,
T. C. Sherwood, Cashier.

CAPITALISTS.

Julius Houseman,
Capitalist and M. C.,
26 Monroe Street.

HOTELS.

Morton House,
Pantlind & Co., Proprietors.

Sweet's Hotel,
H. C. Johnson, Proprietor.

Clarendon Hotel,
Ed. Killean, Proprietor,
Cor. Canal & Bridge Streets,
Grand Rapids.

LIVERY.

J. J. Close,
Livery & Sale Stable,
64 North Ionia St.

MANUFACTURERS.

H. C. Russell,
Grand Rapids Mattress Co.,
Manufacturer of Wire Springs.

M. J. Bond,
Manufacturer and Dealer in Lumber and Shingles; Dealer in City Property, Farms and New Lands.
Office 15 Pearl St.

J. M. Carr,
Manufacturer and Dealer in Lumber and Shingles.
Office, 17 Pierce's Block; Mills at Conger & Morley, on G. R. & I. R. R.

C. C. Comstock,
Manufacturer of Common, Sawed and Dressed Lumber, Pails, Tubs, Woodenware, Sash, Doors; also Dealer in Groceries, Provisions, Boots, Shoes, Clothing, Etc.
331 Canal Street.

L. H. Cutcheon,
Sash, Door and Blind Factory,
Dealer in Lumber, Lath & Shingles.
139 Bridge Street.

A. L. Chubb & Co.
Plow Manufacturers.

Grand Rapids Manufacturing Co.
Manufacturers of Agricultural Implements. Office & Works, Corner Earle and South Front Sts., W. Side.
D. P. Clay, Pres.

Lyman T. Kinney,
Lumber Manufacturer,
109 Ottawa St.

Luther & Sumner Manfg. Co.
Wholesale Manufacturers of Ash and Maple Furniture,
Junction of Det. Gr. H. & M. and C. & W. Mich. R. R.

Powers & Walker,
Manufacturers of Wood Burial Cases and Caskets, also Manufacturers of Patent Sliding Face Lid Casket.
Office and Factories, Nos. 99 to 103 S. Front St.

Widdicomb Furniture Co.
Wholesale Manufacturers of Furniture,
Office, 4th St., near Division St.

Wetzell Bros.
Manufacturers and Wholesale Dealers in Lumber and Shingles,
Office, Pierce's Block.

Wetzell Bros. & Pantlind,
Manufacturers & Wholesale Dealers in Lumber & Shingles,
Room 25, Pierce's Block.

J. H. Wonderly,
Manufacturer of Lumber and Dealer in Pine Lands,
35 Monroe Street.

L. H. Withey & Co.
Lumber Manufacturers,
771 Canal St.

Alvah F. DeVinney,
Manufacturer of Seals, Stencils, Steel Stamps, and Dies, &c., &c.

Smith & Barrett,
Manufacturers and Wholesale Dealers in Pine Lumber, Lath and Shingles, 15 Pearl St.

Keystone Gang Saw Mill,
A. D. Long & Son,
Manufacturers of Lumber and Lath, and 18-inch Shingles.
Office and Mill, North end of Front Street, Grand Rapids, Mich.

F. Raniville,
Manufacturer of Short-Lap, Oak Tanned Leather Belting,
and Dealer in Rubber Belting and Mill Supplies.
No. 1 Pearl Street, Grand Rapids, Mich.

Spiral Spring Buggy Co.
Manufacturers of the Famous Spiral Spring Carriages. Complete and in parts.
The only Spring in the world that can be adjusted to suit the load. The newest and best thing out in Carriage Springs. Absolutely no end pitch or side sway. [illegible] perfectly level no matter where the load is placed. Write for Illustrated Catalogue and Price List.
44 East Bridge St., Grand Rapids, Mich.

PUBLISHERS.

F. W. Ball,
Publisher of
The Democrat.

RAILROADS.

Chic. & W. M. R. R.
Geo. C. Kimball, Gen'l Manager.
A. M. Nichols, Asst. Supt. & Gen. Frt. & Pass. Agent, Grand Rapids.
General offices, Muskegon, Mich.

Grand Rapids & Ind. R. R.
W. O. Hughart, Pres. and Gen'l Manager.
C. L. Lockwood, Gen'l Pass. Agent.

REAL ESTATE.

C. H. Berkey,
Real Estate and Loans,
18 Canal St.

Percy T. Cook,
Lumber and Real Estate,
8 Pierce Block.

G. L. Knight & Sons,
Dealers in Lumber and Pine Lands,
35 Bronson St.

N. W. Northrop,
Real Estate and Loan Office,
Over City National Bank.

H. Walt,
Special Agent for the Sale of Pine Lands in Michigan, Wisconsin, and Minnesota.
Also General Agent for Sale of All Kinds of Wood Working Machinery.
Second-hand Saw & Shingle Mills a Specialty.

UNDERTAKERS.

Jas. Dolbee & Co.
Undertakers and Funeral Furnishers,
114 Monroe Street.

Wholesale Grocers.

Cody, Ball & Co.
Wholesale Grocers.

EVART.

DRUGGISTS.

J. T. Peter & Co.
Druggists and Apothecaries.

J. H. Volter,
Druggist.
Perfumery, Toilet Articles, Etc.

Dealers in Merchandise.

Wolf Bros.
Dealers in General Merchandise.

HOTELS.

Evart House,
F. S. Postal, Propr.;
Fred Postal, Clerk.
Good Sample Rooms for Agents.
Bath Room attached.

PRINTERS.

Hinckle Bros.
Publishers and Proprietors of
"Evart Weekly Review."
Artistic Job Printers, Book Binders and Stationers.

FLINT.

ATTORNEYS.

John H. Hicock,
Attorney At Law.

Lee & Aitken,
Attorneys At Law.

H. R. Lovell,
Attorney, Solicitor, and Counselor,
Flint, Michigan.
Special Attention given to Collections.
In Business since 1863.

BANKS.

Citizens' National Bank,
Robert J. Whaley, Pres.;
H. C. VanDeusen, Cashier.

Medical Institutions.

Institution for Deaf & Dumb,
Dan H. Church, Superintendent.

Flint Medical Institute & Hospital
Dr. S. Carman, Proprietor.

MANUFACTURERS.

Begole, Fox & Co.
Lumber Manufacturers.

W. W. Crapo,
Lumber Manufacturing; also Sash, Doors & Blinds.

Beardslee, Gillies & Co.
Lumber Yard, Planing Mill, and Sash, Door and Blind Manufacturers.

The Flint Wagon Works,
Wholesale Manufacturers of Farm and Freight Wagons. J. H. Whiting, Gen'l Manag'r. Allan Y. Beach, Supt.

A. Randall,
Manufacturer of Carriages, Buggies and Sleighs. General Repairer.

Flint Cabinet Creamery Co.
Manufacturers of
Cabinet Creamery and Wilson's Barrel Churn.

Money Loaner.

Jacob B. Stockdale,
Money Loaner.

REAL ESTATE.

Lyon & Co.,
(Successors to Lyon & Son.)
Dealers and Real Estate Dealers.
[illegible]

LAPEER.

ATTORNEYS.

Geer & Williams,
Attorneys.

City Officers.

Charles W. Brown,
Judge of Probate,
Probate Office.

Dealer in Music, Etc.

G. F. Hartwell,
Dealer in Sewing Machines, Organs, Picture Frames, Stationery, Fancy Goods, and Musical Merchandise,
2 Doors East of Lapeer Bakery.

HOTELS.

Lindner House,
(Formerly Marshall House.) Geo. Lindner Propr.
This House has been Thoroughly Renovated and Refurnished, and is Located in the Business Part of the City.
[illegible] Sample Rooms for Commercial Men. Good Stabling Accommodations. First-class Livery in Connection. Terms, $1 per day.

MILLERS.

Mrs. C. T. Dodge,
Centennial Flouring Mills.

Real Estate.

Jno. Abbott,
Abstract of Titles.

Lansing.

EXECUTIVE DEPARTMENT.

Executive Office,
Josiah W. Begole, Governor;
Wm. Stevenson, Sec'y to Governor.

Department of State,
Harry A. Conant, Sec'y of State.
D. Henry McComas, Deputy.

Auditor General's Office,
Wm. C. Stevens, Auditor General;
Herbert H. Pratt, Deputy.

State Land Office,
Minor S. Newell, Com'r;
H. S. Sleeper, Deputy Com'r.

Michigan State Library,
Mrs. H. A. Tenney, Librarian;
Miss L. L. Parker, Ass't.

Swamp Land Com'r,
Wm. D. Fuller, Commissioner;
W. A. Innes, Clerk.

Office of Superintendent of Public Instruction.
Varnum B. Cochran, Superintendent;
Wm. L. Smith, Dep'y Superintendent.

Insurance Bureau,
Samuel H. Row, Com'r of Insurance,
Henry N. Lawrence, Deputy Com'r.

HOTELS.

Goodrich House,
Strictly Temperance,
Eli Bidelman, Proprietor.

Hudson House,
M. Hudson, Proprietor.

MANUFACTURERS.

Jackson Wagon Works,
Manufacturers of the Celebrated
Jackson Farm Wagons.

E. Bement & Sons,
Agricultural Implements and Stove Manufacturers.

A. Foerster,
Manufacturer of Lager Beer.
Orders for Kegs and Bottled Lager will Receive Prompt Attention.
Grand River Brewery.

John McKinley,
Manufacturer of Fine Carriages, Buggies, Platform Wagons and Sleighs.
Repairing and Painting a Specialty.

REAL ESTATE.

Jones & Porter,
Real Estate Brokers,
Buy and Sell Western Lands.

J. H. Moores,
Real Estate,
130 Washington Ave.

Seymour Foster,
Abstract of Title and Real Estate Dealer.

Monroe.

ATTORNEYS.

Grosvenor & Landon,
Attorneys At Law.

BREWERS.

John Wahl, Jr.,
Lager Beer Brewer and Bottler.

Commercial Printing House.

The Monroe Commercial,
F. D. Hamilton, Publisher.
Job Printing in all its Branches.

GRAIN, ETC.

G. R. Hurd,
Dealer in Grain & Agricultural Implements.

HOTELS.

Park Hotel,
[illegible]
W. B. Plummer, Propr.

Western Hotel,
Best Board and Prompt Attention
$1 per day.
John M. Waidelich, Proprietor.

MANUFACTURERS.

Schrander & Frisble,
[illegible]

Nurserymen.

I. E. Ilgenfritz & Sons,
Nurserymen.

Petersburg P. O.

CLERGY.

Rev. J. P. Wright,
Lambertville P. O.

COURTS.

C. Joslin,
Circuit Judge,
Ypsilanti.

FARMERS.

John Larned,
Ash Tp., Rockwood P. O. 7 Acres.

John Peters,
Farmer and Lumber Dealer,
Summerfield Tp.,
Petersburg P. O.

J. B. Arms,
Farmer,
Dexter P. O., Sec. 10, Webster Tp.
97 Acres.

John Phelps,
Farmer,
Lambertville P. O.

James Ery,
Farmer,
Whiteford Centre P. O.,
Whiteford Tp.

General Dealers.

H. C. McLachlin,
General Dealer,
Petersburg P. O.

HOTELS.

E. H. Plunkett,
Deerfield Hotel. Deerfield Livery and Feed Stable.

PHYSICIANS.

R. B. Kirby, M. D.,
Physician and Surgeon,
Petersburg P. O.

Nazareth Paquette,
Physician and Surgeon,
Petersburg P. O.

PONTIAC.

ATTORNEYS.

R. J. Lowrsbury,
Attorney at Law.

J. E. Sawyer,
Attorney at Law.

Daniel L. Davis,
Law and Collecting, and Dealer in Real Estate.

Taft & Smith,
Attorneys and Counsellors At Law, Levi Taft, Ex-Judge 6th Jud. Circuit, Mich.; Samuel W. Smith, Prosecuting Attorney, Oakland County.

Elmer R. Webster,
Attorney At Law, Justice of the Peace, and County School Examiner.

Aug. C. Baldwin,
Attorney At Law.

BANKS.

First National Bank,
Charles Lawson, Pres.;
John Horton, Cashier.

CAPITALISTS.

Chas. H. Palmer,
Capitalist,

Treasurer.

E. E. Sherwood,
County Treasurer.

Ludington.

ATTORNEYS.

Elsworth & Graves,
Law, Real Estate, and Insurance.

White & McMahon,
Attorneys At Law.

Dry Goods, Etc.

Adam Drach,
Dry Goods, and Boots & Shoes.

Groceries, Etc.

James A. Armstrong,
Dealer in Groceries and Provisions, also Crockery, Lamps, Glassware and Notions.

Iron Works.

Industrial Iron Works,
Robert B. Patterson, Proprietor.

LIVERY.

William Allen,
Livery, Sale and Feed Stable.

John Bethune,
Livery and Boarding Stable,
James St.

Meat Markets.

N. M. Beatly,
Butcher and Meat Market.

Omnibus Lines.

Jas. A. Boyd,
Hack, Omnibus, and Express Line, Hacks and Busses to and from all Trains and Boats.
Telephone Connection.

Real Estate.

Chas. T. Sawyer,
Abstracts and Real Estate.

Danaher, Melendy & Co.
Dealers in Lumber, Pine Lands and General Merchandise.

Marquette.

ATTORNEYS.

D. H. Ball,
Attorney.

F. O. Clark,
Attorney At Law.

W. P. Healy,
Attorney At Law.

AGENTS.

W. W. Manning,
Agent Military Road Lands belonging to the Estate of James C. Ayer.

J. M. Longyear,
Land Agent
for L. S. S. C. R. & L. Co.

Horatio Seymour, Jr.,
Agent M. L. & I. Co. (Limited).

J. Hornby,
Agent M. H. & O. R. R. Land Office.

BANKS.

Peter White,
Banker,
Marquette.

CLERGY.

Rt. Rev. John Vertin,
Roman Catholic Bishop of Marquette.

HOTELS.

Clifton House,
W. H. Voca, Proprietor.

Iron Companies.

Champion Iron Company,
[illegible]

Manufacturers.

Iron Bay Manufacturing Co.
D. H. Merritt, Gen'l Manager.

Lake Superior Powder Co.
Manfrs. of Nitro-Glycerine, Excelsior Blasting and Sporting Powder, Caps, Fuse, and Magnet Batteries, Leading Wire, &c.

REGISTER.

V. B. Cochran,
Register of U. S. Land Office.

Wholesale Dealers.

C. H. Call & Co.
Wholesale and Retail Dealers in Heavy Hardware, Railway and Mining Supplies.

Mt. Clemens.

ATTORNEYS.

Crocker & Hutchins,
Attorneys.

Eldredge & Spiers,
Attorneys.

BANKS.

Ulrich & Crocker,
Bankers.

HOTELS.

The New Avery House,
(Near Depot.)
Open Year Round. The Best Water in America for Rheumatism, Etc.,
For Information, Address P. B. Bruch, Propr.

Real Estate.

Farrar & Laugnshausen,
Abstracts of Titles,

Negaunee.

Banking, Law & Insurance.

M. E. Pearne,
Banking, Life and Fire Insurance.

John Q. Adams,
Law and Insurance.

CAPITALISTS.

Edward Breitung,
Capitalist and M. C.

Furniture, Etc.

Norman McLeod,
Furniture Dealer and Undertaker.

JUDGES.

J. H. Primeau,
Justice of the Peace.

MINES.

Adams & Foley,
Mines and Mining.

Newspapers.

C. J. Griffey,
Proprietor of
"Iron Herald."

Owosso.

ATTORNEYS.

E. B. Hutchins,
Attorney At Law.

HOTELS.

Exchange Hotel,
Centrally Located; Strictly First-Class. Rates $1.00, $1.50 and $2.00 per day; Bus to and from all Trains. Geo. Fasik, Proprietor.

MANUFACTURERS.

Estey Manufacturing Co.
Manufacturers of Furniture.
Cheap Bedroom Sets a Specialty.

Union Mattress Co.
Manufacturers of & Wholesale Dealers in Curled Hair, Wool, Moss, Husk & Excelsior Mattresses, The Celebrated [illegible] Woven Bed, and all Grades of Feathers. M. H. Tuxbury, Proprietor.

Physicians.

S. T. Goddard,
Physician and Surgeon.

REAL ESTATE.

H. O. Williams,
Dealer in Real Estate,
Owosso.

Ishpeming.

ATTORNEYS.

G. W. Hayden,
Lawyer.

E. E. Osborn,
Attorney.

BANKS.

D. F. Wadsworth,
Banker.

FARMERS.

Fred Cota,
Farmer,
Garden Bay Tp., Sec. 5.

HOTELS.

Commercial Hotel,
John Funke, Proprietor.

Mines.

J. Ropes,
P. M. and Pres. Ropes' Gold and Silver Mines.

Recorder.

Conrad Carlson,
Recorder.

HOLLY.

BANKS.

First National Bank,
J. C. Simonson, Pres.,
S. S. Wheeler, Cashier.

Inventors.

Thomas J. Vinton,
Inventor and Patentee of
"Champion Fire Escape."
Descriptive Circulars sent free by addressing Globe Patent Agency, 34 Park Row, New York, or Thomas J. Vinton, Holly, Mich.

Newspapers.

Oakland County Advertiser,
Established in 1877.
Fred Slocum, Editor and Proprietor.
General Weekly.

Real Estate.

Jno. M. Baird,
Real Estate and Insurance Agent.

Students.

Robert P. Brock,
Law Student.

IONIA.

Agriculture.

Barringer & Wentworth,
Agricultural Implements.

Attorneys.

Lemuel Clute,
Lawyer.

John H. Mitchell,
Attorney At Law.

E. B. Stanton,
Attorney At Law.

Wm. O. Webster,
Attorney and Counsellor At Law.

Real Estate.

Frederick Hall,
Real Estate.

CLERKS.

M. B. Taylor,
County Clerk.

SHERIFF.

Wm. Toane,
Sheriff.

St. Louis.

Attorneys.

S. J. Scott,
Attorney.

James Paddock,
Att. At Law, Judge of Probate for Gratiot Co. Collections a Specialty, and Remittances Promptly Made. Rooms 1 and 2 [illegible] Blk. Have a Complete Set of Abstracts to all Lands in Gratiot County.

BANKS.

Harrington, Saviers & Co.
Bankers.
F. G. Kneeland, Cashier.

Builders.

E. A. Gillis,
Architect and Builder, also Furnish Plans, Specifications and Estimates Furnished.

JUDGES.

E. H. Landon,
Justice of the Peace.

Manufacturers.

L. S. Dickey,
Proprietor of the Holcomb Salt Works, Planing Mill and Bromine Works.

Newspapers.

J. V. Johnson & Co.
Publishers of the
"Gratiot County Democrat."

Willard D. Tucker,
Publisher of the
"St. Louis Herald,"
Established in 1867; Terms, $1 per year.

Real Estate.

Wm. A. McOmber,
Real Estate, Loan and Insurance Agent.

St. Ignace.

ATTORNEYS.

Cady & Hoffman,
Lawyers,
St. Ignace.

BANKS.

W. A. Burt & Co.
Bankers,
Life, Fire and Marine Insurance.

HOTELS.

Bay View House,
E. Sherwood, Proprietor.

Newspapers

St. Ignace NEWS,
Chas. Geo. Cavanagh, Proprietor.

Supervisors.

W. P. Preston,
Chairman of Board of Supervisors,
Mackinac County.

Surveyors.

E. B. Chamberlain,
Surveyor.

Miscellaneous.

ATTORNEYS.

A. Plummer,
Attorney At Law,
Benton Harbor, Mich.

Collectors.

Francis Stanton,
City Recorder and Collector
Adrian, Mich.

Contractors.

Alfred J. West,
Contractor.
Capac, Mich.

HOTELS.

Hurd House,
Smith & Hurd, Proprietors,
Jackson, Mich.

Park Hotel,
On The Bluff Overlooking Lake Michigan. Good Accommodations for the Traveling Public and Summer Boarders. A Livery Stable in Connection. J. C. [illegible], Prop. St. Joseph, Michigan.

Herrington Washer.

Herrington Washer,
A Model of Simplicity and Effect. No Rubbing. Will last a lifetime. A child can Use it. Price, express prepaid, $5. [illegible] & Co., Traverse City, Mich.

MANUFACTURERS.

Henry Stevens & Co.
Manufacturers of Lumber,
St. Helen, Roscommon Co.

REAL ESTATE.

Chas. H. Chick,
Dealer in Pine and Farming Lands.
Baldwin, Mich.

www.ingramcontent.com/pod-product-compliance
Lightning Source LLC
Chambersburg PA
CBHW030823270326
41928CB00007B/877
* 9 7 8 3 7 4 3 4 4 8 0 7 0 *